C0-BUZ-574

THE LOEB CLASSI[CAL LIBRARY]

FOUNDED BY JAMES [LOEB]

EDITED BY

E. H. WARMINGTON, M.A., F.R.HIST.SOC.

PREVIOUS EDITORS

† T. E. PAGE, C.H., LITT.D.

† W. H. D. ROUSE, LITT.D.

† E. CAPPS, PH.D., LL.D.

L. A. POST, L.H.D.

PHILO

VII

320

PHILO

IN TEN VOLUMES
(AND TWO SUPPLEMENTARY VOLUMES)

VII

WITH AN ENGLISH TRANSLATION BY
F. H. COLSON, M.A.
LATE FELLOW OF ST. JOHN'S COLLEGE, CAMBRIDGE

CAMBRIDGE, MASSACHUSETTS
HARVARD UNIVERSITY PRESS
LONDON
WILLIAM HEINEMANN LTD
MCMLXVIII

First printed 1937
Reprinted 1950, 1958, 1968

Printed in Great Britain

CONTENTS OF VOLUME VII

CONTENTS

PREFACE TO VOLUME VII

This seventh volume is in a sense a continuation of the sixth, in that both belong to the second main division of Philo's work, the *Exposition of the Laws*. But the contents differ so essentially from the biographical treatises, contained in the last volume, that it seemed advisable to add a General Introduction, which will apply not only to the seventh, but also to a large part of the matter which has to be relegated to the eighth.

The only other thing I need say here is that I wish to acknowledge my debt to the German translators, particularly to the great Philonic scholar, I. Heinemann, whose version of three out of these four treatises and still more the notes appended to them have given me valuable help. I have not always felt able to accept his conclusions and differ from him occasionally as to the meaning of particular sentences and phrases. But I have generally, if not always, recorded these cases, so that scholars will be able to judge between us. His more recent work *Philons griechische und jüdische Bildung*[a] has also

[a] Referred to in the notes as *Bildung*.

proved very useful. I will also note Prof. E. R. Goodenough's *Jewish Jurisprudence in Egypt*, and if I seem to mention it to express disagreement more often than agreement, this does not detract from what I owe to his fresh and illuminating way of treating the many problems which these treatises suggest.

F. H. C.

CAMBRIDGE, *January* 1937.

GENERAL INTRODUCTION

The last volume carried us through the introductory part of the Exposition of the Laws, namely that in which Philo set before his readers the picture of Moses and his predecessors as living embodiments of the laws. In this volume we pass on to the laws themselves. Inevitably he begins with the Ten Commandments, which being given directly by God himself are to be regarded as the general heads under which the specific enactments given through Moses are to be grouped. While he practically accepts our division of the Ten into duty towards God and duty towards our neighbour, he does not divide them into four and six, but, led perhaps by his love of numerical symmetry, into two sets of five, the place of the Fifth in the first group being justified by the close analogy of parenthood to the creative work of God.

The first of the four treatises in this volume, the *De Decalogo*, apart from some preliminary considerations about the theophany on Sinai and a short sketch at the end of the system to be followed in the subsequent treatises, deals with the Ten in their literal meaning. He now passes on to the Special Laws. In all four books the treatment of each commandment begins with a dissertation on the commandment itself in its literal sense, similar to, though fuller than, that in the *De Decalogo,* and then proceeds to a discussion of the particular enactments which he thinks may be set under it. Thus in Book I, which takes the First and Second Commandments, this preliminary dissertation is followed by an account of the regulations about the priests, the sacrifices of various kinds and as appointed for the various feasts and the moral condition required of the sacrificers. As all these are concerned with the right method of worshipping God he considers that they are bound up in the commandment " Thou shalt have none other God but me."

The second Book covers all laws which can be assigned to the next three Commandments. Under the Third come all regulations about oaths and vows ; under the Fourth a very wide assortment of subjects. Philo has to some extent already dealt with the other holydays besides the Sabbath, when he enumerated the sacrifices offered at each, but he now returns to them, not so much as we might expect because the Sabbath is only the chief holyday, but because seven is a sacred number and the feasts are either for seven days or for one which is mystically identified with seven. On the same principle the sabbatical year and the year of Jubile, though social rather than religious ordinances, are here included. Under the Fifth, which is briefly treated, we have apart from the duties of parents and children to each other little more than the duty of paying respect to age in general.

Book III carries on with the Sixth and Seventh Commandments. It discusses many enactments which deal with sexual irregularities and crimes of violence. In Book IV regulations dealing with various forms of dishonesty come under the Eighth Commandment, and minor regulations as to witnesses and just judgement under the Ninth. In dealing with the Tenth, Philo, taking οὐκ ἐπιθυμήσεις to apply to desire in general, reads into it the duty of controlling the appetites and thus finds an opportunity for discussing the Pentateuchal food laws. At this point (iv. 132)[a] he recognizes that there are various precepts and enactments which cannot properly be assigned to any of the Ten but are implied by them all, and in consequence we have here what seems practically a new scheme. The laws in the succeeding part of the Exposition are classified according to the virtues, justice, courage, humanity, etc., which they may severally be said to promote. The last part of Book IV discusses justice in this sense and is followed by a treatise or rather a set of minor treatises bearing the title *De Virtutibus* and this again is supplemented by another (*De Praemiis*), well described as an epilogue, on rewards and penalties there laid down, with another perhaps entirely separate on blessings and cursings. As all these belong to the next volume I need not say more about them here.

It seems to me that on the whole Philo reports with fairness and accuracy the laws which he discusses. They are only a selection and it is not, I think, possible to find any principle on which the selection is based. There is, of course, a great amount of interpretation and justification and in this it will be found that he is influenced by Greek and Roman Law in the same way that he is influenced by Greek Philosophy in the Commentary. In the same way but not to the same extent; for though he was well read in Demosthenes

[a] In fact if it were not for long established tradition the natural arrangement would be to end Book IV here and join the rest of the book with the *De Virtutibus*.

and very probably had a fair knowledge of Attic Law in general, he was not a jurist in the same sense that he was a philosopher. In his statements of the laws themselves there are several cases where either the whole law or some detail in it has no direct scriptural warrant, but many, if not most, of these are reasonable deductions from what is to be found in Scripture [a] and indeed he says this himself of some of these deductions.[b] Sometimes a scriptural law is applied to contemporary circumstances,[c] sometimes a non-scriptural detail is derived from contemporary practice or his own observation,[d] sometimes perhaps he has misinterpreted his text,[e] and sometimes his memory has gone astray,[f] but these last are quite exceptional.[g]

In the first section of the *De Decalogo* Philo promises that if any allegorical meaning should

[a] *e.g.* i. 235, ii. 128, 252, iii. 64, 147 f.

[b] *i.e.* with the phrase "Moses forbade from afar" (πόρρωθεν). See note on iii. 63.

[c] ii. 82, iii. 72.

[d] *e.g.* much of what he says of the temple, i. 71 ff., 166, ii. 175.

[e] iii. 86, 140, 150.

[f] i. 72, iii. 82, 205.

[g] Here may be mentioned Prof. Goodenough's thesis elaborated in his *Jewish Jurisprudence in Egypt*. He believes that "the laws as expounded by Philo are the law of the Jewish courts in Alexandria" and "that what Philo is doing throughout is to rephrase the prescriptions of the Terah, reinterpret them, or even alter them or deny them in a literal sense altogether, so that in the end Jewish law resembles now a law of Rome, now one of Greece, or again one of the few laws we still have from Alexandria" (pp. 13, 14). He sustains this view with a wealth of references to, and citations from, a number of modern as well as ancient authorities, with which I am not really competent to cope. And, when I say that he does not seem to me to prove his point, I do not wish to speak dogmatically. My main criticisms may be put as follows: First, it does not seem to me that we know enough either of the limits of jurisdiction allowed to the Jews in Alexandria, or how they administered what they had, to determine

appear to underlie the laws he discusses he will not fail to state it. The promise is only partially fulfilled. As a matter of fact allegory is almost entirely absent from the *De Dec.*[a] itself and only appears occasionally in the civil or social laws of the *Spec. Leg.*[b] though many of these have been allegorized at length in the Commentary.[c] Here again I cannot see any clear principle on which some particular laws are chosen for such treatment. On the other hand, when he is dealing with the sacrifices in Book I and the feasts in Book II allegory or rather symbolism is almost universal. Naturally enough. For both sacrifices and feasts have little meaning for him except the spiritual.

whether, when Philo departs from the substance of the Terah, he is adjusting it to what was administered or to what he himself thought reasonable. Secondly, that Prof. Goodenough much exaggerates, if not the "rephrasing and reinterpretation," at any rate the "alterations and denials." So that after reading and re-reading the book and with full acknowledgement of the useful and illuminating remarks in which it abounds, I adhere to my view that, with the reservations mentioned above, Philo gives a fair and accurate account of the laws which he discusses.

[a] See, however, § 49.

[b] *Sp. Leg.* i. 8 ff., 327 ff., ii. 29 ff., iii. 178 ff.

[c] Two notable examples are Deut. xxi. 18-21, the stoning of the disobedient son, the allegorical sermon on which occupies a large part of *De Ebr.*, and *ib.* 15-17, the right of the firstborn son of the discarded wife, which is the text for the long allegory in *De Sac.* 19 ff., and again in *De Sob.* 21. These two are treated literally without any hint of allegory in *Sp. Leg.* ii. 232 f. and 135 f. respectively. Still more remarkable is Philo's treatment of Deut. xx. 5-7 (exemption of the newly-married etc. from military service). In *De Agr.* 149 an allegory is suggested on the grounds that the sense of the exemption taken literally is at least doubtful (157). In *De Virt.* 27 ff. it is extolled as a wise measure. A similar inconsistency in dealing with "till the death of the high priest" (Num. xxxv. 28) is pointed out in the note to *Sp. Leg.* iii. 131 (App. p. 638).

What is the purpose of the Exposition? I think it is best expressed in the words of *De Vita Mosis* ii. 44, where he says that if the Jewish people prospered better each nation would abandon its ancestral customs and turn to honouring their laws alone and that these would darken the light of the others as the risen sun darkens the stars. That is to say, by this exposition he wishes to show the world at large how admirable is the Pentateuchal code, and if this is so, the natural answer to the question for whom was the Exposition written will be, primarily at any rate, for Gentiles. In the introduction to the preceding volume I noted characteristics in the treatises on Abraham and Joseph which pointed that way, and nothing in this volume seems to me to imply the contrary,[a] while in his insistence on the duty of honouring and welcoming proselytes and on the universal priesthood of the Jewish race we may see positive signs of a desire to interest and conciliate Gentile readers. It is true that the epilogue, the *De Praemiis*, seems to be addressed mainly to the Jews, but if we expand "primarily for Gentiles" by the addition "and also for Jews though not of the type which delighted in the tortuous meditations of the Commentary," it will probably satisfy the facts. It is quite in accordance with Philo's perpetually shifting mentality that he should have at one moment the first, at another the second class of readers in view.

The impression which the Exposition leaves is by no means uniform. We may naturally be revolted by the ferocity with which he supports the severer

[a] I agree with Goodenough (*Harvard Theological Review*, Apr. 1933, pp. 110 ff.) against Massebieau that such phrases as "Our Nation" (*De Dec.* 1) have no bearing on the question.

sentences of the Pentateuch and sometimes goes beyond it. On the other hand we may well admire the fine liberal spirit shown in the emphasis which he lays on the humaner side of the code and in his constant plea for kindness to the poor, the helpless and the stranger. And the spirituality with which he interprets the baldness of the Levitical ritual, fanciful though it be, does something to illuminate what is the least readable and the least read part of the Old Testament.

Note on the Text

While the ms. authority for *De Dec.* and *Sp. Leg.* iii. is fairly plentiful, something has to be said about the other two treatises in this volume. The somewhat meagre evidence for the text of *Sp. Leg.* i. has received in recent years an important addition by the discovery of a palimpsest which Cohn calls R.[a] The Philo text of this is said to date probably from the 9th century. At a later time there were written across it some commentaries on Aristotle, which sometimes make the original hand hard to read ; so

[a] R as we have it contains also *De Vita Mosis* ii. from § 71-end and the whole of *De Dec.* But as it only came to Cohn's knowledge between the publication in 1902 of his vol. iv (which includes these two treatises), and the publication of vol. v in 1906, while it is regularly cited in the App. Crit. to *Sp. Leg.* i. and ii., it is not so with the App. of the two earlier treatises. In his account of the manuscript in *Sitzungsberichte der kön. preuss. Ak. der Wissenschaften*, 1905, pp. 36 ff. he cites some of its readings in *De Dec.* with approval, most of which I have mentioned in my textual notes, but considers it to be of much less value in that treatise, and still more in *De Vit. Mos.*, than in *Sp. Leg.* Some words, however, suggest that he did not give it the same careful scrutiny in the books which he had already edited as in those which he had still to publish.

that "R, ut videtur" occasionally appears in Cohn's App. Crit. He regards it as of special value, though unfortunately it comes to an end at ii. 95.[a]

The state of the text in Book II is a more complicated matter, and though some of the information here given will be found in the notes, it may be well to supply it more fully here.

The Editio Princeps of Philo contained merely the part dealing with the Third Commandment (§§ 1-38). The Fourth Commandment down to § 214 was added by Hoeschel in 1614. But Hoeschel had MSS. of Philo to hand only for the first part of this, namely down to the end of § 123. From this point he relied on MSS. of Nicetas Serranus, Archbishop of Heraclea,[b] which in the absence of any codex of Philo himself he believed to be the genuine text. These, however, did not include the sections on the law of inheritance (§§ 124-139), nor the conclusion of the Fourth Commandment (the Basket Rite) (§§ 215-223), while the Fifth Commandment section and the concluding remarks were absent altogether.[c]

In the parts which they cover the excerpts supply a considerably abridged[d] version, with a certain

[a] It should also be noted that §§ 177-193 of *Sp. Leg.* i. were absent from the MSS. to which Mangey had access. The result is that in the marginal references in this edition to Mangey's paging p. 240 is not followed by p. 241 till after nine pages of my text instead of after the normal two.

[b] I have no information as to his date. I must apologize for having called him Nicetes in Vol. iii. p. 511 and elsewhere.

[c] Nicetas's excerpts are part of a commentary on St. Luke, this particular set being quoted on ch. xxi. 1 "Now the feast of unleavened bread drew nigh which is called the Passover."

[d] The extent of the abridging may be easily seen from the marginal references to Mangey's pages. A rough calculation will shew that something like half the full text has been omitted in §§ 140-214.

amount of variation. Hoeschel's text was adopted by Mangey and continued to be accepted till 1818, when another manuscript (called M) came to light, containing the full text of the whole book.[a] The total result is that for more than half of the book we have either M alone or at the best M with Nicetas's abridgement.[b]

A few words must be added on the tiresome subject of the traditional divisions, especially in Book I. Here the MS. Headings at different points translated as *De Circumcisione*, *De Monarchia*, etc., are sensible enough, if regarded as indicating the main divisions of the book. But if taken as introducing separate treatises, as they are in Mangey's edition and Yonge's translation, they are misleading in that they disguise the fact that the whole book[c] is a systematic dissertation on the laws which fall under the two first commandments. Unfortunately they are too often used for reference in fairly recent works to be completely ignored.

In Book II the separation of the Third, Fourth and Fifth Commandments is justifiable. But the divisions of the Fourth, as they appear in the MSS., are quite unnecessary. They are disregarded in Cohn's head-

[a] According to Cohn a complete edition of the book from the MSS. was first published by Tischendorf in 1868. Yonge, however, translated "the Basket" and "Honouring parents" in 1855 from what he calls " Schwichest's edition."

[b] M is called a corrupt manuscript by Cohn. But judging from the emendations recorded its text is far purer than that of *De Post.* and *De Som.* ii., where also we have to rely on a single codex.

[c] With the exception of the first 11 sections on circumcision which Philo does not claim to come under a particular commandment.

ings of the pages and partially[a] in his numeration of chapters.

In Book III the headings and divisions need not trouble us, though I have indicated them in the textual notes. They are really quite useless, being introduced at haphazard and rarely applying to more than a few sections of the matter they might be expected to cover. Fortunately Mangey ignores them in the heading of his pages and Cohn also, as well as in his numeration of chapters, though both insert them in the body of the text. It surely cannot be supposed that they, or indeed any of these headings, are due to Philo himself.

[a] See below.

Cohn's Numeration of Chapters—The Special Laws I.

The point at which each fresh numeration begins is indicated in the notes, but to facilitate reference a summary is here appended.

Cohn		This Translation
De Circumcisione . . .	I.-II.	I.-II.
De Monarchia . . .	I.-IX.	III.-XI.
De Templo and De Sacerdotibus	I.-XV.	XII.-XXVI.
(In Mangey called De Monarchia II.)		
De Sacerdotum honoribus .	I.-VI.	XXVII.-XXXII.
De Victimis	I.-XV.	XXXIII.-XLVII.
De Sacrificantibus . . .	I.-XVI.	XLVIII.-LXIII.

Numeration of Chapters—The Special Laws II.

Cohn		This translation
The Third Commandment (No special heading)	I.-IX.	I.-IX.
De Septenario . . .	I.-XXIV.	X.-XXXIII.
The Basket Rite . . (No special heading)	I.-IV.	XXXIV.-XXXVII.
De parentibus colendis	I.-XI	XXXVIII.-XLVIII.

LIST OF PHILO'S WORKS

SHOWING THEIR DIVISION INTO VOLUMES IN THIS EDITION

VOLUME

I. On the Creation (De Opificio Mundi)
Allegorical Interpretation (Legum Allegoriae)

II. On the Cherubim (De Cherubim)
On the Sacrifices of Abel and Cain (De Sacrificiis Abelis et Caini)
The Worse attacks the Better (Quod Deterius Potiori insidiari solet)
On the Posterity and Exile of Cain (De Posteritate Caini)
On the Giants (De Gigantibus)

III. On the Unchangeableness of God (Quod Deus immutabilis sit)
On Husbandry (De Agricultura)
On Noah's Work as a Planter (De Plantatione)
On Drunkenness (De Ebrietate)
On Sobriety (De Sobrietate)

IV. On the Confusion of Tongues (De Confusione Linguarum)
On the Migration of Abraham (De Migratione Abrahami)
Who is the Heir (Quis Rerum Divinarum Heres)
On the Preliminary Studies (De Congressu quaerendae Eruditionis gratia)

V. On Flight and Finding (De Fuga et Inventione)
On the Change of Names (De Mutatione Nominum)
On Dreams (De Somniis)

VI. On Abraham (De Abrahamo)
On Joseph (De Iosepho)
Moses (De Vita Mosis)

LIST OF PHILO'S WORKS

[1] Only two fragments extant.
[2] Extant only in an Armenian version.

THE DECALOGUE
(DE DECALOGO)

INTRODUCTION TO *DE DECALOGO*

The first part of this treatise deals with some questions raised by the law-giving on Sinai. First, why was it given in the desert? Four reasons are suggested: (*a*) because of the vanity and idolatry rampant in cities (2-9), (*b*) because solitude promotes repentance (10-13), (*c*) because it was well that laws needed for civic life should begin before the era of that life began (14), (*d*) that the divine origin of the laws should be attested by the miraculous supply of food in the barren wilderness (15-17). Secondly, observing that the Commandments given by God Himself were ten, we ask why that number, and the answer is given by a disquisition on its perfection as a number (18-31). Thirdly, what was the nature of the voice which announced the commandments?—not God's, for He is not a man, but an invisible kind of speech created for the occasion (32-35). Fourthly, why was the singular number "thou" used? (*a*) Because it emphasizes the value of the individual soul (36-38), (*b*) the personal appeal better secures obedience (39), (*c*) it is a lesson to the great not to despise the humblest (40-44). This part concludes with some words on the grandeur of the scene, particularly the fire from which the voice issued (45-49).

Coming to the Commandments themselves, after noting that they divide into two sets of five (50-51), we pass to the First. Polytheism is denounced, particularly as taking the form of worship given to the elements or heavenly bodies (52-65). Worse than this is the worship of lifeless images forbidden by the Second Commandment. Its absurdity is exposed (66-76) and with it the worse absurdity of Egyptian animal-worship (77-81). The Third Commandment is taken as forbidding principally perjury (82-91), but also reckless swearing (92-95). The Fourth teaches us to set apart a time for philosophy as opposed to practical life (96-101), and reasons are given for the sanctity of seven and the seventh day in particular (102-105). The Fifth stands on the border-line, because parenthood assimilates man to God and to dishonour parents is to dishonour God (106-111). Children owe all to their parents, and in the duty of repaying kindness they may take a lesson from the lower animals (112-120).

The second set of five opens with the prohibition of Adultery (121). Adultery is denounced as (*a*) voluptuous (122), (*b*) involving the sin of another (123-124), (*c*) destructive of family ties (125-127), (*d*) cruel to the children (128-131). The second of the set forbids murder as both unnatural and sacrilegious, since man is the most sacred of God's possessions (132-134). Stealing is forbidden by the third, because theft on the smallest scale may develop into wholesale robbery and usurpation (135-137). The fourth forbids false witness, as opposed in itself to truth and justice, and also in law-courts causing judges to give wrong verdicts and thus break their own oaths (138-141). The last Commandment against " desire " gives Philo an opportunity of discoursing in Stoical terms on the four passions, pleasure, grief, fear, desire, of which the last is the deadliest (142-153).

Sections 154-175 are really a rough synopsis of Books II., III., and IV. 1-131, shewing the nature of the particular laws which will be placed under each commandment. And the concluding sections 176-178 justify the absence of any penalties attached to the commandments on the grounds that God who is the cause of good leaves the punishment for transgression to his subordinates.

ΠΕΡΙ ΤΩΝ ΔΕΚΑ ΛΟΓΩΝ
ΟΙ ΚΕΦΑΛΑΙΑ ΝΟΜΩΝ ΕΙΣΙΝ

[180] 1 I. Τοὺς βίους τῶν κατὰ Μωυσέα σοφῶν ἀνδρῶν,
οὓς ἀρχηγέτας τοῦ ἡμετέρου ἔθνους καὶ νόμους
ἀγράφους αἱ ἱεραὶ βίβλοι δηλοῦσιν, ἐν ταῖς προτέραις συντάξεσι μεμηνυκὼς κατὰ τὰ ἀκόλουθα
ἑξῆς τῶν ἀναγραφέντων νόμων τὰς ἰδέας ἀκριβώσω
μηδ᾽, εἴ τις ὑποφαίνοιτο τρόπος ἀλληγορίας, τοῦτον
παρεὶς ἕνεκα τῆς πρὸς διάνοιαν φιλομαθοῦς ἐπιστήμης, ἣ πρὸ τῶν ἐμφανῶν ἔθος τὰ ἀφανῆ ζητεῖν.
2 Πρὸς δὲ τοὺς ἀποροῦντας, τί δή ποτε οὐκ ἐν
πόλεσιν ἀλλ᾽ ἐν ἐρήμῳ βαθείᾳ τοὺς νόμους ἐτίθει,
λεκτέον πρῶτον μέν, ὅτι αἱ πολλαὶ τῶν πόλεων
[181] ἀμυθήτων κακῶν εἰσι | μεσταί, καὶ τῶν πρὸς τὸ
θεῖον ἀνοσιουργημάτων καὶ τῶν πρὸς ἀλλήλους
3 ἀδικημάτων. οὐδὲν γάρ ἐστιν ὃ μὴ κεκιβδήλευται,
τὰ γνήσια τῶν νόθων παρευημερούντων καὶ τἀληθῆ
τῶν εἰκότων, ἃ φύσει μὲν κατέψευσται, πιθανῶς
4 δ᾽ ὑποβάλλει φαντασίας πρὸς ἀπάτην. ἐν πόλεσιν
οὖν καὶ ὁ πάντων ἐπιβουλότατος φύεται τῦφος, ὃν
τινες τεθήπασι καὶ προσκυνοῦσι τὰς κενὰς δόξας
σεμνοποιοῦντες διὰ χρυσῶν στεφάνων καὶ ἁλουρ-

---

[a] See General Introduction to Vol. VI. pp. ix. f.

[b] See General Introduction to this volume, p. xiii.

[c] Lit. "On account of studious knowledge tending to under-

THE DECALOGUE

I. Having related in the preceding treatises the 1
lives of those whom Moses judged to be men of wisdom, who are set before us in the Sacred Books as founders of our nation and in themselves unwritten laws,[a] I shall now proceed in due course to give full descriptions of the written laws. And if some allegorical interpretation should appear to underlie them, I shall not fail to state it.[b] For knowledge loves to learn and advance to full understanding [c] and its way is to seek the hidden meaning rather than the obvious.

To the question why he promulgated his laws in 2
the depths of the desert instead of in cities we may answer in the first place that most cities are full of countless evils, both acts of impiety towards God and wrongdoing between man and man. For every- 3
thing is debased, the genuine overpowered by the spurious, the true by the specious, which is intrinsically false but creates impressions whose plausibility serves but to delude. So too in cities there arises 4
that most insidious of foes, Pride,[d] admired and worshipped by some who add dignity to vain ideas [e] by means of gold crowns and purple robes and a

standing." I cannot think that the text is right. For further discussion and attempts to emend it see App. p. 609.

[d] Or "vanity." [e] Or "opinions."

γίδων καὶ πλήθους θεραπόντων καὶ ὀχημάτων,
ἐφ᾽ ὧν οἱ λεγόμενοι μακάριοι καὶ εὐδαίμονες
μετέωροι φέρονται, τοτὲ μὲν ὀρεῖς ἢ ἵππους
καταζευγνύντες τοτὲ δὲ καὶ ἀνθρώπους, οἳ τὰ
φορεῖα κατὰ τῶν αὐχένων ἀχθοφοροῦσι τὴν ψυχὴν
πρὸ τοῦ σώματος δι᾽ ὑπερβολὴν ὕβρεως πιεζόμενοι.
5 II. τῦφος καὶ πολλῶν ἄλλων κακῶν δημιουργός
ἐστιν, ἀλαζονείας, ὑπεροψίας, ἀνισότητος[1]· αἱ δ᾽
εἰσὶν ἀρχαὶ ξενικῶν καὶ ἐμφυλίων πολέμων οὐδὲν
μέρος, οὐ κοινόν, οὐκ ἴδιον, οὐ κατὰ γῆν, οὐ κατὰ
6 θάλατταν, ἡσυχάζειν ἐῶσαι. τί δὲ δεῖ
τῶν πρὸς ἀλλήλους ἁμαρτημάτων μεμνῆσθαι;
τύφῳ γὰρ καὶ τὰ θεῖα ἐξωλιγώρηται, καίτοι
νομιζόμενα τῆς ἀνωτάτω τυγχάνειν τιμῆς· τιμὴ
δὲ τίς ἂν γένοιτο, μὴ προσούσης ἀληθείας, ἣ καὶ
ὄνομα καὶ ἔργον ἔχει τίμιον, ἐπεὶ καὶ τὸ ψεῦδος
7 ἔμπαλιν ἄτιμον φύσει; ἡ δ᾽ ὀλιγωρία τῶν θείων
ἐμφανὴς τοῖς ὀξυδερκέστερον ὁρῶσι· μυρίας γὰρ
ὅσας διὰ γραφικῆς καὶ πλαστικῆς μορφώσαντες
ἰδέας ἱερὰ καὶ νεὼς αὐταῖς προσπεριεβάλοντο καὶ
βωμοὺς κατασκευάσαντες ἀγάλμασι καὶ ξοάνοις
καὶ τοιουτοτρόποις ἀφιδρύμασι τιμὰς ἰσολυμπίους
8 καὶ ἰσοθέους ἀπένειμαν, ἅπασιν ἀψύχοις. οὓς
εὐθυβόλως αἱ ἱεραὶ γραφαὶ τοῖς ἐκ πόρνης γεγονόσιν ἀπεικάζουσιν· ὡς γὰρ οὗτοι πάντας, ὅσους
ἐραστὰς ἔσχεν ἡ μήτηρ, ἐπιγράφονται πατέρας
ἑνὸς ἀγνοίᾳ τοῦ φύσει, οὕτω καὶ οἱ κατὰ πόλεις
οὐκ εἰδότες τὸν ὄντα ὄντως ἀληθῆ θεὸν μυρία
9 πλήθη ψευδωνύμων ἐκτεθειώκασιν. εἶτ᾽ ἄλλων
παρ᾽ ἄλλοις τιμωμένων, ἡ περὶ τοῦ ἀρίστου κρα-

great establishment of servants and cars, on which
these so-called blissful and happy people ride aloft,
drawn sometimes by mules and horses, sometimes
by men, who bear the heavy burden on their
shoulders, yet suffer in soul rather than in body
under the weight of extravagant arrogance. II.
Pride is also the creator of many other evils, 5
boastfulness, haughtiness, inequality, and these are
the sources of wars, both civil and foreign, suffering
no place to remain in peace whether public or private,
whether on sea or on land. Yet why 6
dwell on offences between man and man? Pride also
brings divine things into utter contempt, even though
they are supposed to receive the highest honours.
But what honour can there be if truth be not there
as well, truth honourable both in name and function,
just as falsehood is naturally dishonourable? This 7
contempt for things divine is manifest to those of
keener vision. For men have employed sculpture
and painting to fashion innumerable forms which they
have enclosed in shrines and temples and after building altars have assigned celestial and divine honours
to idols of stone and wood and suchlike images, all
of them lifeless things. Such persons are happily 8
compared in the sacred Scriptures to the children of
a harlot[a]; for as they in their ignorance of their one
natural father ascribe their paternity to all their
mother's lovers, so too throughout the cities those
who do not know the true, the really existent God
have deified hosts of others who are falsely so called.
Then as some honour one, some another god, diver- 9

[a] See note on *Spec. Leg.* i. 332.

[1] S ɔ R: other MSS. ἀνοσιότητος.

τήσασα διχόνοια καὶ τὰς πρὸς τὰ ἄλλα πάντα
διαφορὰς ἐγέννησεν. εἰς ἃ πρῶτον ἀπιδὼν ἔξω
πόλεων[1] ἐβουλήθη νομοθετεῖν.

10 Ἐνενόει δὲ κἀκεῖνο δεύτερον, ὅτι τοῦ μέλλοντος
ἱεροὺς νόμους παραδέχεσθαι τὴν ψυχὴν ἀναγκαῖόν
ἐστιν ἀπορρύψασθαι καὶ ἐκκαθήρασθαι τὰς | δυσ-
[182] εκπλύτους κηλῖδας, ἃς μιγάδων καὶ συγκλύδων
ὄχλος ἀνθρώπων κατὰ πόλεις προσετρίψατο. τοῦτο
11 δὲ ἀμήχανον ἑτέρως ἢ διοικισθέντι συμβῆναι, καὶ
οὐκ εὐθὺς ἀλλὰ μακρῷ χρόνῳ ὕστερον, ἕως ἂν
οἱ τῶν ἀρχαίων παρανομημάτων ἐνσφραγισθέντες
τύποι κατὰ μικρὸν ἀμαυρούμενοι καὶ ἀπορρέοντες
12 ἀφανισθῶσι. τοῦτον τὸν τρόπον καὶ οἱ τὴν ἰατρικὴν
ἀγαθοὶ σῴζουσι τοὺς κάμνοντας· οὐ γὰρ πρότερον
σιτία καὶ ποτὰ παρέχειν ἀξιοῦσι, πρὶν ἢ τὰ τῶν
νόσων αἴτια ὑπεξελέσθαι· μενόντων γὰρ ἀνωφελεῖς
αἱ τροφαί, ἀλλὰ καὶ ἐπιζήμιοι, ὗλαι γινόμεναι τοῦ
13 πάθους. III. εἰκότως οὖν ἐκ τῶν κατὰ πόλεις
βλαβερωτάτων συνηθειῶν εἰς ἐρήμην ἀπαγαγών,
ἵνα κενώσῃ τὰς ψυχὰς ἀδικημάτων, ἤρξατο προσφέρειν ταῖς διανοίαις τροφάς· αὗται δὲ τίνες ἂν
εἶεν ὅτι μὴ νόμοι καὶ λόγοι θεῖοι;

14 Τρίτη δέ ἐστιν αἰτία ἥδε· καθάπερ οἱ στελ-
λόμενοι μακρὸν πλοῦν, οὐχ ὅταν ἐπιβάντες τῆς
νεὼς ἀπὸ λιμένος ἐξαναχθῶσιν, ἄρχονται κατασκευάζειν ἱστία καὶ πηδάλια καὶ οἴακας, ἀλλ' ἔτι
μένοντες ἐπὶ γῆς ἕκαστα τῶν συντεινόντων πρὸς
πλοῦν εὐτρεπίζονται, τὸν αὐτὸν τρόπον ἠξίωσεν
οὐ λαβόντας κληρουχίας καὶ τὰς πόλεις οἰκήσαντας
τότε ζητεῖν νόμους, οἷς πολιτεύσονται, ἀλλ'
ἑτοιμασαμένους τοὺς τῆς πολιτείας κανόνας καὶ

[1] mss. πόλεως.

sity of opinion as to which was best waxed strong and engendered disputes in every other matter also. This was the primary consideration which made him prefer to legislate away from cities.

He had also a second object in mind. He who is about 10
to receive the holy laws must first cleanse his soul and purge away the deep-set stains which it has contracted through contact with the motley promiscuous
horde of men in cities. And to this he cannot attain 11
except by dwelling apart, nor that at once, but only long afterwards, and not till the marks which his old transgressions have imprinted on him have gradually
grown faint, melted away and disappeared. In this 12
way too good physicians preserve their sick folk: they think it unadvisable to give them food or drink until they have removed the causes of their maladies. While these still remain, nourishment is useless, indeed harmful, and acts as fuel to the distemper.
III. Naturally therefore he first led them away from 13
the highly mischievous associations of cities into the desert, to clear the sins out of their souls, and then began to set the nourishment before their minds—and what should this nourishment be but laws and words of God?

He had a third reason as follows: just as men 14
when setting out on a long voyage do not begin to provide sails and rudders and tillers when they have embarked and left the harbour, but equip themselves with enough of the gear needed for the voyage while they are still staying on shore, so Moses did not think it good that they should just take their portions and settle in cities and then go in quest of laws to regulate their civic life, but rather should first provide themselves with the rules for that life and gain practice

ἐνασκηθέντας οἷς ἔμελλον οἱ δῆμοι κυβερνᾶσθαι
σωτηρίως τηνικαῦτα εἰσοικίζεσθαι, χρησομένους
εὐθὺς ταῖς τῶν δικαίων παρασκευαῖς ἐν ὁμονοίᾳ
καὶ κοινωνίᾳ καὶ διανομῇ τῶν ἐπιβαλλόντων
ἑκάστοις.
15 IV. Φασὶ δέ τινες καὶ τετάρτην αἰτίαν οὐκ
ἀπῳδὸν ἀλλ᾽ ἐγγυτάτω τῆς ἀληθείας· ἐπειδὴ γὰρ
ἔδει πίστιν ἐγγενέσθαι ταῖς διανοίαις περὶ τοῦ μὴ
εὑρήματα ἀνθρώπου τοὺς νόμους ἀλλὰ θεοῦ
χρησμοὺς σαφεστάτους εἶναι, πορρωτάτω τῶν
πόλεων ἀπήγαγε τὸ ἔθνος εἰς ἐρήμην βαθεῖαν καὶ
ἄγονον οὐ μόνον ἡμέρων καρπῶν ἀλλὰ καὶ ποτίμου
16 ὕδατος, ἵν᾽, ἐὰν ἐν σπάνει γενόμενοι τῶν ἀναγκαίων
καὶ δίψει καὶ λιμῷ διαφθαρῆναι προσδοκήσαντες
ἐξαπιναίως ἀφθονίαν τῶν ἐπιτηδείων ἀπαυτοματι-
σθέντων ἀνευρίσκωσιν, οὐρανοῦ μὲν ὕοντος τροφὰς
τὸ καλούμενον μάννα, προσόψημα δὲ τροφῶν ἀπ᾽[1]
ἀέρος ὀρτυγομήτρας φοράν, ὕδατος δὲ πικροῦ
γλυκαινομένου πρὸς τὸ πότιμον, πέτρας δὲ ἀκρο-
τόμου πηγὰς ἀνομβρούσης, μηκέτι θαυμάζωσιν,
[183] εἰ λόγια θεοῦ συμβέβηκεν | εἶναι τοὺς νόμους,
ἐναργεστάτην βάσανον εἰληφότες ἐκ τῶν χορηγιῶν,
17 ἃς ἐξ ἀπόρων ἔσχον οὐκ ἐλπίσαντες. ὁ γὰρ πρὸς
τὸ ζῆν ἀφθονίαν δοὺς καὶ τὰς πρὸς τὸ εὖ ζῆν
ἀφορμὰς ἐδωρεῖτο· πρὸς μὲν οὖν τὸ ζῆν σιτίων
ἔδει καὶ ποτῶν, ἅπερ ἀνεύρισκον οὐχ ἑτοιμασάμενοι,

[1] So MSS. and Cohn. But I should prefer with Mangey to omit ἀπ᾽. I do not know of any case in which οὐρανός includes the lower air, as the text implies, while on the other hand the index gives thirteen examples where heaven, air, water, earth are named as the four parts of the universe. See *Spec. Leg.* iii. 111, and *cf. ibid.* 152. With ἀπ᾽ omitted each of the four makes its contribution, earth being given by πέτρας.

in all that would surely enable the communities to steer their course in safety, and then settle down to follow from the first the principles of justice lying ready for their use, in harmony and fellowship of spirit and rendering to every man his due.

IV. Some too give a fourth reason which is not out 15
of keeping with the truth but agrees very closely with it. As it was necessary to establish a belief in their minds that the laws were not the inventions of a man but quite clearly the oracles of God, he led the nation a great distance away from cities into the depths of a desert, barren not only of cultivated fruits
but also of water fit for drinking, in order that, 16
if after lacking the necessaries of life and expecting to perish from hunger and thirst they suddenly found abundance of sustenance self-produced—when heaven rained the food called manna and the shower of quails from the air to add relish to their food—when the bitter water grew sweet and fit for drinking and springs gushed out of the steep[a] rock—they should no longer wonder whether the laws were actually the pronouncements of God, since they had been given the clearest evidence of the truth in the supplies which they had so unexpectedly received in their
destitution. For He who gave abundance of the means 17
of life also bestowed the wherewithal of a good life; for mere life they needed food and drink which they found without making provision; for the good life

[a] Or "hard," "flinty." Here, as in *Mos.* i. 210-211, Philo does not stress the connexion of the word (taken from Deut. viii. 15), with ἀκρός as he does elsewhere. See note on *Mos.* i. 210. The events alluded to are found in Ex. xv. and xvi.

πρὸς δὲ τὸ εὖ ζῆν νόμων καὶ διαταγμάτων, οἷς
βελτιοῦσθαι τὰς ψυχὰς ἔμελλον.
18 V. Αἵδ᾿ εἰσὶν ἐν στοχασμοῖς εἰκόσιν αἰτίαι λεγόμεναι περὶ τοῦ διαπορηθέντος· τὰς γὰρ ἀληθεῖς
οἶδεν ὁ θεὸς μόνος. εἰπὼν δ᾿ ἅπερ ἥρμοττε περὶ
τούτων ἑξῆς αὐτοὺς ἀκριβώσω τοὺς νόμους, ἐκεῖνο
κατὰ τὸ ἀναγκαῖον προμηνύσας, ὅτι τῶν νόμων
οὓς μὲν αὐτὸς ὁ θεὸς οὐ προσχρησάμενος ἄλλῳ δι᾿
ἑαυτοῦ μόνου θεσπίζειν ἠξίωσεν, οὓς δὲ διὰ προφήτου Μωυσέως, ὃν ἀριστίνδην ἐκ πάντων ὡς ἐπι-
19 τηδειότατον ἱεροφάντην ἐπελέξατο. τοὺς
μὲν οὖν αὐτοπροσώπως θεσπισθέντας δι᾿ αὐτοῦ
μόνου συμβέβηκε καὶ νόμους εἶναι καὶ νόμων
τῶν ἐν μέρει κεφάλαια, τοὺς δὲ διὰ τοῦ προ-
20 φήτου πάντας ἐπ᾿ ἐκείνους ἀναφέρεσθαι. VI. λέξω
δ᾿, ὡς ἂν οἷός τε ὦ, περὶ ἑκατέρων καὶ πρό-
τερόν γε τῶν κεφαλαιωδεστέρων· ὧν
εὐθέως ἄξιον θαυμάσαι τὸν ἀριθμὸν δεκάδι τῇ
παντελείᾳ περατουμένων, ἣ πάσας μὲν ἀριθμῶν
διαφορὰς ἀρτίων καὶ περιττῶν καὶ ἀρτιοπερίττων,
ἀρτίων μὲν δυοῖν, περιττῶν δὲ τριῶν, ἀρτιοπερίττων δὲ ἕξ,[1] πάσας δὲ λόγων τῶν ἐν ἀριθμοῖς πολυ-
πλασίων καὶ ἐπιμερῶν καὶ ὑποεπιμερῶν περιέχει,
21 πάσας δ᾿ ἀναλογίας, τήν τε ἀριθμητικήν, ἣ τῷ

[1] MSS. πέντε and so Cohn by an oversight afterwards corrected in a note to Treitel's translation. This must be a mistake of the scribe. Philo could not possibly have made it; *cf. Spec. Leg.* ii. 58, and the more elaborate explanation of the even-odds in *De Op.* 13.

they needed laws and ordinances which would bring improvement to their souls.

V. These are the reasons suggested to answer the 18
question under discussion: they are but probable surmises; the true reasons are know to God alone. Having said what was fitting on this subject, I will proceed to describe the laws themselves in order, with this necessary statement by way of introduction, that some of them God judged fit to deliver in His own person alone without employing any other, and some through His prophet Moses whom He chose as of all men the best suited to be the revealer
of verities. Now we find that those which 19
He gave in His own person and by His own mouth alone include both laws and heads summarizing the particular laws, but those in which He spoke through the
prophet all belong to the former class. VI. I will 20
deal with both to the best of my ability, taking those which are rather of the nature of summaries first. Here our admiration is at once aroused by their number, which is neither more nor less than is the supremely perfect,[a] Ten. Ten contains all different kinds of numbers,[b] even as 2, odd as 3, and even-odd as 6, and all ratios, whether of a number to its multiples or fractional, when a number is either increased or diminished by some part of itself.[c]
So too it contains all the analogies or progressions, the 21
arithmetical where each term in the series is greater

[a] For the Pythagorean origin of the term παντέλεια as applied to ten see note on *De Abr.* 244.

[b] This does not seem to mean more than that all the properties and mysteries of numbers must necessarily fall within the decimal system, for "round ten as a turning-point the unlimited series of numbers wheel and retrace their steps," *De Op.* 47.

[c] *i.e.* improper or proper fractions.

ἰσαρίθμῳ ὑπερέχει καὶ ὑπερέχεται, οἷον ἐπὶ τοῦ ἓν
καὶ δύο καὶ τρία, καὶ τὴν γεωμετρικήν, καθ' ἣν
οἷος ὁ λόγος πρὸς τὸν πρῶτον τοῦ δευτέρου, τοιοῦτος καὶ ὁ πρὸς τὸν δεύτερον τοῦ τρίτου, ὡς ἔχει
ἐπὶ τοῦ ἓν καὶ δύο καὶ τέσσαρα, ἔν τε διπλασίοις
καὶ τριπλασίοις καὶ συνόλως πολυπλασίοις καὶ
πάλιν ἐν ἡμιολίοις καὶ ἐπιτρίτοις καὶ τοῖς παραπλησίοις, ἔτι μέντοι καὶ τὴν ἁρμονικήν, καθ' ἣν
ὁ μέσος τῶν ἄκρων τῷ ἴσῳ μορίῳ ὑπερέχει τε καὶ
ὑπερέχεται, ὡς ἔχει ἐπὶ τοῦ τρίτου καὶ τετάρτου
22 καὶ ἕκτου. περιέχει δὲ ἡ δεκὰς καὶ τὰς
τῶν τριγώνων καὶ τετραγώνων καὶ τῶν ἄλλων
πολυγώνων ἐμφαινομένας ἰδιότητας καὶ τὰς τῶν
συμφωνιῶν, τήν τε διὰ τεσσάρων ἐν ἐπιτρίτῳ
[184] λόγῳ, τῷ τέσσαρα | πρὸς τρία, καὶ τὴν διὰ πέντε ἐν
ἡμιολίῳ, τῷ τρία πρὸς δύο, καὶ τὴν διὰ πασῶν ἐν
διπλασίῳ, τῷ δύο πρὸς ἕν, καὶ τὴν δὶς διὰ πασῶν
23 ἐν τετραπλασίῳ, τῷ ὀκτὼ πρὸς δύο. παρό μοι
δοκοῦσι καὶ οἱ πρῶτοι τὰ ὀνόματα τοῖς πράγμασι
θέμενοι—σοφοὶ γὰρ ἦσαν—εἰκότως αὐτὴν προσ-
αγορεῦσαι δεκάδα, ὡσανεὶ δεχάδα οὖσαν, παρὰ τὸ
δέχεσθαι καὶ κεχωρηκέναι τὰ γένη πάντα τῶν
ἀριθμῶν καὶ λόγων τῶν κατ' ἀριθμὸν καὶ ἀνα-
λογιῶν ἁρμονιῶν τε αὖ καὶ συμφωνιῶν.
24 VII. τὴν μέντοι δεκάδα πρὸς τοῖς εἰρημένοις καὶ
διὰ ταῦτα εἰκότως ἄν τις θαυμάσειε περιέχουσαν
τήν τε ἀδιάστατον φύσιν καὶ τὴν διαστηματικήν·
ἡ μὲν οὖν ἀδιάστατος τάττεται κατὰ σημεῖον
μόνον, ἡ δὲ διαστηματικὴ κατὰ τρεῖς ἰδέας γραμμῆς
25 καὶ ἐπιφανείας καὶ στερεοῦ· τὸ μὲν γὰρ δυσὶ
σημείοις περατούμενόν ἐστι γραμμή, τὸ δ' ἐπὶ
δύο διαστατὸν ἐπιφάνεια, ῥυείσης ἐπὶ πλάτος

than the one below and less than the one above
by the same amount,[a] as for example 1 2 3 ; the geometrical where the ratio of the second to the first
term is the same as that of the third to the second,
as with 1 2 4, and this is seen whether the ratio is
double or treble or any multiple, or again fractional
as 3 to 2, 4 to 3, and the like ; once more the harmonic in which the middle term exceeds and is exceeded by the extremes on either side by the same
fraction, as is the case with 3, 4, 6.[b] Ten 22
also contains the properties observed in triangles,
quadrilaterals and other polygons, and also those of
the concords, the fourth, fifth, octave and double
octave intervals, where the ratios are respectively $1\frac{1}{3}$,
i.e. 4 : 3, $1\frac{1}{2}$, *i.e.* 3 : 2, doubled, *i.e.* 2 : 1, fourfold,
i.e. 8 : 2. Consequently it seems to me that those 23
who first gave names to things did reasonably, wise
men that they were, in giving it the name of decad,
as being the dechad, or receiver, because it receives
and has made room for every kind of number and
numerical ratio and progressions and also concords
and harmonies. VII. But indeed apart 24
from what has been said, the decad may reasonably be admired because it embraces Nature as seen
both with and without extension in space. Nature
exists without extension nowhere except in the point ;
with extension in three forms, line, surface, solid.
For space as limited by two points is a line, but, 25
where there are two dimensions, we have a surface,

[a] Lit. "which exceeds and is exceeded by the same number." See App. p. 609.

[b] See the more detailed explanation in *De Op.* 109, where the example given is that 6, 8, 12 are in harmonic progression because 8 exceeds 6 by $\frac{1}{3}$ of 6, and is exceeded by 12 by $\frac{1}{3}$ of 12. Here as often the ordinal is used for the cardinal.

γραμμῆς, τὸ δ᾿ ἐπὶ τρία στερεόν, μήκους καὶ πλάτους βάθος προσλαβόντων, ἐφ᾿ ὧν ἵσταται ἡ φύσις· πλείους γὰρ τριῶν διαστάσεις οὐκ ἐγέννησεν.
26 ἀρχέτυποι δὲ τούτων ἀριθμοὶ τοῦ μὲν ἀδιαστάτου σημείου τὸ ἕν, τῆς δὲ γραμμῆς τὰ δύο, καὶ ἐπιφανείας μὲν τρία, στερεοῦ δὲ τέσσαρα, ὧν ἡ σύνθεσις ἑνὸς καὶ δυοῖν καὶ τριῶν καὶ τεσσάρων ἀποτελεῖ δεκάδα παραφαίνουσαν τοῖς ὁρατικοῖς
27 καὶ ἕτερα κάλλη· σχεδὸν γὰρ ἡ ἀπειρία τῶν ἀριθμῶν ταύτῃ μετρεῖται, διότι οἱ συστήσαντες αὐτὴν ὅροι τέσσαρές εἰσιν, ἓν καὶ δύο καὶ τρία καὶ τέτταρα, οἱ δ᾿ ἴσοι ὅροι ἑκατοντάδα γεννῶσιν ἐκ δεκάδων—δέκα γὰρ καὶ εἴκοσι καὶ τριάκοντα καὶ τεσσαράκοντα γίνονται ἑκατόν—, ὁμοίως δὲ καὶ χιλιάδα ἐξ ἑκατοντάδων καὶ μυριάδα ἐκ χιλιάδων, μονὰς δὲ καὶ δεκὰς καὶ ἑκατοντὰς καὶ χιλιὰς
28 τέσσαρες ὅροι οἱ δεκάδα γεννῶντες· ἥτις δίχα τῶν πρόσθεν εἰρημένων καὶ ἑτέρας ἀριθμῶν ἐμφαίνει διαφοράς, τόν τε πρῶτον κόσμον, ὃς μονάδι μόνῃ μετρεῖται, οὗ παράδειγμα ὁ τρεῖς, ὁ πέντε, ὁ ἑπτά, καὶ τὸν τετράγωνον, τὸν τέσσαρα, τὸν ἰσάκις ἴσον, καὶ μὲν δὴ τὸν κύβον, τὸν ὀκτώ, ὅς ἐστιν ἰσάκις
[185] ἴσος ἰσάκις, καὶ τὸν τέλειον, τὸν ἕξ, ἰσούμενον τοῖς
29 ἑαυτοῦ μέρεσι, τρισὶ καὶ δυσὶ καὶ ἑνί. VIII. | τί δὲ δεῖ καταλέγεσθαι τὰς δεκάδος ἀρετὰς ἀπείρους τὸ πλῆθος, πάρεργον ποιουμένους ἔργον μέγιστον, ὃ καθ᾿ αὑτὸ συμβέβηκεν αὐταρκεστάτην εἶναι ὑπόθεσιν τοῖς περὶ τὰ μαθήματα διατρίβουσι;

---

[a] This seems to be the meaning, though both ὅροι and γεννάω are used in a different sense from what they have in the earlier part of the sentence, where the ὅροι generate by addition to each

as the line has expanded into breadth; where there are three, we have a solid, as length and breadth have acquired depth, and here Nature comes to a halt, for she has not produced more than three dimensions. All these have numbers for their archetypes, 26
1 for the non-extended point, 2 for the line, 3 for the surface, 4 for the solid, and these one, two, three, four added together make the ten which gives a glimpse of other beauties also to those who have eyes to see. For we may say that the infinite series 27
of numbers is measured by ten, because its constituent terms are the four, 1, 2, 3, 4, and the same terms produce the hundred out of the tens, since 10, 20, 30, 40 make a hundred, and similarly the thousand is produced out of the hundreds and the ten thousand or myriad out of the thousands, and these, the unit, the ten, the hundred and the thousand are the four starting-points from each of which springs a ten.[a]
And again, this same ten, apart from what has already 28
been said, reveals other differences in numbers; the order of prime numbers divisible by the unit alone having for its pattern three, five, seven: the square, that is four, the cube, eight, the products respectively of two and three equal numbers, and the perfect number six equal to the sum [b] of its factors 3, 2 and 1. VIII. But why enumerate the 29
virtues of Ten, which are infinite in number, and thus treat perfunctorily a task of supreme greatness which by itself is found to be an all-sufficing subject for

other. Presumably the *μυριάς* is not named as a new starting-point, because Greek has no special term for ten myriads or beyond.

[b] Or perhaps "both the product and sum," *cf. De Op.* 13. But the essence of "perfection" lies in the sum, as exemplified by 28, *cf. Mos.* ii. 84 and note.

τὰς μὲν οὖν ἄλλας ὑπερθετέον, μιᾶς δ' οὐκ ἄτοπον ἴσως ἐπιμνησθῆναι δείγματος ἕνεκα.
30 τὰς γὰρ ἐν τῇ φύσει λεγομένας κατηγορίας δέκα μόνας εἶναί φασιν οἱ ἐνδιατρίβοντες τοῖς τῆς φιλοσοφίας δόγμασιν· οὐσίαν, ποιόν, ποσόν, πρός τι, ποιεῖν, πάσχειν, ἔχειν, κεῖσθαι, τὰ ὧν οὐκ
31 ἄνευ ⟨πάντα⟩, χρόνον καὶ τόπον. οὐδὲν γάρ ἐστι τούτων ἀμέτοχον· οἷον ἐγὼ μετέχω μὲν οὐσίας δανεισάμενος ἀφ' ἑκάστου τῶν στοιχείων, ἐξ ὧν ἀπετελέσθη ὅδε ὁ κόσμος, γῆς καὶ ὕδατος καὶ ἀέρος καὶ πυρός, τὰ πρὸς τὴν ἐμὴν σύστασιν αὐταρκέστατα· μετέχω δὲ καὶ ποιότητος, καθ' ἣν ἄνθρωπός εἰμι, καὶ ποσότητος, ᾗ πηλίκος· γίνομαι δὲ καὶ πρός τι, ὅταν μου πρὸς δεξιοῖς τις ἢ πρὸς εὐωνύμοις ᾖ· ἀλλὰ καὶ ποιῶ, τρίβων τι ἢ κείρων,[1] καὶ πάσχω, κειρόμενος ἢ τριβόμενος ὑφ' ἑτέρων· κἂν τῷ ἔχειν ἐξετάζομαι, ἢ περιβεβλημένος ἢ ὡπλισμένος, κἂν τῷ κεῖσθαι, σχέδην[2] τι καθεζόμενος ἢ κατακεκλιμένος· εἰμὶ δὲ πάντως κἀν τόπῳ καὶ χρόνῳ, τῶν προειρημένων οὐδενὸς δυναμένου χωρὶς ἀμφοῖν ὑφίστασθαι.

32 IX. Ταυτὶ μὲν οὖν ἀποχρώντως λελέχθω, συνυφαίνειν δ' ἀναγκαῖον τὰ ἀκόλουθα. τοὺς δέκα λόγους ἢ χρησμούς, νόμους ἢ θεσμοὺς πρὸς ἀλήθειαν ὄντας, ἀθροισθέντος τοῦ ἔθνους ἀνδρῶν ὁμοῦ καὶ γυναικῶν εἰς ἐκκλησίαν, ὁ πατὴρ τῶν ὅλων ἐθέσπισεν. ἆρά γε φωνῆς τρόπον προέμενος

[1] MSS. *καίων*. Clearly it must correspond with the passive following. But Aristotle in *Categ.* has *καίω* and *καίομαι* as his examples.

[2] So Mangey with most MSS.: Cohn *σχεδόν* with M. Though the addition of *τι* may perhaps rather point to *σχεδόν* I do not see what it can mean here. *σχέδην* regarded as the

students of mathematics? But while we must leave unnoticed the rest, there is one which may without impropriety be mentioned as a sample. Those who study the doctrines of philosophy say 30
that the categories [a] in nature, as they are called, are ten only, substance, quality, quantity, relation, activity, passivity, state, position and the indispensables for all existence, time and place. There 31
is nothing which does not participate in these categories. I have substance, for I have borrowed what is all-sufficient to make me what I am from each of the elements out of which this world was framed, earth, water, air and fire. I have quality in so far as I am a man, and quantity as being of a certain size. I become relative when anyone is on my right hand or my left, I am active when I rub or shave [b] anything, or passive when I am rubbed or shaved. I am in a particular state when I wear clothing or arms and in a particular position when I sit quietly or am lying down, and I am necessarily both in place and time since none of the above conditions can exist without these two.

IX. These points have been sufficiently discussed 32
and may now be left. We must proceed to carry on the discussion to embrace what follows next. The ten words or oracles, in reality laws or statutes, were delivered by the Father of All when the nation, men and women alike, were assembled together. Did He do so by His own utterance in the form of a

[a] On the categories see App. pp. 609-610.

[b] Or "shear." κείρω seems to have been a favourite word for exemplifying the force of the three voices. See note on *De Cher.* 79.

---

adverb of σχέσις, often used by Philo in contrast with κίνησις (see particularly *De Sobr.* 34), seems quite appropriate here.

αὐτός; ἄπαγε, μηδ' εἰς νοῦν ποτ' ἔλθοι τὸν ἡμέτερον· οὐ γὰρ ὡς ἄνθρωπος ὁ θεός, στόματος
33 καὶ γλώττης καὶ ἀρτηριῶν δεόμενος. ἀλλά γέ μοι δοκεῖ κατ' ἐκεῖνον τὸν χρόνον ἱεροπρεπέστατόν τι θαυματουργῆσαι κελεύσας ἦχον ἀόρατον ἐν ἀέρι δημιουργηθῆναι, πάντων ὀργάνων θαυμασιώτερον, ἁρμονίαις τελείαις ἡρμοσμένον, οὐκ ἄψυχον ἀλλ' οὐδ' ἐκ σώματος καὶ ψυχῆς τρόπον ζῴου συνεστηκότα,[1] ἀλλὰ ψυχὴν λογικὴν ἀνάπλεων[2] σαφηνείας καὶ τρανότητος, ἣ τὸν ἀέρα σχηματίσασα καὶ ἐπιτείνασα καὶ πρὸς πῦρ φλογοειδὲς μεταβαλοῦσα καθάπερ πνεῦμα διὰ σάλπιγγος φωνὴν τοσαύτην ἔναρθρον ἐξήχησεν, ὡς τοῖς ἔγγιστα τοὺς πορρω-
[186] τάτω κατ' | ἴσον ἀκροᾶσθαι δοκεῖν. ἀνθρώπων
34 μὲν γὰρ αἱ φωναὶ πρὸς μήκιστον ἀποτεινόμεναι πεφύκασιν ἐξασθενεῖν, ὡς ἀριδήλους τοῖς μακρὰν ἀφεστηκόσι μὴ γίνεσθαι τὰς ἀντιλήψεις ταῖς ἐπεκτάσεσιν ἐκ τοῦ κατ' ὀλίγον ἀμαυρουμένας,
35 ἐπειδὴ καὶ τὰ ὄργανα φθαρτά· τὴν δὲ κεκαινουργημένην φωνὴν ἐπιπνέουσα θεοῦ δύναμις ἤγειρε καὶ ἐζωπύρει καὶ ἀναχέουσα πάντῃ τὸ τέλος τῆς ἀρχῆς ἀπέφαινε τηλαυγέστερον, ἀκοὴν ἑτέραν πολὺ βελτίω τῆς δι' ὤτων ταῖς ἑκάστων ψυχαῖς ἐντιθεῖσα· ἡ μὲν γὰρ βραδυτέρα πως οὖσα αἴσθησις ἀτρεμίζει, μέχρις ἂν ὑπ' ἀέρος πληχθεῖσα διακινηθῇ, φθάνει δ' ἡ τῆς ἐνθέου διανοίας ὀξυτάτῳ τάχει προϋπαντῶσα τοῖς λεγομένοις.

36 X. Φωνῆς μὲν δὴ τῆς θείας πέρι τοσαῦτα. δεόντως δ' ἂν τις ἀπορήσαι, τοῦ χάριν, πλείστων

[1] mss. συνεστηκὼς or -ὸς or -ότα.

[2] Cohn prints ἀνάπλεω, which appears in one ms., but I cannot discover any authority for this form of the acc.

voice? Surely not: may no such thought ever enter our minds, for God is not as a man needing mouth
and tongue and windpipe. I should suppose that 33
God wrought on this occasion a miracle of a truly holy kind by bidding an invisible sound to be created in the air more marvellous than all instruments and fitted with perfect harmonies, not soulless, nor yet composed of body and soul like a living creature, but a rational soul full of clearness and distinctness, which giving shape and tension to the air and changing it to flaming fire, sounded forth like the breath through a trumpet an articulate voice so loud that it appeared to be equally audible to the farthest as well as the
nearest. For it is the nature of men's voices if 34
carried to a great distance to grow faint so that persons afar off have but an indistinct impression which gradually fades away with each lengthening of the extension, since the organism which produces them
also is subject to decay.[a] But the new miraculous voice 35
was set in action and kept in flame by the power of God which breathed upon it and spread it abroad on every side and made it more illuminating in its ending than in its beginning by creating in the souls of each and all another kind of hearing far superior to the hearing of the ears. For that is but a sluggish sense, inactive until aroused by the impact of the air, but the hearing of the mind possessed by God makes the first advance and goes out to meet the spoken words with the keenest rapidity.

X. So much for the divine voice. But we may 36
properly ask why, when all these many thousands were

[a] Or perhaps "just as musical instruments (and therefore the sounds which they make) are subject to decay."

ὅσων μυριάδων εἰς ἓν ἠθροισμένων χωρίον, ἕκαστον θεσπίζειν τῶν δέκα λογίων ἠξίωσεν ὡς οὐχὶ πρὸς πλείους ἀλλ' ὡς πρὸς ἕνα, " οὐ μοιχεύσεις" λέγων, " οὐ φονεύσεις," " οὐ κλέψεις" καὶ τὰ
37 ἄλλα ταύτῃ. λεκτέον οὖν ἓν μέν, ὅτι βούλεται κάλλιστον ἀναδιδάξαι μάθημα τοὺς ἐντυγχάνοντας ταῖς ἱεραῖς γραφαῖς, ὡς ἄρα καθ' αὑτὸν εἷς ἕκαστος, ὅταν ᾖ νόμιμος καὶ θεῷ καταπειθής, ἰσότιμός ἐστιν ὅλῳ ἔθνει πολυανθρωποτάτῳ, μᾶλλον δὲ καὶ πᾶσιν ἔθνεσιν, εἰ δὲ δεῖ περαιτέρω προελθόντα εἰπεῖν,
38 καὶ παντὶ τῷ κόσμῳ. διόπερ ἐν ἑτέροις ἐπαινῶν τινα δίκαιον ἄνδρα φησίν· " ἐγώ εἰμι ὁ θεὸς σός "· ὁ δ' αὐτὸς ἦν καὶ κόσμου θεός, ὡς τοὺς ὑπηκόους τὴν αὐτὴν τεταγμένους τάξιν καὶ ὁμοίως εὐαρεστοῦντας τῷ ταξιάρχῳ τῆς ἴσης ἀποδοχῆς καὶ τιμῆς μεταλαμβάνειν.

39 Δεύτερον δέ, ὅτι κοινῇ μὲν ὡς πλήθει τις ἐκκλησιάζων οὐκ ἐξ ἀνάγκης διαλέγεται ἑνί, ὅτε δὲ προστάττων ἢ ἀπαγορεύων ἰδίᾳ ὡς ἑνὶ ἑκάστῳ, τῶν ἐμφερομένων εὐθὺς ἂν δόξαι τὰ πρακτέα καὶ κοινῇ πᾶσιν ἀθρόοις ὑφηγεῖσθαι· εὐπειθέστερος δὲ ὁ τὰς παραινέσεις αὐτοπροσώπως δεχόμενος, ὁ δὲ συλλήβδην μεθ' ἑτέρων κεκώφωται τὸν ὄχλον ἀφηνιασμοῦ παρακάλυμμα ποιούμενος.

40 Τρίτον, ἵνα μηδείς ποτε βασιλεὺς ἢ τύραννος ἀφανοῦς ἰδιώτου καταφρονήσῃ γεμισθεὶς ἀλαζονείας

---

[a] Gen. xvii. 1 LXX; E.V. "I am God Almighty."

[b] I have punctuated and translated this sentence in the only way which seems to me possible, if the text is to stand, *i.e.* I have placed a comma after ἑκάστῳ instead of (as Cohn) after ἀπαγορεύων, and understand ἐκκλησιάζει or διαλέγεται after ὅτε δὲ and take τῶν ἐμφερομένων as partitive after

collected in one spot, He thought good in proclaiming His ten oracles to address each not as to several persons but as to one, Thou shalt not commit adultery, Thou shalt not kill, Thou shalt not steal, and so too with the rest. One answer which must 37
be given is that He wishes to teach the readers of the sacred scriptures a most excellent lesson, namely that each single person, when he is law-abiding and obedient to God, is equal in worth to a whole nation, even the most populous, or rather to all nations, and if we may go still farther, even to the whole world. And therefore elsewhere, when He praises a certain 38
just man, He says, I am thy God,[a] though He was also the God of the world. And thus we see that all the rank and file who are posted in the same line and give a like satisfaction to their commander, have an equal share of approbation and honour.

A second reason is that a speaker who harangues 39
a multitude in general does not necessarily talk to any one person, whereas if he addresses his commands or prohibitions as though to each individual separately, the practical instructions given in the course of his speech are at once held to apply to the whole body in common also.[b] If the exhortations are received as a personal message, the hearer is more ready to obey, but if collectively with others, he is deaf to them, since he takes the multitude as a cover for disobedience.

A third reason is that He wills that no king or 40
despot swollen with arrogance and contempt should despise an insignificant private person but should study

πρακτέα = "among the contents of his speech." But it is exceedingly awkward and some corruption is probable. For further discussion see App. p. 610.

καὶ ὑπεροψίας, ἀλλ' εἰς τὰ τῶν ἱερῶν νόμων
[187] διδασκαλεῖα φοιτήσας | χαλάσῃ τὰς ὀφρῦς, ἀπομαθὼν οἴησιν εἰκότι μᾶλλον δ' ἀληθεῖ λογισμῷ.
41 εἰ γὰρ ὁ ἀγένητος καὶ ἄφθαρτος καὶ ἀίδιος καὶ οὐδενὸς ἐπιδεὴς καὶ ποιητὴς τῶν ὅλων καὶ εὐεργέτης καὶ βασιλεὺς βασιλέων καὶ θεὸς θεῶν οὐδὲ τὸν ταπεινότατον ὑπεριδεῖν ὑπέμεινεν, ἀλλὰ καὶ τοῦτον εὐωχῆσαι λογίων καὶ θεσμῶν ἱερῶν ἠξίωσεν, ὡς μόνον ἑστιᾶν μέλλων καὶ μόνῳ τὸ συμπόσιον εὐτρεπίζεσθαι πρὸς ψυχῆς ἀνάχυσιν ἱεροφαντουμένης, ᾗ θέμις τὰς μεγάλας τελεῖσθαι τελετάς, ἐμοὶ τῷ θνητῷ τί προσῆκον ὑψαυχενεῖν καὶ πεφυσῆσθαι φρυαττομένῳ πρὸς τοὺς ὁμοίους, οἳ τύχαις μὲν ἀνίσοις ἴσῃ δὲ καὶ ὁμοίᾳ συγγενείᾳ κέχρηνται μίαν ἐπιγραψάμενοι μητέρα τὴν κοινὴν ἁπάντων
42 ἀνθρώπων φύσιν; εὐπρόσιτον οὖν καὶ εὐέντευκτον ἐμαυτὸν παρέξω, κἂν τὸ τῆς γῆς καὶ τῆς θαλάττης κράτος ἀνάψωμαι, τοῖς ἀπορωτάτοις καὶ ἀδοξοτάτοις καὶ οἰκειοτάτης συμμαχίας ἐρήμοις, ἑκατέρου τῶν γονέων ὀρφανοῖς καὶ γυναιξὶ χηρείαν ὑπομενούσαις καὶ πρεσβύταις ἢ μὴ παιδοποιησαμένοις τὸ παράπαν ἢ ἀποβαλοῦσιν ὠκυμόρους
43 οὓς ἐγέννησαν. ἄνθρωπος γὰρ ὢν ὄγκον καὶ σεμνότητα τετραγῳδημένην οὐ δικαιώσω προσίεσθαι, μενῶ δ' ἐντὸς τῆς φύσεως τοὺς ὅρους αὐτῆς μὴ ὑπερβαίνων, ἀλλ' ἐθίζων τὴν ἐμαυτοῦ διάνοιαν ἀνθρωποπαθεῖν, οὐ μόνον διὰ τὰς ἀδήλους πρὸς τἀναντία μεταβολὰς καὶ τῶν εὖ πραττόντων καὶ τῶν ἐν κακοπραγίαις, ἀλλὰ καὶ διὰ τὸ ἁρμόττειν, κἂν ἀτρέπτως καὶ βεβαίως παραμένῃ τὸ εὐτυχεῖν, μὴ ἐπιλανθάνεσθαί τινα ἑαυτοῦ.

in the school of the divine laws and abate his supercilious airs, and through the reasonableness or rather the assured truth of their arguments unlearn his self-
conceit. For if the Uncreated, the Incorruptible, the 41
Eternal, Who needs nothing and is the maker of all, the Benefactor and King of kings and God of gods could not brook to despise even the humblest, but deigned to banquet him on holy oracles and statutes, as though he should be the sole guest, as though for him alone the feast was prepared to give good cheer to a soul instructed in the holy secrets and accepted for admission to the greatest mysteries, what right have I, the mortal, to bear myself proud-necked, puffed-up and loud-voiced, towards my fellows, who, though their fortunes be unequal, have equal rights of kinship because they can claim to be children
of the one common mother of mankind, nature? So 42
then, though I be invested with the sovereignty of earth and sea, I will make myself affable and easy of access to the poorest, to the meanest, to the lonely who have none close at hand to help them, to orphans who have lost both parents, to wives on whom widowhood has fallen, to old men either childless from the first or bereaved by the early death of those whom
they begot. For as I am a man, I shall not deem it 43
right to adopt the lofty grandeur of the pompous stage, but make nature my home and not overstep her limits. I will inure my mind to have the feelings of a human being, not only because the lot both of the prosperous and the unfortunate may change to the reverse we know not when, but also because it is right that even if good fortune remains securely established, a man should not forget what he is.

διὰ ταῦτά μοι δοκεῖ τοὺς χρησμοὺς ἑνικῶς ἀπο-
τεινάμενος ὡς πρὸς ἕνα θεσπίζειν ἐθελῆσαι.
44 XI. Πάντα δ᾽ ὡς εἰκὸς τὰ περὶ τὸν τόπον
ἐθαυματουργεῖτο, κτύποις βροντῶν μειζόνων ἢ
ὥστε χωρεῖν ἀκοάς, ἀστραπῶν λάμψεσιν αὐγοει-
δεστάταις, ἀοράτου σάλπιγγος ἠχῇ πρὸς μήκιστον
ἀποτεινούσῃ, καθόδῳ νεφέλης, ἣ κίονος τρόπον
τὴν μὲν βάσιν ἐπὶ γῆς ἠρήρειστο, τὸ δ᾽ ἄλλο σῶμα
πρὸς αἰθέριον ὕψος ἀνέτεινε, πυρὸς οὐρανίου φορᾷ
καπνῷ βαθεῖ τὰ ἐν κύκλῳ συσκιάζοντος· ἔδει γὰρ
θεοῦ δυνάμεως ἀφικνουμένης μηδὲν τῶν τοῦ
κόσμου μερῶν ἡσυχάζειν, ἀλλὰ πάντα πρὸς
[188] ὑπηρεσίαν | συγκεκινῆσθαι. παρειστήκει δὲ ὁ
45 λεὼς ἁγνεύσας ὁμιλιῶν τῶν πρὸς γυναῖκας καὶ
πασῶν ἡδονῶν ἔξω τῶν πρὸς τροφὰς ἀναγκαίων
ἀποσχόμενος, λουτροῖς τε καὶ περιρραντηρίοις
καθηράμενος ἐκ τριῶν ἡμερῶν, ἔτι καὶ τὰς ἐσθῆτας
ἀποπλυνάμενος, ἐν τοῖς μάλιστα λευχείμων, ἀκρο-
βατῶν καὶ ἀνωρθιακὼς τὰ ὦτα, Μωυσέως προ-
δηλώσαντος εὐτρεπίζεσθαι πρὸς ἐκκλησίαν· ἔγνω
γὰρ αὐτὴν ἐσομένην, ἡνίκα μόνος ἀνακληθεὶς
46 ἐχρησμῳδεῖτο. φωνὴ δ᾽ ἐκ μέσου τοῦ ῥυέντος ἀπ᾽
οὐρανοῦ πυρὸς ἐξήχει καταπληκτικωτάτη, τῆς
φλογὸς εἰς διάλεκτον ἀρθρουμένης τὴν συνήθη τοῖς
ἀκροωμένοις, ᾗ τὰ λεγόμενα οὕτως ἐναργῶς
ἐτρανοῦτο, ὡς ὁρᾶν αὐτὰ μᾶλλον ἢ ἀκούειν δοκεῖν.
47 ἐγγυᾶται δέ μου τὸν λόγον ὁ νόμος, ἐν ᾧ γέγραπται·
"πᾶς ὁ λαὸς ἑώρα τὴν φωνήν"· ἐμφαντικώτατα·

---

[a] For this and the next section see Ex. xix. 14-19.
[b] So LXX, Ex. xx. 18, *cf. De Mig.* 47, *Mos.* ii. 213.

Such was the reason, as it seems to me, why he willed to word the series of his oracles in the singular form, and delivers them as though to one alone.

XI.[a] It was natural that the place should be the scene of all that was wonderful, claps of thunder louder than the ears could hold, flashes of lightning of surpassing brightness, the sound of an invisible trumpet reaching to the greatest distance, the descent of a cloud which like a pillar stood with its foot planted on the earth, while the rest of its body extended to the height of the upper air, the rush of heaven-sent fire which shrouded all around in dense smoke. For when the power of God arrives, needs must be that no part of the world should remain inactive, but all move together to do Him service. 44
Near by stood the people. They had kept pure from intercourse with women and abstained from all pleasures save those which are necessary for the sustenance of life. They had cleansed themselves with ablutions and lustrations for three days past, and moreover had washed their clothes. So in the whitest of raiment they stood on tiptoe with ears pricked up in obedience to the warning of Moses to prepare themselves for a congregation which he knew would be held from the oracular advice he received 45
when he was summoned up by himself. Then from the midst of the fire that streamed from heaven there sounded forth to their utter amazement a voice, for the flame became articulate speech in the language familiar to the audience, and so clearly and distinctly were the words formed by it that they seemed to see 46
rather than hear them. What I say is vouched for by the law in which it is written, " All the people saw the voice," [b] a phrase fraught with much meaning, 47

τὴν μὲν γὰρ ἀνθρώπων ἀκουστὴν εἶναι συμβέβηκεν,
ὁρατὴν δὲ ὡς ἀληθῶς τὴν θεοῦ. διὰ τί; ὅτι ὅσα
ἂν λέγῃ ὁ θεός, οὐ ῥήματά ἐστιν ἀλλ᾿ ἔργα, ἅπερ
48 ὀφθαλμοὶ πρὸ ὤτων δικάζουσι. παγκάλως μέντοι
καὶ θεοπρεπῶς εἴρηται ἐκ τοῦ πυρὸς ἡ φωνὴ
προέρχεσθαι· ἠκρίβωται γὰρ καὶ βεβασάνισται τὰ
49 τοῦ θεοῦ λόγια καθάπερ χρυσὸς πυρί. μηνύει δὲ
καὶ διὰ συμβόλου τι τοιοῦτον· ἐπειδὴ τοῦ πυρὸς τὸ
μὲν φωτίζειν τὸ δὲ καίειν πέφυκεν, οἱ μὲν τοῖς
χρησμοῖς ἀξιοῦντες εἶναι καταπειθεῖς ὡς ἐν ἀσκίῳ
φωτὶ τὸν ἀεὶ χρόνον βιώσονται τοὺς νόμους αὐτοὺς
ἀστέρας ἔχοντες ἐν ψυχῇ φωσφοροῦντας, ὅσοι δ᾿
ἀφηνιασταί, καιόμενοι καὶ κατακαιόμενοι δια-
τελοῦσιν ὑπὸ τῶν ἔνδον ἐπιθυμιῶν, αἳ φλογὸς
τρόπον πορθήσουσι τὸν σύμπαντα τῶν ἐχόντων
βίον.

50 XII. Ἃ μὲν οὖν ἀναγκαῖον ἦν προδηλῶσαι,
ταῦτ᾿ ἐστίν. ἐπ᾿ αὐτὰ δὲ ἤδη τρεπτέον τὰ λόγια
καὶ πάντα τὰ ἐν τούτοις ἐρευνητέον διάφορα.
δέκα τοίνυν ὄντα διένειμεν εἰς δύο πεντάδας, ἃς
δυσὶ στήλαις ἐνεχάραξε, καὶ ἡ μὲν προτέρα πεντὰς
τὰ πρωτεῖα ἔλαχεν, ἡ δ᾿ ἑτέρα δευτερείων ἠξιοῦτο·
καλαὶ δ᾿ ἀμφότεραι καὶ βιωφελεῖς, εὐρείας ὁδοὺς
καὶ λεωφόρους ἑνὶ τέλει περατουμένας ἀνα-
στέλλουσαι πρὸς ἄπταιστον ψυχῆς ἐφιεμένης ἀεὶ
51 τοῦ βελτίστου πορείαν. ἡ μὲν οὖν ἀμείνων πεντὰς
τοιάδε ἦν· περὶ μοναρχίας, ᾗ μοναρχεῖται ὁ κόσμος·
περὶ ξοάνων καὶ ἀγαλμάτων καὶ συνόλως ἀφ-
ιδρυμάτων χειροκμήτων· περὶ τοῦ μὴ λαμβάνειν
ἐπὶ ματαίῳ θεοῦ πρόσρησιν· περὶ τοῦ τὴν ἱερὰν |
[189] ἑβδόμην ἄγειν ἱεροπρεπῶς· περὶ γονέων τιμῆς καὶ
ἰδίᾳ ἑκατέρου καὶ ἀμφοτέρων κοινῇ· ὡς εἶναι τῆς

for it is the case that the voice of men is audible, but the voice of God truly visible. Why so ? Because whatever God says is not words but deeds, which are
judged by the eyes rather than the ears. Admirable 48
too, and worthy of the Godhead, is the saying that the voice proceeded from the fire, for the oracles of God have been refined and assayed as gold is by fire.
And it conveys too, symbolically, some such meaning 49
as this : since it is the nature of fire both to give light and to burn, those who resolve to be obedient to the divine utterances will live for ever as in unclouded light with the laws themselves as stars illuminating their souls, while all who are rebellious will continue to be burnt, aye and burnt to ashes, by their inward lusts, which like a flame will ravage the whole life of those in whom they dwell.

XII. Such are the points which required a pre- 50
liminary treatment. We must now turn to the oracles themselves and examine all the different matters with which they deal. We find that He divided the ten into two sets of five which He engraved on two tables, and the first five obtained the first place, while the other was awarded the second. Both are excellent and profitable for life ; both open out broad highroads leading at the end to a single goal, roads along which a soul which ever desires the best can
travel without stumbling. The superior set of five 51
treats of the following matters : the monarchical principle by which the world is governed : idols of stone and wood and images in general made by human hands : the sin of taking the name of God in vain : the reverent observance of the sacred seventh day as befits its holiness : the duty of honouring parents, each separately and both in common.

μιᾶς γραφῆς τὴν μὲν ἀρχὴν θεὸν καὶ πατέρα καὶ ποιητὴν τοῦ παντός, τὸ δὲ τέλος γονεῖς, οἳ μιμούμενοι τὴν ἐκείνου φύσιν γεννῶσι τοὺς ἐπὶ μέρους. ἡ δ' ἑτέρα πεντὰς τὰς πάσας ἀπαγορεύσεις περιέχει· μοιχείας, φόνου, κλοπῆς, ψευδομαρτυριῶν, ἐπιθυμιῶν.

52 *Ἐπισκεπτέον δὲ μετὰ πάσης ἀκριβείας τῶν λογίων ἕκαστον μηδὲν πάρεργον αὐτῶν ποιουμένους. ἀρχὴ δ' ἀρίστη πάντων μὲν τῶν ὄντων θεός, ἀρετῶν δ' εὐσέβεια· περὶ ὧν ἀναγκαιότατον πρῶτον διεξελθεῖν. πλάνος τις οὐ μικρὸς τὸ πλεῖστον τῶν ἀνθρώπων γένος κατέσχηκε περὶ πράγματος, ὅπερ ἢ μόνον ἢ μάλιστα ἦν εἰκὸς ἀπλανέστατον ταῖς ἑκάστων διανοίαις ἐνιδρῦσθαι.*
53 *ἐκτεθειώκασι γὰρ οἱ μὲν τὰς τέσσαρας ἀρχάς, γῆν καὶ ὕδωρ καὶ ἀέρα καὶ πῦρ, οἱ δ' ἥλιον καὶ σελήνην καὶ τοὺς ἄλλους πλανήτας καὶ ἀπλανεῖς ἀστέρας, οἱ δὲ μόνον τὸν οὐρανόν, οἱ δὲ τὸν σύμπαντα κόσμον· τὸν δ' ἀνωτάτω καὶ πρεσβύτατον, τὸν γεννητήν, τὸν ἄρχοντα τῆς μεγαλοπόλεως, τὸν στρατάρχην τῆς ἀηττήτου στρατιᾶς, τὸν κυβερνήτην, ὃς οἰκονομεῖ σωτηρίως ἀεὶ τὰ σύμπαντα, παρεκαλύψαντο ψευδωνύμους προσρήσεις ἐκείνοις ἐπι-*
54 *φημίσαντες ἑτέρας ἕτεροι. καλοῦσι γὰρ οἱ μὲν τὴν γῆν Κόρην, Δήμητραν, Πλούτωνα, τὴν δὲ θάλατταν Ποσειδῶνα, δαίμονας ἐναλίους ὑπάρχους αὐτῷ προσαναπλάττοντες καὶ θεραπείας ὁμίλους μεγάλους ἀρρένων τε καὶ θηλειῶν, Ἥραν δὲ τὸν ἀέρα καὶ τὸ πῦρ Ἥφαιστον καὶ ἥλιον Ἀπόλλωνα καὶ σελήνην Ἄρτεμιν καὶ ἑωσφόρον Ἀφροδίτην*

Thus one set of enactments begins with God the Father and Maker of all, and ends with parents who copy His nature by begetting particular persons. The other set of five contains all the prohibitions, namely adultery, murder, theft, false witness, covetousness or lust.

We must examine with all care each of the pro- 52
nouncements, giving perfunctory treatment to none. The transcendent source of all that exists is God, as piety is the source of the virtues, and it is very necessary that these two should be first discussed. A great delusion has taken hold of the larger part of mankind in regard to a fact which properly should be established beyond all question in every mind to the exclusion of, or at least above, all
others. For some have deified the four elements, 53
earth, water, air and fire, others the sun, moon, planets [a] and fixed stars, others again the heaven by itself, others the whole world. But the highest and the most august, the Begetter, the Ruler of the great World-city, the Commander-in-Chief of the invincible host, the Pilot who ever steers all things in safety, Him they have hidden from sight by the misleading titles assigned to the objects of worship mentioned above.
Different people give them different names: some 54
call the earth Korē or Demeter or Pluto, and the sea Poseidon, and invent marine deities subordinate to him and great companies of attendants, male and female. They call air Hera [b] and fire Hephaestus, the sun Apollo, the moon Artemis, the morning-star

[a] Greek "the other planets," the sun and moon being regarded as planets.

[b] See App. p. 610.

55 καὶ στίλβοντα Ἑρμῆν· καὶ τῶν ἄλλων ἀστέρων
ἑκάστου τὰς ἐπωνυμίας μυθογράφοι[1] παρέδοσαν, οἳ
πρὸς ἀπάτην ἀκοῆς εὖ τετεχνασμένα πλάσματα
συνυφήναντες ἔδοξαν περὶ τὴν τῶν ὀνομάτων θέσιν
56 κεκομψεῦσθαι· τόν τε οὐρανὸν εἰς ἡμισφαίρια τῷ
λόγῳ διχῇ διανείμαντες, τὸ μὲν ὑπὲρ γῆς, τὸ δ᾽
ὑπὸ γῆς, Διοσκόρους ἐκάλεσαν τὸ περὶ τῆς ἑτερη-
μέρου ζωῆς αὐτῶν προστερατευσάμενοι διήγημα.
57 τοῦ γὰρ οὐρανοῦ συνεχῶς καὶ ἀπαύστως ἀεὶ κύκλῳ
περιπολοῦντος, ἀνάγκη τῶν ἡμισφαιρίων ἑκάτερον
ἀντιμεθίστασθαι παρ᾽ ἡμέραν ἄνω τε καὶ κάτω
γινόμενον ὅσα τῷ δοκεῖν· ἄνω γὰρ καὶ κάτω πρὸς
ἀλήθειαν οὐδὲν ἐν σφαίρᾳ, πρὸς δὲ τὴν ἡμετέραν |
[190] σχέσιν αὐτὸ μόνον εἴωθε λέγεσθαι τὸ μὲν ὑπὲρ
58 κεφαλῆς ἄνω, κάτω δὲ τοὐναντίον. τῷ
δὴ φιλοσοφεῖν ἀνόθως ἐγνωκότι καὶ ἀδόλου καὶ
καθαρᾶς εὐσεβείας μεταποιουμένῳ κάλλιστον καὶ
ὁσιώτατον ὑφηγεῖται παράγγελμα, μηδὲν τῶν τοῦ
κόσμου μερῶν αὐτοκρατῆ θεὸν ὑπολαμβάνειν εἶναι·
καὶ γὰρ γέγονε, γένεσις δὲ φθορᾶς ἀρχή, κἂν
προνοίᾳ τοῦ πεποιηκότος ἀθανατίζηται, καὶ ἦν
ποτε χρόνος, ὅτε οὐκ ἦν· θεὸν δὲ πρότερον οὐκ ὄντα
καὶ ἀπό τινος χρόνου γενόμενον καὶ μὴ διαιωνίζοντα
59 λέγειν οὐ θεμιτόν. XIII. ἀλλὰ γὰρ ἔνιοι
περὶ τὰς κρίσεις ἀπονοίᾳ τοσαύτῃ κέχρηνται, ὡς
οὐ μόνον τὰ εἰρημένα θεοὺς νομίζειν, ἀλλὰ καὶ
ἕκαστον αὐτῶν μέγιστον καὶ πρῶτον θεόν, τὸν

[1] mss. *μυθογράφους* or *-οις*.

---

[a] Or "sparkler," "twinkler." For these non-mythological names of the planets see *Quis Rerum* 224.

Aphrodite and the glitterer [a] Hermes, and each of the 55
other stars have names handed down by the myth-
makers, who have put together fables skilfully contrived to deceive the hearers and thus won a reputation for accomplishment in name-giving. So too in 56
accordance with the theory by which they divided
the heaven into two hemispheres, one above the
earth and one below it, they called them the Dioscuri
and invented a further miraculous story of their
living on alternate days.[b] For indeed as heaven is 57
always revolving ceaselessly and continuously round
and round, each hemisphere must necessarily alternately change its position day by day and become
upper or lower as it appears, though in reality there
is no upper or lower in a spherical figure, and it is
merely in relation to our own position that we are
accustomed to speak of what is above our heads as
upper and the opposite to this as lower.

Now to one who is determined to follow a genuine 58
philosophy and make a pure and guileless piety his
own, Moses gives this truly admirable and religious
command that he should not suppose any of the
parts of the universe to be the omnipotent God.
For the world has become what it is, and its becoming is the beginning of its destruction, even though
by the providence of God it be made immortal, and
there was a time when it was not. But to speak of
God as "not being" at some former time, or having
"become" at some particular time and not existing
for all eternity is profanity. XIII. But 59
there are some whose views are affected with such
folly that they not only regard the said objects as
gods but each of them severally as the greatest and

[b] *Od.* xi. 303. See App. p. 610.

ὄντα ὄντως ἢ οὐκ εἰδότες ἀδιδάκτῳ τῇ φύσει ἢ οὐ
σπουδάζοντες μαθεῖν, ἕνεκα τοῦ μηδὲν ἔξω τῶν
αἰσθητῶν ἀόρατον καὶ νοητὸν αἴτιον ὑπολαμβάνειν
εἶναι, καίτοι σαφεστάτης ἐγγὺς παρακειμένης
60 πίστεως. ψυχῇ γὰρ ζῶντες καὶ βουλευόμενοι καὶ
πάνθ' ὅσα κατὰ τὸν ἀνθρώπινον βίον δρῶντες
οὐδέποτε ψυχὴν ὀφθαλμοῖς σώματος ἴσχυσαν
θεάσασθαι, καίτοι φιλοτιμηθέντες ἂν πάσας φιλο-
τιμίας, εἴ πως ἰδεῖν οἷόν τε ἦν τὸ ἄγαλμα τὸ πάντων
ἱεροπρεπέστατον, ἀφ' οὗ κατὰ μετάβασιν εἰκὸς
ἦν ἔννοιαν τοῦ ἀγενήτου καὶ ἀιδίου λαβεῖν, ὃς
ἅπαντα τὸν κόσμον ἡνιοχῶν σωτηρίως ἀόρατος
61 ὢν κατευθύνει. καθάπερ οὖν τοῦ μεγάλου βασιλέως
τὰς τιμὰς εἴ τις τοῖς ὑπάρχοις σατράπαις ἀπένειμεν,
ἔδοξεν ἂν οὐκ ἀγνωμονέστατος μόνον ἀλλὰ καὶ
ῥιψοκινδυνότατος εἶναι χαριζόμενος τὰ δεσπότου
δούλοις, τὸν αὐτὸν τρόπον [ἂν] τοῖς αὐτοῖς εἴ τις
γεραίρει τὸν πεποιηκότα τοῖς γεγονόσιν, ἴστω
πάντων ἀβουλότατος ὢν καὶ ἀδικώτατος, ἴσα
διδοὺς ἀνίσοις οὐκ ἐπὶ τιμῇ τῶν ταπεινοτέρων ἀλλ'
62 ἐπὶ καθαιρέσει τοῦ κρείττονος. εἰσὶ δ'
οἳ καὶ προσυπερβάλλουσιν ἀσεβείᾳ μηδὲ τὸ ἴσον
ἀποδιδόντες, ἀλλὰ τοῖς μὲν τὰ πάντα τῶν ἐπὶ τιμῇ
χαριζόμενοι, τῷ δ' οὐδὲν νέμοντες ἀλλ' οὐδὲ
μνήμην, τὸ κοινότατον· ἐπιλήθονται γὰρ οὗ μόνον
[191] μεμνῆσθαι προσῆκον ἦν, | ἐπιτηδεύοντες οἱ βαρυ-
63 δαίμονες ἑκούσιον λήθην. ἔνιοι δὲ καὶ στομάργῳ
κατεχόμενοι λύττῃ τὰ δείγματα τῆς ἐνιδρυμένης
ἀσεβείας εἰς μέσον προφέροντες βλασφημεῖν ἐπι-

---

[a] So, I think, rather than as Mangey "utique solius" or Treitel "ausschliesslich," which would rather be *μόνου*.

primal God. Incapacity for instruction or indifference to learning prevents them from knowing the truly Existent because they suppose that there is no invisible and conceptual cause outside what the senses perceive, though the clearest possible proof lies ready
at their hand. For while it is with the soul that they 60
live and plan and carry out all the affairs of human life, they can never see the soul with the eyes of the body, though every feeling of ambition might well have been aroused in the hope of seeing that most august of all sacred objects, the natural stepping-stone to the conception of the Uncreated and Eternal, the invisible Charioteer who guides in safety the
whole universe. So just as anyone who rendered 61
to the subordinate satraps the honours due to the Great King would have seemed to reach the height not only of unwisdom but of foolhardiness, by bestowing on servants what belonged to their master, in the same way anyone who pays the same tribute to the creatures as to their Maker may be assured that he is the most senseless and unjust of men in that he gives equal measure to those who are not equal, though he does not thereby honour the meaner many but deposes the one superior.
And there are some who in a further 62
excess of impiety do not even give this equal payment, but bestow on those others all that can tend to honour, while to Him they refuse even the commonest of all tributes, that of remembering Him. Whom duty bids them remember, if nothing more,[a] Him they forget, a forgetfulness deliberately
practised to their lasting misery. Some again, seized 63
with a loud-mouthed frenzy, publish abroad samples of their deep-seated impiety and attempt to blas-

χειροῦσι τὸ θεῖον, ἀκονησάμενοι κακήγορον γλῶτταν, ἅμα καὶ λυπεῖν ἐθέλοντες τοὺς εὐσεβοῦντας, οἷς ἄλεκτον καὶ ἀπαρηγόρητον εὐθὺς εἰσδύεται πένθος τὴν ὅλην πυρπολοῦν ψυχὴν δι' ὤτων· ἡ γὰρ τῶν ἀνοσίων ἑλέπολις τοῦτ' ἐστίν, ᾧ μόνῳ τοὺς φιλοθέους ἐπιστομίζουσι νομίζοντας ὑπὲρ τοῦ μὴ παροξύνειν ἐν τῷ παρόντι κάλλιστον ἡσυχίαν.

64 XIV. πᾶσαν οὖν τὴν τοιαύτην τερθρείαν ἀπωσάμενοι τοὺς ἀδελφοὺς φύσει μὴ προσκυνῶμεν, εἰ καὶ καθαρωτέρας καὶ ἀθανατωτέρας οὐσίας ἔλαχον —ἀδελφὰ δ' ἀλλήλων τὰ γενόμενα καθὸ γέγονεν, ἐπεὶ καὶ πατὴρ ἁπάντων εἷς ὁ ποιητὴς τῶν ὅλων ἐστίν,—ἀλλὰ καὶ διανοίᾳ καὶ λόγῳ καὶ πάσῃ δυνάμει τῇ τοῦ ἀγενήτου καὶ ἀιδίου καὶ τῶν ὅλων αἰτίου θεραπείᾳ σφόδρα εὐτόνως καὶ ἐρρωμένως ἐπαποδυώμεθα, μὴ ὑποκατακλινόμενοι μηδ' ὑπείκοντες ταῖς τῶν πολλῶν ἀρεσκείαις, ὑφ' ὧν

65 καὶ οἱ δυνάμενοι σῴζεσθαι διαφθείρονται. πρῶτον μὲν οὖν παράγγελμα καὶ παραγγελμάτων ἱερώτατον στηλιτεύσωμεν ἐν ἑαυτοῖς, ἕνα τὸν ἀνωτάτω νομίζειν τε καὶ τιμᾶν θεόν· δόξα δ' ἡ πολύθεος μηδ' ὤτων ψαυέτω καθαρῶς καὶ ἀδόλως ἀνδρὸς εἰωθότος ζητεῖν ἀλήθειαν.

66 Ἀλλ' ὅσοι μὲν ἡλίου καὶ σελήνης καὶ τοῦ σύμπαντος οὐρανοῦ τε καὶ κόσμου καὶ τῶν ἐν αὐτοῖς ὁλοσχερεστάτων μερῶν ὡς θεῶν πρόπολοί τε καὶ θεραπευταί, διαμαρτάνουσι μὲν—πῶς γὰρ οὔ;—τοὺς ὑπηκόους πρὸ τοῦ ἄρχοντος ἀποσεμνύνοντες, ἧττον δὲ τῶν ἄλλων ἀδικοῦσι τῶν ξύλα καὶ λίθους ἄργυρόν τε

---

[a] Mangey strangely says that the brothers are the angels. But clearly they are the heavenly bodies, which are "souls divine and without blemish throughout" (*De Gig.* 8, where

pheme the Godhead, and when they whet the edge of their evil-speaking tongue they do so in the wish to grieve the pious who feel at once the inroad of a sorrow indescribable and inconsolable, which passing through the ears wastes as with fire the whole soul. For this is the battery of the unholy, and is in itself enough to curb the mouths of the devout who hold that silence is best for the time being to avoid giving provocation. XIV. Let us then reject all such im- 64
posture and refrain from worshipping those who by nature are our brothers,[a] even though they have been given a substance purer and more immortal than ours, for created things, in so far as they are created, are brothers, since they have all one Father, the Maker of the universe. Let us instead in mind and speech and every faculty gird ourselves up with vigour and activity to do the service of the Uncreated, the Eternal, the Cause of all, not submitting nor abasing ourselves to do the pleasure of the many who work the destruction even of those who might be saved. Let us, then, engrave deep in our hearts this as the 65
first and most sacred of commandments, to acknowledge and honour one God Who is above all, and let the idea that gods are many never even reach the ears of the man whose rule of life is to seek for truth in purity and guilelessness.

[b] But while all who give worship and service to sun 66
and moon and the whole heaven and universe or their chief parts as gods most undoubtedly err by magnifying the subjects above the ruler, their offence is less than that of the others who have given shape to stocks

see note), though elsewhere, as in *De Op.* 144, admitted to have bodies. Philo always, I think, distinguishes them from angels.

[b] Here begins the Second Commandment.

καὶ χρυσὸν καὶ τὰς παραπλησίους ὕλας μορφω-
σάντων ὡς φίλον ἑκάστοις, εἶτ' ἀγαλμάτων καὶ
ξοάνων καὶ τῶν ἄλλων χειροκμήτων, ὧν πλαστικὴ
καὶ ζωγραφία δημιουργοὶ μεγάλα ἔβλαψαν τὸν
67 βίον τὸν ἀνθρώπινον, καταπλησάντων τὴν οἰκου-
[192] μένην. τὸ γὰρ κάλλιστον ἔρεισμα τῆς | ψυχῆς
ἐξέκοψαν, τὴν περὶ τοῦ ζῶντος ἀεὶ θεοῦ προσήκουσαν ὑπόληψιν, ὥσπερ τε ἀνερμάτιστα σκάφη
σαλεύουσιν ὧδε κἀκεῖσε διαφερόμενοι τὸν αἰῶνα,
μηδέποτ' εἰς λιμένα καταῖραι μηδ' ἐνορμίσασθαι
βεβαίως ἀληθείᾳ δυνάμενοι, τυφλώττοντες περὶ τὸ
θέας ἄξιον, πρὸς ὃ μόνον ὀξυδορκεῖν ἀναγκαῖον
68 ἦν. καί μοι δοκοῦσι τῶν τὰς τοῦ σώματος ὄψεις
πεπηρωμένων ἀθλιώτερον ζῆν· ἐκεῖνοι μὲν γὰρ
ἀκουσίως ἐβλάβησαν ἢ νόσον ὀφθαλμῶν χαλεπὴν
ὑποστάντες ἢ πρὸς ἐχθρῶν ἐπιβουλευθέντες, οἱ δ'
ἑκουσίῳ γνώμῃ τὸ τῆς ψυχῆς ὄμμα οὐκ ἠμαύρωσαν
μόνον ἀλλὰ καὶ παντελῶς ἀποβαλεῖν ἠξίωσαν.
69 ὅθεν τοῖς μὲν ἔλεος ὡς ἠτυχηκόσι, τοῖς δὲ κόλασις
ὡς μοχθηροῖς ἕπεται δικαίως, οἳ μετὰ τῶν ἄλλων
οὐδὲ τὸ προχειρότατον ἐνενόησαν, ὃ καὶ παῖς
" ἔγνω νήπιος," ὅτι τοῦ τεχνιτευθέντος ὁ τεχνίτης
ἀμείνων, καὶ χρόνῳ—πρεσβύτερος γὰρ καὶ τρόπον
τινὰ τοῦ δημιουργηθέντος πατήρ—καὶ δυνάμει· τὸ
γὰρ δρῶν τοῦ πάσχοντος ἐπικυδέστερον.
70 καὶ δέον, εἴπερ ἄρα ἐξημάρτανον, τοὺς ζωγράφους
αὐτοὺς καὶ ἀνδριαντοποιοὺς ὑπερβολαῖς τιμῶν
ἐκτεθειωκέναι, τοὺς μὲν εἴασαν ἀφανεῖς οὐδὲν
πλέον παρασχόντες, τὰ δ' ὑπ' ἐκείνων δημιουρ-

---

[a] *Cf. Iliad*, xvii. 32, and Hesiod, *Op.* 218 παθὼν δέ τε νήπιος ἔγνω, quoted as a proverb Plato, *Symp.* 222 B.

and stones and silver and gold and similar materials each according to their fancy and then filled the habitable world with images and wooden figures and the other works of human hands fashioned by the craftsmanship of painting and sculpture, arts which have wrought great mischief in the life of mankind.
For these idolaters cut away the most excellent 67
support of the soul, the rightful conception of the Ever-living God. Like boats without ballast they are for ever tossed and carried about hither and thither, never able to come to harbour or to rest securely in the roadstead of truth, blind to the one thing worthy of contemplation, which alone demands keen-sighted
vision. To my mind they live a more miserable life 68
than those who have lost the sight of the body, for those have been disabled through no wish of their own but either through suffering from some grievous disease of the eyes or through the malice of their enemies, but these others have of deliberate purpose not only dimmed but without scruple cast away entirely the eye of the soul. And therefore pity for 69
their misfortune waits upon the former, punishment for their depravity quite justly on the latter. In their general ignorance they have failed to perceive even that most obvious truth which even " a witless infant knows,"[a] that the craftsman is superior to the product of his craft both in time, since he is older than what he makes and in a sense its father, and in value, since the efficient element is held in higher esteem than
the passive effect. And while if they 70
were consistent in their sin, they should have deified the sculptors and painters themselves and given them honours on a magnificent scale, they leave them in obscurity and bestow no favour on them, while they

γηθέντα πλάσματα καὶ ζωγραφήματα θεοὺς ἐνό-
71 μισαν. καὶ οἱ μὲν τεχνῖται πολλάκις ἄποροι καὶ
ἄδοξοι κατεγήρασαν ἀτυχίαις ἐπαλλήλοις ἐναπο-
θανόντες, τὰ δὲ τεχνιτευθέντα πορφύρᾳ καὶ
χρυσῷ καὶ ταῖς ἄλλαις πολυτελείαις, ἃς πλοῦτος
χορηγεῖ, σεμνοποιεῖται καὶ θεραπεύεται, οὐ πρὸς
ἐλευθέρων μόνον ἀλλὰ καὶ εὐπατριδῶν καὶ τὸ σῶμα
καλλίστων· ἱερέων γὰρ καὶ τὸ γένος ἐξετάζεται
μετὰ πάσης ἀκριβείας, εἰ ἀνεπίληπτον, καὶ ἡ
κοινωνία τῶν τοῦ σώματος μερῶν, εἰ σύμπασα
72 ὁλόκληρος. καὶ οὔπω τοῦτο δεινόν,
καίτοι δεινὸν ὄν, ἀλλ' ἐκεῖνο παγχάλεπον· ἤδη γάρ
τινας οἶδα τῶν πεποιηκότων τοῖς πρὸς ἑαυτῶν
γεγονόσιν εὐχομένους τε καὶ θύοντας, οἷς πολὺ
βέλτιον ἦν ἑκατέραν τῶν χειρῶν προσκυνεῖν, εἰ δὲ
μὴ βούλοιντο δόξαν φιλαυτίας ἐκτρεπόμενοι, σφύρας
γοῦν καὶ ἄκμονας καὶ γραφίδας καὶ καρκίνους καὶ
τὰ ἄλλα ἐργαλεῖα, δι' ὧν ἐμορφώθησαν αἱ ὗλαι.
73 [193] XV. | καίτοι πρὸς τοὺς οὕτως ἀπονοηθέντας ἄξιον
παρρησιασαμένους εἰπεῖν· εὐχῶν ἀρίστην εἶναι
συμβέβηκεν, ὦ γενναῖοι, καὶ τέλος εὐδαιμονίας τὴν
74 πρὸς θεὸν ἐξομοίωσιν. εὔχεσθε οὖν καὶ ὑμεῖς
ἐξομοιωθῆναι τοῖς ἀφιδρύμασιν, ἵνα τὴν ἀνωτάτω
καρπώσησθε εὐδαιμονίαν, ὀφθαλμοῖς μὴ βλέποντες,
ὠσὶ μὴ ἀκούοντες, μυκτῆρσι μήτε ἀναπνέοντες
μήτε ὀσφραινόμενοι, στόματι μὴ φωνοῦντες μηδὲ
γευόμενοι, χερσὶ μήτε λαμβάνοντες μήτε διδόντες
μήτε δρῶντες, ποσὶ μὴ βαδίζοντες, μηδ' ἄλλῳ τινὶ
τῶν μερῶν ἐνεργοῦντες, ἀλλ' ὥσπερ ἐν εἱρκτῇ τῷ
ἱερῷ φρουρούμενοι καὶ φυλαττόμενοι, μεθ' ἡμέραν
τε καὶ νύκτωρ τὸν ἀπὸ τῶν θυομένων ἀεὶ καπνὸν

regard as gods the figures and pictures made by
their workmanship. The artists have often grown 71
old in poverty and disesteem, and mishap after mis-
hap has accompanied them to the grave, while the works of their art are glorified by the addition of purple and gold and silver and the other costly embellishments which wealth supplies, and are served not merely by ordinary freemen but by men of high birth and great bodily comeliness. For the birth of priests is made a matter for the most careful scrutiny to see whether it is unexceptionable, and the several parts which unite to form the body whether they
make a perfect whole. Horrible as all 72
this is, we have not reached the true horror. The worst is still to come. We have known some of the image-makers offer prayers and sacrifices to their own creations though they would have done much better to worship each of their two hands, or if they were disinclined for that because they shrank from appearing egotistical, to pay their homage to the hammers and anvils and pencils and pincers and the other tools by which their materials were shaped.
XV. Surely to persons so demented we might well say 73
boldly, "Good sirs, the best of prayers and the goal
of happiness is to become like God. Pray you there- 74
fore that you may be made like your images and thus enjoy supreme happiness with eyes that see not, ears that hear not, nostrils which neither breathe nor smell, mouths that never taste nor speak, hands that neither give nor take nor do anything at all, feet that walk not, with no activity in any parts of your bodies,[a] but kept under watch and ward in your temple-prison day and night, ever drinking in the smoke of the

[a] Philo clearly has in mind Ps. cxv. 5-8; *cf. Spec. Leg.* ii. 256.

σπῶντες· ἓν γὰρ μόνον τοῦτ᾽ ἀγαθὸν προσανα-
75 πλάττετε τοῖς ἀφιδρύμασιν. ἀλλ᾽ ἔγωγε νομίζω
ταῦτα ἀκούοντας οὐχ ὡς ἐπ᾽ εὐχαῖς ἀλλ᾽ ὡς ἐπὶ
κατάραις ἀγανακτήσειν καὶ τρέψεσθαι[1] πρὸς λοιδο-
ρίας ἄμυναν ἀντικατηγοροῦντας· ὃ μέγιστον ἂν
εἴη τεκμήριον τῆς ἐπιπολαζούσης ἀσεβείας ἀνθρώπων θεοὺς νομιζόντων, οἷς ὅμοιοί ποτε τὰς φύσεις
76 ἀπεύξαιντ᾽ ἂν γενέσθαι. XVI. μηδεὶς οὖν τῶν
ἐχόντων ψυχὴν ἀψύχῳ τινὶ προσκυνείτω· πάνυ
γὰρ τῶν ἀτόπων ἐστὶ τὰ φύσεως ἔργα πρὸς θεραπείαν τετράφθαι τῶν χειροκμήτων.

Αἰγυπτίοις[2] δ᾽ οὐ μόνον τὸ κοινὸν ἔγκλημα χώρας
ἁπάσης, ἀλλὰ καὶ ἕτερον ἐξαίρετον ἐπάγεται δεόν-
τως· πρὸς γὰρ ξοάνοις καὶ ἀγάλμασιν ἔτι καὶ ζῷα
ἄλογα παραγηόχασιν εἰς θεῶν τιμάς, ταύρους καὶ
κριοὺς καὶ τράγους, ἐφ᾽ ἑκάστῳ μυθικόν τι πλάσμα
77 τετερατευμένοι. καὶ ταῦτα μὲν ἴσως ἔχει τινὰ
λόγον, ἡμερώτατα γὰρ καὶ ὠφελιμώτατα τῷ βίῳ·
ἀροτὴρ ὁ βοῦς αὔλακας ἀνατέμνει καιρῷ σπορᾶς,
ἀλοῆσαι πάλιν, ὅταν δέῃ τὸν καρπὸν καθαίρεσθαι,
δυνατώτατος· ὁ κριὸς τὸ κάλλιστον τῶν σκεπασμά-
των, ἐσθῆτα, παρέχει· γυμνὰ γὰρ ἂν τὰ σώματα
διεφθείρετο ῥᾳδίως, ἢ διὰ θάλπος ἢ διὰ κρύος
ἄμετρον, τοτὲ μὲν τῷ ἀφ᾽ ἡλίου φλογμῷ, τοτὲ
78 δὲ τῇ ἀπ᾽ ἀέρος περιψύξει. νυνὶ δὲ προσυπερ-

[1] MSS. τρέψασθαι.
[2] So Cohn from the αἰγυπτίων of some authorities. The αἰγύπτῳ of the majority agrees well with χώρας, though not so well with the plurals which follow.

[a] Rather a strange phrase for mankind, but justified by

victims. For this is the one good which you imagine
your idols to enjoy." As a matter of fact I expect 75
that such advice would be received with indignation
as savouring of imprecations rather than of prayers
and would call forth abusive repudiations and retorts,
and this would be the strongest proof of the wide
extent of impiety shown by men who acknowledge
gods of such a nature that they would abominate the
idea of resembling them. XVI. Let no one, then, who 76
has a soul worship a soulless thing, for it is utterly
preposterous that the works of nature [a] should turn
aside to do service to what human hands have
wrought. But the Egyptians are rightly
charged not only on the count to which every country
is liable, but also on another peculiar to themselves.
For in addition to wooden and other images, they
have advanced to divine honours irrational animals,[b]
bulls and rams and goats, and invented for each some
fabulous legend of wonder. And with these perhaps 77
there might be some reason, for they are thoroughly
domesticated and useful for our livelihood. The ox
is a plougher and opens up furrows at seed-time and
again is a very capable thresher when the corn has
to be purged; the ram provides the best possible
shelter, namely, clothing, for if our bodies were naked
they would easily perish, either through heat or
through intense cold, in the first case under the
scorching of the sun, in the latter through the re-
frigeration caused by the air. But actually the 78
Egyptians have gone to a further excess and chosen

the antithesis to *χειρόκμητα*. Possibly our "brethren," the stars, which would also have to worship the images, if they were worthy of worship, are included.

[b] For other references to Egyptian animal worship see App. pp. 610-611.

βάλλοντες καὶ τῶν ἀνημέρων τὰ ἀγριώτατα καὶ
ἀτιθασώτατα, λέοντας καὶ κροκοδείλους καὶ ἑρπετῶν τὴν ἰοβόλον ἀσπίδα, γεραίρουσιν ἱεροῖς καὶ
τεμένεσι θυσίαις τε καὶ πανηγύρεσι καὶ πομπαῖς
καὶ τοῖς παραπλησίοις· ἀφ' ἑκατέρου γὰρ τῶν εἰς
[194] χρῆσιν δοθέντων | ἀνθρώποις ὑπὸ θεοῦ, γῆς καὶ
ὕδατος, διερευνησάμενοι τὰ ἀγριώτατα οὔτε ⟨τῶν⟩
χερσαίων λέοντος θηριωδέστερον ἀνεῦρον οὔτε
κροκοδείλου τῶν ἐνύδρων ἀγριώτερον, ἃ σέβουσι
79 καὶ τιμῶσι. πολλὰ μέντοι καὶ ἄλλα ζῷα, κύνας,
αἰλούρους, λύκους, καὶ πτηνὰ ἴβιδας καὶ ἱέρακας,
καὶ πάλιν ἰχθύων ἢ ὅλα τὰ σώματα ἢ μέρη τούτων
ἐκτεθειώκασιν· ὧν τί ἂν γένοιτο καταγελαστότερον;
80 καὶ δὴ τῶν ξένων οἱ πρῶτον εἰς Αἴγυπτον ἀφικό-
μενοι, πρὶν τὸν ἐγχώριον τῦφον εἰσοικίσασθαι ταῖς
διανοίαις, ἐκθνήσκουσι χλευάζοντες· ὅσοι δὲ παιδείας ὀρθῆς ἐγεύσαντο, τὴν ἐπ' ἀσέμνοις πράγμασι
σεμνοποιίαν καταπλαγέντες οἰκτίζονται τοὺς χρωμένους, ἀθλιωτέρους, ὅπερ εἰκός, ὑπολαμβάνοντες
εἶναι τῶν τιμωμένων, μεταβεβληκότας εἰς ἐκεῖνα
τὰς ψυχάς, ὡς ἀνθρωποειδῆ θηρία περινοστεῖν
81 δοκεῖν. ἀνελὼν οὖν ἐκ τῆς ἱερᾶς νομοθεσίας πᾶσαν τὴν τοιαύτην ἐκθέωσιν ἐπὶ τὴν τοῦ
πρὸς ἀλήθειαν ὄντος θεοῦ τιμὴν ἐκάλεσεν, ἑαυτοῦ
τιμῆς οὐ προσδεόμενος—οὐ γὰρ ἑτέρου χρεῖος ἦν
ὁ αὐταρκέστατος ἑαυτῷ—, βουλόμενος δὲ τὸ γένος
τῶν ἀνθρώπων ἀνοδίαις πλαζόμενον εἰς ἀπλανε-
στάτην ἄγειν ὁδόν, ἵν' ἑπόμενον τῇ φύσει τὸ ἄριστον
εὕρηται τέλος, ἐπιστήμην τοῦ ὄντως ὄντος, ὅς ἐστι
τὸ πρῶτον ἀγαθὸν καὶ τελεώτατον, ἀφ' οὗ τρόπον

the fiercest and most savage of wild animals, lions and crocodiles and among reptiles the venomous asp, all of which they dignify with temples, sacred precincts, sacrifices, assemblies, processions and the like. For after ransacking the two elements given by God to man for his use, earth and water, to find their fiercest occupants, they found on land no creature more savage than the lion nor in water than the crocodile
and these they reverence and honour. Many other 79
animals too they have deified, dogs, cats, wolves and among the birds, ibises and hawks; fishes too, either their whole bodies or particular parts. What could be more ridiculous than all this?
Indeed strangers on their first arrival in Egypt 80
before the vanity of the land has gained a lodgement in their minds are like to die with laughing at it, while anyone who knows the flavour of right instruction, horrified at this veneration of things so much the reverse of venerable, pities those who render it and regards them with good reason as more miserable than the creatures they honour, as men with souls transformed into the nature of those creatures, so that as they pass before him,
they seem beasts in human shape. So 81
then He gave no place in His sacred code of laws to all such setting up of other gods, and called upon men to honour Him that truly is, not because He needed that honour should be paid to Him, for He that is all-sufficient to Himself needs nothing else, but because He wished to lead the human race, wandering in pathless wilds, to the road from which none can stray, so that following nature they might win the best of goals, knowledge of Him that truly IS, Who is the primal and most perfect good, from

πηγῆς ἄρδεται τῷ κόσμῳ καὶ τοῖς ἐν αὐτῷ τὰ ἐπὶ
μέρους ἀγαθά.

82 XVII. Διειλεγμένοι καὶ περὶ τῆς δευτέρας παρ-
αινέσεως ὅσα οἷόν τε ἦν, τὴν ἑπομένην κατὰ τὸ ἑξῆς
ἀκριβώσωμεν· ἔστι δὲ μὴ λαμβάνειν ὄνομα θεοῦ
ἐπὶ ματαίῳ. τὰ μὲν οὖν τῆς τάξεως γνώριμα τοῖς
τὴν διάνοιαν ὀξυδορκοῦσιν· ὄνομα γὰρ ἀεὶ δεύτερον
ὑποκειμένου πράγματος, σκιᾷ παραπλήσιον, ἣ παρ-
83 έπεται σώματι. προειπὼν οὖν περὶ τῆς ὑπάρξεως
καὶ τιμῆς τοῦ ἀεὶ ὑπάρχοντος, ἑπομένως τῷ τῆς
ἀκολουθίας εἱρμῷ τὰ πρέποντα καὶ περὶ τῆς
κλήσεως εὐθὺς παρήγγειλε· πολύτροποι γὰρ καὶ
πολυειδεῖς αἱ περὶ τοῦτο τὸ μέρος τῶν ἀνθρώπων
84 ἁμαρτίαι. κάλλιστον δὴ καὶ βιωφελέστατον καὶ ἁρμόττον λογικῇ φύσει τὸ ἀνώμοτον,
[195] οὕτως | ἀληθεύειν ἐφ᾽ ἑκάστου δεδιδαγμένῃ, ὡς
τοὺς λόγους ὅρκους εἶναι νομίζεσθαι. δεύτερος
δέ, φασί, πλοῦς τὸ εὐορκεῖν· ἤδη γὰρ ὅ γε ὀμνὺς
85 εἰς ἀπιστίαν ὑπονοεῖται. μελλητὴς οὖν ἔστω καὶ
βραδύς, εἴ πως ἐνδέχοιτο ταῖς ὑπερθέσεσιν ἀπ-
ώσασθαι τὸν ὅρκον· εἰ δέ τις ἀνάγκη
βιάζοιτο, περισκεπτέον οὐ παρέργως ἕκαστα τῶν
ἐμφερομένων· τὸ γὰρ πρᾶγμα οὐ μικρόν, εἰ καὶ τῷ
86 ἔθει καταφρονεῖται. μαρτυρία γάρ ἐστι θεοῦ περὶ
πραγμάτων ἀμφισβητουμένων ὅρκος· μάρτυρα δὲ
καλεῖν ἐπὶ ψεύδει θεὸν ἀνοσιώτατον. ἴθι γάρ, εἰ
βούλει, τῷ λόγῳ διάκυψον εἰς τὴν τοῦ μέλλοντος
ὀμνύναι διάνοιαν ἐπὶ ψεύδει· θεάσῃ γὰρ αὐτὴν οὐκ

---

[a] See note on *De Som.* i. 44.

Whom as from a fountain is showered the water of each particular good upon the world and them that dwell therein.

XVII. We have now discussed as fully as possible 82
the second commandment. Let us proceed to examine carefully the next in order, not to take God's name in vain. Now the reason for the position of this commandment in the list will be understood by those who have clear-sighted minds, for the name always stands second to the thing which it represents as the
shadow which follows the body. So after speaking 83
first about the existence of the Ever-existent and the honour due to Him as such, He follows it at once in orderly sequence by giving a commandment on the proper use of His title, for the errors of men in this part of their duty are manifold and multiform.

To swear not at all is the best course 84
and most profitable to life, well suited to a rational nature which has been taught to speak the truth so well on each occasion that its words are regarded as oaths; to swear truly is only, as people say, a "second-best voyage,"[a] for the mere fact of his swearing casts suspicion on the trustworthiness of
the man. Let him, then, lag and linger in the hope 85
that by repeated postponement he may avoid the oath altogether. But, if necessity be too strong for him, he must consider in no careless fashion all that an oath involves, for that is no small thing,
though custom makes light of it. For an oath is an 86
appeal to God as a witness on matters in dispute, and to call Him as witness to a lie is the height of profanity. Be pleased, I beg you, to take a look with the aid of your reason into the mind of the intending perjurer. You will see there a mind not at

ἠρεμοῦσαν, ἀλλὰ θορύβου καὶ ταραχῆς μεστήν, κατηγορουμένην καὶ πάσας ὕβρεις καὶ βλασφημίας
87 ὑπομένουσαν. ὁ γὰρ ἑκάστῃ ψυχῇ συμπεφυκὼς καὶ συνοικῶν ἔλεγχος, οὐδὲν εἰωθὼς παραδέχεσθαι τῶν ὑπαιτίων, μισοπονήρῳ καὶ φιλαρέτῳ χρώμενος ἀεὶ τῇ φύσει, κατήγορος ὁμοῦ καὶ δικαστὴς ὁ αὐτὸς ὤν, διακινηθεὶς ὡς μὲν κατήγορος αἰτιᾶται, κατηγορεῖ, δυσωπεῖ, πάλιν δ' ὡς δικαστὴς διδάσκει, νουθετεῖ, παραινεῖ μεταβάλλεσθαι· κἂν μὲν ἰσχύσῃ πεῖσαι, γεγηθὼς καταλλάττεται, μὴ δυνηθεὶς δὲ ἀσπονδεὶ πολεμεῖ μήτε μεθ' ἡμέραν μήτε νύκτωρ ἀφιστάμενος, ἀλλὰ κεντῶν καὶ τιτρώσκων ἀνίατα, μέχρις ἂν τὴν ἀθλίαν καὶ ἐπάρατον ζωὴν ἀπορρήξῃ.

88 XVIII. τί λέγεις, εἴποιμ' ἂν πρὸς τὸν ἐπίορκον, τολμήσεις τινὶ τῶν σεαυτοῦ γνωρίμων φάναι προσελθών· ὦ οὗτος, ἃ μήτ' εἶδες μήτ' ἤκουσας, ὡς ἰδών, ὡς ἀκούσας, ὡς παρηκολουθηκὼς ἅπασιν, ἀφικόμενός μοι μαρτύρησον; ἐγὼ μέν γε[1] οὐκ οἶμαι· μανίας γὰρ ἀθεραπεύτου τὸ ἔργον.
89 ἐπεὶ τίσιν ὀφθαλμοῖς νήφων καὶ ἐν σεαυτῷ δοκῶν εἶναι προσιδὼν τὸν φίλον ἐρεῖς· διὰ τὴν ἑταιρίαν ἀδικοπράγει, παρανόμει, συνασέβει μοι; δῆλον γὰρ ὡς, εἰ ταῦτ' ἀκούσαι, πολλὰ χαίρειν φράσας ἑταιρίᾳ τῇ νομιζομένῃ καὶ κακίσας αὐτόν, ὅτι τὴν ἀρχὴν ἀνδρὶ τοιούτῳ φιλίας ἐκοινώνησεν, ἀποπηδήσεται καθάπερ ἀπὸ θηρὸς ἀγριαίνοντος καὶ
90 λελυττηκότος. εἶτα, πρὸς ἃ μηδὲ φίλον ἄγειν τολμήσεις, ἐπὶ ταῦτα θεὸν μάρτυρα καλῶν οὐκ ἐρυθριᾷς, τὸν πατέρα καὶ ἡγεμόνα τοῦ κόσμου;

[1] See App. p. 611.

---

[a] For this double function of "Conviction" or the "Inward Monitor" *cf. Quod Deus* 135 ff.

peace but full of uproar and confusion, labouring under accusation, suffering all manner of insult and
reviling. For every soul has for its birth-fellow 87
and house-mate a monitor[a] whose way is to admit nothing that calls for censure, whose nature is ever to hate evil and love virtue, who is its accuser and its judge in one. If he be once roused as accuser he censures, accuses and puts the soul to shame, and again as judge, he instructs, admonishes and exhorts it to change its ways. And if he has the strength to persuade it, he rejoices and makes peace. But if he cannot, he makes war to the bitter end, never leaving it alone by day or night, but plying it with stabs and deadly wounds until he breaks the thread of
its miserable and ill-starred life. XVIII. How 88
now! I would say to the perjurer, will you dare to accost any of your acquaintance and say, "Come, sir, and testify for me that you have seen and heard and been in touch throughout with things which you did not see nor hear." My own belief is that you would not, for it would be the act of a hopeless lunatic.
If you are sober and to all appearance in your right 89
mind, how could you have the face to say to your friend, "For the sake of our comradeship, work iniquity, transgress the law, join me in impiety"? Clearly if he hears such words, he will turn his back upon his supposed comradeship, and reproaching himself that there should ever have been the tie of friendship between him and such a person, rush away from him as from a savage and maddened beast.
Can it be, then, that on a matter on which you would 90
not dare to cite even a friend you do not blush to call God to witness, God the Father and Ruler of the

πότερον ἐπιστάμενος, ὅτι πάνθ᾿ ὁρᾷ καὶ πάντων
[196] 91 ἀκούει, ἢ τοῦτ᾿ ἀγνοῶν; | εἰ μὲν οὖν ἀγνοῶν, ἄθεός τις εἶ, πηγὴ δὲ πάντων ἀδικημάτων ἀθεότης· πρὸς δὲ τῷ ἀθέῳ καὶ καταστρατηγεῖς τὸν ὅρκον, ὀμνὺς κατὰ τοῦ μὴ προσέχοντος ὡς ἐπιμελουμένου τῶν ἀνθρωπείων πραγμάτων· εἰ δ᾿ ὅτι προνοεῖ σαφῶς οἶδας, ὑπερβολὴν ἀσεβείας οὐκ ἀπολέλοιπας λέγων, εἰ καὶ μὴ στόματι καὶ γλώττῃ, τῷ γοῦν συνειδότι πρὸς θεόν· τὰ ψευδῆ μοι μαρτύρει, συγκακούργει, συρρᾳδιούργει· μία μοι τοῦ παρ᾿ ἀνθρώποις εὐδοκιμεῖν ἐλπὶς τὸ παρακαλύψασθαί σε τὴν ἀλήθειαν· ὑπὲρ ἑτέρου πονηρὸς γενοῦ, ὑπὲρ τοῦ χείρονος ὁ κρείττων, ὑπὲρ ἀνθρώπου καὶ ταῦτα μοχθηροῦ θεὸς ὁ πάντων ἄριστος.

92 XIX. εἰσὶ δ᾿ οἳ μηδὲ κερδαίνειν τι μέλλοντες ἔθει πονηρῷ κατακόρως καὶ ἀνεξετάστως ὀμνύουσιν ἐπὶ τοῖς τυχοῦσιν, οὐδενὸς ἀμφισβητουμένου τὸ παράπαν, τὰ κενὰ τῶν[1] ἐν τῷ λόγῳ προσαναπληροῦντες ὅρκοις, ὡς οὐκ ἄμεινον ὂν ἀποκοπὴν ῥημάτων μᾶλλον δὲ καὶ ἀφωνίαν ὑποστῆναι παντελῆ· φύεται
93 γὰρ ἐκ πολυορκίας ψευδορκία καὶ ἀσέβεια. διὸ χρὴ τὸν μέλλοντα ὀμνύναι πάντ᾿ ἐπιμελῶς ἐξητακέναι καὶ σφόδρα περιττῶς, τὸ πρᾶγμα, εἰ εὐμέγεθες καὶ εἰ γέγονεν ὄντως καὶ εἰ πραχθὲν κατείληφε παγίως, ἑαυτόν, εἰ καθαρεύει ψυχὴν καὶ σῶμα καὶ γλῶτταν, τὴν μὲν παρανομίας, τὸ δὲ μιασμάτων, τὴν δὲ βλασφημιῶν· οὐ γὰρ ὅσιον, δι᾿

[1] So Cohn by a later correction for MS. τὰ μὲν αὐτῶν. See App. p. 611.

world? Do you do so with the knowledge that He sees and hears all things or in ignorance of this? If in ignorance, you are an atheist, and atheism is 91
the source of all iniquities, and in addition to your atheism you cut the ground from under the oath, since in swearing by God you attribute a care for human affairs to one who in your view has no regard for them. But if you are convinced of His providence as a certainty, there is no further height of impiety which remains for you to reach when you say to God, if not with your mouth and tongue, at any rate with your conscience, "Witness to a falsehood for me, share my evil-doing and my knavery. The one hope I have of maintaining my good name with men is that Thou shouldest disguise the truth. Be wicked for the sake of another, the superior for the sake of the inferior, the Divine, the best of all, for a man, and a bad man to boot."

XIX. There are some who without even any gain in 92
prospect have an evil habit of swearing incessantly and thoughtlessly about ordinary matters where there is nothing at all in dispute, filling up the gaps in their talk with oaths, forgetting that it were better to submit to have their words cut short or rather to be silenced altogether, for from much swearing springs false swearing and impiety. Therefore one who is 93
about to take an oath should have made a careful and most punctilious examination, first of the matter in question, whether it is of sufficient importance, whether it has actually happened, and whether he has a sound apprehension of the facts; secondly, of himself, whether his soul is pure from lawlessness, his body from pollution, his tongue from evil-speaking, for it would be sacrilege to employ the mouth by

οὗ στόματος τὸ ἱερώτατον ὄνομα προφέρεταί τις,
94 διὰ τούτου φθέγγεσθαί τι τῶν αἰσχρῶν. ἐρευνάτω
δὲ καὶ τόπον καὶ καιρὸν ἐπιτήδειον· οἶδα γὰρ οἶδά
τινας ἐν βεβήλοις καὶ ἀκαθάρτοις χωρίοις, ἐν οἷς
οὔτε πατρὸς οὔτε μητρὸς ἀλλ' οὐδὲ τῶν ὀθνείων
πρεσβύτου τινὸς εὖ βεβιωκότος ἄξιον μεμνῆσθαι,
διομνυμένους καὶ ὅλας ῥήσεις ὅρκων συνείροντας,
τῷ τοῦ θεοῦ πολυωνύμῳ καταχρησαμένους ὀνόματι
95 ἔνθα μὴ δεῖ πρὸς ἀσέβειαν. ὁ δὲ τῶν λεχθέντων
ὀλιγώρως ἔχων ἴστω τὸ μὲν πρῶτον μιαρὸς καὶ
ἀκάθαρτος ὤν, εἶθ' ὡς αἰεὶ αἱ μέγισται τῶν
τιμωριῶν ἐφεδρεύουσιν αὐτῷ, τῆς ἐφόρου τῶν
ἀνθρωπείων δίκης ἀτρέπτως καὶ ἀπαρηγορήτως
ἐπὶ τοῖς οὕτω μεγάλοις ἀδικήμασιν ἐχούσης, ἥτις,
ὅταν μὴ παραχρῆμα κολάζειν ἀξιοῖ, ἐπὶ πολλῷ
[197] δανείζειν ἔοικε τὰς τιμωρίας, | ἅς, ὅταν ᾖ καιρός,
ἀναπράττει μετὰ τοῦ κοινῇ συμφέροντος.
96 XX. Τέταρτόν ἐστι παράγγελμα τὸ περὶ τῆς
ἱερᾶς ἑβδόμης, ἵν' εὐαγῶς καὶ ὁσίως ἄγηται.
ταύτην ἔνιαι μὲν τῶν πόλεων ἑορτάζουσιν ἅπαξ τοῦ
μηνὸς ἀπὸ τῆς κατὰ σελ νην[1] νουμηνίας διαριθμού-
μεναι, τὸ δὲ Ἰουδαίων ἔθνος συνεχῶς ⟨ἡμέρας⟩ ἓξ
97 διαλείποντες αἰεί. λόγος δ' ἐστὶν ἀναγραφεὶς ἐν
τοῖς κατὰ τὴν κοσμοποιίαν, περιέχων αἰτίαν
ἀναγκαίαν· ἐν γὰρ ἓξ ἡμέραις φησὶ κτισθῆναι τὸν
κόσμον, τῇ δ' ἑβδόμῃ παυσάμενον τῶν ἔργων τὸν
98 θεὸν ἄρξασθαι τὰ γεγονότα καλῶς θεωρεῖν. ἐκέλευσεν οὖν καὶ τοὺς μέλλοντας ἐν ταύτῃ ζῆν τῇ
πολιτείᾳ καθάπερ ἐν τοῖς ἄλλοις καὶ κατὰ τοῦθ'

[1] Other MSS. θεόν, which Cohn prints, though later he declared for σελήνην, which appears in R. See App. p. 611.

[a] See App. p. 611.

which one pronounces the holiest of all names, to utter any words of shame. And let him seek for a 94
suitable time and place. For I know full well that there are persons who, in profane and impure places where it would not be fitting to mention either a father or mother or even any good-living elder outside his family, swear at length and make whole speeches consisting of a string of oaths and thus, by their misuse of the many forms of the divine name in places where they ought not to do so, show their impiety. Anyone who treats what I have said with 95
contempt may rest assured, first, that he is polluted and unclean, secondly, that the heaviest punishments are waiting to fall upon him. For justice, who surveys human affairs, is inflexible and implacable towards such grave misdeeds, and when she thinks well to refrain from immediate chastisement, be sure that she does but put out her penalties to loan at high interest, only to exact them when the time comes to the common benefit of all.

XX. The fourth commandment deals with the 96
sacred seventh day, that it should be observed in a reverent and religious manner. While some states celebrate this day as a feast once a month,[a] reckoning it from the commencement as shown by the moon, the Jewish nation never ceases to do so at continuous intervals with six days between each. There is an 97
account recorded in the story of the Creation containing a cogent reason for this : we are told that the world was made in six days and that on the seventh God ceased from His works and began to contemplate what had been so well created, and therefore
He bade those who should live as citizens under this 98
world-order follow God in this as in other matters.

ἕπεσθαι θεῷ, πρὸς μὲν ἔργα τρεπομένους ἐφ' ἡμέρας ἕξ, ἀνέχοντας δὲ τῇ ἑβδόμῃ καὶ φιλοσοφοῦντας καὶ θεωρίαις μὲν τῶν τῆς φύσεως σχολάζοντας, ἐπισκοποῦντας δὲ καὶ εἴ τι μὴ καθαρῶς ἐν ταῖς προτέραις ἐπράχθη, λόγον καὶ εὐθύνας ὧν εἶπον ἢ ἔδρασαν παρ' ἑαυτῶν λαμβάνοντας ἐν τῷ τῆς ψυχῆς βουλευτηρίῳ, συνεδρευόντων καὶ συνεξεταζόντων τῶν νόμων εἴς τε τὴν τῶν παροραθέντων κατόρθωσιν καὶ πρὸς τὴν τοῦ μηδὲν
99 αὖθις ἐξαμαρτάνειν προφυλακήν. ἀλλ' ὁ μὲν θεὸς ἅπαξ κατεχρήσατο ταῖς ἓξ ἡμέραις πρὸς τὴν τοῦ κόσμου τελείωσιν μήκους χρόνων οὐ προσδεόμενος· ἀνθρώπων δ' ἕκαστος ἅτε θνητῆς φύσεως μετέχων καὶ μυρίων ἐνδεὴς ὢν πρὸς τὰς ἀναγκαίας τοῦ βίου χρείας ὀφείλει μὴ κατοκνεῖν ἐκπορίζειν τὰ ἐπιτήδεια μέχρι τελευτῆς τοῦ βίου διαναπαυόμενος
100 τὰς ἱερὰς ἑβδομάδας. ἆρ' οὐ παγκάλη παραίνεσις καὶ πρὸς πᾶσαν ἀρετὴν ἱκανωτάτη προτρέψασθαι καὶ διαφερόντως εἰς εὐσέβειαν; "ἕπου" φησίν "αἰεὶ θεῷ· παράδειγμα προθεσμίας ἔστω σοι πράξεων ἓν ἑξαήμερον[1] αὐταρκέστατον, ἐν ᾧ τὸν κόσμον ἐδημιούργει· παράδειγμα καὶ τοῦ δεῖν φιλοσοφεῖν ἡ ἑβδόμη, καθ' ἣν ἐπιδεῖν λέγεται ἃ εἰργάσατο, ὅπως καὶ αὐτὸς ἐπιθεωρῇς τὰ φύσεως καὶ τὰ ἴδια ὅσα συντείνει πρὸς εὐδαιμονίαν."
101 τοιοῦτον οὖν ἀρχέτυπον τῶν ἀρίστων βίων, πρακτικοῦ τε καὶ θεωρητικοῦ, μὴ παρέλθωμεν, ἀλλ' αἰεὶ πρὸς αὐτὸ βλέποντες ἐναργεῖς εἰκόνας καὶ τύπους ταῖς ἑαυτῶν διανοίαις ἐγχαράττωμεν ἐξομοιοῦντες θνητὴν φύσιν ὡς ἔνεστιν ἀθανάτῳ κατὰ

[1] MSS. ἓν ἑξάμετρον or ἑξὰς μέτρον.

So He commanded that they should apply themselves to work for six days but rest on the seventh and turn to the study of wisdom, and that while they thus had leisure for the contemplation of the truths of nature they should also consider whether any offence against purity had been committed in the preceding days, and exact from themselves in the council-chamber of the soul, with the laws as their fellow-assessors and fellow-examiners, a strict account of what they had said or done in order to correct what had been neglected and to take precaution against repetition
of any sin. But while God once for all made a final 99
use of six days for the completion of the world and had no further need of time-periods, every man being a partaker of mortal nature and needing a vast multitude of things to supply the necessaries of life ought never to the end of his life to slacken in providing what he requires, but should rest on the sacred
seventh days. Have we not here a most admirable 100
injunction full of power to urge us to every virtue and piety most of all? "Always follow God," it says, "find in that single six-day period in which, all-sufficient for His purpose, He created the world, a pattern of the time set apart to thee for activity. Find, too, in the seventh day the pattern of thy duty to study wisdom, that day in which we are told that He surveyed what He had wrought, and so learn to meditate thyself on the lessons of nature and all that in thy
own life makes for happiness." Let us not then 101
neglect this great archetype of the two best lives, the practical and the contemplative, but with that pattern ever before our eyes engrave in our hearts the clear image and stamp of them both, so making mortal nature, as far as may be, like the immortal by saying

[198] τὸ λέγειν καὶ πράττειν ἃ χρή. πῶς δὲ | λέγεται ἐν ἓξ ἡμέραις γεγενῆσθαι τὸν κόσμον ὑπὸ θεοῦ τοῦ μηδὲ χρόνων εἰς τὸ ποιεῖν δεομένου, μεμήνυται διὰ τῶν ἀλληγορηθέντων ἐν ἑτέροις.

102 XXI. Τὴν μέντοι προνομίαν, ἧς ἐν τοῖς οὖσιν ἑβδομὰς ἠξίωται, δηλοῦσιν οἱ περὶ τὰ μαθήματα διατρίψαντες, ἐπιμελῶς πάνυ καὶ πεφροντισμένως αὐτὴν ἐξιχνεύσαντες. ἥδε γάρ ἐστιν ἡ ἐν ἀριθμοῖς παρθένος, ἡ ἀμήτωρ φύσις, ἡ μονάδος οἰκειοτάτη καὶ ἀρχῆς, ἡ ἰδέα τῶν πλανήτων, ἐπεὶ καὶ τῆς ἀπλανοῦς σφαίρας μονάς· ἐκ γὰρ μονάδος καὶ ἑβδομάδος οὐρανὸς ὁ ἀσώματος, τὸ παράδειγμα

103 τοῦ ὁρατοῦ. πέπηγε δ' ὁ οὐρανὸς ἔκ τε τῆς ἀμερίστου φύσεως καὶ τῆς μεριστῆς· ἡ μὲν οὖν ἀμέριστος τὴν πρώτην καὶ ἀνωτάτω καὶ ἀπλανῆ περιφορὰν εἴληχεν, ἣν μονὰς ἐπισκοπεῖ, ἡ δὲ μεριστὴ τὴν καὶ δυνάμει καὶ τάξει δευτέραν, ἧς ἐπιτροπεύει ἑβδομάς, ἥτις ἑξαχῇ διανεμηθεῖσα τοὺς ἐπικαλουμένους ἑπτὰ πλάνητας εἰργάσατο·

104 οὐκ ἐπειδὴ πεπλάνηταί τι τῶν κατὰ τὸν οὐρανὸν θείας καὶ μακαρίας καὶ εὐδαίμονος φύσεως μετεσχηκότων, οἷς πᾶσι τὸ ἀπλανὲς οἰκειότατον—τὴν γοῦν ἐν ὁμοίῳ ταυτότητα σῴζοντα δολιχεύει τὸν

[a] *i.e.* in *Leg. All.* i. 2-4: "Moses wished to exhibit things mortal and immortal as having been formed in a way corresponding to their proper numbers" (§ 4). The reason why six is the appropriate number for mortal things, as seven for immortal, is given just before.

[b] For the Pythagorean origin of these epithets see note on *Mos.* ii. 210.

[c] Or "archetype."

[d] For the mystical identity of One and Seven *cf. De Post.* 64, *Quod Deus* 11, and § 159 below.

[e] This whole section, like its parallel, *De Cher.* 22, is based

and doing what we ought. But in what sense the world is said to have been created by God in six days when no time-period of any kind was needed by Him for his work has been explained elsewhere in our allegorical expositions.[a]

XXI. As for the number seven, the precedence 102
awarded to it among all that exists is explained by the students of mathematics, who have investigated it with the utmost care and consideration. It is the virgin[b] among the numbers, the essentially motherless, the closest bound to the initial Unit, the "idea"[c] of the planets, just as the unit is of the sphere of the fixed stars, for from the Unit and Seven springs the incorporeal heaven which is the pattern of the visible.[d]

Now the substance from which the 103
heaven has been framed is partly undivided and partly divided. To the undivided belongs the primal, highest and undeviating revolution presided over by the unit; to the divided another revolution, secondary both in value and order, under the governance of Seven, and this by a sixfold partition has produced
the seven so-called planets, or wanderers.[e] Not that 104
any of the occupants of heaven wander, for sharing as they do in a blessed and divine and happy nature, they are all intrinsically free from any such tendency. In fact they preserve their uniformity unbroken and

upon Plato, *Timaeus* 36 C–D, where the heaven is conceived of as consisting of two revolving circles, the exterior, the sphere of the fixed stars, and the interior subdivided into seven concentric circles, one for each planet. "The exterior motion he called the motion of the Same (ταὐτόν, *cf.* Philo's ταυτότης), the interior the motion of the Other" (so in *De Cher.*). The terms for "undivided" and "he divided" are ἄσχιστος and σχίσας, but Plato has ἀμέριστος and μεριστὴ οὐσία a little before (35 A).

αἰῶνα μηδεμίαν ἐνδεχόμενα τροπὴν καὶ μεταβολὴν —, ἀλλ᾿ ὅτι περιπολοῦνται ὑπεναντίως τῇ ἀμερίστῳ καὶ ἐξωτάτω σφαίρᾳ, πλάνητες ὠνομάσθησαν οὐ κυρίως ὑπ᾿ ἀνθρώπων εἰκαιοτέρων, οἳ τὴν ἰδίαν πλάνην τοῖς οὐρανίοις ἐπεφήμισαν, ἃ τὴν τοῦ θείου
105 στρατοπέδου τάξιν οὐδέποτε λείπει. διὰ μὲν δὴ ταῦτα καὶ ἔτι πλείω τετίμηται ἡ ἑβδομάς· ἐπ᾿ οὐδενὶ δ᾿ οὕτω προνομίας ἔτυχεν ἢ τῷ μάλιστα τὸν ποιητὴν καὶ πατέρα τῶν ὅλων ἐμφαίνεσθαι δι᾿ αὐτῆς· ὡς γὰρ διὰ κατόπτρου φαντασιοῦται ὁ νοῦς θεὸν δρῶντα καὶ κοσμοποιοῦντα καὶ τῶν ὅλων ἐπιτροπεύοντα.

106 XXII. Μετὰ δὲ τὰ περὶ τῆς ἑβδόμης παραγγέλλει πέμπτον παράγγελμα τὸ περὶ γονέων τιμῆς τάξιν αὐτῷ δοὺς τὴν μεθόριον τῶν δυοῖν πεντάδων· τελευταῖον γὰρ ὂν τῆς προτέρας, ἐν ᾗ τὰ ἱερώτατα προστάττεται,[1] συνάπτει καὶ τῇ δευτέρᾳ περιεχούσῃ
107 τὰ πρὸς ἀνθρώπους δίκαια. αἴτιον δ᾿ ὡς οἶμαι τόδε· τῶν γονέων ἡ φύσις ἀθανάτου καὶ θνητῆς οὐσίας ἔοικεν εἶναι μεθόριος, θνητῆς μὲν διὰ τὴν
[199] πρὸς | ἀνθρώπους καὶ τὰ ἄλλα ζῷα συγγένειαν κατὰ τὸ τοῦ σώματος ἐπίκηρον, ἀθανάτου δὲ διὰ τὴν τοῦ γεννᾶν πρὸς θεὸν τὸν γεννητὴν τῶν ὅλων
108 ἐξομοίωσιν. ἤδη μὲν οὖν τινες τῇ ἑτέρᾳ μερίδι προσκληρώσαντες ἑαυτοὺς ἔδοξαν τῆς ἑτέρας ὀλιγωρεῖν· ἄκρατον γὰρ ἐμφορησάμενοι τὸν εὐσεβείας πόθον, πολλὰ χαίρειν φράσαντες ταῖς ἄλλαις

[1] So Cohn for MS. πρὸς τὰ πέντε. See App. pp. 611-612.

run their round to and fro for all eternity admitting no swerving or alteration. It is because their course is contrary to that of the undivided and outermost sphere that the planets gained their name which was improperly applied to them by the more thoughtless people, who credited with their own wanderings the heavenly bodies which never leave their posts
in the divine camp.[a] For these reasons and many 105
others beside Seven is held in honour. But nothing so much assures its predominance as that through it is best given the revelation of the Father and Maker of all, for in it, as in a mirror, the mind has a vision of God as acting and creating the world and controlling all that is.

XXII. After dealing with the seventh day, He 106
gives the fifth commandment on the honour due to parents. This commandment He placed on the border-line between the two sets of five; it is the last of the first set in which the most sacred injunctions are given and it adjoins the second set which contains
the duties of man to man. The reason I consider is 107
this: we see that parents by their nature stand on the border-line between the mortal and the immortal side of existence, the mortal because of their kinship with men and other animals through the perishableness of the body; the immortal because the act of generation assimilates them to God, the generator
of the All. Now we have known some 108
who associate themselves with one of the two sides and are seen to neglect the other. They have drunk of the unmixed wine of pious aspirations and turning their backs upon all other concerns devoted their

[a] *Cf.* Plato, *Laws* 821 C-D, where the name of "wanderers" is said to be a blasphemy.

πραγματείαις ὅλον ἀνέθεσαν τὸν οἰκεῖον βίον θερα-
109 πείᾳ θεοῦ. οἱ δ᾽ οὐδὲν ἔξω τῶν πρὸς ἀνθρώπους
δικαιωμάτων ἀγαθὸν ὑποτοπήσαντες εἶναι μόνην
τὴν πρὸς ἀνθρώπους ὁμιλίαν ἠσπάσαντο, τῶν τε
ἀγαθῶν τὴν χρῆσιν ἐξ ἴσου πᾶσι παρέχοντες διὰ
κοινωνίας ἵμερον καὶ τὰ δεινὰ κατὰ δύναμιν
110 ἐπικουφίζειν ἀξιοῦντες. τούτους μὲν οὖν φιλ-
ανθρώπους, τοὺς δὲ προτέρους φιλοθέους ἐνδίκως
ἂν εἴποι τις, ἡμιτελεῖς τὴν ἀρετήν· ὁλόκληροι γὰρ
οἱ παρ᾽ ἀμφοτέροις εὐδοκιμοῦντες. ὅσοι δὲ μήτ᾽
ἐν τοῖς πρὸς ἀνθρώπους ἐξετάζονται, συνηδόμενοι
μὲν ἐπὶ τοῖς κοινοῖς ἀγαθοῖς, συναλγοῦντες δ᾽ ἐπὶ
τοῖς ἐναντίοις, μήτ᾽ εὐσεβείας καὶ ὁσιότητος περιέχονται, μεταβεβληκέναι δόξαιεν ἂν εἰς θηρίων
φύσιν· ὧν τῆς ἀγριότητος οἴσονται τὰ πρωτεῖα οἱ
γονέων ἀλογοῦντες, ἑκατέρας μερίδος ὄντες ἐχθροὶ
καὶ τῆς πρὸς θεὸν καὶ τῆς πρὸς ἀνθρώπους.
111 XXIII. ἐν δυσὶν οὖν δικαστηρίοις, ἃ δὴ μόνα ἐστὶν
ἐν τῇ φύσει, μὴ ἀγνοείτωσαν ἑαλωκότες, ἀσεβείας
μὲν ἐν τῷ θείῳ, διότι τοὺς ἐκ τοῦ μὴ ὄντος εἰς τὸ
εἶναι παραγαγόντας καὶ κατὰ τοῦτο μιμησαμένους
θεὸν οὐ περιέπουσι, μισανθρωπίας δ᾽ ἐν τῷ κατ᾽
112 ἀνθρώπους. τίνα γὰρ ἕτερον εὖ ποιήσουσιν οἱ τῶν
συγγενεστάτων καὶ τὰς μεγίστας παρασχομένων
δωρεὰς ὀλιγωροῦντες, ὧν ἔνιαι δι᾽ ὑπερβολὴν οὐδ᾽
ἀμοιβὰς ἐνδέχονται; πῶς γὰρ ἂν ὁ γεννηθεὶς
ἀντιγεννῆσαι δύναιτο τοὺς σπείραντας, κλῆρον
ἐξαίρετον τῆς φύσεως χαρισαμένης πρὸς παῖδας
γονεῦσιν εἰς ἀντίδοσιν ἐλθεῖν οὐ δυναμένον; ὅθεν

personal life wholly to the service of God. Others 109
conceiving the idea that there is no good outside doing justice to men have no heart for anything but companionship with men. In their desire for fellowship they supply the good things of life in equal measure to all for their use, and deem it their duty to alleviate by anything in their power the dreaded hardships. These may be justly called lovers of 110
men, the former sort lovers of God. Both come but halfway in virtue; they only have it whole who win honour in both departments. But all who neither take their fit place in dealings with men by sharing the joy of others at the common good and their grief at the reverse, nor cling to piety and holiness, would seem to have been transformed into the nature of wild beasts. In such bestial savagery the first place will be taken by those who disregard parents and are therefore the foes of both sides of the law, the godward and the manward.

XXIII. Let them not then fail to understand that 111
in the two courts, the only courts which nature has, they stand convicted; in the divine court, of impiety because they do not show due respect to those who brought them forth from non-existence to existence and in this were imitators of God; in the human court, of inhumanity. For to whom else will they show 112
kindness if they despise the closest of their kinsfolk who have bestowed upon them the greatest boons, some of them far exceeding any possibility of repayment? For how could the begotten beget in his turn those whose seed he is, since nature has bestowed on parents in relation to their children an estate of a special kind which cannot be subject to the law

καὶ σφόδρα προσῆκεν ἀγανακτεῖν, εἰ μὴ πάντα
ἔχοντες ἀντιχαρίζεσθαι μηδὲ τὰ κουφότατα ἐθε-
113 λήσουσιν. οἷς δεόντως ἂν εἴποιμι· τὰ
θηρία πρὸς ἀνθρώπους[1] ἡμεροῦσθαι δεῖ· καὶ πολ-
λάκις ἔγνων ἡμερωθέντας λέοντας, ἄρκτους, |
[200] παρδάλεις, οὐ μόνον πρὸς τοὺς τρέφοντας διὰ
τὴν ἐπὶ τοῖς ἀναγκαίοις χάριν, ἀλλὰ καὶ πρὸς
τοὺς ἄλλους, ἕνεκά μοι δοκῶ τῆς πρὸς ἐκείνους
ὁμοιότητος· καλὸν γὰρ ἀεὶ τῷ κρείττονι τὸ
114 χεῖρον ἀκολουθεῖν διὰ βελτιώσεως ἐλπίδα. νυνὶ δ᾽
ἀναγκασθήσομαι τἀναντία λέγειν· μιμηταὶ θηρίων
ἐνίων, ἄνθρωποι, γίνεσθε. τοὺς ὠφεληκότας ἀντ-
ωφελεῖν ἐκεῖνα οἶδε καὶ πεπαίδευται· κύνες οἰκουροὶ
προασπίζουσι καὶ προαποθνήσκουσι τῶν δεσποτῶν,
ὅταν κίνδυνός τις ἐξαπιναίως καταλάβῃ· τοὺς δ᾽
ἐν ταῖς ποίμναις φασὶ προαγωνιζομένους τῶν
θρεμμάτων ἄχρι νίκης ἢ θανάτου παραμένειν ὑπὲρ
115 τοῦ διατηρῆσαι τοὺς ἀγελάρχας ἀζημίους. εἶτ᾽
οὐκ αἰσχρῶν ἐστιν αἴσχιστον, ἐν χαρίτων ἀμοιβαῖς
ἄνθρωπον ἡττηθῆναι κυνός, τοῦ θηρίων θρασυτάτου
τὸ ἡμερώτατον ζῷον; ἀλλ᾽ εἰ μὴ τοῖς
χερσαίοις ἀναδιδασκόμεθα, πρὸς τὴν πτηνὴν καὶ
ἀεροπόρον μετίωμεν φύσιν ἃ χρὴ παρ᾽ αὐτῆς
116 μαθησόμενοι. τῶν πελαργῶν οἱ μὲν γηραιοὶ κατα-
μένουσιν ἐν ταῖς νεοττιαῖς ἀδυνατοῦντες ἵπτασθαι,
οἱ δὲ τούτων παῖδες ὀλίγου δέω φάναι γῆν καὶ

[1] MSS. ἀνθρώπων.

---

[a] Clearly an allusion to the Attic law by which a citizen nominated to perform a "leiturgia" might call upon a person not so nominated whom he considered to be wealthier than himself to exchange properties with him. Here, as often,

of "exchange"[a]? And therefore the greatest indignation is justified if children, because they are unable
to make a complete return, refuse to make even the
slightest. Properly,[b] I should say to them, 113
"beasts ought to become tame through association
with men." Indeed I have often known lions and
bears and panthers become tame, not only with those
who feed them, in gratitude for receiving what they
require, but also with everybody else, presumably
because of the likeness to those who give them food.[c]
That is what should happen, for it is always good for
the inferior to follow the superior in hope of improvement. But as it is I shall be forced to say the opposite 114
of this, "You men will do well to take some beasts
for your models." They have been trained to know
how to return benefit for benefit. Watch-dogs guard
and die for their masters when some danger suddenly
overtakes them. Sheep-dogs, they say, fight for their
charges and hold their ground till they conquer or
die, in order to keep the herdsmen unscathed. Is it 115
not, then, a very scandal of scandals that in returning
kindnesses a man should be worsted by a dog, the
most civilized of living creatures by the most auda-
cious of brutes? But, if we cannot learn
from the land animals, let us turn for a lesson in
right conduct to the winged tribe that ranges the air.
Among the storks[d] the old birds stay in the nests 116
when they are unable to fly, while their children fly,
I might almost say, over sea and land, gathering

Philo shews his knowledge of Attic law, as he found it in Demosthenes.

[b] The sense is "the natural and proper thing is for beasts to learn from men; in this case men have to learn from beasts."

[c] *i.e.* these animals come to associate the human form with kindness.

[d] See App. p. 612.

θάλατταν ἐπιποτώμενοι πανταχόθεν ἐκπορίζουσι
117 τοῖς γονεῦσι τὰ ἐπιτήδεια· καὶ οἱ μὲν ἀξίως τῆς
ἡλικίας ἠρεμοῦντες ἐν ἀφθονίᾳ διατελοῦσι τῇ πάσῃ
τρυφῶντες, οἱ δὲ τὰς εἰς τὸν πορισμὸν κακοπαθείας
ἐπελαφριζόμενοι τῷ εὐσεβεῖν καὶ τῷ προσδοκᾶν
ἐν γήρᾳ τὰ αὐτὰ πείσεσθαι ὑπὸ τῶν ἐκγόνων
ἀναγκαῖον ὄφλημα ἀντεκτίνουσιν, ἐν καιρῷ καὶ
λαβόντες αὐτὸ καὶ ἀνταποδιδόντες, ὅτ' οὐδέτεροι
τρέφειν αὑτοὺς δύνανται, παῖδες μὲν ἐν ἀρχῇ τῆς
γενέσεως, γονεῖς δ' ἐπὶ τελευτῇ τοῦ βίου· ὅθεν
αὐτοδιδάκτῳ τῇ φύσει νεοττοτροφηθέντες γηρο-
118 τροφοῦσι χαίροντες. ἆρ' οὐκ ἄξιον ἐπὶ
τούτοις ἀνθρώπους, ὅσοι γονέων ἀμελοῦσιν, ἐγκαλύπτεσθαι καὶ κακίζειν ἑαυτούς, ὠλιγωρηκότας
ὧν ἢ μόνων ἢ πρὸ τῶν ἄλλων ἀναγκαῖον ἦν
πεφροντικέναι, καὶ ταῦτ' οὐ διδόντας μᾶλλον ἢ
ἀποδιδόντας; παίδων γὰρ ἴδιον οὐδέν, ὃ μὴ
γονέων ἐστίν, ἢ οἴκοθεν ἐπιδεδωκότων ἢ τὰς αἰτίας
119 τῆς κτήσεως παρασχομένων. εὐσέβειαν δὲ καὶ
ὁσιότητα, τὰς ἀρετῶν ἡγεμονίδας, ἆρά γ' ἐντὸς
ὅρων ἔχουσι τῶν ψυχῶν; ὑπερορίους μὲν οὖν ἀπ-
εληλάκασι καὶ πεφυγαδεύκασι· θεοῦ γὰρ ὑπηρέται
[201] πρὸς | τέκνων σπορὰν οἱ γονεῖς· ὁ δ' ὑπηρέτην
120 ἀτιμάζων συνατιμάζει καὶ τὸν ἄρχοντα. τῶν δ'
εὐτολμοτέρων ἀποσεμνύνοντες τὸ γονέων ὄνομά
φασί τινες, ὡς ἄρα πατὴρ καὶ μήτηρ ἐμφανεῖς εἰσι
θεοί, μιμούμενοι τὸν ἀγένητον ἐν τῷ ζῳοπλαστεῖν·

[a] See App. p. 612.

from every quarter provision for the needs of their
parents; and so while they in the inactivity justi- 117
fied by their age continue to enjoy all abundance of luxury, the younger birds making light of the hardships sustained in their quest for food, moved by piety and the expectation that the same treatment will be meted to them by their offspring, repay the debt which they may not refuse—a debt both incurred and discharged at the proper time—namely that in which one or other of the parties is unable to maintain itself, the children in the first stage of their existence, the parents at the end of their lives. And thus without any teacher but their natural instinct they gladly give to age the nurture which
fostered their youth. With this example 118
before them may not human beings, who take no thought for their parents, deservedly hide their faces for shame and revile themselves for their neglect of those whose welfare should necessarily have been their sole or their primary care, and that not so much as givers as repayers of a due? For children have nothing of their own which does not come from their parents, either bestowed from their own resources or acquired by means which originate from
them. Piety and religion are the queens among the 119
virtues. Do they dwell within the confines of such souls as these? No, they have driven them from the realm and sent them into banishment. For parents are the servants of God for the task of begetting children, and he who dishonours the servant dishonours also the Lord. Some bolder spirits,[a] glorify- 120
ing the name of parenthood, say that a father and a mother are in fact gods revealed to sight who copy the Uncreated in His work as the Framer of life. He,

ἀλλὰ τὸν μὲν εἶναι τοῦ κόσμου θεόν, τοὺς δὲ μόνων ὧν ἐγέννησαν. ἀμήχανον δ' εὐσεβεῖσθαι τὸν ἀόρατον ὑπὸ τῶν εἰς τοὺς ἐμφανεῖς καὶ ἐγγὺς ὄντας ἀσεβούντων.

121 XXIV. Τοσαῦτα καὶ περὶ γονέων τιμῆς φιλοσοφήσας τέλος ἐπιτίθησι τῇ ἑτέρᾳ καὶ θειοτέρᾳ πεντάδι. τὴν δ' ἑτέραν ἀναγραψάμενος περιέχουσαν ἀπαγορεύσεις τῶν πρὸς ἀνθρώπους ἀπὸ μοιχείας ἄρχεται, μέγιστον ἀδικημάτων τοῦτ' εἶναι ὑπο-
122 λαβών. πρῶτον μὲν γὰρ πηγὴν ἔχει φιληδονίαν, ἣ καὶ τὰ σώματα θρύπτει τῶν ἐχόντων καὶ τοὺς τῆς ψυχῆς ἐκλύει τόνους καὶ τὰς οὐσίας διαφθείρει πάντα δίκην ἀσβέστου πυρὸς ὧν ἂν προσάψηται καταφλέγουσα καὶ μηδὲν σῷον ἀπολείπουσα τῶν
123 κατὰ τὸν ἀνθρώπινον βίον. ἔπειτ' ἀναπείθει τὸν μοιχὸν οὐκ ἀδικεῖν μόνον ἀλλὰ καὶ διδάσκειν συναδικεῖν ἐν ἀκοινωνήτοις πράγμασι κοινωνίαν τιθέμενον· οἴστρου γὰρ [τοῦ][1] κατασχόντος, ἀμήχανον λαβεῖν τέλος δι' ἑνὸς μόνου τὰς ὀρέξεις, ἀλλὰ δεῖ πάντως δύο κοινοπραγῆσαι, τὸν μὲν ὑφηγητοῦ τὸν δὲ γνωρίμου τάξιν λαβόντα, πρὸς ἀκρασίας καὶ λαγνείας βεβαίωσιν, αἰσχίστων
124 κακῶν. οὐδὲ γὰρ τοῦτ' ἔνεστιν εἰπεῖν, ὡς τὸ σῶμα μόνον διαφθείρεται τῆς μοιχευομένης γυναικός, ἀλλ', εἰ δεῖ τἀληθὲς εἰπεῖν, ἡ ψυχὴ πρὸ τοῦ σώματος εἰς ἀλλοτρίωσιν ἐθίζεται διδασκομένη πάντα τρόπον ἀποστρέφεσθαι καὶ μισεῖν τὸν ἄνδρα.
125 καὶ ἧττον ἂν ἦν δεινόν, εἰ τὸ μῖσος ἐπεδείκνυτο ἐμφανές—τὰ γὰρ ἐν περιόπτῳ ῥᾷον φυλάξασθαι·—νυνὶ δὲ δυσυπονόητον καὶ δυσθήρατόν

[1] Or, as Mangey, read τούτου.

they say, is the God or Maker of the world, they of those only whom they have begotten, and how can reverence be rendered to the invisible God by those who show irreverence to the gods who are near at hand and seen by the eye?

XXIV. With these wise words on honouring 121
parents He closes the one set of five which is more concerned with the divine. In committing to writing the second set which contains the actions prohibited by our duty to fellow-men, He begins with adultery, holding this to be the greatest of crimes. For in the 122
first place it has its source in the love of pleasure which enervates the bodies of those who entertain it, relaxes the sinews of the soul and wastes away the means of subsistence, consuming like an unquenchable fire all that it touches and leaving nothing wholesome in human life. Secondly, it persuades the 123
adulterer not merely to do the wrong but to teach another to share the wrong by setting up a partnership in a situation where no true partnership is possible. For when the frenzy has got the mastery, the appetites cannot possibly gain their end through one agent only, but there must necessarily be two acting in common, one taking the position of the teacher, the other of the pupil, whose aim is to put on a firm footing the vilest of sins, licentiousness and lewdness. We cannot even say that it is only the body of the 124
adulteress which is corrupted, but the real truth is that her soul rather than her body is habituated to estrangement from the husband, taught as it is to feel complete aversion and hatred for him.

And the matter would be less terrible if the hatred 125
were shown openly, since what is conspicuous is more easily guarded against, but in actual fact it easily

ἐστι, πανούργοις τέχναις συσκιαζόμενον καὶ τὴν ἐναντίαν ἔστιν ὅτε τοῦ φιλεῖν δόξαν ἐμποιοῦν
126 γοητείαις τισὶ καὶ ἀπάταις. ἀναστάτους γε μὴν τρεῖς ἀποδείκνυσιν[1] οἴκους, τόν τε τοῦ παρασπονδουμένου ἀνδρός, ὃς τὰς ἐπὶ γάμοις εὐχὰς καὶ τὰς ἐπὶ γνησίοις παισὶν ἐλπίδας περικόπτεται, καὶ δύο δ᾽ ἑτέρους τόν τε τοῦ μοιχοῦ καὶ τὸν τῆς γυναικός, καὶ γὰρ τούτων ἑκάτερος ὕβρεως καὶ ἀτιμίας καὶ τῶν μεγίστων ὀνειδῶν ἀναπίμπλαται.
127 κἂν πολυάνθρωποι μὲν τύχωσιν αἱ συγγένειαι διὰ τὰς ἐπιγαμίας καὶ τὰς ἄλλων πρὸς ἄλλους ἐπιμιξίας, ἅψεται καὶ τῆς πόλεως ἁπάσης ἐν κύκλῳ
128 βαδίζον τἀδίκημα. παγχάλεπόν γε μὴν
[202] | καὶ ὁ τῶν τέκνων ἐπαμφοτερισμός· μὴ γὰρ ἁγνευούσης γυναικός, ἀμφίδοξον καὶ ἄδηλον, τὰ ἀποκυόμενα τίνος ἐστὶ τῇ ἀληθείᾳ πατρός· εἶτα λανθάνοντος τοῦ πράγματος, οἱ μοιχίδιοι τὴν τῶν γνησίων παρασπασάμενοι τάξιν ἀλλοτρίαν γενεὰν νοθεύουσι καὶ κλῆρον ὅσον τῷ δοκεῖν πατρῷον
129 οὐδὲν προσήκοντα διαδέξονται. καὶ ὁ μὲν μοιχὸς ἐφυβρίσας καὶ ἐναπερυγὼν τὸ πάθος, ἐπίληπτον σπορὰν σπείρας, ὅταν ἀποπλησθῇ τῆς ἐπιθυμίας, οἰχήσεται καταλιπών, γέλωτα θέμενος τὴν τοῦ παρανομηθέντος ἄγνοιαν· ὁ δ᾽ οἷα τυφλὸς μηδὲν τῶν ὑποικουρημένων ἐπιστάμενος ὡς οἰκειότατα ἔκγονα τὰ ἐκ τῶν πολεμιωτάτων θεραπεύειν
130 ἀναγκασθήσεται. φανερὸν δ᾽ εἰ γένοιτο τἀδίκημα, κακοδαιμονέστατοι γένοιντ᾽ ἂν οἱ μηδὲν ἠδικηκότες

[1] Cohn with some MSS. ἀποδεικνύουσιν, but the MS. authority is almost as good for the singular, which seems better suited

eludes suspicion and detection, shrouded by artful knavery and sometimes creating by deceptive wiles the opposite impression of affection. Indeed it makes 126
havoc of three families : of that of the husband who suffers from the breach of faith, stripped of the promise of his marriage-vows and his hopes of legitimate offspring, and of two others, those of the adulterer and the woman, for the infection of the outrage and dishonour and disgrace of the deepest kind extends to the family of both. And if their connexions include 127
a large number of persons through intermarriages and widespread associations, the wrong will travel all round and affect the whole State. Very 128
painful, too, is the uncertain status of the children, for if the wife is not chaste there will be doubt and dispute as to the real paternity of the offspring. Then if the fact is undetected, the fruit of the adultery usurp the position of the legitimate and form an alien and bastard brood and will ultimately succeed to the heritage of their putative father to which they have no right. And the adulterer having in 129
insolent triumph vented his passions and sown the seed of shame, his lust now sated, will leave the scene and go on his way mocking at the ignorance of the victim of his crime, who like a blind man knowing nothing of the covert intrigues of the past will be forced to cherish the children of his deadliest foe as his own flesh and blood. On the other hand, if 130
the wrong becomes known, the poor children who have done no wrong will be most unfortunate, unable

to the context than the plural, which would presumably have ἀπάται or τέχναι for its subject. The sequel refers to adultery in general rather than the deceptions which usually accompany it.

ἄθλιοι παῖδες, μηδετέρῳ γένει προσνεμηθῆναι
δυνάμενοι, μήτε τῷ τοῦ γήμαντος μήτε τῷ τοῦ
131 μοιχοῦ. τοιαύτας συμφορὰς ἀπεργαζομένης τῆς
ἐκνόμου μίξεως, εἰκότως στυγητὸν καὶ θεομίσητον
πρᾶγμα, μοιχεία, πρῶτον ἀδικημάτων ἀνεγράφη.
132 XXV. Δεύτερον δὲ πρόσταγμα μὴ ἀνδροφονεῖν.
ἀγελαστικὸν γὰρ καὶ σύννομον ζῷον τὸ ἡμερώτατον
ἄνθρωπον ἡ φύσις γεννήσασα πρὸς ὁμόνοιαν καὶ
κοινωνίαν ἐκάλεσε, λόγον δοῦσα συναγωγὸν εἰς
ἁρμονίαν καὶ κρᾶσιν ἠθῶν. ὁ δὴ κτείνων τινὰ μὴ
ἀγνοείτω νόμους φύσεως καὶ θεσμοὺς ἀνατρέπων
133 καλῶς καὶ συμφερόντως ἅπασι γραφέντας. ἴστω
μέντοι καὶ ἱεροσυλίας ἔνοχος ὢν τὸ ἱερώτατον τῶν
τοῦ θεοῦ κτημάτων σεσυληκώς· τί γὰρ σεμνότερον
ἢ ἁγιώτερον ἀνάθημα ἀνθρώπου; χρυσὸς μὲν καὶ
ἄργυρος καὶ λίθοι πολυτελεῖς καὶ ὅσαι ἄλλαι
τιμαλφέσταται ὗλαι κόσμος οἰκοδομημάτων ἐστίν,
134 ἄψυχος ἀψύχων· ἄνθρωπος δέ, ζῷον ἄριστον κατὰ
τὸ κρεῖττον τῶν ἐν αὐτῷ, τὴν ψυχήν, συγγενέ-
στατος τῷ καθαρωτάτῳ τῆς οὐσίας οὐρανῷ, ὡς δ᾽
ὁ τῶν πλείστων λόγος, καὶ τῷ τοῦ κόσμου πατρί,
τῶν ἐπὶ γῆς ἁπάντων οἰκειότατον ἀπεικόνισμα
καὶ μίμημα τῆς ἀιδίου καὶ εὐδαίμονος ἰδέας τὸν
νοῦν λαβών.
135 XXVI. Τρίτον δ᾽ ἐστὶ τῆς δευτέρας πεντάδος
παράγγελμα μὴ κλέπτειν. ὁ γὰρ τοῖς ἀλλοτρίοις
ἐπικεχηνὼς κοινὸς πόλεως ἐχθρός, βουλήσει μὲν
τὰ πάντων δυνάμει δὲ τά τινων ὑφαιρούμενος, τῷ
τὴν μὲν πλεονεξίαν ἐπὶ μήκιστον ἐκτείνεσθαι, τὸ

---

[a] Literally "blending of temperaments or characteristics." See note on *Mos.* ii. 256.

to be classed with either family, either the husband's
or the adulterer's. Such being the disasters wrought 131
by illicit intercourse, naturally the abominable and
God-detested sin of adultery was placed first in the
list of wrongdoing.

XXV. The second commandment is to do no 132
murder. For nature, who created man the most
civilized of animals to be gregarious and sociable,
has called him to shew fellowship and a spirit of
partnership by endowing him with reason, the bond
which leads to harmony and reciprocity of feeling.[a]
Let him, then, who slays another know full well that
he is subverting the laws and statutes of nature so
excellently enacted for the well-being of all. Further, 133
let him understand that he is guilty of sacrilege,
the robbery from its sanctuary of the most sacred of
God's possessions. For what votive offering is more
hallowed or more worthy of reverence than a man?
Gold and silver and costly stones and other substances of highest price serve as ornaments to buildings which are as lifeless as the ornaments themselves.
But man, the best of living creatures, through that 134
higher part of his being, namely, the soul, is most
nearly akin to heaven, the purest thing in all that
exists, and, as most admit, also to the Father of the
world, possessing in his mind a closer likeness and
copy than anything else on earth of the eternal and
blessed Archetype.

XXVI. The third commandment in the second 135
five forbids stealing, for he who gapes after what
belongs to others is the common enemy of the
State, willing to rob all, but able only to filch from
some, because, while his covetousness extends in-

δʼ ἀσθενὲς ὑστερίζον εἰς βραχὺ στέλλεσθαι καὶ
[203] μόνον | φθάνειν ἐπʼ ὀλίγους. ὅσοι τοίνυν τῶν
136 κλεπτῶν ἰσχὺν προσέλαβον ὅλας συλῶσι πόλεις ἀλογοῦντες τιμωριῶν διὰ τὸ ἐπικυδέστεροι τῶν νόμων εἶναι δοκεῖν· οὗτοι δʼ εἰσὶν οἱ ὀλιγαρχικοὶ τὰς φύσεις, οἱ τυραννίδων καὶ δυναστειῶν ἐπιθυμοῦντες, οἱ τὰς μεγάλας ἐργαζόμενοι κλοπάς, σεμνοῖς ὀνόμασι τοῖς ἀρχῆς καὶ ἡγεμονίας ἐπι-
137 κρύπτοντες λῃστείαν τἀληθὲς ἔργον. ἐκ πρώτης οὖν ἡλικίας ἀναδιδασκέσθω τις μηδὲν λάθρα τῶν ἀλλοτρίων ὑφαιρεῖσθαι, κἂν βραχύτατον ᾖ, διότι ἐγχρονίζον ἔθος φύσεως κραταιότερόν ἐστι καὶ τὰ μικρὰ μὴ κωλυόμενα φύεται καὶ ἐπιδίδωσι πρὸς μέγεθος συναυξανόμενα.

138 XXVII. Κλέπτειν δʼ ἀπειπὼν ἑξῆς ψευδομαρτυρεῖν ἀπαγορεύει, πολλοῖς καὶ μεγάλοις καὶ πᾶσι χαλεποῖς τοὺς ψευδομάρτυρας ἐνόχους εἰδώς. τὸ μὲν γὰρ πρῶτον φθείρουσι τὴν σεμνὴν ἀλήθειαν, ἧς οὐκ ἔστιν ἐν βίῳ κτῆμα ἱερώτερον,[1] ἡλίου τρόπον φῶς τοῖς πράγμασι περιτιθείσης, ἵνα μηδὲν αὐτῶν
139 ἐπισκιάζηται. δεύτερον δὲ πρὸς τῷ ψεύδεσθαι καὶ τὰ πράγματα οἷα νυκτὶ καὶ σκότῳ βαθεῖ περιαμπίσχουσι καὶ συμπράττουσι μὲν τοῖς ἁμαρτάνουσιν, ἐπιτίθενται δὲ τοῖς ἀδικουμένοις, ἃ μήτʼ εἶδον μήτʼ ἤκουσαν μήτʼ ἴσασι παγίως εἰδέναι καὶ σφόδρα κατειληφέναι διαβεβαιούμενοι.
140 προσεξεργάζονται δὲ καὶ τρίτον παρανόμημα τῶν προτέρων ἀργαλεώτερον· ὅταν γὰρ σπάνις ἀποδείξεων ᾖ διὰ λόγων ἢ διὰ γραμμάτων, ἐπὶ μάρ-

definitely, his feebler capacity cannot keep pace with it but restricted to a small compass reaches only to a few. So all thieves who have acquired the strength 136
rob whole cities, careless of punishment because their high distinction seems to set them above the laws. These are oligarchically-minded persons, ambitious for despotism or domination, who perpetrate thefts on a great scale, disguising the real fact of robbery under the grand-sounding names of government and leadership. Let a man, then, learn from 137
his earliest years to filch nothing by stealth that belongs to another, however small it may be, because custom in the course of time is stronger than nature, and little things if not checked grow and thrive till they attain to great dimensions.

XXVII. Having denounced theft, he next pro- 138
ceeds to forbid false witness, knowing that false witnesses are guilty under many important heads, all of them of a grave kind. In the first place, they corrupt truth, the august, the treasure as sacred as anything that we possess in life, which like the sun pours light upon facts and events and allows none of them to be kept in the shade. Secondly, apart from 139
the falsehood, they veil the facts as it were in night and profound darkness, take part with the offenders and against those who are wronged, by affirming that they have sure knowledge and thorough apprehension of things which they have neither seen nor heard. And indeed they commit a 140
third transgression even more heinous than the first two. For when there is a lack of proofs, either verbal or written, disputants have resort to

[1] So R, other MSS. ἱερώτατον: Cohn proposes as an alternative <κάλλιον>, ἱερώτατον agreeing with φῶς.

τυρας καταφεύγουσιν οἱ τὰς ἀμφισβητήσεις ἔχοντες, ὧν τὰ ῥήματα κανόνες εἰσὶ τοῖς δικασταῖς περὶ ὧν μέλλουσιν ἀποφαίνεσθαι· μόνοις γὰρ τούτοις ἐπανέχειν ἀνάγκη, μηδενὸς ὄντος ἑτέρου τῶν εἰς ἔλεγχον· ἐξ οὗ συμβαίνει, τοὺς μὲν καταμαρτυρουμένους ἀδικεῖσθαι νικᾶν δυναμένους, τοὺς δὲ προσέχοντας δικαστὰς ἀδίκους καὶ παρανόμους
141 ψήφους ἀντὶ νομίμων καὶ δικαίων γράφειν. τὸ μέντοι πανούργημα φθάνει καὶ πρὸς ἀσέβειαν· οὐ γὰρ ἀνωμότοις δικάζειν ἔθος, ἀλλὰ μετὰ φρικωδεστάτων ὅρκων, οὓς παραβαίνουσι πρὸ τῶν ἀπατωμένων οἱ φενακίζοντες, ἐπειδὴ τῶν μὲν τὸ σφάλμα οὐ κατὰ γνώμην, οἱ δ' ἐπιστήμῃ καταστρατηγοῦσι καὶ ἐκ προνοίας ἁμαρτάνοντες καὶ τοὺς κυρίους τῆς ψήφου συνεξαμαρτάνειν ἀναπείθοντες οὐκ εἰδότας ὃ δρῶσιν ἐπὶ τιμωρίᾳ τῶν
[204] οὐδεμιᾶς ἀξίων κολάσεως. | διὰ μὲν δὴ ταῦτά μοι δοκεῖ ψευδομαρτυρίαν ἀπειπεῖν.

142 XXVIII. Τελευταῖον δ' ἐπιθυμεῖν ἀπαγορεύει νεωτεροποιὸν καὶ ἐπίβουλον τὴν ἐπιθυμίαν εἰδώς. πάντα μὲν γὰρ τὰ ψυχῆς πάθη χαλεπά, κινοῦντα καὶ σείοντα αὐτὴν παρὰ φύσιν καὶ ὑγιαίνειν οὐκ ἐῶντα, χαλεπώτατον δ' ἐπιθυμία· διὸ[1] τῶν μὲν ἄλλων ἕκαστον θύραθεν ἐπεισιὸν καὶ προσπῖπτον

[1] Perhaps read, as Cohn later, διότι. See note *d*.

---

[a] *i.e.* the jurymen.

[b] Perhaps understand the jurymen, but the analogy of § 91 points rather to "oaths."

[c] It will be seen that Philo extends the meaning of the word from covetousness of what is another's to desire in general, and this enables him to enter on a disquisition on the four passions of the Stoics. Driver notes that the Hebrew

witnesses whose words are taken by the jurymen as standards in determining the verdicts they are about to give, since they are obliged to fall back on these alone if there is no other means of testing the truth. The result is that those against whom the testimony is given suffer injustice when they might have won their case, and the judges who listen to the testimony record unjust and lawless instead of just and lawful votes. In fact, the knavery of the action amounts to 141
impiety, for it is the rule that jurymen must be put on their oaths and indeed oaths of the most terrific character which are broken not so much by the victims [a] as by the perpetrators of the deception, since the former do not err intentionally, while the latter with full knowledge set the oaths at nought.[b] They deliberately sin themselves and persuade those who have control of the voting to share their sin and, though they know not what they do, punish persons who deserve no chastisement. It was for these reasons, I believe, that He forbade false witness.

XXVIII. The last commandment is against covet- 142
ousness or desire [c] which he knew to be a subversive and insidious enemy. For all the passions of the soul which stir and shake it out of its proper nature and do not let it continue in sound health are hard to deal with, but desire is hardest of all. And therefore [d] while each of the others seems to be involuntary, an

word also is general and only gets its bad sense from the context. For some analogies with Stoic phraseology see App. p. 612.

[d] The logic of "therefore" is not at all clear; neither, however, is Cohn's later substitute of "because." Perhaps however χαλεπά may be taken = "baneful" or "evil," and Philo is, as so often, insisting on the difference in guilt between voluntary and involuntary sins.

ἔξωθεν ἀκούσιον εἶναι δοκεῖ, μόνη δ' ἐπιθυμία τὴν ἀρχὴν ἐξ ἡμῶν αὐτῶν λαμβάνει καὶ ἔστιν ἑκούσιος.
143 τί δ' ἐστὶν ὃ λέγω; τοῦ παρόντος καὶ νομισθέντος ἀγαθοῦ φαντασία διεγείρει καὶ διανίστησι τὴν ψυχὴν ἠρεμοῦσαν καὶ σφόδρα μετέωρον ἐξαίρει καθάπερ ὀφθαλμοὺς φῶς ἀναστράψαν· καλεῖται δὲ τουτὶ τὸ πάθος αὐτῆς ἡδονή.
144 τὸ δ' ἐναντίον ἀγαθῷ κακόν, ὅταν εἰσβιασάμενον[1] πληγὴν ἐπενέγκῃ καίριον, συννοίας καὶ κατηφείας εὐθὺς αὐτὴν ἀναπίμπλησιν ἄκουσαν· ὄνομα δὲ
145 [καὶ] τούτῳ τῷ πάθει λύπη. ὅταν δὲ τὸ κακὸν μήπω μὲν εἰσῳκισμένον θλίβῃ, μέλλῃ δ' ἀφικνεῖσθαι καὶ παρευτρεπίζηται, πτοίαν καὶ ἀγωνίαν, ἀποφράδας ἀγγέλους, προεκπέμπει δειματοῦντας· φόβος δὲ προσαγορεύεται τὸ πάθος.
146 ἐπειδὰν δὲ λαβών τις ἔννοιαν ἀγαθοῦ μὴ παρόντος ὀρέγηται τυχεῖν αὐτοῦ, πρὸς μήκιστον τὴν ψυχὴν ἐλαύνων[2] καὶ ἐπὶ πλεῖστον ἐκτείνων, ψαῦσαι τοῦ ποθουμένου γλιχόμενος, ὥσπερ ἐπὶ τροχοῦ κατατείνεται, σπεύδων μὲν συλλαβεῖν, ἐφικνεῖσθαι δ' ἀδυνατῶν καὶ ταὐτὸν πεπονθὼς τοῖς τοὺς ἐξαναχωροῦντας διώκουσιν ἐλάττονι μὲν τάχει προθυμίᾳ δ' ἀνανταγωνίστῳ.
147 ὅμοιον δέ τι καὶ περὶ τὰς αἰσθήσεις ἔοικε συμβαίνειν· ὀφθαλμοί τε γὰρ πολλάκις ὁρατοῦ τινος πάνυ μακρὰν ἀφεστῶτος εἰς κατάληψιν ἐλθεῖν ἐπειγόμενοι, τείνοντες αὐτούς, εὖ μάλα καὶ πλέον τῆς δυνάμεως ἐνεχθέντες, ὤλισθον κατὰ κενοῦ περὶ τὴν ἀκριβῆ τοῦ ὑποκειμένου γνῶσιν σφαλέντες καὶ

[1] So Cohn by a later correction for ἐκβιασάμενον, in which the prefix seems very inappropriate. One MS. gives ἐμβ-. No

extraneous visitation, an assault from outside, desire alone originates with ourselves and is voluntary.
What is it that I mean? The presenta- 143
tion to the mind of something which is actually with us and considered to be good, arouses and awakes the soul when at rest and like a light flashing upon the eyes raises it to a state of great elation. This sensation of the soul is called pleasure. And 144
when evil, the opposite of good, forces its way in and deals a home thrust to the soul, it at once fills it all against its will with depression and dejection. This sensation is called grief, or pain. When 145
the evil thing is not yet lodged inside nor pressing hard upon us but is on the point of arriving and is making its preparation, it sends in its van trepidation and distress, messengers of evil presage, to sound the alarm. This sensation is called fear. But 146
when a person conceives an idea of something good which is not present and is eager to get it, and propels his soul to the greatest distance and strains it to the greatest possible extent in his avidity to touch the desired object, he is, as it were, stretched upon a wheel, all anxiety to grasp the object but unable to reach so far and in the same plight as persons pursuing with invincible zeal, though with inferior speed, others who retreat before them. We 147
also find a similar phenomenon in the senses. The eyes are often eager to obtain apprehension of some very far off object. They strain themselves and carry on bravely and indeed beyond their strength, then hit upon a void and there slip, failing to get an accurate knowledge of the object in question,

---

such verb is known to the dictionaries, but it has the analogy of ἐμβάλλω.

[2] MSS. ἐλαύνει.

προσέτι τὴν ὄψιν τῷ βιαίῳ καὶ συντόνῳ τῆς
ἀτενοῦς προσβολῆς ἀσθενήσαντες ἀμαυροῦνται.[1]
148 καὶ θροῦ πάλιν ἀσαφοῦς ἐκ μακροῦ
διαστήματος φερομένου, τὰ ὦτα ἀνεγερθέντα καὶ
ἐπουρίσαντα ἵεται καὶ σπεύδει προσελθεῖν εἰ οἷόν
τε ἐγγυτέρω, πόθῳ τοῦ τρανωθῆναι ταῖς ἀκοαῖς
149 τὸν ἦχον· ὁ δ'—ἔτι γὰρ ἀμαυρὸς ὡς ἔοικε προσ-
πίπτει—οὐδὲν τῶν εἰς γνῶσιν τηλαυγέστερον
ἐπιδίδωσιν, ὡς ἔτι μᾶλλον τὸν ἀνήνυτον καὶ ἀ-
διεξίτητον ἐπιτείνεσθαι τοῦ καταλαβεῖν ἵμερον,
Ταντάλειον τιμωρίαν ἐπιφερούσης τῆς ἐπιθυμίας·
ἐκεῖνός τε γὰρ ὧν ὀρεχθείη πάντων ὁπότε μέλλοι
ψαύσειν, ἀπετύγχανεν, ὅ τε κρατηθεὶς ἐπιθυμίᾳ,
[205] διψῶν ἀεὶ τῶν ἀπόντων, οὐδέποτε πληροῦται περὶ
150 κενὴν ἰλυσπώμενος τὴν ὄρεξιν. ὥσπερ τε τὰ
ἑρπηνώδη τῶν νοσημάτων, εἰ μὴ προανακρουσθείη
τομαῖς ἢ καύσεσιν, ἐπιθέοντα σύμπασαν ἐν κύκλῳ
καταλαμβάνει τὴν τοῦ σώματος κοινωνίαν οὐδὲν
ἀπαθὲς μέρος ἐῶντα, οὕτως, εἰ μὴ λόγος ὁ κατὰ
φιλοσοφίαν ἰατροῦ δίκην ἀγαθοῦ ῥέουσαν τὴν
ἐπιθυμίαν ἐπίσχοι, πάντ' ἐξ ἀνάγκης τὰ τοῦ βίου
πράγματα κινηθήσεται παρὰ φύσιν· οὐδὲν γάρ
ἐστιν ὑπεξῃρημένον ὃ διαφεύγει τὸ πάθος, ἀλλ'
ὅταν ἄδειαν λάβῃ καὶ ἐκεχειρίαν, ἐπινέμεται καὶ
151 σίνεται[2] πάντα διὰ πάντων. εὔηθες ἴσως
μακρηγορεῖν ἐστι περὶ τῶν οὕτως ἐμφανῶν, ἃ τίς
ἀνὴρ ἢ πόλις ἀγνοεῖ καθ' ἑκάστην οὐχ ἡμέραν
μόνον ἀλλὰ καὶ ὥραν ὡς ἔπος εἰπεῖν ἔλεγχον
ἐναργῆ παριστάντα; χρημάτων ἔρως ἢ γυναικὸς
ἢ δόξης ἤ τινος ἄλλου τῶν ἡδονὴν ἀπεργαζομένων

[1] For text see App. p. 613.
[2] mss. γίνεται.

and furthermore they lose strength and their power of sight is dimmed by the intensity and violence of their steady gazing.
And again when an in- 148
distinct noise is carried from a long distance the ears are roused and pressed forward at high speed[a] and are eager to go nearer if they could, in their longing
to have the sound made clear to the hearing. The 149
noise however, whose impact evidently continues to be dull, does not shew any increase of clearness which might make it knowable, and so a still greater intensity is given to the ceaseless and indescribable longing for apprehension. For desire entails the punishment of Tantalus ; as he missed everything that he wished for just when he was about to touch it, so the person who is mastered by desire, ever thirsting for what is absent remains unsatisfied,
fumbling around his baffled appetite. And just as 150
diseases of the creeping type, if not arrested in time by the knife or cautery, course round all that unites to make the body and leave no part uninjured, so unless philosophical reasoning, like a good physician, checks the stream of desire, all life's affairs will be necessarily distorted from what nature prescribes. For there is nothing so secreted that it escapes from passion, which when once it finds itself in security and freedom spreads like a flame and works universal
destruction. It may perhaps be foolish 151
to dilate at this length on facts so obvious, for what man or city does not know that they provide clear proof of their truth, not only every day but almost every hour ? Consider the passion whether for money or a woman or glory or anything else that produces

[a] For the use of ἐπουρίζω (here intransitive) see note on *De Ab.* 20 and *Mos.* i. 283.

ἆρά γε μικρῶν καὶ τῶν τυχόντων αἴτιος γίνεται
152 κακῶν; οὐ διὰ τοῦτον[1] συγγένειαι μὲν ἀλλοτριοῦνται
τὴν φυσικὴν εὔνοιαν μεθαρμοζόμεναι πρὸς ἀνήκεστον ἔχθραν, χῶραι δὲ μεγάλαι καὶ πολυάνθρωποι στάσεσιν ἐμφυλίοις ἐρημοῦνται, γῆ δὲ καὶ θάλαττα πληροῦται τῶν καινουργουμένων αἰεὶ συμφορῶν
153 ναυμαχίαις[2] καὶ πεζαῖς στρατιαῖς; οἱ γὰρ Ἑλλήνων
καὶ βαρβάρων πρός τε ἑαυτοὺς καὶ πρὸς ἀλλήλους τραγῳδηθέντες πόλεμοι πάντες ἀπὸ μιᾶς πηγῆς ἐρρύησαν, ἐπιθυμίας ἢ χρημάτων ἢ δόξης ἢ ἡδονῆς· περὶ γὰρ ταῦτα κηραίνει τὸ τῶν ἀνθρώπων γένος.
154 XXIX. Ἅλις μὲν δὴ τούτων. χρὴ δὲ μηδ'
ἐκεῖνο ἀγνοεῖν, ὅτι οἱ δέκα λόγοι κεφάλαια νόμων εἰσὶ τῶν ἐν εἴδει παρ' ὅλην τὴν νομοθεσίαν ἐν ταῖς
155 ἱεραῖς βίβλοις ἀναγραφέντων. ὁ μὲν πρῶτος τῶν
περὶ μοναρχίας· οὗτοι δὲ δηλοῦσιν, ὅτι ἓν αἴτιον τοῦ κόσμου καὶ ἡγεμὼν καὶ βασιλεὺς εἷς ὁ ἡνιοχῶν καὶ κυβερνῶν τὰ ὅλα σωτηρίως, ὀλιγαρχίαν ἢ ὀχλοκρατίαν, ἐπιβούλους πολιτείας φυομένας παρ' ἀνθρώποις τοῖς κακίστοις ἐξ ἀταξίας καὶ πλεονεξίας, ἐξεληλακὼς ἐκ τοῦ καθαρωτάτου τῆς
156 οὐσίας, οὐρανοῦ. ὁ δὲ δεύτερος κεφά-
λαιόν ἐστι πάντων, ὅσα περὶ χειροκμήτων ἐνομοθετεῖτο, ἀγάλματα καὶ ξόανα καὶ συνόλως ἀφιδρύματα, ὧν γραφικὴ καὶ πλαστικὴ βλαβεραὶ δημιουργοί, κατασκευάζειν οὐκ ἐῶν οὐδ' ὅσα μύθων πλάσματα προσίεσθαι, θεογαμίαν καὶ θεο-
[206] γονίαν καὶ τὰς ἀμφοτέραις ἑπομένας | ἀμυθήτους

[1] MSS. τοῦτο.
[2] Cohn (in note to Treitel's translation) ναυμαχικαῖς. But,

pleasure: are the evils which it causes small or
casual? Is it not the cause why kinsmen become 152
estranged and change their natural goodwill to deadly hatred, why great and populous countries are desolated by internal factions, and land and sea are filled with ever-fresh calamaties wrought by
battles on sea and campaigns on land? For all the 153
wars of Greeks and barbarians between themselves or against each other, so familiar to the tragic stage, are sprung from one source, desire, the desire for money or glory or pleasure. These it is that bring disaster to the human race.

XXIX. Enough on this subject, but also we must 154
not forget that the Ten Covenants are summaries of the special laws which are recorded in the Sacred Books and run through the whole of the legislation.
The first summarizes the laws on God's monarchical 155
rule. These laws declare that there is one First Cause of the World, one Ruler and King, Who guides the chariot and steers the bark of the universe in safety, and has expelled from the purest part of all that exists, namely heaven, those mischievous forms of government, oligarchy and mob-rule, which arise among the vilest of men, produced by disorder and covetousness. The second sums 156
up all the enactments made concerning the works of men's hands. It forbids the making of images or wooden busts and idols in general produced by the baneful craftsmanship of painting and sculpture, and also the acceptance of fabulous legends about the marriages and pedigrees of deities and the numberless and very grave scandals associated with both

---

even if the word exists, which seems doubtful, I see no reason for the change.

157 καὶ ἀργαλεωτάτας κῆρας. τῷ δὲ τρίτῳ
ὑποστέλλει τά τε ἀνώμοτα πάντα καὶ ἐφ᾿ οἷς
ὀμνύναι δεῖ καὶ ὁπότε καὶ ὅπου χρὴ καὶ τίνα καὶ
πῶς ἔχοντα κατά τε ψυχὴν καὶ σῶμα καὶ ὅσα ἐπ᾿
εὐόρκοις καὶ τοὐναντίον ἐχρήσθη.

158 XXX. Τὸ δὲ τέταρτον, τὸ περὶ τῆς ἑβδομάδος,
οὐδὲν ἀλλ᾿ ἢ κεφάλαιον νομιστέον ἑορτῶν καὶ τῶν
διατεταγμένων εἰς ἑκάστην ἁγνευτικῶν, περιρραντηρίων τε αἰσίων καὶ ἐπηκόων εὐχῶν καὶ θυσιῶν
159 τελείων, αἷς ἡ λατρεία ἐγίνετο. ἑβδόμην δὲ λέγω
καὶ τὴν σὺν ἑξάδι τῇ γονιμωτάτῃ καὶ τὴν ἄνευ
ἑξάδος, ἐπιπροσθοῦσαν αὐτῇ, μονάδι ὁμοιουμένην,
ὧν ἑκατέρᾳ τὰς ἑορτὰς παραριθμεῖ· μονάδι μὲν
τήν τε ἱερομηνίαν, ἣν σάλπιγξιν ὑποσημαίνουσι,
καὶ νηστείαν, ἐν ᾗ σιτίων καὶ ποτῶν ἀποχὴ
διείρηται, καὶ ἣν Ἑβραῖοι πατρίῳ γλώττῃ Πάσχα
προσαγορεύουσιν, ἐν ᾗ θύουσι πανδημεὶ αὐτῶν[1]
ἕκαστος τοὺς ἱερεῖς αὐτῶν οὐκ ἀναμένοντες,
ἱερωσύνην τοῦ νόμου χαρισαμένου τῷ ἔθνει παντὶ

[1] Cohn suggests αὐτὸς on the ground that the stress lies on each man sacrificing himself.

---

[a] Or "the number seven." See App. p. 613.

[b] Six is the most creative of numbers, because its factors 2 and 3 represent the odd (or male) and the even (or female) principle. See *De Op.* 13.

[c] The seventh (or seven) which does not include six, seems to mean that in view of the mystical identity of seven and one (see on § 102) a feast which occupies one day only may be regarded as coming under the law of the seventh day.

[d] Or perhaps "supersedes it." The verb, derived from the adverb ἐπίπροσθεν, seems to be used of a thing which gets in front of something else and obscures it (*Spec. Leg.* iv. 52). So here the idea may be that the unit or monad does not need six to make it equivalent to seven.

of these. Under the third he includes 157
directions as to all the cases where swearing is forbidden and as to the time, place, matters, persons, state of soul and body which justify the taking of an oath, and all pronouncements concerning those who swear truthfully or the reverse.

XXX. The fourth, which treats of the seventh day,[a] 158
must be regarded as nothing less than a gathering under one head of the feasts and the purifications ordained for each feast, the proper lustrations and the acceptable prayers and flawless sacrifices with which the ritual was carried out. By the seventh I mean 159
both the seventh which includes the most creative of numbers, six,[b] and that which does not include it[c] but takes precedence of it[d] and resembles the unit. Both these are employed by him in reckoning the feast-times.[e] The unit is taken in the case of the holy-month-day[f] which they announce with trumpets, and the fast-day on which abstinence from food and drink is commanded, and the day called by the Hebrews in their own tongue the Pasch on which the whole people sacrifice, every member of them, without waiting for their priests, because the law has granted to the whole nation for

[e] The seven feasts which follow are enumerated again in *Spec. Leg.* ii. 41 and described at length in the following sections. They appear there, however, in the order in which they occur in the year and are not classified according to the number of days observed. Also there are three which do not appear in this list, the Sabbath itself, the feast of "Every Day" and the monthly New Moon. The first of these is of course implied here, and the omission of the second is not unnatural, but it is curious that the New Moon should be left out. Has τὴν νουμηνίαν fallen out before τήν τε ἱερομηνίαν?

[f] Or opening of the holy month, see App. pp. 613-614.

κατὰ[1] μίαν ἡμέραν ἐξαίρετον ἀνὰ πᾶν ἔτος εἰς
160 αὐτουργίαν θυσιῶν· καὶ ἔτι τὴν ἐν ᾗ προσφέρεται δράγμα χαριστήριον εὐγονίας καὶ φορᾶς τῆς πεδιάδος δι' ἀσταχύων πληρώσεως· καὶ τὴν ἀπὸ ταύτης καταριθμουμένην ἑπτὰ ἑβδομάσι πεντηκοστὴν ἡμέραν, ἐν ᾗ προσάγειν ἄρτους ἔθος, οἳ καλοῦνται πρωτογεννημάτων ἐτύμως, ἐπειδήπερ εἰσὶν ἀπαρχὴ γεννημάτων καὶ καρπῶν ἡμέρου τροφῆς, ἣν ἀνθρώπῳ τῷ ἡμερωτάτῳ ζῴων ἀπένειμεν ὁ θεός.
161 ἑβδομάδι δὲ τὰς μεγίστας καὶ πολυημέρους ἑορτὰς προσένειμε κατὰ τὰς τοῦ ἔτους ἰσημερίας, ἐαρινὴν καὶ μετοπωρινήν, δύο δυσὶν ἀναθείς, ἑκατέραν ἐφ' ἡμέρας ἑπτά, τὴν μὲν κατὰ τὸ ἔαρ ἐπὶ τελειώσει τῶν σπειρομένων, τὴν δὲ μετοπωρινὴν ἐπὶ συγκομιδῇ καρπῶν ἁπάντων, οὓς καὶ τὰ δένδρα ἤνεγκεν· ἑπτὰ δ' ἡμέραι ἀπενεμήθησαν εἰκότως ἑπτὰ μησὶ τῆς ἰσημερίας ἑκατέρας, ἵνα μὴν ἕκαστος λαμβάνῃ γέρας ἐξαίρετον μίαν ἱερὰν ἡμέραν· ἑορτώδη πρὸς εὐθυμίαν καὶ ἀπόλαυσιν
162 ἐκεχειρίας. ἐμφέρονται δὲ καὶ ἄλλοι νόμοι πάνυ καλῶς τεθέντες, εἰς ἡμερότητα καὶ κοινωνίαν ἀτυφίαν τε καὶ ἰσότητα προκαλούμενοι· τούτων οἱ μέν εἰσι περὶ τοῦ λεγομένου ἑβδοματικοῦ,[2] καθ'
[207] ὃ διείρηται πᾶσαν ἀργὴν | τὴν χώραν ἐᾶν μήτε σπείροντας μήτε ἀροῦντας μήτε δένδρα διακαθαίροντας ἢ τέμνοντας ἢ ὅσ' ἄλλα τῶν κατὰ γεωργίαν
163 ἐπιτελοῦντας· ἓξ γὰρ ἐνιαυτοῖς τήν τε πεδιάδα

[1] mss. καί.

[2] Perhaps, as Mangey suggests, ἔτους (or ἐνιαυτοῦ) has fallen out. *Cf.* Josephus, *Ant.* xi. 8. 6 τὸ ἑβδοματικὸν ἔτος . . . οὐδὲ γὰρ αὐτοὺς σπείρειν ἐν αὐτῷ. But why add λεγομένου? It sug-

one special day in every year the right of priesthood and of performing the sacrifices themselves.
Also the day on which a sheaf is brought as a 160
thanksgiving for fertility and for the produce of the lowlands as shown in the full corn in the ear; then by reckoning seven sevens after this the fiftieth day, when it is the custom to bring loaves the nature of which is properly described by their title of "loaves of the first-products," as they are the sample of the crops and fruits produced by civilized cultivation which God has assigned for his nourishment to man,
the most civilized of living things. To seven he gives 161
the chief feasts prolonged for many days, two feasts,[a] that is, for the two equinoxes, each lasting for seven days, the first in the spring to celebrate the ripeness of the sown crops, the second in the autumn for the ingathering of all the tree-fruits; also seven days were naturally assigned to the seven months of each equinox,[b] so that each month may have, as a special privilege, one festal day consecrated to cheerfulness
and enjoyment of leisure. Other laws, too, come 162
under the same head, admirable enactments exhorting men to gentleness and fellowship and simplicity and equality. Some of them deal with the hebdomadal year, as it is called, in which the land is ordered to be left entirely idle without any sowing or ploughing or purging or pruning of trees or any other opera-
tion of husbandry. For when both the lowlands and 163

[a] *i.e.* Unleavened Bread and Tabernacles, but the latter had eight days. See *Spec. Leg.* ii. 211.

[b] According to the ordinary inclusive reckoning each equinox occurs in the 7th month after the preceding.

---

gests rather that the simple τὸ ἑβδ. had become a recognized phrase for the sabbatical year.

καὶ τὴν ὀρεινὴν εἰς καρπῶν γένεσιν καὶ δασμῶν ἐτήσιον φορὰν πονηθείσας ἀνέσεως ἠξίωσε τοῦ διαπνεῦσαι χάριν καὶ ἀπελευθεριάσαι χρησαμένας[1]
164 ἀνεπικελεύστῳ τῇ φύσει. ἕτεροι δ' εἰσὶ περὶ τοῦ πεντηκοστοῦ ἔτους, ἐν ᾧ τά τε λεχθέντα ἀρτίως ἐπιτελεῖται καὶ—τὸ ἀναγκαιότατον—τῶν κληρουχιῶν ἀποκατάστασις εἰς τοὺς ἐξ ἀρχῆς λαχόντας οἴκους, πρᾶγμα φιλανθρωπίας καὶ δικαιοσύνης μεστόν.

165 XXXI. Τὸ δὲ πέμπτον, τὸ περὶ γονέων τιμῆς, πολλοὺς καὶ ἀναγκαίους νόμους ὑπαινίττεται, τοὺς ἐπὶ πρεσβύταις καὶ νέοις ἀναγραφέντας, τοὺς ἐπ' ἄρχουσι καὶ ὑπηκόοις, τοὺς ἐπ' εὐεργέταις καὶ εὖ πεπονθόσι, τοὺς ἐπὶ δούλοις καὶ δεσπόταις.
166 γονεῖς μὲν γὰρ ἐν τῇ κρείττονι τῶν εἰρημένων εἰσὶ τάξει, ἐν ᾗ πρεσβύτεροι, ἡγεμόνες, εὐεργέται, δεσπόται, παῖδες δὲ ἐν τῇ καταδεεστέρᾳ, ἐν ᾗ
167 νεώτεροι, ὑπήκοοι, εὖ πεπονθότες, δοῦλοι. πολλὰ δὲ καὶ ἄλλα προστέτακται, νέοις μὲν εἰς ἀποδοχὴν γήρως, πρεσβύταις δ' εἰς ἐπιμέλειαν νεότητος, καὶ ὑπηκόοις μὲν εἰς πειθαρχίαν ἡγεμόνων, ἡγεμόσι δ' εἰς ὠφέλειαν τῶν ἀρχομένων, καὶ εὖ μὲν πεπονθόσιν εἰς χαρίτων ἀμοιβάς, ἄρξασι δὲ δωρεῶν εἰς τὸ μὴ ζητεῖν καθάπερ ἐν δανείοις ἀπόδοσιν, καὶ θεράπουσι μὲν εἰς ὑπηρεσίαν φιλοδέσποτον, δεσπόταις δ' εἰς ἠπιότητα καὶ πρᾳότητα, δι' ὧν ἐξισοῦται τὸ ἄνισον.

168 XXXII. Καὶ ἡ μὲν προτέρα πεντὰς ἐν τούτοις περατοῦται[2] κεφαλαιώδη τύπον περιέχουσα, τῶν δ' ἐν εἴδει νόμων οὐκ ὀλίγος ἀριθμός. τῆς δ' ἑτέρας πρῶτόν ἐστι κεφάλαιον τὸ κατὰ μοιχῶν, ᾧ ὑπο-

[1] mss. χρησάμενος. [2] mss. περαιοῦται.

the uplands have been worked for six years to bring forth fruits and pay their annual tribute, he thought well to give them a rest to serve as a breathing-space in which they might enjoy the freedom of undirected
nature. And there are other laws about the fiftieth 164
year which is marked not only by the course of action just related, but also by the restoration of inheritance to the families which originally possessed them, a very necessary procedure abounding in humanity and justice.

XXXI. In the fifth commandment on honouring 165
parents we have a suggestion of many necessary laws drawn up to deal with the relations of old to young, rulers to subjects, benefactors to benefited, slaves to
masters. For parents belong to the superior class 166
of the above-mentioned pairs, that which comprises seniors, rulers, benefactors and masters, while children occupy the lower position with juniors, subjects,
receivers of benefits and slaves. And there are many 167
other instructions given, to the young on courtesy to the old, to the old on taking care of the young, to subjects on obeying their rulers, to rulers on promoting the welfare of their subjects, to recipients of benefits on requiting them with gratitude, to those who have given of their own initiative on not seeking to get repayment as though it were a debt, to servants on rendering an affectionate loyalty to their masters, to masters on showing the gentleness and kindness by which inequality is equalized.

XXXII. The first set having each of them the form 168
of a summary contains these five and no more, while the number of the special laws is considerable. In the other set the first head is that against adultery,

τέτακται πλεῖστα διατάγματα, τὸ κατὰ φθορέων, τὸ κατὰ παιδεραστῶν, τὸ κατὰ τῶν λαγνίστερον βιούντων ὁμιλίαις τε καὶ μίξεσιν ἐκνόμοις καὶ
169 ἀκολάστοις χρωμένων. τὰς δὲ ἰδέας ἀναγέγραφεν
[208] οὐχ ὑπὲρ τοῦ μηνῦσαι τὸ | πολύχουν καὶ πολύτροπον τῆς ἀκρασίας, ἀλλ' ὑπὲρ τοῦ τοὺς ἀσχημόνως ζῶντας ἐμφανέστατα δυσωπεῖν ἐπαντλοῦντα[1] τοῖς ὠσὶν αὐτῶν ἀθρόα ὀνείδη, δι' ὧν ἐρυθριάσουσι.
170 δεύτερον δὲ κεφάλαιον ἡ τοῦ μὴ ἀνδροφονεῖν ἀπαγόρευσις, ὑφ' ἣν εἰσι πάντες οἱ περὶ βιαίων, ὕβρεως, αἰκίας, τραυμάτων, πηρώσεως ἀναγκαῖοι νόμοι καὶ σφόδρα κοινωφελεῖς.
171 τρίτον δὲ τὸ περὶ τοῦ μὴ κλέπτειν, ᾧ ὑποτέτακται τὰ ἐπὶ χρεωκοπίαις ὁρισθέντα καὶ ἐξάρνοις παρακαταθηκῶν καὶ ἀκοινωνήτῳ κοινωνίᾳ καὶ ἀναισχύντοις ἁρπαγαῖς καὶ συνόλως πλεονεξίαις, ὑφ' ὧν πείθονταί τινες φανερῶς ἢ λάθρα τἀλλότρια
172 νοσφίζεσθαι. τέταρτον δὲ τὸ περὶ τοῦ μὴ ψευδομαρτυρεῖν, ᾧ πολλὰ ἐμφέρεται, τὸ μὴ ἀπατᾶν, τὸ μὴ συκοφαντεῖν, τὸ μὴ τοῖς ἐξαμαρτάνουσι συμπράττειν, τὸ μὴ ποιεῖσθαι προκάλυμμα πίστιν ἀπιστίας, ἐφ' οἷς ἅπασι νόμοι προσήκοντες
173 ἐτέθησαν. πέμπτον δὲ τὸ ἀνεῖργον τὴν τῶν ἀδικημάτων πηγήν, ἐπιθυμίαν, ἀφ' ἧς ῥέουσιν αἱ παρανομώταται πράξεις, ἴδιαι καὶ κοιναί, μικραὶ καὶ μεγάλαι, ἱεραὶ[2] καὶ βέβηλοι, περί τε σώματα

[1] So Cohn for MS. ἐπαντλοῦντας. But strict grammar requires ἐπαντλῶν.

[2] Mangey corrected to ἀνίεραι (ἀνίεροι?), "neque sane actiones ἱεραὶ possunt ab impuro fonte cupiditatis profluere." But an antithesis is clearly required and the deed may remain "sacred" though done from an impure motive.

[a] I understand this to refer to cases where a man repays a

under which come many enactments against seducers and pederasty, against dissolute living and indulgence
in lawless and licentious forms of intercourse. The 169
characteristics of these he has described, not to show the multiform varieties which incontinence assumes, but to bring to shame in the most open way those who live a disreputable life by pouring into their ears a flood of reproaches calculated to make them blush.
The second head forbids murder, and 170
under it come the laws, all of them indispensable and of great public utility, about violence, insult, outrage,
wounding and mutilation. The third is 171
that against stealing under which are included the decrees made against defaulting debtors, repudiations of deposits, partnerships which are not true to their name, shameless robberies and in general covetous feelings which urge men openly or secretly to appropriate the possessions of others. The 172
fourth against bearing false witness embraces many prohibitions. It forbids deceit, false accusation, co-operation with evil-doers and using honesty as a screen for dishonesty,[a] all of which have been the subjects of appropriate laws.
The fifth blocks that fount of injustice, desire, from 173
which flow the most iniquitous actions, public and private, small and great, dealing with things sacred or things profane, affecting bodies and souls and what

small sum or returns a small deposit in order to induce the other party to entrust him with something greater which he can embezzle. Philo has referred to this form of dishonesty in *De Cher.* 14 and *De Plant.* 101. One would expect it to come under the head of stealing, but Philo notes it in *Spec. Leg.* iv. 67 under the ninth commandment. Possibly, however, it may refer more generally to the false assumption of a truthful air.

καὶ ψυχὰς καὶ τὰ λεγόμενα ἐκτός· διαφεύγει γὰρ
οὐδέν, ὡς καὶ πρότερον ἐλέχθη, τὴν ἐπιθυμίαν,
ἀλλ' οἷα φλὸξ ἐν ὕλῃ νέμεται δαπανῶσα πάντα
174 καὶ φθείρουσα. πολλὰ δὲ καὶ τῶν ὑποπιπτόντων
αὐτῇ διατέτακται πρός τε νουθεσίας ἐπανόρθωσιν
ἐνδεχομένων καὶ πρὸς κόλασιν ἀφηνιαστῶν ὅλον
τὸν βίον ἐνδεδωκότων τῷ πάθει.

175 XXXIII. Τοσαῦτα καὶ περὶ τῆς δευτέρας πεντάδος ἀποχρώντως λέλεκται πρὸς ἐκπλήρωσιν τῶν
δέκα λογίων, ἅπερ ἱεροπρεπῶς ἔχρησεν αὐτὸς ὁ
θεός. ἦν γὰρ ἁρμόττον αὐτοῦ τῇ φύσει, κεφάλαια
μὲν τῶν ἐν εἴδει νόμων αὐτοπροσώπως θεσπίσαι,
νόμους δὲ τοὺς ἐν τῷ μέρει διὰ τοῦ τελειοτάτου
τῶν προφητῶν, ὃν ἐπικρίνας ἀριστίνδην καὶ ἀνα-
πλήσας ἐνθέου πνεύματος ἑρμηνέα τῶν χρησμῳ-
δουμένων εἵλετο.

176 Μετὰ δὲ ταῦτα λέγωμεν τὴν αἰτίαν, δι' ἣν τοὺς
δέκα λόγους ἢ νόμους ἀπεφήνατο ψιλαῖς προστάξεσι
καὶ ἀπαγορεύσεσι κατὰ τῶν παραβησομένων, ὡς
ἔθος νομοθέταις, μηδὲν ὁρίσας ἐπιτίμιον· θεὸς ἦν,
εὐθὺς δὲ κύριος ἀγαθός, μόνων ἀγαθῶν αἴτιος,
177 κακοῦ δ' οὐδενός. οἰκειότατον οὖν ὑπολαβὼν αὐτοῦ
τῇ φύσει τὰ σωτήρια κελεύειν ἀμιγῆ καὶ ἀμέτοχα
[209] τιμωρίας, ἵνα μή πως | φόβῳ τις ἄφρονι συμβούλῳ
χρησάμενος ἄκων ἀλλ' ἔμφρονι λογισμῷ καθ'
ἑκούσιον γνώμην αἱρῆται τὰ βέλτιστα, μετὰ

---

[a] Or "fuel."

[b] I do not think that Treitel and Mangey bring out the full sense of this. The essential characteristic of God as θεός is goodness, *cf. e.g. Spec. Leg.* i. 307. It is in His other aspect of κύριος that He gives the commandments, and is indeed the κολαστικὴ δύναμις, but the goodness of θεός is so

are called external things. For nothing escapes desire, and as I have said before, like a flame in the forest,[a] it spreads abroad and consumes and destroys everything. And there are many ordinances which 174
come under this head intended for the admonition of those who are capable of reformation and the punishment of the rebellious who have made a lifelong surrender to passion.

XXXIII. This is all that need be said regarding 175
the second five to complete our account of the ten oracles which God gave forth Himself as well befitted His holiness. For it was in accordance with His nature that the pronouncements in which the special laws were summed up should be given by Him in His own person, but the particular laws by the mouth of the most perfect of the prophets whom He selected for his merits and having filled him with the divine spirit, chose him to be the interpreter of His sacred utterances.

Next let us pass on to give the reason why He ex- 176
pressed the ten words or laws in the form of simple commands or prohibitions without laying down any penalty, as is the way of legislators, against future transgressors. He was God, and it follows at once that as Lord[b] He was good, the cause of good only and of nothing ill. So then He judged that it was 177
most in accordance with His being to issue His saving commandments free from any admixture of punishment, that men might choose the best, not involuntarily, but of deliberate purpose, not taking senseless fear but the good sense of reason for their counsellor.

far extended to κύριος that the execution of punishment, and indeed here the sentencing, is entrusted to subordinates. For a similar thought to this *cf. De Fuga* 66.

κολάσεως οὐκ ἠξίωσε θεσπίζειν, οὐκ ἀσυλίαν τοῖς ἀδικοπραγοῦσι διδούς, ἀλλ' εἰδὼς τὴν πάρεδρον αὐτῷ δίκην καὶ τῶν ἀνθρωπίνων ἔφορον πραγμάτων οὐκ ἠρεμήσουσαν ἅτε φύσει μισοπόνηρον καὶ ὥσπερ τι συγγενὲς ἔργον ἐκδεξομένην τὴν κατὰ
178 τῶν ἁμαρτανόντων ἄμυναν. ἐμπρεπὲς γὰρ ὑπηρέταις μὲν καὶ ὑπάρχοις θεοῦ καθάπερ τοῖς πολέμου στρατηγοῖς ἐπὶ λιποτάκταις οἳ λείπουσι τὴν τοῦ δικαίου τάξιν ἀμυντηρίοις χρῆσθαι, τῷ δὲ μεγάλῳ βασιλεῖ τὴν κοινὴν ἀσφάλειαν ἐπιγεγράφθαι τοῦ παντός, εἰρηνοφυλακοῦντι καὶ τὰ τῆς εἰρήνης ἀγαθὰ πάντα τοῖς πανταχοῦ πᾶσιν ἀεὶ πλουσίως καὶ ἀφθόνως χορηγοῦντι· τῷ γὰρ ὄντι ὁ μὲν θεὸς πρύτανις εἰρήνης, οἱ δ' ὑποδιάκονοι πολέμων ἡγεμόνες εἰσίν.

He therefore thought right not to couple punishment with His utterances, though He did not thereby grant immunity to evil-doers, but knew that justice His assessor, the surveyor of human affairs, in virtue of her inborn hatred of evil, will not rest, but take upon herself as her congenital task the punishment of
sinners. For it befits the servants and lieutenants of 178
God, that like generals in war-time they should bring vengeance to bear upon deserters who leave the ranks of justice. But it befits the Great King that the general safety of the universe should be ascribed to Him, that He should be the guardian of peace and supply richly and abundantly the good things of peace, all of them to all persons in every place and at every time. For indeed God is the Prince of Peace while His subalterns are the leaders in war.

THE SPECIAL LAWS
(DE SPECIALIBUS LEGIBUS)

INTRODUCTION TO *DE SPECIALIBUS LEGIBUS*, I

This treatise opens with a discussion of circumcision and its hygienic value (1-7), followed by its allegorical interpretation as signifying the excision of voluptuousness and conceit (8-11). The treatment of the First Commandment which follows (12-20) is much on the lines of that in *De Dec.*, as also is that of the Second (21-31) with the addition that it interprets "idols" symbolically also, as representing the vain things, such as wealth, which humanity worships.

In 32-35 the proof of God's existence, and in 36-50 the value of meditation on the Divine nature, inscrutable though it is, are set forth. While proselytes are to be welcomed, apostates must be put to death without mercy, as in the story of Phinehas (51-57). The prohibition of divination and like practices, for which the prophetic gift is the divinely-assigned substitute, concludes what he has to say about the laws which inculcate a proper conception of God (58-65). The rest of the treatise down to 298 is concerned with regulations of worship.

These begin with the Temple itself; the reasons that there is but one (66-70), a general description of it (71-75), its revenues (76-78); then the priests and Levites, the bodily qualifications required of them (79-81), their dress (82-83), and that of the high priest with the spiritual lessons symbolized by it (84-97), their abstinence from intoxicants while officiating (98-100), rules about their marriage, including some special rules applying only to the high priest (101-111), restrictions as to contact with dead bodies (112-116), and use of the sacrificial meats (117-130).

The revenues of the priests consist partly of tithes, including the ransom of the first-born (131-144), and the portions of the sacrifices allotted to them (145-155), similarly the revenues of the Levites or temple-attendants include the tithes as well as their forty-eight cities (156-161).

The animals allowed for sacrifices are doves, pigeons, sheep, goats, and oxen, all of which must be flawless (162-167). The various offerings follow as prescribed, daily or on the Sabbath (168-176), on the new moons (177-179), on the other feasts (180-189). There is also required on each occasion a he-goat as a sin-offering (190-193). These sacrifices may be classified as (*a*) whole-burnt-offerings, (*b*) "preservation" (or "peace") offerings, (*c*) sin-offerings

(194-197). The first class, whose motive is the honouring of God, is described in detail with full explanation of its symbolism (198-211). So, too, the second, which is a prayer for human betterment, with some reflections on the significance of the parts of the victim (212-223), and on a subdivision of them called "praise-offering" (224-225). The third, the sin-offering, which asks for pardon of the past, varies with the class of person offering it and whether the sin is voluntary or involuntary (226-246). Finally, we have an account of the special case of the Nazirite or "great" vow in which the offering of the Self partakes of the nature of all the three described above (247-254). In all these the offering has been given by laymen, but the priests also must make their oblation of fine flour (255-256).

What is required of the worshipper himself? Purity of soul (257-260), also of the body, but the method used of sprinkling with hyssop dipped in water poured on the ashes of a heifer is really a symbol of soul-purification (261-272). The same is shown by the superiority assigned to the altar of incense as against that on which animals are immolated (273-279), and by the prohibition of bringing the harlot's hire into the temple (280-284), and the high qualities required in the altar of the worshipper's soul are shown by the fire maintained on the altar (285-288), and the order that salt should always and honey and leaven never be used in the oblation (289-295). The next point, that the lamp on the sacred candlestick is to be kept alight all night as a thank-offering for the blessings of sleep seems somewhat irrelevant (296-298).

The spiritual lessons given above are all conveyed in the form of symbolical ritual. We pass on to the exhortations to virtue given in Deuteronomy (299-318). This leads him on to *ibid.* xxiii. 18, which he understands to be directed against "mysteries" as opposed to open preaching of righteousness (319-323), and then to *ibid.* 1-3, where various classes are excluded from the congregation (324-326).

A long allegory concludes the treatise. The five classes which he finds there symbolized are (*a*) the deniers of the Platonic Forms or Ideas (327-329), (*b*) atheists (330), (*c*) polytheists (331-332), (*d*) those who honour the human mind (333-336), or (*e*) human senses (337-343), rather than God, to whom the true disciple of Moses looks (344-345).

For Cohn's Numeration of Chapters see Gen. Int. p. xvii.

ΠΕΡΙ ΤΩΝ ΕΝ ΜΕΡΕΙ ΔΙΑΤΑΓΜΑΤΩΝ

ΠΕΡΙ ΤΩΝ ΑΝΑΦΕΡΟΜΕΝΩΝ ΕΝ ΕΙΔΕΙ ΝΟΜΩΝ ΕΙΣ ΔΥΟ ΚΕΦΑΛΑΙΑ ΤΩΝ ΔΕΚΑ ΛΟΓΙΩΝ, ΤΟ ΤΕ ΜΗ ΝΟΜΙΖΕΙΝ ΕΞΩ ΤΟΥ ΕΝΟΣ ΘΕΟΥΣ ΕΤΕΡΟΥΣ ΑΥΤΟΚΡΑΤΕΙΣ ΚΑΙ ΤΟ ΜΗ ΧΕΙΡΟΚΜΗΤΑ ΘΕΟΠΛΑΣΤΕΙΝ

[210]
1 I. Τὰ μὲν γένη τῶν ἐν εἴδει νόμων, οἱ προσαγο-
ρευόμενοι δέκα λόγοι, διὰ τῆς προτέρας ἠκρίβωνται
συντάξεως, τὰ δ' ἐν μέρει διατάγματα κατὰ τὴν τῆς
γραφῆς ἀκολουθίαν νῦν ἐπισκεπτέον. ἄρξομαι δ'
2 ἀπὸ τοῦ γελωμένου παρὰ τοῖς πολλοῖς. γελᾶται δὲ
ἡ τῶν γεννητικῶν περιτομή. πρᾶγμα σπουδαζό-
μενον οὐ μετρίως καὶ παρ' ἑτέροις ἔθνεσι καὶ
μάλιστα τῷ Αἰγυπτιακῷ, ὃ καὶ πολυανθρωπότατον
καὶ ἀρχαιότατον καὶ φιλοσοφώτατον εἶναι δοκεῖ.
3 παρὸ καὶ προσῆκον ἦν παιδικὴν χλεύην μεθεμένους
φρονιμώτερον καὶ σεμνότερον ἀναζητῆσαι τὰς αἰ-

---

[a] Or "gods with absolute powers," see § 13.

[b] In the MSS. this chapter is headed Περὶ περιτομῆς.

[c] Or (as Mangey and Heinemann) "in the order indicated in the scriptures," *i.e.* though the laws are not actually grouped in the Pentateuch under the Ten Commandments, such an order is suggested by the Decalogue. γραφή, however, in this sense seems to be regularly coupled with ἱερά.

the earliest men [a] held that the unseen and superior element to which the concepts of the mind owe their existence should have assimilated to it the visible and apparent, the natural parent of the things perceived by sense. The fourth and most vital reason is its 7
adaptation to give fertility of offspring, for we are told that it causes the semen to travel aright without being scattered or dropped into the folds of the foreskin, and therefore the circumcised nations appear to be the most prolific and populous.

II. These are the explanations handed down to us 8
from the old-time studies of divinely gifted men who made deep research into the writings of Moses. To these I would add that I consider circumcision to be a symbol of two things most necessary to our well-being. One is the excision of pleasures which be- 9
witch the mind. For since among the love-lures of pleasure the palm is held by the mating of man and woman, the legislators thought good to dock the organ which ministers to such intercourse, thus making circumcision the figure of the excision of excessive [b] and superfluous pleasure, not only of one pleasure but of all the other pleasures signified by one, and that the most imperious. The other 10
reason is that a man should know himself and banish from the soul the grievous malady of conceit. For there are some who have prided themselves on their power of fashioning as with a sculptor's cunning the fairest of creatures, man, and in their braggart pride assumed godship, closing their eyes to the Cause of all that comes into being, though they might find

[b] The equation of περιτομή with περιττῆς ἐκτομή is of course an intentional play upon words; or even perhaps an etymology.

11 ἐπανορθώσασθαι τὴν ἀπάτην δυνάμενοι· πολλοὶ μὲν
γὰρ παρ' αὐτοῖς εἰσιν ἄνδρες ἄγονοι, πολλαὶ δὲ
στεῖραι γυναῖκες, ὧν ἀτελεῖς αἱ ὁμιλίαι καταγηρα-
σάντων ἐν ἀπαιδίᾳ. πονηρὰν οὖν δόξαν ἐκτμητέον
τῆς διανοίας καὶ τὰς ἄλλας ὅσαι μὴ φιλόθεοι.
12 Τούτων μὲν δὴ πέρι τοσαῦτα· τρεπτέον δ' ἐπὶ
τοὺς κατὰ μέρος ἤδη νόμους καὶ πρώτους, ἀφ' ὧν
[213] ἄρχεσθαι καλόν, τοὺς περὶ μοναρχίας ὁρισθέντας.[a]
13 III. Τινὲς ἥλιον καὶ σελήνην καὶ τοὺς ἄλλους
ἀστέρας ὑπέλαβον εἶναι θεοὺς αὐτοκράτορας, οἷς
τὰς τῶν γινομένων ἁπάντων αἰτίας ἀνέθεσαν.
Μωυσεῖ δ' ὁ κόσμος ἔδοξεν εἶναι καὶ γενητὸς καὶ
καθάπερ πόλις ἡ μεγίστη, ἄρχοντας ἔχουσα καὶ
ὑπηκόους, ἄρχοντας μὲν τοὺς ἐν οὐρανῷ πάντας
ὅσοι πλάνητες καὶ ἀπλανεῖς ἀστέρες, ὑπηκόους δὲ
τὰς μετὰ σελήνην ἐν ἀέρι καὶ περιγείους φύσεις·
14 τοὺς δὲ λεχθέντας ἄρχοντας οὐκ αὐτεξουσίους, ἀλλ'
ἑνὸς τοῦ πάντων πατρὸς ὑπάρχους, οὗ μιμουμένους
τὴν ἐπιστασίαν κατορθοῦν πρυτανεύοντος[1] κατὰ
δίκην καὶ νόμον ἕκαστον τῶν γεγονότων· τοὺς δὲ
μὴ βλέποντας τὸν ἐπιβεβηκότα ἡνίοχον τοῖς ὑπ-
εζευγμένοις ὡς αὐτουργοῖς τῶν ἐν τῷ κόσμῳ γινο-
15 μένων ἀνάψαι τὰς αἰτίας. ὧν τὴν ἄγνοιαν ὁ
ἱερώτατος νομοθέτης εἰς ἐπιστήμην μεθαρμόζεται
λέγων ὧδε· "μὴ ἰδὼν τὸν ἥλιον καὶ τὴν σελήνην
καὶ τοὺς ἀστέρας καὶ πάντα τὸν κόσμον τοῦ οὐρανοῦ

[1] The variant πρυτανεύοντας is adopted by Heinemann, but see § 207.

---

[a] At this point the MSS. insert the heading Οἱ περὶ μοναρχίας νόμοι, *i.e.*, the laws about the sole sovereignty (of God), and the chapters which follow down to the end of § 65 are treated by

in their familiars a corrective for their delusion. For 11
in their midst are many men incapable of begetting and many women barren, whose matings are ineffective and who grow old childless. The evil belief, therefore, needs to be excised from the mind with any others that are not loyal to God.

So much for these matters. We must now turn 12
to the particular laws, taking those first with which it is well to begin, namely those the subject of which is the sole sovereignty of God.

III. [a] Some have supposed that the sun and moon 13
and the other stars were gods with absolute powers and ascribed to them the causation of all events. But Moses held that the universe was created and is in a sense the greatest of commonwealths, having magistrates and subjects; for magistrates, all the heavenly bodies, fixed or wandering; for subjects, such beings as exist below the moon, in the air or on
the earth. The said magistrates, however, in his view 14
have not unconditional powers, but are lieutenants of the one Father of All, and it is by copying the example of His government exercised according to law and justice over all created beings that they acquit themselves aright; but those who do not descry the Charioteer mounted above attribute the causation of all the events in the universe to the team that draw the chariot as though they were sole agents.
From this ignorance our most holy lawgiver would 15
convert them to knowledge with these words: "Do not when thou seest the sun and the moon and the stars and all the ordered host of heaven go astray and

Mangey and others as a separate treatise. Cohn observes this in his numeration of the chapters but not of the sections; see Gen. Introd. p. xviii.

πλανηθεὶς προσκυνήσῃς αὐτοῖς.ᵃ" εὐθυβόλως πάνυ
καὶ καλῶς πλάνον εἶπε τὴν τῶν εἰρημένων ὡς θεῶν
16 ἀποδοχήν. οἱ γὰρ ἰδόντες ἡλίου μὲν προσόδοις καὶ
ἀναχωρήσεσι τὰς ἐτησίους ὥρας συνισταμένας, ἐν
[214] αἷς αἱ | ζῴων καὶ φυτῶν καὶ καρπῶν γενέσεις
ὡρισμέναις χρόνων περιόδοις τελεσφοροῦνται, σελήνην δ' ὑπηρέτιν καὶ διάδοχον ἡλίου νύκτωρ τὴν
ἐπιμέλειαν καὶ προστασίαν ἀνειληφυῖαν ὧν μεθ'
ἡμέραν ἥλιος, καὶ τοὺς ἄλλους ἀστέρας κατὰ τὴν
πρὸς τὰ ἐπίγεια συμπάθειαν μυρία τῶν ἐπὶ διαμονῇ
τοῦ παντὸς ἐνεργοῦντάς τε καὶ δρῶντας, πλάνον
ἐπλανήθησαν ἀνήνυτον μόνους εἶναι τούτους θεοὺς
17 ὑποτοπήσαντες. εἰ δ' ἐσπούδασαν διὰ τῆς ἀ-
πλανοῦς βαδίζειν ὁδοῦ, κἂν εὐθὺς ἔγνωσαν ὅτι,
καθάπερ αἴσθησις ὑποδιάκονος νοῦ γέγονε, τὸν
αὐτὸν τρόπον καὶ οἱ αἰσθητοὶ πάντες ὑπηρέται τοῦ
νοητοῦ κατέστησαν, ἀγαπήσαντες εἰ δευτερείων
18 ἐφίξονται. παγγέλοιον γὰρ οἴεσθαι, ὅτι ὁ μὲν νοῦς
ὁ ἐν ἡμῖν βραχύτατος ὢν καὶ ἀόρατος ἡγεμὼν τῶν
αἰσθητικῶν ὀργάνων ἐστίν, ὁ δὲ τοῦ παντὸς ὁ
μέγιστος καὶ τελειότατος οὐχὶ βασιλεὺς βασιλέων
19 εἶναι πέφυκε, βλεπομένων οὐ βλεπόμενος. πάντας
οὖν τοὺς κατ' οὐρανὸν οὓς αἴσθησις ἐπισκοπεῖ θεοὺς
οὐκ αὐτοκρατεῖς νομιστέον, τὴν ὑπάρχων τάξιν
εἰληφότας, ὑπευθύνους μὲν φύσει γεγονότας, ἕνεκα
20 δ' ἀρετῆς εὐθύνας οὐχ ὑφέξοντας. ὥσθ' ὑπερβάντες
τῷ λογισμῷ πᾶσαν τὴν ὁρατὴν οὐσίαν ἐπὶ τὴν τοῦ
ἀειδοῦς καὶ ἀοράτου καὶ μόνῃ διανοίᾳ καταληπτοῦ
τιμὴν ἴωμεν, ὃς οὐ μόνον θεὸς θεῶν ἐστι νοητῶν τε

ᵃ Deut. iv. 19.

worship them." [a] Well indeed and aptly does he call the acceptance of the heavenly bodies as gods a going astray or wandering. For those who see the sun 16
with its advances and retreats producing the yearly seasons in which the animals and plants and fruits are brought at fixed periods of time from their birth to maturity, and the moon as handmaid and successor to the sun taking over at night the care and supervision of all that he had charge of by day, and the other stars in accordance with their sympathetic affinity to things on earth acting and working in a thousand ways for the preservation of the All, have wandered infinitely far in supposing that they alone are gods. But if they had been at pains to walk in 17
that road where there is no straying, they would at once have perceived that just as sense is the servitor of mind, so too all the beings perceived by sense are the ministers of Him who is perceived by the mind. It is enough for them if they gain the second place. For it is quite ridiculous to deny that if the mind in 18
us, so exceedingly small and invisible, is yet the ruler of the organs of sense, the mind of the universe, so transcendently great and perfect, must be the King of kings who are seen by Him though He is not seen by them. So all the gods which sense descries in 19
Heaven must not be supposed to possess absolute power but to have received the rank of subordinate rulers, naturally liable to correction, though in virtue of their excellence never destined to undergo it. Therefore carrying our thoughts beyond all the realm 20
of visible existence let us proceed to give honour to the Immaterial, the Invisible, the Apprehended by the understanding alone, who is not only God of gods, whether perceived by sense or by mind, but

καὶ αἰσθητῶν ἀλλὰ καὶ πάντων δημιουργός. ἐὰν δέ τις τὴν τοῦ ἀιδίου καὶ ποιητοῦ θεραπείαν ἄλλῳ προσνέμῃ νεωτέρῳ καὶ γενητῷ, φρενοβλαβὴς ἀναγεγράφθω καὶ ἔνοχος ἀσεβείᾳ τῇ μεγίστῃ.

21 IV. Εἰσὶ δέ τινες οἳ χρυσὸν καὶ ἄργυρον ἀνδριαντοποιοῖς ὡς θεοπλαστεῖν ἱκανοῖς παρέδοσαν· οἱ δὲ λαβόντες ἀργὴν ὕλην θνητῷ παραδείγματι προσχρησάμενοι, τὸ παραλογώτατον, θεοὺς ὅσα τῷ δοκεῖν ἐμόρφωσαν· καὶ νεὼς κατασκευάσαντες καὶ ἱδρυσάμενοι βωμοὺς ἐδείμαντο[1] θυσίαις τε καὶ πομπαῖς καὶ ταῖς ἄλλαις ἱερουργίαις τε καὶ ἁγιστείαις ἐπιμελῶς πάνυ καὶ πεφροντισμένως γεραίρουσιν, ἱερέων τε καὶ ἱερειῶν τὸν περὶ ταῦτα τῦφον ὡς ἔνι μάλιστα
22 σεμνοποιούντων. οἷς ὁ τῶν ὅλων πατὴρ προαγορεύει λέγων· "οὐ ποιήσετε μετ' ἐμοῦ[2] θεοὺς ἀργυροῦς καὶ χρυσοῦς," μόνον οὐκ ἄντικρυς ἀναδιδάσκων, ὅτι οὐδ' ἐξ ἑτέρας ὕλης χειρόκμητον οὐδὲν τὸ παράπαν θεοπλαστήσετε διακωλυθέντες ἐκ τῶν ἀρίστων· ἄργυρος γὰρ καὶ χρυσὸς τὰ πρωτεῖα
23 τῶν ἐν ὕλαις φέρονται. δίχα δὲ τῆς ῥητῆς ἀπαγορεύσεως καὶ ἕτερον αἰνίττεσθαί μοι δοκεῖ τῶν πρὸς ἠθοποιΐαν μάλιστα συντεινόντων, διελέγχων
[215] οὐ μετρίως τοὺς φιλοχρημάτους, | οἳ πανταχόθεν μὲν ἀργύριον καὶ χρυσίον ἐκπορίζουσι, τὸ δὲ

[1] Perhaps omit ἐδείμαντο; the sentence is clearer without it.
[2] MSS. μετ' ἐμὲ or ἐμοὶ or ὑμῖν or omit. Cohn's adoption of μετ' ἐμοῦ is based on *Leg. All.* i. 51, where the verse is quoted in most MSS. with μετ' ἐμοῦ, but in one μετ' ἐμέ. The LXX has ὑμῖν αὐτοῖς. In this uncertainty I print Cohn's text, but cannot follow his reasoning. Philo does not by any means always keep the same form in his quotations.

[a] Here Philo begins the consideration of the second commandment, though no special heading is given in the MSS.

also the Maker of all. And if anyone renders the worship due to the Eternal, the Creator, to a created being and one later in time, he must stand recorded as infatuated and guilty of impiety in the highest degree.

IV. [a] There are some who put gold and silver in the hands of sculptors as though they were competent to fashion gods; and the sculptors taking the crude material and furthermore using mortal form for their model, to crown the absurdity shape gods, as they are supposed to be. And after erecting and establishing temples they have built altars and in their honour hold sacrifices and processions with other religious rites and ceremonies conducted with the most elaborate care, and the vain shew is treated by priests and priestesses with the utmost possible solemnity. 21
Such idolaters are warned by the Ruler of All in these words: "Ye shall not make with Me gods of silver and gold," and the lesson conveyed is little less than a direct command,[b] "Neither shall ye make gods the work of your hands from any other material if you are prevented from using the best," for silver and gold hold first place among the sculptor's materials. 22
But apart from the literal prohibition, He seems to me to suggest another thought of great value for the promotion of morality,[c] and to condemn strongly the money-lovers who procure gold and silver coins from every side and treasure their hoard like a 23

[b] Ex. xx. 23. The argument appears to be "if gold and silver idols are forbidden, still more are idols of inferior materials."

[c] *i.e.* in the sphere of human conduct, as opposed to our relation to God, to which the commandment in the literal sense belongs. *Cf.* the antithesis of ἠθική and φυσική (in the sense of theological), *Mos.* ii. 96.

πορισθὲν ὡς ἄγαλμα θεῖον ἐν ἀδύτοις θησαυροφυλακοῦσιν, ἀγαθῶν αἴτιον καὶ τῆς συμπάσης εὐ-
24 δαιμονίας τοῦτ' εἶναι νομίζοντες. καὶ ὅσοι μέντοι τῶν ἀπόρων κεκράτηνται χαλεπῇ νόσῳ, φιλαργυρίᾳ, οὐκ ἔχοντες ἴδιον πλοῦτον, ὃν θεραπείας ἀξιώσουσι, τὸν τῶν πλησίον τεθηπότες καὶ προσκυνοῦντες ἕωθεν εἰς τὰς τῶν περιουσιαζόντων οἰκίας ἀφικνοῦνται καθάπερ εἰς ἱερὰ μέγιστα, προσευξόμενοι καὶ τἀγαθὰ παρὰ τῶν δεσποτῶν ὡς θεῶν αἰτησόμενοι.
25 πρὸς οὓς καὶ ἐν ἑτέροις φησίν· "οὐκ ἐπακολουθήσετε εἰδώλοις καὶ θεοὺς χωνευτοὺς οὐ ποιήσετε," διὰ συμβόλων ἀναδιδάσκων, ὅτι πλούτῳ τιμὰς ἰσοθέους ἀπονέμειν οὐ προσήκει· πλούτου γὰρ αἱ περιβόητοι ὗλαι χρυσὸς καὶ ἄργυρος χεῖσθαι[1] πεφύκασιν, αἷς ἀκολουθοῦσιν οἱ πολλοὶ τὰ τοῦ λεγομένου τυφλοῦ πλούτου μόνα ἢ μάλιστα εὐδαιμονίας αἴτια
26 νομίζοντες. τάδ' ἐστὶν ἅ φησιν "εἴδωλα," σκιαῖς ἐοικότα καὶ φάσμασιν, οὐδενὸς ἠρτημένα ἰσχυροῦ καὶ βεβαίου· φέρεται γὰρ πνεύματος τρόπον ἀστάτου τροπὰς καὶ μεταβολὰς παντοίας ἐνδεχόμενα. σημεῖον δ' ἐστὶ τούτων ἐναργές· μὴ προλαβόντων ἐξαπιναίως ἔστιν ὅτε προσέπτη, παγίως ἐνειλῆφθαι νομιζόντων πάλιν ἀπεπήδησε, καὶ ὅτε μέντοι πάρεστι, καθάπερ τὰ διὰ τῶν κατόπτρων εἴδωλα φαντάζεται τὴν αἴσθησιν ἀπατῶντα καὶ καταγοη-

[1] This is the reading of two out of four MSS. supported by κεῖσθαι of the other two. Cohn, relying on the superior authority of R, on which see Gen. Introd. pp. xv f., prints εἶναι. I have retained χεῖσθαι, as it seems to me needed to bring out the full sense.

[a] Lev. xix. 4.

divine image in a sanctuary, believing it to be a
source of blessing and happiness of every kind. And 24
further, all the needy who are possessed by that grievous malady, the desire for money, though they have no wealth of their own on which they may bestow worship as its due, pay awe-struck homage to that of their neighbours, and come at early dawn to the houses of those who have abundance of it as though they were the grandest temples, there to make their prayers and beg for blessing from the
masters as though they were gods. To such he says 25
elsewhere "Ye shall not follow idols and ye shall not make molten gods,"[a] thus teaching them in a figure that it is not fitting to assign divine honours to wealth. For it is the nature of the far-famed materials of wealth, gold and silver, to melt,[b] and they are followed by the multitude who think that what "blind"[c] wealth has to give is the sole or the chief source of
happiness. It is these that he calls "idols," like to 26
shadows and phantoms, with nothing firm or strong to which they can cling. They are borne along like a restless wind, subject to every kind of change and alteration. And of this we have a clear proof. Sometimes they suddenly light on one who has never owned them ere now: then again, when he thinks that they are firmly grasped, they spring away. And indeed when they are present, the apparition is like idols or images seen through mirrors, deceiving and

[b] The argument is "since gold and silver, substances which *melt*, are the chief materials of the *phantom* wealth, idols (*i.e.* phantoms) and *molten* gods may be understood to indicate riches." If εἶναι is read instead of χεῖσθαι, the point of χωνευτοὺς is lost.

[c] The addition of λεγομένου indicates that the phrase is proverbial or a quotation. See App. pp. 615-616.

τεύοντα καὶ ὡς ἂν ὑφεστηκότα τὰ μὴ ὑπομένοντα.
27 καὶ τί δεῖ τὸν ἀνθρώπινον πλοῦτον ἢ τῦφον, ὃν ἀναζωγραφοῦσιν αἱ κεναὶ δόξαι, δηλοῦν ὡς ἔστιν ἀβέβαιος; ἤδη γάρ τινες καὶ τὰ ἄλλα πάντα ζῷα καὶ φυτά, ὧν γένεσίς ἐστι καὶ φθορά, συνεχῶς μὲν καὶ ἀπαύστως φασὶ ῥεῖσθαι, τῆς δ' ἀπορροίας ἀδηλοτέραν αἴσθησιν εἶναι, ἀεὶ νικώσης τῆς περὶ τὴν ῥύσιν[1] ὀξύτητος τὴν δι' ὄψεως ἀκριβῆ προσβολήν.

28 V. Ἀλλ' οὐ μόνον πλοῦτος καὶ δόξα καὶ τὰ τοιοῦτα εἴδωλα καὶ ἀμενηναὶ σκιαί, ἀλλὰ καὶ[2] πάντες, οὓς οἱ μυθογράφοι διαπλάσαντες ἐξετύφωσαν ἐπιτειχίσαντες τὰς ψευδεῖς δόξας κατὰ τῆς ἀληθείας, θεοὺς καινοὺς ὥσπερ ἀπὸ μηχανῆς εἰσαγαγόντες ἕνεκα τοῦ τὸν ἀίδιον καὶ ὄντα ὄντως θεὸν λήθῃ παραδοθῆναι. πρὸς δὲ τὸ εὐπαράγωγον μέλεσι καὶ ῥυθμοῖς καὶ μέτροις ἐνηρμόσαντο τὸ ψεῦδος, νομίζοντες ῥᾳδίως καταγοητεύσειν τοὺς
29 ἐντυγχάνοντας. οὐ μὴν ἀλλὰ καὶ πλαστικὴν καὶ
[216] ζωγραφίαν συνεργοὺς τῆς ἀπάτης | προσπαρέλαβον, ἵνα χρωμάτων καὶ σχημάτων καὶ ποιοτήτων εὖ δεδημιουργημέναις ἰδέαις ὑπαγάγωνται τοὺς ὁρῶντας καὶ τὰς ἡγεμονίδας αἰσθήσεις ὄψιν καὶ ἀκοὴν δελεάσαντες, τὴν μὲν ἀψύχοις εὐμορφίαις, τὴν δ' εὐφωνίᾳ ποιητικῇ, συναρπάσωσι τὴν ψυχὴν ἀ-
30 βέβαιον καὶ ἀνίδρυτον αὐτὴν ἀπεργασάμενοι. διὰ

[1] MSS. φύσιν or φορὰν.
[2] Cohn suggests (μῦθοι) πάντες, and so apparently Heinemann. It seems to me needless and less forcible. *Cf.* ii. 164 θεῶν . . . οὓς τὸ ποιητικὸν γένος ἐμύθευσε. Mangey reads with two MSS. ἄλλαι ἀπάται ἃς.

[a] Particularly Heracleitus and his followers. See App p. 616.

bewitching the sense and seeming to subsist when they have no abiding substance. And why need we 27
prove that human riches or human vanity, which empty-headed thinking paints in such bright colours, are unstable? For we know that some[a] assert that all other living creatures and plants which are born and perish are in a constant and ceaseless state of flux, though our perception of the effluence is indistinct, because the swiftness of its course always defeats the efforts of the eyesight to observe it with exactness.

V. But not only wealth and glory and the like 28
are idols and unsubstantial shadows, but also all those personages, which the myth-makers have invented and spread delusion therewith, building up their false imaginations into a stronghold to menace the truth, and staging as by machinery[b] new gods, in order that the eternal and really existing God might be consigned to oblivion. And to promote the seductiveness they have fitted the falsehood into melody, metre and rhythm,[c] thinking to cajole their audience thereby. Further, too, they have brought 29
in sculpture and painting to co-operate in the deception, in order that with the colours and shapes and artistic qualities wrought by their fine workmanship they may enthrall the spectators and so beguile the two leading senses, sight and hearing—sight through lifeless shapes of beauty, hearing through the charm of poetry and music—and thus make the soul unsteady and unsettled and seize it for their prey.

[b] I do not know how to translate this phrase. It is said to denote "a sudden or unexpected event," but this seems to me inadequate. See App. p. 616.

[c] The regular triple division of music. See note on *De Som.* i. 205.

τοῦτ' ἐπιστάμενος ἐπὶ μέγα δυνάμεως προεληλυθότα τὸν τῦφον καὶ δορυφορούμενον ὑπὸ τοῦ πλείστου γένους ἀνθρώπων οὐκ ἐξ ἀνάγκης ἀλλ' ἑκουσίοις γνώμαις, εὐλαβηθεὶς μή ποτε καὶ οἱ ζηλωταὶ τῆς ἀδεκάστου καὶ ἀληθοῦς εὐσεβείας καθάπερ ὑπὸ χειμάρρου παρασυρῶσιν, ἐνσφραγίζεται βαθεῖς τύπους ταῖς διανοίαις ἐγχαράττων ὁσιότητος, ὑπὲρ τοῦ μὴ συγχυθέντας ἢ ἐπιλεανθέντας ἀμαυρωθῆναί ποτε χρόνῳ, καὶ συνεχῶς ἐπᾴδει ποτὲ μὲν λέγων ὅτι θεὸς εἷς ἐστι καὶ κτίστης καὶ ποιητὴς τῶν ὅλων, ποτὲ δὲ ὅτι κύριος τῶν γεγονότων, ἐπειδὴ τὸ βέβαιον καὶ πάγιον καὶ τὸ
31 κῦρος ὡς ἀληθῶς περὶ αὐτὸν μόνον πέφυκε. λέλεκται δ' ὅτι "οἱ προσκείμενοι τῷ ὄντι θεῷ ζῶσι πάντες."[a] ἆρ' οὐχ οὗτός ἐστιν ὁ τρισμακάριος καὶ τρισευδαίμων βίος, ἀγαπητικῶς ἔχεσθαι τῆς θεραπείας τοῦ πρεσβυτάτου πάντων αἰτίου καὶ μὴ τοὺς ὑποδιακόνους καὶ πυλωροὺς πρὸ τοῦ βασιλέως θεραπεύειν ἀξιοῦν; ἀθάνατος ἥδε ἡ ζωὴ καὶ μακραίων ἐν ταῖς τῆς φύσεως στήλαις ἀναγέγραπται· ταυτὶ δὲ τὰ γράμματα τῷ κόσμῳ συνδιαιωνίζειν ἀναγκαῖον.

32 VI. Δυστόπαστος μὲν οὖν καὶ δυσκατάληπτος ὁ πατὴρ καὶ ἡγεμὼν τῶν συμπάντων ἐστίν, ἀλλ' οὐ διὰ τοῦτ' ἀποκνητέον τὴν ζήτησιν αὐτοῦ. δύο δ' ἐν ταῖς περὶ θεοῦ ζητήσεσι τὰ ἀνωτάτω ταῦτ' ἐπαπορεῖ ἡ διάνοια τοῦ φιλοσοφοῦντος ἀνόθως· ἓν μὲν εἰ ἔστι τὸ θεῖον, ἕνεκα τῶν ἐπιτηδευσάντων ἀθεότητα, κακιῶν τὴν μεγίστην· ἕτερον δὲ τὸ τί ἐστι κατὰ τὴν οὐσίαν. τὸ μὲν οὖν πρότερον οὐ

---

[a] Deut. iv. 4. The meaning of the original is that all those

Therefore knowing that vanity had attained high 30
power and was championed by the greater part of the human race, not under compulsion but of their own free will, and fearing lest the devotees of piety, true and incorruptible, might be swept away as by a torrent, he stamped upon their minds as with a seal deep imprints of holiness, so that no fusion or smoothing in the course of years should ever blur their distinctness. This lesson he continually repeats, sometimes saying that God is one and the Framer and Maker of all things, sometimes that He is Lord of created beings, because stability and fixity and lordship are by nature vested in Him alone. We are 31
told, too, that "those who cling to the God that IS all live."[a] Is not this the thrice-happy and thrice-blessed life, to cling lovingly to the service of the most ancient Cause of all and to reject the thought of serving the menials and the door-keepers rather than the King? This true life stands inscribed on the tables of nature as deathless and agelong, and the writing that records it must endure with the universe to all eternity.

VI. Doubtless hard to unriddle and hard to ap- 32
prehend is the Father and Ruler of all, but that is no reason why we should shrink from searching for Him. But in such searching two principal questions arise which demand the consideration of the genuine philosopher. One is whether the Deity exists, a question necessitated by those who practise atheism, the worst form of wickedness, the other is what the Deity is in essence. Now to answer the first question

who took God's side when the others followed Baal Peor are still alive. Philo has given the same extension of the meaning in *De Fuga* 56, and again in § 345 below.

πολὺς πόνος ἰδεῖν, τὸ δὲ δεύτερον οὐ χαλεπὸν μόνον ἀλλὰ καὶ ἴσως ἀδύνατον. ἐπισκεπτέον δ' ἑκάτερον.
33 ἀεὶ τοίνυν γνωρίσματα τῶν δημιουργῶν πέφυκέ πως εἶναι τὰ δημιουργηθέντα· τίς γὰρ ἀνδριάντας ἢ γραφὰς θεασάμενος οὐκ εὐθὺς ἐνενόησεν ἀνδριαντοποιὸν ἢ ζωγράφον; τίς δὲ ἐσθῆτας ἢ ναῦς ἢ οἰκίας ἰδὼν οὐκ ἔννοιαν ἔλαβεν ὑφάντου καὶ ναυπηγοῦ καὶ οἰκοδόμου; παρελθὼν δέ τις εἰς πόλιν εὔνομον, ἐν ᾗ τὰ τῆς πολιτείας σφόδρα καλῶς διακεκόσμηται, τί ἕτερον ὑπολήψεται ἢ ὅτι ἐπ-
[217] ιστατεῖται ἥδε ἡ πόλις ὑπ' ἀρχόντων | ἀγαθῶν;
34 τὸν οὖν ἀφικόμενον εἰς τὴν ὡς ἀληθῶς μεγαλόπολιν, τόνδε τὸν κόσμον, καὶ θεασάμενον τὴν ὀρεινὴν καὶ πεδιάδα βρίθουσαν[1] ζῴων καὶ φυτῶν καὶ ποταμῶν αὐθιγενῶν καὶ χειμάρρων φορὰς καὶ πελαγῶν ἀναχύσεις καὶ εὐκρασίας ἀέρος καὶ τῶν ἐτησίων ὡρῶν τροπάς, εἶτα ἥλιον καὶ σελήνην, τοὺς ἡμέρας καὶ νυκτὸς ἡγεμόνας, καὶ τὰς τῶν ἄλλων πλανήτων τε καὶ ἀπλανῶν καὶ τοῦ σύμπαντος οὐρανοῦ περιπολήσεις καὶ χορείας, οὐκ εἰκότως, μᾶλλον δὲ ἀναγκαίως, ἔννοιαν λήψεσθαι δεῖ τοῦ ποιητοῦ καὶ
35 πατρὸς καὶ προσέτι ἡγεμόνος; οὐδὲν γὰρ τῶν τεχνικῶν ἔργων ἀπαυτοματίζεται· τεχνικώτατον δὲ καὶ ἐπιστημονικώτατον ὅδε ὁ κόσμος, ὡς ὑπό τινος τὴν ἐπιστήμην ἀγαθοῦ καὶ τελειοτάτου πάντως δεδημιουργῆσθαι. τοῦτον τὸν τρόπον ἔννοιαν ἐλάβομεν ὑπάρξεως θεοῦ.
36 VII. Τὴν δ' οὐσίαν, εἰ καὶ δυσθήρατον καὶ

[1] So Cohn from R in preference to the πλήθουσαν or πληθύουσαν of the other MSS. It seems to me doubtful. βρίθω more especially = "laden with," and so Philo, *De Op.* 85 κριοὶ βρίθοντες βαθέσι μαλλοῖς.

does not need much labour, but the second is not only difficult but perhaps impossible to solve. Still,
both must be examined. [a] We see then that any 33
piece of work always involves the knowledge of a workman. Who can look upon statutes or painting without thinking at once of a sculptor or painter? Who can see clothes or ships or houses without getting the idea of a weaver and a shipwright and a house-builder? And when one enters a well-ordered city in which the arrangements for civil life are very admirably managed, what else will he suppose but
that this city is directed by good rulers? So then 34
he who comes to the truly Great City, this world, and beholds hills and plains teeming with animals and plants, the rivers, spring-fed or winter torrents, streaming along, the seas with their expanses, the air with its happily tempered phases, the yearly seasons passing into each other,[b] and then the sun and moon ruling the day and night, and the other heavenly bodies fixed or planetary and the whole firmament revolving in rhythmic order, must he not naturally or rather necessarily gain the conception of the Maker
and Father and Ruler also? For none of the works 35
of human art is self-made, and the highest art and knowledge is shewn in this universe, so that surely it has been wrought by one of excellent knowledge and absolute perfection. In this way we have gained the conception of the existence of God.

VII. As for the divine essence, though in fact it is 36

[a] For illustration of the argument in this and the next section see App. p. 616.

[b] For this use of *τροπαί* for the transitions of the four seasons rather than for the two solstices *cf.* *τροπὰς τέσσαρας* *Mos.* ii. 124.

δυσκατάληπτον εἶναι συμβέβηκεν, ὅμως καθ᾽ ὅσον
ἐνδέχεται διερευνητέον. ἄμεινον γὰρ οὐδὲν τοῦ
ζητεῖν τὸν ἀληθῆ θεόν, κἂν ἡ εὕρεσις αὐτοῦ δια-
φεύγῃ δύναμιν ἀνθρωπίνην, ἐπειδὴ καὶ ἡ περὶ τὸ
βούλεσθαι μαθεῖν σπουδὴ καθ᾽ αὑτὴν ἀλέκτους
37 ἡδονὰς καὶ εὐφροσύνας ἐργάζεται. μάρτυρες δὲ οἱ
μὴ χείλεσιν ἄκροις γευσάμενοι φιλοσοφίας, ἀλλὰ
τῶν λόγων καὶ δογμάτων αὐτῆς ἐπὶ πλέον ἑστια-
θέντες· τούτων γὰρ ὁ λογισμὸς ἀπὸ γῆς ἄνω
μετέωρος ἀρθεὶς αἰθεροβατεῖ καὶ συμπεριπολῶν
ἡλίῳ καὶ σελήνῃ καὶ τῷ σύμπαντι οὐρανῷ, τἀκεῖ
πάντα γλιχόμενος ἰδεῖν, ἀμυδροτέραις χρῆται ταῖς
προσβολαῖς, ἀκράτου καὶ πολλοῦ φέγγους ἐκ-
χεομένου, ὡς τὸ τῆς ψυχῆς ὄμμα ταῖς μαρμαρυγαῖς
38 σκοτοδινιᾶν. ἀλλ᾽ οὐ διὰ τοῦτο προκαμὼν ἀπαγορεύει, γνώμῃ δ᾽ ἀηττήτῳ πρὸς τὴν ἐνδεχομένην
θέαν ἵεται, καθάπερ ἐν ἄθλοις δευτερείων μετα-
ποιούμενος, ἐπειδὴ τῶν πρώτων ἐσφάλη. φαντασίας
δ᾽ ἀληθοῦς δεύτερά ἐστιν εἰκασία καὶ στοχασμὸς
καὶ ὅσα εἰς τὴν τῶν εὐλόγων καὶ πιθανῶν ἰδέαν
39 ἀνάγεται. καθάπερ οὖν οἷός ἐστι τῶν ἀστέρων
ἕκαστος κατὰ τὴν οὐσίαν εἰλικρινῶς οὔτ᾽ εἰδότες
οὔτε δυνάμενοι σαφῶς διαγνῶναι ζητεῖν ὅμως
προθυμούμεθα, τερπόμενοι τοῖς εἰκόσι λόγοις ἕνεκα
40 τοῦ φύσει φιλομαθοῦς, τὸν αὐτὸν τρόπον, εἰ καὶ τῆς
κατὰ τὸν ὄντως ὄντα θεὸν ἐναργοῦς φαντασίας
ἀμοιροῦμεν, ὀφείλομεν μὴ ἀπολείπεσθαι τῆς ζητή-
σεως αὐτοῦ, διὰ τὸ τὴν σκέψιν καὶ ἄνευ τῆς εὑρέσεως καθ᾽ αὑτὴν τριπόθητον εἶναι, ἐπεὶ καὶ τοὺς
[218] τοῦ | σώματος ὀφθαλμοὺς οὐδεὶς αἰτιᾶται, παρόσον
ἥλιον αὐτὸν ἰδεῖν ἀδυνατοῦντες τὴν φερομένην
ἀπόρροιαν τῶν ἀκτίνων ἐπὶ γῆν ὁρῶσιν, ἡλιακῶν

hard to track and hard to apprehend, it still calls for all the inquiry possible. For nothing is better than to search for the true God, even if the discovery of Him eludes human capacity, since the very wish to learn, if earnestly entertained, produces untold joys
and pleasures. We have the testimony of those who 37
have not taken a mere sip of philosophy but have feasted more abundantly on its reasonings and conclusions. For with them the reason soars away from earth into the heights, travels through the upper air and accompanies the revolutions of the sun and moon and the whole heaven and in its desire to see all that is there finds its powers of sight blurred, for so pure and vast is the radiance that pours therefrom that the soul's eye is dizzied by the flashing of the rays.
Yet it does not therefore faintheartedly give up the 38
task, but with purpose unsubdued presses onwards to such contemplation as is possible, like the athlete who strives for the second prize since he has been disappointed of the first. Now second to the true vision stands conjecture and theorizing and all that can be brought into the category of reasonable
probability. So then just as, though we do not know 39
and cannot with certainty determine what each of the stars is in the purity of its essence, we eagerly persist in the search because our natural love of learning
makes us delight in what seems probable, so too, 40
though the clear vision of God as He really is is denied us, we ought not to relinquish the quest. For the very seeking, even without finding, is felicity in itself, just as no one blames the eyes of the body because when unable to see the sun itself they see the emanation of its rays as it reaches the earth, which is but the extremity of the brightness which the beams of

41 αὐγῶν ἔσχατον φέγγος. VIII. εἰς ἅπερ
ἀπιδὼν ὁ ἱεροφάντης καὶ θεοφιλέστατος Μωυσῆς
ἱκετεύει τὸν θεὸν λέγων· "ἐμφάνισόν μοι σαυτόν,"
μόνον οὐ κατασχεθεὶς καὶ ἐκβοῶν ἄντικρυς, ὅτι
"τοῦ μὲν εἶναί σε καὶ ὑπάρχειν διδάσκαλος καὶ
ὑφηγητής μοι γέγονεν ὅδε ὁ κόσμος, καὶ ὡς υἱὸς
ἀναδιδάξας με περὶ τοῦ πατρὸς καὶ ὡς ἔργον περὶ
τοῦ τεχνίτου· τίς δὲ κατὰ τὴν οὐσίαν τυγχάνεις ὢν
διαγνῶναι ποθῶν οὐδένα τούτου τοῦ μαθήματος
ὑφηγητὴν ἐν οὐδενὶ τῶν τοῦ παντὸς μερῶν ἀν-
42 ευρίσκω. διὸ δὴ δέομαι καὶ ποτνιῶμαι προσέσθαι
τὴν ἱκεσίαν ἀνδρὸς ἱκέτου καὶ φιλοθέου καὶ μόνον
σὲ θεραπεύειν ἀξιοῦντος· ὡς γὰρ τὸ φῶς ὑφ' ἑτέρου
μὴ γνωριζόμενον αὐτὸ ἑαυτοῦ γνώρισμά ἐστιν,
οὕτως καὶ σὺ σεαυτὸν μόνος ἂν φῆναι δύναιο. διὸ
συγγνώμης ἀξιῶ τυχεῖν, εἰ σπάνει τοῦ διδάξοντος
ἐπὶ σὲ καταφυγεῖν ἐθάρρησα περὶ σοῦ σπεύδων
43 μαθεῖν." ὁ δὲ "τὴν μὲν προθυμίαν" φησίν "ἐπαινετὴν οὖσαν ἀποδέχομαι, τὸ δ' αἴτημα οὐδενὶ τῶν
εἰς γένεσιν ἡκόντων ἐφαρμόζει. χαρίζομαι δ' ἐγὼ
τὰ οἰκεῖα τῷ ληψομένῳ· οὐ γὰρ ὅσα μοι δοῦναι
ῥᾴδιον καὶ ἀνθρώπῳ λαβεῖν δυνατόν· ὅθεν ὀρέγω
τῷ χάριτος ἀξίῳ πάσας ὅσας ἂν οἷός τε ᾖ δέξασθαι
44 δωρεάς. τὴν δ' ἐμὴν κατάληψιν οὐχ οἷον ἀνθρώπου
φύσις ἀλλ' οὐδ' ὁ σύμπας οὐρανός τε καὶ κόσμος

---

[a] §§ 41-50 are a meditation on Ex. xxxiii. 13-23. The divine answer to the first petition, "Reveal thyself to me" (*v.* 13), is not reproduced by Philo, but the words of § 43, "I freely bestow," etc., are an interpretation of part of God's answer to the second petition, "I will be gracious to whom I will be gracious, and will shew mercy on whom I will shew

the sun give forth. VIII. It was this 41
which Moses the sacred guide, most dearly beloved of God, had before his eyes when he besought God with the words, "Reveal Thyself to me."[a] In these words we may almost hear plainly the inspired cry "This universe has been my teacher, to bring me to the knowledge that Thou art and dost subsist. As Thy son, it has told me of its Father, as Thy work of its contriver. But what Thou art in Thy essence I desire to understand, yet find in no part of the All any to
guide me to this knowledge. Therefore I pray and 42
beseech Thee to accept the supplication of a suppliant, a lover of God, one whose mind is set to serve Thee alone; for as knowledge of the light does not come by any other source but what itself supplies, so too Thou alone canst tell me of Thyself. Wherefore I crave pardon if, for lack of a teacher, I venture to appeal to Thee in my desire to learn of Thee."
He replies, "Thy zeal I approve as praiseworthy, but 43
the request cannot fitly be granted to any that are brought into being by creation. I freely bestow what is in accordance with the recipient; for not all that I can give with ease is within man's power to take, and therefore to him that is worthy of My grace I extend all the boons which he is capable of receiving.
But the apprehension of Me is something more than 44
human nature, yea even the whole heaven and

mercy." In the second petition (*v.* 18), which Philo reads, in accordance with some MSS. of the LXX, as "Shew me thy glory" (so also E.V.), glory is interpreted to mean the Powers as distinguished from the Self-existent, and God's answer, "Thou shalt see the things behind me," LXX τὰ ὀπίσω μου (A.V. "my back parts," R.V. "my back"), is taken to mean "Thou shalt see what lies behind the Powers, *i.e.* their manifestation in the sensible world." The same interpretation of the verse is given in *De Fuga* 165, *De Mut.* 9, *De Post.* 169.

δυνήσεται χωρῆσαι. γνῶθι δὴ σαυτὸν καὶ μὴ
συνεκφέρου ταῖς ὑπὲρ δύναμιν ὁρμαῖς καὶ ἐπιθυμίαις, μηδέ σε τῶν ἀνεφίκτων ἔρως αἱρέτω καὶ
μετεωριζέτω· τῶν γὰρ ἐφικτῶν οὐδενὸς ἀμοιρή-
45 σεις." ταῦτα ἀκούσας ἐπὶ δευτέραν
ἱκεσίαν ἦλθε καί φησι· " πέπεισμαι μὲν ταῖς σαῖς
ὑφηγήσεσιν, ὅτι οὐκ ἂν ἴσχυσα δέξασθαι τὸ τῆς σῆς
φαντασίας ἐναργὲς εἶδος. ἱκετεύω δὲ τὴν γοῦν περὶ
σὲ δόξαν θεάσασθαι· δόξαν δὲ σὴν εἶναι νομίζω τὰς
περὶ σὲ δορυφορούσας δυνάμεις, ὧν διαφεύγουσα ἡ
κατάληψις ἄχρι τοῦ παρόντος οὐ μικρὸν ἐνεργάζεταί
46 μοι πόθον τῆς διαγνώσεως." ὁ δὲ ἀμείβεται καί
φησιν· " ἃς ἐπιζητεῖς δυνάμεις εἰσὶν ἀόρατοι καὶ
νοηταὶ πάντως ἐμοῦ τοῦ ἀοράτου καὶ νοητοῦ· λέγω
δὲ νοητὰς οὐχὶ τὰς[1] ἤδη ὑπὸ νοῦ καταλαμβανομένας,
ἀλλ' ὅτι εἰ καταλαμβάνεσθαι οἷαί τε εἶεν, οὐκ ἂν
αἴσθησις αὐτὰς ἀλλ' ἀκραιφνέστατος νοῦς κατα-
47 λαμβάνοι. πεφυκυῖαι δ' ἀκατάληπτοι κατὰ τὴν
οὐσίαν ὅμως παραφαίνουσιν ἐκμαγεῖόν τι καὶ ἀπεικόνισμα τῆς ἑαυτῶν ἐνεργείας· οἷαι αἱ παρ' ὑμῖν
σφραγῖδες—ὅταν ⟨γὰρ⟩ προσενεχθῇ κηρὸς ἤ τις
ὁμοιότροπος ὕλη, μυρίους ὅσους τύπους ἐναπομάτ-
[219] τονται, μηδὲν ἀκρωτηριασθεῖσαι μέρος, | ἀλλ' ἐν
ὁμοίῳ μένουσαι,—τοιαύτας ὑποληπτέον καὶ τὰς
περὶ ἐμὲ δυνάμεις περιποιούσας ἀποίοις ποιότητας
καὶ μορφὰς ἀμόρφοις καὶ μηδὲν τῆς ἀιδίου φύσεως
48 μήτ' ἀλλαττομένας μήτε μειουμένας. ὀνομάζουσι

[1] For *οὐχὶ τὰς* I suggest *οὐχ ὡς*. See note *a*.

[a] This must be the meaning if the text is to stand, but what are "the powers which are now discerned by mind"? The

universe will be able to contain. Know thyself, then,
and do not be led away by impulses and desires beyond
thy capacity, nor let yearning for the unattainable
uplift and carry thee off thy feet, for of the obtainable
nothing shall be denied thee." When 45
Moses heard this, he addressed to Him a second
petition and said, "I bow before Thy admonitions,
that I never could have received the vision of Thee
clearly manifested, but I beseech Thee that I may at
least see the glory that surrounds Thee, and by Thy
glory I understand the powers that keep guard around
Thee, of whom I would fain gain apprehension, for
though hitherto that has escaped me, the thought of
it creates in me a mighty longing to have knowledge
of them." To this He answers, "The powers which 46
thou seekest to know are discerned not by sight but
by mind even as I, Whose they are, am discerned by
mind and not by sight, and when I say 'they are discerned by mind' I speak not of those [a] which are now
actually apprehended by mind but mean that if these
other powers could be apprehended it would not be
by sense but by mind at its purest. But while in their 47
essence they are beyond your apprehension, they
nevertheless present to your sight a sort of impress
and copy of their active working. You men have
for your use seals which when brought into contact
with wax or similar material stamp on them any
number of impressions while they themselves are not
docked in any part thereby but remain as they were.
Such you must conceive My powers to be, supplying
quality and shape to things which lack either and yet
changing or lessening nothing of their eternal nature.

sense to be expected is "I do not mean that they are now discerned," and so Heinemann and Mangey.

δ' αὐτὰς οὐκ ἀπὸ σκοποῦ τινες τῶν παρ' ὑμῖν ἰδέας, ἐπειδὴ ἕκαστα τῶν ὄντων εἰδοποιοῦσι[1] τὰ ἄτακτα τάττουσαι καὶ τὰ ἄπειρα καὶ ἀόριστα καὶ ἀσχημάτιστα περατοῦσαι καὶ περιορίζουσαι καὶ σχηματίζουσαι καὶ συνόλως τὸ χεῖρον εἰς τὸ ἄμεινον
49 μεθαρμοζόμεναι. μήτ' οὖν ἐμὲ μήτε τινὰ τῶν ἐμῶν δυνάμεων κατὰ τὴν οὐσίαν ἐλπίσῃς ποτὲ δυνήσεσθαι καταλαβεῖν. τῶν δ' ἐφικτῶν, ὡς εἶπον, ἑτοίμως καὶ προθύμως μεταδίδωμι· ταῦτα δ' ἐστὶν ἐπὶ τὴν τοῦ κόσμου καὶ τῶν ἐν αὐτῷ καλέσαι θέαν, ἣν οὐ σώματος ὀφθαλμοῖς ἀλλὰ τοῖς διανοίας ἀκοιμήτοις ὄμμασι συμβαίνει καταλαμβάνεσθαι.
50 μόνον ὁ σοφίας ἵμερος συνεχὴς ἔστω καὶ πυκνός, ὃς δογμάτων ἀοιδίμων καὶ περικαλλεστάτων ἀναπίμπλησι τοὺς φοιτητὰς καὶ γνωρίμους αὐτῆς." ταῦτα ἀκούσας οὐκ ἐπαύσατο τῆς ἐπιθυμίας, ἀλλ' ἔτι τὸν ἐπὶ τοῖς ἀοράτοις πόθον ἐζωπύρει.
51 IX. Καὶ πάντας τοὺς ὁμοιοτρόπους εἴτ' οὖν φύντας ἐξ ἀρχῆς εἴτε καὶ ἐκ τοῦ μεταβάλλεσθαι πρὸς τὴν ἀμείνω τάξιν κρείττους γεγονότας ἀποδέχεται, τοὺς μὲν ὅτι τὴν εὐγένειαν οὐ κατέλυσαν, τοὺς δ' ὅτι πρὸς εὐσέβειαν ἠξίωσαν μεθορμίσασθαι[2] —τούτους δὲ καλεῖ προσηλύτους ἀπὸ τοῦ προσεληλυθέναι καινῇ καὶ φιλοθέῳ πολιτείᾳ,—οἳ μυθικῶν μὲν ἀλογοῦσι πλασμάτων, περιέχονται δὲ ἀκραιφ-

[1] Or, as some MSS., ἰδιοποιοῦσι, "give individuality." It would be quite in Philo's way to associate ἴδιος with ἰδέα.

[2] MSS. μεθαρμόσασθαι, a word less suitable here and often confused in MSS. with μεθορμίσ. See Cohn, *Hermes*, 1908, p. 186.

Some among you call them not inaptly 'forms' or 48
'ideas,' [a] since they bring form into everything that is, giving order to the disordered, limit to the unlimited, bounds to the unbounded, shape to the shapeless, and in general changing the worse to something better.
Do not, then, hope to be ever able to apprehend Me 49
or any of My powers in Our essence. But I readily and with right goodwill will admit you to a share of what is attainable. That means that I bid you come and contemplate the universe and its contents, a spectacle apprehended not by the eye of the body but
by the unsleeping eyes of the mind.[b] Only let there 50
be the constant and profound longing for wisdom which fills its scholars and disciples with verities glorious in their exceeding loveliness." When Moses heard this, he did not cease from his desire but kept the yearning for the invisible aflame in his heart.

IX. All of like sort to him, all who spurn idle fables 51
and embrace truth in its purity, whether they have been such from the first or through conversion to the better side have reached that higher state, obtain His [c] approval, the former because they were not false to the nobility of their birth, the latter because their judgement led them to make the passage to piety. These last he calls "proselytes," or newly-joined, because they have joined the new and godly common-

[a] This and § 323 below seem to be the only places where Philo definitely identifies the δυνάμεις with the Platonic ἰδέαι, though perhaps *De Cher.* 51 αἱ τυποῦσαι δυνάμεις τὰ ἐν μέρει may imply it.

[b] *i.e.* the contemplation must be philosophical, "looking through nature to nature's God."

[c] The subject of ἀποδέχεται is certainly God, but that of καλεῖ and the verbs that follow is more likely Moses. Rapid changes of this kind are not, I think, unusual in Philo.

52 νοῦς ἀληθείας. ἰσοτιμίαν γοῦν ἅπασιν ἐπηλύταις διδοὺς καὶ χαρισάμενος ὅσα καὶ τοῖς αὐτόχθοσι παραινεῖ τοῖς εὐπατρίδαις, μὴ μόνον αὐτοὺς τιμαῖς γεραίρειν ἀλλὰ καὶ ἐξαιρέτῳ φιλίᾳ καὶ εὐνοίᾳ περιττῇ. καὶ μήποτ' εἰκότως· "ἀπολελοιπότες" φησί "πατρίδα καὶ φίλους καὶ συγγενεῖς δι' ἀρετὴν καὶ ὁσιότητα μὴ ἀμοιρείτωσαν ἑτέρων πόλεων καὶ οἰκείων[1] καὶ φίλων, ἀλλ' ἔστωσαν ἔφεδροι καταφυγαὶ τοῖς πρὸς εὐσέβειαν αὐτομολοῦσι· φίλτρον γὰρ ἀνυσιμώτατον καὶ δεσμὸς ἄλυτος εὐνοίας ἑνωτικῆς ἡ τοῦ ἑνὸς θεοῦ τιμή."

53 προστάττει δὲ μή, παρόσον αὐτοῖς ἰσονομίαν καὶ ἰσοτέλειαν [ἐπηλύταις][2] παρέχει κατεγνωκόσι τοῦ πατρῴου καὶ προγονικοῦ τύφου, στομαργίᾳ χρήσασθαι καὶ ἀχαλίνῳ γλώσσῃ βλασφημοῦντας οὓς ἕτεροι νομίζουσι θεούς, ἵνα μὴ κἀκεῖνοι διακινηθέντες ἃ μὴ θέμις φθέγξωνται κατὰ [220] τοῦ ὄντως ὄντος· ἀγνοίᾳ γὰρ τῆς | διαφορᾶς, ἅτε τὸ ψεῦδος ὡς ἀληθὲς προμαθόντες ἐκ παίδων καὶ σύντροφον ἔχοντες, ἐξαμαρτήσονται.

54 Τῶν δ' ἀπὸ τοῦ ἔθνους εἴ τινες καθυφίενται τὴν

[1] MSS. οἰκιῶν.

[2] So Cohn: Mangey on the other hand expunges αὐτοῖς, which is absent in three MSS., and retains ἐπηλύταις. Against Cohn it may be said that it is not clear why the order which follows should be addressed to the proselytes instead of to Israel (unless on the ground that converts or perverts are apt to be particularly severe to their former co-religionists). If ἐπηλύταις is retained a fair sense can be obtained. The honours awarded by God to converts from the outside religions might naturally be regarded as a signal evidence of the abhorrence which these religions deserve.

[a] See Lev. xix. 33, 34; Deut. x. 18, 19; E.V. "strangers."

wealth.[a] Thus, while giving equal rank 52
to all in-comers with all the privileges which he gives
to the native-born, he exhorts the old nobility to
honour them not only with marks of respect but with
special friendship and with more than ordinary goodwill.[b] And surely there is good reason for this ; they
have left, he says, their country, their kinsfolk and
their friends for the sake of virtue and religion. Let
them not be denied another citizenship or other ties
of family and friendship, and let them find places of
shelter standing ready for refugees to the camp of
piety. For the most effectual love-charm, the chain
which binds indissolubly the goodwill which makes
us one is to honour the one God. Yet he 53
counsels them that they must not, presuming on the
equal privilege and equal rank which He grants them
because they have denounced the vain imaginings
of their fathers and ancestors, deal in idle talk or revile
with an unbridled tongue the gods whom others
acknowledge,[c] lest they on their part be moved to
utter profane words against Him Who truly IS. For
they know not the difference, and since the falsehood
has been taught to them as truth from childhood and
has grown up with them, they will go astray.
But if any members of the nation betray the honour 54

The word of course does not imply conversion to the religion of Israel, as Philo might have seen from "ye were proselytes in Egypt."

[b] "Thou shalt love him as thyself," Lev. xix. 34.

[c] This is no doubt mainly based on Ex. xxii. 28, "Thou shalt not revile God," where the LXX has θεούς. See *Mos.* ii. 203 and note, with references to Josephus. But that passage shews that he gave the same interpretation to Lev. xxiv. 15, "whosoever curseth God shall bear the guilt of his sin," on the grounds that as this is treated as a lesser sin than naming the name of the Lord, it could not refer to the true God.

τοῦ ἑνὸς τιμήν, ὡς λιπόντες τὴν ἀναγκαιοτάτην τάξιν εὐσεβείας καὶ ὁσιότητος ταῖς ἀνωτάτω τιμωρίαις ὀφείλουσι κολάζεσθαι, σκότος αἱρούμενοι πρὸ αὐγοειδεστάτου φωτὸς καὶ τυφλὴν ἀπεργαζό-
55 μενοι διάνοιαν ὀξὺ καθορᾶν δυναμένην. καὶ ἐπιτετράφθαι δὲ καλὸν ἅπασι τοῖς ζῆλον ἔχουσιν ἀρετῆς ἐκ χειρὸς ἀναπράττειν ἀνυπερθέτως τὰς τιμωρίας, μήτ' εἰς δικαστήριον μήτ' εἰς βουλευτήριον μήτε συνόλως ἐπ' ἀρχὴν ἄγοντας, ἀλλὰ τῷ παραστάντι μισοπονήρῳ πάθει καὶ φιλοθέῳ καταχρῆσθαι πρὸς τὰς τῶν ἀσεβῶν ἀπαραιτήτους κολάσεις, νομίσαντας αὑτοὺς ὑπὸ τοῦ καιροῦ τὰ πάντα γεγενῆσθαι, βουλευτάς, δικαστάς, στρατηγούς, ἐκκλησιαστάς, κατηγόρους, μάρτυρας, νόμους, δῆμον, ἵνα μηδενὸς ὄντος ἐμποδὼν ἄφοβοι σὺν ἀδείᾳ πολλῇ
56 προαγωνίζωνται ὁσιότητος. X. ἀναγέγραπταί τις ἐν τοῖς νόμοις τὸ καλὸν τοῦτο τόλμημα τολμήσας. ἐπειδὴ γὰρ ἐθεάσατό τινας ἀλλοφύλοις συνόντας γυναιξὶ καὶ ἕνεκα τῶν πρὸς αὐτὰς φίλτρων ἀλογοῦντας μὲν τῶν πατρίων, τελουμένους δὲ τὰς μυθικὰς τελετάς, ἕνα τὸν ἔξαρχον καὶ ἡγεμόνα τῆς παρανομίας καταθαρροῦντα ἤδη παρεπιδείκνυσθαι δημοσίᾳ τὸ ἀνοσιούργημα καὶ θυσίας ἀγάλμασι καὶ ξοάνοις ἀθύτους[1] φανερῶς ἐπιτελοῦντα παρόντος ἅπαντος τοῦ πλήθους ἐνθουσιῶν, ἀνείρξας τοὺς παρ'

[1] MSS. ἀθύτοις.

---

[a] For this section *cf.* Deut. xiii. 12 ff., and xvii. 6 ff., though there a stricter inquiry is enjoined than what is suggested here. On this and Jewish lynching in general see App. pp. 616-618.

due to the One they should suffer the utmost penalties. They have abandoned their most vital duty, their service in the ranks of piety and religion, have chosen darkness in preference to the brightest light and blindfolded the mind which had the power of keen
vision. [a]And it is well that all who have a zeal for 55
virtue should be permitted to exact the penalties offhand and with no delay, without bringing the offender before jury or council or any kind of magistrate at all, and give full scope to the feelings which possess them, that hatred of evil and love of God which urges them to inflict punishment without mercy on the impious. They should think that the occasion has made them councillors, jurymen, high sheriffs,[b] members of assembly, accusers, witnesses, laws, people, everything in fact, so that without fear or hindrance they may champion religion in full security.

X. There is recorded in the Laws 56
the example of one who acted with this admirable courage.[c] He had seen some persons consorting with foreign women and through the attraction of their love-charms spurning their ancestral customs and seeking admission to the rites of a fabulous religion. One in particular he saw, the chief ringleader of the backsliding, who had the audacity to exhibit his unholy conduct in public and was openly offering sacrifices, a travesty of the name, to images of wood and stone in the presence of the whole people. So, seized with inspired fury, keeping back the throng of spectators

[b] Or "governor (of a nome)." See note on *De Ios.* 3. Goodenough, "Roman magistrates."

[c] See Num. xxv. ff. The story of Phinehas, used for allegorical purposes in *De Post.* 182 ff., *De Ebr.* 73 ff., *De Conf.* 57, has been given in much the same terms as here, though more fully, in *Mos.* i. 301 ff.

ἑκάτερα ἐπὶ τὴν θέαν ἠθροισμένους, οὐδὲν εὐλαβηθεὶς ἀναιρεῖ σὺν τῇ γυναικί, τὸν μὲν ἕνεκα τῆς
εὐμαθείας ⟨τῶν⟩ ἃ λυσιτελὲς ἀπομανθάνειν, τὴν δ'
57 ὅτι διδάσκαλος κακῶν ἐγένετο. τουτὶ τὸ ἔργον
ἐξαίφνης δρασθὲν ἐν θερμῷ παραστήματι μυρίους
ἐνουθέτησε τῶν ἐπὶ ταῦτα παρασκευαζομένων.
ἐπαινέσας οὖν ὁ θεὸς τὴν ἀριστείαν αὐτοκελεύστῳ
καὶ ἐθελουργῷ σπουδῇ γενομένην διτταῖς αὐτὸν
ἀναστέφει δωρεαῖς, εἰρήνῃ καὶ ἱερωσύνῃ, τῇ μὲν
κρίνας ἄξιον ἀπολέμου μεταποιεῖσθαι βίου τὸν
ἀράμενον τοὺς ὑπὲρ θεοῦ τιμῆς ἀγῶνας, τῇ δ' ὅτι
γέρας οἰκειότατον εὐσεβοῦς ἀνδρὸς ἱερωσύνη θεραπείαν ἐπαγγελλομένη τοῦ πατρός, ᾧ τὸ δουλεύειν
οὐκ ἐλευθερίας μόνον ἀλλὰ καὶ βασιλείας ἄμεινον.
58 ἔνιοι δὲ τοσαύτῃ κέχρηνται μανίας
ὑπερβολῇ, ὥστ' οὐδ' ἀναχώρησιν αὐτοῖς εἰς μετά-
[221] νοιαν | ἀπολείποντες ἵενται πρὸς δουλείαν τῶν
χειροκμήτων, γράμμασιν αὐτὴν ὁμολογοῦντες, οὐκ
ἐν χαρτιδίοις, ⟨ἀλλ'⟩, ὡς ἐπὶ τῶν ἀνδραπόδων ἔθος,
[ἀλλ'] ἐν τοῖς σώμασι καταστίζοντες αὐτὰ σιδήρῳ
πεπυρωμένῳ πρὸς ἀνεξάλειπτον μονήν· οὐδὲ γὰρ
χρόνῳ ταῦτα ἀμαυροῦται.[a]
59 XI. Τὴν δ' ὁμοίαν προαίρεσιν ὁ ἱερώτατος
Μωυσῆς καὶ ἐπὶ τῶν ἄλλων ἅπαξ ἁπάντων σῴζειν
ἔοικεν ἀληθείας ἐραστὴς ὢν καὶ διδάσκαλος, ἣν καὶ
πᾶσι τοῖς γνωρίμοις ἐγχαράττειν καὶ ἐνσφραγίζε-
σθαι ποθεῖ τὰς ψευδεῖς δόξας μακρὰν τῆς διανοίας

[a] The allusion is to Lev. xix. 28 (*cf. ib.* xxi. 5, Deut. xiv. 1), "Ye shall not make any cuttings in your flesh for the dead (LXX ἐπὶ ψυχῇ), nor print any marks upon you," which Philo takes to refer to idolatrous practices. Such connexion as there is with the preceding section lies in the antithesis between bondage to God and bondage to idols. See App. p. 618.

on either side, he slew without a qualm him and her, the man because he listened to lessons which it were a gain to unlearn, the woman because she had been the instructor in wickedness. This deed suddenly 57
wrought in the heat of excitement acted as a warning to multitudes who were preparing to make the same apostasy. So then God, praising his high achievement, the result of zeal self-prompted and whole-hearted, crowned him with a twofold award, the gifts of peace and priesthood, the first because He judged the champion who had battled for the honour of God worthy to claim a life free from war, the second because the guerdon most suitable to a man of piety is the priestly office which professes the service of the Father, bondage to Whom is better not only than freedom but also than kingship. [a] But 58
some labour under a madness carried to such an extravagant extent that they do not leave themselves any means of escape to repentance, but press to enter into bondage to the works of men and acknowledge it by indentures not written on pieces of parchment, but, as is the custom of slaves, branded on their bodies with red-hot iron. And there they remain indelibly, for no lapse of time can make them fade.

XI. The like principle [b] is clearly maintained in 59
the case of everything else by the most holy Moses, who loves and teaches the truth which he desires to engrave and stamp on all his disciples, dislodging and banishing false opinions to a distance from their

[b] Not very clear. It obviously cannot refer to the preceding section, nor very appropriately to §§ 56, 57. For Philo does not go on to suggest that the persons now described should be lynched or even judicially executed, but merely excluded, though Lev. xx. 6 and 27 sanction the penalty of death. See App. p. 618.

60 αὐτῶν ἀποικίζων. ἐπιστάμενος γοῦν τῷ πλάνῳ τῶν πολλῶν βίῳ συμπράττουσαν οὐ μετρίως εἰς ἀνοδίαν μαντικήν, οὐδενὶ τῶν εἰδῶν αὐτῆς ἐᾷ χρῆσθαι, πάντας δὲ τοὺς κολακεύοντας αὐτὴν ἐλαύνει τῆς ἰδίου[1] πολιτείας, θύτας, καθαρτάς, οἰωνοσκόπους, τερατοσκόπους, ἐπᾴδοντας, κλη-
61 δόσιν ἐπανέχοντας. στοχασταὶ γὰρ πάντες οὗτοι πιθανῶν καὶ εἰκότων, ἄλλοτε ἄλλας ἀπὸ τῶν αὐτῶν φαντασίας λαμβάνοντες, διὰ τὸ μήτε τὰ ὑποκείμενα φύσιν ἔχειν πάγιον μήτε τὴν διάνοιαν ἀκριβῆ βάσανον περιπεποιῆσθαι, ᾗ βασανισθήσεται τὰ
62 δόκιμα. παρασκευαὶ δὲ πάντα ταῦτ' εἰσὶν ἀσεβείας· διὰ τί; ὅτι ὁ προσέχων καὶ πειθόμενος αὐτοῖς ἀλογεῖ τοῦ πάντων αἰτίου μόνα ταῦθ' ὑπολαμβάνων ἀγαθῶν εἶναι καὶ κακῶν αἴτια, καὶ οὐκ αἰσθάνεται τὰς τοῦ βίου φροντίδας ἐξάπτων ἀβεβαιοτάτων πεισμάτων, ὀρνίθων καὶ πτερῶν καὶ φορᾶς ἐν ἀέρι τῆς ὧδε κἀκεῖσε καὶ χαμαιζήλων ἑρπετῶν, ἃ τῶν φωλεῶν ἀνέρπει πρὸς ζήτησιν τροφῆς, ἔτι δὲ σπλάγχνων καὶ αἵματος καὶ νεκρῶν σωμάτων, ἃ στερόμενα ψυχῆς εὐθὺς ἐπισυμπίπτει καὶ συγχεῖται καὶ ἑτεροιούμενα τὰς οἰκείας φύσεις ἐξαλλάττει
63 πρὸς τὴν χείρω μεταβολήν. ἀξιοῖ γὰρ τὸν ἐγγραφόμενον τῇ κατὰ τοὺς νόμους πολιτείᾳ "τέλειον" εἶναι, μὴ ἐν οἷς οἱ πολλοὶ πεπαιδοτρίβηνται, μαντείαις καὶ κληδόσι καὶ πιθαναῖς εἰκασίαις, ἀλλ'

[1] mss. ἰδίας or mostly ἀιδίου. The adjective has -ος, -α, -ον or -ος, -ον indifferently.

[a] These terms are largely drawn from Deut. xviii. 10 f. where we have περικαθαίρων τὸν υἱὸν ἐν πυρί, κληδονιζόμενος, οἰωνιζόμενος, φαρμακὸς ἐπαείδων ἐπαοιδήν, τερατοσκόπος. Philo's καθαρτής, which Heinemann translates by "Sühnepriester,"

understanding. Thus, knowing that the erring life 60
of the multitude is greatly helped on its way into the wilds by the art of divination, he forbids them to use any of its forms and expels from his own commonwealth all its fawning followers, haruspices, purificators, augurs, interpreters of prodigies, incantators,[a] and those who put their faith in sounds and voices.
For all these are but guessing at what is plausible and 61
probable, and the same phenomena present to them ideas which differ at different times because the things on which they are based have no natural stability nor has the understanding acquired any accurate touchstone by which the genuine can be
tested and approved. All these pave the way for 62
impiety. Why so? Because he who pays attention and puts confidence in them is spurning the Cause of all in his belief that they are the sole causes of good and evil and fails to perceive that the anchors on which he moors his life and its cares are utterly insecure, such as birds and wings and their flight hither and thither through the air, and grovelling reptiles which crawl out of their holes to seek their food; and again entrails and blood and corpses which deprived of life at once collapse and decompose and in this process exchange their natural properties
for others of worse condition. Moses demands that 63
one who is registered in the commonwealth of the laws should be perfect not in the lore, in which the many are schooled, of divination and voices and

evidently corresponds to the *περικαθαίρων* of Deut. (E.V. "makes his son to pass through fire"). *κληδόσι*, *cf. Mos.* i. 287, may mean "omens" generally. The "haruspex" naturally has no place in Deut., as the O.T., I believe, shews no trace of divining by entrails of victims. *θύτης* is given in L. & S. revised as "diviner," but is clearly more specific.

ἐν τοῖς πρὸς θεὸν οὐδὲν ἔχουσιν ἐπαμφοτερίζον ἢ
ἀμφίβαλον ἀλλ' ἀνενδοίαστον καὶ γυμνὴν ἀλήθειαν.
64 ἐπεὶ δὲ πᾶσιν ἀνθρώποις ἔρως τῆς τῶν
μελλόντων ἐπιστήμης ἐνίδρυται καὶ διὰ τὸν ἔρωτα
τοῦτον ἐπὶ θυτικὴν καὶ τὰ ἄλλα εἴδη τρέπονται
μαντικῆς, ὡς δι' αὐτῶν τὸ σαφὲς ἀνευρήσοντες, τὰ
δ' ἀσαφείας γέμει πολλῆς καὶ ἐξ ἑαυτῶν ἀεὶ
διελέγχεται, τούτοις μὲν σφόδρα εὐτόνως ἐπ-
ακολουθεῖν ἀπαγορεύει, φησὶ δ' ὅτι, ἐὰν ἀκλινῶς
[222] εὐσεβῶσιν, οὐκ | ἀμοιρήσουσι τῆς τῶν μελλόντων
65 ἐπιγνώσεως, ἀλλά τις ἐπιφανεὶς ἐξαπιναίως προφήτης θεοφόρητος θεσπιεῖ καὶ προφητεύσει, λέγων
μὲν οἰκεῖον οὐδέν—οὐδὲ γάρ, εἰ λέγει, δύναται
καταλαβεῖν ὅ γε κατεχόμενος ὄντως καὶ ἐνθουσιῶν,
—ὅσα δ' ἐνηχεῖται, διελεύσεται καθάπερ ὑποβάλ-
λοντος ἑτέρου· ἑρμηνεῖς γάρ εἰσιν οἱ προφῆται θεοῦ
καταχρωμένου τοῖς ἐκείνων ὀργάνοις πρὸς δήλωσιν
ὧν ἂν ἐθελήσῃ. ταῦτα καὶ τὰ τούτοις παραπλήσια
περὶ τῆς τοῦ ἑνὸς θεοῦ καὶ ὄντως ὄντος ἐννοίας
ὑπειπών, ὃν χρὴ τρόπον ἀπονέμειν αὐτῷ τὰς τιμὰς
ἑξῆς ὑπογράφει.
66 XII.[1] Τὸ μὲν ἀνωτάτω καὶ πρὸς ἀλήθειαν ἱερὸν θεοῦ
νομίζειν τὸν σύμπαντα χρὴ κόσμον εἶναι, νεὼ μὲν
ἔχοντα τὸ ἁγιώτατον τῆς τῶν ὄντων οὐσίας μέρος,
οὐρανόν, ἀναθήματα δὲ τοὺς ἀστέρας, ἱερέας δὲ τοὺς
ὑποδιακόνους αὐτοῦ τῶν δυνάμεων ἀγγέλους, ἀσωμάτους ψυχάς, οὐ κράματα ἐκ λογικῆς καὶ ἀλόγου

[1] Here the mss. insert the heading Περὶ ἱεροῦ.

---

[a] See Deut. xviii. 15-18.

[b] So (*v.* 18), "I will put my words in his mouth and he shall speak unto them all that I shall command him."

[c] For the idea of insistence and reiteration in ἐνηχεῖν (in

plausible conjectures, but in his duties towards God in which there is nothing doubtful or ambiguous but undoubted, naked truth. [a] But since a 64 longing to know the future is ingrained in all men, which longing makes them turn to haruspication and the other forms of divination in the prospect of finding certainty thereby, though actually they are brimful of uncertainty and constantly convict themselves of falsehood—while he very earnestly forbids them to follow such, yet he tells them that if they do not swerve from piety they will not be denied the full knowledge of the future. A prophet possessed 65 by God will suddenly appear and give prophetic oracles.[b] Nothing of what he says will be his own, for he that is truly under the control of divine inspiration has no power of apprehension when he speaks but serves as the channel for the insistent[c] words of Another's prompting. For prophets are the interpreters of God, Who makes full use of their organs of speech to set forth what He wills. These and the like are his injunctions as to the conception of the one truly existing God. Having opened with them, he next proceeds to indicate how the honours due to Him should be paid.

XII.[d] The highest, and in the truest sense the holy, 66 temple of God is, as we must believe, the whole universe, having for its sanctuary the most sacred part of all existence, even heaven, for its votive ornaments the stars, for its priests the angels who are servitors to His powers, unbodied souls, not compounds

colloquial English "to drum or din into one") see note on *De Mut.* 57. For the general sense of the passage *cf. Quis Rerum* 265 f.

[d] The MSS. insert the heading "Of the temple," and Cohn begins a fresh numeration of chapters.

φύσεως, οἵας τὰς ἡμετέρας εἶναι συμβέβηκεν, ἀλλ' ἐκτετμημένας τὸ ἄλογον, ὅλας δι' ὅλων νοεράς,
67 λογισμοὺς ἀκραιφνεῖς, μονάδι ὁμοιουμένας. τὸ δὲ χειρόκμητον· ἔδει γὰρ ὁρμὰς ἀνθρώπων μὴ ἀνακόψαι φορὰς τὰς εἰς εὐσέβειαν συντελούντων καὶ θυσίαις βουλομένων ἢ ἐπὶ τοῖς συμβαίνουσιν ἀγα-
[223] θοῖς εὐχαριστεῖν ἢ ἐφ' οἷς | ἂν ἁμαρτάνωσι συγγνώμην καὶ παραίτησιν αἰτεῖσθαι. προὐνόησε δ' ὡς οὔτε πολλαχόθι οὔτ' ἐν ταὐτῷ πολλὰ κατασκευασθήσεται ἱερά, δικαιώσας, ἐπειδὴ εἷς ἐστιν ὁ
68 θεός, καὶ ἱερὸν ἓν εἶναι μόνον. εἶτα τοῖς βουλομένοις ἐν ταῖς οἰκίαις αὐτῶν ἱερουργεῖν οὐκ ἐφίησιν, ἀλλ' ἀνισταμένους ἀπὸ περάτων γῆς εἰς τοῦτ' ἀφικνεῖσθαι κελεύει, ἅμα καὶ τῶν τρόπων ἀναγκαιοτάτην λαμβάνων βάσανον· ὁ γὰρ μὴ μέλλων θύειν εὐαγῶς οὐκ ἂν ὑπομείναι ποτὲ πατρίδα καὶ φίλους καὶ συγγενεῖς ἀπολιπὼν ξενιτεύειν, ἀλλ' ἔοικεν ὑπὸ δυνατωτέρας ὁλκῆς ἀγόμενος τῆς πρὸς εὐσέβειαν ὑπομένειν τῶν συνηθεστάτων καὶ φιλτάτων ὥσπερ τινῶν ἡνωμένων μερῶν ἀπαρτᾶσθαι.
69 καὶ τοῦδε σαφεστάτη πίστις τὰ γινόμενα· μυρίοι γὰρ ἀπὸ μυρίων ὅσων πόλεων, οἱ μὲν διὰ γῆς, οἱ δὲ διὰ θαλάττης, ἐξ ἀνατολῆς καὶ δύσεως καὶ ἄρκτου καὶ μεσημβρίας καθ' ἑκάστην ἑορτὴν εἰς τὸ ἱερὸν καταίρουσιν οἷά τινα κοινὸν ὑπόδρομον καὶ καταγωγὴν ἀσφαλῆ πολυπράγμονος καὶ ταραχωδεστάτου βίου, ζητοῦντες εὐδίαν εὑρεῖν καὶ φροντίδων ἀνεθέντες, αἷς ἐκ πρώτης ἡλικίας καταζεύγνυνται καὶ πιέζονται, βραχύν τινα διαπνεύ-
70 σαντες χρόνον ἐν ἱλαραῖς διάγειν εὐθυμίαις· ἐλπίδων

[a] *Cf. Mos.* ii. 288.

of rational and irrational nature, as ours are, but with the irrational eliminated, all mind through and through, pure intelligences, in the likeness of the monad.[a] There is also the temple made by hands; for 67
it was right that no check should be given to the forwardness of those who pay their tribute to piety and desire by means of sacrifices either to give thanks for the blessings that befall them or to ask for pardon and forgiveness for their sins. But he provided that there should not be temples built either in many places or many in the same place, for he judged that since God is one, there should be also only one temple.[b]
Further, he does not consent to those who wish to 68
perform the rites in their houses, but bids them rise up from the ends of the earth and come to this temple. In this way he also applies the severest test to their dispositions. For one who is not going to sacrifice in a religious spirit would never bring himself to leave his country and friends and kinsfolk and sojourn in a strange land, but clearly it must be the stronger attraction of piety which leads him to endure separation from his most familiar and dearest friends who form as it were a single whole with himself.
And we have the surest proof of this in what actually 69
happens. Countless multitudes from countless cities come, some over land, others over sea, from east and west and north and south at every feast. They take the temple for their port as a general haven and safe refuge from the bustle and great turmoil of life, and there they seek to find calm weather, and, released from the cares whose yoke has been heavy upon them from their earliest years, to enjoy a brief breathing-space in scenes of genial cheerfulness. Thus filled 70

[b] See Deut. xii. 5-7, 11-14, 17-18. See also App. p. 618.

τε χρηστῶν γεμισθέντες σχολάζουσι τὴν ἀναγκαιοτάτην σχολὴν ὁσιότητι καὶ τιμῇ θεοῦ, φιλίαν καὶ πρὸς τοὺς τέως ἀγνοουμένους συντιθέμενοι καὶ κρᾶσιν ἠθῶν ἐπὶ θυσιῶν καὶ σπονδῶν εἰς βεβαιοτάτην πίστιν ὁμονοίας ποιούμενοι.

71 XIII. Τούτου τοῦ ἱεροῦ ὁ μὲν ἐξωτάτω περίβολος καὶ μήκει καὶ πλάτει μέγιστος ὢν τέσσαρσι στοαῖς εἰς πολυτέλειαν ἠσκημέναις ὠχύρωται· διπλῆ δ' ἐστὶν αὐτῶν ἑκάστη, ξύλων καὶ λίθων ὕλαις καὶ χορηγίαις ἀφθόνοις καὶ δημιουργῶν ἐμπειρίαις καὶ τῶν ἐφεστηκότων ἐπιμελείαις κατεσκευασμένη, τελειότατον ἔργον· οἱ δ' εἴσω βραχύτεροι μέν,
72 αὐστηροτέραν δ' ἔχοντες τὴν κατασκευήν. κατὰ δὲ τὸ μεσαίτατον αὐτὸς ὁ νεὼς παντὸς λόγου κρείττων, ὡς ἐκ τῶν φαινομένων ἔστι τεκμήρασθαι· τὰ γὰρ ἔνδον ἀόρατα παντί τῳ πλὴν ἑνὶ τῷ ἀρχιερεῖ, καὶ τούτῳ μέντοι, δι' ἔτους ἐπιτετραμμένον ἅπαξ εἰσιέναι, πάντ' ἐστὶν ἀθέατα· πυρεῖον γὰρ ἀνθράκων πλῆρες καὶ θυμιαμάτων εἰσκομίζει, πολλῆς δ' ἀναδιδομένης ὡς εἰκὸς ἀτμίδος κατέχεται τἀν κύκλῳ πάντα καὶ ἡ ὄψις ἐπισκιάζεται καὶ ἀνακοπὴν ἴσχει
73 πρόσω χωρεῖν ἀδυνατοῦσα. μέγιστος δὲ ὢν καὶ

---

[a] Lit. "they are at leisure with the most necessary leisure." For this use of ἀναγκαῖος *cf.* § 54 above. Possibly, however, "the leisure which they are compelled by the nature of the circumstances to have," and so perhaps Heinemann ("unentbehrlicher"). But the cognate accusative, as used by Philo, seems to me to point clearly to the rendering in the translation.

[b] Here the MSS. insert a heading Περὶ τοῦ ἱεροῦ, and Cohn begins a fresh numeration of the chapters, as in § 12. For a note on the description which follows see App. pp. 618-619.

[c] *i.e.* with two rows of pillars (so Heinemann).

with comfortable hopes they devote the leisure, as is their bounden duty,[a] to holiness and the honouring of God. Friendships are formed between those who hitherto knew not each other, and the sacrifices and libations are the occasion of reciprocity of feeling and constitute the surest pledge that all are of one mind.

XIII. [b]This temple is enclosed by an outermost 71
wall of very great length and breadth, which gains additional solidity by four porticos so adorned as to present a very costly appearance. Each of them is twofold,[c] and the stone and timber used as its materials and supplied in abundance, combined with the skill of experienced craftsmen and the care bestowed on it by the master-builders, have produced a very perfect piece of work. The inner walls are smaller and in a severer style of architecture.
Right in the very middle stands the sanctuary itself 72
with a beauty baffling description, to judge from what is exposed to view. For all inside is unseen except by the high priest alone, and indeed he, though charged with the duty of entering once a year, gets no view of anything.[d] For he takes with him a brazier full of lighted coals and incense,[e] and the great quantity of vapour which this naturally gives forth covers everything around it, beclouds the eyesight and prevents it from being able to penetrate
to any distance. The huge size and height of the 73

[d] See Lev. xvi. 34 and *cf.* Hebrews ix. 7, and in Philo, *De Ebr.* 136, *De Gig.* 52. Philo, however, seems to make a strange mistake, as it is only "the holy place within the veil" to which this applies. In § 274 and § 296 below he clearly states that the other priests had access to the rest of the sanctuary.

[e] See Lev. xvi. 12, 13.

ὑψηλότατος, καίτοι[1] ἐν χθαμαλωτέρῳ κείμενος, τῶν
[224] περιμηκεστάτων ὀρῶν οὐδενὸς | ἀποδεῖ. τὰ μὲν
οὖν ἐν οἰκοδομίαις ὑπερβολὰς ἔχοντα περίβλεπτά τ' ἐστὶ καὶ θαυμάζεται πρὸς τῶν ὁρώντων καὶ μάλιστα τῶν ἐπιφοιτώντων ξένων, οἳ συγκρίνοντες ταῖς οἰκιῶν δημοσίων κατασκευαῖς ἐκπλήττονται τό τε
74 κάλλος ὁμοῦ καὶ τὴν πολυτέλειαν. ἄλσος[a]
δὲ οὐδέν ἐστιν ἐν τῷ περιβόλῳ προστάξει νόμου, διὰ πολλά· πρῶτον μὲν ὅτι οὐχ ἡδονὴν καὶ τέρψιν εὐδιάγωγον ἐπιζητεῖ τὸ πρὸς ἀλήθειαν ἱερὸν ἀλλ' αὐστηρὰν ἁγιστείαν· δεύτερον δ' ὅτι τὰ συντείνοντα πρὸς τὴν τῶν δένδρων χλόην οὐ θέμις εἰσκομίζεσθαι, τὰ δ' ἐστὶν ἀνθρώπων καὶ ζῴων ἀλόγων περιττώματα· τρίτον δ' ὅτι τὰ μὲν τῆς ἀγρίας ὕλης πρὸς οὐδὲν ὄφελος, "ἄχθος" δ' ὡς οἱ ποιηταί φασι "γῆς," τὰ δὲ τῆς ἡμέρου, καρπῶν ἡμέρων οἰστικά, μεθέλξει τοὺς ὀλιγόφρονας ἀπὸ τῆς περὶ τὴν
75 ἱερουργίαν σεμνότητος. πρὸς δὲ τούτοις λάσια
χωρία καὶ δρυμοὶ βαθεῖς κακούργων εἰσὶν ἐνδιαιτήματα τὴν ἐκ τοῦ συσκιάζεσθαι ποριζομένων ἀσφάλειαν καὶ τὰς ἐξ ἐνέδρας καθ' ὧν ἂν ἐθελήσωσιν αἰφνιδίους ἐπιθέσεις. αἱ δ' εὐρυχωρίαι καὶ τὸ ἀναπεπταμένον καὶ τὸ ἀνειμένον πάντῃ, μηδενὸς τὰς ὄψεις ἐμποδίζοντος, πρὸς τὴν τῶν εἰσιόντων καὶ ἐνδιατριβόντων ἀκριβῆ θέαν ἱερῷ πρεπωδέστατον.[2]

[1] MSS. καὶ.

[2] MSS. ἱεροπρεπωδέστατον.

---

[a] See Deut. xvi. 21. LXX ἄλσος, R.V. Asherah. Hecataeus in his description of the temple (see on § 274) notes the absence of anything like a grove.

sanctuary make it in spite of its comparatively low situation as prominent an object as any of the highest mountains. In fact, so vast are the buildings that they are seen conspicuously and strike the eye with admiration, especially in the case of foreign visitors, who compare them with the architecture of their own public edifices and are amazed both at their beauty and magnificence.

But there is no grove within the walled area by 74
order of the law, for many reasons. [a] First, because the temple which is truly holy does not seek to provide pleasure and hours of easy enjoyment but the austerity of religion; secondly, because the means used to promote the verdure of trees, being the excrements of men and irrational animals, cannot be brought in there without profanity; thirdly, because the plants of the wild kind of vegetation are of no use, but only, as the poets say, "a burden to the soil," [b] while those of the cultivated variety which produce fruits of the same quality will distract the weak-minded from the solemnity of the
sacred rites. Furthermore, overgrown places and 75
dense thickets are the resort of malefactors, who use their obscurity for their own safety and as an ambush whence they can suddenly attack whomsoever they wish. Broad spaces and openness and absence of restriction on every side, where there is nothing to hinder the sight, are most suitable to a temple, to enable those who enter and spend their time there to have an accurate view.

[b] *Ibid.* xviii. 104, *Od.* xx. 379; in both cases ἄχθος ἀρούρης. Plato, however, has the form γῆς ἄχθη, *Theaet.* i. 176 D. In all these cases it is applied to human beings, and so by Philo, *Mos.* i. 30, *De Cong.* 171; but see *Spec. Leg.* iii. 50.

76 XIV. Προσόδους δ᾿ ἔχει τὸ ἱερὸν οὐ μόνον ἀπο-
τομὰς γῆς ἀλλὰ καὶ πολὺ μείζους ἑτέρας, αἳ μηδενὶ
χρόνῳ φθαρήσονται· ἐφ᾿ ὅσον γὰρ τὸ ἀνθρώπων
γένος διαμενεῖ—διαμενεῖ δ᾿ εἰς ἀεί,—καὶ αἱ πρόσοδοι τοῦ ἱεροῦ φυλαχθήσονται συνδιαιωνίζουσαι
77 παντὶ τῷ κόσμῳ. προστέτακται γὰρ ἕκαστον ἀνὰ
πᾶν ἔτος ἀπαρχὰς εἰσφέρειν ἀπὸ εἰκοσαετίας ἀρξά-
μενον. αἱ δ᾿ εἰσφοραὶ "λύτρα" προσονομάζονται·
διὸ καὶ προθυμότατα ποιοῦνται τὰς ἀπαρχάς,
φαιδροὶ καὶ γεγηθότες, ὡς ἅμα τῇ καταθέσει
μέλλοντες ἢ δουλείας ἀπαλλαγὴν ἢ νόσων ἄκεσιν
εὑρίσκεσθαι καὶ βεβαιοτάτην ἐλευθερίαν ὁμοῦ καὶ
78 σωτηρίαν εἰς ἅπαν καρποῦσθαι. πολυανθρωποτάτου δ᾿ ἔθνους ὡς εἰκὸς καὶ τὰς ἀπαρχὰς
ἀφθονωτάτας εἶναι συμβέβηκε· σχεδὸν γοῦν ἀνὰ
πᾶσαν πόλιν ταμεῖα τῶν ἱερῶν χρημάτων ἐστίν,
εἰς ἃ παραγινομένοις ἔθος ἀπάρχεσθαι· καὶ χρόνοις
ὡρισμένοις ἱεροπομποὶ τῶν χρημάτων ἀριστίνδην
ἐπικριθέντες, ἐξ ἑκάστης οἱ δοκιμώτατοι, χειρο-
τονοῦνται, σώους τὰς ἐλπίδας ἑκάστων παρα-
πέμψοντες· ἐν γὰρ ταῖς νομίμοις ἀπαρχαῖς αἱ
τῶν εὐσεβούντων ἐλπίδες εἰσίν.

[225] 79 XV. | [1] Φυλαὶ μέν εἰσι τοῦ ἔθνους δώδεκα, μία δ᾿
ἐκ πασῶν ἀριστίνδην ἐπικριθεῖσα ἱερᾶται, γέρας
ἀνδραγαθίας καὶ φιλοθέου σπουδῆς τουτὶ λαβοῦσα,
καθ᾿ ὃν καιρὸν ἔδοξεν ἡ πληθὺς ἁμαρτεῖν ἀπ-

[1] Here the mss. insert the heading Περὶ ἱερέων.

---

[a] See Ex. xxx. 12-16, where the "ransom" is to be paid at the census to avert the plague, which might be expected to follow such a proceeding (see Driver).

[b] Here the mss. give the heading "Of the priests," but Cohn does not begin a new numeration of chapters.

[c] The allusion is of course to the slaughter of the Calf-

XIV. The revenues of the temple are derived not 76
only from landed estates but also from other and far greater sources which time will never destroy. For as long as the human race endures, and it will endure for ever, the revenues of the temple also will remain secure co-eternal with the whole universe. For it is 77
ordained that everyone, beginning at his twentieth year, should make an annual contribution of first-fruits.[a] These contributions are called "ransom money," and therefore the first-fruits are given with the utmost zeal. The donors bring them cheerfully and gladly, expecting that the payment will give them release from slavery or healing of diseases and the enjoyment of liberty fully secured and also complete preservation from danger. As the nation is 78
very populous, the offerings of first-fruits are naturally exceedingly abundant. In fact, practically in every city there are banking places for the holy money where people regularly come and give their offerings. And at stated times there are appointed to carry the sacred tribute envoys selected on their merits, from every city those of the highest repute, under whose conduct the hopes of each and all will travel safely. For it is on these first-fruits, as prescribed by the law, that the hopes of the pious rest.

XV.[b] The nation has twelve tribes, but one out 79
of these was selected on its special merits for the priestly office, a reward granted to them for their gallantry and godly zeal on an occasion[c] when the multitude was seen to have fallen into sin through

worshippers by the Levites in Ex. xxxii. As to the statement that the Levites received their consecration as a reward for this, a statement made by Philo also in his longer account of the event in *Mos.* ii. 160 f. and repeated in *Spec. Leg.* iii. 125 f., see App. p. 619.

ακολουθήσασα γνώμαις ἐνίων ἀγνώμοσιν, οἳ τὴν Αἰγυπτιακὴν ἔπεισαν ζηλοῦν ἠλιθιότητα καὶ τὸν ἐγχώριον τῦφον, ὃν ἐπ' ἀλόγοις ζῴοις καὶ μάλιστα ταύροις μυθοπλαστοῦσι· τοὺς γὰρ ἡγεμόνας τῆς ἀπονοίας ἅπαντας ἡβηδὸν αὐτοκέλευστοι κατακτείναντες εὐαγὲς ἔδοξαν ἔργον εἰργάσθαι, τοὺς ὑπὲρ εὐσεβείας ἀγῶνας διαθλήσαντες.

80 XVI. Νόμοι δὲ ἱερέων εἰσὶν οἵδε. παντελῆ καὶ ὁλόκληρον εἶναι τὸν ἱερέα προστέτακται, μηδεμίαν ἐν τῷ σώματι λώβην ἔχοντα, μήτε κατ' ἔνδειαν ἐπιλείποντος ἢ ἀκρωτηριασθέντος μέρους μήτε κατὰ πλεονασμὸν ἅμα τῇ γενέσει περιττεύσαντος ἢ ὕστερον ἐκ νόσου προσφύντος μήτε τῆς χρόας μεταβαλούσης εἰς λέπραν ἢ λειχῆνας ἀγρίους ἢ μυρμηκίας ἤ τινας ἄλλας ἐξανθημάτων ἐκφύσεις· ἅ μοι δοκεῖ πάντα σύμβολα τῆς περὶ ψυχὴν εἶναι
81 τελειότητος. εἰ γὰρ τὸ φύσει θνητὸν σῶμα τοῦ ἱερέως ἐπισκεπτέον, ἵνα περὶ μηδὲν ἀτύχημα κηραίνῃ, πολὺ πλέον ψυχὴν τὴν ἀθάνατον, ἥν φασι τυπωθῆναι κατὰ τὴν εἰκόνα τοῦ ὄντος· λόγος δ' ἐστὶν εἰκὼν θεοῦ, δι' οὗ σύμπας ὁ κόσμος ἐδημιουργεῖτο.

82 Μετὰ δὲ τὴν ἐξ εὐπατριδῶν εὐγένειαν καὶ παντέλειαν τὴν ἔν τε σώμασι καὶ ψυχαῖς περὶ ἐσθῆτος, ἣν ἀναλαμβάνειν χρὴ τὸν ἱερέα μέλλοντα λειτουρ-
83 γεῖν τὰς ἱερὰς λειτουργίας, νενομοθέτηται. ἡ δ' ἐσθής ἐστι χιτὼν λινοῦς καὶ περίζωμα, τὸ μὲν εἰς αἰδοίων σκέπην, ἃ μὴ πρὸς τῷ θυσιαστηρίῳ γυ-

[a] See Lev. xxi. 17-21 and xxii. 4. On "redundant" see App. p. 619.

following the ill-judged judgement of some who persuaded them to emulate the foolishness of Egypt and the vainly imagined fables current in that land, attached to irrational animals and especially to bulls. For the men of this tribe at no bidding but their own made a wholesale slaughter of all the leaders of the delusion and thus carrying to the end their championship of piety were held to have done a truly religious deed.

XVI. With regard to the priests there are the 80
following laws. It is ordained that the priest should be perfectly sound throughout, without any bodily deformity.[a] No part, that is, must be lacking or have been mutilated, nor on the other hand redundant, whether the excrescence be congenital or an aftergrowth due to disease. Nor must the skin have been changed into a leprous state or into malignant tetters or warts or any other eruptive growth. All these seem to me to symbolize perfection of soul. For if 81
the priest's body, which is mortal by nature, must be scrutinized to see that it is not afflicted by any serious misfortune, much more is that scrutiny needed for the immortal soul, which we are told was fashioned after the image of the Self-existent.[b] And the image of God is the Word through whom the whole universe was framed.

After providing for his pure descent from a noble 82
stock and his perfection both of body and soul, the legislation deals with the dress which the priest must assume when he is about to carry out the sacred rites. It consists of a linen tunic and short breeches, the 83
latter to cover the loins, which must not be exposed

[b] Gen. i. 27. See note on § 171.

μνουσθαι θέμις, ὁ δὲ χιτὼν ἕνεκα τῆς πρὸς τὴν ὑπηρεσίαν ὀξύτητος· ἀνείμονες γὰρ ἐν μόνοις χιτωνίσκοις τά τε ἱερεῖα καὶ τὰς εὐχὰς[1] καὶ τὰς σπονδὰς καὶ ὅσα ἄλλα θυσίαις χρήσιμα προσ-
84 άγουσιν εἰς ἀνυπέρθετον τάχος ἠσκημένοι. τῷ δ' ἀρχιερεῖ διείρηται μὲν τὴν παραπλησίαν ἐσθῆτα ἀναλαμβάνειν, ἡνίκα ἂν εἰς τὰ ἄδυτα ἐπιθυμιάσων εἰσίῃ, διὰ τὸ τὴν ὀθόνην ἐκ μηδενὸς τῶν ἀποθνῃσκόντων ὥσπερ τὰ ἔρια γεννᾶσθαι, προστέτακται δὲ καὶ ἑτέρᾳ χρῆσθαι πάνυ ποικίλην ἐχούσῃ κατασκευήν, ὡς ἀπεικόνισμα καὶ μίμημα τοῦ κόσμου
85 δοκεῖν εἶναι. σαφὴς δὲ πίστις ἡ κατασκευή. πρῶτον μὲν γὰρ ἔνδυμα περιφερές ἐστιν, ὅλον δι' ὅλων ὑακίνθινον, ποδήρης χιτών, ἀέρος σύμβολον, ἐπειδήπερ ὁ ἀὴρ καὶ φύσει μέλας ἐστὶ καὶ τρόπον τινὰ ποδήρης, ἄνωθεν ἀπὸ τῶν μετὰ σελήνην
[226] | τόπων ταθεὶς ἄχρι τῶν κατωτάτω γῆς μυχῶν.
86 εἶθ' ὕφασμα θωρακοειδὲς ἐπὶ τούτῳ, σύμβολον οὐρανοῦ· δύο τε γὰρ ἐπὶ τῶν ἀκρωμίων λίθοι σμαράγδου τῆς τιμαλφεστάτης ὕλης εἰσίν, ὁ μὲν ἔνθεν, ὁ δ' ἔνθεν, εἷς ἑκατέρωθεν, περιφερεῖς, δείγματα τῶν ἡμισφαιρίων, ὧν τὸ μὲν ὑπὲρ γῆν τὸ δ'

[1] καὶ τὰς εὐχὰς is omitted in the other MSS. and appears in R as καὶ τὰς followed by a word which Cohn prints as εὐχὰς?. He does not say anything about the Armenian. See App. p. 620.

---

[a] See Ex. xxviii. 40-43.
[b] For the word ἀνείμονες see note on *De Som.* i. 99.
[c] See App. p. 620.
[d] Lev. xvi. 4. The linen garment worn on this special occasion is not mentioned in the account of *Mos.* ii. 109 ff.,

at the altar, while the tunic is to make them nimble in their ministry.[a] For in this undress,[b] with nothing more than the short tunics, they are attired so as to move with unhampered rapidity when they bring the victims and the votive offerings [c] and the libations and all other things needed for the sacrifices. The 84
high priest is bidden to put on a similar dress [d] when he enters the inner shrine to offer incense, because its fine linen is not, like wool, the product of creatures subject to death, and also to wear another, the formation of which is very complicated.[e] In this it would seem to be a likeness and copy of the universe. This is clearly shewn by the design. In the first 85
place, it is a circular garment of a dark blue colour throughout, a tunic with a full-length skirt, thus symbolizing the air, because the air is both naturally black and in a sense a full-length robe stretching from the sublunar region above to the lowest recesses of the earth. Secondly, on this is set a piece 86
of woven work in the shape of a breastplate, which symbolizes heaven. For on the shoulder-points there are two emerald stones, a kind of substance which is exceedingly valuable. There is one of these on each side and both are circular, representing the hemispheres, one of which is above and one under

but its significance is pointed out at length in *De Ebr.* 86 ff. *Cf. Leg. All.* ii. 56.

[e] §§ 84-94. This account and interpretation of the long robe (see Ex. xxviii.) follow closely that of *Mos.* ii. 109-135, and the differences, mainly in the treatment of the two mysterious objects called in the LXX Clear shewing and Truth (E.V. Urim and Thummim), § 88, and of the Bells, § 93, were, together with a comparison of the interpretation of the Bells in *De Mig.* 102 f., discussed in the note in Vol. VI. p. 609, and the discussion need not be repeated here.

87 ὑπὸ γῆν ἐστιν. εἶτα πρὸς τοῖς στέρνοις δώδεκα
λίθοι πολυτελεῖς τὰς χρόας διαφέροντες, ἐκ τριῶν
τεταγμένοι τετραστοιχεί, πρὸς παράδειγμα τοῦ
ζῳδιακοῦ τυπωθέντες· καὶ γὰρ ἐκεῖνος ἐκ δώδεκα
συνεστὼς ζῳδίων τὰς ἐτησίους τέτταρας ὥρας ἀπο-
88 τελεῖ τρία νείμας εἰς ἑκάστην. σύμπας δ'
ὁ τόπος καλεῖται λογεῖον ἐτύμως, ἐπειδὴ τὰ ἐν οὐρανῷ πάντα λόγοις καὶ ἀναλογίαις δεδημιούργηται
καὶ συντέτακται· τῶν γὰρ ἐκεῖ τὸ παράπαν ἄλογον
οὐδέν. ἐπὶ δὲ τοῦ λογείου διττὰ ὑφάσματα κατα-
ποικίλλει προσαγορεύων τὸ μὲν δήλωσιν, τὸ δὲ
89 ἀλήθειαν. αἰνίττεται δὲ διὰ μὲν τῆς ἀληθείας, ὅτι
οὐρανοῦ τὸ παράπαν ψεῦδος ἐπιβαίνειν οὐ θεμιτόν,
ἀλλὰ τοῦθ' ἅπαν εἰς τὸν περίγειον πεφυγάδευται
χῶρον ψυχαῖς ἐναγῶν ἀνθρώπων εἰσοικιζόμενον,
διὰ δὲ τῆς δηλώσεως, ὅτι αἱ κατ' οὐρανὸν φύσεις
ἕκαστα δηλοῦσι τῶν παρ' ἡμῖν, ἃ καθ' αὑτὰ πάντως
90 ἂν ἦν ἄγνωστα. σημεῖον δ' ἐναργέστατον· εἰ μὴ
φῶς ἡλίου[1] ἀνέλαμψε, πῶς ἂν αἱ τῶν σωμάτων
ἀμύθητοι ποιότητες διεφάνησαν, πῶς δ' ἂν αἱ
πολύμορφοι τῶν χρωμάτων καὶ σχημάτων ἰδέαι;
ἡμέρας δὲ καὶ νύκτας μῆνάς τε καὶ ἐνιαυτοὺς καὶ
συνόλως χρόνον τίς ἀνέδειξεν ὅτι μὴ σελήνης καὶ
ἡλίου καὶ τῶν ἄλλων ἀστέρων αἱ ἐναρμόνιοι καὶ
91 παντὸς λόγου κρείττους περιφοραί; τίς δὲ τὴν

[1] So R and the Armenian. The other MSS. have φῶς ἥλιος or φῶς ἥλιος δ'. Cohn prints φῶς, ἡλίου ἥλιος, appealing to § 279 below, but there the "sun's sun" is God. He also cites (*Hermes*, 1908, p. 187) *De Op.* 31 as representing light as the source of the sun, but that light is the φῶς νοητόν, an idea which is not, I think, suited to this passage. For further discussion see App. p. 620.

the earth. Then on the breast there are twelve 87
precious stones of different colours, arranged in four rows of three each, set in this form on the model of the zodiac, for the zodiac consisting of twelve signs makes the four seasons of the year by giving three
signs to each. [a]This part of the dress as 88
a whole is significantly called the reason-seat, because heaven and its contents are all framed and ordered on rational principles and proportions, for nothing there is irrational. On the reason-seat he embroidered two pieces of woven work, one of which
he called Clear Shewing and the other Truth. By 89
Truth he suggests the thought that no falsehood is allowed to set foot in heaven but has been banished entirely to the earthly regions and has its lodging in the souls of accursed men : by Clear Shewing that the heavenly beings make clear all things that we are or do, which in themselves would be altogether
unknown. Here is a self-evident proof. If the light 90
of the sun had never shone, how could the numberless qualities of bodily things have been perceived ? Or the multiform varieties of colours and shapes? [b]Who else could have shewn us nights and days and months and years and time in general except the revolutions, harmonious and grand beyond all description, of the
sun and the moon and the other stars? How but 91

[a] If I understand Philo aright, this description of the dress identifies what in *Mos.* ii. 109 is called the ἐπωμίς (there translated "ephod") with the λογεῖον or "oracle of judgement" (for the translation "reason-seat" see note on *Mos.* ii. 112), while there the λογεῖον is attached by chains to the ἐπωμίς.

[b] For the general sense of what follows *cf. De Op.* 58-62; also the eulogy of sight, *De Abr.* 158, 159, all of them deriving originally from Plato, *Timaeus* 47.

ἀριθμοῦ φύσιν εἰ μὴ τὰ λεχθέντα κατὰ τὰς τῶν μερῶν τοῦ χρόνου συνθέσεις; τίς δὲ τὰς ἐν θαλάσσῃ καὶ τοσούτοις πελάγεσιν ὁδοὺς ἀνέτεμε καὶ διέδειξε πλωτῆρσιν εἰ μὴ αἱ τῶν ἀστέρων στροφαὶ
92 καὶ περίοδοι; σοφοὶ δ' ἄνδρες καὶ μυρία ἄλλα παρατηρήσαντες ἀνέγραψαν, ἐκ τῶν οὐρανίων σημειωσάμενοι νηνεμίας καὶ βίας πνευμάτων, φορὰς καὶ ἀφορίας καρπῶν, ἀνειμένα καὶ φλογωδέστατα θέρη, χειμῶνας ἐξαισίους καὶ ἐαρίζοντας, αὐχμοὺς καὶ ἐπομβρίας, εὐγονίας ζῴων καὶ φυτῶν καὶ τοὐναντίον ἑκατέρων ἀγονίας καὶ ὅσα τοιουτότροπα· πάντων γὰρ ἐστηλίτευται τῶν ἐπὶ γῆς ἐν οὐρανῷ τὰ σημεῖα.

93 XVII. Πρὸς δὲ τοῖς κατωτάτω μέρεσι τοῦ ποδήρους ἀπῃώρηνται χρυσοῖ ῥοΐσκοι κώδωνές τε καὶ ἄνθινα· τὰ δ' ἐστὶ σύμβολα γῆς καὶ ὕδατος, γῆς μὲν τὰ ἄνθινα, παρόσον βλαστάνει καὶ ἀνθεῖ πάντα ἐκ ταύτης, ὕδατος δὲ οἱ ῥοΐσκοι λεχθέντες ἐτύμως παρὰ τὴν ῥύσιν, τὴν δ' ἁρμονίαν καὶ συμφωνίαν καὶ συνήχησιν τῶν τοῦ κόσμου μερῶν οἱ κώδωνες
94 ἐμφαίνουσιν. εὖ δ' ἔχει καὶ ἡ θέσις· ἀνωτάτω μέν, ἐν ᾧ οἱ λίθοι, τὸ καλούμενον περιστήθιον, οὐρανοῦ μίμημα, διότι καὶ ὁ οὐρανὸς ἀνωτάτω, ὁ δὲ ποδήρης
[227] ὑπ' αὐτῷ, ὅλος δι' ὅλων ὑακίνθινος, ἐπειδὴ | καὶ ὁ ἀὴρ μέλας ὢν τὴν μετ' οὐρανὸν δευτέραν τάξιν κεκλήρωται, τὰ δ' ἄνθινα καὶ οἱ ῥοΐσκοι πρὸς τοῖς ἐσχάτοις, διότι γῆ καὶ ὕδωρ τὴν κατωτάτω τοῦ
95 παντὸς μοῖραν ἔλαχον. ἥδ' ἐστὶν ἡ τῆς ἱερᾶς ἐσθῆτος κατασκευή, μίμημα τοῦ παντός, θαυμάσιον

through the same heavenly bodies teaching us to compute the divisions of time could we have learnt the nature of number? Who could have opened and shewn to the voyager his path through the seas and all the expanses of the deep had not the stars as they wheel and revolve in their courses done the work?
Numberless other phenomena have been observed and 92
recorded by wise men who by study of the heavenly bodies have marked the signs of calm weather and stormy winds, of plentifulness and scarcity of crops, of mild and scorching summers, of sinister and spring-like winters, of droughts and rainy seasons, of fecundity in animals and plants and on the other hand of sterility in both and all other matters of the same kind. For of all the things that happen upon earth, the signs are graven in the face of heaven.

XVII. At the very lowest part of the skirt there 93
are appended golden pomegranates and bells and flower-work, symbols of earth and water: the flower patterns of earth because they grow and flower out of it, the pomegranate or flowing fruit, of water, the name preserving its derivation from "flowing," while the bells shew forth the harmony and concord and
unison of the parts of the universe. The order in 94
which the parts are arranged is also admirable. At the very top is what he calls the breastpiece in which are placed the stones, a copy of heaven because heaven also is at the top. Then under it the full-length skirt, dark blue right through because the air also is black and occupies the second position below the heaven, and the flower-work and pomegranates at the extremities because to earth and water is
allotted the lowest place in the universe. Such is 95
the form in which the sacred vesture was designed,

ἔργον καὶ ὀφθῆναι καὶ νοηθῆναι· καὶ γὰρ ὄψιν ἔχει καταπληκτικωτάτην οἵαν οὐδὲν ὕφασμα τῶν παρ' ἡμῖν ἕνεκα ποικιλίας ὁμοῦ καὶ πολυτελείας καὶ
96 νόησιν τὴν περὶ τῶν αὐτῆς μερῶν φιλόσοφον. βούλεται γὰρ τὸν ἀρχιερέα πρῶτον μὲν εἰκόνα τοῦ παντὸς ἔχειν ἐμφανῆ περὶ ἑαυτόν, ἵν' ἐκ τῆς συνεχοῦς θέας ἄξιον παρέχῃ τὸν ἴδιον βίον τῆς τῶν ὅλων φύσεως, ἔπειθ' ὅπως ἐν ταῖς ἱερουργίαις συλλειτουργῇ πᾶς ὁ κόσμος αὐτῷ· πρεπωδέστατον δὲ τὸ τὸν ἱερωμένον τῷ τοῦ κόσμου πατρὶ καὶ τὸν υἱόν, τὸ πᾶν,[1] ἐπάγεσθαι πρὸς θεραπείαν τοῦ δε-
97 δημιουργηκότος καὶ γεγεννηκότος. ἔστι δὲ καὶ τρίτον τι τῆς ἱερᾶς ἐσθῆτος σύμβολον ἀναγκαῖον μὴ ἡσυχασθῆναι· τῶν μὲν γὰρ ἄλλων οἱ ἱερεῖς ὑπὲρ οἰκείων καὶ φίλων καὶ πολιτῶν αὐτὸ μόνον εἰώθασι τάς τε εὐχὰς καὶ θυσίας ἐπιτελεῖν, ὁ δὲ τῶν Ἰουδαίων ἀρχιερεὺς οὐ μόνον ὑπὲρ ἅπαντος ἀνθρώπων γένους ἀλλὰ καὶ ὑπὲρ τῶν τῆς φύσεως μερῶν, γῆς, ὕδατος, ἀέρος, πυρός, τάς τε εὐχὰς καὶ τὰς εὐχαριστίας ποιεῖται, τὸν κόσμον, ὅπερ ἐστὶ ταῖς ἀληθείαις, ἑαυτοῦ πατρίδα εἶναι νομίζων, ὑπὲρ ἧς ἱκεσίαις καὶ λιταῖς εἴωθεν ἐξευμενίζεσθαι τὸν ἡγεμόνα ποτνιώμενος τῆς ἐπιεικοῦς καὶ ἵλεω φύσεως αὐτοῦ μεταδιδόναι τῷ γενομένῳ.

98 XVIII. Ταῦθ' ὑπειπὼν προσνομοθετεῖ κελεύων τὸν προσιόντα τῷ βωμῷ καὶ ψαύοντα θυσιῶν, ἐν ᾧ χρόνῳ τέτακται τὰς ἱερὰς λειτουργίας ἐπιτελεῖν, μήτ' οἶνον μήτε τι ἄλλο μέθυσμα πίνειν, τετταρων

[1] So Cohn combining the τὸν υἱὸν of some authorities with the τὸ πᾶν of others. On ἱερωμένον see App. p. 620.

[a] See Lev. x. 8-11, and *cf. De Ebr.* 130 f.

a copy of the universe, a piece of work of marvellous beauty to the eye and the mind. To the eye it presents a most amazing appearance transcending any woven work that we possess in variety and costliness, to the mind the philosophical conceptions which its parts suggest. For it expresses the wish first 96
that the high priest should have in evidence upon him an image of the All, that so by constantly contemplating it he should render his own life worthy of the sum of things, secondly that in performing his holy office he should have the whole universe as his fellow-ministrant. And very right and fit it is that he who is consecrated to the Father of the world should take with him also that Father's son, the universe, for the service of the Creator and Begetter.

There is also a third truth symbolized 97
by the holy vesture which must not be passed over in silence. Among the other nations the priests are accustomed to offer prayers and sacrifices for their kinsmen and friends and fellow-countrymen only, but the high priest of the Jews makes prayers and gives thanks not only on behalf of the whole human race but also for the parts of nature, earth, water, air, fire. For he holds the world to be, as in very truth it is, his country, and in its behalf he is wont to propitiate the Ruler with supplication and intercession, beseeching Him to make His creature a partaker of His own kindly and merciful nature.

XVIII.[a] After saying this by way of prelude, he 98
proceeds to lay down another statute commanding that he who approaches the altar and handles the sacrifices should not during the time in which it is his duty to perform the sacred rites drink wine or any other intoxicant, and this for four most cogent reasons :

ἕνεκα τῶν ἀναγκαιοτάτων, ὄκνου καὶ λήθης καὶ
99 ὕπνου καὶ ἀφροσύνης. ἄκρατος γὰρ τὰς μὲν τοῦ
σώματος δυνάμεις ἀνιεὶς δυσκινητότερα τὰ μέλη
ποιεῖ καὶ ὀκνηροτέρους ἀπεργάζεται καὶ βίᾳ κατα-
δαρθάνειν ἀναγκάζει, τοὺς δὲ τῆς ψυχῆς τόνους
ἐπιχαλῶν λήθης ὁμοῦ καὶ ἀφροσύνης αἴτιος γίνεται·
νήφοντος δὲ τά τε μέρη τοῦ σώματος ἐπελαφρι-
ζόμενα εὐκινητότερα αἵ τε αἰσθήσεις καθαρώτεραι
καὶ εἰλικρινέστεραι ὅ τε νοῦς ἐξυωπέστερος, ὡς καὶ
προϊδέσθαι πράγματα δύνασθαι καὶ ἃ πρότερον
100 εἶδεν ἀπομνημονεῦσαι. συνόλως μὲν οὖν τὴν οἴνου
χρῆσιν ἅπασι τοῖς κατὰ τὸν βίον ἀλυσιτελεστάτην
ὑποληπτέον, ψυχῆς πιεζομένης, αἰσθήσεων ἀμαυ-
ρουμένων, βαρυνομένου σώματος—ἐλεύθερον γὰρ
καὶ ἄφετον οὐδὲν ἐᾷ τῶν παρ' ἡμῖν, ἀλλ' ἑκάστῳ
πρὸς ὃ πέφυκεν ἐμπόδιός ἐστιν,—ἐν δὲ ταῖς ἁγι-
[228] στείαις καὶ ἱερουργίαις τὸ βλάβος | ἀργαλεώτερον,
ὅσῳ καὶ τὸ περὶ θεὸν ἐξαμαρτεῖν τοῦ περὶ ἄνθρωπον
ἀφορητότερον. ὅθεν εἰκότως προστέτακται νηφα-
λίους[1] θύειν, "εἰς διαστολὴν καὶ διάκρισιν ἁγίων καὶ
βεβήλων καὶ καθαρῶν καὶ ἀκαθάρτων" καὶ νομίμων
καὶ παρανόμων.

101 XIX. Ἐπεὶ δ' ὁ ἱερεὺς πολὺ πρότερον ἀνήρ ἐστι
καὶ ταῖς πρὸς συνουσίαν ὁρμαῖς ἐξ ἀνάγκης ὀφείλει
χρῆσθαι, γάμον αὐτῷ μνᾶται παρθένου καθαρᾶς καὶ
ἐκ καθαρῶν γονέων καὶ πάππων καὶ προγόνων εἴς
τε καλοκἀγαθίαν καὶ εὐγένειαν ἀριστίνδην ἐπι-

[1] mss. νηφάλια.

[a] The words in inverted commas are an almost exact

the dangers of slackness, forgetfulness, sleep and
foolish behaviour. For strong drink enervates the 99
bodily faculties, and makes the limbs more difficult
to move, increases the tendency to sluggishness in
a man, and irresistibly forces him to fall asleep, while
by relaxing the sinews of the soul it produces both
forgetfulness and foolish conduct. When he is sober,
his bodily parts are buoyant and easier to move, the
senses are clearer and brighter and the mind keener-
sighted, so that it can foresee events and recount what
it has seen in the past. In general, indeed, wine 100
must be regarded as very unprofitable for every side
of life, since it presses hard upon the soul, dulls the
senses and weighs down the body, leaving none of
our faculties free and untrammelled but hampering
the natural activity of each. But in religious rites
and ceremonies the mischief is graver in the same
degree as it is more intolerable to offend against our
duty to God than our duty to man. Thus it is a very
proper enactment that the officiants at the sacrifice
should fast from wine, "to discern and distinguish
between holy and profane, clean and unclean," lawful
and unlawful.[a]

XIX. Since a priest is a man well before he[b] is 101
a priest and must and should feel the instinct for
mating, Moses arranges for his marriage with a pure
virgin whose parents and grandparents and ancestors
are equally pure, highly distinguished for the excel-

quotation of Lev. x. 10, but the addition "lawful and unlawful," also represents *v.* 11 "to teach the sons of Israel all the statutes" (LXX νόμιμα).

[b] Or "primarily a man, and only secondarily a priest," πολὺ πρότερον not indicating time or even importance, but that the genus comes before the species.

102 κριθέντων. πόρνῃ μὲν γὰρ καὶ βεβήλῳ σῶμα καὶ ψυχὴν οὐδὲ προσελθεῖν[1] ἐᾷ, κἂν τὴν ἐργασίαν ἀποθεμένη σχῆμα κόσμιον καὶ σῶφρον ὑποδύηται, διὰ τὸ τὴν ἀρχαίαν προαίρεσιν ἀνίερον αὐτῇ γενέσθαι. αὕτη δὲ πρὸς μὲν τὰ ἄλλα ἐπιτιμίαν ἐχέτω σπουδάσασα μιασμάτων καθαρεῦσαι· μετάνοια γὰρ ἀδικημάτων ἐπαινετόν· καὶ μηδεὶς ἕτερος αὐτὴν ἄγεσθαι κεκωλύσθω, ἱερεῖ δὲ μὴ προσίτω· τὰ γὰρ ἱερωσύνης ἐξαίρετα δίκαια συμφωνίαν ἐπιζητούσης τὴν ἀπὸ γενέσεως [ἀρχῆς] ἄχρι τελευτῆς ἀνυπαίτιον.
103 εὔηθες γὰρ διὰ μὲν τὰς ἐκ τῶν τραυμάτων ἐπιγενομένας οὐλὰς ἐν τοῖς σώμασιν εἴργεσθαί τινας ἱερωσύνης, αἳ σύμβολον ἀτυχίας, οὐ μοχθηρίας, εἰσί, τὰς δὲ μὴ κατ' ἀνάγκην μόνον ἀλλ' ἔστιν ὅτε καὶ ἑκουσίοις γνώμαις πεπρακυίας τὴν ἰδίαν ὥραν, ἐπειδήπερ ὀψὲ καὶ μόλις μετέγνωσαν, εὐθὺς ἀπὸ ἐραστῶν ἱερεῦσιν ἁρμόζεσθαι καὶ ἀπὸ χαμαιτυπείων εἰς ἱερὰ χωρία μετοικίζεσθαι· μένουσι γὰρ οὐδὲν ἧττον ἐν ταῖς ψυχαῖς τῶν μετανοούντων οὐλαὶ
104 καὶ τύποι τῶν ἀρχαίων ἀδικημάτων. εὖ καὶ παγκάλως ἐν ἑτέροις διείρηται "μηδὲ μίσθωμα πόρνης εἰσκομίζειν εἰς τὸ ἱερόν"· καίτοι τό γε νόμισμα καθ' αὑτὸ οὐκ ἔνοχον, ἀλλὰ διὰ τὴν λαβοῦσαν καὶ τὴν πρᾶξιν ἐφ' ᾗ δέδοται. σχολῇ γ'

[1] MSS. προσιδεῖν.

---

[a] See Lev. xxi. 7 (not as Cohn, 13, 14, which refer to the high priest), "They shall not take a woman that is a harlot or profane, or a woman put away from her husband." By a "pure virgin" Philo, as appears from § 108, means that if she is unmarried she must be pure. The instruction to inquire into her lineage has no scriptural authority. But Josephus, *Contra Apion.* i. 31, entirely supports it as a

lence of their conduct and lineage.[a] For a harlot is 102
profane in body and soul, even if she has discarded her trade and assumed a decent and chaste demeanour, and he is forbidden even to approach her, since her old way of living was unholy. Let such a one indeed retain in other respects her civic rights as she has been at pains to purge herself from her defilements, for repentance from wrongdoing is praiseworthy. Nor let anyone else be prevented from taking her in marriage, but let her not come near to the priest. For the rights and duties of the priesthood are of a special kind, and the office demands an even tenor
of blamelessness from birth to death. It would be 103
foolish if, while the bodily scars which wounds leave behind them, marks of misfortune and not of depravity, preclude one from the priesthood, the women who have sold their personal charms not only under compulsion but sometimes by free and deliberate choice, should just because of a belated and reluctant repentance pass straight from their lovers to wedlock with the priests and exchange the stews for a lodging in holy ground. For in the souls of the repentant there remain, in spite of all, the scars and prints of
their old misdeeds.[b] It is well and admirably said in 104
another place,[c] " Neither shall the hire of a harlot be brought into the Temple," though the coins are not guilty in themselves but only because of the recipient and the business for which it was given her. Surely

practice, "He must inquire into her pedigree, obtaining the genealogy from the archives and producing a number of witnesses." Josephus goes on to say that the practice is observed among the Jews of Egypt, Babylonia, and elsewhere, as much as in Palestine.

[b] See App. p. 620.

[c] Deut. xxiii. 18.

ἂν ἔτι προσοῖτό τις εἰς κοινωνίαν ἱερέων γυναῖκας, ὧν καὶ τὰ χρήματα βέβηλα καὶ παράσημα, εἰ καὶ ταῖς ὕλαις καὶ τοῖς χαρακτῆρσι δόκιμα.

105 XX. Τὰ μὲν οὖν περὶ γάμον οὕτως ἠκρίβωται τῷ ἀρχιερεῖ, ὥστ᾿ οὐδὲ χήραν ἐφεῖται γαμεῖν αὐτῷ, οὔτε τετελευτηκότος ἀνδρὸς μονωθεῖσαν οὔτε ἀπηλλαγμένην ἔτι ζῶντος, ἵνα πρῶτον μὲν εἰς ἄβατον καὶ καθαρὰν ἄρουραν ὁ ἱερὸς σπόρος χωρῇ καὶ μηδεμίαν κρᾶσιν αἱ γοναὶ πρὸς ἑτέραν οἰκίαν λαμβάνωσιν, εἶτα δ᾿ ὅπως ἀκακωτάταις καὶ ἀδιαστρόφοις ταῖς ψυχαῖς συνερχόμενοι ῥᾳδίως δια-
[229] πλάττωσι τὰ | ἤθη καὶ τοὺς τρόπους αὐτῶν· ὁλκοὶ γὰρ καὶ εὐάγωγοι διάνοιαι παρθένων πρὸς ἀρετήν,
106 εἰς διδασκαλίαν ἑτοιμόταται· ἡ δ᾿ ἑτέρου πεῖραν ἀνδρὸς λαβοῦσα κατὰ τὸ εἰκὸς ἀπειθεστέρα πρὸς μάθησιν, ἅτε τὴν ψυχὴν ἀκραιφνεστάτην οὐκ ἔχουσα καθάπερ τινὰ λελειασμένον κηρὸν εἰς τρανότητα τῶν ἐγγραφησομένων δογμάτων, ἀλλὰ τραχεῖαν ὑπὸ τῶν προεγχαραχθέντων τύπων, οἳ δυσεξάλειπτοι παραμένοντες ἢ οὐ παραδέχονται σφραγῖδας ἑτέρας ἢ παραδεξάμενοι συγχέουσι ταῖς ἑαυτῶν ἀνωμα-
107 λίαις. παρθένον οὖν ὁ ἀρχιερεὺς ἀγέσθω γάμων ἁγνήν· λέγω δὲ παρθένον οὐ μόνον ᾗ μὴ ἕτερος ὡμίλησεν, ἀλλὰ καὶ ἐφ᾿ ᾗ μηδεὶς ἄλλος ἀνὴρ ὠνομάσθη διά τινων ὁμολογιῶν, κἂν ἁγνεύῃ τὸ σῶμα.

---

[a] Lev. xxi. 13, 14.

[b] *i.e.* successive high priests. The use of the plural is odd and might suggest that it refers to the couple; and so

one would not care to admit to partnership with the priests the women whose very money is profane and regarded as base, even though the metal and the stamp is true.

XX. [a] So strict are the regulations laid down for the 105
marriage of the high priest that he is not even permitted to marry a widow, whether her isolation is due to the death of her husband or divorce from him while still alive. This is laid down first in order that the holy seed may pass into pure and untrodden soil and the issue receive no admixture with another family. Secondly, that by mating with souls entirely innocent and unperverted they [b] may find it easy to mould the characters and dispositions of their wives, for the minds of virgins are easily influenced and attracted to virtue and very ready to be taught.
But she who has had experience of another husband 106
is naturally less amenable to instruction. For her soul is not one of the completely simple kind like a sheet of wax levelled to show clearly the lessons to be inscribed upon it, but rather like one roughened by the imprints already scored upon it, which resist effacement and either do not yield to the dint of other seals or, if they do, confuse them with their own in-
dentations. Let the high priest then take a virgin 107
who is innocent of marriage. And when I say " virgin " I exclude not only one with whom another man has had intercourse but also one with whom any other has been declared to have an agreement of betrothal, even though her body is that of a maid intact.[c]

apparently Heinemann takes it, but it seems to me impossible that Philo should be supposing that the high priest's character is moulded by his wife.

[c] See on *Spec. Leg.* iii. 72 (App.).

108 XXI. Τοῖς δὲ κατὰ μέρος ἱερεῦσι τὰ μὲν ἄλλα
περὶ γάμων διατέτακται ταὐτὰ ἃ καὶ τοῖς τὴν
μεγίστην ἔχουσιν ἱερωσύνην, ἐφεῖται δ' οὐ μόνον
παρθένους ἀλλὰ καὶ χήρας, οὐ πάσας ἀλλ' ὧν τε-
τελευτήκασιν ἄνδρες, μετ' ἀδείας ἄγεσθαι. φιλο-
νεικίας γὰρ καὶ στάσεις ἐκ τοῦ βίου τῶν ἱερέων
οἴεται δεῖν ὁ νόμος ἀναιρεῖν· πρὸς μὲν οὖν τοὺς
ζῶντας γένοιντ' ἂν ἴσως ἔριδες ἐκ πάθους γυναι-
κείου, ζηλοτυπίας, τοῖς δ' ἀποθανοῦσι συναποθνῄ-
σκει καὶ τὰ τῆς πρὸς τοὺς δευτέρους ἄνδρας ἔχθρας.
109 ἄλλως τε τὸν ἀρχιερέα πλείονος ἐδικαίωσεν ἁγιστείας καὶ καθάρσεως ὥσπερ ἐν ἅπασι τοῖς ἄλλοις
καὶ ἐν γάμου κοινωνίᾳ μεταλαχεῖν, οὐκ ἐάσας ὅτι
μὴ κόρην ἄγεσθαι· τοῖς δὲ τῆς δευτέρας τάξεως
ὑπανῆκε τὰ περὶ συνόδους γυναικῶν, ἐφιεὶς καὶ
πεπειραμένας ἑτέρων ἀνδρῶν ἐγγυᾶσθαι.
110 XXII. πρὸς δὲ τούτῳ καὶ τὸ γένος ἠκρίβωσε τῶν
μελλουσῶν γαμεῖσθαι, προστάξας τῷ μὲν ἀρχιερεῖ
μνᾶσθαι μὴ παρθένον μόνον ἀλλὰ καὶ ἱέρειαν ἐξ
ἱερέων, ἵν' ἐκ μιᾶς οἰκίας καὶ τρόπον τινὰ τοῦ
αὐτοῦ αἵματος ὦσι νυμφίος τε καὶ νύμφη πρὸς
ἁρμονίαν ἐπιδειξάμενοι παρ' ὅλον τὸν βίον κρᾶσιν
111 ἠθῶν βεβαιοτάτην. ἐπετράπη δὲ τοῖς ἄλλοις καὶ

[a] Or "ordinary." So Heinemann; Mangey "privatis." But all these are strange uses for the phrase which should mean the several or particular priests, like οἱ κατὰ μέρος νόμοι. Possibly it means the priests who stood by themselves as a μέρος of the whole class, the other μέρος being the high priest, and so almost = "as a class." So perhaps ἄρχοντος ἐν μέρει, § 226.

[b] Lev. xxi. 7. The permission is reasonably deduced from the prohibition to marry the divorced.

XXI. As for the subordinate[a] priests, while the other marriage regulations are the same for them as for those who hold the highest priesthood, they are permitted to wed with immunity not only virgins but widows,[b] though only such as have lost their husbands by death. This limitation is due to the desire of the law to remove animosities and feuds from the lives of the priests. While the first husband lives, quarrels might be engendered by the feminine proclivity to jealousy.[c] His death carries with it the death of any hostility to the second husband. As for 109
the distinction between priests and high priests, the view of the law was that the greater sanctity and purity required of the latter in all other matters should be extended to his choice of a partner in marriage, and therefore it forbade him to take to wife any but a maiden. But to those of the second rank it made concessions as to their relations with women and permitted them to espouse such as had had experience of other husbands.

XXII. Further, it made clear distinctions as to the 110
birth of the intended wives. The high priest must not propose marriage save to one who is not only a virgin but a priestess descended from priests,[d] so that bride and bridegroom may be of one house and in a sense of the same blood and so, harmoniously united, shew a lifelong blending of temperament firmly established. But the rest are permitted to marry 111

[c] As the jealousy is clearly that felt by one or both of the husbands, I do not see the point of "feminine" unless it means that such a feeling is natural in a woman, but disgraceful to a man. Some word expressing "excited by a passion for women," like γυναικομανοῦς, seems to be wanted.

[d] So Philo interprets Lev. xxi. 14 ἐκ τοῦ γένους αὐτοῦ and in the next verse, ἐκ τοῦ λαοῦ αὐτοῦ (E.V. "of his own people").

μὴ ἱερέων γαμεῖν θυγατέρας, τῇ μὲν ὅτι μικρὰ τούτων καθάρσια, τῇ δ' ὅτι τὸ ἔθνος οὐκ ἐβουλήθη γενεᾶς εἰς ἅπαν ἱερατικῆς ἀμοιρῆσαί τε καὶ παντελῶς ἀπεζεῦχθαι.[1] δι' ἣν αἰτίαν οὐκ ἐκώλυσε τοὺς ἄλλους ἱερέας ἐπιγαμίας ποιεῖσθαι πρὸς τοὺς ἀπὸ
[230] τοῦ ἔθνους, | αἵπερ εἰσὶ δεύτεραι συγγένειαι· γαμβροὶ γὰρ ἀνθ' υἱῶν πενθεροῖς καὶ ἀντὶ πατέρων γαμβροῖς πενθεροί.

112 XXIII. Τὰ μὲν δὴ περὶ γάμου ταῦτα καὶ τὰ τούτοις ὅμοια χάριν παίδων γενέσεως. ἐπεὶ δ' ἕπεται γενέσει φθορά, καὶ τοὺς ἐπὶ τελευταῖς ἀνέγραψε τοῖς ἱερεῦσι νόμους, κελεύσας μὴ ἐφ' ἅπασιν αὐτοὺς μιαίνεσθαι τοῖς ὁπωσοῦν ἢ κατὰ φιλίαν ἢ κατὰ συγγένειαν ᾠκειωμέναις, ἀλλ' ἐπὶ μόνοις πατράσι καὶ μητράσιν, υἱοῖς καὶ θυγατράσιν,
113 ἀδελφοῖς καὶ ἀδελφαῖς παρθένοις. τὸν δ' ἀρχιερέα παντὸς πένθους ὑπεξείλετο· καὶ μήποτ' εἰκότως· τὰς μὲν γὰρ τῶν ἄλλων ἱερέων ὑπηρεσίας ἀνθ' ἑτέρων ἕτεροι λειτουργεῖν δύνανται, ὡς, κἂν πενθῶσί τινες, μηδὲν τῶν ἐξ ἔθους ὑστερίζειν, τὰς δὲ τοῦ ἀρχιερέως οὐδενὶ δρᾶν ἐφεῖται. παρ' ἣν αἰτίαν ἀμίαντος ἀεὶ διατελείτω μὴ προσαπτόμενος νεκροῦ σώματος, ὅπως τὰς ὑπὲρ τοῦ ἔθνους εὐχὰς καὶ θυσίας ἕτοιμος ὢν ἐν καιροῖς τοῖς προσήκουσιν
114 ἀκωλύτως ἐπιτελῇ. καὶ γὰρ ἄλλως προσκεκληρωμένος θεῷ καὶ τῆς ἱερᾶς τάξεως γεγονὼς ταξίαρχος ὀφείλει πάντων ἀλλοτριοῦσθαι τῶν ἐν γενέσει, μὴ

[1] MSS. ἀποζεῦξαι.

---

[a] Deduced from the absence of the prohibition which Philo believes to be imposed on the high priest.

[b] καθάρσια usually means purificatory rites, but here, like

the daughters of others than priests [a] partly because the restrictions required to [b] maintain their purity are slight, partly because the law did not wish that the nation should be denied altogether a share in the priestly clanship or be entirely excluded from it. This was the reason why he did not forbid the other priests to intermarry with the laity of the nation, for intermarriage is kinship in the second degree. Sons-in-law are sons to their fathers-in-law, and the latter are fathers to the former.

XXIII. These and similar regulations as to mar- 112
riage are intended to promote the generation of children, but since generation is followed by dissolution, he has laid down laws for the priests dealing with deaths.[c] In these he ordains that they should not incur defilement for all connected with them by friendship or kinship whatever the degree, but only for fathers and mothers, sons and daughters, brothers
and maiden sisters. But the high priest is precluded 113
from all outward mourning and surely with good reason.[d] For the services of the other priests can be performed by deputy, so that if some are in mourning none of the customary rites need suffer. But no one else is allowed to perform the functions of a high priest and therefore he must always continue undefiled, never coming in contact with a corpse, so that he may be ready to offer his prayers and sacrifices at the proper time without hindrance on behalf of the
nation. Further, since he is dedicated to God and 114
has been made captain of the sacred regiment, he ought to be estranged from all the ties of birth and

κάθαρσις in § 109, seems to be used of what keeps a person pure.

[c] See Lev. xxi. 1-3. [d] See Lev. xxi. 10-12.

γονέων, μὴ τέκνων, μὴ ἀδελφῶν εὐνοίας οὕτως ἡττώμενος, ὡς ἢ παρελθεῖν ἢ ὑπερθέσθαι τι τῶν
115 ὁσίων, ὃ πραχθῆναι πάντως αὐτίκα ἄμεινον. κελεύει δὲ μήτε τὰ ἱμάτια περιρρήττειν ἐπὶ τοῖς οἰκειοτάτοις ἀποθανοῦσι μήτε ἀφαιρεῖν ἀπὸ τῆς κεφαλῆς τὰ παράσημα τῆς ἱερωσύνης μήτε συνόλως ἐκ τῶν ἁγίων ἐξιέναι κατὰ πρόφασιν πένθους, ἵνα καὶ τὸν τόπον αἰδούμενος καὶ τὰ περὶ ἑαυτὸν προκοσμήματα οἷς ἀνέστεπται, κρείττων οἴκτου γενό-
116 μενος, ἄλυπος εἰς ἀεὶ διατελῇ. βούλεται γὰρ αὐτὸν ὁ νόμος μείζονος μεμοιρᾶσθαι φύσεως ἢ κατ' ἄνθρωπον, ἐγγυτέρω προσιόντα τῆς θείας, μεθόριον, εἰ δεῖ τἀληθὲς λέγειν, ἀμφοῖν, ἵνα διὰ μέσου τινὸς ἄνθρωποι μὲν ἱλάσκωνται θεόν, θεὸς δὲ τὰς χάριτας ἀνθρώποις ὑποδιακόνῳ τινὶ χρώμενος ὀρέγῃ καὶ χορηγῇ.

117 XXIV. Ταῦτ' εἰπὼν ἑξῆς εὐθὺς[1] νομοθετεῖ περὶ τῶν χρησομένων ταῖς ἀπαρχαῖς. ἐὰν οὖν τις, φησί, τῶν ἱερέων ὀφθαλμοὺς ἢ χεῖρας ἢ βάσεις ἤ τι μέρος ἄλλο πηρωθῇ τοῦ σώματος ἢ καί τινα μῶμον ἐνδέξηται, λειτουργιῶν μὲν ἀνεχέτω διὰ τὰς ἐγγενομένας κῆρας, τὰ δὲ κοινὰ τῶν ἱερέων γέρα
118 καρπούσθω διὰ τὴν ἀνυπαίτιον εὐγένειαν. ἐὰν μέντοι λέπραι τινὸς ἐξανθήσασαι κατάσχωσιν ἢ καὶ γονορρυὴς τις γένηται τῶν ἱερέων, μήτε τραπέζης ἱερᾶς ψαυέτω μήτε τῶν προκειμένων ἄθλων τῷ γένει, μέχρις ἂν ἥ τε ῥύσις ἐπίσχῃ καὶ ἡ λέπρα μεταβαλοῦσα τῷ τῆς ὑγιοῦς σαρκὸς ἐξομοιωθῇ

[1] Some MSS. ἑξῆς, others εὐθύς.

[a] *Cf. De Som.* ii. 188.

[b] See Lev. xxi. 17 f., already cited on § 80. Here the stress

not be so overcome by affection to parents or children or brothers as to neglect or postpone any one of the religious duties which it were well to perform without any delay. He forbids him also either to rend his 115
garments for his dead, even the nearest and dearest, or to take from his head the insignia of the priesthood, or on any account to leave the sacred precincts under the pretext of mourning. Thus, showing reverence both to the place and to the personal ornaments with which he is decked, he will have his feeling of pity under control and continue throughout free from sorrow. For the law desires him to be endued with 116
a nature higher than the merely human and to approximate to the Divine, on the border-line,[a] we may truly say, between the two, that men may have a mediator through whom they may propitiate God and God a servitor to employ in extending the abundance of His boons to men.

XXIV. These rules are followed directly by his 117
legislation on those who are to share in the first-fruits. [b] If any of the priests, he tells us, has lost the use of his eyes or hands or feet or any part of his body, or suffers from any defect, he must refrain from officiating because of the afflictions which have befallen him, but he may enjoy the privileges common to the priests because his pure lineage still remains without reproach. [c] If, however, leprous eruptions 118
appear upon him or he is suffering from seminal issue, the priest must not touch the holy table or any of the prizes to which his clan is entitled until in the one case the issue has ceased, in the other the leprosy is converted into a resemblance to the hue of healthy flesh.

is on *v.* 22 "the gifts of God are most holy and he shall eat of the holy" (LXX).

[c] See Lev. xxii. 4-7.

119 χρώματι. κἂν προσάψηται μέντοι τις ὅτου δήποτε
[231] τῶν | ἀκαθάρτων ἱερεὺς ἢ καὶ νύκτωρ, οἷα φιλεῖ
πολλάκις, ὀνειρώξῃ, τὴν ἡμέραν ἐκείνην μηδὲν
προσφερέσθω τῶν καθιερωθέντων, λουσάμενος δ'
ἐπιγενομένης ἑσπέρας χρῆσθαι μὴ κεκωλύσθω.
120 πάροικος δ' ἱερέως καὶ μισθωτὸς εἰργέσθω τῶν
ἀπαρχῶν, ὁ μὲν πάροικος, ἐπειδὴ γείτονες τὰ πολλὰ[1]
συνέστιοι καὶ ὁμοτράπεζοι· δέος γάρ, μὴ προῆταί
τις τὰ καθιερωθέντα προφάσει καταχρησάμενος εἰς
ἀσέβειαν ἀκαίρῳ φιλανθρωπίᾳ· μεταδοτέον γὰρ οὐ
πᾶσι πάντων, ἀλλὰ τῶν ἐφαρμοζόντων τοῖς ληψο-
μένοις· εἰ δὲ μή, τὸ κάλλιστον καὶ λυσιτελέστατον
τῶν ἐν τῷ βίῳ, τάξις, ἀναιρεθήσεται ὑπὸ τοῦ
121 βλαβερωτάτου παρευημερηθεῖσα, συγχύσεως. εἰ
γὰρ ἴσον μὲν μέρος[2] ἐν ὁλκάσιν οἴσονται ναῦται
κυβερνήταις, ἴσον δὲ ἐν ταῖς μακραῖς τριήρεσι
τριηράρχοις[3] καὶ ναυάρχοις ἐρέται καὶ τὸ ἐπιβατικόν,
ἐν δὲ στρατοπέδοις ἴσον ἱππεῖς μὲν ἱππάρχοις,
ὁπλῖται δὲ ταξιάρχοις, λοχαγοὶ δὲ στρατηγοῖς, ἐν
δὲ πόλεσι κρινόμενοι δικασταῖς καὶ βουλευταὶ προ-
βούλοις καὶ συνόλως ἄρχουσιν ἰδιῶται, ταραχαὶ καὶ
στάσεις γενήσονται καὶ ἡ ⟨διὰ⟩ λόγων ἰσότης τὴν
δι' ἔργων ἀνισότητα γεννήσει· τὸ γὰρ τοῖς τὰς ἀξίας
ἀνομοίοις ὅμοια ἀπονέμειν ἄνισον, τὸ δ' ἄνισον
122 πηγὴ κακῶν. οὗ χάριν καὶ τὰ γέρα τῶν ἱερέων οὐ
δοτέον ὥσπερ ἄλλοις οὐδὲ τοῖς παροίκοις ἕνεκα τοῦ

[1] Some mss. μὴ πάντες γείτονες, and so Mangey, who perhaps understood it to mean that if the neighbour is one who habitually shared the table of the priest, the danger would be avoided.

[2] Some mss. omit μὲν, the others μέρος.

[3] Some mss. omit τριήρεσι, the others τριηράρχοις.

Further, if a priest touches any impure object or, as 119
often happens, has an emission during the night, he must not during that day partake of consecrated food but bathe himself, and after sundown he should not be debarred from its use. But the first-fruits must 120
be kept out of the hands of a dweller near the priest[a] or his hired servant ; the first is mentioned because board and hospitality are usually given to neighbours, and there is a danger that the consecrated meats may be profaned[b] through an untimely generosity abused as a pretext for impiety. For we must not share everything with everyone, but restrict our gifts to what are suitable to the recipient. Otherwise the most excellent and valuable thing which life possesses, order, will be destroyed, vanquished by its most mischievous foe, confusion. For if sailors on merchant vessels 121
were remunerated equally with the pilots, or oarsmen and marines on men-of-war with captains and admirals, or cavalry soldiers in armies with their commanders, or rank and file with their officers, or regimental captains with generals, or in cities litigants with judges, councillors with their chairmen, or in general private individuals with rulers, disturbances and factions would arise and the nominal equality would engender an actual inequality. For like pay for unlike worth is inequality, and inequality is the fountain of evil. On the same principle the general 122
law against giving away the prerogatives of the priests should be extended to the neighbours also. Otherwise they will be handling the forbidden meats

[a] See Lev. xxii. 10. Philo evidently takes πάροικος = "neighbour" (a sense which the word no doubt can bear). E.V. "sojourner," presumably meaning a stranger residing temporarily (?) with the priest.

[b] Lit. "lest one throw away."

γειτνιᾶν ἐφαψομένοις ὧν οὐ θέμις· οὐ γὰρ οἰκίας
123 ἀλλὰ γένους ἐστὶν ἡ τιμή. XXV. ὁμοίως
μέντοι μηδὲ μισθωτῷ μηδεὶς παρεχέτω μήτε μισθὸν
μήθ' ὑπηρεσίας ἀμοιβὴν ἱερὸν γέρας· χρήσεται γὰρ
ὁ λαβὼν ἔστιν ὅτε πρὸς ἃ μὴ δεῖ, βέβηλα τὰ τῆς
εὐγενείας ἆθλα καὶ τῆς περὶ τὸν νεὼν λειτουργίας
124 ἀπεργασάμενος. δι' ἣν αἰτίαν οὐδ' ἀλλογενεῖ
συνόλως ὁ νόμος ἐπιτρέπει μεταλαμβάνειν τῶν
ἁγίων, κἂν εὐπατρίδης ὢν τυγχάνῃ τῶν αὐτοχθόνων
καὶ πρὸς ἀνδρῶν καὶ πρὸς γυναικῶν ἀνεπίληπτος
[ὤν], ἵνα αἱ τιμαὶ μὴ νοθεύωνται, μένωσι δ' ἐν τῇ
125 ἱερατικῇ τάξει βεβαίως φυλαττόμεναι. καὶ γὰρ
ἄτοπον τὰς μὲν θυσίας καὶ ἱερουργίας καὶ ὅσα ἄλλα
περὶ τὸν βωμὸν ἁγιστεύεται μὴ πᾶσιν ἀλλὰ τοῖς
ἱερεῦσι μόνοις ἐπιτετράφθαι, τὰ δὲ ἀντὶ τούτων
ἆθλα κοινὰ γίνεσθαι καὶ τῶν ἐπιτυχόντων, ὡς δέον
μὲν πόνοις πολλοῖς καὶ καμάτοις καὶ ταῖς μεθ'
ἡμέραν καὶ νύκτωρ φροντίσιν ἀποτρύχειν τοὺς
ἱερέας, τὰ δ' ἆθλα κοινὰ καὶ τοῖς ἀργοῦσιν ἀπο-
126 φαίνειν. οἰκογενεῖ δέ, φησίν, καὶ ἀργυ-
ρωνήτῳ μεταδιδότω δεσπότης ἱερεὺς σιτίων καὶ
ποτῶν ἐκ τῶν ἀπαρχῶν· πρῶτον μὲν ὅτι θεράποντι
πόρος εἷς ὁ δεσπότης, ὁ δὲ τοῦ δεσπότου κλῆρος αἱ
ἱεραὶ φιλανθρωπίαι, ἐξ ὧν ἀνάγκη τὸν δοῦλον
127 τρέφεσθαι· δεύτερον δ' ὅτι τὰ γενησόμενα πάντως
ἀνάγκη δρᾶν ἑκόντας· οἱ δ' οἰκέται, κἂν μὴ θέ-
λωμεν, ἅτε ἀεὶ συνόντες καὶ συνδιαιτώμενοι, σιτία

[a] See Lev. xxii. 10: LXX *ἀλλογενής*, E.V. "stranger," meaning "one who is not a priest." The word might mean "foreigner," but as the LXX uses the same word in *v.* 12, where Philo interprets it as a non-priest (§ 129), he probably means the same here.

just because they live in the vicinity. For the privilege belongs not to a dwelling-house, but to a caste.
XXV. In the same way no one 123
must bestow the sacred prerogative on a hired servant, either as his hire or in exchange for his service. For he will sometimes use the gift for improper purposes, thus profaning the rewards attached to pure
lineage and the ministry of the sanctuary. This is the 124
reason why no one at all of alien race,[a] even though he be nobly born and of the original stock, without flaw either on the male or the female line, is permitted by the law to share in the sacred things, in order that the privileges may not be tainted with bastardy but remain the securely guarded possessions
of the priestly order. For it would be preposterous 125
that while the sacrifices and sacred rites and all the ceremonies of the altar are committed not to all but to the priests alone, the rewards assigned to these offices should become common property and at the service of chance comers, as though it were right to wear out the priests with toil and labour and the cares that beset them night and day and at the same time to allow their rewards to be shared by idlers.

[b] But the home-bred or purchased slave, he proceeds, 126
should be given his share in food and drink from the first-fruits by the priest, his master. First, because the servant has no resources but his master, and that master's estate consists of the sacred gifts of charity by which the slave must necessarily be maintained.
Secondly, what is sure to come to pass anyhow should 127
most certainly be done voluntarily. Our domestics are always with us and share our lives. They prepare

[b] See Lev. xxii. 11.

[232] | τε καὶ ποτὰ καὶ ὄψα τοῖς δεσπόταις προευτρεπιζόμενοι καὶ τραπέζαις ἐφεστῶτες καὶ τὰ λείψανα ἐκκομίζοντες, κἂν μὴ φανερῶς λαμβάνωσι, λάθρα γοῦν ὑφαιρήσονται, κλέπτειν ὑπὸ τῆς ἀνάγκης βιασθέντες, ὡς ἀνθ' ἑνὸς ἐγκλήματος, εἴπερ ἐστὶν ἀδίκημα τὸ ἐκ τῶν δεσποτικῶν τρέφεσθαι, καὶ ἕτερον προσκατασκευάζεσθαι, κλοπήν, ἵνα οἷα φῶρες πρὸ τῶν[1] ἀνυπαιτίως ζώντων ἀπολαύσωσι
128 τῶν καθιερωθέντων, ὅπερ ἐστὶν ἀτοπώτατον· τρίτον κἀκεῖνο χρὴ λογίζεσθαι, ὅτι τὰ τῶν ἀπαρχῶν οὐ παρόσον ἐπινέμεται τοῖς οἰκέταις ὀλιγωρηθήσεται, διὰ τὸν δεσποτικὸν φόβον· ἱκανὸς γὰρ οὗτος ἐπιστομίζειν τήν τινων εὐχέρειαν ῥᾳθυμεῖν οὐκ ἐφιείς.

129 XXVI. Ταῦθ' ὑπειπὼν φιλανθρωπίας μεστὸν νόμον ἑξῆς ἀναγράφει. ἐὰν θυγάτηρ, φησίν, ἱερέως γημαμένη μὴ ἱερεῖ χηρεύσῃ, τελευτήσαντος ἀνδρὸς ἢ καὶ ἔτι ζῶντος, ἄπαις καταλειφθεῖσα, πάλιν ἐπὶ τὸν πατρῷον οἶκον ἐπανερχέσθω μεταληψομένη τῶν ἀπαρχῶν, ὧν καὶ ἡνίκα παρθένος ἦν ἐκοινώνει· τρόπον γάρ τινα καὶ νῦν ἐστι δυνάμει παρθένος ἡ καὶ ἀνδρὸς καὶ παίδων ἔρημος, οὐδεμίαν ἑτέραν
130 ἔχουσα καταφυγὴν ὅτι μὴ τὸν πατέρα. υἱῶν δὲ ὄντων ἢ θυγατέρων, ἀνάγκη τὴν μητέρα τοῖς τέκνοις συντετάχθαι· υἱοὶ γὰρ[2] καὶ θυγατέρες τῆς τοῦ γεννήσαντος οἰκίας ὄντες εἰς ταύτην συνεφέλκονται καὶ τὴν μητέρα.[3]

131 XXVII. Τοῖς ἱερεῦσιν οὐκ ἀπένειμε χώρας ἀπο-

[1] mss. πρὸς τῶν or τρόπον.
[2] mss. δὲ.
[3] Here the mss. insert the heading Γέρα ἱερέων.

---

[a] *i.e.* if the sacred meats are pilfered and eaten on the sly, they would be treated irreverently; but if they are eaten openly and under supervision, this danger is avoided.

the ordinary food and drink and additional dishes for their masters, stand by the table and carry out the remains. Whether we wish it or not, they will even if they do not take them openly, pilfer them on the sly. Thus they are compelled perforce to steal and instead of a single indictment, if indeed it is an offence to feed off the master's viands, a second is provided, namely, stealing, with the result that the enjoyment of the consecrated meats appears to fall to thieves instead of to those who live a blameless life, which is the height of absurdity. There is a third point for 128
consideration. The dignity of the first-fruits will not be brought into contempt because they are shared by the servants. The fear of the master will prevent this, for by keeping them from idle habits he is able to check any light conduct on their part.[a]

XXVI. As a sequel to this he proceeds to lay down 129
a law full of humane feeling.[b] If the daughter of a priest, he says, is widowed after marrying one who is not a priest, either by his death or divorce during his lifetime, and left without children, she should return to her father to regain the share in the first-fruits which she enjoyed as a virgin. For she is still in a sense virtually a virgin, destitute as she is of both husband and children and with no refuge except her father. But if there are sons or daughters, the mother 130
must take her place with her children.[c] For sons and daughters belong to the house of the male parent and carry with them into it the mother also.[d]

XXVII. The priests were not allotted a section of 131

[b] See Lev. xxii. 13.

[c] A reasonable deduction from the above.

[d] Here the MSS. give the heading " Privileges of the Priests." In Cohn a fresh numeration of chapters.

τομὴν ὁ νόμος, ἵν' ὡς ἕτεροι τὰς ἀπὸ τῆς γῆς καρπούμενοι προσόδους τῶν ἀναγκαίων εὐπορῶσιν, ἀλλ' ὑπερβολῇ χρησάμενος τιμῆς τὸν θεὸν ἔφη κλῆρον αὐτῶν εἶναι, κατ' ἀναφορὰν τὴν ἐπὶ τὰ καθιερούμενα, δυεῖν ἕνεκα, τῆς τε ἀνωτάτω τιμῆς, ἐπεὶ κοινωνοὶ τῶν κατ' εὐχαριστίαν ἀπονεμομένων γίνονται θεῷ, καὶ τοῦ περὶ μόνα πραγματεύεσθαι δεῖν τὰ περὶ τὰς ἁγιστείας ὥσπερ τινὰς κλήρων
[233] ἐπιμελητάς. ἃ δὲ | προτίθησιν ἆθλα καὶ ἀριστεῖα
132 ταῦτ' ἐστί. πρῶτον μὲν ἄπονον καὶ ἀταλαίπωρον τροφὴν ἑτοίμην· κελεύει γὰρ τοὺς σιτοπονοῦντας ἀπὸ παντὸς στέατός τε καὶ φυράματος ἄρτον ἀφαιρεῖν ἀπαρχὴν εἰς ἱερέων χρῆσιν, προνοούμενος ἅμα καὶ τῆς εἰς εὐσέβειαν ἀγούσης ὁδοῦ νομίμῳ
133 διδασκαλίᾳ τῶν ἀφαιρούντων. ἐθιζόμενοι γὰρ ἀεὶ καὶ τῆς ἀναγκαίας τροφῆς ἀπάρχεσθαι τὴν θεοῦ μνήμην ἄληστον ἕξουσιν, οὗ μεῖζον ἀγαθὸν οὐκ ἔστιν εὑρεῖν. πολυανθρωποτάτου δ' ἔθνους ἀναγκαῖον εἶναι καὶ τὰς ἀπαρχὰς ἀφθόνους, ὡς καὶ τὸν ἀπορώτατον τῶν ἱερέων ἕνεκα περιουσίας τροφῶν

---

[a] The reference is to Deut. xviii. 1, 2, "The priests shall have no part nor inheritance with Israel. The offerings (καρπώματα) of the Lord shall be their inheritance, they shall eat them, and they shall have no inheritance among their brethren. The Lord Himself is their inheritance." Philo sees that in this text "the offerings of the Lord are their inheritance" is equivalent to "the Lord is their inheritance," and explains the latter phrase as meaning (1) they share the

territory by the law so that like the others they might reap the proceeds of the land and have abundance of their requisites therefrom. Instead, when referring to the consecrated offerings, it paid them the transcendent honour of saying that God was their inheritance.[a] He is their inheritance for two reasons. One is the supreme honour conferred by sharing with God in the thank-offering rendered to Him. The other is the obligation to concern themselves only with the sacred rites, thus becoming in a sense trustees of inheritances. The prizes and guerdons which the law offers are as follows. [b] First, a main- 132
tenance ready to hand and entailing no labour or trouble. For he commands that from all dough of wheat or other grain,[c] the bakers should set apart a loaf as a first portion for the use of the priests. In this he is also thinking of the avenue to piety provided by the lesson which the law of setting apart gives to those who obey it.
For through being accustomed to make this offering 133
out of their necessary food, they will have God in indelible recollection and no greater blessing can be gained than this. As the nation is very populous, the first-fruits are necessarily also on a lavish scale, so that even the poorest of the priests has so superabundant a maintenance that he seems exceedingly

offerings with the Lord; (2) as consecrating the offerings they are trustees and managers of the "inheritances." ἐπιμεληταὶ τῶν κλ. seems to be a technical term for the commoner ἐπίτροποι = "executors." *Cf.* Diog. Laert. v. 55, 56. In *De Plant.* 63 he explains the phrase "the Lord is their inheritance," which occurs also in Num. xviii. 20 and Deut. x. 9, as meaning simply the priesthood.

[b] See Num. xv. 18-20.

[c] *i.e.* στέαρ is wheaten flour made into dough, φύραμα dough in general.

134 εὐπορώτατον δοκεῖν εἶναι. δεύτερον δὲ προστάττει καὶ ἀπὸ τῆς ἄλλης ἁπάσης κτήσεως ἀπάρχεσθαι, καθ' ἑκάστην μὲν ληνὸν οἶνον, καθ' ἑκάστην δ' ἅλωνα σῖτόν τε καὶ κριθήν, ὁμοίως δ' ἐξ ἐλαιῶν ἔλαιον καὶ ἀπὸ τῶν ἄλλων ἀκροδρύων ἡμέρους καρπούς, ἵνα μὴ τἀναγκαῖα μόνον ἔχοντες αὐχμηρότερον ἀποζῶσιν, ἀλλὰ καὶ τῶν πρὸς ἁβροδίαιτον βίον εὐποροῦντες ἱλαρώτερον ἐξ ἀφθόνων τρυφῶσι μετὰ κόσμου τοῦ προσήκοντος.

135 τρίτον ἐστὶ γέρας τὰ πρωτότοκα ἀρρενικὰ πάντα τῶν χερσαίων ὅσα πρὸς ὑπηρεσίαν καὶ χρῆσιν ἀνθρώπων· ταῦτα γὰρ κελεύει διαδίδοσθαι τοῖς ἱερεῦσι, βοῶν μὲν καὶ προβάτων καὶ αἰγῶν αὐτὰ τὰ ἔκγονα, μόσχους καὶ κριοὺς καὶ χιμάρους, ἐπειδὴ καθαρὰ καὶ πρὸς ἐδωδὴν καὶ πρὸς θυσίας ἐστί τε καὶ νενόμισται, λύτρα δὲ τῶν ἄλλων κατατιθέναι, ἵππων καὶ ὄνων καὶ καμήλων καὶ τῶν παρα-

136 πλησίων, μὴ μειοῦντας τὴν ἀξίαν. ἔστι δὲ καὶ ταῦτα παμπληθῆ· κτηνοτροφοῦσι γὰρ καὶ ζῳοτροφοῦσιν ἐν τοῖς μάλιστα οἱ ἀπὸ τοῦ ἔθνους αἰπόλια καὶ βουκόλια καὶ ποίμνας καὶ μυρίας ἄλλας ἀγέλας

137 παντοδαπῶν ζῴων ἐκνέμοντες. ἤδη μέντοι καὶ προσυπερβάλλων ὁ νόμος οὐ μόνον ἀπὸ τῆς κτήσεως καθ' ἑκάστην ἰδέαν ἀπάρχεσθαι προστάττει, ἀλλὰ καὶ ἀπὸ τῶν οἰκείων ψυχῶν τε καὶ σωμάτων· μέρη γὰρ διαιρετὰ γονέων παῖδές εἰσιν, εἰ δὲ δεῖ τἀληθὲς εἰπεῖν, ἀδιαίρετα, συγγενικῷ αἵματι καὶ λόγοις προγόνων, ἀοράτοις εἴδεσιν, εἰς

[a] There is some dispute as to the texts to which Philo refers. See notes in Heinemann (Translation, pp. 49, 50); *Bildung*, pp. 35, 36. The references given in Cohn are Ex. xxii. 29, xxxiv. 26, Num. xviii. 13, Deut. xviii. 4, xxvi. 2 ff.

well-to-do. [a] Secondly, he ordains that 134
first-fruits should be paid of every other possession; wine from every winepress, wheat and barley from every threshing-floor, similarly oil from olives, and fruits from the other orchard-trees, so that the priests may not have merely bare necessaries, just keeping themselves alive in comparatively squalid conditions, but enjoy abundance of the luxuries of life and pass their days amid cheerful and unstinted comfort in the style which befits their
position. A third perquisite is the first- 135
born males of all land animals suitable for the use and service of men.[b] These he orders to be distributed to the priests: in the case of kine and sheep and goats the actual offspring, male calves and lambs and kids, since they are "clean" for the purposes both of eating and sacrificing, and are recognized as such. For the others, horses and asses and camels and the like, compensation is to be paid without chaffering
about the value. All these are very numerous, for 136
the men of the nation are noted particularly as graziers and stock-breeders, and keep flocks and herds of goats and oxen and sheep and of every kind of animal
in vast numbers. And this is not all. We 137
find the laws carrying the principle to a further extent by commanding that first-fruits should be paid not only from possessions of every kind but also from their own souls and bodies. For children are separable parts of their parents, or rather to speak more truly, inseparable parts, joined to them by kinship of blood, by the thoughts and memories of ancestors, invisible presences still alive among their descendants,

[b] See Ex. xxii. 30, Num. xviii. 15-20.

ἐκγόνους διήκουσι φίλτροις τε ἑνωτικῆς εὐνοίας καὶ
138 φύσεως δεσμοῖς ἀλύτοις ἡρμοσμένοι. ἀλλ' ὅμως
καὶ τούτων τοὺς πρωτοτόκους ἄρρενας τρόπον
ἀπαρχῆς καθιεροῖ, χαριστήρια εὐτεκνίας καὶ εὐγονίας οὔσης τε καὶ ἐλπιζομένης, καὶ ἅμα βουλόμενος οὐ μόνον ἀμέμπτους ἀλλὰ καὶ σφόδρα
ἐπαινετοὺς εἶναι τοὺς γάμους. ἐξ ὧν ὁ πρῶτος
βλαστήσας καρπὸς καθιεροῦται· ὅπερ χρὴ λογιζο-
μένους καὶ ἄνδρας καὶ γυναῖκας σωφροσύνης καὶ
οἰκουρίας καὶ ὁμονοίας περιέχεσθαι καὶ συμπνέοντας
ἀλλήλοις ἔν τε λόγῳ καὶ ἔργῳ τὴν λεγομένην
139 κοινωνίαν ἀληθείᾳ παγίως[1] βεβαιοῦσθαι. τῆς δὲ
[234] τῶν πρωτοτόκων | υἱῶν καθιερώσεως,[2] ὑπὲρ τοῦ
μήτε γονεῖς τέκνων μήτε τέκνα γονέων διαζεύγνυ-
σθαι, τιμᾶται τὴν ἀπαρχὴν ἀργυρίῳ ῥητῷ, προστάξας ἴσον εἰσφέρειν καὶ πένητα καὶ πλούσιον, οὐ
πρὸς ἀξίωμα τῶν εἰσφερόντων οὐδὲ πρὸς εὐεξίαν
καὶ κάλλος τῶν γεννηθέντων ἀπιδών, ἀλλ' ὅσον
δυνατὸν εἰσενεγκεῖν καὶ τῷ λίαν ἀπόρῳ σταθμησά-
140 μενος. ἐπειδὴ γὰρ ἡ παίδων γένεσις ἐν ἴσῳ καὶ
τοῖς λαμπροτάτοις καὶ τοῖς ἀφανεστάτοις εἴωθε
συμβαίνειν, ἴσην ἐδικαίωσε καὶ τὴν εἰσφορὰν
νομοθετῆσαι στοχασάμενος, ὡς ἔφην, μάλιστα τοῦ

[1] MSS. παγίω (=παγίῳ).

[2] Cohn considers this genitive as impossible, and following καθιέρωσιν in F and the apparent insertion of ἀλλὰ before τιμᾶται in the Armenian, suggests τὴν . . . καθιέρωσιν <οὐ δέχεται> . . . <ἀλλὰ> τιμᾶται. See *Hermes*, 1908, p. 189. I

by the love-ties of the affection which unites them, by the indissoluble bonds of nature.[a] Yet even 138
parents have their first-born male children consecrated as a first-fruit, a thank-offering for the blessings of parenthood realized in the present and the hopes of fruitful increase in the future. At the same time he shews his wish that the marriages, the first produce of which is a fruit sacred to His service, should be not only blameless but worthy of the highest praise. And reflection on this should lead both husbands and wives to cherish temperance and domesticity and unanimity, and by mutual sympathy shewn in word and deed to make the name of partnership a reality securely founded on truth. [b] But to 139
prevent the parents being separated from the children and the children from their parents, he assessed the first-fruit arising from the consecration of the first-born sons at a fixed sum of money, and ordered rich and poor to make the same contribution. He did not take into consideration either the dignity of the contributors or the good condition and beauty of the offspring, but fixed the payment at an amount which was within the power of even the very poor. For 140
since the birth of children is an event equally common with the grandest and the meanest, he considered it just to enact that the contribution should be equal also, aiming, as I have said, as nearly as possible at a

[a] See Ex. xiii. 2, xxii. 29.

[b] See Num. xviii. 15, 16, where "the fixed sum of money" is given as five shekels.

see no great difficulty in taking καθιερώσεως either as a genitive of respect or as depending on ἀπαρχήν.

141 πᾶσι δυνατοῦ. XXVIII. μετὰ δὲ ταῦτα
καὶ ἄλλον πόρον οὐ βραχὺν ἐπινέμει τοῖς ἱερεῦσιν,
ἕκαστον τῶν προσόδων ἀπάρχεσθαι κελεύσας, ἀπό
τε σίτου καὶ οἴνου καὶ ἐλαίου καὶ ἔτι θρεμμάτων
ἐπιγονῆς κατά τε ποίμνας καὶ βουκόλια καὶ αἰπόλια
καὶ τὰς ἄλλας ἀγέλας. ὅση δὲ καὶ τούτων ἐστὶν
ἀφθονία, τεκμήραιτ' ἄν τις ἐκ τῆς περὶ τὸ ἔθνος
142 πολυανθρωπίας. ἐξ ὧν ἁπάντων δῆλόν ἐστιν, ὅτι
βασιλέων σεμνότητα καὶ τιμὴν περιάπτει τοῖς
ἱερεῦσιν ὁ νόμος· ὡς γοῦν ἡγεμόσι φόρους ἀπὸ
παντὸς μέρους κτήσεως δίδοσθαι κελεύει, καὶ
δίδονται τὸν ἐναντίον τρόπον ἢ ὃν αἱ πόλεις τοῖς
143 δυνάσταις εἰσφέρουσιν· αἱ μὲν γὰρ ἐξ ἀνάγκης καὶ
μόλις, ἐπιστένουσαι, τοὺς ἐκλογεῖς τῶν χρημάτων
ὡς κοινοὺς λυμεῶνας ὑποβλεπόμεναι καὶ προφάσεις
ἄλλοτε ἀλλοίας σκηπτόμεναι καὶ τῶν προθεσμιῶν
ἀλογοῦσαι τὰ ὁρισθέντα τέλη καὶ δασμοὺς κατα-
144 τιθέασιν· οἱ δ' ἀπὸ τοῦ ἔθνους [τὰ ἱερατικὰ] γεγηθότες, χαίροντες, τοὺς αἰτοῦντας φθάνοντες, τὰς
προθεσμίας ἐπιτέμνοντες, λαμβάνειν ἀλλ' οὐ διδόναι νομίζοντες, μετ' εὐφημίας καὶ εὐχαριστίας
καθ' ἑκάστην τῶν ἐτησίων ὡρῶν ποιοῦνται τὰς
εἰσφοράς, ἄνδρες ὁμοῦ καὶ γυναῖκες, αὐτοκελεύστῳ
προθυμίᾳ καὶ ἑτοιμότητι καὶ σπουδῇ παντὸς λόγου
κρείττονι.

145 XXIX. Καὶ ταῦτα μὲν ἀπὸ τῆς ἑκάστου κτήσεως
ἐπινέμεται· ἄλλαι δέ εἰσιν ἐξαίρετοι πρόσοδοι

---

[a] Cohn gives Num. xviii. 12 as the reference for this tax which appears to differ from those of §§ 134 and 135 in being paid not as a first-fruit on each form of produce in its first stage or on the first-born of the animals, but on the final

sum within the means of all. XXVIII. 141
[a] After that he assigns another considerable source of wealth to the priests when he commands everyone to give first-fruits of his revenues from corn and wine and oil, and again of the increase of their livestock levied on their flocks and herds, of sheep and oxen and goats and other animals, and how great an abundance the nation possesses of these may be
judged from the magnitude of the population. From 142
all this it is clear that the law invests the priests with the dignity and honours of royalty. Thus he commands that tribute should be given from every part of a man's property as to a ruler, and the way in which the tribute is paid is a complete contrast to the spirit in which the cities make their payments to their
potentates. The cities pay under compulsion and 143
reluctantly and groan under the burden. They look askance at the tax-collectors as general agents of destruction. They trump up different excuses to suit the occasion, and when they discharge the appointed dues and assessments they do so without
regard to the time limits allowed. But our people 144
pay gladly and cheerfully. They anticipate the demand, abridge the time limits and think that they are not giving but receiving. And so at each of the yearly seasons they make their contributions with benediction and thankfulness, men and women alike, and with a zeal and readiness which needs no prompting and an ardour which no words can describe.

XXIX. These are the contributions levied on the 145
personal possessions of every individual, but the priests have also other special incomings drawn very

harvest or property as a whole. For further discussion see Heinemann *ad loc.*

πρεπωδέσταται ἱερεῦσιν αἱ ἀπὸ τῶν ἀναγομένων θυσιῶν. παντὸς γὰρ ἱερείου προστέτακται δύο τοῖς ἱερεῦσιν ἀπὸ δυεῖν δίδοσθαι μελῶν, βραχίονα μὲν ἀπὸ χειρὸς δεξιᾶς, ἀπὸ δὲ τοῦ στήθους ὅσον πῖον, τὸ μὲν ἰσχύος καὶ ἀνδρείας καὶ πάσης νομίμου πράξεως ἔν τε τῷ διδόναι καὶ λαμβάνειν καὶ ἐνεργεῖν σύμβολον, τὸ δὲ τῆς περὶ τὸν θυμὸν ἵλεω
146 πραότητος. ἐνοικεῖν γὰρ αὐτὸν λόγος ἔχει τοῖς στήθεσιν, ἐπειδὴ χωρίον οἰκειότατον ἡ φύσις ἀπένειμε τὰ στέρνα θυμῷ πρὸς ἐνδιαίτησιν, ᾧ καθάπερ στρατιώτῃ περιέβαλεν εἰς τὸ δυσάλωτον ἕρκος ὀχυρώτατον, τὸν ἐπικαλούμενον θώρακα, ὃν ἐκ πολλῶν καὶ συνεχῶν καὶ κραταιοτάτων ὀστέων
[235] ἀπειργάσατο | σφίγξας αὐτὸν εὖ μάλα νεύροις
147 ἀρραγέσιν. ἀπὸ δὲ τῶν ἔξω τοῦ βωμοῦ θυομένων ἕνεκα κρεωφαγίας τρία προστέτακται τῷ ἱερεῖ δίδοσθαι, βραχίονα καὶ σιαγόνας καὶ τὸ ἔνυστρον καλούμενον, τὸν μὲν βραχίονα διὰ τὴν ὀλίγῳ πρότερον εἰρημένην αἰτίαν, τὰς δὲ σιαγόνας τοῦ τε κυριωτάτου τῶν μελῶν, κεφαλῆς, καὶ λόγου τοῦ κατὰ προφορὰν ἀπαρχήν, οὗ τὸ νᾶμα ῥεῖν ἔξω δίχα τῆς τούτων κινήσεως οὐκ ἂν δύναιτο· σειομένων γὰρ —ἀφ᾿ οὗ καὶ προσωνομάσθησαν ἐτύμως—ὅταν πληχθῶσιν ὑπὸ γλώττης, ἅπασα ἡ τῆς φωνῆς
148 ὀργανοποιΐα συνηχεῖ. τὸ δὲ ἔνυστρον ἔκφυσις κοιλίας ἐστί· κοιλίαν δὲ φάτνην ἀλόγου θρέμματος,

---

[a] Lev. vii. 31-34 (LXX 21-24). There, however, the fat on the breast is to be burnt, and not, as here implied, taken as a perquisite by the priest. (This discrepancy is not noticed by Cohn or Heinemann, and there may perhaps be some explanation of it.)

[b] Or "needed to control" (the *θυμός*). For a similar thought as to the breast being the seat of *θυμός* *cf. Leg. All*

appropriately from the sacrifices offered. [a] It is ordained that with every victim two gifts should be presented to the priest from two of its parts, the arm or shoulder from the right side and all the fat from the breast, the former as a symbol of strength and manliness and of all lawful operations in giving and receiving and general activity, the latter of gentle mildness applied to the spirited element.[b] For it is 146
held that this element resides in the breast, since nature has appointed the chest as the most suitable place for its mansion and girded it like a soldier armed against attack with the stoutest of fenceworks called the thorax, or breastplate, which she has formed of a number of bones one upon another, strong and hard, and bound them tight with unbreakable sinews. But 147
of animals sacrificed away from the altars as meat for private consumption, three portions are appointed to be given to the priests, the shoulder and the jaws and the maw, as it is called.[c] The shoulder for the reason mentioned a little above, the jaws both as belonging to that master-limb, the head, and as a first-fruit of the uttered word which needs their movement to make possible the outflow of its stream. The jaws are shaken—and thence the derivation of their name [d]—when the tongue strikes upon them and then the whole vocal mechanism joins with them in producing sound. The maw is an excrescence of the 148
belly, and it is the fate of the belly to be the manger

iii. 115. Since gentleness is brought into play by being needed to control θυμός, it also is placed in the breast. In much the same way, as reason is needed to curb high spirit, the λογεῖον or reason-seat is placed on Aaron's breast (*ibid.* 119). See further App. pp. 620-621.

[c] See Deut. xviii. 3.

[d] *i.e.* σιαγών is derived from σείω.

ἐπιθυμίας, εἶναι συμβέβηκεν, ἥτις ὑπ᾿ οἰνοφλυγίας καὶ ὀψοφαγίας ἀρδομένη τροφαῖς ἐπαλλήλοις σιτίων ὁμοῦ καὶ ποτῶν ἀεὶ κατακλύζεται καὶ συὸς τρόπον ἐν βορβόρῳ διαιτωμένη χαίρει· παρὸ καὶ τόπος ἀπενεμήθη σφόδρα οἰκειότατος ὁ τῶν περιττωμάτων ἀκολάστῳ καὶ ἀπρεπεστάτῳ θρέμματι
149 ἀντίπαλον δὲ ἐπιθυμίας ἐγκράτεια, ἣν ἀσκητέον καὶ διαπονητέον καὶ σπουδαστέον μηχανῇ πάσῃ περιποιεῖσθαι ὡς μέγιστον ἀγαθὸν καὶ τελειότατον ἰδίᾳ
150 τε καὶ κοινῇ συμφέρον. ἐπιθυμία μὲν οὖν βέβηλος καὶ ἀκάθαρτος καὶ ἀνίερος οὖσα πέρα τῶν ἀρετῆς ὅρων ἐλήλαται καὶ πεφυγάδευται δεόντως· ἐγκράτεια δέ, καθαρὰ καὶ ἀκηλίδωτος ἀρετή, πάντων ὅσα πρὸς βρῶσιν καὶ πόσιν ἀλογοῦσα καὶ ἐπάνω τῶν γαστρὸς ἡδονῶν αὐχοῦσα ἵστασθαι, βωμῶν ἱερῶν ψαυέτω καὶ[1] τὴν πρόσφυσιν ἐπιφερομένη τῆς κοιλίας, ὑπόμνημα τοῦ καταφρονητικῶς ἔχειν ἀπληστίας καὶ λαιμαργίας καὶ πάντων ὅσα τὰ εἰς
151 τὰς ἐπιθυμίας ἀναφλέγει. XXX. ἐφ᾿ ἅπασι μέντοι καὶ τὰς τῶν ὁλοκαυτωμάτων—ἀμύθητα δὲ ταῦτ᾿ ἐστί—δορὰς προστάττει τοὺς ὑπηρετοῦντας ταῖς θυσίαις ἱερεῖς λαμβάνειν, οὐ βραχεῖαν ἀλλ᾿ ἐν τοῖς μάλιστα πολυχρήματον δωρεάν. ἐξ ὧν δῆλόν ἐστιν, ὅτι κλῆρον ἕνα μὴ παρασχὼν τῇ ἱερωμένῃ φυλῇ κατὰ ταὐτὰ ταῖς ἄλλαις τοῦ πασῶν ἔδωκε σεμνότερον πόρον[2] καὶ ἁγιώτερον, κατὰ πρόφασιν ἀπαρχῶν τῶν ἐξ ἅπαντος θυσίας εἴδους.

[1] Perhaps omit καὶ. [2] MSS. τρόπον (or τόπον).

[a] The phrase is taken from Plato, *Timaeus* 70 E "They (*i.e.* God's agents) constructed the part between the midriff and the navel as a manger (φάτνη), for the sustenance of the

of that irrational animal, desire,[a] which drenched by wine-bibbing and gluttony, is perpetually flooded with relays of food and drink administered to it, and like a sow rejoices to make its home in the mire. And therefore the place of dregs and leavings has been assigned as by far the fittest for a licentious and most unseemly animal. But the opposite of desire is con- 149
tinence, the acquisition of which is a task to be practised and pressed forward by every possible means as the greatest and most perfect of blessings promoting personal and public welfare alike. So 150
then desire, profane, impure and unholy, has been expelled outside the confines of virtue and well deserved is its banishment. But let continence, that pure and stainless virtue which disregards all concerns of food and drink and claims to stand superior to the pleasures of the stomach, touch the holy altars and bring with it the appendage of the belly as a reminder that it holds in contempt gluttony and greediness and all that inflames the tendencies to lust. XXX. [b] In addition to all the rest it ordains that 151
the priests who minister at the holy sacrifices should receive the hides of the whole-burnt-offerings, the number of which is incalculable, and this is no small gift, but represents a very large sum of money. From these things it is clear that the law did not provide the consecrated tribe with a single portion, like the others, but gave it, under the guise of first-fruits from every kind of sacrifice, a source of revenue of greater dignity and sanctity than that of them all put together. But that none of the 152

body, and then they chained it (*i.e.* the part of the soul which lusts after meat and drink) like a wild beast" (κατέδησαν ὡς θρέμμα ἄγριον).

[b] See Lev. vii. 8 (LXX vi. 38).

152 ὑπὲρ δὲ τοῦ μηδένα τῶν διδόντων ὀνειδίζειν τοῖς λαμβάνουσι, κελεύει τὰς ἀπαρχὰς εἰς τὸ ἱερὸν
[236] κομίζεσθαι πρότερον, εἶτ' | ἐνθένδε τοὺς ἱερεῖς λαμβάνειν· ἥρμοττε γὰρ θεῷ μὲν τοὺς εὐεργετουμένους ἐν ἅπασι τοῖς κατὰ τὸν βίον χαριστηρίους ἀνάγειν ἀπαρχάς, τὸν δὲ ἅτε μηδενὸς ἐπιδεᾶ τοῖς ἀμφὶ τὸ ἱερὸν ὑπηρέταις καὶ λειτουργοῖς χαρίζεσθαι μετὰ σεμνότητος καὶ τιμῆς τῆς ἁπάσης· τὸ γὰρ μὴ παρ' ἀνθρώπων ἀλλὰ παρὰ τοῦ πάντων εὐεργέτου δοκεῖν λαμβάνειν ἀδυσώπητον ἔχει δωρεάν.

153 XXXI. Τοσούτων οὖν προκειμένων ἄθλων, ἐάν τινες ἀπορῶσι τῶν ἱερέων κοσμίως καὶ ἀνυπαιτίως ζῶντες, τῆς ἡμετέρας παρανομίας ἐφεστᾶσι κατήγοροι, κἂν ἡσυχάζωσιν· εἰ γὰρ ἐπειθαρχοῦμεν τοῖς κελευσθεῖσι καὶ τὰς ἀπαρχὰς ἐποιούμεθα ᾗ προστέτακται, οὐκ ἂν μόνον ἐκεῖνοι τῶν ἀναγκαίων εὐπόρουν, ἀλλὰ καὶ τῶν ἄλλων ὅσα πρὸς ἁβροδιαί-
154 τους χορηγίας ἀνεπίμπλαντο. κἂν ἄρα ποτὲ αὖθις ἡ φυλὴ τῶν ἱερέων ἐν ἅπασι τοῖς κατὰ τὸν βίον ἀφθόνοις ἐξετάζηται, μέγα δεῖγμα γενήσεται τοῦτο κοινῆς ὁσιότητος καὶ τῆς τῶν νομίμων ἐπ' ἀκριβὲς εἰς ἅπαν φυλακῆς. ἀλλ' ἤ τινων ὀλιγωρία—ἅπαντας γὰρ οὐκ ἀσφαλὲς αἰτιᾶσθαι—γέγονεν αἰτία πενίας τοῖς ἱερωμένοις, εἰ δὲ δεῖ τἀληθὲς εἰπεῖν, καὶ αὐτοῖς
155 ἐκείνοις. τὸ γὰρ παρανομεῖν ἐπιζήμιον τοῖς παρανομοῦσι, κἂν πρὸς ὀλίγον δελεάζῃ χρόνον· τὸ δὲ ἕπεσθαι τοῖς τῆς φύσεως νόμοις ὠφελιμώτατον, κἂν παραυτίκα αὐστηρὸν ᾖ καὶ μηδὲν προσηνὲς ἐμφαίνῃ.

[a] Deduced from the language of Num. xviii. 8-19, particularly *v.* 19, where the offerings described in detail are said to be the gift of God to the priests.

donors should taunt the recipients, it ordered the first-fruits to be first brought into the temple and then taken thence by the priests.[a] It was the proper course that the first-fruits should be brought as a thank-offering to God by those whose life in all its aspects is blessed by His beneficence, and then by Him, since He needs nothing at all, freely bestowed with all dignity and honour on those who serve and minister in the temple. For if the gift is felt to come not from men but from the Benefactor of all, its acceptance carries with it no sense of shame.

XXXI. Since, then, the prospective rewards are so 153
great, if any of the priests who live a decent and blameless life are in need, they confront us as accusers of our disobedience to the law, even though they bring no charge. For if we obeyed the commandment and gave the first-fruits as it is ordained, they would have not only abundance of mere necessaries but a full measure of all else that the luxurious can
require. And on the other hand if the priestly tribe 154
shall in the course of the future be found to possess all the means of life in abundance, it will be strong evidence that the practice of religion is general and the law carefully observed in all respects. But the neglectfulness of some[b]—for it would not be safe to accuse all—has brought about the impoverishment of the consecrated class and indeed, it is true to say,
of the defaulters themselves. Disobedience to the 155
law, for all its short-lived seductiveness, recoils upon the disobedient. But in compliance with the laws of nature, though for the moment it is stern and wears a grim aspect, there is the greatest of rewards.

[b] This rather modifies the glowing statement of § 144.

156 XXXII. Τοσαύτας προσόδων ἀφορμὰς χαρισάμενος τοῖς ἱερεῦσιν οὐδὲ τῶν ἐν τῇ δευτέρᾳ τάξει κατωλιγώρησεν· εἰσὶ δὲ νεωκόροι. τούτων οἱ μὲν ἐπὶ θύραις ἵδρυνται παρ᾽ αὐταῖς ταῖς εἰσόδοις πυλωροί, οἱ δ᾽ εἴσω κατὰ τὸ πρόναον ὑπὲρ τοῦ μή τινα ὧν οὐ θέμις ἑκόντα ἢ καὶ ἄκοντα ἐπιβῆναι, οἱ δ᾽ ἐν κύκλῳ περινοστοῦσιν ἐν μέρει διακληρωσάμενοι νύκτα καὶ ἡμέραν, ἡμεροφύλακες καὶ νυκτοφύλακες, ἕτεροι δὲ τὰς στοὰς καὶ τὰ ἐν ὑπαίθρῳ κοροῦντες τὸν φορυτὸν ἐκκομίζουσιν ἐπιμελούμενοι καθαριότητος· οἷς ἅπασι μισθὸς ὡρίσθησαν αἱ
157 δεκάται, κλῆρος γὰρ νεωκόρων οὗτος. οὐ πρότερον γοῦν εἴασεν ὁ νόμος αὐταῖς χρῆσθαι τοὺς λαβόντας ἢ πάλιν ἄλλας δεκάτας ὡς ἀπὸ κτημάτων ἰδίων ἀπάρξασθαι καὶ δοῦναι τοῖς τῆς ἀμείνονος τάξεως ἱερεῦσι· τηνικαῦτα γὰρ ἐφῆκεν ἀπολαύειν, πρότερον
158 δ᾽ οὐκ ἐᾷ. ἀπένειμε δὲ καὶ πόλεις αὐτοῖς ὀκτὼ πρὸς ταῖς τεσσαράκοντα καὶ καθ᾽ ἑκάστην προάστεια εἰς δισχιλίους πήχεις ἐν κύκλῳ πρὸς νομὰς θρεμμάτων καὶ τὰς ἄλλας ὧν δεῖ πόλεσιν ἀναγκαίας ὑπηρεσίας. ἐκ δὲ τούτων ἀπεκληρώθησαν ἕξ, αἱ μὲν ἐκτὸς αἱ δὲ ἐντὸς Ἰορδάνου τοῦ ποταμοῦ, τρεῖς ἑκατέρωθεν, εἰς καταφυγὴν τοῖς
159 ἀκούσιον φόνον δράσασιν. ἐπειδὴ γὰρ | τὸν ὁπω-
[237] σοῦν γενόμενον ἀνθρώπῳ τελευτῆς παραίτιον οὐκ ἦν εὐαγὲς εἴσω περιρραντηρίων παρέρχεσθαι χρώμενον πρὸς ἀσφάλειαν καταφυγῇ τῷ ἱερῷ, τὰς εἰρημένας ἀνῆκε πόλεις, ἱερὰ δεύτερα, πολλὴν

---

[a] See Num. xviii. 21. [b] See Num. xviii. 26-28.

[c] See Num. xviii. 32, "ye shall not bear sin by reason of it (*i.e.* eating the fruits), because ye shall have offered an offering of first-fruits from it." (LXX.)

XXXII. After bestowing these great sources of 156
revenue on the priests, he did not ignore those of the
second rank either, namely the temple attendants.
Some of these are stationed at the doors as gate-
keepers at the very entrances, some within in front
of the sanctuary to prevent any unlawful person from
setting foot thereon, either intentionally or unintentionally. Some patrol around it turn by turn in relays
by appointment night and day, keeping watch and
guard at both seasons. Others sweep the porticoes
and the open court, convey away the refuse and
ensure cleanliness. [a] All these have the tithes appointed as their wages, this being the portion settled
on them as temple attendants. [b] It should be noted 157
that the law does not allow them to avail themselves
of these tithes until they have rendered other tithes
from them treated as their own property as first-
fruits to the priests of the superior class. [c] Only when
this condition has been fulfilled are they allowed to
enjoy their income. [d] He also assigned 158
them forty-eight cities with a frontage of land each
to the depth of 2000 cubits to graze their cattle and
carry on other kinds of business necessary for the
service of the cities. [e] Of these there were six allotted,
three on the near side and three on the far side of the
river Jordan, as a refuge for the perpetrators of involuntary homicide. For since it would be sacrilege 159
for a person responsible for the death of a man, however it was caused, to come within the sacred precincts, and use the temple as a refuge from danger, he
made over to them the aforesaid cities as secondary

[d] See Num. xxxv. 2-8.

[e] For the sequel to the end of § 161 see Num. xxxv. 9-28.

ἀσυλίαν ἐχούσας ἕνεκα τῆς περὶ τοὺς οἰκήτορας προνομίας τε καὶ τιμῆς, οἳ τοὺς ἱκέτας διασῴζειν ἔμελλον, εἰ βιάζοιτό τις ἐχυρωτέρα δύναμις, οὐ παρασκευαῖς ταῖς εἰς πόλεμον οὔσαις, ἀλλ' ἀξιώμασι καὶ προνομίαις, ἅπερ ἐκ τῶν νόμων διὰ τὴν
160 σεμνότητα τῆς ἱερωσύνης εἶχον. ὁ δὲ φυγὰς ἐντὸς ὅρων τῆς πόλεως, εἰς ἣν πεφυγάδευται, κατακεκλείσθω διὰ τοὺς ἐφέδρους κολαστάς, οἳ γένει προσήκοντες τῷ τεθνεῶτι πόθῳ τοῦ συγγενοῦς, κἂν μὴ ὑφ' ἑκόντος ἀναιρεθῇ, κατὰ τοῦ κτείναντος φονῶσι, νικῶντος τοῦ οἰκείου πάθους τὸν ἀκριβῆ τῶν δικαίων λογισμόν. ἔξω δὲ προϊὼν ἐπ' ὀλέθρῳ ἀνενδοιάστῳ προελευσόμενος ἴστω· λήσεται γὰρ οὐδένα τῶν ἀφ' αἵματος, ὑφ' ὧν αὐτίκα λίνοις καὶ
161 πάγαις σαγηνευθεὶς οἰχήσεται. προθεσμία δ' ἔστω τῆς φυγῆς ὁ βίος τοῦ μεγάλου ἱερέως, οὗ τελευτήσαντος ἀμνηστίας ἀξιωθεὶς κατίτω.

Ταῦτα καὶ τὰ τούτοις παραπλήσια νομοθετήσας περὶ τῶν ἱερέων ἑξῆς ἀναδιδάσκει περὶ ζῴων, ἃ
162 πρὸς θυσίας ἐστὶν ἐπιτήδεια. XXXIII. [1] τῶν εἰς τὰς ἱερουργίας ζῴων τὰ μέν ἐστι χερσαῖα, τὰ δὲ ἀεροπόρα. τὰ μὲν οὖν τῶν πτηνῶν ἔθνη μυρία ὅσα παρελθὼν δύο μόνα ἐξ ἁπάντων εἵλετο, περιστερὰν καὶ τρυγόνα, διότι περιστερὰ μὲν τῶν
[238] φύσει | τιθασῶν καὶ ἀγελαστικῶν ἡμερώτατον,

[1] Here the MSS. insert a new heading Περὶ ζῴων τῶν εἰς ἱερουργίας καὶ τίνα τῶν θυσιῶν τὰ εἴδη.

[a] A new heading in MSS., "Of the sacrificial animals and

temples, well secured from violation through the privileged and honourable position of the inhabitants, who, if any stronger power should attempt to use force against the suppliants, would keep them safe, not with warlike preparations, but through the dignities and privileges conferred on them by the laws in virtue of the reverence attached to the priestly
office. But the fugitive must remain shut up within 160
the confines of the city to which he has come as a refuge because of the avengers waiting at the door, whose relationship to the dead makes them seek the blood of the slayer in their bitterness at the loss of their kinsman, even though the fatal act was involuntary. For strong family feeling overpowers the sense of justice which strict reason would give. But if he advances outside he must understand that his movements will entail certain destruction, for they will not be unobserved by any member of the family, and enmeshed in their nets and snares he will be a
lost man. The time limit of his banishment is to 161
coincide with the life of the high priest, at whose death he may return with immunity assured as his due.

After making these and other similar enactments he next proceeds to give instructions as to the
animals suitable for sacrifice. XXXIII. [a] Of the 162
animals used for this purpose some are confined to the dry land and others travel in the air. The winged creatures are divided into numberless tribes, all of which he ignored except two, the pigeon and the turtle-dove,[b] the pigeon because it is the gentlest of those whose nature is tame and gregarious, the dove

the different kinds of sacrifice." Cohn begins a fresh numeration of chapters.

[b] See Lev. i. 14.

τρυγὼν δὲ τῶν φύσει μονωτικῶν τιθασώτατον.
163 τὰς δὲ τῶν χερσαίων ἀμυθήτους ἀγέλας, ὧν οὐδ' ἀριθμὸν εὑρεῖν εὔπορον, ὑπερβὰς τρεῖς ἀριστίνδην ἐπέκρινε, βοῶν καὶ προβάτων καὶ αἰγῶν· ἡμερώταται γὰρ αὗται καὶ χειροηθέσταται· βουκόλια γοῦν μεγάλα καὶ ποίμνια καὶ αἰπόλια πρὸς ἑνὸς ἄγεται τοῦ τυχόντος, οὐκ ἀνδρὸς μόνον ἀλλὰ καὶ κομιδῇ νηπίου παιδός, εἴς τε νομὴν ἐξιόντα καὶ ὁπότε δέοι πάλιν εἰς σηκοὺς ὑποστρέφοντα ἐν
164 κόσμῳ. τῆς δ' ἡμερότητος πολλὰ μὲν καὶ ἄλλα σημεῖα, σαφέστατα δὲ ταυτί· τό τε πάντα εἶναι χλοηφάγα καὶ μηδὲν αὐτῶν σαρκοβόρον καὶ τὸ μήτε γαμψοὺς ἔχειν ὄνυχας μήτε τὴν ἔκφυσιν τῶν ὀδόντων παντελῆ· τὸ γὰρ ἀνωτέρω φάτνιον οὐκ ὀδοντοφυεῖ, ἀλλ' ὅσοι τομίαι τῶν ὀδόντων κατ'
165 αὐτὸ ἐπιλελοίπασι. πρὸς δὲ τούτοις καὶ βιωφελέστατα τῶν ζῴων ἐστί· κριοὶ μὲν εἰς ἐσθῆτας, τὴν ἀναγκαιοτάτην σκέπην σωμάτων, βόες δὲ εἰς τὸ ἀρόσαι γῆν καὶ προετοιμάσασθαι πρὸς σπόρον καὶ τὸν γενόμενον ἀλοῆσαι καρπὸν εἰς μετουσίαν καὶ ἀπόλαυσιν τροφῆς, αἰγῶν δὲ αἱ τρίχες καὶ δοραὶ συνυφαινόμεναί τε καὶ συρραπτόμεναι φορηταὶ γεγόνασιν ὁδοιπόροις οἰκίαι καὶ μάλιστα τοῖς ἐν στρατείαις, οὓς ἔξω πόλεως ἐν ὑπαίθρῳ τὰ πολλὰ
166 διατρίβειν ἀναγκάζουσιν αἱ χρεῖαι. XXXIV. πάντα δ' ὁλόκληρα, περὶ μηδὲν μέρος κηραίνοντα τοῦ σώματος, ὅλα δι' ὅλων ἀσινῆ, μώμων ἀμέτοχα· τοσαύτη γοῦν ἐστι πρόνοια, οὐ μόνον τοῖς ἀνάγουσι

---

[a] Oxen, Lev. i. 3 f.; sheep and goats, i. 10 f.
[b] See Lev. xxii. 19-24.
[c] No scriptural authority is quoted for this. As Cohn

because it is the tamest of those which are naturally fond of solitude. The land animals collect in vast 163
multitudes and the number of their varieties is almost incalculable. All these he passed over after selecting three as of superior merit, namely, oxen, sheep and goats.[a] For these are the gentlest and the most docile. We see great herds and flocks of each kind led by a single person, it matters not who. He may even be not a grown man, but the merest child, and under his guidance they go out to the pasture and when required return back in order to their pens.
This tameness is shewn by many other indications, 164
but most clearly by the following facts. All of them are eaters of grass, none eat flesh ; none of them have crooked talons nor a full supplement of teeth, for the upper gum does not lend itself to the growth of teeth, but all the incisors are missing there. Further- 165
more, in the whole animal kingdom they are the most serviceable for human life. The rams produce raiment, the indispensable shelter for the body, the ox ploughs the soil and prepares it for the seed, and when the crop is produced threshes it, thus making it into food which can be shared and enjoyed, while the skin and hair of the goat, when woven or sewn together, supply portable houses for travellers and particularly for campaigners who are compelled by the exigencies of their life to spend most of their time outside the city and in the open air. XXXIV. 166
[b] All the animals selected must be perfect, with no affliction troubling any part of their body, scathless throughout and free from fault or flaw. [c] In fact, so great is the forethought exercised not only by those

suggests, Philo may be relying on personal observation (or hearsay ?).

τὰς θυσίας ἀλλὰ καὶ τοῖς ἱερωμένοις, ὥστε οἱ δοκιμώτατοι τῶν ἱερέων ἀριστίνδην ἐπικριθέντες εἰς τὴν τῶν μώμων ἐπίσκεψιν ἀπὸ κεφαλῆς ἄχρι ποδῶν ἄκρων ἐρευνῶσιν ὅσα τε ἐμφανῆ καὶ ὅσα ὑπὸ γαστρὶ καὶ μηροῖς ἀποκέκρυπται, μή που τις βραχεῖα λώβη
167 διαλέληθε. τὸ δ' ἀκριβὲς καὶ περιττὸν τῆς ἐξετάσεως οὐχ ἕνεκα τῶν καταθυομένων ἀλλὰ τοῦ περὶ τοὺς καταθύοντας ἀνυπαιτίου γίνεται· βούλεται γὰρ αὐτοὺς ἀναδιδάξαι διὰ συμβόλων, ὁπότε προσέρχοιντο βωμοῖς ἢ εὐξόμενοι ἢ εὐχαριστήσοντες, μηδὲν ἀρρώστημα ἢ νόσημα ἢ πάθος ἐπιφέρεσθαι τῇ ψυχῇ, πειρᾶσθαι δ' ὅλην δι' ὅλων ἀκηλίδωτον ἁγιάζειν, ὡς ἰδόντα μὴ ἀποστραφῆναι θεόν.

168 XXXV. Ἐπεὶ δὲ τῶν θυσιῶν αἱ μέν εἰσιν ὑπὲρ ἅπαντος τοῦ ἔθνους, εἰ δὲ δεῖ τἀληθὲς εἰπεῖν, ὑπὲρ
[239] ἅπαντος ἀνθρώπων γένους, αἱ δ' ὑπὲρ ἑκάστου | τῶν ἱερουργεῖν ἀξιούντων, λεκτέον πρότερον περὶ τῶν κοινῶν. θαυμαστὴ τούτων ἡ τάξις ἐστίν· αἱ μὲν γὰρ ἀνάγονται καθ' ἑκάστην ἡμέραν, αἱ δὲ ταῖς ἑβδόμαις, αἱ δὲ νουμηνίαις καὶ ἱερομηνίαις, αἱ δὲ
169 νηστείαις, αἱ δὲ τρισὶ καιροῖς ἑορτῶν. καθ' ἑκάστην μὲν οὖν ἡμέραν δύο ἀμνοὺς ἀνάγειν διείρηται, τὸν μὲν ἅμα τῇ ἕῳ, τὸν δὲ δείλης ἑσπέρας, ὑπὲρ εὐχαριστίας ἑκάτερον, τὸν μὲν ὑπὲρ τῶν μεθ' ἡμέραν, τὸν δ' ὑπὲρ τῶν νύκτωρ εὐεργεσιῶν, ἃς ἀπαύστως καὶ ἀδιαστάτως ὁ θεὸς τῷ γένει τῶν
170 ἀνθρώπων χορηγεῖ. ταῖς δ' ἑβδόμαις διπλασιάζει

---

[a] See Num. xxviii. 3, 4. They are offered ἐνδελεχῶς, and in *v.* 6 are called a ὁλοκαύτωμα ἐνδελεχισμοῦ, whence Philo's ἐνδελεχεία in § 170.

who bring the sacrifices but also by the officiants, that the most highly approved of the priests, selected as most suitable for such inspection, examine them from the head to the extremities of the feet, both the visible parts and those which are concealed under the belly and thighs, for fear that some small blemish has passed unobserved. The examination is carried 167
out with this excessive minuteness in consideration not of the victims offered but of the innocence of those who offer them. For the law would teach them under this symbol that when they approach the altar to offer either prayers or thanks they must come with no infirmity or ailment or evil affection in the soul, but must endeavour to have it sanctified and free throughout from defilement, that God when He beholds it may not turn away His face from the sight.

XXXV. But since the sacrifices are of two kinds, 168
some offered for the whole nation, or rather, it would be correct to say, for all mankind, others for each separate individual among those whose sense of duty makes them worshippers, we must first speak of those which are general. The system on which they are arranged is admirable. Some are offered 169
daily, others on the seventh days, others at the new moons or the beginnings of the sacred month, others at the fasts, others at the three festal seasons. [a] Every day two lambs are to be brought to the altar, one at dawn, the other towards dusk. Both these are thank-offerings, one for the benefactions of the day-time, the other for those of the night, given to the human race ceaselessly and constantly by the bounty of God. [b] On the seventh days he doubles the number 170

[b] See Num. xxviii. 9, 10.

τὸν τῶν ἱερείων ἀριθμόν, ἴσα προστιθεὶς ἴσοις, ἰσότιμον ἡγούμενος αἰῶνι τὴν ἑβδόμην, ἣν καὶ γενέθλιον τοῦ κόσμου παντὸς ἀνέγραψεν· οὗ χάριν τὴν τῆς ἑβδόμης θυσίαν ἐξομοιῶσαι τῇ "ἐνδε-
171 λεχείᾳ" τῶν ἡμερησίων ἀμνῶν διενοήθη. δὶς δὲ καθ' ἑκάστην ἡμέραν ἐπιθυμιᾶται τὰ πάντων εὐωδέστατα θυμιαμάτων εἴσω τοῦ καταπετάσματος, ἀνίσχοντος ἡλίου καὶ δυομένου, πρό τε τῆς ἑωθινῆς θυσίας καὶ μετὰ τὴν ἑσπερινήν, ὡς εἶναι τὰ μὲν ἔναιμα εὐχαριστίαν ὑπὲρ ἡμῶν τῶν ἐναίμων, τὰ δὲ θυμιάματα ὑπὲρ τοῦ ἡγεμονικοῦ, τοῦ ἐν ἡμῖν λογικοῦ πνεύματος, ὅπερ ἐμορφώθη πρὸς ἀρχέ-
172 τυπον ἰδέαν εἰκόνος θείας. ἄρτοι δὲ προτίθενται ταῖς ἑβδόμαις ἐπὶ τῆς ἱερᾶς τραπέζης ἰσάριθμοι τοῖς μησὶ τοῦ ἐνιαυτοῦ, δυσὶ θέμασιν ἀνὰ ἕξ, [δώδεκα,] κατὰ τὸν λόγον τῶν ἰσημεριῶν ἑκάτερα—δύο γάρ εἰσιν ἀνὰ πᾶν ἔτος, ἐαρινή τε καὶ μετοπωρινή, αἳ μησὶν ἓξ καταριθμοῦνται·—δι' ἣν αἰτίαν * * * ⟨ἐαρινῇ μὲν⟩[1] τὰ σπαρτὰ πάντα τελειογονεῖται, καθ' ὃν χρόνον τὰ δένδρα γεννᾶν ἄρχεται, μετοπωρινῇ δὲ καὶ ὁ τῶν δένδρων καρπὸς τελεσφορεῖται, ἐν ᾧ καιρῷ πάλιν ἀρχὴ σπορᾶς. οὕτως δολιχεύουσα ἡ φύσις τὸν αἰῶνα ἄλλας ἐπ' ἄλλαις ἀμείβει δωρεὰς ἀνθρώπων γένει, ὧν εἰσι σύμβολα
173 αἱ διτταὶ τῶν προκειμένων ἄρτων ἑξάδες. αἰνίττονται δὲ καὶ τὴν ὠφελιμωτάτην τῶν ἀρετῶν

[1] There is clearly a lacuna after δι' ἣν αἰτίαν, which must have ended with ἐαρινῇ μὲν or something like it. For Cohn's suggestion for filling it see App. p. 621.

---

[a] See on *Spec. Leg.* ii. 59.

[b] See Ex. xxx. 7, 8, and note on § 276 below.

[c] *i.e.* the lower part of the ψυχή, *cf. Quis Rerum* 55 with its quotation of Lev. xvii. 11 ψυχὴ πάσης σαρκὸς αἷμά ἐστιν,

of the victims. He makes this addition of a number equal to the original because he considers the seventh day, called also in his records the birthday of the whole world,[a] to be of equal value to eternity, and therefore he purposes to assimilate the sacrifice of the seventh day to the "perpetuity" of the daily offering of lambs.
[b] Twice too every day the perfume of the most fragrant 171
kinds of incense is exhaled within the veil at sunrise and at sunset, both before the morning and after the evening sacrifice. Thus the blood offerings serve as thanksgivings for the blood elements in ourselves[c] and the incense offerings for our dominant part, the rational spirit-force within us which was shaped according to the archetypal form of the divine image.[d]

[e] But on each seventh day loaves are 172
exposed on the holy table equal in number to the months of the year in two layers of six each, each layer corresponding to the equinoxes. For there are two equinoxes in each year, in spring and autumn, with intervals, the sum of which is six months. For this reason * * * At the spring equinox all the seed crops come to their fulness just when the trees begin to produce their fruit, and at the autumn equinox that same fruit is brought to maturity and it is the season when the sowing begins again. Thus nature running its agelong round alternates its gifts to the human race, symbolized by the two sets of six loaves
exposed upon the table. They are also emblematic 173
of that most profitable of virtues, continence, which

rather than as Heinemann "our bodies." Possibly, however, τῶν ἐναίμων agrees with ἡμῶν, *i.e.* "the animals with blood are for us who share it with them."

[d] *i.e.* the Logos, which, being the εἰκών of God, becomes the ἀρχέτυπος ἰδέα of the human spirit. *Cf.* § 81 above and note on *De Som.* ii. 45.

[e] See Lev. xxiv. 5-8.

ἐγκράτειαν, ᾗ δορυφορεῖται πρὸς εὐτελείας καὶ εὐκολίας καὶ ὀλιγοδεΐας, διὰ τὸν ἐξ ἀκολασίας καὶ πλεονεξίας βλαβερώτατον ἐπιτειχισμόν· ἄρτος γὰρ ἐραστῇ σοφίας διαρκὴς τροφή, παρέχουσα καὶ τὰ σώματα ἄνοσα καὶ τὸν λογισμὸν ὑγιῆ καὶ ἐν τοῖς
174 μάλιστα νηφάλιον· ὄψα δὲ καὶ μελίπηκτα καὶ ἡδύσματα καὶ ὅσα σιτοπόνων καὶ ὀψαρτυτῶν περιεργίαι τεχνιτεύουσι καταγοητεύουσαι τὴν ἄμουσον καὶ ἀφιλόσοφον καὶ ἀνδραποδωδεστάτην τῶν αἰσθήσεων γεῦσιν, ὑπηρετοῦσαν καλῷ μὲν οὐδενὶ θεάματι ἢ ἀκούσματι, γαστρὸς δὲ τῆς ταλαίνης ἐπιθυμίαις, νόσους σώματι καὶ ψυχῇ κατασκευάζει
175 πολλάκις ἀνιάτους. συνεπιτίθεται δὲ τοῖς ἄρτοις
[240] λιβανωτὸς καὶ | ἅλες, ὁ μὲν σύμβολον τοῦ μηδὲν ἥδυσμα εὐωδέστερον ὀλιγοδεΐας εἶναι καὶ ἐγκρατείας παρὰ σοφίᾳ δικαζούσῃ, οἱ δ' ἅλες διαμονῆς τε τῶν συμπάντων—οἷς γὰρ ἂν παραπασθῶσι δια-
176 τηροῦσι—καὶ ἱκανοῦ προσοψήματος. οἶδ' ὅτι γέλωτα καὶ χλεύην ταῦτα θήσονται οἱ περὶ τὰ συμπόσια καὶ τὰς εὐωχίας πραγματευόμενοι καὶ πολυτελεῖς τραπέζας μεταδιώκοντες, οἱ ὀρνέων καὶ ἰχθύων καὶ κρεῶν καὶ τῆς ὁμοιοτρόπου φλυαρίας ἄθλιοι δοῦλοι, μηδ' ὄναρ ἀληθοῦς ἐλευθερίας γεύσασθαι δυνάμενοι. ὧν ὀλίγα φροντιστέον τοῖς κατὰ θεὸν καὶ πρὸς τὴν τοῦ ὄντως ὄντος ἀρέσκειαν ζῆν ἐγνωκόσιν, οἳ τῶν σαρκὸς ἀλογεῖν ἡδονῶν πεπαιδευμένοι τὰς διανοίας χαρὰς καὶ εὐπαθείας θεωρίᾳ τῶν τῆς φύσεως ἐνασκούμενοι μεταδιώκουσι.

---

[a] For the general sense of the next sections *cf. De Som.* ii. 48-51.

has simplicity and contentment and frugality for its bodyguard against the baleful assaults engineered by incontinence and covetousness. [a] For bread to a lover of wisdom is sufficient sustenance, making the body proof against disease and the reason sound and sober
in the highest degree. But dainty dishes and honey- 174
cakes and relishes and all the elaborate preparations with which the skill of pastrycooks and other experts at the art bewitches the taste, that most slavish of all the senses, a stranger to culture and philosophy, a servant not to things beautiful to see or hear but to the lusts of the wretched belly, create distempers
of soul and body which are often past all cure. On 175
the loaves there are placed also frankincense and salt,[b] the former as a symbol that in the court of wisdom no relish is judged to be more sweet-savoured than frugality and temperance, the salt to shew the permanence of all things, since it preserves whatever it is sprinkled on, and its sufficiency as a condiment.
All this I know will excite the mockery and ridicule 176
of those to whom banquetings and high feasting are a matter of much concern, who run in search of richly laden tables, miserable slaves to birds and fishes and fleshpots and similar trash, unable even in their dreams to taste the flavour of true freedom. All these things should be held in little account by those who are minded to live with God for their standard and for the service of Him that truly IS—men who, trained to disregard the pleasures of the flesh and practised in the study of nature's verities, pursue the joys and sweet comforts of the intellect.

[b] So LXX, Lev. xxiv. 7. Not in the Hebrew, *cf. Mos.* ii. 104.

177 Ταῦτα περὶ τῆς ἑβδόμης διαταξάμενος ταῖς νουμηνίαις φησὶ δεῖν θύειν ὁλόκαυτα δέκα τὰ σύμπαντα· μόσχους δύο, κριὸν ἕνα, ἀμνοὺς ἑπτά. ἐπειδὴ γὰρ ὁ μὴν τέλειος, ἐν ᾧ σελήνη τὸν ἑαυτῆς κύκλον περατοῦται,[1] τέλειον ἀριθμὸν ζῴων ἠξίωσεν
178 ἱερουργεῖσθαι. ἡ δεκὰς δὲ παντελὴς ἀριθμός, ὃν εὖ μάλα διένειμεν εἰς τὰ λεχθέντα, τοὺς μὲν δύο μόσχους, ἐπειδὴ δύο κινήσεις εἰσὶ σελήνης ἀεὶ διαυλοδρομούσης, ἡ μὲν κατ᾿ αὔξησιν ἄχρι πλησιφαοῦς, ἡ δὲ κατὰ μείωσιν ἄχρι συνόδου, τὸν δ᾿ ἕνα κριόν, ἐπειδὴ λόγος εἷς ἐστι, καθ᾿ ὃν αὔξεταί τε καὶ μειοῦται τοῖς ἴσοις διαστήμασι καὶ φωτιζομένη καὶ ἐπιλείπουσα, τοὺς δὲ ἑπτὰ ἀμνούς, ὅτι καθ᾿ ἑβδομάδας ἐπιδέχεται τοὺς τελείους σχηματισμούς, πρώτῃ μὲν ἑβδομάδι τῇ ἀπὸ συνόδου τὸν διχότομον, δευτέρᾳ δὲ τὸν πλησιφαῆ, καὶ ὅταν ἀνακάμπτῃ πάλιν, εἰς διχότομον τὸ πρῶτον, ἔπειτ᾿ εἰς σύνοδον
179 ἀπολήγει. μετὰ δὲ τῶν ἱερείων σεμίδαλιν ἀναδεδευμένην ἐλαίῳ προσφέρειν καὶ οἶνον εἰς σπονδὰς μέτροις ⟨ὡρισμέν⟩οις[2] διετάξατο, διότι καὶ ταῦτα σελήνης περιόδοις κατὰ τὰς ἐτησίους ὥρας τελεσφορεῖται διαφερόντως τοὺς καρποὺς πεπαινούσης, σῖτος δὲ καὶ οἶνος καὶ ἔλαιον, βιωφελέσταται οὐσίαι καὶ πρὸς χρῆσιν ἀνθρώποις ἀναγκαιόταται, πάσαις εἰκότως θυσίαις συγκαθιεροῦνται.

[1] So Cohn: MSS. περαιοῦται. I feel very doubtful about the correction. The use of περαιοῦμαι for "cross," "pass over" is common enough, and the association with a cycle, if rather strange, is not impossible. On the other hand, while περατοῦσθαι in a passive sense is common, I have not seen any example of its use as a transitive middle.

[2] So Cohn. Perhaps μέτροις οἷς ⟨ἔδει or δεῖ⟩ διετάξατο.

[a] See Num. xxviii. 11-14.

Having given these orders with regard to the 177
seventh days, he deals with the new moons. [a] At
these times whole-burnt-offerings must be sacrificed,
ten in all, two calves, one ram, and seven lambs.
For since the month in which the moon fulfils its
cycle is a complete or perfect whole,[b] he considered
that the number of animals to be sacrificed should be
perfect. Now ten is a perfect number, and he dis- 178
tributed it excellently among the above-mentioned
items ; two calves because the moon as she runs for
ever her race forwards and backwards has two
motions, one as she waxes till she becomes full, one
as she wanes to her conjunction with the sun ; one
ram because there is one law or principle by which
she waxes and wanes at equal intervals, both when
her light grows and when it fails ; seven lambs because the complete changes of form to which she is
subject are measured in sevens.[c] In the first seven
from the conjunction we have the half moon, in the
second the full moon, and when she is reversing her
course she passes first into the half moon and then
dies away into the conjunction. With the victims 179
he ordered that fine meal, soaked in oil, should be
brought, and wine for libations in stated quantities,
because these also are brought to their fullness by
the revolutions of the moon at the various seasons
of the year, and especially by its effect upon the
ripening of the fruits, and corn, oil and wine are
things possessing qualities most profitable to life and
most necessary for human use and therefore are
naturally consecrated with all the sacrifices.

[b] Or "since the month (*i.e.* the past month) is completed," and so Heinemann, but the context suggests that it is the month which is coming which is under consideration.

[c] *Cf. De Op.* 101.

180 Τῇ δ' ἱερομηνίᾳ διττὰ θύματα προσάγεται προσηκόντως, ἐπεὶ καὶ διττὸς ὁ περὶ αὐτῆς λόγος, ὁ μὲν ὡς νουμηνίας, ὁ δὲ ὡς ἱερομηνίας. ᾗ μὲν οὖν νουμηνία, τὰ ἴσα ταῖς ἄλλαις ἱερουργεῖσθαι διείρηται, ᾗ δὲ καὶ ἱερομηνία, διπλασιάζεται τὰ δῶρα, δίχα τῶν μόσχων· εἷς γὰρ ἀντὶ δυεῖν προσάγεται, τοῦ βραβευτοῦ δικαιώσαντος ἀδιαιρέτῳ φύσει μονάδος πρὸ διαιρετῆς δυάδος χρήσασθαι ἐν ἀρχῇ τοῦ ἐνιαυτοῦ.

181 Ἐν δὲ τῷ πρώτῳ καιρῷ—πρῶτον δὲ καιρὸν τὴν ἐαρινὴν ὥραν καὶ ἰσημερίαν καλεῖ—προστάξας ἑπτὰ ἡμέρας ἑορτὴν ἄγειν τὴν ἐπικαλουμένην τῶν ἀζύμων ἰσοτίμους ἀπέφηνε πάσας ἐν ταῖς ἱερουργίαις· δέκα γὰρ ὅσα καὶ ταῖς νουμηνίαις θύειν καθ' ἑκάστην κελεύει, τὰ σύμπαντα ὁλόκαυτα, δίχα τῶν

182 περὶ πλημμελείας, ἀριθμὸν ἑβδομήκοντα. τὸν γὰρ αὐτὸν ἔχειν ᾠήθη λόγον πρὸς μῆνα νουμηνίαν ὃν πρὸς ἰσημερίαν ἑβδόμῳ μηνὶ γινομένην τὰς ἑπτὰ τῆς ἑορτῆς ἡμέρας, ἵν' ἀποφήνῃ καὶ τὴν ἀρχὴν ἑκάστου μηνὸς ἱερὰν καὶ ἀθρόων τῶν ἑπτὰ τὰς ἰσαρίθμους ταῖς νουμηνίαις ἡμέρας.

183 Μεσοῦντος δὲ ἔαρος ἄμητος ἐνίσταται, καθ' ὃν καιρὸν χαριστήρια μὲν ἀνάγεται τῷ θεῷ τῆς πεδιά-

---

[a] See Num. xxix. 1-6. On the term ἱερομηνία see on *De Dec.* 159 (App.).

[b] See App. p. 621.

[c] See Num. xxviii. 17-24.

[d] Implied though not actually stated in Ex. xxiii. 14, "Three times (καιρούς) in the year keep a feast for Me." Then after enumerating the three great feasts "three times (καιρούς) shall all thy males appear before the Lord thy God."

[e] In § 172 Philo based the number of sacrifices on the *six* months between the equinoxes; here on the fact that each equinox occurs in the *seventh* month before the next.

[a] At the beginning of the sacred month double 180
sacrifices are offered in accordance with its double aspect, first as new moon simply, secondly as the opening of the sacred month. Regarding it as new moon, the sacrifices ordered are the same as those of other new moons. Taking it as a sacred-month-day the oblations are doubled except in the case of the calves : only one of these is offered, the awarder having judged that at the beginning of the year [b] the monad whose nature is indivisible is preferable to the divisible dyad.

[c] At the first season, which name [d] he gives to the 181
springtime and its equinox, he ordained that what is called the feast of unleavened bread should be kept for seven days, all of which he declared should be honoured equally in the ritual assigned to them. For he ordered ten sacrifices to be offered each day as at the new moons, whole-burnt-offerings amounting
to seventy in all apart from the sin-offerings. He 182
considered, that is, that the seven days of the feast bore the same relation to the equinox which falls in the seventh month [e] as the new moon does to the month. Thus he assigned the same sanctity both to the beginning of each month considered singly and to the seven days of the feast, which being of the same number as the new moons represented them collectively.

[f] In the middle of the spring comes the corn harvest. 183
At this season thank-offerings are brought for the

[f] See for the Feast of Weeks Lev. xxiii. 15 ff.-Num. xxviii. 26 ff. There is some discrepancy as to the details. The name πρωτογεννημάτων and the lambs for the "preservation-offering" (E.V. "peace-offering") come from the former. The name πρωτ. is also given to it in Ex. xxiii. 16.

δος ἐπὶ τῷ πλήρη τὸν καρπὸν ἐνηνοχέναι καὶ τὰ θέρη συγκομίζεσθαι, δημοτελεστάτη δ' ἄγεται ἑορτὴ προσαγορευομένη πρωτογεννημάτων ἐτύμως ἀπὸ τοῦ συμβεβηκότος, ἐπειδὴ τῶν γεννημάτων τὰ
184 πρῶτα, αἱ ἀπαρχαί, τότε καθιεροῦνται. προστέτακται δ' ἀνάγειν θυσίας μόσχους δύο, κριὸν ἕνα καὶ ἑπτὰ ἀμνούς, ταῦτα μὲν δέκα ἱερεῖα ὁλόκαυτα, δύο δ' ἀμνοὺς εἰς βρῶσιν ἱερέων, οὓς ἐπικαλεῖ σωτηρίου διὰ τὸ τὰς τροφὰς ἀνθρώποις ἐκ πολλῶν καὶ παντοδαπῶν διασεσῶσθαι· φθοραὶ γὰρ εἰώθασι καταλαμβάνειν, αἱ μὲν ἐπομβρίαις, αἱ δ' αὐχμοῖς, αἱ δ' ἄλλαις ἀμυθήτοις νεωτεροποιΐαις, αἱ δ' αὖ χειροποίητοι κατ' ἐφόδους ἐχθρῶν τὴν τῶν πέλας γῆν
185 δῃοῦν ἐπιχειρούντων. εἰκότως οὖν τὰ σῶστρα τῷ πάσας ἀποσκεδάσαντι τὰς ἐπιβουλὰς ἀνάγεται χαριστήρια καὶ ἀνάγεται ἄρτοις, οὓς προσενεγκόντες τῷ βωμῷ καὶ ἄνω πρὸς οὐρανὸν ἀνατείναντες ἐπιδιανέμουσι τοῖς ἱερεῦσι μετὰ τῶν κρεῶν τῆς τοῦ σωτηρίου θυσίας εἰς ἱεροπρεπεστάτην εὐωχίαν.

186 Ὅταν δ' ὁ τρίτος ἐνστῇ καιρὸς ἐν τῷ ἑβδόμῳ μηνὶ κατ' ἰσημερίαν μετοπωρινήν, ἐν ἀρχῇ μὲν ἱερομηνία ἄγεται προσαγορευομένη σαλπίγγων, περὶ ἧς ἐλέχθη πρότερον, δεκάτῃ δ' ἡ νηστεία, περὶ ἣν ἐσπουδάκασιν οὐ μόνον οἷς ζῆλος εὐσεβείας καὶ ὁσιότητος, ἀλλὰ καὶ οἷς κατὰ τὸν ἄλλον βίον εὐαγὲς οὐδὲν δρᾶται· πάντες γὰρ ἡττώμενοι τοῦ περὶ αὐτὴν

---

[a] *i.e.* in § 180. For the name "feast of trumpets" see Lev. xxiii. 24 E.V. "a memorial of blowing of trumpets" (LXX *μνημόσυνον σαλπίγγων*).

[b] For the "Fast" or "Day of Atonement" see Num. xxix. 7-11.

lowlands because they have borne fruit in full and the summer crops are being gathered in. This feast, which is universally observed, is called the feast of first-products, a name which expresses the facts, because the first specimens of the produce, the sample oblations, are then consecrated. The sacrifices 184
ordered on this occasion are two calves, one ram and seven lambs, these ten as victims to be entirely consumed by fire, and also two lambs to be eaten by the priests. These last he calls preservation-offerings because mankind has had its food preserved from many vicissitudes of every kind. For that food is commonly subject to destructive forces, sometimes rain-storms, sometimes droughts, or numberless other violent changes in nature, sometimes again from human activities through the invasions of enemies who attempt to lay waste the land of their neighbours. Naturally, therefore, the thank-offerings for preserva- 185
tion are brought to Him Who has scattered all the forces which threatened mischief. They are also brought in the form of loaves which the worshippers carry to the altar and after holding them with outstretched arms up to heaven distribute to the priests together with the flesh of the preservation-offering to regale them in a way well worthy of their sacred office.

When the third special season has come in the 186
seventh month at the autumnal equinox there is held at its outset the sacred-month-day called trumpet day, of which I have spoken above.[a] On the tenth day is the fast,[b] which is carefully observed not only by the zealous for piety and holiness but also by those who never act religiously in the rest of their life. For all stand in awe, overcome by the sanctity of the

ἱεροπρεποῦς τεθήπασι καὶ οἱ χείρους τοῖς βελτίοσι τότε γοῦν εἰς ἐγκράτειαν καὶ ἀρετὴν ἁμιλλῶνται.
187 διττοὺς δ᾽ ἔχει λόγους τὸ ἀξίωμα τῆς ἡμέρας, τοὺς μὲν ὡς ἑορτῆς, τοὺς δὲ ὡς καθάρσεως καὶ φυγῆς ἁμαρτημάτων, ἐφ᾽ οἷς ἀμνηστία δέδοται χάρισι τοῦ ἵλεω θεοῦ μετάνοιαν ἐν ἴσῳ τῷ μηδὲ[1] ἁμαρτάνειν
188 τετιμηκότος. τὰς μὲν οὖν ὡς ἑορτῆς θυσίας ἰσαρίθμους ἀπέφηνε ταῖς τῶν ἱερομηνιῶν, μόσχον καὶ κριὸν καὶ ἑπτὰ ἄρνας, ἀνακερασάμενος μονάδα ἑβδομάδι καὶ πρὸς ἀρχὴν τὸ τέλος ἀπευθύνας—τέλος μὲν γὰρ ἔργων ἑβδομάς, ἀρχὴν δὲ μονὰς κεκλήρωται,—τὰς δ᾽ ὡς καθάρσεως ⟨τρεῖς⟩· προστάττει γὰρ δύο χιμάρους ἀνάγειν καὶ κριόν, εἶτά φησι δεῖν τὸν μὲν ὁλοκαυτοῦν, διακληροῦν δὲ τοὺς χιμάρους, καὶ τὸν μὲν λαχόντα τῷ θεῷ θύειν, τὸν δ᾽ ἕτερον εἰς ἀτριβῆ καὶ ἄβατον ἐρημίαν ἐκπέμπειν ἐφ᾽ ἑαυτῷ κομίζοντα τὰς ὑπὲρ τῶν πλημμελησάντων ἀράς, οἳ μεταβολαῖς ταῖς πρὸς τὸ βέλτιον ἐκαθάρθησαν, εὐνομίᾳ καινῇ παλαιὰν ἀνομίαν ἐκνιψάμενοι.

189 Τῇ δὲ πεντεκαιδεκάτῃ τῆς πλησιφαοῦς σελήνης ἄγεται ἡ ἐπικαλουμένη σκηνῶν ἑορτή, καθ᾽ ἣν πλείους εἰσὶν αἱ χορηγίαι τῶν θυσιῶν· καταθύονται γὰρ ἐφ᾽ ἡμέρας ἑπτὰ μόσχοι μὲν ἑβδομήκοντα, κριοὶ δὲ τέσσαρες καὶ δέκα, ἄρνες δὲ δυοῖν δεόντων ἑκατόν, ἅπαντα ζῷα ὁλόκαυτα. προστέτακται δὲ καὶ τὴν ὀγδόην ἱερὰν νομίζειν, περὶ ἧς ἀκριβωτέον,

[1] MSS μηδέν. Cohn's correction is perhaps due to a feeling that τὸ μηδὲν ἁμαρτεῖν would indicate complete sinlessness, which is not possible for the ordinary man. *Cf. De Virt.* 177, *De Fuga* 157.

day, and for the moment the worse vie with the better
in self-denial and virtue. The high dignity of this 187
day has two aspects, one as a festival, the other as a time of purification and escape from sins, for which indemnity is granted by the bounties of the gracious God Who has given to repentance the same honour as to innocence from sin. Treating it as a festival day, he made the sacrifices of the same number as those of the sacred-month-days, namely a calf and a ram and seven lambs, thus blending the one with the seven and putting the completion in a line with the beginning. For to seven belongs the completion
of actions, to one their beginning. Treating it as a 188
purification, he added three more and bade them bring two kids and a ram, ordering that the last-named should be consumed entirely by fire and that a lot should be cast for the kids. [a] The one on whom the lot fell was to be sacrificed to God, the other was to be sent out into a trackless and desolate wilderness bearing on its back the curses which had lain upon the transgressors who have now been purified by conversion to the better life and through their new obedience have washed away their old disobedience to the law.

[b] On the fifteenth day of this month at the full moon 189
is held the feast of tabernacles, as it is called, and on this the supply of sacrificial offerings is on a larger scale, for during seven days there are sacrificed seventy calves, fourteen rams and ninety-eight lambs. All these animals are consumed entirely by fire. [c] It is also commanded that the eighth day is to be observed as holy. This last must be treated in detail when

[a] See Lev. xvi. 9, 10.
[b] See Num. xxix. 12-34.
[c] See Num. xxix. 36.

ὅταν σύμπας ὁ περὶ τῶν ἑορτῶν ἐξετάζηται λόγος, ἐν ᾗ προσάγεται ὅσα καὶ ἐν ταῖς ἱερομηνίαις.

190 Αἱ μὲν οὖν ὑπὲρ τοῦ ἔθνους ἢ κυριώτερον εἰπεῖν ὑπὲρ παντὸς ἀνθρώπων γένους κοιναὶ καὶ ὁλόκαυτοι θυσίαι κατ' ἐμὴν δύναμιν εἴρηνται. ταῖς δ' ὁλοκαύτοις καθ' ἑκάστην ἡμέραν ἑορτῆς παρέπεται χίμαρος, ὃς καλεῖται μὲν περὶ ἁμαρτίας, καταθύεται δὲ εἰς ἁμαρτημάτων ἄφεσιν, οὗ τὰ κρέα τοῖς
191 ἱερεῦσιν εἰς ἐδωδὴν ἀπονέμεται. τίς οὖν αἰτία;[1] ἢ ὅτι ἑορτὴ καιρός ἐστιν εὐφροσύνης, ἡ δ' ἀψευδὴς καὶ πρὸς ἀλήθειαν εὐφροσύνη φρόνησίς ἐστιν ἐνιδρυμένη ψυχῇ βεβαίως, φρόνησιν δ' ἀκλινῆ λαβεῖν οὐκ ἔνεστιν ἄνευ θεραπείας ἁμαρτημάτων καὶ παθῶν ἐκτομῆς; ἄτοπον γὰρ ἕκαστον μὲν τῶν ὁλακαυτουμένων ἀσινὲς καὶ ἀβλαβὲς ἀνευρισκόμενον καθιεροῦσθαι, τὴν δὲ τοῦ θύοντος διάνοιαν μὴ οὐ κεκαθάρθαι πάντα τρόπον καὶ πεφαιδρύνθαι λουτροῖς καὶ περιρραντηρίοις χρησαμένην, ἅπερ ὁ τῆς φύσεως ὀρθὸς λόγος δι' ὑγιαινόντων καὶ ἀδια-
192 φθόρων ὤτων ψυχαῖς φιλοθέοις ἐπαντλεῖ. πρὸς δὲ τούτῳ κἀκεῖνο δεόντως ἂν λέγοιτο· αἱ ἑορτώδεις ἀνέσεις αὗται καὶ ἐκεχειρίαι μυρίας ἤδη πολλάκις ἁμαρτημάτων ὁδοὺς ἀνέτεμον· ἄκρατος γὰρ καὶ αἱ μετ' οἰνοφλυγίας ὀψοφαγίαι τὰς γαστρὸς ἀκορέστους ἐπιθυμίας ἐγείρουσαι προσαναφλέγουσι καὶ τὰς ὑπὸ γαστέρα, καὶ ῥέουσαι καὶ χεόμεναι πάντῃ φορὰν ἀμυθήτων ἀπεργάζονται κακῶν τὸ τῆς

[1] So Cohn punctuates. Better perhaps τίς οὖν αἰτία ἢ ὅτι, "What is the cause but that . . .?" *Cf.* iii. 34.

---

[a] See ii. 211.

[b] The mention of the sin-offering occurs regularly in Num.

the subject of the feasts as a whole comes up for discussion.[a] The number of offerings brought are the same as on the sacred-month-days.

The general sacrifices in the form of burnt-offerings 190
performed on behalf of the nation or, to speak more correctly, on behalf of the human race, have now been described to the best of my ability. But these burnt-offerings are accompanied on each day of a feast by the sacrifice of a kid called the sin-offering offered for the remission of sins, its flesh being put aside to be
eaten by the priests.[b] What is the reason for this 191
addition? Is it that a feast is a season of joy, and the true joy in which there is no illusion is wisdom firmly established in the soul, and the wisdom that is stable cannot be acquired without applying medicine to the sin and surgery to the passions? For it would be a strange inconsistency if, while each of the victims consumed in the burnt-offering is only dedicated when found to be free from mischief and blemish, the mind of the worshipper should not be purified in every way and washed clean and fair by the ablutions and lustrations, which the right reason of nature pours into the souls of those who love God through ears that are
sound in health and free from corruption. But be- 192
sides this something else may be justly said. These festal occasions of relaxation and cessation from work have often ere now opened up countless avenues to transgressions. For strong drink and gross eating accompanied by wine-bibbing, while they awaken the insatiable lusts of the belly, inflame also the lusts seated below it, and as they stream along and overflow on every side they create a torrent of evils in-

xxviii. and xxix. for the separate occasions (xxviii. 15, 22, 30; xxix. 5, 11, 22, 25, 28, 31, 34, 38).

ἑορτῆς ἀδεὲς ὁρμητήριον ἔχουσαι καὶ πρὸς τὸ μηδὲν
193 παθεῖν καταφυγήν. ἅπερ συνιδὼν οὐκ ἐφῆκε κατὰ
τὰ αὐτὰ τοῖς ἄλλοις ἑορτάζειν, ἀλλ' ἐν αὐτῷ τῷ τῆς
εὐφροσύνης καιρῷ πρῶτον μὲν ἐκέλευσεν ἁγνεύειν
ἐπιστομίζοντας τὰς ἐφ' ἡδονὴν ὁρμάς, εἶτα εἰς τὸ
ἱερὸν ἐπὶ μετουσίαν ὕμνων καὶ εὐχῶν καὶ θυσιῶν
ἐκάλεσεν, ἵνα κἀκ τοῦ τόπου κἀκ τῶν ὁρωμένων καὶ
λεγομένων διὰ τῶν κυριωτάτων αἰσθήσεων, ὄψεως
καὶ ἀκοῆς, ἐγκρατείας ἅμα καὶ εὐσεβείας ἐρασθῶσιν, εἶτ' ἐπὶ πᾶσιν ὑπέμνησε τοῦ μὴ ἁμαρτάνειν διὰ
τῆς θυσίας τοῦ περὶ ἁμαρτίας· ὁ γὰρ ἀμνηστίαν ἐφ'
οἷς ἥμαρτεν αἰτούμενος οὐχ οὕτως ἐστὶ κακοδαίμων
ὥστ' ἐν ᾧ χρόνῳ παλαιῶν ἀδικημάτων αἰτεῖται
λύσιν ἕτερα καινοτομεῖν.

194 XXXVI. Τοσαῦτα περὶ τούτων διαλεχθεὶς ἄρχεται διαιρεῖν τὰ τῶν θυσιῶν γένη καὶ τέμνων εἰς
εἴδη τρία τὰ ἀνωτάτω τὸ μὲν ὁλόκαυτον καλεῖ, τὸ
δὲ σωτήριον, τὸ δὲ περὶ ἁμαρτίας· εἶθ' ἕκαστον τοῖς
ἁρμόττουσιν ἐπικοσμεῖ τοῦ πρέποντος ἅμα καὶ
195 εὐαγοῦς οὐ μετρίως στοχασάμενος. παγκάλη δὲ
καὶ προσφυεστάτη τοῖς πράγμασιν ἡ διαίρεσις
ἀκολουθίαν ἔχουσα καὶ εἱρμόν· εἰ γὰρ βούλοιτό τις
ἐξετάζειν ἀκριβῶς τὰς αἰτίας, ὧν ἕνεκα τοῖς πρώτοις ἔδοξεν ἀνθρώποις ἐπὶ τὰς διὰ θυσιῶν εὐχαριστίας ὁμοῦ καὶ λιτὰς ἐλθεῖν, εὑρήσει δύο τὰς
ἀνωτάτω· μίαν μὲν τὴν πρὸς θεὸν τιμήν, τὴν ἄνευ
τινὸς ἑτέρου δι' αὐτὸν μόνον γινομένην ὡς ἀναγκαῖον ⟨καὶ⟩ καλόν, ἑτέραν δὲ τὴν τῶν θυόντων

numerable, because they have the immunity of the feast for their headquarters and refuge from retribution. All this the lawgiver observed and therefore 193
did not permit his people to conduct their festivities like other nations, but first he bade them in the very hour of their joy make themselves pure by curbing the appetites for pleasure. Then he summoned them to the sanctuary to take their part in hymns and prayers and sacrifices, that the place and the spectacles there presented and the words there spoken, working through the lordliest of the senses, sight and hearing, may make them enamoured of continence and piety. Last of all by the sin-offering he warned them against continuing in sin, for he who asks for absolution of the sins he has committed is not so lost a wretch as to embark on other new offences at the very time when he asks for remission of the old.

XXXVI. After having discoursed to this extent 194
on these subjects he begins to classify the kinds of sacrifices. He divides them into three principal classes which he calls respectively the whole-burnt-offering, the preservation-offering and the sin-offering. To each of these he adds the adornment of suitable ritual, in which he succeeds admirably in combining decorum with reverence. His classification is quite 195
excellent and perfectly fits the facts to which it shews a logical sequence. For if anyone cares to examine closely the motives which led men of the earliest times to resort to sacrifices as a medium of prayer and thanksgiving, he will find that two hold the highest place. One is the rendering of honour to God for the sake of Him only and with no other motive, a thing both necessary and excellent. The other is the signal benefit which the worshipper

προηγουμένην ὠφέλειαν· διττή δ᾽ ἐστίν, ἡ μὲν ἐπὶ
196 μετουσίᾳ ἀγαθῶν, ἡ δὲ ἐπὶ κακῶν ἀπαλλαγῇ. τῇ
μὲν οὖν κατὰ θεὸν καὶ δι᾽ αὐτὸν μόνον γινομένῃ
προσήκουσαν ὁ νόμος ἀπένειμε θυσίαν τὴν ὁλόκαυτον, ὁλοκλήρῳ καὶ παντελεῖ μηδὲν ἐπιφερομένῃ
τῆς θνητῆς φιλαυτίας ὁλόκληρον καὶ παντελῆ· τὴν
δὲ χάριν ἀνθρώπων, ἐπειδὴ διαίρεσιν ἐπεδέχετο ἡ
δόξα, καὶ αὐτὸς διεῖλε, κατὰ μὲν τὴν μετουσίαν τῶν
ἀγαθῶν ὁρίσας θυσίαν ἣν ὠνόμασε σωτήριον, τῇ δὲ
197 φυγῇ τῶν κακῶν ἀπονείμας τὴν περὶ ἁμαρτίας. ὡς
τρεῖς εἶναι δεόντως ἐπὶ τρισί, τὴν μὲν ὁλόκαυτον δι᾽
[241] αὐτὸν μόνον τὸν | θεόν, ὃν καλὸν τιμᾶσθαι, μὴ δι᾽
ἕτερον, τὰς δ᾽ ἄλλας δι᾽ ἡμᾶς, τὴν μὲν σωτήριον ἐπὶ
σωτηρίᾳ καὶ βελτιώσει τῶν ἀνθρωπίνων πραγμάτων, τὴν δὲ περὶ ἁμαρτίας ἐπὶ θεραπείᾳ ὧν
ἐπλημμέλησεν ἡ ψυχή.

198 XXXVII. Λεκτέον δὲ περὶ ἑκάστης τὰ νομο-
θετηθέντα τὴν ἀρχὴν ποιησαμένους ἀπὸ τῆς ἀρίστης·
ἀρίστη δ᾽ ἐστὶν ἡ ὁλόκαυτος. ἔστω δή, φησί,
πρῶτον μὲν τὸ ἱερεῖον ἄρρεν, ἐκ τῶν πρὸς τὰς
θυσίας ἀριστίνδην ζῴων ἐπικριθέντων, μόσχος ἢ
ἀμνὸς ἢ ἔριφος· ἔπειτα δ᾽ ἀπονιψάμενος ὁ προσάγων
199 τὰς χεῖρας ἐπιφερέτω τῇ τοῦ ἱερείου κεφαλῇ· καὶ
μετὰ ταῦτα λαβών τις τῶν ἱερέων καταθυέτω καὶ
φιάλην ἕτερος ὑποσχὼν καὶ δεξάμενος τοῦ αἵματος
ἐν κύκλῳ περιϊὼν τὸν βωμὸν ἐπιρραινέτω, καὶ τὸ
ἱερεῖον ἀποδαρὲν εἰς ὁλόκληρα μέλη[1] διανεμέσθω,
κοιλίας ἀποπλυνομένης καὶ ποδῶν· εἶτα σύμπαν τῷ
ἱερῷ πυρὶ τοῦ βωμοῦ παραδιδόσθω, γεγονὸς καὶ ἐξ

[1] MSS. μέρη.

[a] See Lev. i. 3 ff.

receives, and this is twofold, on one side directed to obtaining a share in blessings, on the other to release
from evils. To the God-ward motive which has Him 196
alone in view he assigned the whole-burnt-offering, for, whole and complete in itself as it is, it fits in well with the same qualities in the motive which carries with it no element of mortal self-interest; but where human interests were concerned, since the idea admitted of division, the lawgiver also made a division, and appointed what he called a preservation-offering to correspond to the aspiration for participation in blessings, while he assigned the sin-
offering for avoidance of evils. Thus very properly 197
there are three offerings for three objects, the whole-burnt-offering having no other in view but God Himself alone Whom it is good to honour, the other two having ourselves in view, the preservation-offering for the safe preserving and bettering of human affairs, the sin-offering for the healing of the trespasses which the soul has committed.

XXXVII. We must now describe the ordinances 198
dealing with each of these sacrifices, beginning with the best, which is the whole-burnt-offering. [a] First of all, he says the victim must be a male specimen of the animals selected as best for the purpose, namely, a calf or lamb or kid. Secondly, the giver must wash his hands and lay them on the head of the victim,
and after this one priest must take and slay it while 199
another priest holds a vial below and after catching some of the blood goes all round the altar and sprinkles it thereon. The victim after being flayed must be divided into parts complete in themselves, while the belly and feet are washed, and then the whole must be given over to the sacred fire of the altar. Thus

200 ἑνὸς πολλὰ καὶ ἐκ πολλῶν ἕν. ταῦτα μὲν ἡ ῥητὴ πρόσταξις περιέχει. μηνύεται δὲ καὶ νοῦς ἕτερος αἰνιγματώδη λόγον ἔχων τὸν διὰ συμβόλων· σύμβολα δ' ἐστὶ τὰ λεχθέντα φανερὰ ἀδήλων καὶ ἀφανῶν. ἄρρεν εὐθέως τὸ ὁλόκαυτον ἱερεῖον, ἐπειδὴ τοῦ θήλεος καὶ τελειότερον καὶ ἡγεμονικώτερον καὶ συγγενέστερον αἰτίῳ δραστικῷ· τὸ γὰρ θῆλυ ἀτελές, ὑπήκοον, ἐν τῷ πάσχειν
201 μᾶλλον ἢ ποιεῖν ἐξεταζόμενον. δυοῖν δ' ὄντων, ἐξ ὧν ἡ ἡμετέρα ψυχὴ συνέστη, λογικοῦ τε καὶ ἀλόγου, τὸ μὲν λογικὸν τῆς ἄρρενος γενεᾶς ἐστιν, ὅπερ νοῦς καὶ λογισμὸς κεκλήρωται, τὸ δ' ἄλογον τῆς πρὸς γυναικῶν, ὅπερ ἔλαχεν αἴσθησις. νοῦς δὲ αἰσθήσεως, ὡς ἀνὴρ γυναικός, καθ' ὅλον γένος ἀμείνων, ὃς ἄμωμος ὢν καὶ καθαρθεὶς καθάρσεσι ταῖς ἀρετῆς τελείας[1] αὐτός ἐστιν ἡ εὐαγεστάτη θυσία καὶ ὅλη
202 δι' ὅλων εὐάρεστος θεῷ. τὰς δὲ ἐπιτιθεμένας τῇ τοῦ ζῴου κεφαλῇ χεῖρας δεῖγμα σαφέστατον εἶναι συμβέβηκε πράξεων ἀνυπαιτίων καὶ βίου μηδὲν ἐπιφερομένου τῶν εἰς κατηγορίαν ἀλλὰ τοῖς τῆς φύσεως νόμοις καὶ θεσμοῖς συνᾴδοντος.
203 βούλεται γὰρ τοῦ θύοντος πρῶτον μὲν τὸν νοῦν ὡσιῶσθαι γνώμαις ἀγαθαῖς καὶ συμφερούσαις ἐνασκούμενον, ἔπειτα δὲ τὸν βίον ἐξ ἀρίστων συνεστάναι πράξεων, ὡς ἅμα τῇ τῶν χειρῶν ἐπιθέσει δύνασθαί τινα παρρησιασάμενον ἐκ καθαροῦ τοῦ
204 συνειδότος τοιαῦτα εἰπεῖν· αἱ χεῖρες αὗται οὔτε δῶρον ἐπ' ἀδίκοις ἔλαβον οὔτε τὰς ἐξ ἁρπαγῆς καὶ
[242] πλεονεξίας διανομὰς οὔτε αἵματος | ἀθῴου προσ-

[1] MSS. τελείαις.

the one in it has become many and the many one.[a]
These are the contents of the ordinance taken 200
literally. But another meaning also is indicated of the mystical character which symbols convey; words in their plain sense are symbols of things latent and obscure. In the first place the victim of the whole-burnt-offering is a male because the male is more complete, more dominant than the female, closer akin to causal activity, for the female is incomplete and in subjection and belongs to the category of the passive rather than the active. So 201
too with the two ingredients which constitute our life-principle, the rational and the irrational; the rational which belongs to mind and reason is of the masculine gender, the irrational, the province of sense, is of the feminine. Mind belongs to a genus wholly superior to sense as man is to woman; unblemished and purged, as perfect virtue purges, it is itself the most religious of sacrifices and its whole being is highly pleasing to God. In the 202
laying of hands on the head of the animal we find the clearest possible type of blameless actions and of a life saddled with nothing that leads to censure but in harmony with the laws and statutes of nature. For 203
the law desires, first, that the mind of the worshipper should be sanctified by exercise in good and profitable thoughts and judgements; secondly, that his life should be a consistent course of the best actions, so that as he lays his hands on the victim, he can boldly and with a pure conscience speak in this wise:
"These hands have taken no gift to do injustice, nor 204
shared in the proceeds of plunder or overreaching, nor been soiled with innocent blood. None have

[a] *Cf.* § 208.

ἥψαντο, οὐ πήρωσιν, οὐχ ὕβριν, οὐ τραῦμα, οὐ βίαν ἐξειργάσαντο, οὐκ ἄλλο τὸ παράπαν οὐδὲν τῶν κατηγορίαν καὶ ψόγον ἐχόντων ὑπηρέτησαν, ἀλλ' ὑποδιάκονοι πάντων ἐγένοντο τῶν καλῶν καὶ συμφερόντων, ἃ παρὰ σοφίᾳ καὶ νόμοις καὶ σοφοῖς καὶ νομίμοις ἀνδράσι τετίμηται. XXXVIII.

205 τὸ δ' αἷμα κύκλῳ προσχεῖται τῷ βωμῷ, διότι κύκλος σχημάτων ⟨τὸ⟩ τελειότατον καὶ ὑπὲρ τοῦ μέρος μηδὲν ἔρημον καὶ κενὸν ἀπολειφθῆναι ψυχικῆς σπονδῆς· ψυχῆς γὰρ κυρίως εἰπεῖν ἐστι σπονδὴ τὸ αἷμα. συμβολικῶς οὖν ἀναδιδάσκει τὴν διάνοιαν ὅλην δι' ὅλων ἐν κύκλῳ χορεύουσαν ἐν πάσαις ἰδέαις λόγων καὶ βουλευμάτων καὶ ἔργων ἐπιδείκνυσθαι τὴν πρὸς τὸν θεὸν ἀρέσκειαν.

206 ἀποπλύνεσθαι δὲ κοιλίαν καὶ πόδας διείρηται, πάνυ συμβολικῶς· διὰ μὲν γὰρ τῆς κοιλίας αἰνίττεται τὴν ἐπιθυμίαν, ἣν ἐκνίπτεσθαι συμφέρον κηλίδων καὶ μιασμάτων καὶ μέθης καὶ παροινίας μεστήν, κακὸν βλαβερώτατον ἐπὶ λύμῃ τοῦ βίου τῶν ἀνθρώπων

207 συγκροτούμενόν τε καὶ συνασκούμενον· διὰ δὲ τοῦ τοὺς πόδας ἀπολούεσθαι τὸ μηκέτι βαίνειν ἐπὶ γῆς, ἀλλ' αἰθεροβατεῖν· ἡ γὰρ τοῦ φιλοθέου ψυχὴ πρὸς ἀλήθειαν ἀπὸ γῆς ἄνω πρὸς οὐρανὸν πηδᾷ καὶ πτερωθεῖσα μετεωροπολεῖ συντάττεσθαι γλιχομένη καὶ συγχορεύειν ἡλίῳ καὶ σελήνῃ καὶ τῇ τῶν ἄλλων ἀστέρων ἱερωτάτῃ καὶ παναρμονίῳ στρατιᾷ, ταξιαρχοῦντος καὶ ἡγεμονεύοντος τοῦ θεοῦ τοῦ τὴν ἀνανταγώνιστον καὶ ἀναφαίρετον βασιλείαν ἔχοντος,

208 δι' ἧς ἐνδίκως ἕκαστα πρυτανεύεται. ἡ δὲ εἰς μέλη τοῦ ζῴου διανομὴ δηλοῖ, ἤτοι ὡς ἓν τὰ

---

[a] *i.e.* the ψυχή in its lower sense (*cf.* § 177) is an apposite symbol of the higher ψυχή, "the mind."

they maimed or wounded, no deed of outrage or violence have they wrought. They have done no service of any other kind at all which might incur arraignment or censure, but have made themselves humble ministers of things excellent and profitable, such as are held in honour in the sight of wisdom and law and wise and law-abiding men."

XXXVIII. The blood is poured in a circle round the 205
altar because the circle is the most perfect of figures, and in order that no part should be left destitute of the vital oblation. For the blood may truly be called a libation of the life-principle. So, then, he teaches in this symbol that the mind, whole and complete, should, as it moves with measured tread passing circle-wise through every phase of word and intention and deed, shew its willingness to do God's service.[a]

The direction to wash the belly and the 206
feet is highly symbolical. Under the figure of the belly he signifies the lust which it is well to clean away, saturated as it is with stains and pollutions, with wine-bibbing and sottishness, a mighty force for ill, trained and drilled to work havoc in the life of
men. By the washing of the feet is meant that his 207
steps should be no longer on earth but tread the upper air. For the soul of the lover of God does in truth leap from earth to heaven and wing its way on high, eager to take its place in the ranks and share the ordered march of sun and moon and the all-holy, all-harmonious host of the other stars, marshalled and led by the God Whose kingship none can dispute or usurp, the kingship by which everything is justly
governed. The division of the animal 208
into its limbs indicates either that all things are one

πάντα ᾗ ὅτι ἐξ ἑνός τε καὶ εἰς ἕν, ὅπερ οἱ μὲν κόρον καὶ χρησμοσύνην ἐκάλεσαν, οἱ δ᾽ ἐκπύρωσιν καὶ διακόσμησιν, ἐκπύρωσιν μὲν κατὰ τὴν τοῦ θερμοῦ[1] δυναστείαν τῶν ἄλλων ἐπικρατήσαντος, διακόσμησιν δὲ κατὰ τὴν τῶν τεττάρων στοιχείων
209 ἰσονομίαν, ἣν ἀντιδιδόασιν ἀλλήλοις. ἐμοὶ δὲ εὐθυβολώτερον σκοπουμένῳ δοκεῖ τοῦτο δηλοῦσθαι· ἡ τιμῶσα ψυχὴ τὸ ὂν δι᾽ αὐτὸ τὸ ὂν ὀφείλει μὴ ἀλόγως μηδ᾽ ἀνεπιστημόνως ἀλλὰ σὺν ἐπιστήμῃ καὶ λόγῳ τιμᾶν. ὁ δὲ περὶ αὐτοῦ λόγος τομὴν ἐπιδέχεται καὶ διαίρεσιν καθ᾽ ἑκάστην τῶν θείων δυνάμεων καὶ ἀρετῶν· ὁ γὰρ θεὸς ἀγαθός τέ ἐστι καὶ ποιητὴς καὶ γεννητὴς τῶν ὅλων καὶ προνοητικὸς ὧν ἐγέννησε, σωτήρ τε καὶ εὐεργέτης, μακαριότητος καὶ πάσης εὐδαιμονίας ἀνάπλεως· ὧν ἕκαστον καὶ καθ᾽ αὑτὸ ἰδίᾳ σεμνὸν καὶ ἐπαινετὸν καὶ μετὰ τῶν ὁμογενῶν ἐξεταζόμενον.
210 ἔχει δὲ καὶ τὰ ἄλλα ταύτῃ. ὅταν | βουληθῇς, ὦ
[243] διάνοια, εὐχαριστῆσαι περὶ γενέσεως κόσμου θεῷ, καὶ περὶ τοῦ ὅλου ποιοῦ τὴν εὐχαριστίαν καὶ περὶ τῶν ὁλοσχερεστάτων αὐτοῦ μερῶν ὡς ἂν ζῴου

[1] So R. The one other MS. which contained the sentence had θεοῦ, which was the accepted reading before the discovery of R, and it is so quoted by Arnim and others. Presumably they understood it as expressing the view of Heracleitus that the Deity was fire.

[a] The terms belong to the philosophy of Heracleitus, *cf. Leg. All.* iii. 7 and note. Whatever Heracleitus meant by them, Philo clearly here equates κόρος to ἐκπύρωσις and χρησμοσύνη to διακόσμησις.

or that they come from and return to one, an alternation which is called by some Fullness and Want,[a] by others a General Conflagration and Reconstruction,[b] the Conflagration being the state when the supremacy of heat has prevailed over the rest, the Reconstruction when the four elements, by concession to each other, obtain equilibrium. My own reflections 209
lead me to think the following a more correct explanation. The soul which honours the Existent having the Existent Himself only in view, ought to honour Him not irrationally nor ignorantly, but with knowledge and reason. And when we reason about Him we recognize in Him partition and division into each of the Divine powers and excellences. For God is good, He is the maker and begetter of the universe and His providence is over what He has begotten; He is a saviour and a benefactor, and has the plenitude of all blessedness and all happiness. Each of these attributes calls for veneration and praise, both separately in itself and when ranked with its congeners. So, too, it is with the rest.[c] 210
When, my mind, thou wishest to give thanks to God for the creation of the universe, give it both for the sum of things and for its principal parts, thinking of them as the limbs of a living creature of the utmost

[b] For *ἐκπύρωσις* see *Quis Rerum* 228 and note. *διακόσμησις* should perhaps rather be translated by "disposal" or "distribution," without the "re-". Since fire is the primary substance (*τὸ ἕν*), creation itself was a *διακόσμησις*. So too *ἐκπύρωσις* though regularly translated "general conflagration" is rather "resolution into fire." See further App. p. 621.

[c] Or perhaps *ταύτῃ* = "as follows," as not unfrequently; see note on *De Mut.* 129. By "the rest" he means that the universe and the man himself are to be "divided" in the same way as God's attributes have been in the previous section.

τελειοτάτου μελῶν, οἷον οὐρανοῦ λέγω καὶ ἡλίου καὶ σελήνης, πλανήτων καὶ ἀπλανῶν ἀστέρων, εἶτα γῆς καὶ τῶν ἐν αὐτῇ ζῴων καὶ φυτῶν, εἶτα πελαγῶν καὶ ποταμῶν αὐθιγενῶν τε καὶ χειμάρρων καὶ τῶν ἐν αὐτοῖς, ἔπειτα ἀέρος καὶ τῶν κατ' αὐτὸν μεταβολῶν· χειμὼν γὰρ καὶ θέρος, ἔαρ τε καὶ μετόπωρον, αἱ ἐτήσιοι καὶ βιωφελέσταται ὧραι, παθήματα ἀέρος γεγόνασιν ἐπὶ σωτηρίᾳ τῶν μετὰ σελήνην
211 τρεπομένου. κἂν ἄρα ποτὲ περὶ ἀνθρώπων εὐχαριστῇς, μὴ μόνον περὶ τοῦ γένους ἀλλὰ καὶ περὶ τῶν εἰδῶν καὶ ἀναγκαιοτάτων μερῶν εὐχαρίστει, ἀνδρῶν, γυναικῶν, Ἑλλήνων, βαρβάρων, τῶν ἐν ἠπείροις, τῶν τὰς νήσους εἰληχότων· κἂν περὶ ἑνὸς ἀνδρός, τέμε τῷ λόγῳ τὴν εὐχαριστίαν, μὴ εἰς τὰ λεπτότατα μέχρι τῶν ἐσχάτων, ἀλλὰ εἰς τὰ συνεκτικώτατα, σῶμα καὶ ψυχὴν τὸ πρῶτον, ἐξ ὧν συνέστηκεν, εἶτα εἰς λόγον καὶ νοῦν καὶ αἴσθησιν· οὐ γὰρ ἂν γένοιτο ἀναξία θεοῦ ἀκοῆς καὶ ἡ ὑπὲρ ἑκάστου τούτων εὐχαριστία καθ' αὑτήν.

212 XXXIX. Ἀπόχρη τοσαῦτα περὶ τῆς ὁλοκαύτου θυσίας λελέχθαι. τὴν δὲ τοῦ σωτηρίου λεγομένην ἑξῆς ἐπισκεπτέον. ἐπὶ ταύτης ἀδιαφορεῖ, ἐάν τε ἄρρεν ᾖ τὸ ἱερεῖον ἐάν τε καὶ θῆλυ. σφαγέντος δὲ τρία ταῦτα ὑπεξαιρεῖται τῷ βωμῷ, τὸ στέαρ καὶ λοβὸς ἥπατος καὶ νεφροὶ δύο· τὰ δ' ἄλλα τῷ κατα-
213 θύσαντι εὐωχία. διὰ τί δὲ τὰ μέρη ταῦτα τῶν ἐντοσθιδίων καθιεροῦται, μετὰ ἀκριβείας ἐπισκεπτέον ἐκεῖνο μὴ παρελθόντας· διαλογιζόμενος ἐν ἐμαυτῷ πολλάκις ταῦτα καὶ διερευνώμενος ἐπηπό-

---

[a] E.V. "peace-offering." See Lev. iii. 1 ff.
[b] E.V. "the caul upon the liver."

perfection. Such parts are heaven and sun and moon and the planets and fixed stars; then again earth and the living creatures or plants thereon, then the sea and rivers, whether spring-fed or winter courses, and all they contain: then the air and its phases, for winter and summer, spring and autumn, those seasons which recur annually and are so highly beneficial to our life, are different conditions in the air which changes for the preservation of sublunar things. And if thou givest 211
thanks for man, do not do so only for the whole genus but for its species and most essential parts, for men and women, for Greeks and barbarians, for dwellers on the mainland and those whose lot is cast in the islands. And if it is for a single person, divide the thanksgiving as reason directs, not into every tiny part of him down to the very last, but into those of primary importance, first of all into body and soul of which he is composed, then into speech and mind and sense. For thanks for each of these will by itself be not unworthy to obtain audience with God.

XXXIX. Enough has now been said on the whole 212
burnt-offering. We must now consider in its turn the preservation-offering.[a] In this case it is a matter of indifference whether the victim is male or female. When it has been slain these three, the fat, the lobe[b] of the liver and the two kidneys, are set apart for the altar, while the rest serves as a feast to be enjoyed
by the person who has offered the sacrifice. But why 213
these parts of the inwards are consecrated must be carefully considered, not neglecting the following point. In the course of my reflections I have often pondered deeply on this question also; what could

ρησα, τί δήποτε λοβὸν μὲν ἥπατος καὶ νεφροὺς καὶ στέαρ ἀπαρχὰς τῶν καταθυομένων ζῴων ὑπεξείλετο ὁ νόμος, οὔτε δὲ καρδίαν οὔτε ἐγκέφαλον, τοῦ
214 ἡγεμονικοῦ τῷ ἑτέρῳ τούτων ἐνδιαιτωμένου. τὸ δ' αὐτὸ νομίζω καὶ ἄλλους οὐκ ὀλίγους τῶν διανοίᾳ μᾶλλον ἢ ὀφθαλμοῖς ταῖς ἱεραῖς γραφαῖς ἐντυγχανόντων ἐπιζητήσειν· ἐὰν μὲν οὖν ἐπισκεψάμενοι πιθανωτέραν αἰτίαν εὕρωσιν, ἑαυτούς τε καὶ ἡμᾶς ὠφελήσουσιν· εἰ δὲ μή, τὴν ἐπινοηθεῖσαν ὑφ' ἡμῶν ἐπικρινάτωσαν, εἰ δόκιμος. ἔστι δὲ ἥδε· τὸ ἡγεμονικὸν μόνον τῶν ἐν ἡμῖν ἀφροσύνην καὶ ἀδικίαν καὶ δειλίαν καὶ τὰς ἄλλας κακίας δέχεταί[1] τε καὶ
[244] χωρεῖ· τούτου δὲ οἶκος τὸ ἕτερον τῶν λεχθέντων
215 ἐστίν, | ἐγκέφαλος ἢ καρδία. ἐδικαίωσεν οὖν ὁ ἱερὸς λόγος τῷ τοῦ θεοῦ βωμῷ, δι' οὗ πάντων ἁμαρτημάτων καὶ παρανομημάτων ἀπολύσεις γίνονται καὶ παντελεῖς ἀφέσεις, μὴ προσφέρειν ἀγγεῖον, ἐν ᾧ ποτε φωλεύσας ὁ νοῦς ἐπὶ τὴν ἀδικίας καὶ ἀσεβείας ἀνοδίαν ἐχώρησεν ἐκτραπόμενος τὴν ἐπ' ἀρετὴν καὶ καλοκἀγαθίαν ἄγουσαν ὁδόν· εὔηθες γὰρ τὰς θυσίας ὑπόμνησιν ἁμαρτημάτων ἀλλὰ μὴ λήθην αὐτῶν κατασκευάζειν. τοῦτ' αἴτιον εἶναί μοι δοκεῖ τοῦ μηδέτερον τῶν ἡγεμονίαν ἐχόντων, ἐγκέφαλον ἢ καρδίαν, προσφέρεσθαι.

216 Ἃ δὲ διείρηται, λόγον ἔχει προσήκοντα· τὸ μὲν στέαρ, ὅτι καὶ πιότατον καὶ τῶν σπλάγχνων φυλακτήριον—ἐπαμπίσχει γὰρ αὐτὰ καὶ πιαίνει καὶ τῇ μαλακότητι τῆς ἐπαφῆς ὠφελεῖ—, οἱ δὲ νεφροὶ

[1] MSS. δύναται.

[a] See the very similar passage in *De Sac.* 136, and the note there on the question whether τὸ ἡγεμονικόν resided in the brain or in the heart.

be the reason why the law, when setting apart the lobe of the liver and the kidneys and the fat as a tribute reserved from the animals sacrificed, did not include either the heart or the brains, since the dominant principle resides in one or other of them.[a] And I 214
expect the same question will present itself to not a few of those who read the holy scriptures with their understanding rather than with their eyes. If such persons after examination find a more convincing reason, they will benefit both themselves and me; if not I beg them to consider whether that which has commended itself to my mind will stand the test. It is as follows. The dominant principle is the only part of us which admits and retains folly and injustice and cowardice and the other vices, and the home of this principle is one or other of the two just mentioned, namely, the brain and the heart. The holy word, 215
therefore, thought good that the altar of God, by which is given absolution and complete remission of all sins and transgressions, should not be approached by the container in which mind had its lair when it came forth to tread the pathless wilds of injustice and impiety, turning away from the road which leads to virtue and noble conduct. For it would be foolish to have the sacrifices working remembrance instead of oblivion of sin. This seems to me the reason why neither of the parts which hold the pre-eminence, the brain or the heart, is brought to the altar.

As for the parts which are actually prescribed, 216
appropriate reasons can be given for the choice. The fat is the richest part and acts as a protection to the inwards, serving as a covering and a source of richness to them and benefiting them by the softness of its contact. The kidneys are chosen because of their

διὰ τοὺς παραστάτας καὶ τὰ γεννητικά, οἷς παροικοῦντες ἀγαθῶν τρόπον γειτόνων βοηθοῦσι καὶ συμπράττουσιν, ὅπως ὁ τῆς φύσεως σπόρος εὐοδῇ, μηδενὸς τῶν πλησίον ἐμποδίζοντος—αὐτοὶ μὲν γὰρ αἱμοειδεῖς εἰσι δεξαμεναί, οἷς ἡ τῶν περιττωμάτων ὑγρὰ κάθαρσις ἀποκρίνεται, οἱ δὲ παραστάται πλησίον, δι' ὧν ἄρδεται ὁ σπόρος—, λοβὸς δ' ἥπατος τοῦ κυριωτάτου τῶν σπλάγχνων ἐστὶν ἀπαρχή, δι' οὗ τὴν τροφὴν ἐξαιματοῦσθαι συμβέβηκε καὶ ἐποχετευομένην τῇ καρδίᾳ φέρεσθαι διὰ φλεβῶν εἰς τὴν
217 τοῦ ὅλου σώματος διαμονήν. στόμαχος μὲν γὰρ παρακείμενος τῇ καταπόσει τὴν ὑπὸ τῶν ὀδόντων τμηθεῖσαν πρότερον καὶ λεανθεῖσαν αὖθις τροφὴν ὑποδέχεται καὶ προκατεργάζεται κοιλίᾳ· κοιλία δὲ παρὰ στομάχου λαμβάνουσα τὴν δευτέραν ὑπηρεσίαν ἐπιτελεῖ, πρὸς ἣν ὑπὸ φύσεως ἐτάχθη, χύλωσιν ἀπεργαζομένη τῆς τροφῆς· αὐλοὶ δὲ δύο τῆς κοιλίας σωληνοειδεῖς ἐκπεφύκασιν εἰς ἧπαρ ἐπαντλοῦντες
218 ταῖς διαπεφυκυίαις ἐν αὐτῷ δεξαμεναῖς. ἔχει δὲ διττὴν δύναμιν ἧπαρ, διακριτικήν τε καὶ τὴν πρὸς ἐξαιμάτωσιν· ἡ μὲν οὖν διακριτικὴ πᾶν ὅσον ἀτέραμνον καὶ δυσκατέργαστον εἰς τὸ παρακείμενον χολῆς ἀγγεῖον ἀποκρίνει, ἡ δ' ἑτέρα τὸ καθαρὸν καὶ διηθημένον τῷ περὶ αὐτὴν φλογμῷ τρέπει μὲν εἰς αἷμα ζωτικώτατον, ἀναθλίβει δ' εἰς καρδίαν, ἀφ' ἧς ὡς ἐλέχθη ταῖς φλεψὶν ἐποχετευόμενον διὰ παντὸς εἰλεῖται τοῦ σώματος γινόμενον αὐτῷ τροφή.

relation to the testicles and generative organs; situated beside them they give them neighbourly assistance, and co-operate in promoting the easy passage of nature's seed unimpeded by any of the adjacent parts. For the kidneys themselves are blood-coloured receptacles in which the moist off-scouring of the excrement is secreted, and contiguous to them are the testicles which create the stream of the semen. The lobe is a sample tribute from the most important of the inwards, the liver, by which the food is converted into blood and then being sluiced into the heart, is conveyed through the veins for the conservation of the whole body. For the 217
orifice of the stomach being adjacent to the gullet receives the food which has been first bitten off by the teeth and afterwards masticated, and by its action prepares it for the stomach itself. This receives it from the orifice and performs the second office to which it has been appointed by nature, by turning it into juice. And from the stomach there are two pipe-shaped channels extending to the liver and draining the food into the receptacles which lie at intervals therein. Now the liver has two properties: 218
it acts both as a sifter and a creator of blood. As a sifter it secretes all the hard and callous stuff into the adjacent bile-vessel, while in its other capacity by means of the heat which it contains it turns the pure liquid which has been strained off into blood full of life-giving powers, then presses this blood into the heart, whence, as we have said, it is sluiced into the veins, and coursing through the whole body becomes

219 πρόσεστι δὲ κἀκεῖνο τοῖς εἰρημένοις·
τὴν τοῦ ἥπατος φύσιν μετέωρον καὶ λειοτάτην
οὖσαν [καὶ] διὰ λειότητα φανοτάτου κατόπτρου
λόγον ἔχειν συμβέβηκεν, ἵν' ἐπειδὰν τῶν ἡμερινῶν
φροντίδων ἀναχωρήσας ὁ νοῦς, ὕπνῳ μὲν παρ-
ειμένου τοῦ σώματος, μηδεμιᾶς δὲ τῶν αἰσθήσεων
[245] | ἱσταμένης ἐμποδών, ἀνακυκλεῖν αὑτὸν ἄρξηται καὶ
τὰ νοήματα καθαρῶς ἐφ' αὑτοῦ σκοπεῖν, οἷα εἰς
κάτοπτρον ἀποβλέπων τὸ ἧπαρ ἕκαστα εἰλικρινῶς
καταθεᾶται τῶν νοητῶν καὶ περιβλεπόμενος ἐν
κύκλῳ τὰ εἴδωλα, μή τι πρόσεστιν αἶσχος, [ἵνα] τὸ
μὲν φύγῃ, τὸ δ' ἐναντίον ἕληται, καὶ πάσαις ταῖς
φαντασίαις εὐαρεστήσας προφητεύῃ διὰ τῶν ὀνεί-
ρων τὰ μέλλοντα.

220 XL. Δυσὶ δὲ μόναις ἡμέραις ἐπιτρέπει τὴν χρῆσιν
τῆς τοῦ σωτηρίου θυσίας ποιεῖσθαι μηδὲν εἰς τὴν
τρίτην ἀπολείποντας, πολλῶν χάριν· ἑνὸς μὲν ὅτι τὰ
τῆς ἱερᾶς τραπέζης πάντα καιρίως δεῖ προσφέρεσθαι σπουδὴν ποιουμένους, ὡς μὴ μεταβάλῃ μήκει
χρόνου· κρεῶν δὲ ἑώλων εὔσηπτος ἡ φύσις, κἂν
221 ἡδύσμασι παραρτυθῇ. ἑτέρου δ' ὅτι τὰς θυσίας

[a] This section is based on Plato, *Timaeus* 71 (see Archer-Hind's translation), and certainly reproduces the main idea of that curious passage, that the liver acts as a mirror "which receives outlines of the thoughts from the brain and exhibits reflections from them," sometimes of a bitter nature, while sometimes "the part of the soul settled about the liver is enabled to secure a sober amusement at night, enjoying divination during sleep in recompense for its deprivation of intelligence and wisdom." Whether Philo has otherwise understood Plato correctly I do not presume to say.

[b] I do not understand what Philo means by μετέωρος ("high up"). Plato's description of the liver is that God set it in the dwelling-place of the lusting (ἐπιθυμητικόν) part of the soul and made it "dense and smooth and bright, with a share of

its sustenance. [a] There is another point to 219
be added to these statements. The liver has been made so as to lie high [b] and be exceedingly smooth, and in virtue of its smoothness it plays the part of a mirror of the utmost brightness. In consequence when the mind withdrawing from its daytime cares, with the body paralyzed in sleep and the obstruction of every sense removed, begins to turn itself about and concentrate upon the pure observation of its concepts, it looks into the liver as into a mirror where it gains a lucid view of all that mind can perceive and, while its gaze travels round the images to see whether they contain any ugly defect, it eschews all such and selects their opposites, and so, well satisfied [c] with all the visions presented to it, prophesies future events through the medium of dreams.

XL. [d] Two days only are allowed for the use of the 220
preservation-offering as food, and nothing is to be left over till the third day. This for several reasons. One is, that all the meats of the sacred table must be eaten without undue delay, care being taken that they should not deteriorate through lapse of time. It is the nature of stale flesh to decay rapidly, even
though seasoned with spices as preservatives. Another 221

bitterness." Some stress is laid on its position, but there is nothing corresponding to μετέωρος. Can the word mean here "with changing moods," "temperamental," and refer to the mixture of sweetness and bitterness ascribed to it by Plato?

[c] So Mangey and Heinemann for εὐαρεστήσας. This use of the verb, however, seems later. Its common meaning is "well-pleasing to," and so apparently always elsewhere in Philo (εὐαρεστητέον in *De Praem.* 34 may be the verbal of εὐαρεστοῦμαι). This regular meaning is perhaps not altogether impossible here, "it has become a satisfactory medium for all the (good) visions."

[d] See Lev. xix. 5, 6.

ἀταμιεύτους εἶναι προσήκει καὶ πᾶσιν εἰς μέσον προκεῖσθαι τοῖς δεομένοις· εἰσὶ γὰρ οὐκέτι τοῦ τεθυκότος, ἀλλ' ᾧ τέθυται τὸ ἱερεῖον, ὃς εὐεργέτης καὶ φιλόδωρος ὢν κοινωνὸν ἀπέφηνε τοῦ βωμοῦ καὶ ὁμοτράπεζον τὸ συμπόσιον τῶν τὴν θυσίαν ἐπιτελούντων, οἷς παραγγέλλει μὴ νομίζειν ἑστιᾶν· ἐπίτροποι γὰρ εὐωχίας εἰσίν, οὐχ ἑστιάτορες, ὁ δ' ἑστιάτωρ ἐστὶν οὗ συμβέβηκεν εἶναι καὶ τὴν παρασκευήν, ἣν οὐ θέμις ἀποκρύπτειν φειδωλίαν, ἀνελεύθερον κακίαν, φιλανθρωπίας, ἀρετῆς εὐγενοῦς,
222 προκρίνοντας. τελευταίου δ' ὅτι τὴν τοῦ σωτηρίου θυσίαν ὑπὲρ δυεῖν προσάγεσθαι συμβέβηκε, ψυχῆς τε καὶ σώματος, ὧν ἑκατέρῳ μίαν ἡμέραν ἀπένειμεν εἰς εὐωχίαν τῶν κρεῶν· ἥρμοττε γὰρ ἰσάριθμον χρόνον ὁρισθῆναι τοῖς πεφυκόσι σῴζεσθαι τῶν ἐν ἡμῖν, ὡς τῇ μὲν προτεραίᾳ λαμβάνειν ἅμα τῇ βρώσει τῆς ψυχικῆς σωτηρίας ὑπόμνησιν, τῇ δ'
223 ὑστεραίᾳ τῆς κατὰ τὸ σῶμα ὑγείας. ἐπεὶ δὲ τρίτον οὐδὲν ἦν ὃ κυρίως πέφυκε σωτηρίαν ἐνδέχεσθαι, τὴν εἰς τὴν τρίτην ἡμέραν χρῆσιν ἀνὰ κράτος ἀπηγόρευσε προστάξας, εἰ καὶ τύχοι τι κατ' ἄγνοιαν ἢ λήθην ἀπολειφθέν, εὐθὺς ἀναλίσκεσθαι πυρί. τὸν δὲ γευσάμενον αὐτὸ μόνον ἔνοχον ἀποφαίνει καί φησιν αὐτῷ· τεθυκέναι νομίζων, ὦ καταγέλαστε, οὐ τέθυκας· οὐ προσηκάμην[1] ἀθύτων, ἀνιέρων, βε-

[1] προσηκάμην followed by a genitive is irregular, and Cohn proposes some insertion, *e.g.* θοίνην.

---

[a] See Lev. xix. 7, 8. Philo's close following of the text should be noticed, LXX ἐὰν δὲ βρώσει βρωθῇ . . . ἄθυτόν (E.V. "abomination") ἐστιν, οὐ δεχθήσεται. His γευσάμενον αὐτὸ μόνον interprets βρώσει βρωθῇ ("be eaten at all"), though else-

reason is, that the sacrificial meals should not be hoarded, but be free and open to all who have need, for they are now the property not of him by whom but of Him to Whom the victim has been sacrificed, He the benefactor, the bountiful, Who has made the convivial company of those who carry out the sacrifices partners of the altar whose board they share. And He bids them not think of themselves as the entertainers, for they are the stewards of the good cheer, not the hosts. The Host is He to Whom the material provided for the feast has come to belong, and this must not be stowed away out of sight, and niggardliness, the vice of the slave, preferred to kindliness, the
virtue of gentle birth. The final reason is, that the 222
preservation-offering is in fact made in behalf of two, namely soul and body, to each of which he assigned one day for feasting on the flesh. For it was meet that an equal space of time should be appointed for those elements of our nature which are capable of being preserved, so that on the first day as we eat we obtain a reminder of the soul's preservation, on the
morrow of the body's good health. And since there 223
is no third thing which, properly speaking, could be the subject of preservation, he strictly forbade the use of the oblation as food on the third day, and commanded that if anything was left over through ignorance or inadvertence, it should immediately be consumed by fire. [a] Even him who had tasted it and nothing more he declares to be guilty. "Poor fool," he says to him, "thou thinkest to have sacrificed, though thou hast not done so. Sacrilegious, unholy, profane, impure, is the meat which thou hast dressed.

where he does not seem to understand the Hebrew idiom thus rendered in Greek.

βήλων, ἀκαθάρτων, ὧν ἥψηκας κρεῶν, ὦ γαστρίμαργε, θυσιῶν οὐδ᾽ ὄναρ ἐπῃσθημένος.

224 XLI. Τῆς δὲ τοῦ σωτηρίου θυσίας ἐν εἴδει περιλαμβάνεται ἡ λεγομένη τῆς αἰνέσεως, ἥτις λόγον ἔχει τοιόνδε· ὁ μηδενὶ τὸ παράπαν ἀβουλήτῳ περιπεσών, μήτε κατὰ σῶμα μήτε κατὰ τὰ ἐκτός, ἀλλ᾽ ἀπολέμῳ καὶ εἰρηνικῷ βίῳ χρώμενος ἐν εὐπαθείαις τε καὶ εὐτυχίαις ἐξεταζόμενος, ἀπήμων καὶ ἄπταιστος ὢν καὶ τὸ μακρὸν τοῦ βίου πέλαγος εὐθύνων ἐν εὐδίᾳ καὶ γαλήνῃ πραγμάτων, ἐπι-
[246] πνεούσης ἀεὶ κατ᾽ οἰάκων εὐπραγίας, | ἀναγκαίως ὀφείλει τὸν κυβερνήτην θεὸν καὶ ἄνοσον μὲν σωτηρίαν ἀζημίους δ᾽ ὠφελείας καὶ συνόλως ἀμιγῆ κακῶν τὰ ἀγαθὰ δωρούμενον ὕμνοις τε καὶ εὐδαιμονισμοῖς καὶ εὐχαῖς θυσίαις τε καὶ ταῖς ἄλλαις εὐχαριστίαις εὐαγῶς ἀμείβεσθαι· ἃ δὴ πάντα ἀθρόα
225 συλλήβδην ἓν ὄνομα τὸ αἰνέσεως ἔλαχε. ταύτην τὴν θυσίαν οὐχ ὥσπερ τὴν προτέραν τοῦ σωτηρίου δυσὶν ἡμέρας ἀναλίσκεσθαι προστάττει, μιᾷ δ᾽ αὐτὸ μόνον, ἵν᾽ οἱ ἐπιτυχόντες ἑτοίμων καὶ προχείρων εὐεργεσιῶν ἑτοίμην καὶ ἀνυπέρθετον ποιῶνται τὴν μετάδοσιν.

226 XLII. Ταῦτα μὲν ἐπὶ τοσοῦτον. τὴν δὲ τρίτην ἑξῆς ἐπισκεπτέον, ἣ καλεῖται περὶ ἁμαρτίας. αὕτη τέτμηται πολλαχῇ, κἀν τοῖς προσώποις κἀν τοῖς τῶν ἱερείων εἴδεσι, προσώποις μὲν ἀρχιερέως καὶ

---

[a] See Lev. vii. 2 f. (E.V. 12 f.). It is embraced in the preservation-offering because it is called θυσία αἰνέσεως σωτηρίου (E.V. "the sacrifice of his peace-offerings for thanksgiving").

I accept it not, base glutton, who even in thy dreams hast caught no glimpse of what sacrifice means."

XLI. Under the head of the preservation-offering 224
is embraced what is called the praise-offering.[a] The principle of this is as follows. He who has never at all met with any untoward happening, either of soul or body or things external, who lives a life of peace undisturbed by war, placed in an environment of every comfort and good fortune, free from disaster and cause of stumbling, sailing in straight course over the long sea of life amid the sunshine and calm of happy circumstances, with the breeze of prosperity ever behind the helm, has as his bounden duty to requite God his pilot, Who gives him safety untouched by disease, benefits carrying no penalty and in general good unmixed with evil—requite Him, I say, with hymns and benedictions and prayers and sacrifices and the other expressions of gratitude as religion demands. All these collected and summed up have
obtained the single name of praise. [b] For the con- 225
sumption of this sacrifice one day only is allowed, not two as in the former case of the preservation-offering, that those into whose hands benefits have fallen so readily should make repayment with readiness and without delay.

XLII. So much for these. We must next examine 226
the third kind of sacrifice which bears the name of sin-offering. [c] Here we have several divisions, both according to the persons concerned and the kinds of victims. As to persons, the high priest is distin-

[b] See Lev. vii. 5 (E.V. 15).

[c] See Lev. iv. for the high priest (E.V. "anointed priest"), *v.* 3; for the nation, *v.* 13; for the ruler, *v.* 22; for the commoner, *v.* 27.

τοῦ σύμπαντος ἔθνους καὶ ἄρχοντος ἐν μέρει καὶ ἰδιώτου, ἱερείοις δὲ μόσχου καὶ χιμάρου καὶ χι-
227 μαίρας ἢ ἀμνάδος. διακέκριται δὲ καὶ μάλιστ' ἦν ἀναγκαῖον διακεκρίσθαι τά θ' ἑκούσια καὶ ἀκούσια, τροπὰς λαμβανόντων τὰς πρὸς τὸ βέλτιον τῶν δοξάντων ἁμαρτεῖν καὶ κακιζόντων μὲν αὑτοὺς ἐφ' οἷς ἐπλημμέλησαν, μεθορμιζομένων δὲ πρὸς ζωὴν
228 ἀνυπαίτιον. τὰ μὲν οὖν τοῦ ἀρχιερέως ἁμαρτήματα καὶ τοῦ ἔθνους ἰσοτίμῳ καθαίρεται ζῴῳ—μόσχον γὰρ ἀνάγεσθαι περὶ ἑκατέρου προστέτακται—, τὰ δὲ τοῦ ἄρχοντος ἐλάττονι μέν, ἄρρενι δὲ καὶ τούτῳ—χίμαρος γάρ ἐστι τὸ ἱερεῖον—, τὰ δὲ τοῦ ἰδιώτου καταδεεστέρῳ τὸ εἶδος—θῆλυ γὰρ ἀλλ' οὐκ ἄρρεν
229 θῦμα, χίμαιρα,[1] καταθύεται—. ἔδει γὰρ ἰδιώτου μὲν πλέον ἄρχοντα φέρεσθαι κἀν ταῖς ἱερουργίαις, ἄρχοντος δὲ τὸ ἔθνος, ἐπεὶ τὸ ὅλον τοῦ μέρους ἀεὶ κρεῖττον εἶναι δεῖ, τὸν δ' ἀρχιερέα τῷ ἔθνει τῆς αὐτῆς ἠξιῶσθαι προνομίας ἐν τῷ καθαίρεσθαι καὶ παρὰ τῆς ἵλεω τοῦ θεοῦ δυνάμεως ἀμνηστίαν ἀδικημάτων αἰτεῖσθαι· τὸ δ' ἰσότιμον οὐ δι' αὑτόν, ὡς ἔοικε, καρποῦται μᾶλλον ἢ διότι τοῦ ἔθνους ὑπηρέτης ἐστὶ τὰς κοινὰς ὑπὲρ ἁπάντων ποιούμενος εὐχαριστίας ἐν ταῖς ἱερωτάταις εὐχαῖς καὶ ἐν ταῖς
230 εὐαγεστάταις θυσίαις. σεμνὴ δὲ καὶ θαυμάσιος καὶ ἡ περὶ ταῦτα διάταξις· "ἐὰν" φησίν "ὁ ἀρχιερεὺς ἄκων ἁμάρτῃ," καὶ προστίθησιν "ὥστε τὸν λαὸν

[1] Some MSS. *θῦμα* only, the others *χίμαιρα* only.

---

[a] Philo finds the term *ἄρχων* in the LXX, and does not attempt to explain it. For *ἐν μέρει* see on *κατὰ μέρος*, § 208. Possibly it may mean here, "ruler over some particular part," *i.e.* of the whole nation.

guished from the whole nation and the rulers [a] as a class from the men of the common people. As to victims, they may be a male calf, a he-goat, a she-goat or ewe-lamb. Another distinction made is one 227
which is most essential between voluntary and involuntary sins. For those who have acknowledged their sin are changing their way for the better, and while they reproach themselves for their errors are seeking a blameless life as their new goal. The sins, 228
then, of the high priest and those of the whole nation are purged with an animal of the same value; in both cases it is directed that a male calf should be brought. For the sins of the ruler one of less value is ordered, though this too is a male, namely a he-goat; for the sins of the commoner, one still more inferior in kind, a female offering instead of a male, that is, a she-goat. For it was proper that in matters of sacrifice the ruler 229
should fare better than the commoner and the nation than the ruler, since the whole should always be superior to the part; also that the high priest should be adjudged the same precedence as the nation in their purification and supplication for forgiveness of wrongdoings from the merciful power of God. But the equality of honour which the high priest enjoys is evidently not so much on his own account as because he is the servant of the nation also, giving thanks in common for all through the holiest of prayers and the purest of sacrifices. Deeply and wonderfully 230
impressive is the form of command in this matter. [b] "If the high priest," it says, "sins involuntarily," and then adds, "so that the people sin," words which

[b] See Lev. iv. 3. A.V. "according to the sin of the people." R.V. "so as to bring guilt on the people." The LXX has not got ἄκων in this verse, but Philo infers it from ἀκουσίως (R.V. "unwittingly") in *v.* 2.

ἁμαρτεῖν," μόνον οὐκ ἄντικρυς ἀναδιδάσκων, ὅτι ὁ πρὸς ἀλήθειαν ἀρχιερεὺς καὶ μὴ ψευδώνυμος ἀμέτοχος ἁμαρτημάτων ἐστίν, εἰ δ' ὀλισθήσοι ποτέ, πείσεται τοῦτο οὐ δι' αὐτόν, ἀλλὰ διὰ κοινὸν τοῦ ἔθνους σφάλμα· τὸ δὲ σφάλμα οὐκ ἀνίατον, ἀλλὰ
231 ῥᾳδίως τὴν θεραπείαν ἐνδεχόμενον. ὅταν οὖν σφαγιασθῇ ὁ μόσχος, κελεύει τοῦ αἵματος ἐπιρραίνειν ἑπτάκις τῷ δακτύλῳ ἀντικρὺ τοῦ πρὸς τοῖς ἀδύτοις καταπετάσματος, ἐσωτέρω τοῦ προτέρου, καθ' ὃν τόπον ἵδρυται τὰ ἱερώτατα σκεύη, κἄπειτα
[247] ⟨τὰ⟩ τοῦ | θυμιατηρίου τέτταρα κέρατα—τετράγωνον γάρ ἐστι—χρίειν καὶ ἐπαλείφειν, τὸ δ' ἄλλο αἷμα προσχεῖν παρὰ τῇ βάσει τοῦ ἐν ὑπαίθρῳ
232 βωμοῦ· ἐφ' ὃν ἀναφέρειν τρία διείρηται, στέαρ καὶ λοβὸν ἥπατος καὶ διττοὺς νεφρούς, κατὰ τὴν ἐπὶ τοῦ σωτηρίου διάταξιν, δορὰν δὲ καὶ κρέα καὶ σύμπαν ἀπὸ κεφαλῆς ἄχρι ποδῶν τὸ ἄλλο σῶμα τοῦ μόσχου μετὰ τῶν ἐντοσθιδίων προφέρειν[1] ἔξω καὶ κατακαίειν ἐν χωρίῳ καθαρῷ, ἔνθα τὴν ἱερὰν ἀπὸ τοῦ βωμοῦ τέφραν ἐκκομίζεσθαι συμβέβηκε. τὰ δ' αὐτὰ νομοθετεῖ καὶ περὶ παντὸς τοῦ ἔθνους ἁμαρ-
233 τόντος. εἰ δέ τις ἄρχων πλημμελήσειε, χιμάρῳ ποιεῖται τὴν κάθαρσιν, ὡς εἶπον, ἐὰν δὲ ἰδιώτης, χιμαίρᾳ ἢ ἀμνάδι· τῷ μὲν γὰρ ἄρρεν, τῷ δ' ἰδιώτῃ θῆλυ ζῷον ἀπένειμε, τὰ δ' ἄλλα διαταξάμενος ἐπ' ἀμφοῖν ὅμοια, χρίσαι τὰ κέρατα τοῦ ἐν ὑπαίθρῳ βωμοῦ τῷ αἵματι, στέαρ καὶ λοβὸν ἥπατος καὶ διττοὺς νεφροὺς ἀνενεγκεῖν, τὰ δ' ἄλλα τοῖς ἱερεῦσι

[1] MSS. προσφέρειν.

[a] See Lev. iv. 6-12.

almost amount to a plain statement from which we may learn that the true high priest who is not falsely so-called is immune from sin, and if ever he slips, it will be something imposed on him not because of what he does himself, but because of some lapse common to the nation. And that lapse is not incurable but admits easily of healing treatment. [a] So 231
when the calf has been slaughtered he bids the priest to sprinkle some of the blood with his finger seven times over against the veil at the inner shrine, beyond the first veil, at the place where the most sacred chattels have been set, and then anoint and smear the four horns of the altar of incense, corresponding to its four sides, and pour the rest of the blood at the foot of the altar in the open air. To this altar he 232
is commanded to bring three things, the fat and the lobe of the liver and the two kidneys, as in the ordinance of the preservation-offering. But the skin and the flesh and all the rest of the body of the calf from head to foot, with the inwards, are to be carried outside and burnt in a clear and open space[b] whither the holy ashes from the altar also are conveyed. The same rules are laid down by law in the case where the sin lies with the whole nation. But if a trespass is 233
committed by a ruler, he purges himself with a he-goat, as I have said; if by one of the common people, with a she-goat or a ewe-lamb. For he assigned the male animal to the ruler, the female to the commoner, while the other regulations which he made are similar for both persons, namely, that the horns of the open-air altar should be anointed with the blood, the fat and the lobe of the liver and the two kidneys offered at the altar and the rest given to the priests to eat.

[b] Or as E.V. "a clean place." See on § 268.

234 παρασχεῖν ἐδωδήν. XLIII. ἐπεὶ δὲ τῶν ἁμαρτημάτων τὰ μὲν εἰς ἀνθρώπους, τὰ δ' εἰς ἱερὰ καὶ ἅγια δρᾶται, περὶ μὲν τῶν εἰς ἀνθρώπους γινομένων ἀκουσίως διείλεκται, τὴν δ' ἐπὶ τοῖς ἱεροῖς κάθαρσιν[1] ἱλάσκεσθαι κριῷ νομοθετεῖ, πρότερον ἀποτίσαντας ἐκεῖνο περὶ ὃ γέγονεν ἡ πλημμέλεια, τὸ πέμπτον προσεπιτιθέντας τῆς ἀξίας τιμῆς.

235 Ταῦτα καὶ τὰ τούτοις ὅμοια νομοθετήσας ἐπὶ τοῖς ἀκουσίοις καὶ περὶ τῶν ἑκουσίων ἑξῆς διατάττεται. ἐάν τις, φησί, ψεύσηται περὶ κοινωνίας ἢ περὶ παρακαταθήκης ἢ ἁρπαγῆς ἢ εὑρέσεως ὧν ἀπώλεσεν ἕτερος καὶ ὑπονοηθείς, ὅρκου προταθέντος, ὀμόσῃ καὶ δόξας ἐκπεφευγέναι τὸν ἀπὸ τῶν κατηγόρων ἔλεγχον αὐτὸς ἑαυτοῦ γένηται κατήγορος, ἔνδον ὑπὸ τοῦ συνειδότος ἐλεγχθείς, καὶ κακίσῃ μὲν ἑαυτὸν ὧν ἠρνήσατο καὶ ἐπιώρκησεν, ὁμολογῶν δ' ἄντικρυς τὸ πραχθὲν ἀδίκημα συγγνώμην αἰτῆται,

236 κελεύει τῷ τοιούτῳ παρέχειν ἀμνηστίαν, ἐπαληθεύσαντι τὴν μετάνοιαν οὐχ ὑποσχέσει ἀλλ' ἔργοις, ἀποδόσει τῆς παρακαταθήκης καὶ ὧν ἥρπασεν ἢ εὗρεν ἢ συνόλως ἐσφετερίσατο τοῦ πλησίον, προσαποτίσας[2] καὶ τὸ ἐπίπεμπτον εἰς παρηγορίαν τοῦ

237 πλημμεληθέντος. ὅταν δὲ ἱλάσηται τὸν ἠδικημένον πρότερον, ἴτω, φησί, μετὰ ταῦτα καὶ εἰς τὸ ἱερὸν αἰτησόμενος ὧν ἐξήμαρτεν ἄφεσιν, ἐπαγόμενος

[1] A very strange expression, unless κάθαρσιν can be regarded as a sort of cognate accusative. Cohn suggests ἁμαρτίαι. Possibly ἀκαθαρσίαν.

[2] This ungrammatical nominative is either a slip or should be corrected to -σαντι.

---

[a] See Lev. v. 15, 16.

XLIII. [a]But since sins are sometimes committed 234
against men, sometimes against things sacred and holy, besides the regulations already stated for dealing with involuntary offences against men, he lays down that in the case of the holy things the purificatory propitiation should be made with a ram, the offenders having first made full compensation for the subject of the trespass with the addition of a fifth part of its proper value.

These and similar regulations for involuntary 235
offences are followed by his ordinances for such as are voluntary.[b] "If," he says, "a man lies about a partnership or a deposit or a robbery or as to finding the lost property of someone else, and, being suspected and put upon his oath, swears to the falsehood —if then after having apparently escaped conviction by his accusers he becomes, convicted inwardly by his conscience, his own accuser, reproaches himself for his disavowals and perjuries, makes a plain confession of the wrong he has committed and asks for
pardon—then the lawgiver orders that forgiveness be 236
extended to such a person on condition that he verifies his repentance not by a mere promise but by his actions, by restoring the deposit or the property which he has seized or found or in any way usurped from his neighbour, and further has paid an additional fifth
as a solatium for the offence. And when he has thus 237
propitiated the injured person he must follow it up, says the lawgiver, by proceeding to the temple to ask for remission of his sins, taking with him as his

[b] See Lev. vi. 2-7. Where, however, it is not suggested that the offender has made a voluntary confession, Philo as also Josephus, *Ant.* iii. 232, and indeed modern commentators, infers it from the probability that the convicted criminal would not get off so lightly.

παράκλητον οὐ μεμπτὸν τὸν κατὰ ψυχὴν ἔλεγχον, ὃς ἀνιάτου συμφορᾶς αὐτὸν ἐρρύσατο τὴν θανατοῦσαν[1] νόσον ἀνεὶς καὶ πρὸς ὑγείαν παντελῆ μεταβαλών.
238 κριὸν δ' εἶναι[2] καὶ τούτῳ διείρηται σφάγιον,
[248] καθὰ | καὶ τῷ πρὸς τὰ ἅγια πλημμελήσαντι· τὸ γὰρ ἐν τοῖς ἁγίοις ἀκούσιον ἁμάρτημα ἰσότιμον ἀπέφηνε τῷ περὶ τὰ ἀνθρώπινα ἑκουσίῳ, εἰ μὴ ἄρα καὶ τοῦτ' ἐστί τι ἅγιον, ἐπειδὴ προσγέγονεν ὅρκος, ὃν οὐκ ἐφ' ὑγιεῖ γενόμενον ἐπηνωρθώσατο τροπῇ τῇ πρὸς τὸ βέλτιον.

239 Παρατηρητέον δ' ὅτι τὰ μὲν ἐπιφερόμενα τῷ βωμῷ ἐκ τοῦ περὶ ἁμαρτίας ἱερείου ταὐτά ἐστιν ἃ καὶ ἐπὶ τῆς τοῦ σωτηρίου θυσίας, λοβὸς ἥπατος καὶ στέαρ καὶ νεφροί· τρόπον γάρ τινα καὶ ὁ μετανοῶν σῴζεται, τὴν χαλεπωτέραν τῶν ἐν τῷ σώματι
240 παθῶν νόσον ψυχῆς ἐκτρεπόμενος. τὰ δ' ἄλλα μέρη τοῦ ζῴου πρὸς ἐδωδὴν ἀπονέμεται διαφερόντως. ἐν τρισὶ δ' ἡ διαφορά· τόπῳ, χρόνῳ, τοῖς λαμβάνουσι· τόπος μὲν οὖν τὸ ἱερόν, χρόνος δὲ ἀντὶ δυεῖν ἡμερῶν μία, οἱ δὲ μεταλαμβάνοντες ἱερεῖς,
241 ἀλλ' οὐχ ὧν ἐστιν ἡ θυσία, καὶ ἱερέων ἄρσενες. ἔξω μὲν οὖν οὐκ ἐᾷ τοῦ ἱεροῦ προφέρειν βουλόμενος, εἴ τι τῷ μετανοοῦντι πρότερον ἡμάρτηται, μὴ περίφημον εἶναι βασκάνων καὶ φιλαπεχθημόνων γνώμαις ἀγνώμοσι καὶ στόμασιν ἀχαλίνοις, ἐπ' ὀνείδει καὶ

[1] So Cohn for MS. θανατῶσαν or θανατώσασαν. See note on *Spec. Leg.* iii. 102 (App.).

[2] MSS.: so Cohn: κριὸν δεῖν R ("ut videtur" adds Cohn), κριὸν ἀναγαγεῖν F: κριὸν δ' ἄγειν κελεύει, καὶ τοῦτο A.H.

[a] See Lev. vi. 25, 26, 29. But there is no order there that it should be eaten in one day. (So also Jos. *Ant.* iii. 232 αὐθημερόν.)

irreproachable advocate the soul-felt conviction which has saved him from a fatal disaster, allayed a deadly disease, and brought him round to complete health. For him, too, the sacrifice prescribed is a ram, as also for the offender in sacred matters. For the lawgiver
rated the involuntary sin in the sacred sphere as equal 238
to voluntary sin in the human, though indeed this last also is perhaps a desecration, since it is supplemented by an oath sworn under dishonest conditions, though rectified by the man's conversion to the better course.

It must be noticed, however, that while the parts
of the sin-offering laid upon the altar are the same 239
as in the case of the preservation-offering, namely the lobe of the liver, the fat and the kidneys—a natural arrangement because the penitent also is preserved or saved by escape from the soul-sickness which is
more grievous than any which affects the body—the 240
conditions under which the other parts of the animal are appointed to serve for food are different. The difference is threefold, in the place, in the time and in the recipients.[a] The place is the temple, the time one day instead of two, and the participants are priests, not those who offer the sacrifices : also they are male
priests.[b] The prohibition against carrying the flesh 241
outside the temple is due to his wish that any sin which the penitent has previously committed should not be made notorious through the ill-judged judgements and unbridled tongues of malicious and acrimonious persons, and blazed abroad as a subject for

[b] This seems to me to indicate that Philo rightly or wrongly takes "every male among the priests," to mean that apart from this prohibition the women of the priestly clan would be entitled to eat it. In § 110 he has called them "priestesses."

διαβολαῖς ἐκδεδομένον, ἀλλ᾿ ἐντὸς ὅρων ἱερῶν, ἐν
242 οἷς καὶ ἡ κάθαρσις γέγονεν, εἶναι. XLIV. τοῖς δ᾿
ἱερεῦσιν εὐωχεῖσθαι τὴν θυσίαν κελεύει διὰ πολλά· πρῶτον[1] μὲν ἵνα τιμήσῃ τοὺς τεθυκότας, ἡ γὰρ τῶν ἑστιωμένων ἀξίωσις ἐπικοσμεῖ τοὺς ἑστιάτορας· δεύτερον δὲ ἵνα βεβαιότατα πιστεύσωσιν, ὅτι οἷς ἁμαρτημάτων εἰσέρχεται μεταμέλεια ἵλεω τὸν θεὸν ἔχουσιν· οὐ γὰρ ἂν τοὺς προσπόλους αὐτοῦ καὶ θεράποντας ἐπὶ μετουσίαν τῆς τοιαύτης τραπέζης ἐκάλεσεν, εἰ μὴ παντελὴς ἐγεγένητο ἀμνηστία· τρίτον δ᾿ ὅτι λειτουργεῖν οὐδενὶ τῶν ἱερέων ἔξεστιν, ὃς ἂν μὴ ὁλόκληρος ᾖ· καὶ γὰρ τῷ βραχυτάτῳ
243 μώμῳ σκορακίζεται. παρηγορεῖ δὴ τοὺς μηκέτι
τὴν τῶν ἀδικημάτων ὁδὸν ἰόντας ὡς ἱερατικοῦ γένους ἕνεκα προαιρέσεως καθαρᾶς μεταλαχόντας καὶ πρὸς ἱερέων ἰσοτιμίαν ἐπαχθέντας. ὅθεν καὶ μιᾷ ἡμέρᾳ τὸ περὶ ἁμαρτίας ἱερεῖον ἀναλίσκεται, ὡς δέον ὑπερτίθεσθαι μὲν τὸ ἁμαρτάνειν μέλλοντας ἀεὶ πρὸς αὐτὸ καὶ βραδύνοντας, πρὸς δὲ τὸ κατορθοῦν
244 ἐπεσπευσμένῳ τάχει χρῆσθαι. τὰ δ᾿
ὑπὲρ τοῦ ἀρχιερέως ἢ τοῦ ἔθνους ἕνεκα πλημμελείας σφαγιαζόμενα πρὸς μὲν ἐδωδὴν οὐ σκευάζεται, κατακαίεται δ᾿ ἐπὶ τῆς ἱερᾶς τέφρας, ὡς ἐλέχθη· κρείττων γὰρ οὐδεὶς ἀρχιερέως ἢ τοῦ ἔθνους ἐστίν, ὃς ἁμαρτησάντων γενήσεται παρ-
245 αιτητής. εἰκότως οὖν ἀναλίσκεται τὰ κρέα πυρί,

[1] MSS. πρότερον.

[a] The point presumably is that the exclusion of the priests who suffer from defects and therefore cannot have taken part

contumelious and censorious talk, but be confined
within the sacred precincts which have also been the
scene of the purification. XLIV. The command that 242
the sacrifice should serve as a feast for the priests is
due to several reasons. First, to do honour to the
givers of the sacrifice, for the dignity of the guests reflects glory on their entertainers ; secondly, to secure
them firmly in the belief that the graciousness of God
extends to those who feel remorse for their sin. For
He would never have called His servitors and ministers
to share the hospitality of such a table if full pardon
had not been given. Thirdly, because none of the
priests is permitted to perform the rites if he is not
wholly sound, for the slightest blemish causes him to
be thrust from office.[a] In fact he encourages those 243
who no longer tread the path of wrongdoing with the
thought that their resolution to purify themselves
has given them a place in the sacerdotal caste and
advanced them to equal honour with the priest. For
a similar reason the flesh of the sin-offering is consumed in a single day, showing that in sin we should
procrastinate and be slow and dilatory in approaching
it, but when the achievement of righteousness is our
goal, act with speed and promptitude.
The victims immolated in behalf of the high priest 244
or the nation as atonement for trespassing are not
dressed to serve as food but are consumed by fire on
the sacred ashes, as I have said. [b]For there is no one
superior to the high priest or the nation to act as
intercessor for the sinners. It is natural therefore 245
that the flesh should be consumed by fire in imitation

in the sacrifice enhances the honour of the providers of the feast. But see App. p. 621.

[b] *i.e.* in § 232.

κατὰ μίμησιν τῶν ὁλοκαυτουμένων, ἐπὶ τιμῇ τῶν προσώπων, οὐχ ὅτι πρὸς ἀξίωσιν αἱ ἱεραὶ γίνονται κρίσεις, ἀλλ' ὅτι τῶν τὰς ἀρετὰς μεγάλων καὶ ὡς ἀληθῶς ἁγίων ἁμαρτήματα τοιαῦτά ἐστιν, ὡς
246 ἑτέρων κατορθώματα νομίζεσθαι. καθάπερ γὰρ ἡ
[249] βαθεῖα καὶ | ἀρετῶσα πεδιάς, κἂν ἀφορήσῃ ποτέ, τῆς λυπρόγεω φύσει καρπὸν φέρει πλείονα, τὸν αὐτὸν τρόπον καὶ τῶν σπουδαίων καὶ φιλοθέων συμβαίνει τὰς πρὸς καλοκἀγαθίαν ἀφορίας ἀμείνους εἶναι ὧν ἐκ τύχης οἱ φαῦλοι κατορθοῦσι· γνώμῃ γὰρ οὐδὲν ὑγιὲς δρᾶν ὑπομένουσι.

247 XLV. Ταῦτα διαταξάμενος περὶ ἑκάστης ἰδέας τῶν θυσιῶν ἐν μέρει, τῆς τε ὁλοκαύτου καὶ σωτηρίου καὶ περὶ ἁμαρτίας, ἄλλην προσνομοθετεῖ κοινὴν τῶν τριῶν, ἵνα ταύτας ἐπιδείξῃ φίλας καὶ συγγενεῖς οὔσας· ἡ δὲ συναγωγὸς αὐτῶν εὐχὴ μεγάλη κα-
248 λεῖται. διὰ τί δὲ ταύτης ἔτυχε τῆς προσρήσεως, λεκτέον· ὅταν ἀπάρξωνταί τινες ἀπὸ παντὸς μέρους κτήσεως, πυρούς, κριθάς, ἔλαιον, οἶνον, τὰ κάλλιστα τῶν ἀκροδρύων, ἔπειτα τῶν ζῴων τὰ πρωτότοκα ἀρρενικά, τὰ μὲν ἐκ τῶν καθαρῶν καθιερώσαντες, τὰ δ' ἐκ τῶν μὴ καθαρῶν κατ' ἀξίαν τιμησάμενοι, μηκέτ' ἔχοντες ὕλας, ἐν αἷς διαθήσονται τὴν εὐσέβειαν, αὑτοὺς ἀνατιθέασι καὶ καθιεροῦσιν, ἄλεκτον ἐπιδεικνύμενοι ὁσιότητα καὶ ὑπερβολήν τινα γνώμης φιλοθέου. διὸ καὶ μεγάλη

---

[a] Such actions would hardly be *κατορθώματα* in the strict Stoic sense. See note on *Quod Deus* 100.

[b] See Num. vi. 1-12. The "Great Vow" is the name regularly applied to the vow of the Nazirite from *v.* 2, ὃς ἂν

of the whole-burnt-offerings to do honour to the persons concerned, not because God's holy judgements are given by considerations of position but because the sins of the greatly virtuous and the truly sacred are such as to be regarded as acts of righteousness if done by others. For as the fields where the 246
soil is deep and rich, even if they are sometimes unproductive, bear more fruit than those where it is naturally thin and poor, so too we find in virtuous and God-loving persons that their unproductiveness of positive goodness is better than the fortuitous righteous actions[a] of the bad whose nature does not allow them ever to act intentionally in an honest way.

XLV. After laying down these ordinances about 247
each particular kind of sacrifice, whole-burnt-offering, preservation-offering and sin-offering, he institutes rules for another which partakes of the three, to shew the friendship and kinship which exists between them. This connecting link between them is called the Great
Vow.[b] I must explain why it has acquired this name. 248
When people have paid first-fruits of every part of their property, in wheat, barley, oil, wine and their finest orchard-fruits and also in the first-born males of their livestock, consecrated in the case of the clean species and valued at an adequate compensation in the case of the unclean, as they have no more material resources with which to give a pledge of their piety, they dedicate and consecrate themselves, thus shewing an amazing sanctification and a surpassing devotion to God. And therefore it is fitly called the Great Vow,

μεγάλως εὔξηται εὐχὴν ἀφαγνίσασθαι ἁγνείαν (E.V. "made a special vow, the vow of a Nazirite, to separate himself"). The allegorical meaning, as Philo understood it, has been given on special details in several places, and more fully in *Quod Deus* 87 ff.

προσηκόντως εὐχὴ καλεῖται· κτημάτων γὰρ τὸ
μέγιστον αὐτός τίς ἐστιν αὐτῷ· οὗ παραχωρεῖ καὶ
249 ἐξίσταται. ποιησαμένῳ δὲ τὴν εὐχὴν τάδε διαγο-
ρεύει· πρῶτον μὲν ἄκρατον μὴ προσφέρεσθαι μηδ'
" ὅσα ἐκ σταφυλῆς κατεργάζεται " μηδ' ἄλλο τι
μέθυσμα πίνειν ἐπὶ καθαιρέσει λογισμοῦ, νομίζοντα
τὸν χρόνον ἐκεῖνον ἱερᾶσθαι· καὶ γὰρ τοῖς λει-
τουργοῖς τῶν ἱερέων δίψαν ἀκουμένοις ὕδατι τὰ
250 περὶ μέθην ἀπείρηται· δεύτερον δὲ τὰς τρίχας τῆς
κεφαλῆς μὴ ἀποκείρεσθαι, σύμβολον ἐναργὲς τοῖς
ὁρῶσι παρέχοντα[1] τοῦ μὴ παρακόπτειν τὸ νόμισμα
τῆς εὐχῆς· τρίτον δὲ τὸ σῶμα φυλάττειν καθαρὸν
καὶ ἀμίαντον, ὡς μὴ γονεῦσιν ἐπεισιέναι τετελευ-
τηκόσι μηδ' ἀδελφοῖς, τὴν φυσικὴν εὔνοιαν καὶ
συμπάθειαν πρὸς τὰ οἰκεῖα καὶ φίλτατα νικώσης
εὐσεβείας, ἣν ἀεὶ νικᾶν καλὸν ὁμοῦ καὶ συμφέρον.
251 XLVI. ἡκούσης δὲ τῆς προθεσμίας,
τρία ζῷα κελεύει προσάγειν ἐπὶ λύσει τῆς εὐχῆς,
ἄρνα καὶ ἀμνάδα καὶ κριόν, τὸν μὲν εἰς ὁλοκαύ-
τωσιν, τὴν δὲ περὶ ἁμαρτίας, τὸν δὲ κριὸν εἰς θυσίαν
252 τοῦ σωτηρίου. πᾶσι γὰρ τούτοις ἐμφέρεταί[2] πως ὁ
εὐξάμενος, τῇ μὲν ὁλοκαύτῳ θυσίᾳ διὰ τὸ μὴ τῶν
ἄλλων μόνον ἀπαρχῶν ἀλλὰ καὶ ἑαυτοῦ παρα-
χωρεῖν, τῇ δὲ περὶ ἁμαρτίας διὰ τὸ ἄνθρωπος εἶναι
—καὶ γὰρ ὁ τέλειος ᾗ γενητὸς οὐκ ἐκφεύγει τὸ
διαμαρτάνειν—, τῇ δὲ τοῦ σωτηρίου, διότι τὸν
σωτῆρα ὄντως θεὸν ἐπιγέγραπται τῆς σωτηρίας

[1] MSS. παρέχοντας.

[2] If this reading is right, we may suppose that the verb takes the meaning of the common adjective ἐμφερής = " like," but I do not know of any parallel. The other reading συμφέρεται, *i.e.* " corresponds with," has less MS. authority, but seems otherwise more suitable.

for his own self is the greatest possession which anyone has, and this self he forgoes and puts himself outside it. When he has made the vow, the lawgiver 249
gives him the following instructions. First, he must not take any strong drink nor anything " which he makes from the grape " nor drink any other intoxicant to the overthrow of his reason, but hold himself to be serving as priest during that time. For indeed such priests as are performing the rites have to quench their thirst with water and are forbidden intoxicants.
Secondly, he must not shave the hairs of his head, thus 250
giving a clear symbol to the eye that he does not debase the sterling coinage of his vow. Thirdly, he must keep his body pure and undefiled to the extent of abstaining from contact with parents or brothers after death, thus letting his kindly affection and fellow-feeling with the closest and dearest yield to piety that victory which it is both honourable and profitable that it should always win.

[a] XLVI. When the final day as appointed has come, 251
the law bids him bring, to release him from his vow, three animals, a he-lamb, a ewe-lamb and a ram, the first for a whole-burnt-offering, the ewe-lamb as a sin-offering, and the ram as a preservation-offering.
For all these find their likeness in the maker of the vow: 252
the whole-burnt-offering, because he surrenders not only the other first-fruits and gifts but also his own self; the sin-offering, because he is a man, since even the perfect man, in so far as he is a created being, never escapes from sinning; the preservation-offering, because he has acknowledged and adopted the real preserver, God, as the author of his preservation

[a] See Num. vi. 13 f.

αἴτιον, ἀλλ᾽ οὐκ ἰατροὺς καὶ τὰς παρ᾽ αὐτοῖς
[250] δυνάμεις· οἱ | μὲν γὰρ ἐπίκηροι καὶ θνητοὶ μηδ᾽ αὑτοῖς ὑγείαν ἱκανοὶ παρασχεῖν, αἱ δ᾽ οὔτε πάντας οὔτ᾽ ἀεὶ τοὺς αὐτοὺς ὠφελοῦσιν, ἀλλ᾽ ἔστιν ὅτε καὶ μέγα βλάπτουσιν, ἐπειδὴ τὸ κῦρος ἕτερος ἀνῆπται καὶ τῶν δυνάμεων καὶ τῶν χρωμένων αὐταῖς.

253 ἐκπλήττει δέ με τὸ τῶν τριῶν ζῴων προσαγομένων εἰς διαφερούσας θυσίας μηδὲν εἶναι ἑτερογενές, ἀλλὰ ταὐτοῦ γένους τὰ πάντα, κριὸν καὶ ἄρνα καὶ ἀμνάδα· βούλεται γάρ, ὅπερ ἔφην μικρῷ πρότερον, διὰ τούτου παραστῆσαι, ὅτι ἀδελφαὶ καὶ συγγενεῖς εἰσιν αἱ τρεῖς ἰδέαι τῶν θυσιῶν, τῷ καὶ τὸν μετανοοῦντα σῴζεσθαι καὶ τὸν σῳζόμενον ἐκ τῶν ψυχικῶν ἀρρωστημάτων μετανοεῖν καὶ ἑκάτερον σπεύδειν πρὸς ὁλόκληρον καὶ παντελῆ διάθεσιν, ἧς ἡ ὁλόκαυτος θυσία σύμβολον.

254 ἐπεὶ δ᾽ αὐτὸν ηὔξατο προσαγαγεῖν, τὸν δ᾽ ἱερὸν βωμὸν οὐ θέμις αἵματι ἀνθρωπίνῳ μιαίνεσθαι, ἔδει δέ τι πάντως μέρος ἱερουργηθῆναι, μέρος ἐσπούδασε λαβεῖν, ὅπερ ἀφαιρεθὲν οὔτ᾽ ἀλγηδόνας οὔτε λώβην ἀπεργάζεται· τοῦ γὰρ κατὰ τὸ σῶμα φυτικοῦ καθάπερ δένδρου περιττοὺς κλάδους τὰς τῆς κεφαλῆς τρίχας ἀπέκειρε καὶ παρέδωκε πυρί, ᾧ τὰ κρέα τῆς τοῦ σωτηρίου θυσίας ἕψεται· προσηκόντως, ἵνα τι τῶν τοῦ εὐξαμένου μέρος, ὃ μὴ

[a] Lit. "the part of the body which has 'growth' like a tree," *φύσις* in this special sense being opposed on the one hand to *ἕξις* ("cohesion") as in stones, and on the other to *ψυχή* ("life").

instead of the physicians and their faculties of healing For the physicians are mortals ready to perish, unable to secure health even for themselves, and their faculties are not beneficial to all persons nor always to the same persons, but sometimes do great harm: there is Another who is invested with lordship over such faculties and those who exercise them.

I note, and it is a very striking point, that in the three 253
animals brought for the different sacrifices there is no difference of species. They are all of the same species, a ram, a he-lamb and a ewe-lamb. For the law wishes to show in this way what I mentioned a little before, that the three kinds of sacrifice are sisters of one family, because the penitent is preserved and the person preserved from the maladies of his soul repents, and both of them are pressing forward to that perfect and wholly sound frame of mind of which the whole-burnt-offering is a symbol.

Another point—the votary has vowed to bring him- 254
self, and while it would be sacrilege that the altar should be defiled by human blood, it was quite necessary that some part of him should be sacrificially offered. The part, therefore, which his zeal prompted him to take was one which can be removed without causing either pain or mutilation. He cut off the hairs of his head, which are to the body like the superfluous branches in the vegetation of a tree,[a] and gave them to the fire in which the flesh of the preservation-offering is cooked, a fitting proceeding to secure that at least some part of the votary's self which cannot be

[a] *Cf. Leg. All.* ii. 22, with note giving references to *S.V.F.* ii. 457-460. There we had δύναμις ἑκτική, φυτική, ψυχική, and Philo goes on to say that our bones have ἕξις, and our nails and hair φύσις. *Cf.* also the fuller explanation of the terms in *Quod Deus* 35 ff.

ἐπιφέρειν ἔξεστι τῷ βωμῷ, θυσίας γοῦν εἴδει συνανακραθῇ, γενόμενον ὕλη φλογὸς ἱερᾶς.

255 XLVII. Ταῦτα μὲν κοινὰ τῶν ἄλλων. ἔδει δὲ καὶ τοὺς ἱερεῖς ἀπάρξασθαί τι τῷ βωμῷ, μὴ νομίσαντας ἀσυλίαν εὑρῆσθαι τὰς ὑπηρεσίας καὶ λειτουργίας ἐφ' ὧν ἐτάχθησαν. ἡ δ' ἀπαρχὴ πρέπουσα ἱερεῦσιν ἀπ' οὐδενὸς τῶν ἐναίμων, ἀλλ' ἀπὸ
256 τοῦ καθαρωτάτου τῆς ἀνθρωπίνης τροφῆς· σεμίδαλις γάρ ἐστιν ἡ ἐνδελεχὴς αὐτῶν θυσία, μέτρου ἱεροῦ τὸ δέκατον καθ' ἑκάστην ἡμέραν, οὗ τὸ μὲν ἥμισυ πρωΐας, τὸ δὲ ἥμισυ δείλης προσάγεται, ταγηνισθὲν ἐν ἐλαίῳ, μηδενὸς εἰς βρῶσιν ὑπολειφθέντος· χρησμὸς γάρ ἐστι, πᾶσαν θυσίαν ἱερέως ὁλόκαυτον εἶναι καὶ μηδὲν αὐτῆς εἰς ἐδωδὴν ἀπονέμεσθαι.

Εἰρηκότες οὖν, ὡς οἷόν τε ἦν, τὰ περὶ θυσιῶν ἑξῆς καὶ περὶ τῶν θυόντων λέξομεν.

[251]
257 XLVIII. | [1] Βούλεται τὸν ἀνάγοντα θυσίας ὁ νόμος καθαρὸν εἶναι σῶμα καὶ ψυχήν, ψυχὴν μὲν ἀπό τε τῶν παθῶν καὶ νοσημάτων καὶ ἀρρωστημάτων καὶ κακιῶν τῶν ἔν τε λόγοις καὶ πράξεσι,
258 τὸ δὲ σῶμα ἀφ' ὧν ἔθος αὐτῷ μιαίνεσθαι. κάθαρσιν δ' ἐπενόησεν ἑκατέρῳ τὴν προσήκουσαν, ψυχῇ μὲν διὰ τῶν πρὸς τὰς θυσίας εὐτρεπιζομένων ζῴων, σώματι δὲ διὰ λουτρῶν καὶ περιρραντηρίων, περὶ ὧν μικρὸν ὕστερον ἐροῦμεν· ἄξιον γὰρ τῷ κρείττονι καὶ ἡγεμονικωτέρῳ τῶν ἐν ἡμῖν, ψυχῇ, καὶ τὰ τῶν

[1] Here the mss. insert the heading Περὶ τῶν θυόντων.

---

[a] The Greek phrase is vague. Heinemann "mit einem Stück des Opfers sich vermischte"; Mangey only "sacrificia admiscentur." I understand it to mean that it comes to belong to the same εἶδος or species as an ordinary sacrifice.

lawfully brought to the altar should be merged in and share the nature of sacrifice [a] by serving as fuel to a holy flame.

XLVII. These rules apply to the laity in common, 255
but the priests also had to make offerings of first-fruits to the altar, and not suppose that the services and ministrations to which they were appointed entitled them to immunity. [b] The first-fruits suitable for the priest are not taken from any animal with blood in its veins, but from the purest form of human food. Fine flour constitutes their perpetual 256
sacrifice, a tenth part of the sacred measure for every day, half offered in the morning and half in the evening. It is fried in oil and none of it is left over to be eaten. For it is a divine command that every sacrifice offered by a priest should be wholly consumed by fire and none of it set apart for food.

We have described to the best of our ability the regulations for sacrifices and will next proceed to speak of those who offer them.

XLVIII. [c] The law would have such a person pure 257
in body and soul, the soul purged of its passions and distempers and infirmities and every viciousness of word and deed, the body of the defilements which commonly beset it. For each it devised the purifica- 258
tion which befitted it. For the soul it used the animals which the worshipper is providing [d] for sacrifice, for the body sprinklings and ablutions of which we will speak a little later. For precedence in speech as well as elsewhere must be given to the higher and

[b] See Lev. vi. 20-22. For "perpetual" see on § 170.

[c] Heading in MSS. "Of those who sacrifice," and fresh numeration of chapters in Cohn.

[d] The stress is on *εὐτρεπιζομένων*. The fact of his providing the victims shews the purity of his motives.

259 λόγων ἀπονεῖμαι πρεσβεῖα. τίς οὖν ἡ ταύτης
κάθαρσις; ἴδε, φησίν, ὦ οὗτος, ὃ προσάγεις
ἱερεῖον, ὡς ἔστιν ὁλόκληρον καὶ παντελῶς μώμων
ἀμέτοχον, ἐπικριθὲν ἐκ πολλῶν ἀριστίνδην διανοίαις
μὲν ἀδεκάστοις ἱερέων ὀξυωπεστάταις δ' αὐτῶν
ὄψεσι καὶ τῷ συνεχεῖ τῆς ἀσκήσεως συγκεκροτη-
μέναις εἰς ἀνυπαίτιον ἐπίσκεψιν· ἐὰν γὰρ μὴ τοῖς
ὀφθαλμοῖς μᾶλλον ἢ τῷ λογισμῷ τοῦτο κατίδῃς,
ἐκνίψῃ τὰ ἁμαρτήματα καὶ ὅσας ἐν ἅπαντι τῷ βίῳ
κηλῖδας ἀπεμάξω,[1] τὰ μὲν ἀβουλήτοις συντυχίαις,
260 τὰ δὲ καθ' ἑκούσιον γνώμην. εὑρήσεις γὰρ τὴν
τοσαύτην περὶ τὸ ζῷον ἀκριβολογίαν αἰνιττομένην
διὰ συμβόλου τὴν τῶν σῶν βελτίωσιν ἠθῶν· οὐ γὰρ
ὑπὲρ ἀλόγων ὁ νόμος, ἀλλ' ὑπὲρ τῶν νοῦν καὶ λόγον
ἐχόντων, ὥστε οὐ τῶν θυομένων φροντίς ἐστιν, ἵνα
μηδεμίαν ἔχῃ λώβην, ἀλλὰ τῶν θυόντων, ἵνα περὶ
261 μηδὲν πάθος κηραίνωσι. τό γε μὴν σῶμα,
ὡς εἶπον, λουτροῖς καὶ περιρραντηρίοις καθαίρει
καὶ οὐκ ἐᾷ περιρρανάμενον εἰς ἅπαξ ἢ ἀπολουσά-
μενον εὐθὺς εἴσω περιβόλων ἱερῶν παρέρχεσθαι,
ἀλλὰ ἑπτὰ ἡμέρας ἔξω διατρίβειν κελεύει καὶ δὶς
περιρραίνεσθαι τῇ τρίτῃ καὶ ἑβδόμῃ καὶ μετὰ
ταῦτα λουσαμένῳ παρέχει τάς τε εἰσόδους καὶ τὰς
262 ἱερουργίας ἀδεεῖς. XLIX. | ὅσον δὲ κἂν τούτῳ
[252] τὸ προμηθὲς καὶ φιλόσοφον, ἐπισκεπτέον. οἱ
μὲν ἄλλοι σχεδὸν ἅπαντες ἀμιγεῖ ὕδατι περιρραί-
νονται, θαλάττῃ μὲν οἱ πολλοί, τινὲς δὲ ποταμοῖς,
οἱ δὲ καὶ κάλπεσιν ἐκ πηγῶν ἀρυόμενοι· Μωυσῆς δε
τέφραν προετοιμασάμενος ὑπολειφθεῖσαν ἐξ ἱεροῦ

[1] MSS. ἀνεμάξω.

---

[a] See Num. xix. 11 f. [b] See Num. xix. 17, 18.

more dominant element in ourselves, the soul. How 259
then is the soul purified? "Note, friend," says the lawgiver, "how perfect and utterly free from blemish is the victim which you bring selected as the best of many by the priests with all impartiality of mind and clearness of vision, the result of the continued practice which has trained them to faultless discrimination. For if you observe this with your reason rather than with your eyes you will proceed to wash away the sins and defilements with which you have besmeared your whole life, some involuntary and accidental, some due to your own free will. For 260
you will find that all this careful scrutiny of the animal is a symbol representing in a figure the reformation of your own conduct, for the law does not prescribe for unreasoning creatures, but for those who have mind and reason. It is anxious not that the victims should be without flaw but that those who offer them should not suffer from any corroding passion. [a] As for the body, it purifies it 261
with ablutions and sprinklings and does not allow the person to be sprinkled and washed once for all and then pass straightway within the sacred precincts, but bids him stay outside for seven days and be twice sprinkled on the third and seventh day, and after that, when he has bathed himself, it gives him full security to come within and offer his sacrifice.
XLIX. The following regulation also shews a far- 262
sighted wisdom which should be noted. In almost all other cases men used unmixed water for the sprinkling. By most people it is taken from the sea, by others from the rivers, and by others it is drawn in ewers from the wells.[b] But Moses first provided ashes, the remnants of the sacred fire, obtained in a

πυρὸς—ὃν δὲ τρόπον, αὐτίκα δηλωθήσεται—ἀπὸ ταύτης φησὶ δεῖν ἀναιρεῖσθαι καὶ ἐμβάλλοντας εἰς ἀγγεῖον αὖθις ὕδωρ ἐπιφέρειν, εἶτα ἐκ τοῦ κράματος βάπτοντας ὑσσώπου κλάδους τοῖς καθαιρομένοις
263 ἐπιρραίνειν. αἰτία δ᾿ οὐκ ἀπὸ σκοποῦ λέγοιτ᾿ ἂν ἥδε· βούλεται τοὺς ἐπὶ τὴν τοῦ ὄντος θεραπείαν ἰόντας γνῶναι πρότερον ἑαυτοὺς καὶ τὴν ἰδίαν οὐσίαν· ὁ γὰρ ἀνεπιστήμων ἑαυτοῦ πῶς ἂν δυνηθείη καταλαβεῖν τὴν ἀνωτάτω καὶ πάνθ᾿ ὑπερβάλλουσαν
264 θεοῦ δύναμιν; ἔστιν οὖν ἡμῶν ἡ κατὰ τὸ σῶμα οὐσία, γῆ καὶ ὕδωρ, ἧς ὑπομιμνήσκει διὰ τῆς καθάρσεως, αὐτὸ τοῦθ᾿ ὑπολαμβάνων εἶναι τὴν ὠφελιμωτάτην κάθαρσιν, τὸ γνῶναί τινα ἑαυτὸν καὶ ἐξ οἵων ὡς οὐδεμιᾶς σπουδῆς ἀξίων, τέφρας καὶ
265 ὕδατος, συνεκράθη. τοῦτο γὰρ ἐπιγνοὺς τὴν ἐπίβουλον οἴησιν εὐθὺς ἀποστραφήσεται καὶ καθελὼν τὸ ὑπέραυχον εὐαρεστήσει θεῷ καὶ μεταποιήσεται τῆς ἵλεω δυνάμεως αὐτοῦ ⟨τοῦ⟩ μισοῦντος ἀλαζονείαν. εἴρηται γάρ που καλῶς, ὅτι ὁ ἐγχειρῶν ὑπεραύχοις ἢ λόγοις ἢ ἔργοις οὐκ ἀνθρώπους μόνον ἀλλὰ καὶ "θεὸν παροξύνει" τὸν ἰσότητος καὶ
266 παντὸς τοῦ ἀρίστου δημιουργόν. ἐν οὖν τῷ περιρραίνεσθαι πληττομένοις καὶ διεγειρομένοις μόνον οὐκ ἄντικρυς αὐτὰ τὰ στοιχεῖα, γῆ καὶ ὕδωρ, φωνὴν ἀφιέντα φησίν· ἡμεῖς ἐσμεν ἡ τοῦ σώματος ὑμῶν οὐσία, ἡμᾶς ἡ φύσις κερασαμένη θείᾳ τέχνῃ διέπλασεν εἰς ἀνθρωπόμορφον ἰδέαν, ἐξ ἡμῶν παγέντες, ὅτε ἐγένεσθε, πάλιν εἰς ἡμᾶς ἀναλυθήσεσθε, ὅταν δέῃ θνῄσκειν· οὐδὲν γὰρ εἰς τὸ

---

[a] See Num. xv. 30 καὶ ψυχὴ ἥτις ποιήσῃ ἐν χειρὶ ὑπερηφανίας . . τὸν θεὸν οὗτος παροξυνεῖ (LXX).

manner which will be explained shortly. Some of these, he says, are to be taken and thrown into a vessel and afterwards have water poured upon them. Then the priests are to dip branches of hyssop in the mixture and sprinkle with it those who are being
purged. The reason for this may be aptly stated as 263
follows. Moses would have those who come to serve Him that IS first know themselves and of what substance these selves are made. For how should he who has no knowledge of himself be able to apprehend the power of God which is above all and trans-
cends all? Now the substance of which our body 264
consists is earth and water, and of this he reminds us in the rite of purging. For he holds that the most profitable form of purification is just this, that a man should know himself and the nature of the elements of which he is composed, ashes and water, so little
worthy of esteem. For if he recognizes this, he will 265
straightway turn away from the insidious enemy, self-conceit, and abasing his pride become well-pleasing to God and claim the aid of His gracious power Who hates arrogance. For that is a good text[a] which tells us that he who sets his hand to words and deeds of pride "provokes" not only men, but also "God," the
author of equality and all that is most excellent. So 266
then, whilst they are being thus sprinkled, deeply moved and roused as they are, they can almost hear the voice of the elements themselves, earth and water, say plainly to them, "We are the substance of which your body consists: we it is whom nature blended and with divine craftsmanship made into the shape of human form. Out of us you were framed when you came into being and into us you will be resolved again when you have to die. For nothing is so made

μὴ ὂν φθείρεσθαι πέφυκεν, ἀλλ᾿ ἐξ ὧν ἡ ἀρχή, πρὸς ταῦτα καὶ τὸ τέλος.

267 L. Ἤδη δ᾿ ἀναγκαῖον καὶ τὴν ὑπόσχεσιν ἀποδοῦναι τῆς περὶ τὴν τέφραν ταύτην ἰδιότητος· ἔστι γὰρ οὐ ξύλων αὐτὸ μόνον δαπανηθέντων ὑπὸ πυρός, ἀλλὰ καὶ ζῴου πρὸς τὴν τοιαύτην κάθαρσιν ἐπι-
268 τηδείου. κελεύει γὰρ δάμαλιν πυρρὰν ἄζυγον ἄμωμον ἀχθεῖσαν σφαγιασθῆναι μὲν ἔξω πόλεως, τὸν δ᾿ ἀρχιερέα λαμβάνοντα ἀπὸ τοῦ αἵματος ἑπτάκις ἐπιρραίνειν ἀντικρὺ τοῦ νεὼ πάντα, εἶθ᾿ ὅλην κατακαίειν σὺν δορᾷ καὶ κρέασι καὶ αἵματι καὶ πλήρει τῇ κοιλίᾳ περιττωμάτων· ἤδη δ᾿ ὑπο-
[253] μαραινομένης τῆς φλογὸς εἰς τὸ μεσαίτατον | τρία ταῦτα ἐμβάλλειν, ξύλον κέδρινον καὶ ὕσσωπον καὶ κόκκινον, κελεύει, εἶτ᾿ ἐὰν ἀποσβεσθῇ, τὴν τέφραν συλλέγειν καθαρὸν ἄνθρωπον καὶ ἀποτιθέναι πάλιν
269 ἔξω πόλεως ἐν χωρίῳ καθαρῷ. τίνα δὲ διὰ τούτων ὡς διὰ συμβόλων αἰνίττεται, δι᾿ ἑτέρων ἠκριβώσαμεν ἀλληγοροῦντες. ἀναγκαῖον οὖν τοὺς μέλλοντας φοιτᾶν εἰς τὸ ἱερὸν ἐπὶ μετουσίᾳ θυσίας τό τε σῶμα φαιδρύνεσθαι καὶ τὴν ψυχὴν πρὸ τοῦ σώματος· δεσπότις γὰρ καὶ βασιλὶς καὶ ἐν ἅπασι κρείττων ἅτε θειοτέρας φύσεως μεταλαχοῦσα. τὰ δὲ φαιδρύνοντα διάνοιάν ἐστι σοφία καὶ τὰ σοφίας δόγματα πρὸς τὴν θεωρίαν τοῦ κόσμου καὶ τῶν ἐν αὐτῷ ποδηγετοῦντα καὶ ὁ τῶν ἄλλων ἀρετῶν ἱερὸς χορὸς καὶ αἱ κατ᾿ ἀρετὰς καλαὶ καὶ σφόδρα ἐπαινε-

---

[a] See Num. xix. 2-9.

[b] Here the juxtaposition of the clean man shews that Philo must have taken καθαρῷ χωρίῳ as "clean," and not as "open," though it does not follow that he did so in the passages cited in the note on *Mos.* ii. 72, or even in § 232 above.

[c] No such account survives. Heinemann suggests that it

as to disappear into non-existence. Whence it came in the beginning, thither will it return in the end."

L. I must now also fulfil my promise to describe 267
the special qualities of these ashes. They are not merely the ashes of wood consumed by fire but also of a living creature well-suited to a rite of purification
such as this. [a] He orders a red heifer which has never 268
been yoked and without blemish to be taken outside the city and there slaughtered. Then the high priest is to take of the blood and sprinkle it seven times over everything in front of the sanctuary, then burn it wholly to ashes with the skin and flesh and blood and the belly filled with its ordure. When the flame is dying down, he is to cast right into the middle these three things, cedar wood and hyssop and scarlet wool. Then if it is quite extinguished, a clean man is to collect the ashes and deposit them outside
the city in a clean place.[b] What these things sym- 269
bolically indicate has been described in full elsewhere where we have expounded the allegory.[c] So we see that they who mean to resort to the temple to take part in sacrifice must needs have their bodies made clean and bright,[d] and before their bodies their souls. For the soul is queen and mistress, superior to the body in every way because a diviner nature has been allotted to it. The mind is cleansed by wisdom and the truths of wisdom's teaching which guide its steps to the contemplation of the universe and all that is therein, and by the sacred company of the other virtues and by the practice of them shewn in noble

belongs to the *Quaestiones* of which we have nothing beyond Exodus.

[d] φαιδρύνω is more than simply "clean," in colloquial English to make "smart" or "spick and span," = διακεκοσμημένος in § 270.

270 ταὶ πράξεις. ὁ μὲν οὖν τούτοις διακεκοσμημένος ἴτω θαρρῶν εἰς οἰκειότατον αὐτῷ τὸν νεών, ἐνδιαίτημα πάντων ἄριστον, ἱερεῖον ἐπιδειξόμενος αὑτόν· ὅτῳ δ' ἐγκάθηνται καὶ ἐλλοχῶσιν αἱ πλεονεξίαι καὶ ἐπιθυμίαι τῶν ἀδικιῶν, ἐγκαλυψάμενος ἠρεμείτω τὴν ἀναίσχυντον ἀπόνοιαν καὶ τὸ λίαν θράσος ἐν οἷς εὐλάβεια λυσιτελὲς ἐπισχών· τὸ γὰρ τοῦ ὄντως
271 ὄντος ἱερὸν ἀνιέροις ἄβατον.[1] θυσίαις, εἴποιμ' ἄν, ὦ γενναῖε, ὁ θεὸς οὐ χαίρει, κἂν ἑκατόμβας ἀνάγῃ τις· κτήματα γὰρ αὐτοῦ τὰ πάντα, κεκτημένος ὅμως[2] οὐδενὸς δεῖται· χαίρει δὲ φιλοθέοις γνώμαις καὶ ἀνδράσιν ἀσκηταῖς ὁσιότητος, παρ' ὧν ψαιστὰ καὶ κριθὰς καὶ τὰ εὐτελέστατα ὡς τιμιώτατα πρὸ
272 τῶν πολυτελεστάτων ἄσμενος δέχεται· κἂν μέντοι μηδὲν ἕτερον κομίζωσιν, αὑτοὺς φέροντες πλήρωμα καλοκἀγαθίας τελειότατον τὴν ἀρίστην ἀνάγουσι θυσίαν, ὕμνοις καὶ εὐχαριστίαις τὸν εὐεργέτην καὶ σωτῆρα θεὸν γεραίροντες, τῇ μὲν διὰ τῶν φωνητηρίων ὀργάνων, τῇ δὲ ἄνευ γλώττης καὶ στόματος, μόνῃ ψυχῇ τὰς νοητὰς ποιούμενοι διεξόδους καὶ ἐκβοήσεις, ὧν ἓν μόνον οὖς ἀντιλαμβάνεται τὸ θεῖον· αἱ γὰρ τῶν ἀνθρώπων οὐ φθάνουσιν ἀκοαὶ συναισθέσθαι.

273 LI. Ὡς δ' ἀψευδής ἐστιν οὗτος ὁ λόγος καὶ οὐκ ἐμὸς ἀλλὰ τῆς φύσεως, μαρτυρεῖ μέν πως καὶ ἡ

[1] Cohn punctuates with full stop after *θυσίαις*. I follow Heinemann's punctuation. *εἴποιμ' ἄν* in cases like this generally, if not always, is inserted parenthetically, *e.g.* ii. 96.

[2] Cohn (*Hermes*, 1908, p. 190) thinks that *ὅμως* makes no sense and suggests *κεκτημένος δ' οὐδ' ὅλως*; but see note *a*.

[a] I understand the connexion of thought to be "though He possesses all, He needs it not, and therefore how much more are the gifts of men unneeded."

and highly praiseworthy actions. He, then, who is 270
adorned with these may come with boldness to the sanctuary as his true home, the best of all mansions, there to present himself as victim. But anyone whose heart is the seat of lurking covetousness and wrongful cravings should remain still and hide his face in confusion and curb the shameless madness which would rashly venture where caution is profitable. For the holy place of the truly Existent is
closed ground to the unholy. To such a one I would 271
say, "Good sir, God does not rejoice in sacrifices even if one offer hecatombs, for all things are His possessions, yet though He possesses[a] He needs none of them, but He rejoices in the will to love Him and in men that practise holiness, and from these He accepts plain meal or barley,[b] and things of least price, holding them most precious rather than those of highest
cost." And indeed though the worshippers bring 272
nothing else, in bringing themselves they offer the best of sacrifices, the full and truly perfect oblation of noble living,[c] as they honour with hymns and thanksgivings their Benefactor and Saviour, God, sometimes with the organs of speech, sometimes without tongue or lips, when within the soul alone their minds recite the tale or utter the cry of praise. These one ear only can apprehend, the ear of God, for human hearing cannot reach to the perception of such.

LI. That what I have said above is true and is the 273
word not of myself but of nature is attested not only

[b] Or "barley ground or unground."

[c] Or, taking πλήρωμα in apposition with αὐτούς, "when bringing themselves, that is, the full oblation," etc. In either case "bringing themselves" is explained in the next few words as the heartfelt thanksgiving of the lips and soul.

ἐνάργεια τρανὴν παρέχουσα πίστιν τοῖς μὴ διὰ τὸ φιλόνεικον ἐπιτηδεύουσιν ἀπιστίαν, μαρτυρεῖ δὲ καὶ ὁ νόμος προστάξας δύο κατασκευασθῆναι βωμοὺς καὶ ταῖς ὕλαις καὶ τοῖς τόποις καὶ ταῖς χρείαις
274 διαφέροντας· ὁ μὲν γὰρ ἐκ λίθων λογάδων ἀτμήτων συνῳκοδόμηται καὶ ἐν ὑπαίθρῳ παρὰ ταῖς τοῦ νεὼ προσβάσεσιν ἵδρυται καὶ γέγονε πρὸς χρείαν τὴν τῶν ἐναίμων· ὁ δὲ χρυσοῦ μὲν τοῦ καθαρωτάτου κατεσκεύασται, ἵδρυται δ᾿ ἐν ἀδύτοις εἴσω τοῦ προτέρου καταπετάσματος, ὃς οὐδενὶ τῶν ἄλλων
[245] ἐστὶν | ὁρατὸς ὅτι μὴ τοῖς ἁγνεύουσι τῶν ἱερέων καὶ
275 γέγονε πρὸς χρείαν τὴν τῶν θυμιαμάτων. ἐξ οὗ δῆλόν ἐστιν, ὅτι καὶ βραχύτατον λιβανωτὸν παρ᾿ ἀνδρὸς ὁσίου τιμιώτερον ὁ θεὸς νομίζει μυρίων θρεμμάτων, ὅσα ἂν τις ἱερουργῇ μὴ σφόδρα ἀστεῖος ὤν· ὅσῳ γάρ, οἶμαι, λίθων μὲν εἰκαίων ἀμείνων χρυσός, τὰ δ᾿ ἐν ἀδύτοις τῶν ἐκτὸς ἁγιώτερα, τοσούτῳ κρείττων ἡ διὰ τῶν ἐπιθυμιωμένων εὐ-
276 χαριστία τῆς διὰ τῶν ἐναίμων. ὅθεν οὐ μόνον ὕλης πολυτελείᾳ καὶ κατασκευῇ καὶ τόπῳ τετίμηται ὁ τῶν θυμιαμάτων βωμός, ἀλλὰ καὶ τῷ πρότερον καθ᾿ ἑκάστην ἡμέραν ὑπηρετεῖν ταῖς πρὸς θεὸν ἀνθρώπων εὐχαριστίαις· οὐ γὰρ ἐφεῖται τὴν ὁλόκαυτον θυσίαν ἔξω προσαγαγεῖν, πρὶν ἔνδον περὶ βαθὺν

[a] The two altars are described respectively in Ex. xxvii. and xxx. There, however, they are both made of acacia wood, LXX ἄσηπτον, "incorruptible," though the second is overlaid with gold. The "unhewn stones" seems to be

by its self-evident certitude which provides clear grounds of belief to those who do not out of contentiousness cultivate disbelief, but also by the law which commanded two altars to be constructed differing in materials and situations and in the use
to which they were applied.[a] For one of these was 274
built of stones picked up and left unhewn, and it was set in the open air beside the avenues to the sanctuary and was to be used for blood-offerings. The other was formed of the purest gold ; it was set in the inner shrine within the first veil, not to be seen by any except such priests as were in a state of purity,[b] and
it was to be used for frankincense-offerings. This 275
clearly shews that even the least morsel of incense offered by a man of religion is more precious in the sight of God than thousands of cattle sacrificed by men of little worth. For as gold is better than casual stones and all in the inner shrine more sacred than what stands outside, so and in the same measure is the thank-offering of incense superior to that of the
blood of beasts. And therefore the altar of incense 276
receives special honour, not only in the costliness of its material, its construction and its situation, but by taking every day the earlier place in subserving the thanksgiving which men render to God. For it is not permitted to bring the victim of the whole-burnt-offering outside until the incense has been offered

drawn from Ex. xx. 25, "And if thou make me an altar of stone thou shalt not build it of hewn stones." Philo's description may be derived from personal observation, for Josephus, *Contra Apion.* i. 198 quotes a passage ascribed to Hecataeus (4th-3rd century B.C.), in which he states, when speaking of the temple at Jerusalem, that the altar is built of heaped up stones unhewn and unwrought. But see App. pp. 621-622.

[b] And therefore permitted to officiate.

277 ὄρθρον ἐπιθυμιᾶσαι. τὸ δ' ἐστὶ σύμβολον οὐχ ἑτέρου τινὸς ἢ τοῦ παρὰ θεῷ μὴ τὸ πλῆθος τῶν καταθυομένων εἶναι τίμιον, ἀλλὰ τὸ καθαρώτατον τοῦ θύοντος πνεῦμα λογικόν· εἰ μὴ ἄρα δικαστὴς μέν, ᾧ μέλει τῆς ὁσίας κρίσεως, παρά τινος τῶν κρινομένων οὐκ ἂν λάβοι δῶρα ἢ λαβὼν ἔνοχος ἔσται δωροδοκίᾳ, οὐδ' ἀνὴρ ἀστεῖος παρὰ μοχθηροῦ τινος, ἄνθρωπος παρ' ἀνθρώπου πλουτοῦντος αὐτὸς ἴσως δεόμενος, σὺ δ' ᾠήθης τὸν θεὸν δεκάζεσθαι, τὸν αὐταρκέστατον ἑαυτῷ καὶ μηδενὸς τῶν ἐν γενέσει χρεῖον, ὅστις ὢν τὸ πρῶτον ἀγαθόν, τὸ τελειότατον, ἡ ἀέναος πηγὴ φρονήσεως καὶ δικαιοσύνης καὶ πάσης ἀρετῆς, ἀποστρέφεται τὰς
278 παρὰ τῶν ἀδίκων δωρεάς. ὁ δὲ κομίζων οὐ πάντων ἀναισχυντότατος ἐξ ὧν ἔκλεψεν ἢ ἥρπασεν ἢ ἠρνήσατο ἢ ἀπεστέρησε μέρος ὡς κοινωνῷ τῆς ἑαυτοῦ κακίας καὶ πλεονεξίας διδούς; πάντων κακοδαιμονέστατε, εἴποιμ' ἂν τῷ τοιούτῳ, δυοῖν θάτερον ἢ λήσεσθαι προσδοκᾷς ἢ καταφανήσεσθαι·
279 λήσεσθαι μὲν οὖν ὑπολαμβάνων ἀνεπιστήμων εἶ θεοῦ δυνάμεως, καθ' ἣν ἅμα πάντα ὁρᾷ καὶ πάντων ἀκούει· νομίζων δ' ἐμφανήσεσθαι θρασύτατος εἶ· δέον ἐφ' οἷς ἥμαρτες ἐγκαλύπτεσθαι, προφέρεις εἰς μέσον τὰ δείγματα ὧν ἠδίκησας καὶ ἐπισεμνυνόμενος διανέμῃ πρὸς θεόν, ἀπαρχὰς αὐτῷ κομίζων

---

[a] The same statement has been made in § 171. See Ex. xxx. 7, where the LXX says that the incense-offering is to be made πρωῒ πρωΐ, which Philo presumably takes as = βαθὺς ὄρθρος, and earlier than the πρωΐ of Ex. xxix. 39 and Num. xxviii. 4 (which he renders here and in § 169 by ἅμα τῇ ἕῳ). The statement in § 171 that the evening incense-offering was

inside at the first glimpse of day.[a] The 277
symbolical meaning is just this and nothing else: that what is precious in the sight of God is not the number of victims immolated but the true purity of a rational spirit in him who makes the sacrifice. Can you think that if the judge whose heart is set on giving righteous judgement will not take gifts from any of the litigants, or if he does take them will be open to the charge of bribery; if again the good man will not receive them from the bad, though both are men, and the one perhaps in need and the other rich—can you think, I say, that God can be corrupted, God Who is absolutely sufficient to Himself and needs nothing of anything created, and being as He is the primal good, the consummation of perfection, the perennial fountain of wisdom and justice and every virtue, turns His face from the gifts of the unjust?
And is not he who proffers them the most shameless 278
of men when he gives to God a share of the profits of his thefts or robbery or denial of a just debt or refusal to pay it, and treats Him as a partner in his wickedness and greed? To such a one I would say "Most miserable of wretches, there are only two alternatives: You expect that your conduct will
either be unobserved by God or patent to Him. If 279
the former, you little know the power by which He sees all and hears all: if the latter, your audacity is beyond measure. When you should hide your face in shame for the sins you have committed, you make an open show of the outward signs of your iniquity and, priding yourself on them, assign a share to God. You bring Him the first-fruits of unholiness and have

after the evening sacrifice would seem to be opposed to the argument in this passage.

ἀνοσίους, καὶ οὐκ ἐλογίσω τοῦθ' ὅτι οὔτε νόμος ἀνομίαν παραδέχεται οὔτε φῶς ἡλιακὸν σκότος. ὁ δὲ θεὸς καὶ νόμων ἐστὶ παράδειγμα ἀρχέτυπον καὶ ἡλίου ἥλιος, νοητὸς αἰσθητοῦ, παρέχων ἐκ τῶν ἀοράτων πηγῶν ὁρατὰ φέγγη τῷ βλεπομένῳ.

[264]
280 [1]Πάνυ καλῶς ἐν ταῖς ἱεραῖς τοῦ νόμου στήλαις κἀκεῖνο ἀναγέγραπται, μίσθωμα πόρνης εἰς τὸ ἱερὸν μὴ κομίζειν πεπρακυίας τὴν ἰδίαν ὥραν, ἑλομένης
281 ἕνεκα λημμάτων αἰσχρῶν ἐπονείδιστον βίον. εἰ δὲ τὰ παρὰ γυναικὸς ἡταιρηκυίας δῶρα ἀνίερα, πῶς οὐχὶ μᾶλλον τὰ παρὰ ψυχῆς πεπορνευμένης, ἥτις
[265] παρέρριψεν | ἑαυτὴν ἐπ' αἰσχύνῃ καὶ ὕβρεσι ταῖς ἐσχάταις, οἰνοφλυγίαις, ὀψοφαγίαις, φιλαργυρίαις, φιλοδοξίαις, φιληδονίαις, ἄλλαις μυρίαις παθῶν τε αὖ καὶ νοσημάτων καὶ κακιῶν ἰδέαις; ὧν τὰ μιάσματα ἐκεῖνα τίς ἂν ἐκνίψαι χρόνος; ἔγωγε οὐκ
282 οἶδα. τῶν μὲν γὰρ ἑταιρῶν τὴν ἐργασίαν κατέλυσε πολλάκις γῆρας, ἐπειδήπερ ἐξώροις γενομέναις οὐδεὶς ἔτι πρόσεισιν, ἀπομαρανθείσης ὥσπερ τινῶν ἀνθῶν τῆς ἀκμῆς· ψυχῆς δὲ πορνείαν ἀκολασίᾳ συντρόφῳ καὶ συνήθει πεπαιδοτριβημένης τίς ἂν αἰὼν μεταβάλοι πρὸς εὐκοσμίαν; αἰὼν μὲν οὔ, θεὸς δὲ μόνος, ᾧ δυνατὰ τὰ παρ' ἡμῖν ἀδύνατα.
283 δεῖ δὴ τὸν μέλλοντα θύειν σκέπτεσθαι, μὴ εἰ τὸ

[1] At this R has the heading Περὶ τοῦ μίσθωμα πόρνης εἰς τὸ ἱερὸν μὴ κομίζειν, though A and H transfer it with the five sections that follow to the end of this treatise, and make them the introduction to a separate treatise, composed of the material already printed in Vol. II. pp. 106-119, *De Sac.* 20-33. See Introduction to that treatise, p. 93.

[a] The heading here introduced in MSS., "Of bringing the hire of a harlot into the temple," is of course in copies which do not transfer these sections as described in note 1 quite

not reflected that the law does not admit of lawlessness nor sunlight of darkness. But God is the archetype on which laws are modelled : He is the sun of the sun, in the realm of mind what that is in the realm of sense, and from invisible fountains He supplies the visible beams to the sun which our eyes behold."

[a] There is a very excellent ordinance inscribed in 280
the sacred tables of the law, that the hire of a harlot should not be brought into the temple ;[b] the hire, that is, of one who has sold her personal charms and chosen a scandalous life for the sake of the wages of
shame. But if the gifts of one who has played the 281
harlot are unholy, surely more unholy still are the gifts of the soul which has committed whoredom, which has thrown itself away into ignominy and the lowest depths of outrageous conduct, into winebibbing and gluttony, into the love of money, of reputation, of pleasure, and numberless other forms of passion and soul-sickness and vice. What length of time can purge away the stains of these ? None,
to my knowledge. The harlots' traffic indeed is 282
often brought to a close by old age, since when the freshness of their charm is passed, all cease to seek them now that their bloom is faded like the bloom of flowers. But as for the soul, when by constant familiarity with incontinence it has been schooled into harlotry, what agelong stretch of years can convert it to decent living ? Not even the longest, but only God, with Whom that is possible which is
impossible with us. So he who intends to sacrifice 283
must consider not whether the victim is unblemished

absurd. The point of the harlot's hire is merely introduced as an illustration of the moral enforced.

[b] See Deut. xxiii. 18.

ἱερεῖον ἄμωμον, ἀλλ᾿ εἰ ἡ διάνοια ὁλόκληρος αὐτῷ καὶ παντελὴς καθέστηκε. διερευνάτω μέντοι καὶ τὰς αἰτίας, ὧν ἕνεκα ἀνάγειν ἀξιοῖ θυσίας· ἤτοι γὰρ εὐχαριστῶν ἐπὶ προϋπηργμέναις εὐεργεσίαις ἢ βεβαιότητα παρόντων ἢ μελλόντων κτῆσιν ἀγαθῶν αἰτούμενος ἢ κακῶν παρόντων ἢ προσδοκωμένων ἀποτροπήν, ἐφ᾿ οἷς ἅπασιν ὑγείαν καὶ σωτηρίαν
284 ἐκπορίζειν ὀφείλει τῷ λογισμῷ. εἴτε γὰρ ἐπὶ προϋπηργμένοις εὐχαριστεῖ, μὴ ἀχαριστησάτω φαῦλος γενόμενος—σπουδαίῳ γὰρ ἐδόθησαν αἱ χάριτες—, εἴτε βεβαιούμενος τὰ παρόντα ἀγαθὰ καὶ χρηστὰ περὶ τῶν μελλόντων προσδοκῶν, ἄξιον αὐτὸν παρεχέτω τῶν εὐπραγιῶν ἀστεῖος ὤν, εἴτε κακῶν τινων φυγὴν αἰτούμενος, μὴ δράτω κολάσεων ἐπάξια καὶ τιμωριῶν.

[254] LII. [1] Πῦρ, φησίν, ἐπὶ τοῦ θυσιαστηρίου καυθή-
285 σεται διὰ παντὸς ἄσβεστον· εἰκότως, οἶμαι, καὶ προσηκόντως· ἐπειδὴ γὰρ αἱ τοῦ θεοῦ χάριτες ἀέναοι καὶ ἀνελλιπεῖς καὶ ἀδιάστατοι, ὧν μεθ᾿ ἡμέραν καὶ νύκτωρ οἱ ἄνθρωποι τυγχάνουσιν, καὶ τὸ σύμβολον τῆς εὐχαριστίας, ἡ ἱερὰ φλόξ, ζωπυρεί-
[255] σθω καὶ ἀεὶ ἄσβεστος | ἔστω. τάχα μέντοι καὶ διὰ
286 τοῦδε[2] βούλεται τὰς παλαιὰς ταῖς νέαις θυσίαις ἁρμόσασθαι καὶ ἑνῶσαι τῇ μονῇ καὶ παρουσίᾳ τοῦ αὐτοῦ πυρός, ᾧ πᾶσαι καθιεροῦνται, πρὸς ἔνδειξιν

[1] Here the MSS. interpolate the heading Τὰ ἄλλα περὶ τὸ θυσιαστήριον (or τὸν βωμόν).
[2] MSS. τόδε. Perhaps ·καὶ διὰ τόδε· βούλεται, as Heinemann suggests, citing § 309.

---

[a] The heading here introduced, "Of the other matters concerning the altar," which, as no later heading is given, presumably extends to the rest of the treatise, is almost as

but whether his own mind stands free from defect and imperfection. Further, let him examine the motives which determine him to make the offering. For either he is giving thanks for benefits already received or is asking for security in his tenure of present blessings or for acquisition of others to come, or for deliverance from evils, either present or expected, and all these demand that he should put himself into a condition of mental health and safety.
For if he is offering thanks for what has already been 284
granted, let him not shew ingratitude by falling from the state of virtue in which he received these boons. Or if he is securing present blessings or has bright expectations for the future, let him shew himself by good conduct worthy of such happy events. Or if he is seeking to escape from some ills, let none of his actions be deserving of chastisement and punishment.

LII. [a] The fire on the altar, he tells us, will burn 285
continuously and not be extinguished.[b] That, I think, is natural and fitting, for since the gracious gifts of God granted daily and nightly to men are perennial, unfailing and unceasing, the symbol of thankfulness also, the sacred flame, should be kept
alight and remain unextinguished for ever. Perhaps 286
also he wishes in this way to employ the abiding presence of the same fire by which all the sacrifices are consecrated to unite them, old and new alike,[c] and thus shew that they carry out perfectly the duty

absurd as the last. At the best it only serves for a description of §§ 285-295. In §§ 296-298 we pass on to the lamps, and after that to general reflections on the morality enjoined in the cult. Cohn ignores both this and the preceding heading in his numeration of chapters.

[b] See Lev. vi. 9, 12, 13.

[c] *i.e.* those of the past, and those of the present and future.

τοῦ τελείας ἐν εὐχαριστίαις εἶναι, κἂν ἀπὸ μυρίων ὅσων ἀφορμῶν γίνωνται κατὰ περιουσίας ἀφθόνους ἢ τοὐναντίον ἐνδείας τῶν προσαγομένων.[1]

287 τὰ μὲν ῥητὰ ταῦτα [σύμβολα νοητῶν], τὰ δὲ πρὸς διάνοιαν τοῖς τῆς ἀλληγορίας κανόσιν ἐπισκεπτέον· πρὸς ἀλήθειαν τοῦ θεοῦ θυσιαστήριόν ἐστιν ἡ εὐχάριστος τοῦ σοφοῦ ψυχὴ παγεῖσα ἐκ τελείων ἀρετῶν ἀτμήτων καὶ ἀδιαιρέτων· οὐδὲν γὰρ μέρος

288 ἀρετῆς ἀχρεῖον. ἐπὶ ταύτης ἀεὶ τὸ ἱερὸν φῶς ἀνακαίεται φυλαττόμενον ἄσβεστον· διανοίας δὲ φῶς ἐστι σοφία, ἐπεὶ καὶ τοὐναντίον σκότος ψυχῆς ἀφροσύνη· ὅπερ γὰρ αἰσθητὸν φῶς ὀφθαλμοῖς[2] πρὸς κατάληψιν σωμάτων, τοῦτ᾽ ἐπιστήμη λογισμῷ πρὸς θεωρίαν τῶν ἀσωμάτων καὶ νοητῶν, ἧς ἀεὶ τὸ φέγγος ἐπιλάμπει μηδέποτε ἀμαυρούμενον ⟨ἢ⟩ σβεννύμενον.[3]

289 LIII. Μετὰ ταῦτά φησιν· "ἐπὶ παντὸς δώρου προσοίσετε ἅλα," δι᾽ οὗ, καθάπερ καὶ πρότερον εἶπον, τὴν εἰς ἅπαν διαμονὴν αἰνίττεται· φυλακτήριον γὰρ οἱ ἅλες σωμάτων, τετιμημένοι ψυχῆς δευτερείοις· ὡς γὰρ αἰτία τοῦ μὴ διαφθείρεσθαι τὰ σώματα ψυχή, καὶ οἱ ἅλες ἐπὶ πλεῖστον αὐτὰ

290 συνέχοντες καὶ τρόπον τινὰ ἀθανατίζοντες. διὸ καὶ κέκληκε θυσιαστήριον, ἴδιον καὶ ἐξαίρετον ὄνομα θέμενος αὐτῷ παρὰ τὸ διατηρεῖν, ὡς ἔοικε, τὰς θυσίας, καίτοι τῶν κρεῶν ἀναλισκομένων ὑπὸ πυρός. ὡς εἶναι σαφεστάτην πίστιν, ὅτι οὐ τὰ ἱερεῖα θυσίαν ἀλλὰ τὴν διάνοιαν καὶ προθυμίαν ὑπο-

[1] Cohn (*Hermes*, 1908, pp. 190, 191) corrects to προσαγόντων. It is certainly more natural, but does not seem to me necessary.

[2] MSS. εἰς ὀφθαλμούς.

[3] R ἀμαυρούμενον only. The others σβεννύμενον only.

of giving thanks, however numberless are the differences in the resources on which they are based, according as the oblations are lavishly abundant or
on the other hand scanty. This is the 287
literal account: the inner meaning must be observed by the laws of allegory. The true altar of God is the thankful soul of the Sage, compacted of perfect virtues unsevered[a] and undivided, for no part of virtue
is useless. On this soul-altar the sacred light is ever 288
burning and carefully kept unextinguished, and the light of the mind is wisdom, just as the darkness of the soul is folly. For knowledge is to the reason what the light of our senses is to the eye: as that gives the apprehension of material things, so does knowledge lead to the contemplation of things immaterial and conceptual, and its beam shines for ever, never dimmed nor quenched.

LIII. After this he says, "On every gift ye shall 289
offer salt,"[b] by which he signifies, as I have said before, complete permanence. Salt acts as a preservative to bodies, ranking in this as second in honour to the life-principle. For just as the life-principle causes bodies to escape corruption, so does salt, which more than anything else keeps them together and makes
them in a sense immortal. From the same point of 290
view he called the altar a sacrifice-keeper,[c] evidently giving it that special and distinctive name from its preserving the sacrifices, though the flesh is consumed by fire. And thus we have the clearest proof that he holds the sacrifice to consist not in the victims but in the offerer's intention and his zeal which derives

[a] An allusion to the unhewn stones of which the altar was built; see § 274.

[b] See Lev. ii. 13.

[c] τηρεῖν = "keep," θυσίας = "sacrifices." *Cf. Mos.* ii. 106.

λαμβάνει τοῦ καταθύοντος εἶναι, ἐν ᾗ τὸ μόνιμον
291 καὶ βέβαιον ἐξ ἀρετῆς. προσέτι κἀκεῖνο προσνομοθετεῖ, κελεύων πᾶσαν θυσίαν δίχα ζύμης καὶ
μέλιτος προσάγεσθαι, μηδέτερον ἀξιῶν ἀναφέρειν
ἐπὶ τὸ θυσιαστήριον· μέλι μὲν ἴσως, ἐπειδήπερ ἡ
συναγωγὸς αὐτοῦ μέλιττα ζῷόν ἐστιν οὐ καθαρόν,
ἐκ σήψεως καὶ φθορᾶς νεκρῶν, ὡς ὁ λόγος, βοῶν
γεννώμενον, καθὰ καὶ οἱ σφῆκες ἐξ ἱππείων σω-
292 μάτων· ἢ κατὰ σύμβολον τοῦ πᾶσαν ἀνίερον εἶναι
τὴν περιττὴν ἡδονήν, τὰ μὲν περὶ τὴν κατάποσιν
γλυκαίνουσαν, πικρὰς δὲ καὶ δυσιάτους αὖθις ἐπι-
φέρουσαν ἀλγηδόνας, ὑφ᾿ ὧν ἀνάγκη τὴν ψυχὴν
σείεσθαι καὶ κλονεῖσθαι παγίως ἱδρυθῆναι μὴ
293 δυναμένην· ζύμην δὲ διὰ τὴν γινομένην ἔπαρσιν ἐξ
[256] αὐτῆς, πάλιν συμβολικῶς, | ἵνα μηδεὶς προσιὼν τῷ
θυσιαστηρίῳ τὸ παράπαν ἐπαίρηται φυσηθεὶς ὑπ᾿
ἀλαζονείας, ἀλλ᾿ εἰς τὸ τοῦ θεοῦ μέγεθος ἀποβλέπων
αἴσθησιν λαμβάνῃ τῆς περὶ τὸ γενητὸν ἀσθενείας,
κἂν εὐτυχίαις ἑτέρων διαφέρῃ, καὶ τὸν εἰκότα
ποιησάμενος λογισμὸν στέλλῃ τὸ τοῦ φρονήματος
294 ὑπέραυχον ὕψος, τὴν ἐπίβουλον οἴησιν καθαιρῶν. εἰ
γὰρ ὁ τῶν ὅλων κτίστης καὶ ποιητὴς καὶ πάντων
ἀνεπιδεὴς ὧν ἐγέννησεν, οὐ πρὸς τὰς ὑπερβολὰς τοῦ
κράτους αὐτοῦ καὶ τῆς ἐξουσίας ἀπιδὼν ἀλλὰ πρὸς
τὴν σὴν ἀσθένειαν, μεταδίδωσί σοι τῆς ἵλεω δυνάμεως αὐτοῦ τὰς ἐνδείας ἀναπληρῶν αἷς κέχρησαι,
σὲ τί ποιεῖν ἁρμόττει πρὸς ἀνθρώπους τοὺς φύσει
συγγενεῖς καὶ ἀπὸ τῶν αὐτῶν στοιχείων σπαρέντας,
τὸν μηδὲν εἰς τὸν κόσμον ἀλλὰ μηδὲ σαυτὸν εἰσ-
295 ενηνοχότα; γυμνὸς μὲν γάρ, θαυμάσιε, ἦλθες,

its constancy and permanence from virtue. He
adds, too, a further enactment by which he orders 291
every sacrifice to be offered without honey or leaven.[a]
Both these substances he considers unfit to be brought to the altar: honey perhaps because the bee which collects it is an unclean animal, bred from the putrescence and corruption of dead oxen, we are told, just as wasps are from the carcasses of horses[b];
or else he forbids it as a symbol of the utter unholiness 292
of excessive pleasure which tastes sweet as it passes through the throat but afterwards produces bitter and persistent pains which of necessity shake and agitate the soul and make it unable to stand firmly
in its place. Leaven is forbidden because of the 293
rising which it produces. Here again we have a symbol of the truth, that none as he approaches the altar should be uplifted or puffed up by arrogance; Rather gazing on the greatness of God, let him gain a perception of the weakness which belongs to the creature, even though he may be superior to others in prosperity; and having been thus led to the reasonable conclusion, let him reduce the overweening exaltation of his pride by laying low that pestilent
enemy, conceit. For if the Creator and Maker of the 294
universe, though needing nothing of all that He has begotten, has regard to your weakness and not to the vastness of His might and sovereignty, makes you a partaker in His gracious power and fills up the deficiencies that belong to your life, how ought you to treat other men, your natural kinsfolk, seedlings from the same elements as yourself, you who brought
nothing into the world, not even yourself? For naked 295
you came into the world, worthy sir, and naked will

[a] See Lev. ii. 11. [b] See App. p. 622.

γυμνὸς δὲ πάλιν ἄπεις, τὸν μεταξὺ χρόνον γενέσεως καὶ θανάτου παρὰ τοῦ θεοῦ χρῆσιν λαβών, ἐν ᾧ τί ποιεῖν προσῆκον ἦν ἢ κοινωνίας καὶ ὁμονοίας ἰσότητός τε καὶ φιλανθρωπίας καὶ τῆς ⟨ἄλλης⟩ ἀρετῆς ἐπιμελεῖσθαι, ἀποβαλλόμενον τὴν ἄνισον καὶ ἄδικον καὶ ἀσύμβατον κακίαν, ἣ τὸ ἡμερώτατον φύσει ζῷον, ἄνθρωπον, ὠμὸν καὶ ἀτίθασον ἐργάζεται;

296 LIV. *Πάλιν ἀφ' ἑσπέρας ἕως πρωίας προστάττει καίεσθαι λύχνους ἐπὶ τῆς ἱερᾶς λυχνίας εἴσω τοῦ καταπετάσματος, πολλῶν χάριν· ἑνὸς μὲν ἵνα ἐκ διαδοχῆς τοῦ μεθημερινοῦ φωτὸς καταλάμπηται τὰ ἅγια γινόμενα ἀεὶ σκότους ἀμέτοχα καθ' ὁμοιότητα τῶν ἀστέρων· καὶ γὰρ οὗτοι δύντος ἡλίου τὸ ἴδιον ἀναφαίνουσι φέγγος ἣν ἐτάχθησαν ἐν τῷ κόσμῳ*
297 *τάξιν οὐ λείποντες· ἑτέρου δὲ τοῦ καὶ νύκτωρ ἀδελφόν τι καὶ συγγενὲς ταῖς μεθημεριναῖς θυσίαις ἐπιτελεῖσθαι πρὸς ἀρέσκειαν θεοῦ καὶ μηδένα χρόνον ἢ καιρὸν εὐχαριστίας παραλείπειν· ἐπιτηδειοτάτη δὲ καὶ προσφυεστάτη νυκτὶ τῆς εὐχαριστίας θυσία—θυσίαν γὰρ αὐτὴν ἄξιον καλεῖν—ἡ τοῦ*
298 *ἱερωτάτου φέγγους ἐν τοῖς ἀδύτοις αὐγή· τρίτου δὲ καὶ σφόδρα ἀναγκαίου· ἐπειδὴ γὰρ οὐ μόνον ἐγρηγορότες εὖ πάσχομεν ἀλλὰ καὶ καθεύδοντες, τοῦ φιλοδώρου θεοῦ μεγάλην ἐπικουρίαν, ὕπνον, τῷ θνητῷ γένει παρασχόντος ἐπ' ὠφελείᾳ σώματός τε καὶ ψυχῆς, τοῦ μὲν σώματος τῶν μεθημερινῶν πόνων ἀφιεμένου, τῆς δὲ ψυχῆς ἐπικουφιζομένης τὰς φροντίδας καὶ ἀναχωρούσης εἰς ἑαυτὴν ἀπὸ τοῦ τῶν αἰσθήσεων ὄχλου καὶ θορύβου καὶ δυναμένης τότε γοῦν ἰδιάζειν καὶ ἐνομιλεῖν ἑαυτῇ, προσ-*

[a] See Ex. xxvii. 21, Lev. xxiv. 3, 4.

you again depart, and the span of time between your birth and death is a loan to you from God. During this span what can be meet for you to do but to study fellow-feeling and goodwill and equity and humanity and what else belongs to virtue, and to cast away the inequitable, unrighteous and unforgiving viciousness which turns man, naturally the most civilized of creatures, into a wild and ferocious animal !

LIV. Again he commands that the lamps on the 296
sacred candlestick within the veil should be kept burning from evening till early morning.[a] He has several objects in this. One is, that the holy places should be illuminated when the daylight leaves them and thus remain ever exempt from darkness, in this resembling the stars. For they when the sun has set display their own light instead and do not forsake
their place in the cosmic order. A second 297
object was, that at night-time also some rites of the same kith and kin as those of the day-time should be performed for the service of God, and that no time or season should omit its thanksgiving. And to shew our thankfulness the sacrificial offering, for sacrificial it may quite properly be called, most suitable and appropriate to the night is the radiance of that most
sacred light in the inner shrine. There is a third 298
reason, a very cogent one : Not only in our waking hours do we experience blessings, but also in our slumbers. For God the bountiful has provided our mortal race with a great support in the form of sleep, whereby both body and soul are benefited. The body is released from the labours of the day, the soul relaxes its anxious cares and retreats into itself, away from the press and clamour of the senses, and can then, if at no other time, enjoy privacy and commune

ηκόντως ἐδικαίωσεν ὁ νόμος τὰς εὐχαριστίας διακληρῶσαι, ὑπὲρ μὲν ἐγρηγόρσεως διὰ τῶν προσαγομένων ἱερείων, ὑπὲρ δὲ ὕπνου καὶ τῶν ἀπὸ τοῦδε ὠφελειῶν διὰ τῆς τῶν ἱερῶν λύχνων ἐξάψεως.

299 LV. | [a]Ἃ μὲν οὖν πρὸς εὐσέβειαν νομοθετεῖται
[257] κατὰ προστάξεις καὶ ἀπαγορεύσεις, ταῦτα καὶ τὰ τούτοις παραπλήσιά ἐστιν· ἃ δὲ κατὰ τὰς φιλοσόφους ὑποθήκας καὶ παραινέσεις, ὧδε λεκτέον. αἰτεῖται γάρ, φησίν, ὦ διάνοια, παρὰ σοῦ ὁ θεὸς οὐδὲν βαρὺ καὶ ποικίλον ἢ δύσεργον ἀλλὰ ἁπλοῦν
300 πάνυ καὶ ῥᾴδιον. ταῦτα δ᾽ ἐστὶν ἀγαπᾶν αὐτὸν ὡς εὐεργέτην, εἰ δὲ μή, φοβεῖσθαι γοῦν ὡς ἄρχοντα καὶ κύριον, καὶ διὰ πασῶν ἰέναι τῶν εἰς ἀρέσκειαν ὁδῶν καὶ λατρεύειν αὐτῷ μὴ παρέργως ἀλλὰ ὅλῃ τῇ ψυχῇ πεπληρωμένῃ γνώμης φιλοθέου καὶ τῶν ἐντολῶν αὐτοῦ περιέχεσθαι καὶ τὰ δίκαια τιμᾶν.
[ἐξ ὧν ἁπάντων αὐτὸς μὲν ἐν ὁμοίᾳ μένει φύσει μὴ τρεπόμενος. τί δὲ[1] τῶν ἄλλων ὅσα κατὰ τὸν κόσμον ἐστι βελτίωσιν ἴσχει, ἥλιος ἢ σελήνη ἢ τὸ πλῆθος τῶν ἄλλων ἀστέρων ἢ ὁ σύμπας οὐρανός;

[1] Cohn ἔτι δὲ with R (ut videtur), AH εἴ τι δὲ. The Armenian is not stated.

---

[a] Here Philo begins his homily on the moral and religious lessons in Deuteronomy. See Deut. x. 12 f.

[b] That the rest of this section from "Among all these" cannot possibly be in its right place, as it is quite irrelevant to the context, is, as Cohn and Heinemann agree, quite indisputable. But it seems to me that it does not make sense in itself, and that Heinemann's admission that it is not "ganz klar" understates the facts. As Cohn prints it, as indicated in the textual notes, it appears to state that all the other parts of the universe (except God?) "have betterment," and to illustrate this we are told that the mountains rise to a very great height, the plains get wider, etc. (In this part it is hard to see why ἤ is used instead of καί.) At the end it appears that

with itself. Rightly therefore did the law determine so to apportion the thank-offerings that thankfulness is expressed for our waking time by the victims brought to the altar, for sleep and the benefits which it gives by the lighting of the sacred lamps.

LV. These and similar injunctions to piety are 299
given in the law in the form of direct commands and prohibitions. Others which have now to be described are of the nature of homilies giving admonitions and exhortations. Addressing himself to the mind of man he says,[a] "God asks nothing from thee that is heavy or complicated or difficult, but only something quite simple and easy. And this is just to love Him 300
as a benefactor, or failing this to fear Him at least as a ruler and lord, and to tread in every way that will lead thee to please Him, to serve Him not half-heartedly but with thy whole soul filled with the determination to love Him and to cling to His commandments and to honour justice."

[b] [Among all these things God Himself remains with a nature which changes not. But of all else that is in the universe, what is there that changes for the better? Sun or moon or the multitude of the other stars or the whole heaven?

contrary to what has been said (μὲν οὖν) they remain exactly as they were from the first.

The corrections I have made are, apart from the punctuation, very slight, τί δὲ for ἔτι δὲ and πλεῖον for πλεῖστον. For R's περιμηκέστερον is, in Cohn's view, as well as, if not better supported, than -τατον. But they seem to me to convey a thought which, however irrelevant to the context, is well worthy of Philo. The preceding words have probably spoken of the perpetual movement and change in the universe, from which God alone is exempt, But does this flux imply βελτίωσις? The ἀρετή of mountains is their height, of the plains their width. Do they grow higher or wider? And so with everything else. The one thing in the universe which is capable of betterment is the soul of man.

ἀλλὰ καὶ τῆς γῆς τὰ μὲν ὄρη πρὸς ὕψος αἴρεται περιμηκέστερον,[1] ἡ δὲ πεδιὰς ὥσπερ αἱ χυταὶ οὐσίαι ἐπὶ πλεῖον[2] εὐρύνεται, καὶ ἡ θάλαττα μεταβάλλει πρὸς πότιμον ἢ οἱ ποταμοὶ πελαγῶν ἐξισοῦνται μεγέθεσιν; ἐπὶ μὲν οὖν τῶν αὐτῶν ὅρων ἕκαστον ἵδρυται ἐφ᾽ οἷς εὐθὺς ἐξ ἀρχῆς ὅτε ἐποίησεν ἐτάχθη· σὺ δὲ βελτίων ἔσῃ ζῶν ἀνυπαιτίως.]

301 τί δὴ τούτων ἀργαλέον ἐστὶν ἢ ἐπίπονον; οὐκ ἄπλωτα πελάγη δεῖ περαιοῦσθαι καὶ μέσου χειμῶνος κλύδωνι καὶ βίαις ἐναντίων πνευμάτων κλονουμένους[3] ἄνω καὶ κάτω θαλαττεύειν ἢ τραχείας καὶ ἀτριβεῖς πεζεύειν ἀνοδίας, οὐχ ὁδούς, ληστῶν ἢ θηρίων ἐφόδους ἀεὶ κατεπτηχότας ἢ τειχοφυλακεῖν ἐν ὑπαίθρῳ νυκτερεύοντας, ἐφεδρευόντων πολεμίων καὶ τοὺς ἀνωτάτω κινδύνους ἀπειλούντων—ἄπαγε, μηδὲν ἐπὶ καλοῖς λεγέσθω τῶν ἀηδῶν· εὐφημητέον
302 ἐπὶ τοῖς οὕτω συμφέρουσιν. ἐπινεῦσαι μόνον δεῖ τὴν ψυχήν, καὶ πάρεστιν ἐν ἑτοίμῳ τὰ πάντα. ἢ τοῦτο ἀγνοεῖς, ὅτι τοῦ θεοῦ καὶ ὁ αἰσθητός ἐστιν οὐρανὸς καὶ ὁ νοητός, ὁ κυρίως, εἴποι τις ἄν, "οὐρανὸς οὐρανοῦ," καὶ πάλιν ἡ γῆ καὶ τὰ ἐν αὐτῇ καὶ σύμπας ὁ κόσμος, ὅ τε ὁρατὸς καὶ ὁ ἀόρατος καὶ ἀσώματος, τὸ παράδειγμα τοῦ ὁρατοῦ οὐρανοῦ;
303 LVI. ἀλλ᾽ ὅμως καὶ ἐξ ἅπαντος ἀνθρώπων γένους τοὺς πρὸς ἀλήθειαν ἀνθρώπους ἀριστίνδην ἐπιλέξας εἵλετο καὶ προνομίας[4] ἠξίωσε τῆς πάσης, ἐπὶ τὴν θεραπείαν καλέσας ἑαυτοῦ, τὴν ἀέναον τῶν καλῶν

[1] So R: Cohn περιμηκέστατον with AH.
[2] MSS. πλεῖστον. (Cohn places full stops after οὐρανός and μεγέθεσιν instead of the marks of interrogation printed above.)
[3] MSS. κυκλουμένους.
[5] MSS. προνοίας.

[a] Here the homily brings in Deut. xxx. 11-14, but returns in § 302 to Deut. x. 14 f.

And on earth do the mountains grow to a loftier height or the lowlands widen forth as liquids spread when poured out? Is the sea converted into fresh water or do the rivers become equal in magnitude to the seas? No, each remains firmly stayed in the same limits in which they were set at the very first when He made them. But thou, by living a blameless life, wilt change for the better.]

[a] Which of these is painful or laborious? You have 301
not to cross great waters where no ship has sailed and in the heart of winter to brave the deep, tossed up and down by the surging of the waves and the violence of opposing winds, or to foot it over rough and untrodden wilds where no road is, in perpetual dread of assault from robbers or wild beasts, or to pass the night unsheltered as a sentry on the walls, threatened with the gravest perils from the enemy ever watchful for their chance. No, away with such thoughts. In good matters let there be no talk of discomfort, nothing but happy words to describe things so profitable. Only must the soul give its assent and every- 302
thing is there ready to your hand. Do you not know that to God belongs both the heaven perceived by sense and that known to thought alone, which may quite properly be called the "heaven of heaven,"[b] again the earth and its contents and all the universe, both the visible and the invisible and immaterial, the
pattern of the visible? LVI. Yet out of the whole 303
human race He chose as of special merit and judged worthy of pre-eminence over all, those who are in a true sense men,[c] and called them to the service of Himself, the perennial fountain of things excellent,

[b] So Deut. x. 14, "the heaven and the heaven of heavens."

[c] The selection of Israel in *v.* 15 is here interpreted as the selection of the worthiest. The meaning thus given to οἱ πρὸς ἀλήθειαν ἄνθρωποι is unusual. Generally "the true man" is the reasonable mind or conscience in the individual man.

πηγήν, ἀφ' ἧς καὶ τὰς ἄλλας ὤμβρησεν ἀρετὰς καὶ ἀνέχεεν[1] εἰς ἀπόλαυσιν ὠφελιμωτάτην, νέκταρος
304 μᾶλλον ἢ οὐχ ἧττον ἀθανατίζον ποτόν. οἰκτροὶ δὲ καὶ κακοδαίμονες ὅσοι μὴ τὸν ἀρετῆς πότον εὐωχήθησαν καὶ κακοδαιμονέστατοι διετέλεσαν οἱ εἰς ἅπαν ἄγευστοι καλοκἀγαθίας, παρὸν καὶ ἐν-
[258] ευφρανθῆναι καὶ | ἐντρυφῆσαι δικαιοσύνῃ καὶ ὁσιότητι· ἀλλ' εἰσὶν ἀπερίτμητοι τὴν καρδίαν, ᾗ φησιν ὁ νόμος, καὶ διὰ σκληρότητα τρόπων ἀφηνιασταί, σκιρτῶντες αὐθαδῶς καὶ ἀπαυχενίζοντες·
305 οὓς νουθετεῖ φάσκων· "περιτέμνεσθε τὴν σκληροκαρδίαν," τὸ δέ ἐστι, τὰς περιττευούσας φύσεις τοῦ ἡγεμονικοῦ, ἃς αἱ ἄμετροι τῶν παθῶν ἔσπειράν τε καὶ συνηύξησαν ὁρμαὶ καὶ ὁ κακὸς ψυχῆς γεωργὸς ἐφύτευσεν, ἀφροσύνη, μετὰ σπουδῆς ἀποκείρασθε.
306 καὶ ὁ τράχηλος, φησίν, ὑμῶν μὴ σκληρὸς ἔστω, τουτέστι, μὴ ἀκαμπὴς ὁ νοῦς καὶ αὐθαδέστατος, μηδ' ὑπὸ τῆς ἄγαν σκαιότητος ἐπιτηδευέτω τὴν βλαβερωτάτην ἀμαθίαν, ἀλλὰ τὸ φύσει δύσκολον καὶ δύστροπον ἀποθέμενος ὡς ἐχθρὸν μεταβαλλέτω
307 πρὸς τὸ εὔκολον,[2] πειθαρχήσων νόμοις φύσεως. ἢ οὐχ ὁρᾷς, ὅτι περὶ τὸ ὂν αἱ πρῶται καὶ μέγισται τῶν δυνάμεών εἰσιν, ἥ τε εὐεργέτις καὶ κολαστήριος; καὶ προσηγόρευται ἡ μὲν εὐεργέτις θεός, ἐπειδὴ κατὰ ταύτην ἔθηκε καὶ διεκόσμησε τὸ πᾶν, ἡ δὲ ἑτέρα κύριος, καθ' ἣν ἀνῆπται τῶν ὅλων τὸ

[1] MSS. ἀνενεχθεὶς.
[2] MSS. εἰκὸς.

[a] The figure of the divine watering of the soul is perhaps suggested by the promise of the water from heaven to irrigate the land in Deut. viii. 7 and xi. 11.

[b] Or "they," *i.e.* those just mentioned.

[c] The phrase comes from Lev. xxvi. 41, though of course

from which He sends the shower of the other virtues gushing forth to give drink, delicious and most beneficial, and conferring immortality as much as or more
than nectar.[a] Pitiable and miserable are all those 304
who have not feasted to the full on virtue's draught, and greatest is the lasting misery of those who have never tasted the cup of noble living when they might revel in the delights of righteousness and holiness.

But some[b] are uncircumcised in heart, says the law,[c] and through their hardness of temper disobedient to the rein, plunging in unruly fashion
and fighting against the yoke. These he admonishes 305
with the words, "Circumcise the hardness of your hearts!" make speed, that is, to prune away from the ruling mind the superfluous overgrowths[d] sown and raised by the immoderate appetites of the passions and planted by folly, the evil husbandman of the soul.
And let not your neck be hard, he continues : that is, 306
let not your mind be unbending and exceedingly unruly, nor in its much frowardness pursue that wilful ignorance which is so fraught with mischief, but casting aside as an enemy all that is naturally indocile and intractable, change over to docility, ready to obey
the laws of nature. [e] Cannot you see that the primal 307
and chief powers belonging to the Existent are the beneficent and the punitive ? And the beneficent is called God because by this He set out[f] and ordered the world ; the other is called Lord, being that by which He is invested with the sovereignty of all that

implied in Deut. x. 16, which is the text for the next two sections.

[d] περιτέμνεσθε . . . περιττευούσας. The same play as in § 9.

[e] See Deut. x. 17.

[f] Another allusion to the accepted derivation of θεός from τίθημι. See notes on *De Abr.* 121 and *De Conf.* 137 (App.).

κράτος. θεὸς δὲ οὐκ ἀνθρώπων μόνον ἀλλὰ καὶ θεῶν ἐστι θεός, καὶ ἄρχων οὐκ ἰδιωτῶν μόνον ἀλλὰ καὶ ἀρχόντων, μέγας τέ ἐστιν ὢν ὄντως καὶ
308 ἰσχυρὸς καὶ κραταιός. LVII. ἀλλ᾿ ὅμως ὁ τοσοῦτος ἐν ἀρεταῖς καὶ δυνάμεσιν ἔλεον καὶ οἶκτον λαμβάνει τῶν ἐν ἐνδείαις ἀπορωτάτων, οὐκ ἀπαξιῶν γενέσθαι κριτὴς προσηλύτοις ἢ ὀρφανοῖς ἢ χήραις, ἀλλὰ βασιλέων καὶ τυράννων καὶ τῶν ἐν μεγάλαις δυναστείαις ὑπεριδὼν τὸ ταπεινὸν τῶν
309 λεχθέντων ἀξιοῖ προνοίας.[1] τῶν μὲν ἐπηλύτων διὰ τόδε· καταλιπόντες οὗτοι τὰ πάτρια οἷς ἐνετράφησαν ψευδῶν πλασμάτων γέμοντα καὶ τύφου, γενόμενοι ἀτυφίας καὶ ἀληθείας ἐρασταὶ γνήσιοι, μετεχώρησαν πρὸς εὐσέβειαν, ἱκέται τε καὶ θεραπευταὶ τοῦ ὄντως ὄντος ἀξίως ὄντες τῆς προνοίας τῆς ἁρμοττούσης εἰκότως μεταλαγχάνουσι, καρπὸν εὑράμενοι τῆς ἐπὶ τὸν θεὸν καταφυγῆς
310 τὴν ἀπ᾿ αὐτοῦ βοήθειαν. ὀρφανῶν δὲ καὶ χηρῶν, ἐπειδὴ κηδεμόνας ἀφῄρηνται, οἱ μὲν γονεῖς, αἱ δὲ ἄνδρας, καταφυγὴ δ᾿ οὐδεμία τοῖς οὕτως ἐρήμοις ἐξ ἀνθρώπων ἀπολείπεται· διὸ τῆς μεγίστης ἐλπίδος οὐκ ἀμοιροῦσι, τοῦ θεοῦ, διὰ τὴν ἵλεω φύσιν αὐτοῦ τὴν πρόνοιαν καὶ ἐπιμέλειαν μὴ απο-
311 στραφέντος τῶν οὕτως ἐρήμων. ἔστω δή, φησί, μόνος θεὸς αὔχημά σου καὶ μέγιστον κλέος, καὶ μήτ᾿ ἐπὶ πλούτῳ μήτε δόξῃ μήτε ἡγεμονίᾳ μήτε σώματος εὐμορφίᾳ μήτε ῥώμῃ μήτε τοῖς παραπλησίοις, ἐφ᾿ οἷς εἰώθασιν οἱ κενοὶ φρενῶν ἐπαίρεσθαι, σεμνυνθῇς, λογισάμενος ὅτι πρῶτον μὲν ἀμέτοχα

[1] MSS. προνομίας.

[a] See Deut. x. 18 f.

is. But He is the God not only of men but also of gods, and the ruler not only of commoners but of rulers, and being truly existent, He is great and
strong and mighty. LVII. [a] Yet vast as are his excel- 308
lences and powers, he takes pity and compassion on those most helplessly in need, and does not disdain to give judgement to strangers or orphans or widows. He holds their low estate worthy of His providential care, while of kings and despots and great potentates
He takes no account. He provides for 309
the incomers because forsaking the ancestral customs in which they were bred, customs packed with false inventions and vanity, they have crossed over to piety in whole-hearted love of simplicity and truth, and rendering to Him that truly exists the supplication and service which are His right, partake in due course of His protecting care in the measure that fits their case, and gain in the help that He gives the fruit of
making God their refuge. He provides 310
for the orphans and widows because they have lost their protectors, in the first case parents, in the second husbands, and in this desolation no refuge remains that men can give; and therefore they are not denied the hope that is greatest of all, the hope in God, Who in the graciousness of His nature does not refuse the task of caring for and watching over them in this
desolate condition. [b] Let God alone be thy boast 311
and thy chief glory, he continues, and pride thyself neither on riches nor on reputation nor dominion nor comeliness nor strength of body, nor any such thing, whereby the hearts of the empty-minded are wont to be lifted up. Consider in the first place that these things have nothing in them of the nature of the true

[b] See Deut. x. 21.

ταῦτ᾿ ἐστὶ τῆς ⟨τοῦ⟩ ἀγαθοῦ φύσεως, ἔπειτα δ᾿ ὅτι καιρὸν ὀξὺν ἔχει τῆς μεταβολῆς, μαραινόμενα
312 τρόπον τινά, πρὶν ἀνθῆσαι βεβαίως. ὃ δὴ πάγιον καὶ ἄτρεπτον καὶ ἀμετάβλητον ἀγαθὸν μετα-
[259] διώκωμεν καὶ τῆς | ἱκεσίας καὶ θεραπείας αὐτοῦ περιεχώμεθα. καὶ μήτε κρατήσαντες ἐχθρῶν ζηλώσωμεν τὰς ἐκείνων ἐν αἷς εὐσεβεῖν δοκοῦσιν ἀσεβείας υἱοὺς καὶ θυγατέρας τοῖς αὐτῶν
313 κατακαίοντες θεοῖς—οὐχ ὅτι τὰ τέκνα πᾶσι τοῖς βαρβάροις ἐμπιμπράναι δι᾿ ἔθους ἐστίν· οὐ γὰρ οὕτως ἐξηγρίωνται τὰς φύσεις, ὡς, ἃ μηδὲ πολεμίους καὶ ἐχθροὺς ἀσυμβάτους ἐν πολέμῳ, ταῦτα τοὺς φιλτάτους καὶ οἰκειοτάτους ἐν εἰρήνῃ δρᾶν ὑπομένειν· ἀλλ᾿ ὅτι τὰς ψυχὰς τῷ ὄντι καταφλέγουσι καὶ διαφθείρουσιν ὧν ἐγέννησαν ἐξ ἔτι σπαργάνων ἁπαλαῖς ἔτι μὴ ἐγχαράττοντες τὰς[1] ἀληθείας δόξας περὶ τοῦ ἑνὸς καὶ πρὸς ἀλήθειαν ὄντος θεοῦ— μήτ᾿ οὖν ἡττηθέντες ἀναπέσωμεν καὶ ὑπαχθῶμεν ταῖς ἐκείνων εὐτυχίαις ὡς δι᾿ εὐσέβειαν
314 νενικηκότων· πολλοῖς γὰρ ἐπ᾿ ἐνέδρᾳ συμβαίνουσιν αἱ παραυτίκα εὐπραγίαι δέλεαρ σφοδρῶν καὶ ἀνιάτων οὖσαι κακῶν· εἰκὸς δὲ καὶ ἀναξίους ὄντας κατορθοῦν, μὴ δι᾿ ἑαυτούς, ἀλλὰ ὑπὲρ τοῦ λυπεῖσθαι καὶ ἀνιᾶσθαι σφοδρότερον ἡμᾶς οὐχ ὅσια δρῶντας, οἳ γεννηθέντες ἐν πολιτείᾳ φιλοθέῳ καὶ ἐντραφέντες νόμοις ἐπὶ πᾶσαν ἀρετὴν ἀλείφουσι καὶ ἐκ πρώτης ἡλικίας παιδευόμενοι τὰ κάλλιστα παρὰ θεσπεσίοις ἀνδράσι τῶν μὲν ὀλιγωροῦμεν, τῶν δ᾿ ὡς ἀληθῶς

[1] MSS. τῆς.

[a] See Deut. xii. 29-31.

[b] The warning against misunderstanding the lesson of defeat does not appear to have any clear parallel in Deutero-

good ; secondly, how quickly comes the hour of their passing, how they wither away, as it were, before their flower has come to its strength. Let us follow 312
after the good that is stable, unswerving, unchangeable, and hold fast to our service as His suppliants and worshippers.[a] So if we are victorious over our enemies, let us not affect their impious ways in which they think to show their piety by burning their sons and daughters to their gods. This does 313
not mean that all the outside nations have a custom of giving their children to the fire. They have not become so savage in nature as to bring themselves to do in peace to their nearest and dearest what they would not do in wartime to their enemies in the field or to the objects of their implacable hatred. Rather the words refer to that consuming fire in which they veritably destroy the souls of their offspring right from the cradle by failing to imprint on their still tender souls truth-giving conceptions of the one, the truly existent God. [b] Nor yet if defeated let us lose heart or be overcome by their successes as though the victory were due to their piety. To 314
many their temporary pieces of good fortune have proved to be a pitfall, a trap baited with evils vast and fatal. And it may well be that the triumph of the unworthy comes to pass not for their own sake but that we should be more abundantly distressed and afflicted for our unholy deeds ; we who, born as citizens of a godly community, reared under laws which incite to every virtue, trained from our earliest years under divinely gifted men, show contempt for their teaching and cling to what truly deserves our

nomy, though there are various passages which threaten foreign conquest or enslavement as the punishment for forsaking God, *e.g.* xxviii. 49-57.

ὀλιγωρίας ἀξίων περιεχόμεθα, παιδιὰν μὲν τὰ
σπουδαῖα, σπουδὴν δὲ τὰ παιδιᾶς ἄξια ἡγούμενοι.
315 LVIII. Κἂν μέντοι τις ὄνομα καὶ σχῆμα προ-
φητείας ὑποδύς, ἐνθουσιᾶν καὶ κατέχεσθαι δοκῶν,
ἄγῃ πρὸς τὴν τῶν νενομισμένων κατὰ πόλεις
θρησκείαν θεῶν, οὐκ ἄξιον προσέχειν ἀπατωμένους
ὀνόματι προφήτου· γόης γὰρ ἀλλʼ οὐ προφήτης
ἐστὶν ὁ τοιοῦτος, ἐπειδὴ ψευδόμενος λόγια καὶ
316 χρησμοὺς ἐπλάσατο. κἂν ἀδελφὸς ἢ υἱὸς ἢ θυγάτηρ
ἢ γυνὴ ἡ οἰκουρὸς ἢ γνήσιος φίλος ἤ τις ἕτερος
εὔνους εἶναι δοκῶν εἰς τὰ ὅμοια ἐνάγῃ προτρέπων
συνασμενίζειν[1] τοῖς πολλοῖς καὶ ἐπὶ τὰ αὐτὰ ἱερὰ καὶ
τὰς αὐτὰς σπονδάς τε καὶ θυσίας ἀφικνεῖσθαι,
κολαστέον ὡς δήμιον καὶ κοινὸν ἐχθρὸν ὄντα ὀλίγα
φροντίσαντας οἰκειότητος καὶ τὰς παραινέσεις αὐτοῦ
διαγγελτέον πᾶσι τοῖς εὐσεβείας ἐρασταῖς, οἳ
ἀνυπερθέτῳ τάχει ταῖς κατʼ ἀνδρὸς ἀνοσίου τιμωρίαις ἐπιδραμοῦνται κρίνοντες εὐαγὲς τὸ κατʼ αὐτοῦ
317 φονᾶν. ἔστω γὰρ ἡμῖν μία οἰκειότης καὶ φιλίας ἓν
σύμβολον ἡ πρὸς θεὸν ἀρέσκεια καὶ τὸ πάντα λέγειν
τε καὶ πράττειν ὑπὲρ εὐσεβείας· αἱ δʼ ἐκ προγόνων
ἀφʼ αἵματος αὗται λεγόμεναι συγγένειαι καὶ αἱ
κατʼ ἐπιγαμίας ἤ τινας ἄλλας ὁμοιοτρόπους αἰτίας
οἰκειότητες ἀπορριπτέσθωσαν, εἰ μὴ πρὸς τὸ αὐτὸ
τέλος ἐπείγονται, τὴν τοῦ θεοῦ τιμήν, ἣ πάσης
ἑνωτικῆς εὐνοίας ἄλυτος δεσμός ἐστιν· ἀντιλήψονται
[260] γὰρ οἱ τοιοῦτοι σεμνοτέρας καὶ | ἱεροπρεπεστέρας

[1] MSS. ἐνασμενίζειν.

[a] See Deut. xiii. 1-11 and note on § 55 (App. pp. 616-618).

contempt, count the serious side of life as child's-play and what befits the playground as matters of serious import.

LVIII. [a] Further if anyone cloaking himself under 315
the name and guise of a prophet and claiming to be possessed by inspiration lead us on to the worship of the gods recognized in the different cities, we ought not to listen to him and be deceived by the name of prophet. For such a one is no prophet, but an impostor, since his oracles and pronouncements are falsehoods invented by himself. And if a brother or 316
son or daughter or wife or a housemate or a friend however true, or anyone else who seems to be kindly disposed, urge us to a like course, bidding us fraternize with the multitude, resort to their temples, and join in their libations and sacrifices, we must punish him as a public and general enemy, taking little thought for the ties which bind us to him ; and we must send round a report of his proposals to all the lovers of piety, who will rush with a speed which brooks no delay to take vengeance on the unholy man, and deem it a religious duty to seek his death. For we should have one tie of affinity, one accepted 317
sign of goodwill, namely the willingness to serve God and that our every word and deed promotes the cause of piety. But as for these kinships, as we call them, which have come down from our ancestors and are based on blood-relationship, or those derived from intermarriage or other similar causes, let them all be cast aside if they do not seek earnestly the same goal, namely, the honour of God, which is the indissoluble bond of all the affection which makes us one. For those who are so minded will receive in exchange kinships of greater dignity and sanctity. This 318

318 συγγενείας. βεβαιοῦται δέ μου τὴν ὑπόσχεσιν ὁ νόμος λέγων, ὅτι οἱ " τὸ ἀρεστὸν " τῇ φύσει δρῶντες καὶ " τὸ καλὸν " υἱοί εἰσι τοῦ θεοῦ, φησὶ γάρ· " υἱοί ἐστε κυρίῳ τῷ θεῷ ὑμῶν," δηλονότι προνοίας καὶ κηδεμονίας ἀξιωθησόμενοι τῆς ὡς ἐκ πατρός· ἡ δὲ ἐπιμέλεια τοσοῦτον διοίσει τῆς[1] ἀπ' ἀνθρώπων, ὅσονπερ, οἶμαι, καὶ ὁ ἐπιμελούμενος διαφέροι.

319 LIX. Πρὸς τούτοις ἔτι τὰ περὶ τελετὰς καὶ μυστήρια καὶ πᾶσαν τὴν τοιαύτην τερθρείαν καὶ βωμολοχίαν ἐκ τῆς ἱερᾶς ἀναιρεῖ νομοθεσίας, οὐκ ἀξιῶν τοὺς ἐν τοιαύτῃ πολιτείᾳ τραφέντας ὀργιάζεσθαι καὶ μυστικῶν πλασμάτων ἐκκρεμαμένους ὀλιγωρεῖν ἀληθείας καὶ τὰ νύκτα καὶ σκότος προσκεκληρωμένα μεταδιώκειν παρέντας τὰ ἡμέρας καὶ φωτὸς ἄξια. μηδεὶς οὖν μήτε τελείτω μήτε τελείσθω τῶν Μωυσέως φοιτητῶν καὶ γνωρίμων· ἑκάτερον γὰρ καὶ τὸ διδάσκειν καὶ τὸ μανθάνειν
320 τελετὰς οὐ μικρὸν ἀνοσιούργημα. τί γάρ, εἰ καλὰ ταῦτ' ἐστίν, ὦ μύσται, καὶ συμφέροντα, συγκλεισάμενοι ἑαυτοὺς ἐν σκότῳ βαθεῖ τρεῖς ἢ τέτταρας μόνους ὠφελεῖτε, παρὸν ἅπαντας ἀνθρώπους ἐν

[1] MSS. ἰδίοις τοῖς. The correction is stated to be probably supported by the Armenian.

---

[a] See Deut. xiii. 18 and xiv. 1 ἐὰν ἀκούσῃς τῆς φωνῆς Κυρίου τοῦ Θεοῦ σου . . . ποιεῖν τὸ καλὸν καὶ τὸ ἀρεστὸν ἐναντίον Κυρίου τοῦ θεοῦ σου. υἱοὶ ἐστε Κυρίου τοῦ θεοῦ ὑμῶν. Philo treats

promise of mine is confirmed by the law, where it says that they who do " what is pleasing " to nature and what is " good " are sons of God.[a] For it says, " Ye are sons to your Lord God," clearly meaning that He will think fit to protect and provide for you as would a father. And how much this watchful care will exceed that of men is measured, believe me, by the surpassing excellence of Him who bestows it.

LIX. Furthermore, he banishes from the sacred 319
legislation[b] the lore of occult rites and mysteries and all such imposture and buffoonery. He would not have those who were bred in such a commonwealth as ours take part in mummeries and clinging on to mystic fables despise the truth and pursue things which have taken night and darkness for their province, discarding what is fit to bear the light of day. Let none, therefore, of the followers and disciples of Moses either confer or receive initiation to such rites. For both in teacher and taught such action is gross sacrilege. For tell me, ye mystics, if these things 320
are good and profitable, why do you shut yourselves up in profound darkness and reserve their benefits for three or four alone, when by producing them in the midst of the market-place you might extend

the last six words, which are really the beginning of the new paragraph, as part of the previous sentence. See also App. p. 622.

[c] Philo's authority in Deuteronomy for this section is xxiii. 17, 18, where, after the words "there shall be no harlot of the daughters of Israel, neither shall there be a sodomite (LXX fornicator) of the sons of Israel," the LXX adds, "there shall be no τελεσφόρος among the daughters, nor τελισκόμενος among the sons." L. & S. (1936) give for τελεσφόρος "sorceress," and for τελισκόμενος "initiate" or ἱερόδουλος. Whatever the LXX means, Philo clearly understood both words as referring to initiation into the mysteries.

ἀγορᾷ μέσῃ τὰ τῆς ὠφελείας προθέντας, ἵνα πᾶσιν ἀδεῶς ἐξῇ βελτίονος καὶ εὐτυχεστέρου κοινωνῆσαι
321 βίου; φθόνος γὰρ ἀρετῆς διῴκισται. οἱ μὲν γὰρ τὰ βλαβερὰ πράττοντες αἰσχυνέσθωσαν καὶ καταδύσεις ἐπιζητοῦντες καὶ γῆς μυχοὺς καὶ βαθὺ σκότος ἐπικρυπτέσθωσαν τὴν πολλὴν ἀνομίαν αὐτῶν ἐπισκιάζοντες, ὡς μηδεὶς ἴδοι· τοῖς δὲ τὰ κοινωφελῆ δρῶσιν ἔστω παρρησία καὶ μεθ' ἡμέραν διὰ μέσης ἴτωσαν ἀγορᾶς ἐντευξόμενοι πολυανθρώποις ὁμίλοις, ἡλίῳ καθαρῷ τὸν ἴδιον βίον ἀνταυγάσοντες καὶ διὰ τῶν κυριωτάτων αἰσθήσεων τοὺς συλλόγους ὀνήσοντες, ὁρῶντας μὲν ἡδίστας ὁμοῦ καὶ καταπληκτικωτάτας ὄψεις, ἀκούοντας δὲ καὶ ἑστιωμένους λόγων ποτίμων, οἳ τὰς διανοίας
322 τῶν μὴ σφόδρα ἀμούσων εἰώθασιν εὐφραίνειν. ἢ οὐχ ὁρᾷς, ὅτι καὶ ἡ φύσις τῶν ἑαυτῆς ἀοιδίμων καὶ παγκάλων ἔργων οὐδὲν ἀπέκρυψεν, ἀλλὰ ἀστέρας μὲν καὶ τὸν σύμπαντα οὐρανὸν εἴς τε τὴν δι' ὄψεως τέρψιν καὶ πρὸς φιλοσοφίας ἵμερον ἀπέφηνεν, πελάγη δὲ καὶ πηγὰς καὶ ποταμοὺς καὶ τὰς ἀέρος εὐκρασίας δι' ἀνέμων τε καὶ αὐρῶν[1] εἰς τὰς ἐτησίους ὥρας, φυτῶν τε καὶ ζῴων ἔτι δὲ καρπῶν ἀμυθήτους ἰδέας εἰς χρῆσιν καὶ ἀπόλαυσιν ἀνθρώ-
323 πων; εἶτ' οὐκ ἐχρῆν καὶ ἡμᾶς ἑπομένους τοῖς ἐκείνης βουλήμασι πάνθ' ὅσα ἀναγκαῖα καὶ χρήσιμα
[261] | προτιθέναι πᾶσι τοῖς ἀξίοις ἐπ' ὠφελείᾳ; νῦν δὲ

[1] Cohn δι' ἀνέμων τε καὶ πνευμάτων: Mangey with A and H ἀνέμων τε. R has διανέμοντες αὐτῶν and, as ς' in R is a common symbol for καί, the first word clearly stands for δι' ἀνέμων τε καὶ. Why, however, Cohn adopted πνευμάτων (for which I have substituted the obvious αὐρῶν to represent R's αὐτῶν), I do not understand. *Cf.* ii. 172 ἀέρος εὐκρασίαι ζωτικωτάταις αὔραις ἐπιπνέοντος, and much the same in *De Virt.* 93. See also App. p. 622.

them to every man and thus enable all to share in
security a better and happier life? For virtue has 321
no room in her home for a grudging spirit.[a] Let those
who work mischief feel shame and seek holes and corners of the earth and profound darkness, there lie hid and keep the multitude of their iniquities veiled out of the sight of all. But let those whose actions serve the common weal use freedom of speech and walk in daylight through the midst of the market-place, ready to converse with crowded gatherings, to let the clear sunlight shine upon their own life and through the two most royal senses, sight and hearing, to render good service to the assembled groups, who through the one behold spectacles as marvellous as they are delightful,[b] and through the other feast on the fresh sweet draught of words[c] which are wont to gladden the minds of such as are not wholly averse
to learning. Cannot you see that nature also does 322
not conceal any of her glorious and admirable works, but displays the stars and the whole heaven to delight us by the sight and to foster the love of philosophy; so too the seas and fountains and rivers and the air so happily tempered by winds and breezes to make the yearly seasons, and the countless varieties of plants and animals and again of fruits—all for the use and
enjoyment of men? Were it not well, then, that we 323
should follow her intentions and display in public all that is profitable and necessary for the benefit of those who are worthy to use it? As it is, we often

[a] *Cf. Phaedrus* 247 A and ii. 249 below.

[b] The meaning presumably is that a good man's life is a finer spectacle than those which united with the mystic liturgy to charm, and at the same time awe, the initiated.

[c] *Cf. Phaedrus* 243 A and see App. p. 622.

συμβαίνει πολλάκις τῶν μὲν ἀγαθῶν ἀνδρῶν μηδένα μυεῖσθαι, λῃστὰς δ' ἔστιν ὅτε καὶ καταποντιστὰς καὶ γυναικῶν θιάσους βδελυκτῶν καὶ ἀκολάστων, ἐπειδὰν ἀργύριον παράσχωσι τοῖς τελοῦσι καὶ ἱεροφαντοῦσιν. ὑπερόριοι δὴ πάντες οὗτοι φυγαδευέσθωσαν πόλεως καὶ καταστάσεως, ἐν ᾗ τὸ καλὸν καὶ ἡ ἀλήθεια δι' αὐτὰ τιμᾶται. ταῦτα μὲν ἐπὶ τοσοῦτον.

324 LX. Κοινωνίας δὲ καὶ φιλανθρωπίας εἰσηγητὴς ὢν ἐν τοῖς μάλιστα ὁ νόμος ἑκατέρας ἀρετῆς τήν τε ἀξίωσιν καὶ τὴν σεμνότητα διετήρησεν, οὐδενὶ τῶν ἀνιάτως ἐχόντων ἐπιτρέψας καταφυγεῖν ἐπ' αὐτάς,

325 ἀλλὰ πορρωτάτω σκορακίσας. ἐπιστάμενος γοῦν ἐν ταῖς ἐκκλησίαις οὐκ ὀλίγους τῶν μοχθηρῶν παρεισρέοντας καὶ διὰ τὸ συνειλεγμένον πλῆθος λανθάνοντας, ἵνα μὴ τοῦτο γένηται, προανείργει πάντας τοὺς ἀναξίους ἱεροῦ συλλόγου τὴν ἀρχὴν ποιούμενος ἀπὸ τῶν νοσούντων τὴν θήλειαν νόσον ἀνδρογύνων, οἳ τὸ φύσεως νόμισμα παρακόπτοντες εἰς ἀκολάστων γυναικῶν πάθη καὶ μορφὰς εἰσβιάζονται· θλαδίας γὰρ καὶ ἀποκεκομμένους τὰ γεννητκὰ ἐλαύνει τό τε τῆς ὥρας ταμιεύοντας ἄνθος, ἵνα μὴ ῥᾳδίως μαραίνοιτο, καὶ τὸν ἄρρενα τύπον μεταχαράττοντας εἰς θηλύμορφον ἰδέαν.

326 ἐλαύνει δὲ οὐ μόνον πόρνας ἀλλὰ καὶ τοὺς ἐκ πόρνης, ἐπιφερομένους μητρῷον αἶσχος, [καὶ] διότι ἡ πρώτη σπορὰ καὶ γένεσις αὐτοῖς κεκιβδήλευται καὶ συγκέχυται διὰ τὸ πλῆθος τῶν ὡμιληκότων

find that no person of good character is admitted to the mysteries, while robbers and pirates and associations of abominable and licentious women, when they offer money to those who conduct the initiatory rites, are sometimes accepted. Let all such persons, then, be banished from the confines of any State or constitution in which morality and truth are honoured for their own sakes. So much for this subject.

LX. But while the law stands pre-eminent in en- 324
joining fellowship and humanity, it preserves the high position and dignity of both virtues by not allowing anyone whose state is incurable to take refuge with them, but bidding him avaunt and keep
his distance. Thus, knowing that in assemblies there 325
are not a few worthless persons who steal their way in and remain unobserved in the large numbers which surround them, it guards against this danger by precluding all the unworthy from entering the holy congregation. It begins with the men who belie their sex and are affected with effemination, who debase the currency of nature and violate it by assuming the passions and the outward form of licentious women. For it expels those whose generative organs are fractured or mutilated,[a] who husband the flower of their youthful bloom, lest it should quickly wither, and restamp the masculine cast into a feminine form.
And it banishes not only harlots, but 326
also the children of harlots[b] who carry with them their mother's shame, because their begetting and their birth has been adulterated at the fountain-head and reduced to confusion through the number of their

[a] See Deut. xxiii. 1.
[b] See Deut. xxiii. 2 (E.V. "bastard").

ταῖς μητράσιν, ὡς μὴ δύνασθαι τὸν ἀληθῆ πατέρα διαγνῶναι καὶ διακρῖναι.

327 Ὁ δὲ τόπος οὗτος, εἰ καί τις ἄλλος, ἀλληγορίαν ἐπιδέχεται φιλοσόφου θεωρίας ὧν ἀνάπλεως· τῶν γὰρ ἀσεβῶν καὶ ἀνοσίων οὐχ εἷς τρόπος, ἀλλὰ πολλοὶ καὶ διαφέροντες. οἱ μὲν γὰρ τὰς ἀσωμάτους ἰδέας ὄνομα κενὸν ἀμέτοχον ἀληθοῦς πράγματος εἶναί φασι, τὴν ἀναγκαιοτάτην οὐσίαν ἐκ τῶν ὄντων ἀναιροῦντες, ἥτις ἐστὶν ἀρχέτυπον παράδειγμα πάντων ὅσα ποιότητες οὐσίας, καθ' ἣν
328 ἕκαστον εἰδοποιεῖτο καὶ διεμετρεῖτο. τούτους αἱ ἱεραὶ τοῦ νόμου στῆλαι μηνύουσι "θλαδίας"· ὡς γὰρ τὸ τεθλασμένον ἀφῄρηται τὴν ποιότητα καὶ τὸ εἶδος καὶ οὐδὲν ἕτερόν ἐστιν ἢ κυρίως εἰπεῖν ἄμορφος ὕλη, οὕτως καὶ ἡ ἀναιροῦσα δόξα ἰδέας πάντα συγχεῖ καὶ πρὸς τὴν ἀνωτέρω τῶν στοιχείων
329 οὐσίαν τὴν ἄμορφον καὶ ἄποιον ἐκείνην ἄγει. οὗ τί γένοιτ' ἂν ἀτοπώτερον; ἐξ ἐκείνης γὰρ πάντ' ἐγέννησεν ὁ θεός, οὐκ ἐφαπτόμενος αὐτός—οὐ γὰρ ἦν θέμις ἀπείρου καὶ πεφυρμένης ὕλης ψαύειν τὸν εὐδαίμονα καὶ μακάριον—, ἀλλὰ ταῖς ἀσωμάτοις δυνάμεσιν, ὧν ἔτυμον ὄνομα αἱ ἰδέαι, κατεχρήσατο πρὸς τὸ γένος ἕκαστον τὴν ἁρμόττουσαν λαβεῖν
[262] μορφήν. ἡ δὲ πολλὴν ἀταξίαν | εἰσηγεῖται καὶ σύγχυσιν· ἀναιροῦσα γὰρ ταῦτα, δι' ὧν αἱ ποιότητες, συναναιρεῖ ποιότητας.

330 Ἕτεροι δ' ὡς ἐν ἄθλοις κακίας τὰ ἐπ' ἀσεβείᾳ νικητήρια σπεύδοντες αἴρεσθαι προσυπερβάλλουσιν ἅμα ταῖς ἰδέαις καὶ ὕπαρξιν θεοῦ παρακαλυπτό-

---

[a] For some remarks on the relation of the following sections to the philosophers' schools see App. pp. 622-623.

[b] See note on § 48.

mother's lovers, so that they cannot recognize or distinguish their real father.

[a] This is a topic peculiarly susceptible of allegorical 327
interpretation and full of matter for philosophical study. For the heads under which the impious and unholy can be characterized are not one, but many and different. Some aver that the Incorporeal Ideas or Forms are an empty name devoid of any real substance of fact, and thus they abolish in things the most essential element of their being, namely the archetypal patterns of all qualities in what exists, and on which the form and dimensions of each
separate thing was modelled. These the holy tables 328
of the law speak of as "crushed," for just as anything crushed has lost its quality and form and may be literally said to be nothing more than shapeless matter, so the creed which abolishes the Forms confuses everything and reduces it to the pre-elemental state of existence, that state devoid of shape and
quality. Could anything be more preposterous than 329
this? For when out of that confused matter God produced all things, He did not do so with His own handiwork, since His nature, happy and blessed as it was, forbade that He should touch the limitless chaotic matter. Instead He made full use of the incorporeal potencies [b] well denoted by their name of Forms to enable each kind to take its appropriate shape. But this other creed brings in its train no little disorder and confusion. For by abolishing the agencies which created the qualities, it abolishes the qualities also.

There are others who in the arena of wickedness 330
eagerly compete for the first prize in impiety and go to the further extreme of drawing a curtain over the

μενοι ὡς οὐκ ὄντος λεγομένου δ᾿ εἶναι χάριν τοῦ συμφέροντος ἀνθρώποις, οἳ δὴ δι᾿ εὐλάβειαν τοῦ δοκοῦντος πάντῃ παρεῖναι καὶ πάντα καθορᾶν ὄμμασιν ἀκοιμήτοις [οἷς] ἔμελλον ἀνέξειν ἀδικημάτων. τούτους ὁ νόμος εὐθυβόλως "ἀποκόπους" προσαγορεύει τὴν περὶ τοῦ πάντα γεννῶντος ἐκτετμημένους ὑπόληψιν, ἀγόνους μὲν σοφίας, ἐπιτηδεύοντας δὲ τὴν μεγίστην κακιῶν, ἀθεότητα.

331 Τρίτοι δ᾿ εἰσὶν οἳ τὴν ἐναντίαν ἔτεμον εἰσηγησάμενοι πλῆθος ⟨θεῶν⟩ ἀρρένων τε καὶ θηλειῶν, πρεσβυτέρων τε αὖ καὶ νεωτέρων, πολυαρχίας λόγῳ τὸν κόσμον ἀναπλήσαντες, ἵνα τὴν τοῦ ἑνὸς καὶ ὄντως ὄντος ὑπόληψιν ἐκ τῆς ἀνθρώπων δια-
332 νοίας ἐκτέμωσιν. οὗτοι δ᾿ εἰσὶν οἱ συμβολικῶς "ἐκ πόρνης" ὑπὸ τοῦ νόμου προσαγορευόμενοι· καθάπερ γὰρ ὧν μητέρες πόρναι τὸν μὲν ἀληθῆ πατέρα οὔτε ἴσασιν οὔτ᾿ ἐπιγράψασθαι δύνανται, πολλοὺς δὲ καὶ σχεδὸν ἅπαντας τοὺς ἐραστὰς καὶ ὡμιληκότας, τὸν αὐτὸν τρόπον καὶ οἱ ἀγνοοῦντες τὸν ἕνα καὶ ἀληθινὸν θεὸν πολλοὺς καὶ ψευδωνύμους ἀναπλάττοντες περὶ τὸ ἀναγκαιότατον τῶν ὄντων τυφλώττουσιν, ὅπερ ἢ μόνον ἢ πρώτιστον ἐξ αὐτῶν σπαργάνων εἰκὸς ἦν ἀναδιδάσκεσθαι· τί γὰρ μάθημα κάλλιον ἢ τοῦ ὄντως ὄντος θεοῦ;

333 LXI. Τετάρτους δὲ καὶ πέμπτους ἐλαύνει πρὸς

---

[a] For the application of ἀποκεκομμένος (there including

existence of God as well as of the Forms. They assert that God does not exist, but is alleged to exist for the benefit of men who, it was supposed, would abstain from wrongdoing in their fear of Him Whom they believed to be present everywhere and to survey all things with ever-watchful eyes. These are happily called by the law "mutilated,"[a] for they have lost by castration the conception of the Generator of all things. They are impotent to beget wisdom and practise the worst of wickednesses, atheism.

A third class are those who have shaped their 331
course in the opposite direction, and introduced a numerous company of deities male and female, elder and younger. Thus they have infected the world with the idea of a multiplicity of sovereigns in order to geld from the mind of men the conception of the
one and truly existent Being. It is these who are 332
figuratively called by the law "the children of a harlot."[b] For as anyone who has a harlot for his mother has no knowledge of, and can claim no affiliation to, his real father, but must accept the paternity of most or practically all her lovers and patrons, so too those who know not the one true God but invent a number of deities, false so-called, are blind to the most essential reality with which they should have been indoctrinated from the cradle to the exclusion of or before anything else. For what better theme for the learner can there be than the Being who truly exists, even God?

LXI. The banishment is extended to a fourth and 333

θλαδίας) to atheism *cf. De Mig.* 69. The text is usually applied to unwisdom in general.

[b] For the application of the words to polytheism *cf. De Mig.* 69, *De Dec.* 8, *De Conf.* 144.

μὲν τὸ αὐτὸ τέλος ἐπειγομένους, οὐ μὴν ἀπὸ τῶν αὐτῶν βουλευμάτων· ἀμφότεροι γὰρ ζηλωταὶ μεγάλου κακοῦ, φιλαυτίας, ὄντες ὥσπερ τινὰ κοινὴν οὐσίαν διενείμαντο τὴν ὅλην ψυχὴν ἐκ λογικοῦ καὶ ἀλόγου μέρους συνεστῶσαν· καὶ οἱ μὲν τὸ λογικόν, ὃ δὴ νοῦς ἐστι, διεκληρώσαντο, οἱ δὲ τὸ ἄλογον,
334 ὅπερ εἰς τὰς αἰσθήσεις τέμνεται. οἱ μὲν
οὖν τοῦ νοῦ προστάται τὴν ἡγεμονίαν καὶ βασιλείαν τῶν ἀνθρωπείων πραγμάτων ἀνάπτουσιν[1] αὐτῷ καί φασιν ἱκανὸν εἶναι καὶ τὰ παρεληλυθότα μνήμῃ διασῴζειν καὶ τῶν παρόντων ἐρρωμένως ἀντιλαμβάνεσθαι καὶ τὰ μέλλοντα εἰκότι στοχασμῷ
335 φαντασιοῦσθαί τε καὶ λογίζεσθαι. οὗτος γάρ ἐστιν
ὁ γῆν τὴν βαθύγειον καὶ ἀρετῶσαν τῆς ὀρεινῆς καὶ πεδιάδος κατασπείρας καὶ καταφυτεύσας καὶ τὴν βιωφελεστάτην γεωργίαν εὑρών· οὗτος ὁ ναῦν κατασκευάσας καὶ τὴν χέρσου[2] φύσιν ἐπινοίαις παντὸς λόγου κρείττοσι πλωτὴν ἀπεργασάμενος καὶ

[1] MSS. ἀνάγουσιν.

[2] Heinemann χερσαῖον. See note *a* below.

---

[a] *i.e.* the Ammonites (5th) and the Moabites (4th); see the continuation of the passage quoted from Deut. xxiii. "an Ammonite or a Moabite shall not enter into the assembly of the Lord." Philo does not actually quote the verse, possibly feeling that the arguments which lead him to the identification are too involved for this treatise. But that this is his meaning clearly appears from *Leg. All.* iii. 81, when,

a fifth class also.[a] Both these seek the same goal but have different plans for attaining it. Both classes are votaries of the pestilent vice of self-assertion,[b] but have treated the soul, which is a whole consisting of two parts, the rational and irrational, as if it were a property shared by two persons, and have partitioned it out between them. One class has taken as its portion the rational part, that is the mind, the other has taken the irrational, which is subdivided into the
senses. The champions of mind ascribe 334
to it the leadership and sovereignty of human affairs, and aver that it is competent to preserve the past by means of memory, to gain a firm apprehension of the present, and to envisage and calculate the future
by prognostication of what may be expected. It is 335
mind, they say, which sowed and planted the deep and fertile soil in the uplands and lowlands and so greatly enriched human life by the invention of agriculture. It is mind which constructed a ship, and by devices admirable beyond description turned what was

after noting that Ammon and Moab refused to give food to Israel, he described the Ammonites as deriving their nature from "sense" (*αἴσθησις*) their mother, and the Moabites from "mind" their father, the latter name being interpreted as *ἐκ πατρός* (*cf. De Som.* i. 89 and LXX, Gen. xix. 37, "she called his name Moab, saying *ἐκ τοῦ πατρός μου*"). Philo does not, I think, give any corresponding derivation for Ammon, but Heinemann suggests that he derived it from the Hebrew אם = "mother," see Gen. xix. 38 E.V. "and she called his name Ben-ammi" (LXX *ἐκ τοῦ γένους μου*). *Cf.* also *De Post.* 177. See also App. p. 623 on § 327.

[b] I do not feel that this word (or "self-exaltation") is an adequate word for *φιλαυτία* in this context, but it seems to me better than "self-love" or "selfishness," both of which are restricted to the love of oneself as an individual, and not as a member of the race.

ὁδοὺς ἐν θαλάττῃ πολυσχιδεῖς ἄχρι λιμένων τῶν κατὰ πόλεις καὶ ὑποδρόμων λεωφόρους ἀνατεμὼν καὶ γνωρίσας ἠπειρώτας νησιώτας οὐκ ἄν ποτ' εἰς ἑαυτοὺς ἐλθόντας, εἰ μὴ σκάφος ἐναυπηγήθη· οὗτος ὁ καὶ τῶν βαναύσων καὶ τῶν γλαφυρωτέρων τεχ-
336 νῶν λεγομένων εὑρετής· οὗτος γράμματα καὶ ἀριθμοὺς καὶ μουσικὴν καὶ τὴν ἐγκύκλιον ἅπασαν παιδείαν ἐπενόησε καὶ συνηύξησε καὶ πρὸς τὸ τέλος ἤγαγεν· οὗτος καὶ τὸ μέγιστον ἀγαθόν, φιλοσοφίαν, ἐγέννησε καὶ δι' ἑκάστου τῶν μερῶν αὐτῆς ὠφέλησε τὸν ἀνθρώπινον βίον, διὰ μὲν τοῦ λογικοῦ πρὸς
[263] ἀνεξαπάτητον ἑρμηνείαν, διὰ | δὲ τοῦ ἠθικοῦ πρὸς τὴν τῶν τρόπων ἐπανόρθωσιν, διὰ δὲ τοῦ φυσικοῦ πρὸς ἐπιστήμην οὐρανοῦ τε καὶ κόσμου. καὶ ἄλλα μέντοι παμπληθῆ λέγουσιν ἐγκώμια νοῦ συμφορήσαντές τε καὶ ἀγείραντες ἔχοντα[1] τὴν ἀναφορὰν ἐπὶ τὰ λεχθέντα ἤδη, περὶ ὧν οὐ καιρὸς ἐνοχλεῖν.

337 LXII. οἱ δὲ τῶν αἰσθήσεων προστάται τὸν ἔπαινον αὐτῶν εὖ μάλα σεμνοποιοῦσι διανέμοντες τῷ λόγῳ τὰς ἀπ' αὐτῶν ἐγγινομένας χρείας καί φασιν, ὅτι δύο μὲν αἴτια τοῦ ζῆν ἐστιν, ὄσφρησις καὶ γεῦσις, δύο δὲ τοῦ καλῶς ζῆν, ὅρασις καὶ ἀκοή.

[1] MSS. ἔχοντες.

[a] Or (reading χερσαῖον as Heinemann, or perhaps χέρσοι ἴδιον as suggested by R's χερ . . . διον) "turns the land-creature man into one that floats or swims." Heinemann quotes very appositely *Spec. Leg.* iv. 155, where, in a passage very similar to this, "the most incredible thing is that ἡ χερσαία φύσις διὰ πλωτῆς οἵα τε ᾖ περαιοῦσθαι," also *De Op* 147, where man is said to be χερσαῖον ζῷον on land, and ἔνυδρον when he sails in ships. The analogy with *Spec. Leg*

naturally dry land into a waterway,[a] opened up in the sea routes whose many branches serve as highways to the havens and roadsteads of the different states, and made the inhabitants of the mainland and those of the islands known to each other, who would never have met if a vessel had not been built. It is mind which discovered the mechanical[b] and the finer arts,
as they are called, which devised, fostered and brought 336
to their consummation letters and numbers and music and the whole range of school studies. Mind too was the parent of philosophy, the greatest of blessings, and employed each part of it to benefit human life, the logical to produce absolute exactitude of language, the ethical for the amelioration of character, the physical to give knowledge of heaven and the universe.[c] And besides these they collect and accumulate in honour of mind a vast number of tributes to the same effect as those already mentioned, with which we have no occasion to trouble ourselves
now. LXII. The champions of the senses 337
sound their praises in lofty terms. They discuss and classify them according to the purposes which they serve and tell us that two, smell and taste, are the basis of life, and two, sight and hearing, of good life.

s not quite exact as there πλωτῆς is passive, while here it would be on Heinemann's rendering active. His other argument that dry land does not become a waterway might be met by supposing that Philo is thinking of Xerxes' canal through Mount Athos, on which he enlarges in *De Som.* i. 118. He may not have known of any similar undertaking, but it is quite in his manner to treat a single historical example as a common occurrence.

[b] Or "vulgar."

[c] For the familiar triple division of philosophy see particularly Diog. Laert. vii. 39, and notes on *Leg. All.* 157 and *De Agr.* 14.

338 διὰ μὲν οὖν γεύσεως αἱ τῶν σιτίων τροφαὶ παρα-
πέμπονται, διὰ δὲ μυκτήρων ὁ ἀήρ, οὗ πᾶν ζῷον
ἐξήρτηται· τροφὴ δ' ἐστὶ καὶ οὗτος ἡ συνεχὴς καὶ
ἀδιάστατος, ὃς οὐκ ἐγρηγορότας μόνον ἀλλὰ καὶ
κοιμωμένους διατρέφει τε καὶ διασῴζει· σαφὴς δὲ
πίστις· εἰ γὰρ κἂν βραχύτατον ὁ τῆς ἀναπνοῆς
δίαυλος ἐπισχεθείη κατὰ τὴν τοῦ πεφυκότος ἔξωθεν
ἐποχετεύεσθαι πνεύματος ἀποκοπήν, θάνατος ἀπαρ-
339 αίτητος ἐξ ἀνάγκης ἐπακολουθήσει. τῶν
γε μὴν φιλοσόφων αἰσθήσεων, δι' ὧν περιγίνεται τὸ
εὖ ζῆν, ὅρασις μὲν φῶς τὸ κάλλιστον ἐν τοῖς οὖσιν
ὁρᾷ, ὁρᾷ δὲ διὰ φωτὸς τἆλλα πάντα, ἥλιον, σελήνην,
ἀστέρας, οὐρανόν, γῆν, θάλατταν, φυτῶν καὶ ζῴων
ἀμυθήτους διαφοράς, καὶ συνόλως πάντα σώματα
καὶ σχήματα καὶ χρώματα καὶ μεγέθη, ὧν ἡ θέα
περιττὴν φρόνησιν ἐξειργάσατο καὶ πολὺν ἵμερον
340 ἐπιστήμης ἐγέννησε. παρέχεται δὲ καὶ ἄνευ τούτων ὠφελείας ὅρασις ἡμῖν τὰς μεγίστας, εἴς τε τὴν
οἰκείων καὶ ἀλλοτρίων καὶ φίλων καὶ ἐχθρῶν
διάκρισιν καὶ βλαβερῶν μὲν φυγήν, αἵρεσιν δὲ τῶν
ἐπ' ὠφελείᾳ. γέγονε μὲν οὖν καὶ τῶν ἄλλων
ἕκαστον τοῦ σώματος μερῶν πρὸς ἁρμοττούσας
χρείας καὶ σφόδρα ἀναγκαίας, ὡς βάσεις μὲν πρὸς
περίπατον καὶ δρόμον καὶ τἆλλα ὅσα διὰ σκελῶν
ἐνεργεῖται, χεῖρες δὲ πρὸς τὸ πρᾶξαί τι καὶ δοῦναι
καὶ λαβεῖν· ὀφθαλμοὶ δὲ ὡσπερεί τι κοινὸν ἀγαθὸν
τὴν τοῦ δύνασθαι κατορθοῦν αἰτίαν καὶ τούτοις καὶ
341 τοῖς ἄλλοις ἅπασι παρέχουσιν. ἀψευδέστατοι δ' οἱ
πεπηρωμένοι μάρτυρες, οἳ μήτε χερσὶ μήτε ποσὶ
δύνανται χρῆσθαι κατὰ τὸ βέλτιον τὴν πρόσρησιν

[a] Lit. "use them in the better way," *i.e.* that in which they could be used if supported by sight.

Taste acts as a conductor of the sustenance which 338
food gives, and the nostrils do the same for the air
on which every created being depends. Air too is a
means of sustenance, constant and unceasing, and
nourishes and preserves us not only when awake but
also while we sleep. We have a clear proof of this ;
for if the course of respiration backwards and forwards
is stopped ever so little by the interception of the
natural influx of breath from outside, death will
inexorably and inevitably follow. To 339
turn to the senses which minister to philosophy
and secure for us the good life, sight sees the
light which is the most beautiful of all that is
and by means of the light sees everything else,
sun, moon, stars, heaven, earth, sea, the countless
varieties of plants and animals, in general, all kinds
of bodies, shapes, colours and magnitudes, the contemplation of which creates a subtle intelligence
and generates a great thirst for knowledge. But 340
apart from these benefits sight gives us others of
the highest value, by enabling us to distinguish
between kinsfolk and strangers, friends and enemies,
and to shun the harmful and choose the beneficent. And while it is true that each of the other
members of the body has its appropriate and very
indispensable use, as the feet for walking and
running and the other activities to which the legs are
instrumental, and the hands for doing and giving and
receiving things, the eyes may be said to have a
common value and to create the conditions under
which these members and all the others can operate
successfully. The strongest testimony to this truth 341
is afforded by the blind, who cannot make the proper
use [a] of their hands or feet and thus verify the name

ἐπαληθεύοντες, ἣν οὐκ ἐπ᾽ ὀνείδει μᾶλλον ἢ οἴκτῳ θέσθαι φασὶ τοὺς πρότερον ἀδυνάτους ὀνομάσαντας· ἅμα γὰρ τῇ τῶν ὀμμάτων φθορᾷ καὶ αἱ τοῦ σώματος δυνάμεις οὐχ ὑποσκελίζονται μόνον ἀλλὰ καὶ
342 φθείρονται. θαυμασιώτατον δὲ καὶ ἀκοὴ χρῆμα, δι᾽ ἧς μέλη καὶ μέτρα καὶ ῥυθμοί, ἔτι δὲ ἁρμονίαι καὶ συμφωνίαι καὶ τῶν γενῶν καὶ συστημάτων αἱ μεταβολαὶ καὶ πάνθ᾽ ὅσα κατὰ μουσικὴν ἐπικρίνεται, καὶ λόγων [τε] τῶν κατὰ διεξόδους [καὶ] παμπληθεῖς ἰδέαι δικανικῶν συμβουλευτικῶν ἐγκωμιαστικῶν, ἔτι δὲ τῶν ἐν ἱστορίαις καὶ διαλόγοις καὶ τῶν ἐν ὁμιλίαις ἀναγκαίαις περὶ τῶν ἐν βίῳ πραγμάτων πρὸς τοὺς ἀεὶ πλησιάζοντας· συνόλως γὰρ διὰ φωνῆς διττὴν ἐχούσης δύναμιν, εἴς τε τὸ λέγειν καὶ τὸ ᾄδειν, ἑκάτερα τὰ ὦτα[1] διακρίνει πρὸς
343 ὠφέλειαν ψυχῆς· ᾠδὴ γὰρ καὶ λόγος ὑγιεινὰ καὶ σωτήρια φάρμακα, ἡ μὲν τὰ πάθη κατεπᾴδουσα καὶ τὸ ἄρρυθμον ἐν ἡμῖν ῥυθμοῖς, τὸ δ᾽ ἐκμελὲς μέλεσι, τὸ δ᾽ ἄμετρον μέτροις ἐπιστομίζουσα—ποικίλον δ᾽ ἐστὶ καὶ παντοδαπὸν ἕκαστον, ὡς μουσικοὶ καὶ
[264] ποιηταὶ μαρτυροῦσιν, οἷς | πιστεύειν ἀναγκαῖον ἐπιτήδευμα τοῖς εὖ πεπαιδευμένοις—, ὁ δὲ λόγος ἐπέχων καὶ ἀνακόπτων τὰς ἐπὶ κακίαν ὁρμὰς καὶ τοὺς κεκρατημένους ἀφροσύναις καὶ ἀηδίαις ἐκνοσηλεύων, μαλακώτερον μὲν τοὺς ὑπείκοντας,

[1] MSS. ταῦτα, which Cohn printed but corrected in his Addenda (from the Armenian) to τὰ ὦτα.

[a] *i.e.* in Attic law. See L. & S. (revised), which gives the reference to Aristotle, Ἀθ. Πολ. 49. 4, where we have δοκιμάζει

of incapable[a] given to them in the past, more, we are told, in pity than as a reproach. For when the eyes are destroyed, the capacities of the body are not merely overthrown, but actually perish. In 342
hearing too we have something very marvellous. By means of it we distinguish melodies and metres and rhythm, and with them the harmonies and consonances, and the varieties of genera and systems[b] and all the elements of music; and again, the multitudinous kinds of set speeches delivered in the law-courts, in the senate, in laudations, as well as the language used in historical narrative and dialogues and discussions of matters of business which we are bound to have with those with whom we come in contact from time to time. For we may say in sum that the voice has a twofold capacity for speech and song. Both these are assessed by the ears to the benefit of the soul. For both are medicaments, health-giving and life- 343
preserving. Song charms away the passions and controls the irregular element in us with its rhythm, the discordant with its melodies, the immoderate with its measures. And each of these three assumes every variety of form, as the musicians and poets testify, belief in whom necessarily becomes habitual in those who have received a good education. Speech checks and hampers impulses to vice and effects the cure of those in whom foolish and distressful thoughts have gained the mastery. It deals more gently with

δὲ τοὺς ἀδυνάτους ἡ βουλή. It then appears that the term includes paupers and τοὺς τὸ σῶμα πεπηρωμένους ὥστε μὴ δύνασθαι μηδὲν ἔργον ἐργάζεσθαι. See also the oration of Lysias 24, ὑπὲρ τοῦ ἀδυνάτου, where the defendant argues his right to the privileges.

[b] For the use of these words to translate γένη καὶ συστήματα see note on *De Som.* i. 28.

σφοδρότερον δὲ τοὺς ἀφηνιάζοντας, αἴτιος γίνεται τῶν μεγίστων ὠφελειῶν.

344 LXIII. Τοιαῦτα συνείροντες οἵ τε τοῦ νοῦ θιασῶται καὶ οἱ τῶν αἰσθήσεων οἱ μὲν ἐκεῖνον οἱ δὲ ταύτας θεοπλαστοῦσιν ὑπὸ φιλαυτίας ἐκλαθόμενοι τοῦ πρὸς ἀλήθειαν ὄντος θεοῦ. διὸ πάντας εἰκότως ἀπήλασεν ἱεροῦ συλλόγου, τούς τε τὰς ἰδέας ἀναιροῦντας, "θλαδίας" ὑπειπών, καὶ τοὺς κατὰ τὸ παντελὲς ἀθέους, οἷς ὄνομα οἰκεῖον τὸ "ἀποκόπων" ἔθετο, καὶ τοὺς ἐξ ἐναντίας εἰσηγητὰς θεογονίας, οὓς ἐκάλεσεν "ἐκ πόρνης," καὶ ἐπὶ πᾶσι τοὺς φιλαύτους, ὧν οἱ μὲν τὸν λογισμόν, οἱ δ' ἑκάστην τῶν αἰσθήσεων ἐξεθείωσαν· ἐπείγονται γὰρ πάντες οὗτοι πρὸς τὸ αὐτὸ τέλος, εἰ καὶ ἀπὸ διαφερόντων ἄγονται βουλευμάτων, τὸν ἕνα καὶ ὄντως
345 ὄντα θεὸν παρησυχάζοντες. ἀλλ' ἡμεῖς γε οἱ φοιτηταὶ καὶ γνώριμοι τοῦ προφήτου Μωυσέως τὴν τοῦ ὄντος ζήτησιν οὐ μεθησόμεθα, τὴν ἐπιστήμην αὐτοῦ τέλος εὐδαιμονίας εἶναι νομίζοντες καὶ ζωὴν μακραίωνα, καθὰ καὶ ὁ νόμος φησὶ τοὺς προσκειμένους τῷ θεῷ ζῆν ἅπαντας, δόγμα τιθεὶς ἀναγκαῖον καὶ φιλόσοφον· ὄντως γὰρ οἱ μὲν ἄθεοι τὰς ψυχὰς τεθνᾶσιν, οἱ δὲ τὴν παρὰ τῷ ὄντι θεῷ τεταγμένοι τάξιν ἀθάνατον βίον ζῶσιν.

---

[a] As their particular name (to distinguish them from the θλάδιαι).

[b] See Deut. iv. 4. The meaning of the original is that

the docile, more drastically with the rebellious, and thus becomes the source of the greatest possible benefits.

344 LXIII. Such is the chain of argument which leads the votaries of mind and the votaries of the senses to ascribe divinity to their respective idols, forgetting in their self-assertion the God Who truly exists. And therefore Moses naturally banished them all from the holy congregation, both those who abolish the Forms, who appear under the name of "the crushed," and those who absolutely deny God, to whom he assigned the suitable [a] title of "the mutilated" and those who preach the opposite doctrine of a family of gods, called by him "the children of the harlot," and finally the self-assertive, one party of whom deify the reason, the other each several sense. For these last all press to the same goal, though influenced by different plans for attaining it, and ignore the one and really existing God.

345 But we, the scholars and disciples of Moses, will not forgo our quest of the Existent, holding that the knowledge of Him is the consummation of happiness. It is also agelong life. The law tells us that all who "cleave to God live," [b] and herein it lays down a vital doctrine fraught with much wisdom. For in very truth the godless are dead in soul, but those who have taken service in the ranks of the God Who only IS are alive, and that life can never die.

those who cleave to God when the others followed Baal-Peor are alive to-day. Philo gives this general meaning to the text in *De Fug.* 56 also.

The Third Commandment (1-38).

While swearing at all is to be deprecated, since the simple word should be enough, to swear by parents or heaven and the like is better than using God's name (1-5), which many do recklessly (6-8). When swearing is necessary the oath must be performed, if it can be lawfully (9). To call God to witness a falsehood is impious (10-11). Criminal or vindictive oaths, however, should not be performed (12-17). Philo then condemns the arrogant swearing of the extravagant rich and contrasts them with others who though rich live simply (18-23). He discusses vows and particularly the rule by which widows, unlike virgins and wives, cannot cancel a vow (24-25). This is susceptible of an allegorical interpretation (28-31). This is interrupted by 26-27, which returns to the subject of perjury and the penalties for the perjuror and his accomplices. The Pentateuchal regulations for assessing votive offerings are then discussed, when the votary offers (*a*) himself (32-34), (*b*) an animal (35-36), (*c*) a house (37-38).

The Fourth Commandment (39-222).

Philo begins with a sketch of the way in which he proposes to treat the subject (39), followed by some remarks on the sacred number Seven (41), and a list of the ten feasts (41).

The first feast is the feast of every day. This conception, that the ideal life of the true philosopher is one continuous feast, is worked out with much eloquence (42-49). For its scriptural foundation see note on § 45.

The second feast, the Sabbath itself, after some further remarks on the mystical properties of Seven (56-59), is set forth partly as a necessary respite from toil (60), but still more as a time for exercising the soul in contrast to the body (61-64). The prohibition of fire (65), and the extension of the rest to servants (65-68), and to cattle (69-70) are noted. With the Sabbath we may associate other institutions which bear witness to the sanctity of Seven: (*a*) the cancellation of debts in the seventh year (71-73), and this leads to a denunciation of lending money on interest in general (74-78); (*b*) liberation of slaves in the same year, which provides an occasion for the lesson of treating slaves humanely (79-85); (*c*) the same lesson that consideration should be shewn not only by masters to servants, but by rulers to subjects is taught by the "sabbatical year," which leaves the land fallow in the seventh year (86-103), and also by throwing the fields open encourages generosity to the poor (104-109); (*d*) the same applies to the fiftieth year, in which estates return to the original owners (110-115), with special regulations about houses (116-121) and debtors and purchased slaves (122-123). This is followed by some general remarks (for the connexion see note on § 124) about the laws of inheritance (124-132), and the right of primogeniture (133-139).

The third feast is the New Moon, and some observations on the place of the moon in the system of things is subjoined (140-144). Fourth is the Passover, a feast in which each layman acts as priest, interpreted by Philo as the " Crossing " from the passions to wisdom (145-149). Fifth is " Unleavened Bread," and reasons are given for the time at which it occurs and the nature of the food enjoined (150-161). Sixth, the offering of the " Sheaf," is combined with the two just mentioned. Philo takes this first offering of the harvest in the double aspect of a thank-offering, (*a*) for the whole world (162-167), and (*b*) for Israel, acknowledging how much the harvest owes to nature rather than man (168-175).

Seventh is the Feast of Weeks or Pentecost (179-187). Eighth is the opening of the sacred month, or Feast of Trumpets (188-192). Ninth the Fast or Day of Atonement (193-203). Tenth the Feast of Tabernacles (204-214). All these are accompanied by a number of reflections on their origin and significance. Besides these there is the rite of offering the " Basket," for which no date can be fixed (215-222).

The Fifth Commandment (223-241).

The claims of parents are justified on the grounds that their position as Creators is analogous to that of God, and that they are the seniors, the benefactors, the rulers and the absolute masters or owners of their children (223-236). But the commandment also enjoins respect to age in general (237-238), and also the duty of parents to avoid undue indulgence (239-241).

The treatise concludes with declaring death to be the appropriate punishment for disobedience, to the Fifth (242-248), the Fourth (249-251), the Third (252-254), the Second and First (255-256). The rewards for obedience, except the Fifth, for which a definite reward is mentioned, are to be found in the thought that virtue is its own reward (257-262).

For Cohn's Numeration of Chapters see Gen. Int. p. xviii.

ΠΕΡΙ ΤΩΝ ΑΝΑΦΕΡΟΜΕΝΩΝ ΕΝ ΕΙΔΕΙ ΝΟΜΩΝ ΕΙΣ ΤΡΙΑ ΓΕΝΗ ΤΩΝ ΔΕΚΑ ΛΟΓΙΩΝ, ΤΟ ΤΡΙΤΟΝ, ΤΟ ΤΕΤΑΡΤΟΝ, ΤΟ ΠΕΜΠΤΟΝ· ΤΟ ΠΕΡΙ ΕΥΟΡΚΙΑΣ ΚΑΙ ΣΕΒΑΣΜΟΥ ΤΗΣ ΙΕΡΑΣ ΕΒΔΟΜΗΣ ΚΑΙ ΓΟΝΕΩΝ ΤΙΜΗΣ

[270]
1 I. Ἐν μὲν τῇ πρὸ ταύτης συντάξει δύο κεφάλαια
ἠκρίβωται τῶν δέκα, τό τε περὶ τοῦ μὴ νομίζειν
θεοὺς αὐτοκρατεῖς ἑτέρους καὶ τὸ περὶ τοῦ μηδὲν
θεοπλαστεῖν χειρόκμητον· εἴρηται δὲ καὶ τὰ ἑκατέρῳ τῶν κατὰ μέρος διατεταγμένων ἁρμόττοντα
νόμιμα. νυνὶ δὲ περὶ τριῶν τῶν κατὰ στοῖχον ἑξῆς
διαλεξώμεθα πάλιν ἐφαρμόττοντες τὰ προσήκοντα
2 τῶν ἐν εἴδει. πρῶτον δ' ἐστὶ τῶν τριῶν
τὸ μὴ θεοῦ ὄνομα λαμβάνειν ἐπὶ ματαίῳ. ὁ γὰρ
τοῦ σπουδαίου, φησί, λόγος ὅρκος ἔστω, βέβαιος,
ἀκλινής, ἀψευδέστατος, ἐρηρεισμένος ἀληθείᾳ. κἂν
εἰ ὀμνύναι μέντοι βιάζοιντο αἱ χρεῖαι, πατρὸς ἢ
[271] μητρὸς ζώντων μὲν ὑγείαν καὶ εὐετηρίαν, | τετελευ-
τηκότων δὲ τὴν μνήμην ὅρκον ποιητέον· ἀπεικο-
νίσματα γὰρ οὗτοί γε καὶ μιμήματα θείας δυνάμεώς
εἰσι, τοὺς μὴ ὄντας εἰς τὸ εἶναι παραγαγόντες.

BOOK II

ON THE SPECIAL LAWS WHICH FALL UNDER THREE OF THE TEN GENERAL COMMANDMENTS, NAMELY THE THIRD ON THE DUTY OF KEEPING OATHS,[a] THE FOURTH ON REVERENCING THE SEVENTH DAY, AND THE FIFTH ON HONOURING PARENTS

I. In the preceding treatise we have dealt fully 1
with two of the ten heads, one directed against the acknowledgement of other sovereign gods, the other against giving divine honours to any work of men's hands. And we have described such among the particular enactments of the law as may be properly classed under either head. Let us now discuss the three next in the list, again subjoining those of the special ordinances which belong to them.

The first of the three forbids us to take God's name 2
in vain: the good man's word, it means, should be an oath, firm, unswerving, utterly free from falsehood, securely planted on truth. And if indeed occasion should force us to swear, the oath should be by a father and mother, their good health and welfare if they are alive, their memory if they are dead. For parents are copies and likenesses of the divine power, since they have brought the non-existent into exist-

[a] As the sequel shews, a very inadequate term to describe §§ 1-38.

3 ἀναγέγραπταί τις ἐν τοῖς νόμοις τῶν ἀρχηγετῶν
καὶ ἐπὶ σοφίᾳ μάλιστα θαυμασθέντων ὀμνὺς "κατὰ
τοῦ φόβου τοῦ πατρός," ὑπὲρ ὠφελείας, οἶμαι, τῶν
ἔπειτα καὶ διδαχῆς ἀναγκαίας, ἵνα τοὺς γονεῖς ὃν
χρὴ τρόπον τιμῶσι στέργοντες ὡς εὐεργέτας καὶ
εὐλαβούμενοι ὡς ὑπὸ φύσεως κατασταθέντας ἄρχοντας καὶ μὴ ῥᾳδίως ἐπιχειρῶσιν ὀνομάζειν θεόν.
4 ἄξιον ἐπαινεῖν καὶ τούς, εἴ ποτε βιασθεῖεν ὀμνύναι,
τῷ μέλλειν καὶ βραδύνειν καὶ ἀποκνεῖν ἐμποιοῦντας
δέος οὐ μόνον τοῖς ὁρῶσιν ἀλλὰ καὶ τοῖς προκαλου-
μένοις εἰς τὸν ὅρκον· εἰώθασι γὰρ ἀναφθεγξάμενοι
τοσοῦτον μόνον "νὴ τόν" ἢ "μὰ τόν," μηδὲν
προσπαραλαβόντες, ἐμφάσει τῆς ἀποκοπῆς τρανοῦν
5 ὅρκον οὐ γενόμενον. ἀλλὰ καὶ προσπαραλαβέτω
τις, εἰ βούλεται, μὴ μέντοι τὸ ἀνωτάτω καὶ πρεσβύτατον εὐθὺς αἴτιον, ἀλλὰ γῆν, ἥλιον, ἀστέρας,
οὐρανόν, τὸν σύμπαντα κόσμον· ἀξιολογώτατα γὰρ
ταῦτα ἅτε καὶ πρεσβύτερα τῆς ἡμετέρας γενέσεως
καὶ προσέτι ἀγήρω διαιωνιοῦντα τῇ τοῦ πεποιη-
6 κότος γνώμῃ. II. τοσαύτῃ δέ τινες
εὐχερείᾳ καὶ ῥαθυμίᾳ χρῶνται, ὥστε τὰ ἐν γενέσει
πάντα ταῦθ' ὑπερβάντες ἐπὶ τὸν ποιητὴν καὶ πατέρα
τῶν ὅλων ἀνατρέχειν τῷ λόγῳ τολμῶσι, μὴ τόπους
εἰ βέβηλοι ἢ ἱεροί, μὴ καιροὺς εἰ ἐπιτήδειοι, μὴ
αὑτοὺς εἰ καθαροὶ σῶμα καὶ ψυχήν, μὴ τὰ πράγματα εἰ μεγάλα, μὴ τὰς χρείας εἰ ἀναγκαῖαι
προεξετάσαντες, ἀλλά, τὸ λεγόμενον δὴ τοῦτο,

---

[a] *i.e.* Jacob, see Gen. xxxi. 53. "The fear" really means (see *v.* 42) the God whom Isaac feared; so in R.V. it is printed "Fear." Philo evidently takes it to mean Jacob's own fear of Isaac.

[b] See App. p. 624.

[c] ἐμφάσει is used in the rhetorical sense of the significance

ence. In the laws we read of one of our first founders,[a] 3
who are particularly admired for their wisdom, that he swore by the fear of his father, a fact recorded, I believe, for the benefit of posterity and to teach them the necessary lesson that they should honour their parents in the proper way by showing affection to them as benefactors and awe of them as rulers appointed by nature, and should not lightly essay
to use the name of God. Those persons too deserve 4
praise whose unwillingness, tardiness and shrinking, if they are ever forced to swear, raise qualms not only in the spectators but even in those who are administering the oath: such people are in the habit of saying "Yes, by — " or "No, by—"[b] and add nothing more, and by thus breaking off suggest[c] the clear
sense of an oath without actually making it. But 5
also a person may add to his "Yes" or "No" if he wish, not indeed the highest and most venerable and primal cause, but earth, sun, stars, heaven, the whole universe.[d] For these are worthy of highest respect, since they have precedence in time over our place in creation, and also will remain for ever untouched by age according to the purpose of Him Who made
them. II. But so great is the lightness 6
and heedlessness shown by some that they pass by all these works of creation and allow their words to dash on to the Maker and Father of all, never staying to examine whether the place is profane or holy, whether the occasion is suitable, whether they themselves are pure in body and soul, whether the business is important or the object necessary. Instead,

conveyed by the ἀποκοπή. Heinemann's translation "and so suddenly break off their affirmation so that the oath is not actually effected" misses the full meaning.

[d] Contrast Matthew v. 34 f.

" ἀνίπτοις χερσὶ " πάντα φύροντες, ὡς δέον, ἐπειδὴ γλῶτταν ἡ φύσις αὐτοῖς ἐδωρήσατο, λελυμένῃ
7 χρῆσθαι καὶ ἀχαλινώτῳ πρὸς ἃ μὴ θέμις· οὓς ἐχρῆν
ὀργάνων τῷ καλλίστῳ, ᾧ φωνὴ καὶ λόγος τὰ
βιωφελέστατα καὶ κοινωνίας αἴτια τετράνωται,
πρὸς τιμὴν καὶ σεμνότητα καὶ εὐδαιμονισμὸν κατα-
8 χρῆσθαι τοῦ πάντων αἰτίου. νυνὶ δ' ὑπὸ τῆς ἄγαν
ἀσεβείας περὶ ὧν ἂν τύχῃ τὰς φρικωδεστάτας
ὀνομάζουσι κλήσεις καὶ ἄλλα ἐπ' ἄλλοις ἐπιφέροντες
ὀνόματα σωρηδὸν οὐκ ἐρυθριῶσι, νομίζοντες τῇ
πυκνότητι καὶ τῷ συνεχεῖ τῶν ἐπαλλήλων ὅρκων
οὗ διανοοῦνται περιέσεσθαι, λίαν ὄντες εὐήθεις· οὐ
γὰρ πίστεως ἡ πολυορκία τεκμήριον ἀλλ' ἀπιστίας
ἐστὶ παρὰ τοῖς εὖ φρονοῦσιν.
9 III. Ἐὰν δέ τις ἐκβιασθεὶς ὀμόσῃ περὶ παντὸς
[272] οὑτινοσοῦν, ὃ μὴ νόμος | ἀπείρηκε, παντὶ σθένει καὶ
μηχανῇ πάσῃ τὸν ὅρκον βεβαιούτω μηδὲν ἐμποδὼν
τιθέμενος εἰς τὴν τοῦ γνωσθέντος τελείωσιν, καὶ
μάλιστα ἐπειδὰν μὴ ὀργαὶ ἀτίθασοι ἢ λελυττηκότες
ἔρωτες ἢ ἐπιθυμίαι ἀκάθεκτοι τὴν διάνοιαν ἐκμήνω-
σιν, ὡς ἀγνοῆσαι τὰ λεγόμενα καὶ πραττόμενα,
λογισμῷ δὲ καὶ διανοίᾳ νηφούσῃ ποιῆται τὸν ὅρκον.
10 τί γὰρ ἄμεινον ἢ ἀψευδεῖν παρ' ὅλον τὸν βίον καὶ
ταῦτα μάρτυρι θεῷ χρώμενον; ὅρκος γὰρ οὐδὲν

---

[a] *Il.* vi. 266 " I fear to pour a libation to Zeus with unwashed hands."

[b] Lit. " causes " in antithesis to the " cause " below. But in English we can hardly call " words " the " cause of fellowship." I have introduced " creators " and " created " to preserve something of the antithesis.

[c] καὶ ταῦτα, " and that too," is difficult. The natural mean-

with unwashed hands,[a] as the phrase goes, they make a foul brew of everything, as though Nature's gift of a tongue justified them in using it without
restraint or bridle for unlawful purposes, whereas 7
that most excellent of instruments which gives clear expression to voice and words, those great benefactors of human life and creators[b] of a sense of fellowship, should have been employed to the full by them to ascribe honour and majesty and blessedness to
the Cause Which has created all things. As it is, so 8
highly impious are they that on any chance matter the most tremendous titles are on their lips and they do not blush to use name after name, one piled upon another, thinking that the continual repetition of a string of oaths will secure them their object. A very foolish delusion. For in the eyes of sensible people much swearing is a proof, not of good faith, but of faithlessness.

III. But if anyone has been absolutely compelled 9
to swear on any matter whatever, so long as it is not forbidden by the law, he should use all his strength and every means in his power to make good his oath, and allow nothing to hinder him from carrying out his decision, particularly when he has taken the oath in a reasonable and sober frame of mind, not distraught by savage tempers or frenzied yearnings or uncontrollable desires, so that he does not know what
he says or does. For what is better than to practise 10
a lifelong veracity, and to have God as our witness thereto?[c] For an oath is nothing else than to call

ing is that having taken God as our witness enhances the excellence of keeping to the truth. But this contradicts what he has said against swearing at all. Perhaps in this sentence he passes for a moment from oaths to vows, *i.e.* from swearing *by* God to swearing *to* God.

ἄλλο ἢ μαρτυρία θεοῦ περὶ πράγματος ἀμφισβητουμένου· θεὸν δὲ μὴ ἐπ' ἀληθεῖ[1] καλεῖν πάντων ἀν-
11 οσιώτατον. ὁ γὰρ τοῦτο ποιῶν μόνον οὐκ ἄντικρυς βοᾷ, κἂν ἡσυχάζειν δοκῇ· " σοὶ χρῶμαι τοῦ ἀδικεῖν προκαλύμματι· αἰδουμένῳ μοι τὸ δοκεῖν ἁμαρτάνειν συνέργησον, ἀντ' ἐμοῦ πονηρευομένου τὴν αἰτίαν ὑπόστηθι· μέλει γάρ μοι πλημμελοῦντι μὴ φαύλῳ νομίζεσθαι· σὺ δὲ τῆς παρὰ τοῖς πολλοῖς δόξης ἀλογεῖς οὐδὲν εὐφημίας ἐπιστρεφόμενος." ἅπερ καὶ λέγειν καὶ ἐννοεῖσθαι ἀσεβέστατον· ἀγανακτήσαι γὰρ ἂν οὐχ ὅτι θεὸς ὁ πάσης κακίας ἀμέτοχος, ἀλλὰ καὶ πατὴρ καὶ ὀθνεῖος ἄνθρωπος μὴ τελείως ἀρετῆς ἄγευστος, εἰ τοιαῦτα ἀκούοι.

12 Πάντας μὲν οὖν ὅρκους, ὡς ἔφην, βεβαιωτέον, ὅσοι περὶ καλῶν καὶ συμφερόντων γίνονται πρὸς ἐπανόρθωσιν ἰδίων ἢ κοινῶν πραγμάτων, φρονήσεως καὶ δικαιοσύνης καὶ ὁσιότητος ἡγουμένων.—IV. τούτοις ἐμφέρονται καὶ τῶν εὐχῶν αἱ νομιμώταται διὰ περιουσίαν ἀγαθῶν ἢ παρόντων ἢ προσδοκωμένων γινόμεναι—, τοὺς δ' ἕνεκα τῶν
13 ἐναντίων ἐπικυροῦν οὐκ εὐαγές. εἰσὶ γὰρ οἳ ὀμνύουσιν, ἐὰν τύχῃ, κλοπὰς καὶ ἱεροσυλίας ἢ φθορὰς καὶ μοιχείας ἢ τραύματα καὶ σφαγὰς ἤ τι τῶν ὁμοιοτρόπων κακῶν ἐργάσεσθαι,[2] καὶ ἀνυπερθέτως αὐτὰ δρῶσι ποιούμενοι πρόφασιν τὸ εὐορκεῖν, ὡς οὐκ ἄμεινον[3] καὶ θεῷ κεχαρισμένον μᾶλλον τῆς ⟨οὐ⟩

[1] MSS. ἀληθεία (=ἀληθείᾳ). [2] MSS. ἐργάσασθαι.

[3] ὡς οὐκ ἄμεινον ⟨ὂν⟩ would, I think, be more usual Greek. *Cf. De Dec.* 92.

God to bear witness in a disputed matter, but to call God to witness to a falsehood is the very height of
profanity. To do so is practically to say outright, 11
even though one appear not to utter a word, " I take Thee as a cloak for my wrongdoing. I am ashamed to appear a sinner, be Thou my accomplice ; take the charge of my villainy upon Thyself instead of me. For it is a matter of weight to me in my wickedness not to be thought a rogue, but Thou carest not for the opinion of the multitude and troublest not that men should speak well of Thee." Such words or thoughts are impious in the extreme. To hear them would rouse the indignation, not only of God, Who is exempt from all wickedness, but also of a father or even a stranger who knew anything at all of the flavour of virtue.

So then, as I have said, all oaths must be made good 12
so long as they are concerned with matters honourable and profitable for the better conduct of public or private affairs and are subject to the guidance of wisdom and justice and righteousness, IV. under which head come also the perfectly lawful vows made in acknowledgement of an abundant measure of blessings either present or expected. But when the oaths have objects of the opposite kind in view,
religion forbids us to put them into execution. For 13
there are some who swear at random [a] to commit acts of theft and sacrilege or rape and adultery or assaults and murders or other similar crimes and carry them out without hesitation on the pretext that they must be faithful to their oaths, as though it were not better and more pleasing to God to abstain from wrong-

[a] Or " as opportunity offers."

παραβάσεως[1] τῶν ὅρκων τὸ μηδὲν ἀδικεῖν, ἐπεὶ
δικαιοσύνη καὶ πᾶσα ἀρετὴ νόμος ἐστὶ πάτριος καὶ
θεσμὸς ἀρχαῖος· νόμοι δὲ καὶ θεσμοὶ τί ἕτερον ἢ
φύσεως ἱεροὶ λόγοι τὸ βέβαιον καὶ τὸ πάγιον ἐξ
14 αὑτῶν ἔχοντες, ὡς ὅρκων ἀδιαφορεῖν; ἴστω δὴ πᾶς
ἐνωμότως ἄδικα δρῶν, ὅτι εὐορκεῖ μὲν οὔ, τὸν δὲ
πολλῆς φυλακῆς καὶ ἐπιμελείας ἄξιον ὅρκον ἀνα-
τρέπει, ᾧ τὰ καλὰ καὶ δίκαια ἐπισφραγίζεται·
προστίθησι γὰρ ὑπαίτια ὑπαιτίοις, ἐν οὐ δέοντι
[273] γινομένοις ὅρκοις, οὓς πολὺ | βέλτιον ἦν ἡσυχάζε-
15 σθαι, πράξεις παρανόμους. ἀπεχόμενος οὖν τοῦ
ἀδικοπραγεῖν ποτνιάσθω τὸν θεόν, ἵνα μεταδῷ τῆς
ἵλεω δυνάμεως αὐτῷ συγγνοὺς ἐφ᾽ οἷς ἀβουλίᾳ
χρησάμενος ὤμοσε· διπλάσια γὰρ αἱρεῖσθαι κακά,
δυνάμενον τὴν ἡμίσειαν αὐτῶν ἀποφορτίσασθαι,
16 μανία καὶ φρενοβλάβεια δυσίατος. εἰσὶ δ᾽
οἳ τὴν φύσιν ἄμικτοι καὶ ἀκοινώνητοι δι᾽ ὑπερβολὴν μισανθρωπίας γεγονότες ἢ καὶ ὑπ᾽ ὀργῆς οἷα
χαλεπῆς δεσποίνης ἐκβιασθέντες ὅρκῳ τὴν ἀγριότητα πιστοῦνται τῶν ἠθῶν, οἵτινες οὔ φασιν
ὁμοτράπεζον ἢ ὁμωρόφιον ἕξειν τὸν δεῖνα ἢ τὸν
δεῖνα ἢ πάλιν τῷ δεῖνι μὴ παρέξειν ὠφέλειάν τινα ἢ
παρ᾽ ἐκείνου τι λήψεσθαι μέχρι τελευτῆς· ἔστι δ᾽
ὅτε καὶ μετὰ τὴν τελευτὴν τὸ ἀσύμβατον διαφυλάτ-

[1] Cohn following Mangey prints for the *τῆς παραβάσεως* of the MSS. *βεβαιώσεως*. I have hesitated in making the correction printed above, because it seems strange that anything so obvious should have escaped Mangey, Cohn, Heinemann and others. But I can see nothing against it. The double negative is rather effective than otherwise. The omission of the negative in the MSS. of Philo is common (see in this treatise §§ 129, 132), and Philo was no doubt familiar with the use of *οὐ* with a substantive, as *τὴν τῶν γεφυρῶν . . . οὐ διάλυσιν* in Thuc. i. 137 and elsewhere.

doing than to abstain from breaking their oaths. Justice and every virtue are commanded by the law of our ancestors and by a statute established of old, and what else are laws and statutes but the sacred words of Nature, possessing intrinsically a fixity and stability which makes them equivalent to oaths?
And everyone who commits a wrong because he has 14
sworn to do so may be assured that the act is not one of faithfulness to a pledge but breaks the oath so worthy of all careful observance with which she sets her seal[a] on what is just and excellent. For he adds guilt to guilt when oaths taken for improper purposes which had better have been left unspoken are followed by actions which violate the law. Let him 15
abstain, then, from wrongful conduct and supplicate God, that He may grant him a share of what His gracious power can give and pardon him for what he has sworn so unadvisedly. For to choose a double measure of ill when he could disburden himself of the half of it is the act of one almost hopelessly imbecile and insane. But there are some who, either 16
because through excessive moroseness their nature has lost the sense of companionship and fellow-feeling or because they are constrained by anger which rules them like a stern mistress, confirm the savagery of their temper with an oath. They declare that they will not admit such and such a person to their board or under their roof, or again, that they will not render assistance to so and so or accept anything from him till his life's end. Sometimes they carry on their vindictiveness after that end has come and leave

[a] I take *φύσις* to be the subject of *ἐπισφραγίζεται*. Heinemann takes the verb as passive, but I can find no example of this.

τουσιν οὐδὲ νεκροῖς τοῖς σώμασιν ἐπιτρέποντες ἐν
17 διαθήκαις[1] τὰ νομιζόμενα παρασχεῖν. οἷς παραινέσαιμι ἂν καθάπερ καὶ τοῖς προτέροις, εὐχαῖς καὶ θυσίαις ἐξευμενίζεσθαι τὸν θεόν, ἵνα εὕρωνταί τινα ψυχικῶν ἀρρωστημάτων θεραπείαν ἀναγκαίαν, ἃ μηδεὶς ἀνθρώπων ἱκανὸς ἰάσασθαι.

V. Ἕτεροι δ' εἰσὶ κομπασταὶ τῶν ὑπ' ἀλαζονείας φυσωμένων,[2] οἳ λιμοδοξοῦντες οὐδενὶ τῶν εἰς τὴν ὠφελιμωτάτην ὀλιγοδεΐαν χρῆσθαι δικαιοῦσιν, ἀλλὰ κἂν προτρέπῃ τις ἕνεκα τοῦ τὸν ἀφηνιασμὸν τῶν ἐπιθυμιῶν ἀναχαιτίσαι, τὴν νουθεσίαν ὕβριν εἶναι νομίζουσι καὶ πρὸς τὸν ἁβροδίαιτον ὠθούμενοι βίον ἀλογοῦσι τῶν σωφρονιστῶν, γέλωτα καὶ χλεύην τιθέμενοι τὰς φρονήσεως καλὰς ὁμοῦ καὶ λυσιτελε-
19 στάτας ὑφηγήσεις. εἰ δὲ δὴ καὶ τύχοι τις εἶναι περιουσία καὶ ἀφθονία τῶν περὶ τὸν βίον, ὅρκοις ἐπισφραγίζονται τὴν χρῆσιν καὶ ἀπόλαυσιν τῶν εἰς πολυτέλειαν· οἷον δή τι λέγω· πρῴην τις τῶν οὐκ ὀλίγα κεκτημένων ὑγρὸν καὶ διαρρέοντα βίον ἀσπασάμενος, ἐπειδὴ πρεσβύτης παρὼν συγγενὴς ἢ πατρικὸς ὥς γ' οἶμαι φίλος ἐνουθέτει πρὸς τὸ σεμνότερον καὶ αὐστηρότερον τὴν δίαιταν παρακαλῶν μεταβαλεῖν, τὴν παραίνεσιν οὐ μετρίως δυσχεράνας ὤμοσεν ἀντιφιλονεικῶν, ἕως ἂν τὰς

[1] Mangey preferred *θήκαις*. See note *a*.
[2] Cohn regards *τῶν . . . φυσωμένων* as corrupt, and Heinemann would expunge *κομπασταὶ* as a gloss, but see note *b*.

---

[a] Mangey's suggestion of *θήκαις* (or *ταῖς θήκαις*?) for *διαθήκαις*, *i.e.* "in the tomb" is tempting. That the implacable man should take steps to insure that when he himself is dead his enemy should suffer after *his* death, seems rather absurd.

directions in their wills[a] against even granting the customary rites to his corpse. To such persons I 17
would give the advice which I gave to the former class, that they should propitiate God with prayers and sacrifices to win from Him what their needs demand, namely, the healing treatment of their spiritual distempers which no human power is competent to cure.

V. But there are others, boastful persons,[b] of the 18
sort that is puffed up by arrogance, who in their craving for high position determine to have nothing to do in any way with the frugal, the truly profitable mode of living. Indeed, if any rebuke them in order to rein in the unruliness of their desires, they regard the admonition as an insult, and as they press forward to a career of luxury disregard their correctors and hold the admirable and also highly valuable instructions of wisdom a matter for laughter and mockery. And if they happen to have some abund- 19
ance of resources and means of living on a lavish scale, they employ oaths to set the seal on their use and enjoyment of the wealth which enables them to spend so freely. Here is an instance of what I mean. A short time ago a man of considerable property who had found a loose and dissipated style of living to his taste, was in the presence of an elderly person, a relation or old family friend, I believe, who was reproving him and advising him to make a change and conduct himself with more strictness and seriousness. The other strongly resented this reproof and countered the challenge by swearing that so long as

[b] Cohn's difficulty seems to me imaginary. I understand the κομπασταί to be persons who *talk* in the truculent manner described below. But this is not necessarily true of all who are "puffed up by arrogance."

χορηγίας ἔχῃ καὶ παρασκευάς, μηδενὶ χρήσεσθαι
τῶν εἰς εὐτέλειαν, μὴ κατὰ πόλιν, μὴ κατʼ ἀγρούς,
μὴ πλέων, μὴ πεζεύων, ἀλλʼ ἀεὶ καὶ πανταχοῦ τὸν
πλοῦτον ἐπιδείξεσθαι. πλούτου δὲ ταῦθʼ, ὡς
ἔοικεν, ἐπίδειξις οὐκ ἔστι μᾶλλον ἢ ἀλαζονείας καὶ
20 ἀκρασίας. καίτοι τῶν ἐν ταῖς μεγάλαις
ἡγεμονίαις οὐκ ὀλίγοι μέχρι νῦν εἰσιν οἳ παμπληθεῖς ἔχοντες παρασκευὰς καὶ χορηγίας ἀφθόνους,
ὥσπερ ἐξ ἀενάου τινὸς πηγῆς πλούτου ῥέοντος
αὐτοῖς ἀδιαστάτως, ὅμως ἐφʼ ἃ καὶ οἱ πένητες
ἡμεῖς ἔστιν ὅτε τρέπονται, κεραμεᾶς κύλικας καὶ
[274] ὀβελίας ἄρτους καὶ ἐλαίας ἢ τυρὸν ἢ λάχανα | προσ-
όψημα, καὶ θέρους μὲν περίζωμα καὶ λεπτὴν
ὀθόνην, χειμῶνος δὲ χλαῖναν ἀρραγῆ καὶ στιφρὰν
καὶ τὰ πρὸς τὴν κοίτην ἔστιν ὅτε χαμαίστρωτα,
πολλὰ χαίρειν φράσαντες κλίναις ἐλεφαντίναις ἢ
χελώνης ἢ χρυσοῦ πεποιημέναις καὶ στρωμναῖς
ἀνθοβαφέσι καὶ ἐσθῆσιν ἁλουργίσι καὶ πεμμάτων
μελιπήκτων περιεργίαις καὶ τραπεζῶν πολυτελείαις.
21 αἴτιον δʼ οὐ μόνον, οἶμαι, τὸ φύσεως αὐτοὺς εὐ-
μοίρου λαχεῖν, ἀλλὰ καὶ τὸ παιδείας ὀρθῆς ἐκ
πρώτης ἡλικίας ἐφάψασθαι, ἥτις ἀνεδίδαξε πρὸ τῶν
ἡγεμονικῶν τὰ ἀνθρώπινα τιμᾶν, ἥτις καὶ ἐνδιαιτω-
μένη τῇ ψυχῇ μόνον οὐ καθʼ ἑκάστην ἡμέραν
ὑπομιμνῄσκει τῆς ἀνθρωπότητος ἀπὸ τῶν ὑφηλῶν
καὶ ὑπερόγκων ἀντισπῶσα καὶ στέλλουσα καὶ τὸ
22 ἄνισον ἰσότητι θεραπεύουσα. τοιγαροῦν τὰς πόλεις
εὐθηνίας, εὐπορίας, εὐνομίας, εἰρήνης ἀναπεπλή-

---

[a] For a similar, though much longer, diatribe against luxurious living see *De Som.* ii. 18 ff.

he possessed his incomings and goods in stock he would take no step in the direction of economy, either in town or country, either on shipboard or on the road, but would make display of his wealth always and everywhere. But this is evidently not so much an exhibition of wealth as of arrogance
and intemperance. And yet to this day 20
among those who hold high offices of authority there are not a few who possessing accumulated goods in vast numbers and abundant resources, to whom wealth is ceaselessly flowing in as from a perennial fountain, still sometimes betake themselves to the use of such things as we poor people use.[a] Their cups are earthern, their loaves spit-baked, their extra dishes olives or cheese or greens: in the summer they wear a girdle and a thin shirt and in the winter a stout rent-proof mantle. The floor will sometimes serve for their bedstead: they have nothing to say to beds of ivory-work or made of tortoiseshell and gold, or bedding brocaded with flowers and purple-dyed garments and elaborate honey-cakes and tables spread with costly luxuries.
The reason, I take it, is not only that they are blessed 21
with a fine nature, but also that they have been brought under the influence of a right training from their earliest years. That training has taught them to value the interests of the man before those of the ruler. It makes its abode in their souls, and hardly a day passes but it reminds it of their common humanity and draws them away from lofty and overweening thought, reduces their swollen dimensions,
and medicines their inequality with equality. And 22
therefore they have filled their cities with plenty and abundance, with order and peace; of no good thing

κασιν, ἀγαθὸν μὲν οὐδὲν ὑπεξελόμενοι, πάντα δ' ἀφειδῶς καὶ ἀταμιεύτως χαριζόμενοι. τὰ μὲν δὴ τῶν εὐγενῶν καὶ ὡς ἀληθῶς ἡγεμόνων ἔργα ταῦτα
23 καὶ τὰ τούτοις παραπλήσια. τὰ δὲ τῶν νεοπλούτων ἐκεῖνα πλάνῳ τινὶ τύχης εἰς πολυχρηματίαν περιηκόντων, οἳ[a] τὸν ἀληθῆ καὶ βλέποντα πλοῦτον ἐξ ἀρετῶν τελείων συνεστῶτα καὶ τῶν κατ' ἀρετὰς πράξεων οὐδ' ὄναρ ἴσασι, τῷ δὲ τυφλῷ προσέπταισαν, ἐφ' οὗ[b] σκηριπτόμενοι κατ' ἀναγκαῖον τὴν ἄγουσαν ὁδὸν οὐχ ὁρῶντες εἰς ἀνοδίας ἐκτρέπονται, θαυμάζοντες τὰ μηδεμιᾶς ἄξια σπουδῆς καὶ τὰ φύσει τίμια γελῶντες· οἷς ὁ ἱερὸς λόγος ὅρκον ἐν οὐ δέοντι καιρῷ ποιουμένοις οὐ μετρίως ἐπιτιμᾷ καὶ ὀνειδίζει· δυσκάθαρτοι γὰρ καὶ δυσίατοι, ὡς μηδὲ παρὰ θεῷ τῷ τὴν φύσιν ἵλεῳ συγγνώμης ἀξιοῦσθαι.
24 VI. Παρθένων δὲ καὶ γυναικῶν τὸ περὶ τάς εὐχὰς αὐτοκρατὲς ἀφείλετο, τῶν μὲν παρθένων τοὺς πατέρας κυρίους, τῶν δὲ γυναικῶν τοὺς ἄνδρας ἐπιγνώμονας ἀποφήνας εἴς τε βεβαίωσιν τῶν ὅρκων καὶ λύσιν· καὶ μήποτ' εἰκότως· αἱ μὲν γὰρ διὰ νεότητα δύναμιν ὅρκων οὐκ ἴσασιν, ὡς χρῄζειν τῶν ἐπικρινούντων, αἱ δὲ πολλάκις ὑπ' εὐχερείας ὀμνύουσιν, ἃ μὴ τοῖς ἀνδράσι συνοίσει· διόπερ αὐτοῖς ἀνέθηκε τὴν ἐξουσίαν τοῦ τὰ ὀμοσθέντα[1] φυλάττειν
25 ἢ τοὐναντίον. χῆραι δὲ μὴ ῥᾳδίως ὀμνύτωσαν—οὐ γὰρ ἔχουσι τοὺς παραιτητάς, οὔτε ἄνδρας ὧν δι-

[1] MSS. νομισθέντα or ὀνομασθέντα.

---

[a] See on i. § 25.
[b] Or "stumbled over," but σκηριπτόμενοι seems to suggest

have they mulcted them, all good things have they bestowed freely, unsparingly and unstintedly. These and the like are the actions of noble men, rulers in the true sense.
Far different are the 23
actions of the newly rich who have been wafted into opulence by a freak of fortune. They know nothing, have never even dreamt, of the true wealth which has eyes to see,[a] whose substance is the perfect virtues and the actions which conform with them; it is a blind wealth against which they have struck[b] and taking it for their support they fail of necessity to see the road before them and wander away into pathless wilds, admiring what deserves no serious respect and mocking at what nature would bid them honour. Such persons, when they take a mistimed oath, are rebuked and reproached in no gentle terms by the holy word. Hardly can they be purged and healed, so that even the gracious nature of God deems them unworthy of His pardon.

VI. [c] Virgins and wives are not allowed full control 24
of their vows by the law. It puts the virgins in subjection to their fathers and sets the husbands to judge for their wives whether the oaths are to hold good or to be cancelled. That is surely reasonable, for the former, owing to their youth, do not know the value of oaths, so that they need others to judge for them, and the latter often, through want of sense, swear what would not be to their husbands' advantage; and therefore it gave the husbands power to maintain the promise, or the reverse. [d] Widows who have none 25
to intervene on their behalf, neither husbands from

a blind person (οὐχ ὁρῶντες) coming into collision with another blind person. *Cf.* "shall the blind lead the blind?"

[c] Num. xxx. 4 ff.

[d] Num. xxx. 9 ff.

ἐζεύχθησαν οὔτε πατέρας ἀφ' ὧν μετανέστησαν, ὅτε τὴν πρὸς γάμον ἀποικίαν ἐστέλλοντο—, ἐπειδὴ μένειν τοὺς τούτων ὅρκους ἀναγκαῖον ἐρημίᾳ τῶν
26 κηδομένων βεβαιουμένους.
[275] Ἐὰν δέ τις | ἐπιορκοῦντά τινα εἰδὼς μὴ καταμηνύσῃ ἢ ἀπελέγξῃ φιλίᾳ ἢ αἰδοῖ ἢ φόβῳ διδοὺς πλέον ἢ εὐσεβείᾳ, τοῖς αὐτοῖς ἐπιτιμίοις ἔνοχος ἔστω· διαφέρει γὰρ τοῦ ἀδικεῖν οὐδὲν τὸ συν-
27 επιγράφεσθαι ἀδικοῦντι. δίκαι δὲ κατ' ἐπιόρκων αἱ μὲν ἀνάκεινται τῷ θεῷ, αἱ δὲ ἀνθρώποις, θεῷ μὲν αἱ ἀνωτάτω καὶ μέγισται—ἵλεως γὰρ οὐ γίνεται τοῖς οὕτως ἀσεβοῦσιν, ἀλλὰ μένειν εἰς ἀεὶ δυσκαθάρτους ἐᾷ, δικαίως, οἶμαι, καὶ προσηκόντως· ὁ γὰρ ἀμελήσας τί δεινὸν εἰ ἀντ-
28 αμεληθήσεται, οἷς δίδωσι τὰ ἴσα καρπούμενος;—αἱ δ' ἀπ' ἀνθρώπων διάφοροι, θάνατος ἢ πληγαί, τῶν μὲν ἀμεινόνων καὶ περιττῶν εἰς εὐσέβειαν θανάτου δίκας βεβαιούντων, τῶν δὲ μαλακώτερον χρωμένων ὀργαῖς δημοσίᾳ μάστιγι τυπτόντων ἀναφανδὸν ἐν κοινῷ· εἰσὶ δὲ καὶ πληγαὶ τοῖς μὴ δουλοπρεπέσιν οὐκ ἔλαττον δίκης θανάτου.
29 VII. Ταῦτα μὲν οὖν αἱ ῥηταὶ προστάξεις περιέχουσιν. ἔστι δὲ καὶ ἀλληγορῆσαι τὰ περὶ τὸν

---

[a] Lev. v. 1. R.V. "If anyone sin in that he heareth the voice of adjuration" (A.V. "swearing") "he being a witness, whether he hath seen or known, if he do not utter it then he shall bear his iniquity." The meaning of "adjuration" apparently is a solemn appeal in the name of God to give witness (as in the banns of marriage). Philo takes the Greek word for adjuration *ὁρκισμός* as = "(false) swearing."

[b] Probably (as Heinemann), an allusion to the LXX form of the third commandment, "shall not purify," *οὐ μὴ καθαρίσῃ*, for "shall not hold guiltless."

[c] No definite punishments for perjury, as distinguished

whom they have been parted, nor fathers whom they left behind them when they set out to find a new home in marriage, should be slow to swear, for their oaths stand beyond repeal, the inevitable result of their lack of protectors.

[a] If anyone knows that another has perjured him- 26
self, and influenced by friendship or shame or fear rather than piety, fails to inform against him or bring him to justice, he must be liable to the same penalties as the perjurer. For to range oneself on the side of the wrongdoer is just the same as committing the
wrong. As to the penalties of perjury, some proceed 27
from God, others from man. The highest and greatest are from God, Who is not gentle to such impiety, but suffers the guilty to remain for ever in their well-nigh hopeless uncleanness, a just and fitting penalty, I hold.[b] For he who has ignored God, how can he wonder if he is ignored in his turn and is repaid in his
own coin? The penalties given by men are different, 28
death or the lash.[c] The better kind whose piety is extra-fervent maintain the penalty of death, while those whose feelings of indignation are not so stern have the offenders scourged by order of the State in a public place and in the sight of all. Indeed except to persons of a servile nature, a flogging is as severe a penalty as death.

VII. Such is the sum and substance of these ordin- 29
ances[d] taken literally. But we may also allegorize

from false witness in general, appear in the Pentateuch. See on § 252.

[d] The allegory which follows only applies to §§ 24 and 25, and not to §§ 26-28. Have these sections been misplaced? The subject of vows which occupies the rest of the treatment of the third commandment differs radically from oaths, and the sudden return to the question of perjury is very awkward.

τόπον ἔχοντα θεωρίαν τὴν διὰ συμβόλων. εἰδέναι
τοίνυν προσήκει ὅτι ὁ τῆς φύσεως ὀρθὸς λόγος
πατρὸς ὁμοῦ καὶ ἀνδρὸς ἔχει δύναμιν, ἐπινοίαις
διαφόροις· ἀνδρὸς μέν, ἐπειδὴ τὸν ἀρετῶν σπόρον
ὥσπερ εἰς ἀγαθὴν ἄρουραν τὴν ψυχὴν καταβάλ-
λεται, πατρὸς δ' ὅτι βουλὰς ἀγαθὰς καὶ πράξεις
καλὰς καὶ σπουδαίας γεννᾶν πέφυκε καὶ γεννήσας
ἐκτρέφει ποτίμοις δόγμασιν, ἃ παιδεία καὶ σοφία
30 χορηγοῦσι. διάνοια δ' ἀπεικάζεται τοτὲ μὲν
παρθένῳ, τοτὲ δὲ γυναικὶ ἢ χηρευούσῃ ἢ ἀνδρὶ ἔτι
ἡρμοσμένῃ· παρθένος μὲν διάνοια ἁγνὴν καὶ ἀδιά-
φθορον διαφυλάττουσα ἑαυτὴν ἀπό τε ἡδονῶν καὶ
ἐπιθυμιῶν, ἔτι δὲ καὶ λυπῶν καὶ φόβων, ἐπιβούλων
παθῶν, ἧς τὴν προστασίαν ὁ γεννητὴς ἀνῆπται
πατήρ· τῆς δ' ὡς γυναικὸς ἀστείῳ λόγῳ τῷ κατ'
ἀρετὴν συμβιούσης τὴν ἐπιμέλειαν ὁ αὐτὸς λόγος
οὗτος ἐπαγγέλλεται σπείρων ἀνδρὸς τρόπον ἐννοίας
31 ἀρίστας. ἣ δ' ἂν ἀπορφανισθῇ ψυχὴ καὶ γενεᾶς
τῆς κατὰ τὴν φρόνησιν καὶ ἐπιγαμίας τῆς κατὰ τὸν
ὀρθὸν λόγον, χηρεύουσα τῶν καλλίστων καὶ ἔρημος
οὖσα σοφίας, ὑπαίτιον ἑλομένη ζωήν, ἔνοχος ἔστω
οἷς ἔγνω καθ' ἑαυτῆς, ἰατρὸν ἁμαρτημάτων οὐκ
ἔχουσα οὔθ' ὡς ἄνδρα συμβιωτὴν οὔθ' ὡς πατέρα
γεννητὴν τὸν κατὰ σοφίαν λόγον.

32 VIII. Τῶν δὲ μὴ μόνον τὰς οὐσίας ἢ μέρη τούτων ἀλλὰ καὶ αὐτοὺς ἀνάθημα ποιησαμένων ἐν
εὐχαῖς ὥρισε τιμάς, οὐ πρὸς κάλλος ἢ μέγεθος ἤ τι
[276] τῶν ὁμοιοτρόπων ἀπιδών, | ἀλλὰ πρὸς ἀριθμὸν

---

[a] For §§ 32-34 see Lev. xxvii. 2-8.

such parts of the subject as admit of being studied in a figurative sense. We should know, then, that nature's right reasoning has the functions both of a father and a husband, though the conceptions attached to each are different. It acts as a husband because it deposits the seed of virtue in the soul as in a fertile field. It acts as a father because its nature is to beget good intentions and noble and worthy actions, and then to foster its offspring with the water of the truths which education and wisdom abundantly
supply. The mind is likened on the one hand to a 30
virgin, on the other to a woman either in widowhood, or still united to a husband. As a virgin it keeps itself pure and uncorrupted from the malignant passions, pleasures and desires and griefs and fears. Over this virgin mind the father who begat it has assumed authority. But when, like a wife, it dwells with virtuous reasoning as its worthy mate, that same reasoning promises to take charge of it and impregnates it husband-like with thoughts of highest
excellence. But the soul, which is bereaved of 31
its birth-tie with sound sense or its marriage-tie with right reasoning, is widowed of all that is most excellent and, deserted by wisdom because it has chosen a life of guilt, must stand bound by the decision which it has made to its own undoing. It has none to heal its errors, no reasoning of wisdom, either to live with it as its husband or to act as its father and begetter.

VIII. [a] In dealing with those who have dedicated 32
votive offerings, not only of their property or parts of it, but of themselves, the law laid down a scale of valuation in which no regard is paid to beauty or stature or anything of the kind, but all are assessed

ἴσον, διακρίνας ἄνδρας αὐτὸ μόνον γυναικῶν καὶ
33 νηπίους τελείων. κελεύει γὰρ ἀπὸ μὲν εἰκοσαετίας
ἄχρις ἑξηκονταετίας ἀνδρὸς εἶναι τιμὴν δραχμὰς
διακοσίας νομίσματος ὁλαργύρου, γυναικὸς δὲ
εἴκοσι πρὸς ταῖς ἑκατόν, ἀπὸ δὲ πενταετίας ἄχρις
εἰκοσαετίας τοῦ μὲν ἄρρενος δραχμὰς ὀγδοήκοντα,
τῆς δὲ θηλείας τεσσαράκοντα, ἀπὸ δὲ βρέφους εἰς
πενταετίαν τοῦ μὲν ἄρρενος δραχμὰς εἴκοσι, τοῦ δὲ
θήλεος δώδεκα, τῶν δ᾿ ὑπὲρ ἑξήκοντα ἔτη βεβιω-
κότων πρεσβυτῶν μὲν δραχμὰς ἑξήκοντα, πρεσβυ-
34 τίδων δὲ τεσσαράκοντα. τὰ δ᾿ ἴσα καὶ ἐπ᾿ ἀρρένων
καθ᾿ ἡλικίαν ἑκάστην καὶ ἐπὶ θηλειῶν ὁμοίως
διετάξατο, τριῶν ἕνεκα τῶν ἀναγκαιοτάτων· ἑνὸς
μὲν ὅτι ἴσον ἐστὶ καὶ ὅμοιον τὸ ἀξίωμα τῆς εὐχῆς,
ἐάν τε ὑπὸ μεγάλου τινὸς ἐάν τε καὶ ὑπ᾿ εὐτελοῦς
γίνηται· δευτέρου δ᾿ ὅτι τοὺς εὐξαμένους ἁρμόττον
οὐκ ἦν ταῖς τῶν ἀνδραπόδων ὑποβάλλεσθαι τύχαις
—ἐκεῖνα γὰρ πρὸς τὰς τῶν σωμάτων εὐεξίας καὶ
εὐμορφίας τιμᾶται ἢ τοὐναντίον ἐπευωνίζεται—.
τρίτου δ᾿ ὃ καὶ ἀναγκαιότατον, ὅτι παρὰ μὲν ἡμῖν
ἀνισότης, ἰσότης δὲ παρὰ θεῷ τίμιον.

35 IX. Ταῦτα μὲν ἐπ᾿ ἀνθρώπων, ἐπὶ δὲ κτηνῶν
τάδε νομοθετεῖται· ἐάν τις ἀφορίσῃ κτῆνος, εἰ μὲν
εἴη καθαρὸν ἔκ τινος γένους τῶν τριῶν, ἅπερ εἰς
θυσίαν ἀπενεμήθη, βοῦς ἢ πρόβατον ἢ αἴξ, ἐκεῖνο
καταθυέτω μὴ ὑπαλλαττόμενος μήτε χεῖρον κρείττονος μήτ᾿ ἄμεινον χείρονος· οὐ γὰρ πολυσαρκίᾳ καὶ

[a] E.V. "50 shekels," LXX "50 didrachma," that is, properly speaking, 100 drachmas, but Philo follows the common valuation by which the didrachmon was held to be worth half a shekel. *Cf.* Matt. xvii. 24 (where the R.V. translates δίδραχμον by "half-shekel"), of the temple-tax based on Ex.

equally, the sole distinctions made being between men and women and between children and adults.
It ordained that from 20 years to 60 a man should be 33
valued at 200[a] drachmas of pure silver coinage and a woman at 120 ; from 5 to 20 years, a male at 80 and a woman at 40 drachmas ; from infancy to 5 years, a male at 20 and a female at 12 drachmas, while in the case of old persons who have lived beyond 60, the men are valued at 60 drachmas and the women at 40.
The order that all males and all females should be 34
assessed equally[b] at every age was made for three most cogent reasons. First, because the worth of one person's vow is equal and similar to that of another, whether it is made by a person of great importance or one of mean estate ; secondly, because it was not seemly that the votaries should be subject to the vicissitudes of slaves who are valued at a high price or on the other hand are rated low accordingly as they have or have not a fine condition of body and comeliness ; thirdly, and this is the most convincing of all, that in the sight of men inequality, in the sight of God equality, is held in honour.

IX. These are the regulations laid down by the law 35
in the case of human beings.[c] For livestock we have the following. If a man sets apart a beast from his stock, if it is a clean specimen of one of the three kinds which are allowed for sacrifice, an ox or sheep or goat, he must sacrifice that particular animal without substituting either a better for a worse or a worse for a better. For God does not delight in the

xxx. 13. So too Josephus, *Ant.* iii. 195, says that the shekel is worth 4 Attic drachmas. The same transvaluation is followed throughout this section.

[b] *i.e.* irrespective of the other considerations, beauty and stature, mentioned above.

[c] Lev. xxvii. 9-13.

πιότητι ζῴων χαίρει ὁ θεός, ἀλλ' ἀνυπαιτίῳ τοῦ
εὐξαμένου διαθέσει· ἐὰν δὲ ὑπαλλάττηται, δύο ἀνθ'
ἑνὸς καθιερούτω, τό τε ἀρχαῖον καὶ τὸ ἀντ' ἐκείνου.
36 ἐὰν δέ τις εὔξηταί τι τῶν μὴ καθαρῶν κτηνῶν,
ἀγέτω πρὸς τὸν δοκιμώτατον τῶν ἱερέων· ὁ δὲ
τιμάσθω μὴ ὑπερβάλλων τὴν ἀξίαν, προσεπιτιθεὶς
τῆς τιμῆς καὶ τὸ πέμπτον, ἵν', εἰ δέοι καθαρὸν ἀντὶ
τούτου ζῷον ἱερουργεῖν, μηδὲν ὑστερίζοι τῆς ἀξίας
τιμῆς, καὶ ἄλλως ὑπὲρ τοῦ δυσωπῆσαι τὸν εὐξά-
μενον, ὅτι τὴν εὐχὴν ἐποιήσατο οὐ συλλογισμῷ, τὸ
μὴ καθαρὸν ζῷον ὥς γ' οἶμαι τότε νομίσας εἶναι
καθαρὸν πλάνῳ διανοίας, κεκρατημένος ὑπὸ πάθους.
37 οἰκία δ' εἰ γένοιτο ἀνάθημα, πάλιν ἐχέτω τιμητὴν
ἱερέα· οἱ δ' ὠνούμενοι μὴ τὰ ἴσα κατατιθέτωσαν,
ἀλλ' εἰ μὲν ὁ εὐξάμενος ἀνακομίζεσθαι προέλοιτο,
ἐπιδαψιλευέσθω τὸ πέμπτον, κολάζων τὴν εὐχέρειαν καὶ ἐπιθυμίαν, διττὸν κακόν, ἐν οἷς μὲν
[277] ηὔχετο τὴν εὐχέρειαν, | ἐν οἷς δ' ἐφίεται ὧν πρό-
τερον ἐξέστη τὴν ἐπιθυμίαν, εἰ δ' ἕτερος, μηδὲν
38 πλέον τῆς ἀξίας κατατιθέτω. ὁ δ' εὐξάμενος μὴ
μακροὺς ἐμποιείτω χρόνους πρὸς τὴν ὧν ηὔξατο
τελείωσιν· ἄτοπον γὰρ τὰς μὲν πρὸς ἀνθρώπους

---

[a] In Leviticus simply "the priest."

[b] The meaning of the rule seems to be that if the animal cannot be lawfully dedicated, its owner may sell it for the price fixed by the priest, and give the money, but if he redeems it he must pay the extra fifth. The question of providing a clean animal in its stead does not appear to be considered.

[c] Lit. "mastered by passion." But it is strange to find a mistake or delusion of this kind called a πάθος, though perhaps it falls in with the Stoic theory that the passions are κρίσεις. *Cf.* index in *S.V.F.* to κρίσις, and note on *Leg. All.* ii. 6.

fleshiness or fatness of animals, but in the blameless
intention of the votary. But if he does make any
exchange, he must consecrate two instead of one, both
the original and its substitute. If he has vowed any 36
of his unclean cattle, he must bring it to the most
highly esteemed of the priests,[a] who must assess it not
exceeding its proper value and then add a fifth part
of that value, so that if a clean animal has to be
provided for the sacrifice instead of this one, what is
provided may not fall short of the proper value.[b]
Further, the intention is to discomfit the votary for
having made a vow without reflection under the
impression that the impure animal was on this occasion pure, a mistake presumably due to some mental
aberration which powerfully affected him.[c] If he 37
dedicates his house, again he should take a priest as
assessor, but the sums to be disbursed by the purchasers vary. [d] If the votary determines to redeem
the house, he must spend more freely and add a fifth
as a punishment for two bad things, thoughtlessness
and lust of possession, the former shown in the matter
of his vow, the latter in his desire to regain what he
had surrendered. If the purchaser is other than the
original owner, he should not pay more than the
proper value. The votary must not interpose long 38
delay in accomplishing his vow.[e] It would be a
strange inconsistency if while in our dealings with

[d] Lev. xxvii. 14, 15. Philo omits the regulations about land which follow in *vv.* 16-25.

[e] Deut. xxiii. 21, "If thou shalt vow a vow to the Lord thy God thou shalt not delay (χρονιεῖς) to pay it." The meaning of what follows seems to be that we often anticipate our payments to men, because we know they need it. The fact that God does not need them should not make us treat God with less respect than we shew to men.

ὁμολογίας ἐπιτέμνειν πειρᾶσθαι, τὰς δὲ πρὸς θεὸν τὸν ἀνεπιδεᾶ καὶ οὐδενὸς χρεῖον ἐκπροθέσμους ἀποφαίνειν, μελλήσει καὶ βραδυτῆτι διελέγχοντας αὐτοὺς ἐπὶ τῷ μεγίστῳ τῶν ἀδικημάτων, ὀλιγωρίᾳ τῇ πρὸς αὐτόν, οὗ τὴν θεραπείαν ἀρχὴν καὶ τέλος εὐδαιμονίας εἶναι νομιστέον. ὅρκων μὲν δὴ πέρι καὶ εὐχῶν ἅλις.

39 X. [1] Ἑξῆς ἐστι κεφάλαιον τὸ περὶ τῆς ἱερᾶς ἑβδόμης, ᾧ μυρία καὶ ἀναγκαῖα ἐμφέρεται, τὰ εἴδη τῶν ἑορτῶν, αἱ τῶν φύσει μὲν ἐλευθέρων διὰ δὲ καιροὺς ἀβουλήτους θητευόντων καθ' ἕβδομον ἐνιαυτὸν ἀφέσεις, αἱ πρὸς χρεώστας τῶν συμβαλλόντων φιλοφροσύναι τὰ δάνεια ἑβδόμῳ ἔτει τοῖς ὁμοφύλοις χαριζομένων, αἱ ἀνάπαυλαι τῆς βαθυγείου πεδιάδος τε καὶ ὀρεινῆς, αἳ γίνονται παρ' ἑξαετίαν, τὰ περὶ τοῦ πεντηκοστοῦ ἔτους νομοθετηθέντα· ὧν καὶ ἡ ἄνευ κόπου ψιλὴ διήγησις ἱκανὴ τοὺς μὲν εὐφυεῖς τελειῶσαι πρὸς ἀρετήν, τοὺς δ' ἀφηνιαστὰς καὶ σκληροὺς τὸ ἦθος εὐπειθεστέρους

40 ἀπεργάσασθαι. τὰ μὲν οὖν περὶ τῆς ἐν ἀριθμοῖς ἑβδόμης[2] εἴρηται διὰ μακροτέρων πρότερον, ἥν τε ἔχει φύσιν ἐν δεκάδι καὶ ἣν συγγένειαν

[278] πρός τε αὐτὴν δεκάδα καὶ πρὸς τετράδα, | τὴ

[1] At this point the mss. insert the title Περὶ ἑβδόμης.
[2] Mangey ἑβδομαδὸς.

---

[a] Here begins the fourth commandment. A fresh numeration of the chapters in Cohn. [b] *De Op.* 90-127.

[c] Or "within the series of the first ten numbers." For this see *De Op.* 95-100. The properties "outside the decad

men we try to antedate fulfilment of our promises, in dealing with God, Who lacks and needs nothing, we should extend it beyond the appointed time. By such slowness and procrastination we convict ourselves of the greatest of iniquities, contempt of Him whose service we must hold to be the beginning and consummation of happiness. This is enough on this subject of oaths and vows.

X. [a] The next head is concerned with the sacred 39
seventh day. Under this head are included a great number of matters of vital importance, the different kinds of feasts; the release in the seventh year of persons who were naturally free but through times of adversity are in servitude; the charity shown by creditors to debtors in cancelling loans to their fellow-nationals, this also in the seventh year; the rest allowed both in the lowlands and the uplands to the fertile soil at intervals of six years; and the laws laid down with respect to the fiftieth year. The mere recital of all these is enough to make the naturally gifted perfect in virtue without any effort on their part and to produce some degree of obedience in the rebellious and hard-natured. Now the 40
part played by seven among the numbers has been described at length in an earlier place,[b] where we have discussed the properties which it possesses within the decad,[c] and its close connexion with ten itself[d] and with four, which is the origin and source of

(*ibid.* 91) are explained as those of the seventh term in a series, as in the geometrical progression mentioned here just below.

[d] I do not see anything in *De Op.* which corresponds to this. The "kinship" of 7 to 4 is that $4+3=7$ (*ibid.* 96), and that 4 is the source of 10, because $1+2+3+4=10$, is often brought out, *e.g. ibid.* 47.

δεκάδος ἀρχήν τε καὶ πηγήν, καὶ ὡς συντεθεῖσα μὲν ἀπὸ μονάδος ἑξῆς γεννᾷ τὸν ὀκτὼ καὶ εἴκοσι τέλειον ἀριθμὸν τοῖς αὑτοῦ μέρεσιν ἰσούμενον εἰς δ' ἀναλογίαν ἀχθεῖσα κύβον ὁμοῦ καὶ τετράγωνον ἀποτελεῖ, καὶ ὡς μυρία ἄλλα κάλλη θεωρημάτων ἐξ αὑτῆς ἐπιδείκνυται, περὶ ὧν οὐ καιρὸς μακρηγορεῖν. ἕκαστον δὲ τῶν προκειμένων καὶ ἐμφερομένων εἰδῶν ἐπισκεπτέον, ἀπὸ τοῦ πρώτου τὴν ἀρχὴν ποιησαμένους. ἦν δὲ πρῶτον τὸ περὶ ἑορτῶν.

41 XI. [1] Εἰσὶ τοίνυν ἀριθμῷ δέκα ἑορταί, ἃς ἀναγράφει ὁ νόμος· πρώτη μέν, ἣν ἀκούσας θαυμάσαι τις ἂν ἴσως, αὕτη δ' ἐστὶν ἡμέρα πᾶσα· δευτέρα δὲ ἡ δι' ἓξ ἡμερῶν ἑβδόμη, σάββατον αὐτὴν Ἑβραῖοι πατρίῳ γλώττῃ καλοῦσι· τρίτη δ' ἡ μετὰ σύνοδον τὴν κατὰ σελήνην νέαν νουμηνία· τετάρτη δ' ἡ τῶν διαβατηρίων, ἣ καλεῖται Πάσχα· πέμπτη δ' ἡ τῶν ἀσταχύων ἀπαρχή, τὸ ἱερὸν δράγμα· ἕκτη δ' ἄζυμα· μεθ' ἣν ἡ τῶν ἑβδομάδων ὄντως ἑβδόμη· ὀγδόη δὲ ἱερομηνία· ἐνάτη δὲ νηστεία· δεκάτη δὲ ἡ τῶν σκηνῶν, ἥτις ἐστὶ τῶν ἐτησίων ἑορτῶν συμπέρασμα, εἰς τέλειον ἀριθμὸν δεκάδα τελευτῶσα. ἀρκτέον δὲ ἀπὸ τῆς πρώτης.

42 XII. Ἅπασαν ἡμέραν ἑορτὴν ἀναγράφει ὁ νόμος

[1] Here a title varying in the mss. is inserted, printed by Cohn as Περὶ τῶν δέκα ἑορτῶν.

ten. Also we have shewn how a sevenfold addition of successive numbers beginning with unity produces twenty-eight,[a] a perfect number, equal to the sum of its factors ; again, how when brought into a geometrical progression, it produces simultaneously a square and a cube,[b] besides the numberless other beautiful results which the study of it reveals. On these numerical points we must not linger at the present juncture, but we must examine each specific subject which lies before us included under the general head, beginning with the first; and the first subject, as we saw, is the feasts.

XI. There are in all ten feasts which are recorded 41
in the law. The first, the mention of which may perhaps cause some surprise, is the feast of every day. The second is that held on the seventh day with six days between, called by the Hebrews in their native tongue Sabbath. The third is the new moon which follows the conjunction of the moon with the sun. The fourth is the " Crossing " festival called Pascha. The fifth is the offering of the first ears, the sacred Sheaf. The sixth is the Unleavened Bread. Then comes what is emphatically[c] a seventh, being the feast of Sevens or Weeks. Eighth is the Sacred-month-day, ninth is the Fast, tenth the feast of Tabernacles which concludes the yearly festivals and thus ends up with a perfect number ten. We must begin with the first of these.

XII. When the law records that every day is a 42

[a] *i.e.* $1+2 \ldots +7=28$, the factors of which 1, 2, 4, 7, 14 also $=28$. *Cf. De Op.* 101.

[b] *Cf. ibid.* 92, 93, where $64=4^3$ and 8^2, and $729=27^2$ and 9^3 are given as examples.

[c] Or " truly," *i.e.* it not only comes seventh in the list, but takes its name from the same number.

πρὸς τὸν ἀνεπίληπτον βίον ἁρμοζόμενος ὁσίων[1] ἀνθρώπων ἑπομένων τῇ φύσει καὶ τοῖς ταύτης διατάγμασι. καὶ εἴ γε μὴ παρευημέρησαν αἱ κακίαι καταδυναστεύσασαι τοὺς περὶ τῶν συμφερόντων λογισμοὺς οὓς τῆς ἑκάστων ψυχῆς ἐξῴκισαν, ἀλλ' ἔμειναν αἱ τῶν ἀρετῶν δυνάμεις εἰς ἅπαν ἀήττητοι, μία ἂν ἦν ὁ ἀπὸ γενέσεως ἄχρι τελευτῆς χρόνος ἀδιάστατος ἑορτὴ καὶ αἵ τε οἰκίαι καὶ αἱ πόλεις ἐν ἀδείᾳ καὶ ἐκεχειρίᾳ μεσταὶ πάντων ἂν ἦσαν ἀγαθῶν
43 εὐδίαν ἄγουσαι πραγμάτων. νυνὶ δ' αἱ πλεονεξίαι καὶ ἀντεπιθέσεις, ἃς ἄνδρες ὁμοῦ καὶ γυναῖκες μηχανῶνται κατά τε αὑτῶν καὶ κατ' ἀλλήλων, τὸ συνεχὲς τῆς ἱλαρᾶς διέκοψαν εὐθυμίας. ἐμφανὴς
44 δὲ τοῦ λεγομένου πίστις. ὅσοι γὰρ ἢ παρ' Ἕλ-
[279] λησιν | ἢ παρὰ βαρβάροις ἀσκηταὶ σοφίας εἰσὶν ἀνεπιλήπτως καὶ ἀνυπαιτίως ζῶντες, μήτε ἀδικεῖσθαι μήτε ἀνταδικεῖν αἱρούμενοι, τὰς τῶν φιλοπραγμόνων ὁμιλίας ἐκτρέπονται[2] καὶ τὰ χωρία, ἐν οἷς ποιοῦνται τὰς διατριβάς, προβέβληνται, δικαστήρια καὶ βουλευτήρια καὶ ἀγορὰς καὶ ἐκκλησίας καὶ συνόλως ὅπου τις τῶν εἰκαιοτέρων ἀνθρώπων
45 θίασος ἢ σύλλογος, οἷα βίον ἀπόλεμον καὶ εἰρηναῖον ἐζηλωκότες, θεωροὶ τῆς φύσεως καὶ τῶν ἐν αὐτῇ πάντων ἄριστοι, γῆν καὶ θάλατταν καὶ ἀέρα καὶ

[1] MSS. ὡς τῶν, which does not seem to me as impossible as it does to Cohn. See note *b*.
[2] MSS. ἐκτρεπόμενοι.

---

[a] The idea of the feast of every day comes from Num. xxviii., xxix. In xxviii. 2 we have (LXX) "observe to offer me in my feasts, my gifts" etc. followed by the list of the various offerings. This list begins with the daily sacrifices and continues in the same order as in this book, with the sole exception that the Sheaf is not mentioned. Philo utilizes

festival,[a] it accommodates itself to the blameless life of righteous men [b] who follow nature and her ordinances. And if only the vices had not conquered and dominated the thoughts in us which seek the truly profitable and dislodged them from each soul—if instead the forces of the virtues had remained unvanquished throughout, the time from birth to death would be one continuous feast, and houses and cities dwelling in security and leisure [c] would have been full of all good things with everything tranquil around
them. As it is, the overreaching and the assaults 43
which men and women alike contrive against themselves and each other have cleft a breach in the continuous line of this cheerful gaiety. Here is a clear
proof of what I am saying. All who practise wisdom, 44
either in Grecian or barbarian lands, and live a blameless and irreproachable life, choosing neither to inflict nor retaliate injustice, avoid the gathering of busybodies and abjure the scenes which they haunt, such as law-courts, council-chambers, markets, congregations and in general any gathering or assemblage of
careless men. Their own aspirations are for a life 45
of peace, free from warring. They are the closest observers of nature and all that it contains; earth, sea, air and heaven and the various forms of being

the hint suggested by Numbers to enforce the doctrine, which he bases elsewhere (*De Sac.* 111) on the same text that only the wise man can keep a feast. It is no doubt a consideration with him that the inclusion serves to make the perfect number ten, but he could have obtained this otherwise by including the "Basket," see §§ 215 f.

[b] If the MSS. ὡς τῶν is retained, the meaning will be "the law *assumes* that men follow nature" etc. (which they seldom do). *Cf.* §§ 51, 52.

[c] Or perhaps "peace" (cessation of hostilities), ἐκεχειρία being used in its more technical sense.

οὐρανὸν καὶ τὰς ἐν αὐτοῖς φύσεις διερευνώμενοι, σελήνῃ καὶ ἡλίῳ καὶ τῇ χορείᾳ τῶν ἄλλων ἀστέρων πλανήτων τε καὶ ἀπλανῶν ταῖς διανοίαις συμπεριπολοῦντες, τὰ μὲν σώματα κάτω πρὸς χέρσον ἱδρυμένοι, τὰς δὲ ψυχὰς ὑποπτέρους κατασκευάζοντες, ὅπως αἰθεροβατοῦντες τὰς ἐκεῖ δυνάμεις περιαθρῶσιν, οἷα χρὴ τοὺς[1] τῷ ὄντι κοσμοπολίτας γενομένους, οἳ τὸν μὲν κόσμον ἐνόμισαν εἶναι πόλιν, πολίτας δὲ τοὺς σοφίας ὁμιλητάς, ἀρετῆς ἐγγραφούσης, ᾗ πεπίστευσαι τὸ κοινὸν πολίτευμα πρυ-
46 τανεύειν. XIII. γέμοντες οὖν καλοκἀγαθίας καὶ τῶν περὶ σῶμα κακῶν καὶ τῶν ἐκτὸς ἀλογεῖν ἐθιζόμενοι καὶ ἐξαδιαφορεῖν τὰ ἀδιάφορα μελετῶντες καὶ κατὰ τῶν ἡδονῶν καὶ ἐπιθυμιῶν ἀλειφόμενοι καὶ συνόλως ἐπάνω τῶν παθῶν ἵστασθαι σπουδάζοντες ἀεὶ καὶ τὸν ἐπιτειχισμὸν αὐτῶν πάσῃ δυνάμει καθαιρεῖν παιδευόμενοι καὶ ταῖς τῆς τύχης μὴ καμπτόμενοι προσβολαῖς διὰ τὸ προεκλελογίσθαι τὰς ἐπιθέσεις αὐτῆς—ἐπικουφίζει γὰρ καὶ τὰ βαρύτατα τῶν ἀβουλήτων ἡ πρόληψις, καινὸν οὐδὲν ἔτι τῆς διανοίας τῶν συμβαινόντων ὑπολαμβανούσης, ἀλλ' ὡς ἐπὶ παλαιοῖς καὶ ἑώλοις ἀμαυρὰν τὴν ἀντίληψιν ποιουμένης—, εἰκότως ἐνευφραινόμενοι ταῖς ἀρεταῖς ἅπαντά γε τὸν βίον ἑορτὴν ἄγουσιν.
47 οὗτοι μὲν οὖν ὀλίγος εἰσὶν ἀριθμός, ἐμπύρευμα κατὰ πόλεις ὑποτυφόμενον[2] σοφίας, ἕνεκα τοῦ μὴ κατὰ τὸ παντελὲς σβεσθεῖσαν ἀρετὴν ἐκ τοῦ γένους
48 ἡμῶν ἀφανισθῆναι. εἰ δὲ τοῖς ὀλίγοις συνεφρόνησαν οἱ πανταχοῦ καὶ ἐγένοντο, οἵους βούλεται εἶναι ἡ

[1] MSS. χρηστοὺς

[2] MSS. ὑποτυφόμενοι.

which inhabit them are food for their research, as in mind and thought they share the ranging of the moon and sun and the ordered march of the other stars fixed and planetary. While their bodies are firmly planted on the land they provide their souls with wings, so that they may traverse the upper air and gain full contemplation of the powers which dwell there, as behoves true "cosmopolitans" who have recognized the world to be a city having for its citizens the associates of wisdom, registered as such by virtue to whom is entrusted the headship of the universal
commonwealth. XIII. Such men filled with high 46
worthiness, inured to disregard ills of the body or of external things, schooled to hold things indifferent as indeed indifferent,[a] armed against the pleasures and lusts, ever eager to take their stand superior to the passions in general, trained to use every effort to overthrow the formidable menace which those passions have built up against them, never swerving under the blows of fortune because they have calculated beforehand the force of its assaults, since the heaviest adversities are lightened by anticipation,[b] when the mind ceases to find anything strange in the event and apprehends it but dully as it might some stale and familiar story—such men, we say, in the delight of their virtues, naturally make their whole
life a feast. These are indeed but a small number 47
left in their cities like an ember of wisdom to smoulder, that virtue may not be altogether extinguished and
lost to our race. But if only everywhere men had 48
thought and felt as these few, and become what

[a] *Cf. Quis Rerum* 253, where ἐξαδιαφόρησις τῶν ἀδιαφόρων is coupled with other forms of mental and spiritual exercise, and see note.

[b] See App. p. 624.

φύσις, ἀνεπίληπτοι καὶ ἀνυπαίτιοι πάντες, ἐρασταὶ
φρονήσεως, χαίροντες τῷ καλῷ δι' αὐτὸ τὸ καλὸν
καὶ τοῦτο μόνον ἀγαθὸν ἡγούμενοι, τὰ δ' ἄλλα
πάντα ὑπήκοα καὶ δοῦλα ὡς ἂν ἄρχοντες, εὐδαιμονίας ἂν αἱ πόλεις ἐγένοντο μεσταί, τῶν μὲν ὅσα
λύπης αἴτια καὶ φόβων ἀμέτοχοι, πλήρεις δὲ τῶν
ἀπεργαζομένων χαρὰς καὶ εὐπαθείας, ὡς μηδένα
[280] καιρὸν ἐλλείπειν ἱλαροῦ | βίου, πάντα δὲ τὸν τοῦ
49 ἐνιαυτοῦ κύκλον εἶναι ἑορτήν. XIV. διὸ
παρ' ἀληθείᾳ δικαζούσῃ τῶν φαύλων οὐδεὶς ἀλλ'
οὐδὲ τὸν βραχύτατον χρόνον ἑορτάζει, συνειδήσει
τῶν ἀδικημάτων ἀγχόμενος καὶ τῇ ψυχῇ κατηφῶν,
εἰ καὶ τῷ προσώπῳ μειδιᾶν καθυποκρίνεται. ποῦ
γὰρ ἔχει καιρὸν ἀψευδοῦς εὐφροσύνης κακοβουλό-
τατος ὢν καὶ συζῶν ἀφροσύνῃ καὶ περὶ πάντα
ἀκαιρευόμενος, γλῶτταν, γαστέρα, τὰ γεννητικά;
50 δι' ἧς μὲν γὰρ ἐκλαλεῖ τὰ ἀπόρρητα καὶ ἡσυ-
χαστέα, τὴν δὲ ἀκράτου πολλοῦ καὶ ἐδεσμάτων
ἀμέτρων ἀναπίμπλησιν ὑπὸ λαιμαργίας, τοῖς δὲ
καταχρῆται πρὸς ἐκνομωτάτους οἴστρους καὶ μίξεις
ἀθέσμους, οὐ μόνον ἀλλοτρίοις γάμοις ἐπιμεμηνώς,
ἀλλὰ καὶ παιδεραστῶν καὶ βιαζόμενος τὸν ἄρρενα
τῆς φύσεως χαρακτῆρα παρακόπτειν καὶ μεταβάλλειν εἰς γυναικόμορφον ἰδέαν ἕνεκα τοῦ μεμιασμένῳ
51 καὶ ἐπαράτῳ πάθει χαρίσασθαι. δι' ἣν αἰτίαν ὁ
πάντα μέγας Μωυσῆς τὰς ὑπερβολὰς τοῦ περὶ τὴν
ὄντως ἑορτὴν κάλλους ἰδὼν τελειοτέραν ἢ κατ'
ἀνθρωπίνην φύσιν ὑπέλαβεν εἶναι καὶ ἀνέθηκεν
αὐτὴν θεῷ φήσας κατὰ λέξιν οὕτως· " ἑορταὶ κυ-

nature intended them to be, all of them blameless and guiltless and lovers of sound sense, rejoicing in moral excellence just because it is what it is and counting it the only true good and all the other goods but slaves and vassals, subject to their authority, the cities would have been brimful of happiness, utterly free from all that causes grief and fears, and packed with what produces joys and states of well-being, so that each season as it comes would give full opportunity for cheerful living and the whole cycle of the year would be a feast.

XIV. And there- 49
fore in the judgement of truth none of the wicked keeps a feast, even for the shortest time, tormented as he is by consciousness of wrongdoing and depressed in soul, even though he simulates a smile with his face. For where does the wicked man find a season for true rejoicing? He whose every plan is for evil, whose life-mate is folly, with whom everything, tongue, belly and organs of generation, is against
what is seasonable. For with the first he blurts out 50
matters of secrecy which call for silence, while in his greed he fills the second with viands unlimited and strong drink in great quantities, and as for the third, he misuses them for abominable lusts and forms of intercourse forbidden by all laws. He not only attacks in his fury the marriage-beds of others, but even plays the pederast and forces the male type of nature to debase and convert itself into the feminine form, just to indulge a polluted and accursed passion.
For this reason Moses, great here as ever, seeing how 51
vast was the beauty which belonged to the true feast, held that its perfection was beyond the capacity of human nature to realize, and consecrated it to God with these very words, "The Lord's feasts." For

52 ρίου·" τὸ γὰρ ἐπίλυπον καὶ περιδεὲς τοῦ ἡμετέρου
γένους λογιζόμενος καὶ ὡς ἔστι μυρίων κακῶν
μεστόν, ἃ γεννῶσι μὲν αἱ ψυχῆς πλεονεξίαι, γεννῶσι δὲ καὶ αἱ σώματος κῆρες, προσβάλλουσι δὲ αἱ
τῆς τύχης[1] ἀνωμαλίαι καὶ τῶν συνόντων αἱ ἀντεπιθέσεις μυρία κακὰ δρώντων τε καὶ πασχόντων,
εἰκότως ἐθαύμαζεν, εἰ δύναταί τις ἐν τοσούτῳ
πελάγει πραγμάτων ἑκουσίων τε καὶ ἀκουσίων
φερόμενος καὶ μηδέποτ' ἠρεμῆσαι οἷός τε ὢν μηδ'
ἀκινδύνῳ βίῳ μετ' ἀσφαλείας ἐνορμίσασθαι τὴν μὴ
λεγομένην ἀλλὰ πρὸς ἀλήθειαν οὖσαν ὄντως ἄγειν
ἑορτήν, ἐνευφραινόμενος καὶ ἐντρυφῶν θεωρίᾳ τε
τοῦ κόσμου καὶ τῶν ἐν αὐτῷ καὶ ἀκολουθίᾳ φύσεως
καὶ ἁρμονίᾳ πρὸς ἔργα λόγων καὶ πρὸς λόγους
53 ἔργων. ὅθεν ἀναγκαίως εἶπε τὰς ἑορτὰς εἶναι
μόνου θεοῦ· μόνος γὰρ εὐδαίμων καὶ μακάριος,
παντὸς μὲν ἀμέτοχος κακοῦ, πλήρης δ' ἀγαθῶν
τελείων, μᾶλλον δ', εἰ χρὴ τἀληθὲς εἰπεῖν, αὐτὸς
ὢν τὸ ἀγαθόν, ὃς οὐρανῷ καὶ γῇ τὰ κατὰ μέρος
54 ὤμβρησεν ἀγαθά. παρὸ καὶ τῶν πάλαι
τις ἀρετῶσα διάνοια, γαληνιασάντων αὐτῇ τῶν
παθῶν, ἐνεμειδίασε χαρᾶς ἐγκύμων καὶ ὑπόπλεως
γενομένη· καὶ λογισαμένη παρ' αὐτῇ, μή ποτ' ἄρα
τὸ μὲν χαίρειν ἴδιόν ἐστι μόνου θεοῦ, αὐτὴ δὲ
[281] διαμαρτάνει σφετεριζομένη τὰς ὑπὲρ ἄνθρωπον εὐ-
παθείας, εὐλαβεῖταί τε καὶ τὸν ψυχικὸν | γέλωτα

[1] MSS. ψυχῆς.

[a] Lit. "those who are together"; rather than as Heinemann "our fellowmen."

[b] See Gen. xviii. 11-15. This interpretation of Sarah's laughter and her denial of it, and the answer to that denial "but thou didst laugh," has already been given in *De Abr.* 206, where see note. "Her passions now calmed within her"

when he considered the sorrowful and terror-stricken condition of our race, how charged it is with numberless evils generated by the greedy desires of the soul and also by the infirmities of the body, increased by the vicissitudes of fortune and the mutual onslaughts of neighbours against neighbours[a] who inflict and suffer countless wrongs, he could not but wonder that anyone, tossed about on so vast a sea of events, whether of his own intending or not, and unable to find tranquility or the secure anchorage of a life kept safe from danger, could really hold a feast, not in the sense in which the word is commonly used, but in the true sense; and the true sense is, to find delight and festivity in the contemplation of the world and its contents and in following nature and in bringing words into harmony with deeds and deeds with words. And therefore it was 53
a necessary pronouncement that the feasts belonged to God alone, for God alone is happy and blessed, exempt from all evil, filled with perfect forms of good, or rather, if the real truth be told, Himself *the* good, Who showers the particular goods on heaven and earth.

And so it was that in the days of old 54
a certain mind of rich intelligence, her passions now calmed within her, smiled because joy lay within her and filled her womb.[b] And when, as she considered the matter, it seemed to her that joy might well be the peculiar property of God alone, and that she herself was sinning in taking for her own conditions of well-being above human capacity, she was afraid, and denied the laughter of her soul

is the interpretation often (*e.g. De Fuga* 128) given by Philo of *v.* 11, "it ceased to be with Sarah after the manner of women."

55 ἀρνεῖται μέχρι τοῦ παρηγορηθῆναι· τὸ γὰρ δέος αὐτῆς ἐπικουφίζει ὁ ἵλεως θεὸς χρησμῷ κελεύσας ὁμολογεῖν, ὅτι ἐγέλασεν, ἵν' ἡμᾶς ἀναδιδάξῃ, ὅτι οὐ κατὰ τὸ παντελὲς ἐστέρηται τὸ γενητὸν χαρᾶς, ἀλλ' ἔστιν ἡ μὲν ἀμιγὴς καὶ ἀκραιφνεστάτη, μηδὲν τῶν τῆς ἐναντίας ἐπιδεχομένη φύσεως, ἐξαίρετος θεοῦ, ἡ δ' ἀπ' ἐκείνης ῥυεῖσα μικτή, βραχέσιν ἀνακεκραμένη λυπηροῖς, ἀνδρὸς ἤδη σοφοῦ δωρεὰν μεγίστην λαβόντος τὴν τοιαύτην μῖξιν, ἐν ᾗ πλείω τὰ ἡδέα τῶν ἀηδῶν ἀνακέκραται. ταῦτα μὲν ἐπὶ τοσοῦτον.

56 XV. Μετὰ δὲ τὴν συνεχῆ καὶ ἀδιάστατον καὶ διαιωνίζουσαν ἑορτὴν ἄγεται δευτέρα ἡ δι' ἓξ ἡμερῶν ἱερὰ ἑβδόμη· ἣν οἱ μὲν ὠνόμασαν παρθένον εἰς τὴν ὑπερβάλλουσαν ἁγνείαν ἀπιδόντες αὐτῆς, οἱ δὲ αὐτοὶ καὶ ἀμήτορα, σπαρεῖσαν ἐκ μόνου τοῦ πατρὸς τῶν ὅλων, ἰδέαν τῆς ἄρρενος γενεᾶς, ἀμέτοχον τῆς πρὸς γυναικῶν· ἀνδρειότατος γὰρ καὶ ἀλκιμώτατος ὁ ἀριθμός, πρὸς ἀρχὴν καὶ ἡγεμονίαν εὖ πεφυκώς· ἔνιοι δὲ αὐτὴν καιρὸν προσηγόρευσαν ἀπὸ τῶν αἰσθητῶν τεκμηράμενοι τὴν νοητὴν αὐτῆς
57 οὐσίαν. ὅσα γὰρ τῶν ἐν αἰσθητοῖς ἄριστα, δι' ὧν αἱ ἐτήσιοι ὧραι καὶ τῶν καιρῶν αἱ περίοδοι τεταγμένως ἀποτελοῦνται, μετέσχηκεν ἑβδομάδος, λέγω δὲ πλάνητας ἑπτὰ καὶ ἄρκτον καὶ πλειάδα καὶ σελήνης αὐξομένης τε καὶ μειουμένης ἀνακυκλήσεις

---

[a] See on *De Dec.* 102.

[b] Alternatives for translating the untranslatable καιρός might be "the right season," "the happy hour or moment," or the abstract "timeliness." Heinemann gives "die entscheidende Zeit." In *De Op.* 59 καιρός is defined as χρόνοι κατορθώσεως. The application of it to the number seven is, like the other names, Pythagorean. As Philo understands it

until her doubts were set at rest. For the gracious 55
God allayed her fears by an oracle in which He bade her acknowledge that she laughed, meaning thus to teach us the lesson that joy is not altogether denied to the creature. Joy is of two kinds. One is unmixed and of the utmost purity, admitting nothing whatever of the nature opposite to its own. This joy belongs to God and to no other. The other which flows from it is a mixed stream blended with lesser tributaries of sorrow, and if the blend is such that the pleasant ingredients outnumber the unpleasant, the wise man receives it as the greatest of gifts. So much for this matter.

XV. After this continuous unbroken feast which 56
has neither beginning nor end, the second to be observed is the sacred seventh day, recurring with six days between. Some have given to it the name of virgin,[a] having before their eyes its surpassing chastity. They also call her the motherless,[a] begotten by the father of the universe alone, the ideal form of the male sex with nothing of the female. It is the manliest and doughtiest of numbers, well gifted by nature for sovereignty and leadership. Some give it the name of the "season,"[b] judging its conceptual nature from its manifestation in the realm
of sense. For seven is a factor common to all the 57
phenomena which stand highest in the world of sensible things and serve to consummate in due order transitions of the year and recurring seasons. Such are the seven planets, the Great Bear, the Pleiades and the cycles of the moon, as it waxes and wanes,

here, we may perhaps say that it is personified like τύχη, of which it is the converse, and represents the due order in which events happen. See further App. p. 624.

καὶ τῶν ἄλλων τὰς ἐναρμονίους καὶ παντὸς λόγου
58 κρείττους περιφοράς. Μωυσῆς δὲ ἀπὸ σεμνοτέρου
πράγματος ἐκάλεσεν αὐτὴν συντέλειαν καὶ παντέλειαν, ἑξάδι μὲν τὴν γένεσιν τῶν τοῦ κόσμου μερῶν
ἀναθείς, ἑβδομάδι δὲ τὴν τελείωσιν. ἑξὰς μὲν γὰρ
ἀρτιοπέριττος ἀριθμός, ἐκ τοῦ δὶς τρία παγείς,
ἔχων ἄρρενα μὲν τὸν περιττόν, θῆλυν δὲ τὸν ἄρτιον,
ἐξ ὧν εἰσιν αἱ γενέσεις κατὰ φύσεως θεσμοὺς ἀ-
59 κινήτους. ἑβδομὰς δὲ ἀμιγέστατος καὶ φῶς, εἰ χρὴ
τἀληθὲς εἰπεῖν, ἑξάδος· ἃ γὰρ ἐγέννησεν ἑξάς, ταῦθ'
ἑβδομὰς τελεσφορηθέντα ἐπεδείξατο. παρὸ καὶ
γενέθλιος τοῦ κόσμου δεόντως ἂν προσαγορεύοιτο,
καθ' ἣν τὸ τοῦ πατρὸς ἔργον τέλειον ἐκ τελείων
60 μερῶν ἀνεφάνη· ἐν ᾗ προστέτακται
πάντων ἀνέχειν ἔργων, οὐκ ἐπειδὴ ῥᾳθυμίας ὁ
νόμος εἰσηγητής—ἀεὶ γὰρ ἐθίζει κακοπαθεῖν καὶ
πρὸς πόνον ἀλείφει καὶ τοὺς ἀργεῖν καὶ σχολάζειν
[282] ἐθέλοντας προβέβληται, διείρηται γοῦν | ἓξ ἡμέρας
ἐνεργεῖν—, ἀλλ' ἵνα τοὺς συνεχεῖς καὶ ἀτρύτους
πόνους χαλάσῃ καὶ τὰ σώματα μεμετρημέναις
ἀνέσεσιν ἀνακτησάμενος καινώσῃ πάλιν πρὸς τὰς
αὐτὰς ἐνεργείας· οἱ γὰρ διαπνεύσαντες, οὐκ ἰδιῶται
μόνον ἀλλὰ καὶ ἀθληταί, ῥώμην συλλέγονται καὶ
ἀπὸ κραταιοτέρας δυνάμεως ἀνυπερθέτως ἕκαστα
61 τῶν πρακτέων τλητικῶς ὑπομένουσι. προστάξας
μέντοι μὴ διαπονεῖν τοῖς σώμασι κατὰ τὰς ἑβδόμας

---

[a] *Cf. Mos.* i. 207 (and note), and ii. 210.

and the movements, harmonious and grand beyond
description, of the other heavenly bodies. But 58
Moses from a higher point of view gave it the name
of completion and full perfection when he laid down
six as the number under which the parts of the
universe were brought into being, seven as that
under which they were perfected. For six is even-
odd, formed out of twice three with the odd part
as its male element and the even as its feminine, and
these two, by the immutable laws of nature, are the
sources of generation. But seven is a number en- 59
tirely uncompounded, and may be quite properly
described as the light of six. For seven reveals
as completed what six has produced, and therefore
it may be quite rightly entitled the birthday of the
world,[a] whereon the Father's perfect work, compounded of perfect parts, was revealed as what it
was. On this day we are commanded 60
to abstain from all work, not because the law in-
culcates slackness; on the contrary it always
inures men to endure hardship and incites them
to labour, and spurns those who would idle their
time away, and accordingly is plain in its directions
to work the full six days. Its object is rather
to give men relaxation from continuous and un-
ending toil and by refreshing their bodies with a
regularly calculated system of remissions, to send
them out renewed to their old activities. For a
breathing-space enables not merely ordinary people
but athletes also to collect their strength and
with a stronger force behind them to undertake
promptly and patiently each of the tasks set before
them. Further, when He forbids bodily labour 61
on the seventh day, He permits the exercise of

ἐφῆκε τὰς ἀμείνους πράξεις ἐπιτελεῖν· αὗται δ' εἰσὶν αἱ διὰ λόγων καὶ δογμάτων τῶν κατ' ἀρετήν· προτρέπει γὰρ φιλοσοφεῖν τότε βελτιοῦντας τὴν
62 ψυχὴν καὶ τὸν ἡγεμόνα νοῦν. ἀναπέπταται γοῦν ταῖς ἑβδόμαις μυρία κατὰ πᾶσαν πόλιν διδασκαλεῖα φρονήσεως καὶ σωφροσύνης καὶ ἀνδρείας καὶ δικαιοσύνης καὶ τῶν ἄλλων ἀρετῶν, ἐν οἷς οἱ μὲν ἐν κόσμῳ καθέζονται σὺν ἡσυχίᾳ τὰ ὦτα ἀνωρθιακότες μετὰ προσοχῆς πάσης ἕνεκα τοῦ διψῆν λόγων ποτίμων, ἀναστὰς δέ τις τῶν ἐμπειροτάτων ὑφηγεῖται τὰ ἄριστα καὶ συνοίσοντα, οἷς ἅπας ὁ βίος
63 ἐπιδώσει πρὸς τὸ βέλτιον. ἔστι δ' ὡς ἔπος εἰπεῖν τῶν κατὰ μέρος ἀμυθήτων λόγων καὶ δογμάτων δύο τὰ ἀνωτάτω κεφάλαια, τό τε πρὸς θεὸν δι' εὐσεβείας καὶ ὁσιότητος καὶ τὸ πρὸς ἀνθρώπους διὰ φιλανθρωπίας καὶ δικαιοσύνης· ὧν ἑκάτερον εἰς πολυσχιδεῖς ἰδέας καὶ πάσας ἐπαινετὰς τέμνεται.
64 ἐξ ὧν δῆλόν ἐστιν, ὅτι Μωυσῆς οὐδένα καιρὸν ἀπράκτους ἐᾷ τοὺς χρωμένους αὐτοῦ ταῖς ἱεραῖς ὑφηγήσεσιν· ἀλλ' ἐπειδὴ συνέστημεν ἐκ ψυχῆς καὶ σώματος, ἀπένειμε καὶ τῷ σώματι τὰ οἰκεῖα ἔργα καὶ τῇ ψυχῇ τὰ ἐπιβάλλοντα καὶ ἐφεδρεύειν τὰ ἕτερα τοῖς ἑτέροις ἐσπούδασεν, ἵνα πονοῦντος μὲν τοῦ σώματος ἡ ψυχὴ διαναπαύηται, ἀναπαύλῃ δὲ χρωμένου διαπονῇ, καὶ οἱ ἄριστοι τῶν βίων, ὅ τε θεωρητικὸς καὶ ὁ πρακτικός, ἀμείβωσιν ἀντιπαραχωροῦντες ἀλλήλοις, ὁ μὲν πρακτικὸς λαχὼν

---

[a] The meaning of ὡς ἔπος εἰπεῖν is not quite clear. Generally, if not always, it is applied to a general statement, mostly numerical, to indicate that it is not exact. Perhaps it may

the higher activities, namely, those employed in the study of the principles of virtue's lore. For the law bids us take the time for studying philosophy and thereby improve the soul and the dominant
mind. So each seventh day there stand wide open 62
in every city thousands of schools of good sense, temperance, courage, justice and the other virtues in which the scholars sit in order quietly with ears alert and with full attention, so much do they thirst for the draught which the teacher's words supply, while one of special experience rises and sets forth what is the best and sure to be profitable and will make the whole of life grow to something better.
But among the vast number of particular truths and 63
principles there studied, there stand out practically[a] high above the others two main heads: one of duty to God as shewn by piety and holiness, one of duty to men as shewn by humanity and justice, each of them splitting up into multiform branches, all highly
laudable. These things shew clearly that Moses 64
does not allow any of those who use his sacred instruction to remain inactive at any season. But since we consist of body and soul, he assigned to the body its proper tasks and similarly to the soul what falls to its share, and his earnest desire was, that the two should be waiting to relieve each other. Thus while the body is working, the soul enjoys a respite, but when the body takes its rest, the soul resumes its work, and thus the best forms of life, the theoretical and the practical, take their turn in replacing each other. The practical life has six as

mean here that it would be possible to find more than two main heads, or other than these two. Heinemann translates "so zu sagen," but I do not see what this means here, even if the Greek can be so translated.

ἑξάδα κατὰ τὴν τοῦ σώματος ὑπηρεσίαν, ὁ δὲ θεωρητικὸς ἑβδομάδα πρὸς ἐπιστήμην καὶ τελειότητα διανοίας.

65 XVI. Ἀπείρηται δὲ κατ' αὐτὴν πῦρ ἐναύειν ὡς |
[233] ἀρχὴν καὶ σπέρμα τῶν περὶ βίον πραγματειῶν, ἐπειδήπερ ἄνευ πυρὸς οὐδὲν ἔστι τῶν εἰς τὰς πρὸς τὸ ζῆν ἀναγκαίας χρείας ἐργάσεσθαι· ὡς δι' ἑνὸς τοῦ ἀνωτάτω καὶ πρεσβυτάτου τῶν εἰς τὰς τέχνας
66 καὶ μάλιστα τὰς βαναύσους αἰτίου κεκωλῦσθαι καὶ ⟨τὰ⟩[1] τῶν κατὰ μέρος ὑπηρεσιῶν. ἀλλ' ἔοικε διὰ τοὺς ἀπειθεστέρους καὶ ἥκιστα προσέχοντας τὸν νοῦν τοῖς προσταττομένοις[2] καὶ τὰ ἄλλα προσνομοθετεῖν, οὐ μόνον ἐλευθέρους ἀνέχειν ἔργων ἀξιῶν ταῖς ἑβδόμαις, ἀλλὰ καὶ θεράπουσι καὶ θεραπαίναις ἐφιείς, ἄδειαν καὶ μόνον οὐκ ἐλευθερίαν δι' ἓξ
67 ἡμερῶν προκηρύττων τούτοις, ἵν' ἀμφοτέρους ἀναδιδάξῃ μάθημα κάλλιστον· τοὺς μὲν δεσπότας αὐτουργεῖν ἐθίζεσθαι, μὴ ἀναμένοντας τὰς ἀπὸ τῶν οἰκετῶν λατρείας καὶ ὑπηρεσίας, ἵν', εἴ τινες ἀβούλητοι καιροὶ κατάσχοιεν κατὰ τὰς τῶν ἀνθρωπείων πραγμάτων μεταβολάς, μὴ τῷ ἀήθει τῆς αὐτουργίας προκάμνοντες τοῖς ἐπιτάγμασιν ἀπαγορεύωσιν, ἀλλ' εὐκινητοτέροις χρώμενοι τοῖς τοῦ σώματος μέρεσιν εὐφόρως καὶ μετὰ ῥᾳστώνης

[1] The insertion was made by Tischendorf, though not accepted by Cohn. *Sc.* αἴτια. It seems to me necessary for the construction.

[2] MSS. πραττομένοις.

---

[a] Ex. xxxv. 3, *cf. Mos.* ii. 219 and note.

[b] Or "primary," see on § 82.

[c] For §§ 66-69 see Ex. xx. 10.

[d] This seems to contradict both the foregoing and the

its number allotted for ministering to the body. The theoretical has seven for knowledge and perfection of the mind.

XVI. It is forbidden to light any fire on this day,[a] 65
fire being regarded as the source and origin of life, since without it nothing can be executed which serves the requirements necessary for existence. And thus the prohibition of the highest[b] and earliest instrument needed in the arts, and especially those of the mechanical kind, acts as a barrier to those required
for the particular forms of service. [c]But it would 66
seem that his further enactments were given for the sake of the more disobedient who refused to pay attention to his commandments, when he not only requires the free men to abstain from work on the Sabbath, but gives the same permission to men-servants and handmaids, and sends them a message of security and almost of freedom after every six days, to teach both masters and men an admirable
lesson. The masters must be accustomed to work 67
themselves without waiting for the offices and attentions of their menials,[d] and so in the event of times of difficulty such as occur through the vicissitudes of human affairs, they may not through unfamiliarity with personal service lose heart at the outset and despair of accomplishing the tasks set before them, but use the different parts of their body with more nimbleness and shew a robust and

commandment itself " neither thou . . . nor thy manservant, nor thy maidservant." Philo perhaps means that there are wants which must necessarily receive attention, and that if this attention is rendered by oneself, it is not work in the sense of the commandment, but is work if rendered by another. Strict modern Sabbatarians would probably feel the same.

ἐνεργῶσι, τοὺς δ' οἰκέτας μὴ ἀπογινώσκειν τὰς ἀμείνους ἐλπίδας, ἀλλ' ἔχοντας τὴν δι' ἓξ ἡμερῶν ἄνεσιν ἐμπύρευμά τι καὶ ζώπυρον ἐλευθερίας τὴν εἰς τὸ παντελὲς ἄφεσιν, εἰ διαμένοιεν χρηστοὶ καὶ
68 φιλοδέσποτοι, προσδοκᾶν. ἐκ δὲ τοῦ τοὺς μὲν ἐλευθέρους ὑπομεῖναί ποτε τὰς δούλων ὑπηρεσίας, τοῖς δ' οἰκέταις ἐγγενέσθαι μετασχεῖν ἀδείας, συμβήσεται τὸν τῶν ἀνθρώπων βίον ἐπιδοῦναι πρὸς ἀρετὴν τελειοτάτην, ὑπομιμνῃσκομένων ἰσότητος καὶ ἀντεκτινόντων ἀλλήλοις χρέος ἀναγκαῖον τῶν τε λαμπρῶν εἶναι δοκούντων καὶ τῶν ἀφανεστέρων.

69 ἀλλὰ γὰρ οὐ θεράπουσι μόνον ἐκεχειρίαν ἔδωκεν ὁ νόμος ταῖς ἑβδόμαις, ἀλλὰ καὶ κτήνεσι· καίτοι φύσει θεράποντες μὲν ἐλεύθεροι γεγόνασιν—ἄνθρωπος γὰρ ἐκ φύσεως δοῦλος οὐδείς—, τὰ δ' ἄλογα ζῷα πρὸς τὴν τῶν ἀνθρώπων χρείαν καὶ ὑπηρεσίαν εὐτρεπισθέντα δούλων ἔχει τάξιν· ἀλλ' ὅμως ἀχθοφορεῖν ὀφείλοντα καὶ τοὺς ὑπὲρ τῶν κεκτημένων ὑπομένειν πόνους τε καὶ καμάτους
70 ἀναπαύλας εὑρίσκει ταῖς ἑβδόμαις. καὶ τί δεῖ τῶν ἄλλων μεμνῆσθαι; οὐδὲ γὰρ βοῦς πρὸς τὰ ἀναγκαιότατα καὶ χρησιμώτατα τῶν ἐν τῷ βίῳ γεγονώς, ἄροτον[1] γῆς προετοιμαζομένης εἰς σπορὰν
[284] καὶ πάλιν δραγμάτων συγκομισθέντων | ἀλοητὸν εἰς καρποῦ κάθαρσιν, τότε καταζεύγνυται, τὴν τοῦ κόσμου γενέθλιον ἑορτάζων. οὕτως ἄρα διὰ πάντων τὸ ἱεροπρεπὲς αὐτῆς πεφοίτηκε.

71 XVII. Τοσούτου δ' ἀξιοῖ σεβασμοῦ τὴν ἑβδόμην,

[1] mss. ἄροτρον.

---

[a] See App. pp. 624-625.

[b] The Deuteronomic version of the fourth commandment

easy activity ; while on the other hand the servants are not to refuse to entertain still higher hopes, but should find in the relaxation allowed after six days an ember or spark of freedom, and look forward to their complete liberation if they continue to serve well and loyally. But the result of this occa- 68
sional submission of the free to do the menial offices of the slave, together with the immunity allowed to the slave, will be a step forward in human conduct towards the perfection of virtue, when both the seemingly distinguished and the meaner sort remember equality and repay to each other the debt incumbent on them. But the holiday of 69
the Sabbath is given by the law not only to servants but also to the cattle, though there might well be a distinction. For servants are free by nature, no man being naturally a slave,[a] but the unreasoning animals are intended to be ready for the use and service of men and therefore rank as slaves. Yet all the same, though it is their proper business to carry burdens and undergo toils and labour for their owners, they obtain their respite on the seventh days. There is 70
no need to go through the rest of the list, when even the ox[b] who serves the most useful and indispensable purposes in human life, namely ploughing when the soil is prepared for the sowing, and again thrashing when the sheaves are brought in for the purging of the fruit, is then kept free from the yoke and enjoys the birthday festival of the world. So universally has the sanctity of the day extended its influence.

XVII. So high is the reverence which he assigns 71

(v. 14) has "nor thine ox, nor thine ass, nor any of thy cattle." So also LXX in Ex. xx. 10, though the Hebrew and E.V. have only "nor thy cattle."

ὥστε καὶ ἄλλα ὁπόσα ταύτης μετέχει τετίμηται παρ' αὐτῷ. κατὰ γοῦν ἕβδομον ἐνιαυτὸν ἀεὶ χρεωκοπίαν εἰσηγεῖται πένησιν ἐπικουρῶν καὶ τοὺς πλουσίους ἐπὶ φιλανθρωπίαν προκαλούμενος, ἵνα τῶν ἰδίων μεταδιδόντες ἀπόροις χρηστὰ καὶ περὶ αὑτῶν προσδοκῶσιν, εἴ γένοιτό τι πταῖσμα· πολλὰ δὲ τὰ ἀνθρώπινα καὶ οὐκ ἐπὶ τῶν αὐτῶν ὁ βίος ὁρμεῖ πνεύματος ἀστάτου τρόπον μεταβάλλων πρὸς
72 τὰ ἐναντία. καλὸν μὲν οὖν τὴν ἀπὸ δανειστῶν χάριν ἐπὶ πάντας φθάνειν χρεώστας· ἐπεὶ δ' οὐ πάντες πρὸς μεγαλοφροσύνην πεφύκασιν, ἀλλ' εἰσὶν ἥττους ἔνιοι χρημάτων ἢ οὐ σφόδρα εὔποροι, καὶ τούτους ἐδικαίωσεν εἰσφέρειν ἃ μὴ λυπήσει
73 διδόμενα. παρὰ γὰρ τῶν ὁμοεθνῶν εἰσπράττειν οὐκ ἐάσας ἐφῆκε παρὰ τῶν ἄλλων κομίζεσθαι, τοὺς μὲν καλέσας εὐθυβόλως "ἀδελφούς," ἵνα μηδεὶς φθονῇ τῶν ἰδίων ὡς ἂν ἐκ φύσεως συγκληρονόμοις ἀδελφοῖς, τοὺς δὲ μὴ ὁμοεθνεῖς, ὅπερ εἰκός, "ἀλλοτρίους" ὠνόμασεν. ἡ δ' ἀλλοτριότης ἀκοινώνητον, εἰ μὴ καὶ ταύτην τις ὑπερβολαῖς ἀρετῶν μεθαρμόσαιτο πρὸς συγγενικὴν οἰκειότητα· συνόλως γὰρ ἐν ἀρεταῖς ἡ πολιτεία καὶ νόμοις, οἳ μόνον τὸ
74 καλὸν ἀγαθὸν εἰσηγοῦνται. ὑπαίτιον δὲ τὸ

---

[a] See Deut. xv. 1-3.

[b] Heinemann translates "weniger wohlhabend," apparently taking χρημάτων as a genitive of respect. I think this is impossible.

[c] Meaning perhaps "which must not be allowed to grieve them." *Cf.* Deut. xv. 10, "Thine heart shalt not be grieved (LXX οὐ λυπηθήσῃ) because the Lord will bless thee."

to the seventh day that other things which share in the qualities of the number are honoured in his estimation. Thus he lays down a rule for cancellation of debts in every seventh year,[a] both as a succour to the poor and as a challenge to the rich to shew humanity, in order that by giving some share of their own to the needy they may expect to receive the same kindness themselves, if any disaster befall them. Human vicissitudes are manifold, and life is not always on the same anchorage, but is like an unsteady wind, ever veering round to the opposite quarter.
Now the best course would be that the creditors' 72
liberality should be extended to all debtors. But since they are not all capable of showing magnanimity, some being under the dominion of their money[b] or not very well off, he laid down that they too should make a contribution, the sacrifice of which would
not give them pain.[c] He does not allow them to 73
exact money from their fellow-nationals, but does permit the recovery of dues from the others.[d] He distinguishes the two by calling the first by the appropriate name of brethren, suggesting that none should grudge to give of his own to those whom nature has made his brothers and fellow-heirs. Those who are not of the same nation he describes as aliens,[e] reasonably enough, and the condition of the alien excludes any idea of partnership, unless indeed by a transcendency of virtues he converts even it into a tie of kinship, since it is a general truth that common citizenship rests on virtues and laws which propound the morally
beautiful as the sole good.[f] Now lending 74

[d] Deut. xv. 3. [e] E.V. "foreigner."
See App. p. 625.

δανείζειν ἐπὶ τόκῳ· δανείζεται γάρ τις οὐ περιουσίᾳ
ζῶν, ἀλλὰ δηλονότι χρεῖος ὤν, ὃς[1] ἐπαναγκαζόμενος
τόκους τοῖς ἀρχαίοις προσαποτίνειν ἀπορώτατος ἐξ
ἀνάγκης ἂν γένοιτο καὶ νομίσας ὠφελεῖσθαι ἔτι
βλάπτεται καθάπερ τὰ ὀλιγόφρονα τῶν ζῴων τῷ
75 παρόντι δελέατι. σοὶ δ᾿ εἴποιμ᾿ ἄν, ὦ δανειστά·
τί κοινωνίᾳ τρόπον ἀκοινώνητον συσκιάζεις; τί δὲ
τῷ μὲν δοκεῖν εἶναι χρηστὸς καὶ φιλάνθρωπος προσ-
ποιῇ, ἐν δὲ τοῖς ἔργοις ἀπανθρωπίαν ἐπιδείκνυσαι
καὶ δεινὴν σκαιότητα, πλείω ὧν ἔδωκας ἀναπράτ-
των καὶ ἔστιν ὅπου διπλάσιον, πενιχρότερον ἀπ-
76 εργαζόμενος τὸν πένητα; τοιγάρτοι συναλγεῖ μὲν
οὐδείς, ὅταν ὀρεχθεὶς πλειόνων προσσυναποβάλῃς
[285] καὶ τὰ ὄντα, πάντες | δ᾿ ἐφήδονται τοκογλύφον καὶ
ὀβολοστάτην καὶ τὰ τοιαῦτα ὀνομάζοντες, ὡς
ἔφεδρον ἀλλοτρίων κακῶν καὶ τὴν ἑτέρων ἀτυχίαν
77 ἰδίαν κρίνοντα εὐτυχίαν. ἀλλὰ πηρόν,[2] ὡς ἔφη τις,
ἡ κακία, καὶ ὁ δανείζων τυφλός, τὸν χρόνον τῆς
ἀποδόσεως οὐ βλέπων, ἐν ᾧ μόλις ἢ οὐδ᾿ ὅλως ὧν
ἐκ πλεονεξίας τεύξεσθαι προσεδόκησεν ἐφίξεται.
78 οὗτος μὲν οὖν διδότω δίκας τῆς φιλαργυρίας, ἃ
προήκατο μόνα κομιζόμενος,[3] ἵνα μὴ ἀτυχίας ἀνθρώπων ἐργάζηται προσοδευόμενος ἐξ ὧν οὐ
προσῆκεν· οἱ δὲ χρεῶσται τῆς ἀπὸ τῶν νόμων

[1] MSS. ὡς. [2] MSS. πονηρόν.
[3] MSS. μὴ κομιζόμενος.

---

[a] Ex. xxii. 25, Lev. xxv. 35-37, Deut. xxiii. 19; in the last passage lending money on interest to a foreigner is sanctioned.

[b] The source of the quotation is not known.

[c] ἐργάζηται ἀτυχίας could in itself mean "create or produce misfortunes," as Heinemann seems to take it, though we should expect ἀνθρώποις, but the point is rather that he *uses* people's misfortunes. ἐργάζεσθαι, to "trade" or "make

money on interest is a blameworthy action,[a] for a person who borrows is not living on a superabundance of means, but is obviously in need, and since he is compelled to pay the interest as well as the capital, he must necessarily be in the utmost straits. And while he thinks he is being benefited by the loan, he is actually like senseless animals suffering further damage from the bait which is set before him. I ask you, Sir Moneylender, why do you 75
disguise your want of a partner's feeling by pretending to act as a partner? Why do you assume outwardly a kindly and charitable appearance but display in your actions inhumanity and a savage brutality, exacting more than you lend, sometimes double, reducing the pauper to further depths of poverty? And therefore no one sympathizes when 76
in your eagerness for larger gains you lose your capital as well. In their glee all call you extortioner and money-grubber and other similar terms, you who have lain in wait for the misfortunes of others, and regarded their ill-luck as your own good luck. It has 77
been said[b] that vice has no sense of sight; so too the moneylender is blind, and has no vision of the time of repayment, when it will hardly be possible, if at all, to obtain what he has expected to gain by his greed. Such a person may well pay the penalty 78
of his avarice by receiving back merely what he provided, and learn not to make a trade of other people's misfortunes[c] and enrich himself in improper ways. And the borrowers should be granted the privilege

money," is common enough, and there is a good parallel of this use with the accusative in Demosthenes, p. 794 τὰ τῶν ἄλλων κακὰ τοῦτον τρέφει . . .· ταῦτα γεωργεῖ, ταῦτα ἐργάζεται. (The genitive with ἀπό, or the dative, seems to be commoner, and perhaps we might read ἀπ' ἀτυχίας or ἀτυχίαις.)

φιλανθρωπίας ἀξιούσθωσαν, τόκους καὶ ἐπιτοκίας μὴ τελοῦντες, αὐτὸ δὲ μόνον τὸ ἀρχαῖον ἀποτινύντες· πάλιν γὰρ ἐν καιροῖς τὸν αὐτὸν ἔρανον ἀνταποτίσουσι τοῖς συμβάλλουσιν ἀμειβόμενοι ταῖς ἴσαις ὠφελείαις τοὺς χάριτος ἄρξαντας.

79 XVIII. Τοιαῦτα διαταξάμενος ἑξῆς ἀναγράφει νόμον ἡμερότητος καὶ φιλανθρωπίας μεστόν. ἐάν, φησί, πραθῇ σοί τις τῶν ἀδελφῶν, ἓξ ἔτη δουλευέτω, τῷ δὲ ἑβδόμῳ προῖκα ἐλεύθερος ἀφιέσθω.[a]
80 πάλιν "ἀδελφὸν" τὸν ὁμόφυλον εἶπεν ὑποσπείρων τῇ τοῦ κεκτημένου ψυχῇ διὰ τῆς προσρήσεως τὴν πρὸς τὸν ὑπήκοον συγγένειαν, ἵνα μὴ ὡς ξένου, πρὸς ὃν οὐδὲν φίλτρον ἐστὶν εὐνοίας, κατολιγωρῇ, φιλοίκειον δέ τι προπεπονθὼς πάθος ἐκ διδασκαλίας, ἣν ὁ ἱερὸς λόγος ὑπηχεῖ,[b] μὴ ἀγανακτῇ μέλ-
81 λοντος ἐλευθεροῦσθαι. τοὺς γὰρ τοιούτους δούλους μὲν ὀνομάζεσθαι συμβέβηκε, θῆτας[c] δὲ τῷ ὄντι εἶναι τῶν ἀναγκαίων χάριν ὑπηρετοῦντας, κἂν μυριάκις αὐτεξούσιον δυναστείαν καὶ δεσποτείαν
82 ἀπειλῶσί τινες κατ' αὐτῶν· οὓς τιθασευτέον, ἐπιλέγοντας τὰ χρηστὰ ἐκεῖνα τοῦ νόμου παραγγέλματα· μισθωτός ἐστιν, ὦ ἄνθρωπε, ὁ λεγόμενος δοῦλος, καὶ αὐτὸς ἄνθρωπος ὤν, ἔχων πρὸς σὲ τὴν ἀνωτάτω συγγένειαν, ἔπειτα καὶ ἀπὸ τοῦ αὐτοῦ

[a] See Deut. xv. 12, which follows the passage discussed in §§ 71-73, from which the prohibition of usury was a digression. The limitation of slavery is also enforced in Ex. xxi. 2. But the use of the word "brother" shews that it is Deuteronomy which he has in mind.

[b] For ὑπηχεῖν see note on *De Som.* i. 164.

[c] Or "hired labourers," "wage-earners." The word implies not merely occupation but a definite status, above the δοῦλος, but lower than the other citizens. In § 39 θητεύοντες are opposed to ἐλεύθεροι.

of the law's charity, and pay neither simple nor compound interest, but just the principal. For later, as the proper occasion arise, they will make the same sacrifice to their present creditors and requite with equal assistance those who were the first to bestow the benefit.

XVIII. After ordinances of this sort he follows 79
them by laying down a law which breathes kindness and humanity throughout.[a] "If," he says, "one of your brethren is sold to you, let him continue in slavery for six years but in the seventh be set free without payment." Here again he uses the term 80
brother of a fellow-national, and by this name indirectly sows in the soul of the owner the thoughts of his close relationship to the person in his power. It bids him not despise him as a stranger who has no charm to win his affection, but allow the lesson which the holy word suggests[b] to create a preliminary sense of kinship, and thus feel no resentment at his approaching liberation. For people in this position, 81
though we find them called slaves, are in reality labourers[c] who undertake the service just to procure themselves the necessaries of life, however much some may bluster about the rights of absolute power which they exercise over them. [d]We must abate 82
their truculence by repeating these excellent injunctions of the law. The man whom you call a slave, my friend, is a hired person, himself too a man, ultimately[e] your kinsman, further of the same

[d] §§ 82-85 are a homily on Deut. xv. 12-18.

[e] ἀνωτάτω = "if you go right up to the beginning," "ultimately" or "primarily," as suits the context. So in § 233 and very probably in § 65. *Cf. Mos.* i. 314, he who kills a man is guilty διὰ τὴν ἀνωτάτω καὶ κοινὴν συγγένειαν. Heinemann in "höchsten Sinne" seems to me to miss the sense.

ἔθνους, τάχα δὲ καὶ φυλέτης καὶ δημότης, ἐνδείας
83 χάριν εἰς τουτὶ τὸ σχῆμα ὑπηγμένος. ἀνελὼν οὖν
ἐκ τῆς ψυχῆς ἐπίβουλον κακόν, ἀλαζονείαν, ὡς μισθωτῷ προσφέρου, τὰ μὲν διδούς, τὰ δὲ καὶ λαμβάνων· παρέξει μὲν οὖν ἐκεῖνος ἀοκνότατα τὰς ὑπηρεσίας ἀεὶ καὶ πανταχοῦ, μηδὲν ὑπερτιθέμενος, ἀλλὰ φθάνων τὰς σὰς ἐπικελεύσεις τάχει καὶ προθυμίᾳ· σὺ δ' ἀντιδίδου τὰς τροφὰς καὶ ἐσθῆτα καὶ τὴν ἄλλην ἐπιμέλειαν, μὴ καταζεύξας ὡς ζῷον ἄλογον μηδὲ πλείοσι καὶ βαρυτέροις τῆς δυνάμεως ἄχθεσι πιέζων μηδ' ὑβρίζων μηδὲ ἀπειλαῖς καὶ
[286] ἐπανατάσεσιν εἰς | χαλεπὰς δυσθυμίας ἐφελκόμενος, ἀλλ' ἀναχωρήσεις διδοὺς καὶ ἀνέσεις μεμετρημένας· τὸ γὰρ "μηδὲν ἄγαν" ἐπὶ πάντων ἄριστον καὶ μάλιστα πρὸς οἰκέτας δεσποτῶν.
84 ὑπηρετηθεὶς μέντοι χρόνον αὐταρκέστατον, ἑξαετίαν, ὅταν ὁ ἱερώτατος ἀριθμὸς ἐνίστασθαι μέλλῃ, τὸ ἕβδομον ἔτος, ἐλεύθερον μεθίεσο τὸν ἐλεύθερον φύσει μηδὲν ἐνδοιάσας, ἀλλ', ὦ γενναῖε, καὶ γεγηθὼς δίδου τὴν χάριν, ὅτι καιρὸν ἔλαβες τὸ ζῴων ἄριστον, ἄνθρωπον, ἐν τοῖς μεγίστοις εὐεργετῆσαι· δούλῳ γὰρ οὐκ ἔστι μεῖζον ἐλευθερίας ἀγαθόν.
85 χαίρων οὖν καὶ προσεπιδαψίλευσαί τι τῶν ἰδίων
ἀφ' ἑκάστου μέρους τῆς κτήσεως ἐφοδιάσας τὸν εὐεργετηθέντα· σὸν γὰρ ἐγκώμιον, εἰ μὴ πένης ὢν ἀπαλλάττοιτο τῆς οἰκίας, ἀλλὰ τῶν εἰς τἀναγκαῖα

---

[a] This is a case in which Philo seems to adapt the law to contemporary conditions. We do not hear of δῆμοι in old Israel, but apparently a classification into φυλαί and δῆμοι was in force in Alexandria. See App. p. 625.

[b] See Deut. xv. 18, "It shall not seem hard to thee when thou lettest him go free from thee."

nation, perhaps also of the same tribe and ward,[a] reduced to the guise which he now adopts by actual
need. Expel, then, from your soul that evil and 83
malignant thing, arrogance. Deal with him as your hired servant, both in what you give and what you take. As for the latter, he will render you his services without the slightest backwardness always and everywhere without procrastination, and anticipate your orders with zeal and rapidity. And you must give him in return food and raiment and take care for his other needs. Do not harness him like an unreasoning animal nor oppress him with weights too heavy and too numerous for his capacity, nor heap insults upon him, nor drag him down by threats and menaces into cruel despondency. Rather grant him time and places for respite according to some regular rule. For while " not too much of anything " is an excellent maxim in every case, it is particularly
so as between masters and servants. [b] When however 84
you have received his services for the fullest term required, namely, six years, and when the truly sacred number of the seventh year is about to begin, grant his freedom to him who is naturally free and grant it without hesitation, my friend, and rejoice that you have found an opportunity of benefiting the highest of living creatures, man, in his chief interest. For a
slave can have no greater boon than freedom. [c] Be 85
glad, too, to crown your benefaction by bestowing something of each of your various kinds of property to start him on his way. For it is a praise to you that he should not leave your home penniless but well stocked in resources to procure what is necessary.

[c] *Ibid. v.* 13, " when thou lettest him go free from thee thou shalt not let him go empty."

ἀφορμῶν εὐπορηκώς, ἵνα μὴ πάλιν ὑπ᾿ ἐνδείας εἰς τὴν ἀρχαίαν ἀτυχίαν ὑπαχθῇ δουλεύειν ἀναγκασθεὶς διὰ σπάνιν τῶν περὶ δίαιταν καὶ ἡ σὴ χάρις ἀναιρεθῇ. πενήτων μὲν δὴ πέρι τοσαῦτα.

86 XIX. Κελεύει δ᾿ ἑξῆς ἀργὴν τὴν χώραν ἐᾶν ἔτει ἑβδόμῳ, διὰ πολλά· πρῶτον μέν, ἵνα τὴν ἑβδομάδα τιμήσῃ κατὰ πάντας χρόνους ἡμερῶν καὶ μηνῶν καὶ ἐνιαυτῶν· ἑβδόμη τε γὰρ πᾶσα ἡμέρα ἱερά, τὸ καλούμενον παρ᾿ Ἑβραίοις σάββατον, μηνῶν τε ὁ ἕβδομος κατὰ πᾶν ἔτος ἑορτῶν ἔλαχε τὴν μεγίστην, ὥστ᾿ εἰκότως καὶ ὁ ἕβδομος ἐνιαυτὸς τοῦ περὶ τὸν ἀριθμὸν σεβασμοῦ τυχὼν ἐκτετίμηται.
87 δεύτερον δ᾿ ἐκεῖνο· μὴ πάντα,[1] φησίν, ἴσθι τοῦ κέρδους, ἀλλὰ καὶ ἑκὼν ζημίαν ὑπόμεινον, ἵνα καὶ τὴν ἀκούσιον βλάβην, εἴ ποτε γένοιτο, ῥᾳδίως ἐνέγκῃς, ἀλλὰ μὴ ὡς ἐπὶ καινῷ καὶ ξένῳ δυσχεραίνων ἀθυμήσῃς. εἰσὶ γὰρ τῶν πλουσίων οὕτως ἀτυχεῖς τὰς γνώμας τινές, ὥστε ἀπορίας ἐπισχούσης στένουσι καὶ κατηφοῦσιν οὐδὲν ἧττον ἢ εἰ
88 πᾶσαν ἀφῃρέθησαν τὴν οὐσίαν. ἀλλὰ τῶν Μωυσέως ὁμιλητῶν ὅσοι φοιτηταὶ γνήσιοι καλοῖς ἐνασκούμενοι νομίμοις ἐκ πρώτης ἡλικίας ἐθίζονται τὰς ἐνδείας εὐμαρῶς ὑπομένειν διὰ τοῦ καὶ τὴν ἀρετῶσαν χώραν ἐᾶν ἀργήν, ἅμα καὶ μεγαλοφροσύνην ἀναδιδασκόμενοι καὶ[2] τὰς ὁμολογουμένας

[1] The phrase "do not belong in all things to lucre," seems to me strange, and as the mss. vary between *πάντα, φησίν, ἴσθι* and *παντάπασιν ἴσθι*, one might be inclined to read, as Cohn thinks possible, *παντάπασι, φησί*. Nicetas's paraphrase, however, *ἵνα διδάξῃ μὴ πάντα εἶναι τοῦ κέρδους* is an argument for the form here printed.

[2] Mangey proposed to correct *καὶ* to *διὰ τοῦ*. Heinemann suggests <*διὰ τοῦ*> *καὶ*. See note *a*, p. 362.

Otherwise the same thing may happen again. He may be reduced by need to his old unhappy plight and compelled to undertake slavery again through lack of the means of life, and the boon you bestowed upon him may be cancelled. So much for the poor.

XIX. Then follows a commandment to let the 86
land lie fallow during the seventh year.[a] There are several reasons for this. In the first place he wished to give seven its honourable position in all the series in which time is measured, namely, days, months and years. For every seventh day is holy, a Sabbath as the Hebrews call it, and it is in the seventh month in every year that the chief of all the feasts falls, and therefore naturally the seventh year also has been marked out for a share in the dignity which belongs
to the number. And there is this second reason. 87
Do not, he says, be entirely under the power of lucre, but submit voluntarily to some loss, so that you may find it easy to bear some involuntary injury, if ever it should occur, instead of resenting it as some strange and alien misfortune and falling into despair. For some of the rich are so poor-spirited that when adversity overtakes them, they are as mournful and depressed as if they had
been robbed of their whole substance. But among 88
the followers of Moses all who have been his true disciples, trained in his excellent institutions from their earliest years, by allowing even rich territory to lie idle inure themselves to bear privations calmly and by the lesson of magnanimity thus learned voluntarily and deliberately to let even undoubted

[a] See Ex. xxiii. 11, Lev. xxv. 2 ff.

προσόδους μόνον οὐκ ἐκ τῶν χειρῶν ἑκουσίῳ γνώμῃ
89 μεθιέναι. τρίτον κἀκεῖνο αἰνίττεσθαί μοι
[287] δοκεῖ, τὸ μηδενὶ προσήκειν τὸ | παράπαν ἀνθρώπους ἄχθει βαρύνειν καὶ πιέζειν· εἰ γὰρ τοῖς μέρεσι τῆς γῆς, ἃ μήτε ἡδονῆς μήτε ἀλγηδόνος πέφυκε κοινωνεῖν, μεταδοτέον ἀναπαύλης, πῶς οὐχὶ μᾶλλον ἀνθρώποις, οἷς οὐ μόνον αἴσθησις πρόσεστιν ἡ κοινὴ καὶ τῶν ἀλόγων ζῴων, ἀλλὰ καὶ λογισμὸς ἐξαίρετος, ᾧ τὰ ἐκ πόνων καὶ καμάτων ὀδυνηρὰ
90 τρανοτέραις φαντασίαις ἐντυποῦται; παυσάσθωσαν οὖν οἱ λεγόμενοι δεσπόται τῶν ἐπὶ δούλοις σφοδρῶν καὶ δυσυπομονήτων ἐπιταγμάτων, ἃ καὶ τὰ σώματα κατακλᾷ βιαζόμενα καὶ τὰς ψυχὰς πρὸ τῶν σω-
91 μάτων ἀπαγορεύειν ἀναγκάζει. φθόνος γὰρ οὐδεὶς προστάττειν τὰ μέτρια, δι' ὧν καὶ ὑμεῖς τῆς προσηκούσης ὑπηρεσίας ἀπολαύσετε καὶ οἱ θεράποντες εὐφόρως τὰ κελευσθέντα δράσουσι καὶ τὰς διακονίας οὐ πρὸς ὀλίγον ἅτε προκαμόντες καὶ (εἰ δεῖ τἀληθὲς εἰπεῖν) ἐν τοῖς πόνοις προγηράσαντες ὑπομενοῦσιν, ἀλλὰ πρὸς μήκιστον ἀθλητῶν τρόπον ἀνηβῶντες, οὐ τῶν εἰς πολυσαρκίαν πιαινομένων, ἀλλ' οἷς ἔθος ἐγγυμνάζεσθαι διὰ ξηρῶν ἱδρώτων πρὸς τὴν τῶν περὶ τὸν βίον ἀναγκαίων καὶ χρησί-
92 μων κτῆσιν. παυσάσθωσαν καὶ οἱ τῶν

---

[a] The correction suggested by Mangey and Heinemann (see note 2, p. 360) would make sacrificing revenues parallel to letting the land lie idle. I think the text is better as it stands. Leaving the land idle teaches the poorer to stand the privation, and the richer to sacrifice wealth voluntarily.

[b] The allusion, which neither Cohn nor Heinemann notices, is to Plato, *Phaedrus* 239 c, where ξηροὶ ἱδρῶτες are coupled with πόνοι ἀνδρεῖοι, and contrasted with ἁπαλὴ καὶ ἄνανδρος

sources of wealth fall almost from their very hands.[a]
There is also, I think, this third sug- 89
gestion, that men should absolutely abstain from putting any oppressive burden upon anyone else. For if the different parts of the earth which cannot share in any sensations of pain or pleasure yet have to be given respite, how much more must this be the case with men who not only possess the sense which is common also to the irrational animals but even the special gift of reason through which the painful feelings caused by toil and labour stamp and record themselves in mental pictures, more vivid than mere
sensation! Let so-called masters therefore cease 90
from imposing upon their slaves severe and scarcely endurable orders, which break down their bodies by violent usage and force the soul to collapse before
the body. You need not grudge to moderate your 91
orders. The result will be that you yourselves will enjoy proper attention and that your servants will carry out their orders readily and accept their duties not just for a short time to be abandoned through wearying too quickly, and, indeed, we may say, as if old age had prematurely overtaken them in their labours. On the contrary, they will prolong their youth to the utmost, like athletes, not those who fatten themselves up into full fleshiness, but those who regularly train themselves by "dry sweatings"[b] to acquire what is necessary and useful for
life. So too let rulers of cities cease from 92

δίαιτα. The commentators take the phrase as meaning sweats in the gymnasium as opposed to sweating in the baths, and so with the verb ξηραλοιφεῖν. Philo, however, does not use it in this sense, but for toil-enduring people in general who are in his eyes the true athletes. On the depreciation of athletes see App. pp. 625-626.

πόλεων ἡγεμόνες φόροις καὶ δασμοῖς συνεχέσι καὶ μεγάλοις αὐτὰς ἐκτραχηλίζοντες, οἳ τὰ μὲν ἴδια ταμεῖα πληροῦσιν, ἅμα τοῖς χρήμασι καὶ τὰς ἀνελευθέρους κακίας καὶ τὸν σύμπαντα βίον αὐτῶν
93 ῥυπαινούσας θησαυροφυλακοῦντες. ἀνηλεεστάτους γὰρ καὶ γέμοντας ἀπανθρωπίας τοὺς τῶν φόρων ἐκλογεῖς ἐπίτηδες αἱροῦνται τὰς πρὸς πλεονεξίαν ἀφορμὰς αὐτοῖς ἐνδιδόντες· οἱ δὲ τῇ φυσικῇ σκαιότητι προσειληφότες καὶ τὴν ἐξ ἐπιταγμάτων δεσποτικῶν ἐκεχειρίαν καὶ πάντα ὑπὲρ ἀρεσκείας τῆς ἐκείνων ἐγνωκότες πράττειν οὐδὲν παραλείπουσι τῶν χαλεπωτάτων, ἐπιείκειαν καὶ ἡμερότητα μηδ'
94 ὄναρ εἰδότες· τοιγάρτοι πάντα φύρουσι καὶ συγχέουσιν ἀργυρολογοῦντες, ὡς μὴ μόνον ἐκ τῶν οὐσιῶν ἀναπράττειν, ἀλλὰ καὶ ἐκ τῶν σωμάτων, ὕβρεσιν, αἰκίαις, πρὸς ἀποτομίαν κεκαινουργημέναις βασάνοις· ἤδη δέ τινας ἀκούω μηδὲ νεκρῶν ἀποσχέσθαι δι' ἀγριότητα καὶ παρηλλαγμένην λύτταν, οἳ ἐπὶ τοσοῦτον ἐθηριώθησαν, ὡς καὶ τύπτειν ὑστριχίσι τολμᾶν τοὺς τεθνεῶτας·
95 καὶ ἐπειδή τις τῆς ἄγαν ὠμότητος κατεμέμφετο,[1] εἰ μηδ' ὁ θάνατος, ἡ κακῶν ἁπάντων ἀπαλλαγὴ καὶ ὡς ἀληθῶς τελευτή, περιποιήσει τοῖς ἐκποδὼν τὸ ἀνύβριστον, ἀλλ' ἀντὶ ταφῆς καὶ τῶν νομιζομένων αἰκίας ὑπομενοῦσιν, ἀπολογίᾳ χείρονι κατηγορίας ἐχρῶντο φάσκοντες προπηλακίζειν τοὺς τεθνεῶτας, οὐχ ὑπὲρ τοῦ κωφὴν καὶ ἀναίσθητον κόνιν ὑβρίζειν
[288] —ἀνωφελὲς γάρ—, ἀλλ' ὑπὲρ τοῦ | τοὺς ἢ κατὰ γένος ἢ καθ' ἑταιρίαν προσήκοντας εἰς οἶκτον

[1] At this point R, as we have it, breaks off.

[a] I take αὐτῶν to refer to πόλεις, Heinemann apparently to the ἡγεμόνες.

racking them with taxes and tolls as heavy as they are constant. Such rulers both fill their own coffers and while hoarding money hoard also illiberal vices which defile the whole of civic life.[a] For they pur- 93
posely choose as tax-gatherers the most ruthless of men, brimful of inhumanity, and put into their hands resources for overreaching. These persons add to their natural brutality the immunity they gain from their masters' instructions, and in their determination to accommodate every action to those masters' pleasure they leave no severity untried, however barbarous, and banish mercy and gentleness even from their dreams. And therefore in 94
carrying out their collecting they create universal chaos and confusion and apply their exactions not merely to the property of their victims but also to their bodies, on which they inflict insults and outrages and forms of torture quite original in their savagery. Indeed, I have heard of persons who, actuated by abnormal frenzy and cruelty, have not even spared the dead, persons who become so utterly brutalized that they venture even to flog corpses with whips. And when anyone censured the 95
extraordinary cruelty shewn in refusing to allow even death, the release and in very truth the "end" of all ills, to procure freedom from insult for those who are now beyond its reach, and in causing them to undergo outrage instead of the normal rites of burial, the line of defence adopted was worse than the accusation. They treated the dead, they said, with such contempt not for the useless purpose of insulting the deaf and senseless dust but in order to excite the pity of those who were related to them by birth or some other tie of fellowship, and thus

ἀγαγεῖν καὶ προκαλέσασθαι λύτρα καταθέσθαι τῶν
96 σωμάτων ὑστάτην ἀπονείμαντας χάριν. XX. εἶτα,
ὦ φαυλότατοι πάντων ἀνθρώπων, εἴποιμ᾽ ἂν αὐτοῖς, ἃ διδάσκετε, οὐ προεμάθετε; ἢ προκαλεῖσθαι μὲν εἰς ἔλεον ἑτέρους, εἰ καὶ δι᾽ ὠμοτάτων ἔργων, οἴδατε, τὰ δὲ χρηστὰ καὶ φιλάνθρωπα πάντα τῆς ἑαυτῶν ψυχῆς ἐκτέτμησθε; καὶ ταῦτα μὴ ἀποροῦντες ἀγαθῶν ὑφηγητῶν καὶ μάλιστα τῶν ἡμετέρων νόμων, οἳ καὶ τὴν γῆν μεθεῖσαν φόρων τῶν ἐτησίων ἄνεσιν καὶ ἀνάπαυλαν αὐτῇ παρασχόντες;
97 αὕτη δέ, καίτοι δοκοῦσα ἄψυχος εἶναι,
πρὸς ἀμοιβὴν εὐτρέπισται καὶ χάριτος ἀντίδοσιν, ἣν ἔλαβε δωρεὰν ἀντεκτίνειν ἐπειγομένη· τυχοῦσα γὰρ ἀδείας ἔτει ἑβδόμῳ καὶ μὴ πονηθεῖσα, σύμπαντα δὲ τὸν τοῦ ἐνιαυτοῦ κύκλον ἀπελευθεριάσασα, τῷ μετὰ ταῦτα διπλασίους, ἔστι δ᾽ ὅτε καὶ
98 πολυπλασίους, ὑπ᾽ εὐφορίας[1] ἤνεγκε καρπούς. τὸ
παραπλήσιον μέντοι καὶ τοὺς ἀλείπτας ἔστιν ἰδεῖν δρῶντας ἐπὶ τῶν ἀθλητῶν· ὅταν γὰρ αὐτοὺς συγκροτήσωσιν ἐπαλλήλοις καὶ συνεχέσι γυμνασίαις, πρὶν εἰς ἄκρον καμεῖν, ἀνακτῶνται παρέχοντες ἀνέσεις οὐ μόνον τῶν ἐν ἀθλήσει πόνων ἀλλὰ καὶ τῶν πρὸς ἐδωδὴν καὶ πόσιν, τὸ σκληροδίαιτον χαλῶντες εἴς τε ψυχῆς εὐθυμίαν καὶ εὐπάθειαν
99 σώματος. καὶ οὐ δήπου διδάσκαλοι ῥᾳθυμίας καὶ

[1] MSS. ὑπὲρ εὐφορίας or ὑπὲρ ἐλευθερίας.

---

[a] *i.e.* Philo thinks of the collectors as instructing the relatives on the duty of shewing pity, which they are incompetent to do, as they have no conception of pity themselves A simpler sense might be obtained, particularly if the question marks are dropped and οἳ read for ἢ—" Vilest of men

urge them to ransom the bodies of their friends by making a final gift in payment for them. XX.
Foolish, foolish people, I would say to them, have you 96
not first learnt the lesson which you teach, or are you competent to induce others to shew pity, even with the cruellest actions before them,[a] when you have exscinded all kindly and humane feelings from your own souls? And this you have done, though you had no lack of good advisers, particularly in our laws, which have relieved even the land from its yearly tolls and provided it with a rest and respite. This 97
land, though to all appearance a lifeless thing, is put into a condition to make its requital and to repay a boon which it received as a free gift but is now eager to return. For the immunity which it has during the seventh year and its rest from labour and complete freedom during the whole annual cycle give it a fertility in the next year which causes it to bear twice as much or even many times as much as in the previous years. We may also note that the trainers 98
of athletes take much the same line in dealing with their pupils. When they have thoroughly drilled them by an unbroken course of exercises, before they reach the point of exhaustion, they give them a fresh lease of life by providing relaxations, not only from the labour of the training itself but from the dietary regulations as to food and drink, the hardships of which they abate in order to make the soul cheerful and the body comfortable. And we 99
must not suppose that here we have the professional trainers to hard work appearing as instructors in

you have not first learnt the lesson which you teach; you know how to evoke pity, though with deeds of great cruelty, yet you have exscinded . . ."

τρυφῆς εἰσιν οἷς ἐπάγγελμα τὸ πρὸς πόνους ἀλείφειν, ἀλλὰ μεθόδῳ καὶ τέχνῃ προσποιοῦσιν ἰσχὺν
κραταιοτέραν ἰσχύϊ καὶ δυνάμεις σθεναρωτέρας
δυνάμεσι, τὴν ῥώμην ἀνέσει καὶ ἐπιτάσει καθάπερ
100 ἁρμονίαν συναύξοντες. ἔμαθον δὲ παρὰ τῆς παν-
σόφου ταῦτα φύσεως, ἥτις τὸ ἐπίπονον καὶ καμα-
τηρὸν τοῦ γένους ἡμῶν ἐπισταμένη διένειμε τὸν
χρόνον εἰς ἡμέραν τε καὶ νύκτα, τῇ μὲν ἐγρήγορσιν,
101 νυκτὶ δ' ὕπνον παρασχοῦσα. φροντὶς γὰρ αὐτὴν
οἷα μητέρα κηδεμονικωτάτην εἰσῆλθε τοῦ μὴ τὰ
ἔγγονα ἀποτρύχεσθαι· μεθ' ἡμέραν γὰρ τὰ σώματα
διανίστησι καὶ πρὸς τὰς τοῦ βίου χρείας καὶ ὑπηρεσίας ἁπάσας ἐγείρει κακίζουσα τοὺς ἀργῷ καὶ
ἁβροδιαίτῳ βίῳ σχολάζειν ἐθιζομένους, νύκτωρ δὲ
καθάπερ ἐν πολέμῳ τὸ ἀνακλητικὸν ὑποσημήνασα
πρὸς ἀνάπαυλαν καλεῖ καὶ τὴν τῶν σωμάτων
102 ἐπιμέλειαν. οἱ δ' ἀποθέμενοι πολὺ βάρος πραγματειῶν, ὅσον ἕωθεν εἰς ἑσπέραν ἦσαν ἐπηχθι-
σμένοι, καὶ ἐπανελθόντες οἴκαδε πρὸς ἡσυχίαν
τρέπονται καὶ καταδαρθόντες ὕπνῳ βαθεῖ τὸν
μεθημερινὸν πόνον ἐκνοσηλεύονται, καὶ πάλιν νεα-
λεῖς καὶ ἀκμῆτες γενόμενοι σπεύδουσιν ἕκαστοι
103 πρὸς τὰ οἰκεῖα καὶ συνήθη. τὸν δόλιχον τοῦτον ἡ
φύσις διά τε ὕπνου καὶ ἐγρηγόρσεως ἀπένειμεν |
[289] ἀνθρώποις, ἵν' ἐν μέρει μὲν ἐνεργῶσιν, ἐν μέρει δ'
ἀτρεμίζοντες ἑτοιμότερα καὶ εὐκινητότερα τὰ τοῦ
σώματος ἴσχωσι μέρη.
104 XXI. Πρὸς ἅπερ ἀπιδὼν ὁ τοὺς νόμους ἡμῖν
προφητεύσας ἄνεσιν ἐκήρυξε τῇ χώρᾳ δι' ἑξαετίας
γεωπόνους ἐπισχών. ἀλλὰ γὰρ οὐχ ἕνεκα ὧν εἶποι
αὐτὸ μόνον τοῦτ' εἰσηγήσατο, ἀλλὰ καὶ τῆς

slackness and luxury ; they are following a scientific
method by which further strength and power is given
to what is already strong and powerful, and vigour
enhanced as though it were a harmony by alternating relaxation with tension. This truth I have learnt 100
from the never-failing wisdom of nature who, knowing how toil-worn and weary our race becomes,
divided our time into day and night, giving the hours
of wakefulness to one and of sleep to the other. For, 101
most careful of mothers, her anxious thought was
that her children should not be exhausted. In the
daylight she wakens our bodies and stimulates them
to carry out all the offices and demands of life, and
reproaches those who are making it their practice to
loiter through life in an idle and voluptuous way. But
at night she sounds the recall as in war and summons
them to repose and take care of their bodies. And 102
men casting off all the sore burden of affairs which
has lain heavy upon them from morn till eve, turn
homewards and betake themselves to rest, and in
the deep sleep which falls upon them cast off the distempers of their daylight troubles, and then again
unwearied and full of fresh vigour hasten eagerly
each to his own familiar occupation. This double 103
course nature has assigned to men by means of sleeping and waking with the result that by alternating
activity with inaction they have increased readiness
and nimbleness in the various parts of their bodies.

XXI. These considerations the prophetic author 104
of our laws had before his eyes when he proclaimed
a rest for the land and made the husbandman stay
his work after six years. But he gave this enactment
not only on the grounds which I have mentioned but
also moved by that habitual kindliness which he aims

συνήθους φιλανθρωπίας, ἣν ἅπαντι μέρει τῆς νομοθεσίας συνυφαίνειν ἀξιοῖ τοῖς ἐντυγχάνουσι ταῖς ἱεραῖς γραφαῖς κοινωνικὰ καὶ χρηστὰ ἐνσφραγιζό-
105 μενος ἤθη. κελεύει γὰρ τῷ ἑβδόμῳ ἔτει μηδὲν συγκλείειν χωρίον, ἀλλὰ πάντας ἀμπελῶνας καὶ ἐλαιῶνας ἀναπεπταμένους ἐᾶν καὶ τὰς ἄλλας κτήσεις ὅσαι σπαρτῶν εἰσιν ἢ δένδρων, ἵνα τοῖς ἀπαυτοματισθεῖσι καρποῖς οἱ πένητες ἀδεῶς χρῆσθαι δύνωνται μᾶλλον ἢ οὐχ ἧττον τῶν κεκτημένων.
106 ὅθεν τοῖς μὲν δεσπόταις οὐκ ἐφῆκεν ἐργάζεσθαι στοχασάμενος τοῦ μηδεμιᾶς λύπης αἴτιος αὐτοῖς γενέσθαι ὡς τὰ μὲν ἀναλώματα παρασχοῦσι, τὰς δ' ἀντὶ τούτων προσόδους μὴ λαμβάνουσι, τοὺς δ' ἀπόρους ὡς ἰδίων ἀπολαύειν τότε γοῦν τῶν ἀλλοτρίων εἶναι δοκούντων ἠξίωσε ταπεινοῦ σχήματος αὐτοὺς ἀπαλλάττων καὶ τῶν ἐπὶ μεταίταις ὀνειδῶν.
107 ἆρ' οὐκ ἄξιον ἐρασθῆναι τῶν νόμων, οἳ τοσαύτης γέμουσιν ἡμερότητος; δι' ἣν οἱ μὲν πλούσιοι διδάσκονται μεταδιδόναι καὶ κοινωνεῖν ὧν ἔχουσι, παρηγοροῦνται δ' οἱ πένητες, μὴ πάντοτε ταῖς τῶν εὐπόρων οἰκίαις ἐπιφοιτᾶν ἀναγκαζόμενοι πρὸς ἐπανόρθωσιν ὧν ἐνδεεῖς εἰσιν, ἀλλ' ἔστιν ὅτε καὶ προσοδευόμενοι καθάπερ ἐξ ἰδίων κτημάτων τοὺς ἀπαυτο-
108 ματίζοντας, ὡς ἔφην, καρπούς.
χῆραι καὶ ὀρφανοὶ παῖδες καὶ ὅσοι ἄλλοι τῶν ἠμελημένων καὶ ἀφανῶν ἕνεκα τοῦ μὴ περιουσιάζειν τότε περιουσιάζουσι ταῖς τοῦ θεοῦ δωρεαῖς ἐξαπιναίως πεπλουτηκότες, ὃς αὐτοὺς πρὸς κοινωνίαν ἐκάλεσε τῶν κτητόρων ἐν τῷ τῆς ἱερᾶς ἑβδόμης ἀριθμῷ·

---

[a] Ex. xxiii. 11. In Lev. xxv. 6, 7 the produce of the seventh year is given as food for the household.

at infusing into every part of his legislation, thereby impressing on the readers of the sacred scriptures
the stamp of good and neighbourly customs. For he 105
forbids them to close up any field during the seventh year.[a] All olive-yards and vineyards are to be left wide open and so with the other kinds of property, whether of sown crops or orchard-trees, thus giving an unrestricted use of such fruits as are of natural growth to the poor quite as much, if not more so,
than to the owners. Thus on the one hand he did 106
not allow the masters to do any work of tillage because he wished to avoid giving them the painful feeling that they had incurred the expenditure but did not receive the income in return, and on the other hand he thought fit that the poor should for this year at any rate enjoy as their own what appeared to belong to others, and in this way took from them any appearance of humiliation or possibility of being reproached as beggars. May not our passionate affec- 107
tion well go out to laws charged with such kindly feeling, which teaches the rich to give liberally and share what they have with others and encourages the poor not to be always dancing attendance on the houses of the wealthy, as though compelled to resort thither to make up their own deficiency, but sometimes also to come claiming a source of wealth in the fruits which, as I have said, develop untilled and which they can treat as their own?

Widows and orphans and all others who are
neglected and ignored because they have no surplus 108
of income have at this time such a surplus and find themselves suddenly affluent through the gifts of God, Who invites them to share with the owners
under the sanction of the holy number seven. And
109

109 καὶ ὅσοι μέντοι κτηνοτροφοῦσι, μετ' ἀδείας ἐπὶ
χλοηφαγίας τὰ οἰκεῖα θρέμματα ἄγουσιν ἐκλεγό-
μενοι πεδία εὔχορτα καὶ ἐπιτηδειότατα ἐμβόσκε-
σθαι, καταχρώμενοι τῇ τῆς ἐκεχειρίας ἀδείᾳ· καὶ
φθόνος οὐδεὶς ἀπαντᾶται[1] ἐκ τῶν δεσποτῶν ἅτε
παλαιοτάτῳ ἔθει κεκρατημένων, ὃ σύντροφον ἐκ
μακρῶν χρόνων γενόμενον εἰς φύσιν ἐκνενίκηκεν.

110 XXII. Ἀρχὴν ταύτην βαλλόμενος ὥσπερ θε-
μέλιόν τινα ἐπιεικείας καὶ φιλανθρωπίας ἑπτὰ
ἑβδομάδας ἐτῶν συνθεὶς τὸ πεντηκοστὸν ὅλον
ἀπέφηνεν ἱερόν, ἐξαίρετα καὶ πάντα διαφερόντως
καλὰ νομοθετήσας ἐπ' αὐτῷ παρὰ τὰ κοινωνίαν
111 ἔχοντα.[2] πρῶτον μὲν τόδε· τὰς ἀλλοτριωθείσας
κτήσεις οἴεται δεῖν ἀποδίδοσθαι τοῖς ἐξ ἀρχῆς
κυρίοις, ἵν' αἱ κληρουχίαι τοῖς γένεσι διαφυλάτ-
[290] τωνται | καὶ μηδεὶς τῶν λῆξιν εἰληχότων εἰς ἅπαν
112 στέρηται τῆς δωρεᾶς. ἐπειδὴ γὰρ καιροὶ πολλάκις
προσπίπτουσιν ἀβούλητοι, δι' οὓς ἀναγκάζονταί
τινες πιπράσκειν τὰ ἴδια, καὶ τῆς ἐν δέοντι χρείας
τούτων προὐνόησε καὶ τοὺς ὠνουμένους ἐκώλυσεν
ἀπατᾶσθαι, τοῖς μὲν πιπράσκειν ἐφείς, τοὺς δ' ἐφ'

[1] So Cohn for ἀπαντᾷ ταῖς of M and ἐκ τῶν δεσποτῶν ἀπαντᾷ of F. (The latter he rejects on account of the harsh hiatus before ἅτε, but see on i. 90 (App.).)

[2] According to Cohn and Heinemann corrupt; see note *b*.

---

[a] For the year of Jubile (§§ 110-123) see Lev. xxv. 8-end.

[b] Cohn pronounces these words to be incurably corrupt and supposes them to express something like "confirming the sense of fellow-feeling." I do not think the meaning I have given to them, "those which have a nature common to the others" (and are not ἐξαίρετα), is impossible, though the nearest example I can find, iii. 182 μηδεμίαν ἔχοντα κοινωνίαν, is not quite analogous. For παρά *cf.* παρὰ ταύτας § 216, and for the antithesis ἐξαίρετον—κοινός § 190. Mangey's trans-

indeed all stock-breeders feel at liberty to take out their own cattle in search of pasturage and to select meadow-land of good herbage and particularly suitable for grazing their beasts. Thus they take full advantage of the immunity secured by the time of freedom. And this is not opposed by any grudging on the master's side. They are under the sway of a very ancient custom, which through long familiarity has won its way to the standing of nature.

XXII. While laying down this first foundation of 110
moderation and humanity, he built on it by adding years to the number of seven times seven and consecrated the whole of the fiftieth year.[a] This he made the subject of many special enactments, all of remarkable excellence, apart from those which are common to other seventh years.[b] The first of these 111
enactments is as follows. He considers that alienated estates ought to be restored to their original possessors in order that the apportionments should be secured to the families and that no one to whom they had been allotted should be altogether deprived of the grant.[c] For since times of adversity often arise 112
which make it necessary for some persons to sell their property, he made provision for the just needs of such persons and at the same time took steps to prevent the purchasers being deceived, by accompanying the permission to the vendors to sell with very clear instructions to the purchasers as to the

lation, "supra ea quae ad vulgares annos pertinent," is not unlike mine except that he takes *παρά* = "beyond," and seems to see in *κοινωνίαν* the idea of ordinariness. If my view is right, the reference may be to Lev. xxv. 11, where the rules for the Sabbatical year are repeated, also to the liberation of slaves and remission of debts (*cf.* § 122).

[c] Lev. xxv. 14-16.

113 οἷς ὠνήσονται μάλα σαφῶς ἀναδιδάξας. μὴ γὰρ
δίδοτε, φησί, τὰς ἐπὶ παγκτησίᾳ τιμάς, ἀλλὰ τὰς
πρὸς ἐνιαυτῶν ὡρισμένον ἀριθμόν, οἳ ἐντός εἰσι
πεντηκονταετίας. οὐ γὰρ κτημάτων αἱ πράσεις
ἀλλὰ καρπῶν ὀφείλουσιν εἶναι, διὰ δύο τἀναγκαιό-
τατα· ἓν μὲν ὅτι σύμπασα ἡ χώρα κτῆμα κέκληται
θεοῦ, τῶν δὲ θεοῦ κτημάτων οὐχ ὅσιον ἄλλους
ἐπιγράφεσθαι δεσπότας· ἕτερον δὲ ⟨ὅτι⟩ λῆξις
ἀπονενέμηται ἑκάστῳ τῶν κληρούχων, ἧς στέρε-
114 σθαι τὸν λαχόντα οὐκ ἐδικαίωσεν ὁ νόμος. τὸν μὲν
οὖν ἐντὸς τῆς πεντηκονταετίας δυνάμενον ἀνα-
λαβεῖν τὰ οἰκεῖα ἤ τινα τῶν ἐγγυτάτω γένους
ἀγχιστέων προκαλεῖται πάσῃ μηχανῇ κατατιθέναι
ἣν ἔλαβε τιμὴν καὶ μὴ τῷ πριαμένῳ καθ᾽ ὃν ἔδει
115 καιρὸν ὠφελήσαντι ζημίας αἴτιον γενέσθαι· τῷ δὲ
ἀπόρως ἔχοντι συνεπάθησε καὶ μετέδωκεν ἐλέου
τὴν ἀρχαίαν δωρησάμενος αὖθις περιουσίαν, δίχα
τῶν κατ᾽ εὐχὴν ἀφιερωθέντων ἀγρῶν ἐν τῇ τάξει
τῶν ἀναθημάτων· ἀνάθημα δ᾽ οὐχ ὅσιον ἀκυροῦ-
σθαι χρόνῳ· διὸ προστέτακται τὴν ἀξίαν τιμὴν
τούτων ἐκλέγειν μηδὲν καταχαρισαμένους τῷ
ποιησαμένῳ τὸ ἀνάθημα.

116 XXIII. Ταῦτα μὲν ἐπὶ ταῖς τῆς χώρας διανομαῖς
καὶ κληρουχίαις διατέτακται· ἕτερα δ᾽ ἐπὶ ταῖς
οἰκίαις. ἐπεὶ δὲ [καὶ] τούτων αἱ μὲν κατὰ πόλεις
ἐντὸς τειχῶν εἰσιν, αἱ δ᾽ ἐν ἀγροῖς[1] ἔξω τείχους
ἐπαύλεις, τὰς μὲν ἐν τοῖς χωρίοις ἐπέτρεψεν ὁ νόμος
ἀεὶ λυτροῦσθαι, τὰς δὲ μὴ λυτρωθείσας ἄχρι τοῦ

[1] MSS. ἀγρῷ.

[a] Lev. xxv. 23. [b] Lev. xxvii. 16-21.
[c] Lev. xxv. 29-31.

terms of the transaction. "Do not pay the price," 113
he says, "of complete ownership, but only for a fixed number of years and a lower limit than fifty." For the sale should represent not real property but fruits, and this for two most convincing reasons. One is that the whole country is called God's property,[a] and it is against religion to have anything that is God's property registered under other masters. Another reason is that each of the holders has a portion assigned to him by lot, and that this should be taken from him is contrary to the law's conception of justice.
Anyone, therefore, who before the fifty years are 114
completed has the means to recover his own property, or anyone else very closely related to him, is urged by the lawgiver to take every step to recover the land at the price which he got for it, and not to occasion loss to the purchaser who helped him at the time when he
needed it. On the other hand he sympathized with 115
the poor man and shewed him pity by restoring to him the additional wealth which he originally possessed, excepting fields which had been dedicated by a vow, and therefore rank with votive offerings.[b] Religion forbids that time should affect the validity of a votive offering, and therefore it is ordained that the proper price for such estates should be demanded and that no concessions should be made to the votary.

XXIII. These are the rules for cases where the 116
apportionments and holdings consist of land. There are different regulations as to houses.[c] Houses in some cases belong to cities and are inside the walls, and others are farm-buildings in the country outside the walls. Consequently the law allows the latter to be redeemable at any time, and prescribes that any that have not been ransomed by the fiftieth year

πεντηκοστοῦ ἔτους ἀποδίδοσθαι προῖκα τοῖς πάλαι
κυρίοις, καθάπερ καὶ τὰ κτήματα· μοῖρα γὰρ αἱ
117 ἐπαύλεις κτημάτων. ὅσαι δὲ τειχῶν ἐντός εἰσι,
μέχρι μὲν ἐνιαυτοῦ τὴν ἀναπομπὴν ἐπὶ τοὺς πεπρα-
κότας ἔχουσι, μετὰ δὲ τὸν ἐνιαυτὸν εἰς ἅπαν τοῖς
ὠνησαμένοις βεβαιοῦνται, μηδὲν τῆς τοῦ πεντηκοστοῦ ἔτους ἐκεχειρίας βλαπτούσης τοὺς πρια-
118 μένους. αἴτιον δὲ τὸ βούλεσθαι καὶ ἐπηλύταις
ἱδρύσεως τῆς ἐνταῦθα βεβαίου παρασχεῖν ἀφορμήν·
ἐπειδὴ γὰρ μετουσίαν γῆς οὐκ ἔχουσιν, ἅτε μὴ
καταριθμηθέντες ἐν ταῖς κληρουχίαις, οἰκιῶν αὐτοῖς
[291] κτῆσιν ὁ νόμος ἀπένειμε, φροντίσας τοῦ μὴ | μετ-
ανάστας γενέσθαι τοὺς τῶν νόμων ἱκέτας καὶ πρόσ-
119 φυγας. αἱ γὰρ πόλεις, ὅτε ἐκληροδοτεῖτο ἡ χώρα
κατὰ φυλάς, οὐ διενεμήθησαν, ἀλλ' οὐδὲ τὴν ἀρχὴν
ἦσαν συνῳκοδομημέναι, κατὰ τὰς ἐν ἀγροῖς ἐπαύλεις τῶν οἰκητόρων ποιουμένων τὰς διατριβάς·
ἐξ ὧν ὕστερον ἀναστάντες καὶ συνελθόντες, ἐπίδοσιν
κοινωνίας καὶ φιλίας, ὥσπερ εἰκός, ἐν χρόνῳ μακρῷ
λαμβανούσης, οἰκίας ἐν ταὐτῷ καὶ πόλεις ἐδει-
μαντο, ὧν καὶ ἐπηλύταις, καθάπερ εἶπον, μετ-
έδοσαν, ἵνα μὴ πάντων ἀποροῖεν καὶ τῶν ἐν ἀγροῖς
καὶ τῶν κατὰ πόλεις.

120 XXIV. Περὶ δὲ τῆς ἱερωμένης φυλῆς τάδε νομο-
θετεῖται· γῆς ἀποτομὴν οὐκ ἀπένειμε τοῖς νεω-
κόροις ὁ νόμος, ὑπολαβὼν αὐτάρκη πρόσοδον εἶναι
τούτοις τὰς ἀπαρχάς, ὀκτὼ δὲ καὶ τεσσαράκοντα
πόλεις ἀπεκλήρωσεν εἰς οἴκησιν καὶ δισχιλίους
121 ἑκάστῃ πήχεις προάστειον ἐν κύκλῳ. τὰς οὖν ἐν
ταύταις οἰκίας οὐ τὸν αὐτὸν τρόπον ταῖς ἄλλαις,

[a] Lev. xxv. 32-34.

should be restored without compensation to the former owner as in the case of real property, for farm-buildings are a part of real property. But houses within 117
the walls may be recoverable by the vendors for the space of a year, but after the year are absolutely secured to the purchasers who are not liable to suffer any injury from the general remission in the fiftieth year. His reason is that he wishes to give the 118
newcomers also a basis on which they may feel themselves firmly established in the country. For since they have no apportionment of land as they were not counted when the holdings were distributed, the law assigned to them their houses in fee simple in its anxiety that those who had come as suppliants and refugees to the laws should not be cast adrift. For when the land was apportioned according to the tribes 119
the cities were not distributed, nor indeed built in city form at all, and the inhabitants took for their dwellings the outbuildings in the country. Subsequently when they left these and became concentrated as the feeling of unity and friendship naturally grew stronger in the course of many years, they built houses adjacent to each other, thus forming cities. And of these, as I have said, they assigned a share to the newcomers, to prevent them finding themselves cut off from holding property both in the country and in the cities.

XXIV. The legislation with regard to the conse- 120
crated tribe is as follows.[a] The temple-keepers were not allotted a section of land by the law, which considered that they were sufficiently provided for by the first-fruits, but assigned them instead forty-eight cities to dwell in, with a surrounding frontage in each case of two thousand cubits. Houses within 121
these were not, like the others within the walls,

ὅσαι τειχῶν εἴσω τυγχάνουσιν, ἐβεβαίωσε τοῖς πριαμένοις, ἐντὸς ἐνιαυτοῦ τῶν ἀποδιδομένων κομίσασθαι μὴ δυναμένων, ἀλλ᾽ εἰς ἅπαν ἐφῆκεν αὐτὰς λυτροῦσθαι, καθάπερ καὶ τοῖς ἀπὸ τοῦ ἔθνους τὰς ἐπαύλεις αἷς ἰσοδυναμοῦσιν, ἐπειδὴ μόνας ἐκ τοσαύτης χώρας διεκληρώσαντο τὰς οἰκίας, ὧν οὐκ ᾤετο δεῖν στέρεσθαι τοὺς λαβόντας, καθάπερ οὐδὲ τοὺς κληρούχους τῶν ἐπαύλεων. οἰκιῶν μὲν δὴ πέρι τοσαῦτα.

122 XXV. Τὰ δὲ πρὸς χρεώστας δανειστῶν καὶ πρὸς θεράποντας δεσποτῶν ὅμοια τοῖς πρόσθεν νομοθετεῖται, ὅπως οἱ μὲν δανεισταὶ μὴ ἐκλέγωσι τόκους παρὰ τῶν ὁμοεθνῶν ἀλλ᾽ ὅσον προήκαντο μόνον ἄσμενοι κομίζωνται, οἱ δὲ δεσπόται τοῖς ἀργυρωνήτοις μὴ ὡς φύσει δούλοις ἀλλ᾽ ὡς μισθωτοῖς προσφέρωνται, παρέχοντες ἄδειαν ἐλευθερίας, εὐθὺς μὲν τοῖς ὑπὲρ αὑτῶν λύτρα κατατιθέναι δυναμένοις, αὖθις δὲ τοῖς ἀπόροις ἢ ὅταν ἐπιγένηται ὁ ἀπ᾽ ἀρχῆς δουλείας ἕβδομος ἐνιαυτὸς ἢ ὅταν ὁ πεντηκοστός, κἂν πρὸ μιᾶς ἡμέρας τύχῃ τις εἰς δουλείαν ὑπαχθείς· ἄφεσις γὰρ ὁ χρόνος ἐκεῖνός ἐστι καὶ νενόμισται, πάντων ἐπὶ τὰς ἀρχαίας διαυλοδρομούντων καὶ ἀνακαμπτόντων εὐπραγίας. ἐπι-
123 τρέπει δ᾽ ἐκ τῶν μὴ ὁμοφύλων [οἵτινες ἐξ ἑτέρων ἐθνῶν εἰσιν] οἰκέτας κτᾶσθαι, βουλόμενος πρῶτον μὲν διαφορὰν οἰκείων τε καὶ ἀλλοτρίων εἶναι, ἔπειτα δὲ μὴ κατὰ τὸ παντελὲς ἀναγκαιότατον κτῆμα,

[a] "Lay population" seems to be the meaning required for τοὺς ἀπὸ τοῦ ἔθνους, but I do not know of any similar use of ἔθνος. The phrase is used of the nation in general in i. 54. Possibly ἄλλου has fallen out. (Heinemann strangely translates it by "members of the other tribes," with no hint as to how it is to be obtained from the Greek.)

secured to the purchasers, if the vendors could not find the means to redeem them within the year, but were liable to be redeemed for an unlimited period just as the lay population [a] could redeem the farm buildings, to which the dwelling-houses of the Levites correspond. For these were all that fell to their share in that great territory, and thus he considered that being once received they ought not to be taken back, any more than the farm-buildings in the case of those to whom the holdings were apportioned. So much for the subject of houses.

XXV. Similar rules to those already stated are 122
laid down as to the relations between creditors and debtors and between servants and masters.[b] Creditors are not to exact interest from their fellow-nationals but to be content with recovering what they provided. Masters are to treat their purchased slaves as their hired servants, not as their slaves by nature, and give them secure access to liberty on the spot if they can provide their ransom, or in the case of the needy at a later time, when either the seventh year from the beginning of their slavery or the fiftieth arrives, in the latter case even though only a single day has elapsed since the man was reduced to that condition. For that time is accepted as the remission and actually is such, when all reverse their course and turn back to the prosperity of the past.
But the law does permit the acquisition of slaves 123
from other nations[c] for two reasons; first, that a distinction should be made between fellow-countrymen and aliens; secondly, that that most indispensable possession, domestic service, should not be absolutely

[b] Lev. xxv. 35-41. As Philo observes, the two sections really repeat the substance of §§ 71-85. [c] Lev. xxv. 44.

θεράποντας, ἀνεῖρξαι τῆς αὐτοῦ πολιτείας· μυρία γὰρ τῶν ἐν τῷ βίῳ πραγμάτων ποθεῖ τὰς ἐκ δούλων ὑπηρεσίας.[1]

124 Υἱοὶ κληρονόμοι γονέων ἔστωσαν, εἰ δὲ μὴ εἶεν, θυγατέρες. ὡς γὰρ ἐν τῇ φύσει γυναικῶν ἄνδρες πρωτοστατοῦσι, κἀν ταῖς συγγενείαις ἐχέτωσαν προνομίαν διαδεχόμενοι τὰς οὐσίας καὶ τὴν τῶν τετελευτηκότων τάξιν ἐκπληροῦντες ἀνάγκης νόμῳ κατασχεθέντων[2] οὐδὲν θνητὸν ⟨καὶ⟩ γηγενὲς ἀθανα-

125 τίζοντι. παρθένοι δὲ ἐὰν ἀπολειφθῶσιν ἀνέκδοτοι, προικὸς ὑπὸ ζώντων ἔτι τῶν γονέων μὴ διωρισμένης, ἰσομοιρείτωσαν τοῖς ἄρρεσιν. ἐπιμελείσθω δ' ἡ προεστῶσα ἀρχὴ φυλακῆς τε τῶν ἀπολειφθεισῶν[3] καὶ αὐξήσεως καὶ τῶν εἰς δίαιταν καὶ παιδείαν τὴν ἁρμόττουσαν κόραις ἀναλωμάτων καί, ὁπότε γένοιτο ὥρα, [καὶ] γάμου τοῦ πρέποντος, ἀνδρῶν ἐν[4] ἅπασι δοκίμων ἀριστίνδην ἐπικριθέντων.

126 ἔστωσαν δ' οὗτοι μάλιστα μὲν συγγενεῖς, εἰ δὲ μή, πάντως γοῦν δημόται καὶ φυλέται, χάριν τοῦ μὴ τοὺς κλήρους τοὺς προικιδίους[5] ἐπιγαμίαις ἀλλο-

[1] Here F comes to an end as far as this treatise is concerned, and we are left dependent upon M and the occasional excerpts of Nicetas. As there are no such excerpts from the sections on the law of inheritance which follow down to § 139, they did not appear in Hoeschel's edition, and consequently are also absent in Mangey's, whose p. 291 ends with ὑπηρεσίας and p. 292 begins with ἑπόμενοι καὶ τῇ τάξει, § 140. On a probable lacuna in M at this point see note *a*.

[2] MS. κατασχεθέντες.

[3] MS. ἀπολειφθέντων.

[4] MS. μέν.

[5] MS. πρὸς ἰδίους.

[a] The sections which follow down to § 139 seem entirely out of place here and have nothing to do with the sequence of thought, which has hitherto carried him on from the

excluded from his commonwealth. For the course of life contains a vast number of circumstances which demand the ministrations of slaves.

[a] The heirs of parents are to be sons,[b] or failing sons 124
daughters. For just as in nature men take precedence of women, so too in the scale of relationships they should take the first place in succeeding to the property and filling the position of the departed which they have ceased to hold, debarred by an inevitable law which admits to immortality nothing
that is mortal or earth-born. But if virgins are left 125
without a dower, nothing of the kind having been settled on them by the parents while still alive, they should share equally with the males. The charge of protecting the girls left thus desolate and superintending their development, and the expenses of providing anything required for their maintenance and education as befits maidens should fall upon the head magistrate[c]; also when the time comes, the duty of arranging a suitable marriage and choosing husbands who are selected on their merits and
approved in all respects. And these should be, if 126
possible, of the same family as the girls, or if that cannot be, at any rate of the same ward and tribe, in order that the portions assigned as dowry should not

Sabbath day to the Sabbatical year, and thence to the fiftieth year and the regulations connected with the last two. Cohn thinks that a connexion is to be found in Lev. xxv. 46, where after permitting the purchase of foreign slaves it continues "ye shall make them an inheritance" (LXX καταμεριεῖτε, "ye shall distribute") "to your children." If this is right, it can hardly be doubted, as Cohn says, that some words have fallen out which would shew the connexion.

[b] See Num. xxvii. 8-11, *cf. Mos.* ii. 243 ff.

[c] Or "the chief civil authority." See App. p. 626.

τριοῦσθαι, μένειν δ' ἐν ταῖς ἐξ ἀρχῆς τεταγμέναις
127 κατὰ φυλὰς λήξεσιν. ἐὰν δὲ γενεᾶς ἔρημος ὢν
τυγχάνῃ, παρίτωσαν ἐπὶ τὴν διαδοχὴν ἀδελφοὶ τοῦ
τετελευτηκότος[1]· ἡ γὰρ μεθ' υἱοὺς καὶ θυγατέρας ἐν
συγγενείαις τάξις ἀδελφῶν ἐστιν. εἰ δὲ ἀνάδελφός
τις εἴη τελευτῶν, θεῖοι πρὸς πατρὸς διαδεχέσθωσαν
τὴν οὐσίαν, θείων δὲ μὴ ὄντων, θεῖαι,[2] ⟨εἶτα⟩ τῶν
ἄλλων οἰκείων καὶ συγγενῶν ⟨οἱ⟩ ἐγγυτάτω.[3]
128 σπάνις δ' εἰ καταλάβοι τῆς συγγενείας, ὡς μηδένα
τῶν ἀφ' αἵματος ἀπολειφθῆναι, ἡ φυλὴ κληρονόμος
ἔστω· συγγένεια γάρ τίς ἐστι καὶ ἡ φυλὴ κατὰ
περιγραφὴν μείζονα καὶ τελειοτέραν.
129 ἄξιον μέντοι τὸ διαπορηθὲν ὑπ' ἐνίων ⟨μὴ⟩ ἡσυχα-
σθῆναι· διὰ τί, γάρ φασι, πάντων συγγενῶν καὶ
δημοτῶν καὶ φυλετῶν ἐπιμνησθεὶς ὁ νόμος ἐν ταῖς
τῶν κλήρων διαδοχαῖς γονεῖς μόνους παρεσιώπησεν,
οὓς εἰκὸς ἦν, ὥσπερ κληρονομοῦνται, κληρονομεῖν
τὰ παίδων; ὅτι, ὦ γενναῖε, θεῖος ὢν καὶ τὴν τῆς
φύσεως ἀκολουθίαν αἰεὶ σκοπῶν οὐδὲν ᾠήθη
χρῆναι παλίμφημον εἰσηγεῖσθαι· γονέων μὲν γὰρ
εὐχαί, ζῶντας ἀπολιπεῖν οὓς ἐγέννησαν, διαδεξο-
μένους[4] ὄνομά τε αὐτῶν καὶ γένος καὶ οὐσίαν,
ἐχθρῶν δὲ ἀμειλίκτων ἀραὶ τἀναντία, προαποθνή-
130 σκειν υἱοὺς καὶ θυγατέρας τῶν φυσάντων. ὅπως

[1] MS. τῶν τετελευτηκότων.

[2] As aunts are not mentioned in Num. xxvii. nor in the parallel passage in Philo (*Mos.* ii. 245), θεῖαι might perhaps be expunged. In that case there would be no need for Cohn's insertion of εἶτα.

[3] MS. ἐγγυτέρω.

[4] MS. διαδεξαμένους.

---

[a] See Num. xxxvi. 6 ff. The point that they should, if possible, marry into the same family is not there expressly stated, but might be fairly inferred from *v.* 11, where it is

be alienated by inter-marriage with other tribes, but should retain the place given to them in the allotments originally made on the basis of tribes.[a] But if 127
the deceased has no descendants, the brothers must proceed to the succession, for brothers rank next in tables of relationship with sons and daughters. If the dead man has no brother, the succession must pass to the uncles on the father's side, and if there are no uncles, to the aunts, and then to the next nearest among their other connexions or kinsfolk. But if 128
kinsfolk are so scarce that no blood-relation remains, then the tribe shall be the heir.[b] For the tribe is in a sense a kinship with a wider and more all-embracing compass. [c]One question, however, which 129
is raised by some inquirers should not be passed over in silence. Why, they ask, does the Law when dealing with the regulations of inheritance mention kinsmen of every degree and fellow-wardsmen and fellow-tribesmen, but leaves parents alone unmentioned who would naturally inherit from the children as the children do from them? The answer, good sir, is that the law, God-given as it is, and ever desirous to follow the course of nature, held that no sinister thought should be introduced. Parents pray that they may leave behind them alive the children they have begotten to succeed to their name, race and property, and the imprecations of their implacable enemies are just the opposite, that the sons and daughters may die before their parents. Now he did not 130

said that the daughters of Zelophehad married their first cousins. For "ward and tribe" see on § 82.

[b] Not stated in Num. xxvii. Probably (as Cohn and Heinemann) deduced from the intention of the law to prevent the inheritance passing from one tribe to another (xxxvi. 9).

[c] For §§ 129-132 *cf. Mos.* ii. 244, 245.

οὖν μηδὲν ἀνάρμοστον καὶ ἀσύμφωνον ἐν ἁρμονίᾳ καὶ συμφωνίᾳ, καθ' ἣν διοικεῖται σύμπας ὁ κόσμος, διαγορεύῃ, παίδων μὲν ἀποθνῃσκόντων, γονέων δ' ἐπιβιούντων, ἀναγκαίως ἅμα καὶ πρεπόντως οὐ προσέταξε μητέρας [ἅμα] καὶ πατέρας τὰ υἱῶν καὶ θυγατέρων κληρονομεῖν, εἰδὼς μὴ συνᾷδον τὸ
131 πρᾶγμα βίῳ τε καὶ φύσει. φυλαξάμενος οὖν γυμνοῖς ὀνόμασι καλέσαι γονεῖς ἐπὶ παίδων τετελευτηκότων κληρονομίαν,[1] ὑπὲρ τοῦ μὴ δοκεῖν ἀπευκτὴν ὠφέλειαν προσνέμων ὀνειδίζειν πενθοῦσιν ἢ ὑπομιμνῄσκειν κακοπραγιῶν, ἑτέρῳ τρόπῳ τὰς οὐσίας ἀπένειμεν αὐτοῖς, βραχὺ παρηγόρημα με-
132 γάλου κακοῦ. τίς οὖν ὁ τρόπος; ἀδελφὸν πατρὸς γράφει κληρονόμον ἀδελφιδῶν, ᾗ που διὰ τὸν πατέρα τὸν θεῖον γεραίρων· εἰ μή τις οὕτως ἠλίθιός ἐστιν, ὡς ὑπολαμβάνειν ὅτι ἕτερον τιμῶν ἑτέρου χάριν ἀτιμοῦν ἐκεῖνον προαιρεῖται· μὴ καὶ τοὺς τῶν φίλων γνωρίμους οἱ περιέποντες ἀμελεῖς τῶν ἑταίρων[2] εἰσίν; ἢ ⟨οὐ⟩ πάντων εὐνοϊκώτατοι κηδεμόνες τῶν ἐπὶ τιμῇ καὶ ἑταίρους[2] ἀποδέχονται; τὸν αὐτὸν δὴ τρόπον καὶ ὁ νόμος διὰ πατέρα καλέσας ἀδελφὸν πατρὸς ἐπὶ μετουσίαν κλήρου πολὺ πρότερον πατέρα καλεῖ, φωνῇ μὲν οὔ, διὰ τὰ λεχθέντα, γνωριμωτέρᾳ

[1] MS. κλῆρον. [2] MS. ἑτέρων . . . ἑτέρους.

---

[a] *Cf. Mos.* ii. 245 καὶ τοῦ πρέποντος καὶ τοῦ μὴ τὴν οὐσίαν ἀλλοτριωθῆναι, which suggests that the "necessity" here is to keep the property in the family.

[b] After τιμῇ *sc.* τῶν γνωρίμων. But the whole sentence is very awkward and may contain some corruption besides the omission of οὐ. Heinemann's translation, "lassen sie nicht

wish to speak plainly of anything so out of tune with and discordant to the harmony and concord which prevails throughout the cosmic order as the death of children while the parents survive, and there fore he complied both with necessity and decency [a] in not ordaining that mothers and fathers should inherit from their sons and daughters. He knew that such an event was not in accordance with the ordinary
course of life or with nature. So while he avoided 131
appointing the parents in undisguised terms as heirs to the property of their dead children, lest by assigning to them an acquisition of so undesirable a kind he should seem to be casting a slur upon their mourning or reminding them of their misfortunes, he adopted another way of conveying the ownership to
them, a simple specific for a great mischief. What 132
was this way? He declares the father's brothers to be the heirs of their nephews, a privilege doubtless given to the uncle for the sake of the father, unless anyone is foolish enough to suppose that a person who honours A for the sake of B is deliberately dishonouring B. Is it the case that those who pay court to the acquaintances of their friends are neglecting those friends? Is it not rather the truth that their affectionate care for all that might honour these acquaintances [b] shews regard for the friends also? On the same principle the law, when it nominates the father's brother to share in the inheritance because of his relationship to the father, much more nominates the father, not in actual words it is true for reasons already stated, but with a force more

die Ehrung ihrer Freunde in jeder Weise mit grösster Aufmerksamkeit angelegen sein," does not seem to represent the Greek as it stands.

δὲ φωνῆς δυνάμει τρανούσῃ τὸ βούλημα τοῦ νομοθέτου.

133 Παίδων ὁ πρεσβύτατος οὐκ ἰσομοιρεῖ τοῖς μετ' αὐτόν, ἀλλὰ διπλασίων ἀξιοῦται, διότι τε ἀνὴρ καὶ γυνὴ πρότερον ὑπάρχοντες αὖθις ἐγένοντο πατὴρ καὶ μήτηρ διὰ τὸν φύντα πρῶτον καὶ ἐπειδὴ ὁ ⟨πρῶτος⟩ γενόμενος τούτοις ἀνακαλεῖν ἤρξατο τοῖς ὀνόμασι τοὺς σπείραντας καὶ—τὸ ἀναγκαιότατον—ὅτι ὁ πρὸ τοῦ γενεᾶς ἔρημος οἶκος εὔπαις ἐγένετο πρὸς τὴν τοῦ γένους τῶν ἀνθρώπων διαμονήν, ἧς[1] σπορὰ μὲν γάμος, καρποὶ δὲ τέκνων γενέσεις, ὧν ὁ
134 πρεσβύτατος ἀρχή. διὰ ταύτην γ' οἶμαι τὴν αἰτίαν οἱ πρωτότοκοι τῶν μὲν ἄσπονδα εἰργασμένων ἐχθρῶν, ὡς αἱ ἱεραὶ γραφαὶ δηλοῦσι, μιᾷ νυκτὶ πάντες ἡβηδὸν ἀνῃρέθησαν, τῶν δ' ἀπὸ τοῦ ἔθνους χαριστήριον ἀνετέθησαν θεῷ καθιερωθέντες· ἔδει γὰρ τοὺς μὲν βαρυτάτῳ καὶ ἀπαρηγορήτῳ πένθει βαρῦναι, φθορᾷ τῶν πρωτοστατούντων, γεραίρειν δὲ τὸν σωτῆρα θεὸν ἀπαρχαῖς, αἳ τὴν ἐν τέκνοις
135 ἡγεμονίαν ἔλαχον. ἐπεὶ δ' εἰσί τινες οἳ μετὰ γάμον καὶ παιδοποιίαν ὀψὲ σωφροσύνην ἀπομαθόντες ἐξώκειλαν εἰς ἀκρασίαν καὶ ἐπιμανέντες γυναιξὶν ἑτέραις τὰς προτέρας ἐκάκωσαν καὶ τοῖς ἐξ ἐκείνων οὐκέθ' ὡς πατέρες ἀλλ' ὡς πατρῳοὶ προσηνέχθησαν ἀπομιμησάμενοι τὸ μητρυιῶν εἰς

[1] Cohn in a note to Heinemann's translation would correct to εἰ σπορὰ, but with no improvement of the sense that I can see.

---

[a] This statement is founded on Deut. xxi. 15-17. See App. pp. 626-627. [b] *Cf. Mos.* i. 135.

[c] ἐπεί, which has no logical apodosis, is omitted in the translation.

recognizable than words, leaving no doubt of the intention of the lawgiver.

The eldest son does not share equally with his 133
juniors, but is adjudged a double portion,[a] one reason being that his parents who before were but man and wife, owe to the first-born the fact that they have later become father and mother. Another is that it is their first-born who began to use these names in addressing his parents.[b] The third reason is the most important, that what was before their birth a house of barren stock has become fruitful for the preservation of the human race, a preservation which is sown in marriage and fructified in the birth of
children, starting with the eldest. This was the 134
reason, I suppose, that the first-born sons of the enemies who had shewn themselves so merciless in action, were cut off in wholesale massacre in a single night, as the Holy Scriptures tell us, while the first-born of our nation were dedicated by consecration as a thank-offering to God. For it was just that on the enemy should fall the weight of a blow for which no consolation was possible, namely, the destruction of their foremost rank, while God Who wrought the salvation was honoured by the dedication as first-fruits of those who
headed the line of children. [c]But there 135
are some who after marrying and begetting children unlearn in their later days what they knew of self-restraint and are wrecked on the reef of incontinence. Seized with a mad passion for other women, they maltreat those who hitherto belonged to them and behave to the children they have begotten by them as though they were uncles rather than fathers, copy the unrighteousness shewn

προγονοὺς δυσσεβὲς καὶ ὅλως ἑαυτοὺς καὶ τὰ ἑαυτῶν ἐξέδωκαν ταῖς δευτέραις καὶ παισὶ τοῖς τούτων
ἡδονῆς, αἰσχίστου πάθους, ἥττους γενόμενοι,
χαλινὸν μὲν εἴ πως οἷόν τε ἦν ἐμβαλεῖν ταῖς ἐπιθυμίαις ὑπὲρ τοῦ μὴ ἀνασκιρτᾶν ἐπὶ πλέον οὐκ ἂν
136 ἐμέλλησεν ὁ νόμος. ἐπεὶ δὲ μανίαν ἐξηγριωμένην
οἴστρῳ χαλεπὸν μᾶλλον δ' ἀδύνατον ἰάσασθαι, τὸν
μὲν ὡς ἀθεραπεύτῳ νόσῳ κατεσχημένον ἀπέλιπε,
τὸν δ' ἐκ τῆς διὰ τοὺς νέους ἔρωτας κακωθείσης
υἱὸν οὐχ ὑπερεῖδε κελεύσας αὐτὸν λαμβάνειν διπλάσια τὰ ἐκ τῆς πρὸς τοὺς ἀδελφοὺς διανομῆς.
137 αἴτια δὲ τούτου πολλά· πρῶτον μὲν γὰρ κολάζει
τὸν ὑπαίτιον ἀνάγκην ἐπιθεὶς αὐτῷ ποιεῖν εὖ ὃν
κακῶς διατιθέναι προαιρεῖται, καὶ τῆς ἀγνώμονος
γνώμης ἄκυρον ἀποφαίνει δι' ὧν ὠφελεῖ τὸν κινδυ-
νεύσαντα πρὸς ἐκείνου[1] ζημιωθῆναι τάττων αὐτὸν
ἐν τῇ τάξει τοῦ γεγεννηκότος, ἣν ὁ φύσει πατὴρ ἐπὶ
138 πρεσβυτάτου παιδὸς ἔλιπε. δεύτερον δὲ
ἔλεον καὶ οἶκτον λαμβάνει τῶν ἠδικημένων, οὓς
βαρυτάτης ἀνίας ἐπελαφρίζει μετουσίᾳ χάριτος καὶ
δωρεᾶς· οὐδὲν γὰρ ἧττον τοῦ κληρονομοῦντος υἱοῦ
τὴν διπλασίαν μοῖραν εἰκὸς ἦν ἥδεσθαι τὴν μητέρα,
φιλανθρωπίᾳ νόμου παρηγορηθεῖσαν, ὃς οὐκ εἴασεν
αὐτήν τε καὶ γενεὰν εἰς ἅπαν ἐχθρῶν ἐλαττοῦσθαι.
139 τρίτον δέ· βραβευτὴς ὢν τῶν δικαίων
ἀγαθὸς ἐλογίσατο παρ' ἑαυτῷ, ὅτι τοῖς μὲν ἐκ τῆς
στεργομένης ἐπεδαψιλεύσατο τὰς χορηγίας ὁ πατὴρ

[1] MS. ἐκεῖνο.

---

[a] For the allegorizing of this law (Deut. xxi. 15-17) *cf. De Sac.* 20, *De Sob.* 21 ff.

by stepmothers to the first family and altogether devote themselves and all they have to the second wives and their children, overcome by the vilest of passions, voluptuousness. Such lusts the law would not have hesitated to bridle if it were possible, and prevent them from frisking and plunging still more.
But since it is difficult, or rather impossible, to heal 136
the frenzy goaded into savagery, it left the father to his fate as one in the grip of an incurable disease but did not disregard the son of the wife who was wronged through his passion for another, but bade him take the double portion in the distribution between the
brothers.[a] There are several reasons for this. In 137
the first place, it punishes the culprit by forcing him to give good treatment to the person to whom he intended to give the reverse and renders him incapable of carrying out his ill-judged judgement. This it effects by conferring benefits on the person who was likely to suffer loss at his hands, and by taking upon itself the parental position which had been abandoned by the natural father in so far as
the eldest child was concerned. Secondly, 138
it shews mercy and pity for the victims of injustice whom it relieves of a very grievous trouble by enabling them to share in the boon thus bestowed. For naturally we may suppose that the gratification felt by the son at obtaining the double portion is shared by the mother, encouraged as she is by the humanity of the law which refuses to allow her and her family to lie entirely at the mercy of her
enemies. And there was a third reason. 139
Being gifted with a power to judge justly, it reflected that the father had bestowed his bounties generously on the children of the beloved wife

διὰ τὸν πόθον τῆς γυναικός, τοὺς δ' ἐκ τῆς στυγηθείσης οὐδενὸς [ἢ] παντάπασιν ἠξίωσε διὰ τὸ τῆς μητρὸς ἔχθος, ὡς ἐκείνους μὲν ἔτι ζῶντος[1] προκεκληρονομηκέναι πλείω τῆς ἰσομοιρίας, τούτους δὲ κινδυνεῦσαι καὶ τελευτήσαντος ἁπάντων ἀφαιρεθῆναι τῶν πατρῴων. ἵν' οὖν ἐπανισώσῃ τὴν διανομὴν τοῖς ἐξ ἀμφοτέρων τῶν γυναικῶν, ὥρισε διμοιρίαν τὰ πρεσβεῖα τῷ τῆς ἀπηλλαγμένης παιδί.

[292] τούτων μὲν δὴ ἅλις.

140 XXVI. | Ἑπόμενοι δὲ τῇ τάξει τρίτον εἶδος ἀναγράφομεν ἑορτῆς, ὃ σημανοῦμεν. ἔστι δὲ νουμηνία κατὰ σελήνην, χρόνος[2] ὁ ἀπὸ συνόδου ἐπὶ σύνοδον, ὃν μαθηματικῶν παῖδες εὖ μάλα διηριθμήσαντο. τὴν δ' ἐν ἑορταῖς ἔλαχε τάξιν νουμηνία διὰ πολλά· πρῶτον μὲν ὅτι ἀρχὴ μηνός, ἀρχὴ δὲ καὶ ἀριθμοῦ καὶ χρόνου τίμιον· ἔπειτα δὲ ὅτι κατ' αὐτὴν οὐδὲν ἀφώτιστον ἐν οὐρανῷ· συνόδῳ μὲν γὰρ ὑποδραμούσης ἥλιον σελήνης τὸ πρὸς γῆν μέρος ἐζόφωται, νουμηνίᾳ δὲ πέφυκεν ἀναλάμπειν.

141 τρίτον δὲ ὅτι τῷ ἐλάττονι καὶ ἀσθενεστέρῳ κατ' ἐκεῖνον τὸν χρόνον τὸ κρεῖττον καὶ δυνατώτερον ὠφελείας ἀναγκαίας μεταδίδωσι· νουμηνίᾳ γὰρ ἄρχεται φωτίζειν αἰσθητῷ φέγγει σελήνην ὁ ἥλιος,

[1] MS. ζῶντας.

[2] On the text here see note *b*.

---

[a] *i.e.* in asserting the rights of the eldest son it asserts those of the first family as a whole.

[b] For the New Moon see i. 177. Lit. "it, the new-month-day, according to the moon, the time" etc. *i.e.* the new moon is the time between the conjunctions. This, though unnoticed by Cohn and Heinemann, cannot, as it seems to me, have been stated by Philo. I suggest some such insertion as ἔστι γὰρ ὁ μὴν κατὰ σελήνην, which might

because of his affection for her, but left the children of the hated wife entirely out of consideration owing to his hostility to their mother, so that the former even in his lifetime inherited more than their equal share, and the latter might expect at his death to find themselves robbed of the whole patrimony. And therefore it decreed that the son of the discarded wife should have the eldest son's privilege of the double share, in order to equalize the partition between both families.[a] Enough on these matters.

XXVI. Following the order stated above, we record 140
the third type of feast which we will proceed to explain. This is the New Moon, or beginning of the lunar month,[b] namely the period between one conjunction and the next, the length of which has been accurately calculated in the astronomical schools. The new moon holds its place among the feasts for many reasons. First, because it is the beginning of the month, and the beginning, both in number and in time, deserves honour. Secondly, because when it arrives, nothing in heaven is left without light, for while at the conjunction, when the moon is lost to sight under the sun, the side which faces earth is darkened, when the new month begins it resumes
its natural brightness. The third reason is, that the 141
stronger or more powerful element at that time supplies the help which is needed to the smaller and weaker. For it is just then that the sun begins to illumine the moon with the light which we perceive

easily have fallen out after the preceding *κατὰ σελήνην*. Nicetas, who resumes his excerpts here, has *τρίτην ἑορτὴν ἀναγράφομεν τὴν κατὰ σελήνην νουμηνίαν. πρῶτον μὲν ὅτι κτλ.* Of course in a country where non-lunar months are observed such an explanation is perfectly natural.

ἡ δὲ τὸ ἴδιον κάλλος ἀναφαίνει τοῖς ὁρῶσι. τοῦτο δ' ἐναργής ἐστιν, ὡς ἔοικε, διδασκαλία χρηστότητος καὶ φιλανθρωπίας, ἵνα μηδέποτε τῶν ἰδίων ἀγαθῶν ἄνθρωποι φθονῶσιν, ἀλλὰ μιμούμενοι τὰς ἐν οὐρανῷ μακαρίας καὶ εὐδαίμονας φύσεις ὑπερόριον τῆς ψυχῆς βασκανίαν ἐλαύνωσι καὶ προφέροντες εἰς μέσον τὰ οἰκεῖα κοινοπραγῶσι καὶ χαρίζωνται
142 τοῖς ἀξίοις. τέταρτον δὲ ὅτι τῶν κατ' οὐρανὸν ἁπάντων ἐν ἐλάττονι προθεσμίᾳ σελήνη τὸν ζῳοφόρον περιπολεῖ· μηνιαίῳ γὰρ διαστήματι τὸν κύκλον ἀνύτει. διὸ καὶ τὸ συμπέρασμα τῆς περιόδου, τελευτώσης ἐπὶ τὴν ἀρχὴν ἀφ' ἧς ἤρξατο φέρεσθαι σελήνης,[1] τετίμηκεν ὁ νόμος προσειπὼν ἐκείνην τὴν ἡμέραν ἑορτήν, ὑπὲρ τοῦ πάλιν ἡμᾶς ἀναδιδάξαι μάθημα κάλλιστον, ἵν' ἐν ταῖς τοῦ βίου πράξεσι τὰ τέλη συνῳδὰ ταῖς ἀρχαῖς ἀποφαίνωμεν· γενήσεται δὲ τοῦτ', ἐὰν λογισμῷ τὰς πρώτας ἡνιοχῶμεν ὁρμὰς μὴ ἐπιτρέποντες αὐταῖς ἀφηνιάζειν καὶ ἀνασκιρτᾶν τρόπον θρεμμάτων ἀγελάρχην
143 οὐκ ἐχόντων. ἃς δὲ παρέχεται τοῖς ἐπὶ γῆς[2] ἅπασιν ὠφελείας σελήνη, τί χρὴ διεξιόντα μηκύνειν; ἐμφανεῖς γὰρ αἱ πίστεις. ἢ οὐχὶ ταῖς αὐξήσεσιν αὐτῆς ἀναχέονται ποταμοὶ καὶ πηγαὶ καὶ μειοῦνται πάλιν μειώσεσι, καὶ πελάγη τοτὲ μὲν ἐξαναχωρεῖ καὶ ἀμπωτίζοντα ὑποσύρεται τοτὲ δ' ἐξαπιναίως ἐπιτρέχει κατὰ παλίρροιαν, ὅ τε ἀὴρ αἰθρίαις καὶ νεφώσεσι καὶ ταῖς ἄλλαις μεταβολαῖς παντοίας ἐνδέχεται τροπάς, καρποί τε οἱ σπαρτῶν[3] καὶ δένδρων αὔξονται καὶ τελεσφοροῦνται σελήνης περιόδοις τιθηνουμένης ἕκαστα τῶν φυομένων καὶ πεπαινούσης ἐνδρόσοις καὶ μαλακω-

[1] MS. τελευτῶντος . . . σελήνη (ἀφ' οὗ for ἀφ' ἧς).

and the moon reveals its own beauty to the eye. And this is surely an obvious lesson inculcating kindness and humanity and bidding men never grudge their own good things, but imitating the blessed and happy beings in heaven banish jealousy from the confines of the soul, producing what they have for all to see, treat it as common property,
and give freely to the deserving. The fourth reason 142
is, that the moon traverses the zodiac in a shorter fixed period than any other heavenly body. For it accomplishes that revolution in the span of a single month, and therefore the conclusion of its circuit, when the moon ends its course at the starting-point at which it began, is honoured by the law, which declares that day a feast, again to teach us an admirable lesson, that in the conduct of life we should make the ends correspond with the beginnings. And this will be effected if we keep our primitive appetites under the control of reason and do not permit them to rebel and riot like cattle that have no herdsman.

As for the services that the moon 143
renders to everything on earth, there is no need to dilate upon them. The proofs are perfectly clear. As the moon increases, the rivers and fountains rise, and again diminish as it diminishes. Its phases cause the seas to withdraw and dwindle at the ebb-tide, then suddenly rush back with the returning flood, and the air to undergo all manner of changes as the sky becomes clear or cloudy and alters in other ways. The fruits, both of the sown crops and orchard-trees, grow to their maturity according to the revolutions of the moon, which fosters and ripens everything that grows with the dewy and very gentle breezes

[2] MS. ἐπὶ γῆν.

[3] MS. σπαρτοὶ.

144 τάταις αὔραις; ἀλλ' οὐχὶ καιρός, ὅπερ ἔφην, μακρηγορεῖν ἔπαινον σελήνης διεξιόντα καὶ καταριθμούμενον ἃς παρέχεται ζῴοις καὶ τοῖς ἐπὶ γῆς ἅπασιν ὠφελείας. διὰ μὲν δὴ ταῦτα καὶ τὰ τούτοις παραπλήσια νουμηνία τετίμηται καὶ τάξιν ἔλαχε τὴν ἐν ταῖς ἑορταῖς.

145 XXVII. Μετὰ δὲ τὴν νουμηνίαν ἐστὶν ἑορτὴ τετάρτη, τὰ διαβατήρια, ἣν Ἑβραῖοι Πάσχα πατρίῳ γλώττῃ καλοῦσιν, ἐν ᾗ θύουσι πανδημεὶ πολλὰς μυριάδας ἱερείων ἀρξάμενοι ἀπὸ μεσημβρίας ἄχρι ἑσπέρας, ὁ λεὼς ἅπας, πρεσβῦται καὶ νέοι, κατ' ἐκείνην τὴν ἡμέραν ἱερωσύνης ἀξιώματι τετιμημένοι· τὸν γὰρ ἄλλον χρόνον οἱ ἱερεῖς τάς τε κοινὰς θυσίας καὶ τὰς ἰδίας ἑκάστου προστάξει νόμων ἐπιτελοῦσι, τότε δὲ σύμπαν τὸ ἔθνος μετὰ πάσης ἀδείας ἁγναῖς χερσὶν ἱερουργεῖ[1] καὶ ἱερᾶται.

146 αἴτιον δὲ τόδε· τῆς μεγίστης ἀποικίας ὑπόμνημά ἐστιν ἡ ἑορτὴ καὶ χαριστήριον, ἣν ἀπ' Αἰγύπτου μυριάσιν ὑπὲρ διακοσίας ἀνδρῶν ὁμοῦ καὶ γυναικῶν ἐστείλαντο κατὰ τὰ χρησθέντα λόγια. τότε οὖν, ὡς εἰκός, ἀπολελοιπότες χώραν γέμουσαν ἀπανθρωπίας καὶ ξενηλασίας ἐπιτηδεύουσαν καὶ—τὸ χαλεπώτατον—τὰς τοῦ θεοῦ τιμὰς ἀλόγοις ζῴοις οὐχ ἡμέροις μόνον ἀλλὰ καὶ ἀγρίοις προσνέμουσαν

[1] MS. ἱερουργεῖται.

[a] Philo consistently uses διαβατήρια or διάβασις = πάσχα, and several times, *e.g. Leg. All.* iii. 94, allegorizes it as in § 147, shewing that he traces the name not to the passing over of the Israelites by the destroying angel (Ex. xii. 23 and 27), but to the crossing of Israel itself from Egypt, the type of the body, and no doubt also the crossing of the Red Sea. In classical Greek διαβατήρια are offerings made before crossing a boundary, and also (Plut. *Lucullus*, 24) before

which it brings. But, as I have said, this is not the 144
time to dwell at length on the praises of the moon and record and catalogue the services which it renders to living creatures and everything on earth. It is for these or similar reasons that the New Moon is honoured and obtains its place among the feasts.

XXVII. After the New Moon comes the fourth 145
feast, called the Crossing-feast,[a] which the Hebrews in their native tongue call Pascha. In this festival many myriads of victims from noon till eventide[b] are offered by the whole people, old and young alike, raised for that particular day to the dignity of the priesthood.[c] For at other times the priests according to the ordinance of the law carry out both the public sacrifices and those offered by private individuals. But on this occasion the whole nation performs the sacred rites and acts as priest with pure hands and complete immunity. The reason for this is as follows: the 146
festival is a reminder and thank-offering for that great migration from Egypt which was made by more than two millions[d] of men and women in obedience to the oracles vouchsafed to them. Now at that time they had left a land brimful of inhumanity which made a practice of expelling strangers, and what was worst of all, assigned divine honours to irrational creatures, not merely domesticated animals, but even wild

crossing a swollen river; *cf.* § 147 ἐπικλύζει χειμάρρου ποταμοῦ τρόπον. See also App. p. 627.

[b] See App. p. 627.

[c] *Cf. Mos.* ii. 224.

[d] See Ex. xii. 37, "about six hundred thousand on foot that were men besides children" (LXX "besides the baggage"). So too, Num. xi. 21. "600,000 men implies a total including women and children of at least 2,000,000 souls" (Driver, *ad loc.*).

ὑπὸ τῆς ἄγαν περιχαρείας ἔθυον αὐτοὶ διὰ προθυμίαν ἄλεκτον καὶ τάχος ἐσπευσμένον τοὺς ἱερεῖς
οὐκ ἀναμένοντες. τοῦτο δὴ τότε πραχθὲν αὐτοκελεύστῳ καὶ ἐθελουργῷ πάθει δρᾶν ἐφῆκεν ὁ
νόμος ἅπαξ κατ' ἐνιαυτὸν ἕκαστον εἰς εὐχαριστίας
ὑπόμνησιν. ταῦτα μὲν κατὰ παλαιὰν ἀρχαιολογίαν
147 ἱστορεῖται. οἷς δὲ τὰ ῥητὰ τρέπειν
πρὸς ἀλληγορίαν ἔθος ψυχῆς κάθαρσιν αἰνίττεται
τὰ διαβατήρια· φασὶ γὰρ τὸν σοφίας ἐραστὴν
οὐδὲν ἕτερον ἐπιτηδεύειν ἢ τὴν ἀπὸ τοῦ σώματος
καὶ τῶν παθῶν διάβασιν, ὧν ἕκαστον ἐπικλύζει
χειμάρρου ποταμοῦ τρόπον, εἰ μή τις τοῖς ἀρετῆς
δόγμασιν ἀνακόπτοι καὶ ἀναχαιτίζοι τὴν φοράν.
148 ἑκάστη δὲ οἰκία κατ' ἐκεῖνον τὸν
χρόνον σχῆμα ἱεροῦ καὶ σεμνότητα περιβέβληται,
τοῦ σφαγιασθέντος ἱερείου πρὸς τὴν ἁρμόττουσαν
εὐωχίαν εὐτρεπιζομένου καὶ τῶν ἐπὶ τὰ συσσίτια
συνειλεγμένων ἁγνευτικοῖς περιρραντηρίοις κεκα-
θαρμένων, οἳ παραγεγόνασιν οὐχ ὡς εἰς τὰ ἄλλα
συμπόσια χαριούμενοι γαστρὶ δι' οἴνου καὶ ἐδεσμάτων, ἀλλὰ πάτριον ἔθος ἐκπληρώσοντες μετ'
149 εὐχῶν τε καὶ ὕμνων. ἄξιον μέντοι καὶ τὴν ἡμέραν
παρασημήνασθαι τῆς πανδήμου εὐωχίας· ἄγεται
γὰρ τεσσαρεσκαιδεκάτῃ τοῦ μηνός, ἥτις ἐκ δυεῖν
ἑβδομάδων συνέστηκεν, ἵνα μηδὲν ἀμοιρῇ τῶν
ἀξίων τιμῆς ἑβδομάδος, ἀλλ' αὕτη κατάρχῃ πᾶσιν
ἐπιφανείας καὶ σεμνότητος.
[293] 150 XXVIII. | Συνάπτει δὲ τοῖς διαβατηρίοις ἑορτὴν
διάφορον ἔχουσαν καὶ οὐ συνήθη τροφῆς χρῆσιν,

---

[a] The suggestion that the feast was instituted after the departure is, of course, quite opposed to Ex. xii., where the

beasts. So exceedingly joyful were they that in their vast enthusiasm and impatient eagerness, they naturally enough sacrificed without waiting for their priest.[a] This practice which on that occasion was the result of a spontaneous and instinctive emotion, was sanctioned by the law once in every year to remind them of their duty of thanksgiving. These are the facts as discovered by the study of ancient history.

But to those who are accustomed to turn literal facts 147
into allegory, the Crossing-festival suggests the purification of the soul. They say that the lover of wisdom is occupied solely in crossing from the body and the passions, each of which overwhelms him like a torrent, unless the rushing current be dammed and held back by the principles of virtue. On 148
this day every dwelling-house is invested with the outward semblance and dignity of a temple. The victim is then slaughtered and dressed for the festal meal which befits the occasion. The guests assembled for the banquet have been cleansed by purificatory lustrations, and are there not as in other festive gatherings, to indulge the belly with wine and viands, but to fulfil with prayers and hymns the custom handed down by their fathers. The day on which 149
this national festivity occurs may very properly be noted. It is the 14th of the month, a number formed of the sum of two sevens, thus bringing out the fact that seven never fails to appear in anything worthy of honour but everywhere takes the lead in conferring prestige and dignity.

XXVIII. With the Crossing-feast he combines one 150
in which the food consumed is of a different and un-

blood of the victim is to be smeared on the doorposts to avert the destroying angel.

ἄζυμα, ἀφ' οὗ καὶ ὠνόμασται. διττὸς δὲ ὁ περὶ αὐτῆς λόγος, ὁ μὲν ἴδιος τοῦ ἔθνους ἕνεκα τῆς λεχθείσης ἀποικίας, ὁ δὲ κοινὸς κατὰ φύσεως ἀκολουθίαν καὶ τὴν τοῦ κόσμου παντὸς ἁρμονίαν. ὡς δ' ἀψευδὴς ἡ ὑπόσχεσις, ἐπισκεπτέον. ἕβδομος ὢν ὁ μὴν οὗτος ἀριθμῷ τε καὶ τάξει κατὰ τὸν ἡλιακὸν κύκλον δυνάμει πρῶτός ἐστι, διὸ[1] καὶ πρῶτος ἐν ταῖς ἱεραῖς βίβλοις ἀναγέγραπται.
151 αἴτιον δὲ ὥς γε οἶμαι τόδε· τὴν ἐαρινὴν ἰσημερίαν ἀπεικόνισμά τι καὶ μίμημα συμβέβηκεν εἶναι τῆς ἀρχῆς ἐκείνης, καθ' ἣν ὅδε ὁ κόσμος ἐδημιουργεῖτο· τότε γὰρ διακρινομένων τῶν στοιχείων καὶ τὴν ἐναρμόνιον τάξιν λαμβανόντων πρός τε αὑτὰ καὶ πρὸς ἄλληλα, διεκοσμεῖτο μὲν ὁ οὐρανὸς ἡλίῳ καὶ σελήνῃ καὶ ταῖς τῶν ἄλλων πλανήτων καὶ ἀπλανῶν ἀστέρων χορείαις καὶ περιόδοις, διεκοσμεῖτο δὲ καὶ ἡ γῆ παντοίαις φυτῶν ἰδέαις καὶ ὅση τῆς ὀρεινῆς καὶ πεδιάδος ἀγαθὴ καὶ βαθεῖα πᾶσα
152 ἐτεθήλει καὶ ἐχλοηφόρει. καθ' ἕκαστον οὖν ἐνιαυτὸν ὑπομιμνῄσκων ὁ θεὸς τῆς τοῦ κόσμου γενέσεως ἀνέφηνε τὸ ἔαρ, ἐν ᾧ πάντα ἀνθεῖ καὶ βλαστάνει. διόπερ οὐκ ἀπὸ σκοποῦ πρῶτος ἀναγέγραπται μὴν ἐν τοῖς νόμοις, ἐπειδὴ τρόπον τινὰ τῆς πρώτης ἀρχῆς ἐκμαγεῖόν ἐστιν, ἀπ' ἐκείνης
153 ὥσπερ ἀρχετύπου σφραγῖδος τυπωθείς. ὁ δὲ κατὰ[2] τὴν μετοπωρινὴν ἰσημερίαν τῇ τάξει [πρώτῃ] πρῶτος ὢν ἐν ταῖς ἡλιακαῖς περιόδοις οὐ λέγεται

[1] MS. and Nicetas διότι.
[2] MS. and Nicetas μετὰ.

[a] The feast of Unleavened Bread is regularly distinguished from the Passover, though following immediately after it.

familiar kind, namely, unleavened bread, which also gives its name to the feast.[a] This may be regarded from two points of view, one peculiar to the nation, referring to the migration just mentioned, the other universal, following the lead of nature, and in agreement with the general cosmic order. To show that this affirmation is absolutely true, will require some examination. This month comes seventh in order and number as judged by the cycle of the sun, but in importance it is first, and therefore is described as first in the sacred books.[b] The reason for this I 151
believe to be as follows. In the spring equinox we have a kind of likeness and portraiture of that first epoch in which this world was created. The elements were then separated and placed in harmonious order with reference to themselves and each other. The heaven was adorned with sun and moon and the rhythmic movements and circlings of the other stars, both fixed and planetary. So too the earth was adorned with every manner of plants, and the uplands and lowlands, wherever the soil had depth and goodness, became luxuriant and verdant. So every year God reminds us of the creation of the 152
world by setting before our eyes the spring when everything blooms and flowers. And therefore there is good reason for describing it in the laws as the first month because in a sense it is an image of the primal origin reproduced from it like the imprint from an archetypal seal. But the month of the 153
autumnal equinox, though first in order as measured by the course of the sun, is not called first in the law,

[a] See Lev. xxiii. 5 ff., and also for the details mentioned below *cf.* i. 181 f.

[b] See Ex. xii. 2, and note (App.) on i. 180.

παρὰ τῷ νόμῳ πρῶτος, ὅτι κατ' ἐκεῖνον τὸν χρόνον συγκεκομισμένων τῶν καρπῶν ἁπάντων τὰ δένδρα φυλλορροεῖ καὶ ὅσα ἀκμάζον τὸ ἔαρ ἤνεγκε πάντα [ξηραίνεται] ἀφαναίνεται ξηροῖς πνεύμασι τοῦ ἀέρος αὐχμώδη καταστάντα τοῖς ἀφ' ἡλίου φλογ-
154 μοῖς. πρῶτον μὲν οὖν ἐπιφημίσαι μῆνα, καθ' ὃν ἐστείρωται καὶ ἀγονεῖ ἥ τε ὀρεινὴ καὶ ἡ πεδιάς, παντάπασιν ὑπέλαβεν[1] ἀνάρμοστον καὶ ἀνοίκειον εἶναι· δεῖ γὰρ τοῖς πρώτοις καὶ ἡγεμονίδα τάξιν εἰληχόσι προσεῖναι τὰ κάλλιστα καὶ εὐκταιότατα, δι' ὧν αἱ ζῴων καὶ καρπῶν καὶ φυτῶν γενέσεις καὶ αὐξήσεις εἰσίν, ἀλλ' οὐχ αἱ παλίμφημοι
155 φθοραί. τῆς δὲ ἑορτῆς ἀρχὴ διχόμηνος, ἡ πεντεκαιδεκάτη, καθ' ἣν σελήνη πλησιφαὴς γίνεται, προνοίᾳ τοῦ μηδὲν εἶναι σκότος κατ' ἐκείνην τὴν ἡμέραν, ἀλλὰ φωτὸς ἀνάπλεα πάντα διὰ πάντων, ἡλίου μὲν ἕωθεν εἰς ἑσπέραν ἐπιλάμποντος, σελήνης δὲ ἀφ' ἑσπέρας ἄχρι τῆς ἕω τὰς αὐτὰς[2] . . ., τῶν ⟨δ'⟩ ἀστέρων ἀλλήλοις ἀντιπαραχωρούντων
156 ἀσκίοις φέγγεσιν. ἡ δὲ ἑορτὴ πάλιν ἐφ' ἡμέρας ἑπτὰ ἄγεται δι' ἣν ἔλαχεν ἐν κόσμῳ ὁ ἀριθμὸς προνομίαν τε καὶ τιμήν, ἵνα μηδὲν τῶν εἰς εὐθυμίαν καὶ πάνδημον εὐφροσύνην καὶ εὐχαριστίαν τὴν πρὸς τὸν θεὸν ἀπολείπηται τῆς ἱερᾶς ἑβδομάδος, ἣν ἀρχὴν καὶ πηγὴν ἀνθρώποις

[1] MS. παντάπασι κατέλαβε.

[2] I have reproduced Cohn's text, though it might be as well to omit the signs of a lacuna, as it is quite possible that the corruption may lie in τὰς αὐτὰς itself. Cohn suggests τὰς αὐγὰς ⟨πεμπούσης⟩, Wendland τὰς αὐτὰς ⟨ἐπιτελούσης χρείας⟩. I think the simple correction to ὡσαύτως might be worth considering.

---

[a] Apart from the obvious faultiness of the text, the sentence

because at that time all the fruits have been gathered
in and the trees are shedding their leaves and all the
bloom which the spring brought in its prime already
scorched by the heat of the summer sun is wilting
under the dry currents of air. And so to give the 154
name of " first " to a month in which both uplands
and lowlands are sterilized and unfruitful seemed
to him altogether unsuitable and incongruous. For
things which come first and head the list should be
associated with all the fairest and most desirable
things which are the sources of birth and increase
to animals and fruits and plants, not with the processes of destruction and the dark thoughts which
it suggests. The feast begins at the middle of the 155
month, on the fifteenth day, when the moon is full,
a day purposely chosen because then there is no
darkness, but everything is continuously lighted up
as the sun shines from morning to evening and the
moon from evening to morning and while the stars
give place to each other no shadow is cast upon
their brightness.[a]
Again, the feast is held 156
for seven days to mark the precedence and honour
which the number holds in the universe, indicating
that nothing which tends to cheerfulness and public
mirth and thankfulness to God should fail to be
accompanied with memories of the sacred seven
which He intended to be the source and fountain to

is difficult. The stars, as Heinemann says, do not give place to each other on a night of full moon. He thinks that τῶν ἀστέρων refers to the sun and moon. I hardly think this is possible. Though we find the sun and moon coupled with the "other stars," and included in the "seven stars," there would be no point here in speaking of them as "the stars." Presumably ἀλλήλοις ἀντιπαραχωρούντων is loosely used for "as one gives way to another," and they are mentioned as reinforcing the light of the moon.

157 ἀγαθῶν ἁπάντων εἶναι διενοήθη. τῶν δὲ ἑπτὰ ἡμερῶν δύο, τὴν πρώτην καὶ τὴν ὑστάτην, "ἁγίας" προσεῖπεν, ἀρχῇ καὶ τέλει προνομίαν, ὡς εἰκός, διδοὺς καὶ ἅμα βουλόμενος καθάπερ ἐν ὀργάνῳ μουσικῷ συμφωνίᾳ[1] τῶν ἄκρων τὰς μεθορίους συναρμόσασθαι, τάχα μέντοι καὶ ὑπὲρ τοῦ τόν τε παρελθόντα καὶ μέλλοντα χρόνον συνῳδὸν ἀποφῆναι τῇ ἑορτῇ, τὸν μὲν παρεληλυθότα συνάπτοντα ⟨τῇ πρώτῃ, τὸν δὲ μέλλοντα⟩ τῇ τελευταίᾳ, ὧν ἑκατέρα τὴν ἑαυτῆς καὶ τῆς ἑτέρας δύναμιν εἴληχεν· ἥ τε γὰρ πρώτη τῆς μὲν ἑορτῆς ἐστιν ἀρχή, τέλος δὲ τοῦ παρεληλυθότος χρόνου, ἥ τε ἑβδόμη τέλος μὲν τῆς ἑορτῆς, ἀρχὴ δὲ τοῦ μέλλοντος, ἵν', ὃ καὶ πρόσθεν εἶπον, ἅπας ὁ τοῦ σπουδαίου βίος ἰσότιμος ἑορτῇ νομίζηται λύπην καὶ φόβον καὶ ἐπιθυμίαν καὶ τἆλλα πάθη καὶ νοσήματα τῆς ψυχῆς ἐληλα-
158 κότος. ὁ δ' ἄρτος ἄζυμος, ἤτοι διὰ τὸ τοὺς προγόνους, ἡνίκα θείᾳ πομπῇ τὴν ἀποικίαν ἐστέλλοντο, χρωμένους ἀνυπερβλήτῳ τάχει τὰ φυράματα τοῦ σταιτὸς ἄζυμα ἐπενέγκασθαι ἢ ἐπειδὴ κατὰ τὸν καιρὸν ἐκεῖνον (λέγω δὲ τὴν ἐαρινὴν ὥραν, ἐν ᾗ συμβαίνει τὴν ἑορτὴν ἄγεσθαι) ὁ τοῦ σίτου καρπὸς ἀτελής ἐστι, τῶν πεδίων σταχυηφορούντων καὶ μήπω καιρὸν ἐχόντων εἰς ἄμητον. ἀτελεῖ δὴ τῷ μέλλοντι καρπῷ τελειωθησομένῳ δὲ μικρὸν ὕστερον ἐδικαίωσεν ἐξομοιῶσαι τὴν ἄζυμον τροφὴν—ἀτελὴς γάρ ἐστι καὶ αὕτη—πρὸς ἐλπίδος χρηστῆς ὑπόμνησιν, ὡς ἤδη τῆς φύσεως τὰς ἐτησίους εὐτρεπιζομένης ἀνθρώπων γένει δωρεὰς ἐν τῇ τῶν ἐπιτηδείων ἀφθονίᾳ καὶ

[1] MS. and Nicetas συμφωνίαν.

men of all good things. Two days out of the seven, 157
the first and the last, are declared holy. In this way he gave a natural precedence to the beginning and the end; but he also wished to create a harmony as on a musical instrument between the intermediates and the extremes. Perhaps too he wished to harmonize the feast with a past which adjoins the first day and a future which adjoins the last. These two, the first and the last, have each the other's properties in addition to their own. The first is the beginning of the feast and the end of the preceding past, the seventh is the end of the feast and the beginning of the coming future. Thus, as I have said before,[a] the whole life of the man of worth may be regarded as equivalent to a feast held by one who has expelled grief and fear and desire and the other passions and distempers of the soul.

158 The bread is unleavened either because our forefathers, when under divine guidance they were starting on their migration, were so intensely hurried that they brought the lumps of dough unleavened,[b] or else because at that season, namely, the springtime, when the feast is held, the fruit of the corn has not reached its perfection, for the fields are in the ear stage and not yet mature for harvest. It was the imperfection of this fruit which belonged to the future, though it was to reach its perfection very shortly, that he considered might be paralleled by the unleavened food, which is also imperfect, and serves to remind us of the comforting hope that nature, possessing as she does a superabundant wealth of things needful, is already preparing her yearly gifts to the human

[a] In § 48.

[b] So Ex. xii. 34, 39, and Deut. xvi. 3.

159 περιουσίᾳ. λέγεται δὲ κἀκεῖνο τοῖς ἐξηγηταῖς τῶν ἱερῶν γραμμάτων, ὅτι ἡ μὲν ἄζυμος τροφὴ δώρημα φύσεώς ἐστιν, ἡ δ' ἐζυμωμένη τέχνης ἔργον· ἐπιτηδεύσει γὰρ ἄνθρωποι τὰ ἡδέα τοῖς ἀναγκαίοις[1] ἀναμιγνύναι σπεύδοντες τὸ αὐστηρὸν τῇ
160 φύσει προσηνὲς τέχνῃ κατεσκεύασαν. ἐπεὶ οὖν ἐστιν ἡ ἐαρινὴ ἑορτή, καθάπερ ἐδίδαξα, τῆς τοῦ κόσμου γενέσεως ὑπόμνημα, τοὺς δὲ παλαιτάτους γηγενεῖς τε καὶ ἐκ γηγενῶν ἀναγκαῖον ἦν χρήσασθαι
[294] ταῖς | τοῦ κόσμου δωρεαῖς ἀδιαστρόφοις, μήπω τῆς ἡδονῆς παρευημερούσης, οἰκειοτάτην τροφὴν ἐνομοθέτησε τῷ καιρῷ, βουλόμενος ἀνὰ πᾶν ἔτος τὰ τῆς σεμνῆς καὶ αὐστηρᾶς διαίτης ἐμπυρεύματα ζωπυρεῖν καὶ ἅμα τὸν ἀρχαῖον βίον τῆς ὀλιγοδεΐας καὶ εὐτελείας θαυμάσαι τε καὶ τιμῆσαι πανηγύρεως ἐκεχειρίᾳ καὶ τὸν ἡμῶν καθ' ὅσον οἷόν τε ἦν
161 ἐξομοιῶσαι τῷ παλαιῷ. τὰ λεχθέντα πιστοῦται μάλιστα ἡ τῶν ἰσαρίθμων ταῖς φυλαῖς ἐπὶ τῆς ἱερᾶς τραπέζης ἄρτων δώδεκα πρόθεσις· εἰσὶ γὰρ πάντες ἄζυμοι, δεῖγμα σαφέστατον ἀμιγοῦς τροφῆς οὐ τέχνῃ πρὸς ἡδονὴν ἀλλὰ φύσει πρὸς τὸ τῆς χρήσεως ἀναγκαῖον εὐτρεπισθείσης. ταῦτα μὲν ἐπὶ τοσοῦτον.

162 XXIX. Ἑορτὴ δέ ἐστιν ἐν ἑορτῇ ἡ μετὰ τὴν πρώτην εὐθὺς ἡμέραν, ἥτις ἀπὸ τοῦ συμβεβηκότος ὀνομάζεται δράγμα· τοῦτο γὰρ ἀπαρχὴ προσάγεται τῷ βωμῷ καὶ τῆς χώρας, ἣν ἔλαχε τὸ ἔθνος οἰκεῖν,

[1] MS. δικαίοις.

---

[a] See Lev. xxiv. 5 ff.

[b] See Lev. xxiii. 10 ff.; for "directly after the first day"

race. Another suggestion made by the interpreters 159
of the holy scriptures is that food, when unleavened, is a gift of nature, when leavened is a work of art. For men in their eagerness to temper the barely necessary with the pleasant, have learned through practice to soften by art what nature has made hard.
Since, then, the spring-time feast, as I have laid down, 160
is a reminder of the creation of the world, and its earliest inhabitants, children of earth in the first or second generation, must have used the gifts of the universe in their unperverted state before pleasure had got the mastery, he ordained for use on this occasion the food most fully in accordance with the season. He wished every year to rekindle the embers of the serious and ascetic mode of faring, and to employ the leisure of a festal assembly to confer admiration and honour on the old-time life of frugality and economy, and as far as possible to assimilate our
present-day life to that of the distant past. These 161
statements are especially guaranteed by the exposure of the twelve loaves corresponding in number to the tribes, on the holy table.[a] They are all unleavened, the clearest possible example of a food free from admixture, in the preparation of which art for the sake of pleasure has no place, but only nature, providing nothing save what is indispensable for its use. So much for this.

XXIX. But within the feast there is another feast 162
following directly after the first day. This is called the "Sheaf,"[b] a name given to it from the ceremony which consists in bringing to the altar a sheaf as a first-fruit, both of the land which has been given to

ibid. 11; LXX "on the morrow of the first day"; Hebrew "on the morrow after the sabbath." See App. p. 627.

καὶ τῆς συμπάσης γῆς, ὡς εἶναι τὴν ἀπαρχὴν καὶ τοῦ ἔθνους ἰδίαν καὶ ὑπὲρ ἅπαντος ἀνθρώπων

163 γένους κοινήν. τὸ δ' αἴτιον, ὅτι ὃν λόγον ἔχει πρὸς πόλιν ἱερεύς, τοῦτον πρὸς ἅπασαν τὴν οἰκουμένην τὸ Ἰουδαίων ἔθνος. ἱερᾶται γάρ, εἰ δεῖ τἀληθὲς εἰπεῖν, ἅπασι τοῖς ἁγνευτικοῖς καθαρσίοις χρώμενον καὶ κατὰ σῶμα καὶ κατὰ ψυχὴν ὑφηγήσεσι νόμων θείων, οἳ τάς τε γαστρὸς ἡδονὰς καὶ ὑπογαστρίους ἔστειλαν καὶ τὸν ὄχλον * * *[1] ταῖς αἰσθήσεσιν ἡνίοχον ἀλόγοις λόγον ἐπιστήσαντες, ἔτι δὲ καὶ τὰς τῆς ψυχῆς ἀκρίτους καὶ πλεοναζούσας ὁρμὰς ἀνέκοψαν καὶ ἀνεχαίτισαν, τὰ μὲν μαλακωτέραις ὑφηγήσεσι καὶ φιλοσόφοις προτροπαῖς, τὰ δ' ἐμβριθεστέροις καὶ εὐτονωτέροις ἐλέγχοις καὶ φόβῳ κολάσεως, ὃν ἐπανατείνονται.

164 χωρὶς δὲ τοῦ τὴν νομοθεσίαν τρόπον τινὰ διδασκαλίαν ἱερωσύνης εἶναι καὶ τὸν βιοῦντα κατὰ τοὺς νόμους εὐθὺς ἱερέα, μᾶλλον δ' ἀρχιερέα, παρ' ἀληθείᾳ δικαζούσῃ νομίζεσθαι κἀκεῖνο πρόσεστιν ἐξαίρετον· ἀπερίγραφον καὶ ἀπερίληπτον συμβέβηκεν εἶναι θεῶν πλῆθος τῶν κατὰ πόλεις[2] τιμωμένων ἀρρένων τε καὶ θηλειῶν, οὓς τό τε

[1] Cohn prints here καὶ τὸν ὄχλον <τῆς ψυχῆς ἐχαλίνωσαν, νοῦν> ταῖς αἰσθήσεσι κτλ. I have not followed him, since the insertion is, as he says, only "exempli gratia," and does not seem particularly happy. Philo is amplifying κατὰ σῶμα καὶ κατὰ ψυχήν, and as we take up ψυχή in ἔτι δὲ καὶ κτλ. it seems out of place here. Something is certainly needed after ὄχλον, but αὐτῶν would be in itself enough, or αὐτῶν ἐχαλίνωσαν since ὄχλον contains the notion of turbulence as well as crowd.

[2] MS. πόλιν.

[a] Or "This follows from the fact that," etc. For the following sections *cf.* i. 97, though there it is the high priest, and not the Jewish nation, who prays for the world. Heine-

the nation to dwell in and of the whole earth, so that it serves that purpose both to the nation in particular and for the whole human race in general. The 163
reason of this is[a] that the Jewish nation is to the whole inhabited world what the priest is to the State. For the holy office in very truth belongs to the nation because it carries out all the rites of purification and both in body and soul obeys the injunctions of the divine laws, which restrict the pleasures of the belly and the parts below it and the horde . . . setting reason to guide the irrational senses, and also check and rein in the wild and extravagant impulses of the soul, sometimes through gentler remonstrances and philosophical admonitions, sometimes through severer and more forcible condemnations and the fear of punishment which they hold over it as a deterrent.

But not only is the legislation in a sense 164
a lesson on the sacred office, not only does a life led in conformity with the laws necessarily confer priesthood or rather high priesthood in the judgement of truth, but there is another point of special importance. There is no bound or limit to the number of deities, male and female, honoured in different cities, the vain inven-

mann notes that it is curious that the sections which follow emphasizing the world-priesthood of the Jewish race should be connected with the comparatively insignificant rite of the Sheaf, particularly as Philo in *De Som.* ii. 75 has laid down that the sheaf must be taken from the holy land. But the sheaf is actually the first-fruit of the whole harvest, the accomplishment of which is celebrated in the feasts of Weeks and Tabernacles. Philo does not argue the world-priesthood from the rite, but asserts it as a fact shewn by (1) the obedience of Israel to the divine law; (2) its unique monotheism, and argues from it that the Sheaf, and by implication the other thank-offerings, are world-extensive. That he should attach this argument to the first example is not unnatural.

ποιητικὸν γένος ἐμύθευσε καὶ ⟨ὁ⟩ πολὺς ὅμιλος ἀνθρώπων, οἷς ἄπορος[1] καὶ ἀδιερεύνητος ἡ ζήτησις τῆς ἀληθείας ἐστίν· οὐ μὴν τοὺς αὐτοὺς ἅπαντες ἀλλὰ ἑτέρους ἕτεροι σεμνοποιοῦσι καὶ γεραίρουσιν, ὡς μηδὲ θεοὺς τοὺς ἐπὶ τῆς ἀλλοδαπῆς νομίζειν, ἀλλὰ γέλωτα καὶ χλεύην θέσθαι[2] τὰς ἐκείνων ἀποδοχὰς[3] καὶ καταγινώσκειν τῶν τιμώντων πολλὴν ἠλιθιότητα ὡς ὑγιοῦς διαμαρτανόντων δόξης.
165 εἰ δ' ἔστιν, ὃν μιᾷ γνώμῃ πάντες ὁμολογοῦσιν Ἕλληνες ὁμοῦ καὶ βάρβαροι, ὁ ἀνωτάτω πατὴρ θεῶν τε καὶ ἀνθρώπων καὶ τοῦ σύμπαντος κόσμου δημιουργός, οὗ τὴν φύσιν ἀόρατον καὶ δυστόπαστον οὖσαν οὐ μόνον ὁραθῆναι ἀλλὰ καὶ νοηθῆναι πάντες οἱ περὶ τὰ μαθήματα καὶ τὴν ἄλλην φιλοσοφίαν διατρίβοντες ἀναζητεῖν γλίχονται μηδὲν παρέντες τῶν εἰς εὕρεσιν καὶ [τούτου] θεραπείαν, ἔδει μὲν πάντας ἀνθρώπους ἀνῆφθαι ⟨τούτου⟩ καὶ μὴ καθάπερ ἀπὸ μηχανῆς εἰσποιεῖν ἑτέρους ἐπὶ
166 μετουσίᾳ τῶν ἴσων τιμῶν. ἐπεὶ δὲ περὶ τὸ ἀναγκαιότατον ὤλισθον μέρος, τὸ σφάλμα τῶν ἄλλων ἐπηνωρθώσατο, κυριώτατα φάναι, τὸ Ἰουδαίων ἔθνος, ὅσα μὲν εἰς γένεσιν ἦλθε πάνθ' ὑπερκύψαν ὡς γενητὰ καὶ τῇ φύσει φθαρτά, τοῦ δ' ἀγενήτου

[1] MS. ἄπονος.
[2] MS. ὑποθέσθαι.
[3] MS. ὑποδοχὰς.

[a] This is a remarkable statement, and can hardly mean more than that all acknowledge a creator of some sort. In such a general statement he may perhaps ignore atheists, but the words are not easy to reconcile with what he says elsewhere of polytheists. Or does he think that all the theologies like the Greek and Roman acknowledged one God as above the rest?

[b] Heinemann translates by "Naturforschung." But

tions of the tribe of poets and of the great multitude of men to whom the quest for truth is a task of difficulty and beyond their powers of research. Yet instead of all peoples having the same gods, we find different nations venerating and honouring different gods. The gods of the foreigner they do not regard as gods at all. They treat their acceptance by the others as a jest and a laughing-stock and denounce the extreme folly of those who honour them and the
failure to think soundly shewn thereby. But if He 165
exists Whom all Greeks and barbarians unanimously acknowledge,[a] the supreme Father of gods and men and the Maker of the whole universe, whose nature is invisible and inscrutable not only by the eye, but by the mind, yet is a matter into which every student of astronomical science [b] and other philosophy desires to make research and leaves nothing untried which would help him to discern it and do it service—then it was the duty of all men to cleave to Him and not introduce new gods staged as by machinery [c]
to receive the same honours. When they went 166
wrong in what was the most vital matter of all, it is the literal truth that the error which the rest committed was corrected by the Jewish nation which passed over all created objects because they were created and naturally liable to destruction and chose

μαθήματα, where it is not used quite generally, seems regularly to indicate either mathematics as in § 177 below, or what was regarded as a branch of mathematics, astronomy or astrology. For the latter *cf. De Praem.* 58 τῆς ἐν τοῖς μαθήμασι Χαλδαικῆς τερθρείας and *De Virt.* 212 ἀστρονομικοῦ τῶν περὶ τὰ μαθήματα διατριβόντων. So too μαθηματικός (-ή), § 140 above and *De Mut.* 71 πραγματευόμενον τὰ περὶ φύσεως οὐρανοῦ ὃν μαθηματικὸν ἔνιοι προσαγορεύουσι.

[c] See on i. 28.

καὶ ἀιδίου μόνον τὴν θεραπείαν ἑλόμενον· πρῶτον μὲν ὅτι καλόν, ἔπειτα δ' ὅτι καὶ ὠφέλιμον πρεσβυτέρῳ πρὸ νεωτέρων καὶ ἄρχοντι πρὸ ἀρχομένων καὶ ποιητῇ πρὸ γεγονότων ἀνακεῖσθαί τε καὶ προσ-
167 τίθεσθαι.[1] διὸ καὶ θαυμάζειν ἐπέρχεταί μοι, πῶς τολμῶσί τινες ἀπανθρωπίαν τοῦ ἔθνους κατηγορεῖν, ὃ τοσαύτῃ κέχρηται κοινωνίας καὶ εὐνοίας τῆς[2] πρὸς ⟨τοὺς⟩ πανταχοῦ πάντας ὑπερβολῇ, ὡς τάς τε εὐχὰς καὶ ἑορτὰς καὶ ἀπαρχὰς ὑπὲρ τοῦ κοινοῦ γένους τῶν ἀνθρώπων ἐπιτελεῖν καὶ τὸν ὄντως ὄντα θεὸν θεραπεύειν ὑπέρ τε ἑαυτοῦ καὶ τῶν ἄλλων, οἳ τὰς ὀφειλομένας λατρείας ἀποδεδράκασι.

168 Καὶ ταῦτα μὲν ὑπὲρ τοῦ σύμπαντος ἀνθρώπων γένους. ἰδίᾳ δὲ πάλιν εὐχαριστοῦσι ⟨διὰ⟩ πολλά· πρῶτον μὲν ⟨ὅτι⟩ οὐκ αἰεὶ σποράδην ἀλώμενοι κατά τε νήσους καὶ ἠπείρους διατελοῦσι καὶ ὡς ὀθνεῖοι καὶ ἀνίδρυτοι τὰς ἑτέρων ἐπῳκηκότες καὶ ἀλλοτρίοις ἐφεδρεύοντες ἀγαθοῖς ὀνειδίζονται μηδεμίαν γῆς[3] τοσαύτης ἀποτομὴν τῷ μειονεκτεῖσθαι[4] δανεισάμενοι, χώραν δὲ καὶ πόλεις κτησάμενοι κλῆρον ἴδιον ἐκ πολλοῦ νέμονται, ἀφ' οὗ[5] τὰς
169 ἀπαρχὰς ὅσιόν ἐστι ποιεῖσθαι. δεύτερον δ' ὅτι οὔτε ἀπόβλητον καὶ τὴν ἐπιτυχοῦσαν[6] ἀλλ' ἀγαθὴν καὶ πάμφορον γῆν ἔλαχον πρός τε ζῴων ἡμέρων

[1] MS. προτίθεσθαι. [2] MS. τῇ = τῇ. [3] MS. τῆς.
[4] Cohn prints ⟨ἐπὶ⟩ τῷ μετοικίζεσθαι; see note *a*.
[5] MS. ἀφ' ὧν. [6] MS. ἀποτυχοῦσαν.

---

[a] Cohn in *Hermes*, 1908, p. 200, argues in justification of his correction (see note 4), that it fits in very well with the last words of § 170. This is true, but I cannot follow his

the service only of the Uncreated and Eternal,
first because of its excellence, secondly because it is
profitable to dedicate and attach ourselves to the
elder rather than to the younger, to the ruler rather
than to the subject, to the maker rather than to the
thing created. And therefore it astonishes me to 167
see that some people venture to accuse of inhumanity
the nation which has shewn so profound a sense of
fellowship and goodwill to all men everywhere, by
using its prayers and festivals and first-fruit offerings
as a means of supplication for the human race in
general and of making its homage to the truly existent
God in the name of those who have evaded the service
which it was their duty to give, as well as of itself.

So much for this feast as a thanksgiving for the 168
whole human race. But the nation in particular also
gives thanks for many reasons. First, because they
do not continue for ever wandering broadcast over
islands and continents and occupying the homelands
of others as strangers and vagrants, open to the reproach of waiting to seize the goods of others. Nor
have they just borrowed a section of this great
country for lack of means to purchase,[a] but have
acquired the land and cities for their own property,
a heritage in which they live as long established
citizens and therefore offer first-fruits from it as a
sacred duty. Secondly, the land which has fallen 169
to their lot is not derelict nor indifferent soil, but
good land, well fitted for breeding domestic animals

dictum that μειονεκτεῖσθαι makes no sense. The nation was not like people who borrow or hire a piece of ground because they have not enough to buy it. μειονεκτεῖν is common enough, though I have not found an example of the middle. Heinemann translates μειονεκτεῖσθαι, though he calls the word corrupt.

εὐγονίας καὶ καρπῶν ἀμυθήτων ἀφθονίαν· ἐν αὐτῇ γὰρ οὐδέν ἐστι λυπρόγεων, ἀλλὰ καὶ ὅσα λιθώδη καὶ ἀπόκροτα εἶναι δοκεῖ φλεψὶ μαλακαῖς διέζωσται καὶ σφόδρα βαθείαις, αἳ διὰ πιότητα ζῳοφυτεῖν
170 εἰσιν ἀγαθαί. πρὸς δὲ τούτοις οὐκ ἔρημον χώραν ἔλαβον, ἀλλ' ἐν ᾗ πολυάνθρωπον ἔθνος ἦν καὶ εὐανδροῦσαι μεγάλαι πόλεις· ἀλλ' αἱ μὲν ἐκενώθησαν οἰκητόρων, τὸ δὲ σύμπαν ἔθνος ἔξω μέρους βραχέος ἠφανίσθη, τὰ μὲν πολέμοις, τὰ δὲ καὶ θεηλάτοις προσβολαῖς, διὰ καινὰς[1] καὶ ἐκτόπους ἐπιτηδεύσεις ἀδικημάτων καὶ ὅσα μεγαλουργοῦντες ἐπὶ καθαιρέσει τῶν τῆς φύσεως θεσμῶν ἠσέβουν, ἵνα οἱ ἀντὶ τούτων εἰσοικιζόμενοι τοῖς ἑτέρων σωφρονισθῶσι κακοῖς, ἀναδιδαχθέντες ἔργοις ὅτι ζηλωταὶ μὲν τῶν ⟨κακίας⟩[2] ἔργων γενόμενοι ταὐτὰ πείσονται, τιμήσαντες δ' ἀρετῆς βίον ἕξουσι τὸν ἀπονεμηθέντα κλῆρον, οὐκ ἐν μετοίκοις ἀλλ' ἐν
171 αὐτόχθοσιν ἐξετασθέντες. ὡς μὲν τοίνυν ἀπαρχὴ τὸ δράγμα τῆς τε οἰκείας καὶ τῆς συμπάσης γῆς ἐστιν ἐπ' εὐχαριστίᾳ γινόμενον εὐθηνίας καὶ εὐετηρίας, ᾗ τό τε[3] ἔθνος καὶ τὸ σύμπαν ἀνθρώπων γένος ἐπόθει χρῆσθαι, δεδήλωται. προσήκει δὲ μὴ ἀγνοεῖν, ὅτι πολλὰ διὰ τῆς ἀπαρχῆς καὶ ὠφελιμώτατα παρίσταται· πρῶτον μὲν θεοῦ μνήμη, ἧς οὐκ ἔστιν εὑρεῖν ἀγαθὸν[4] τελειότερον, ἔπειτα δὲ τῷ πρὸς ἀλήθειαν αἰτίῳ τῆς εὐκαρπίας ἀμοιβὴ
172 δικαιοτάτη. τὰ μὲν γὰρ ἀπὸ τέχνης γεωργικῆς

[1] MS. κενὰς. [2] On Cohn's insertion of ⟨κακίας⟩ see note *a*. [3] MS. περί τε. [4] MS. ἀγαθῶν.

---

[a] The insertion of κακίας is very doubtful, and perhaps weakens the sense. I suspect that there is a play, not reproducible in English, on two different meanings of ἔργα: (*a*)

and bearing fruits in vast abundance. For in it there is no poverty of soil and even such parts as seem to be stony or stubborn are intersected by soft veins of very great depth, the richness of which adapts them for producing life. But besides this it 170
was no uninhabited land which they received, but one which contained a populous nation and great cities filled with stalwart citizens. Yet these cities have been stripped of their inhabitants and the whole nation, except for a small fraction, has disappeared, partly through wars, partly through heaven-sent visitations, a consequence of their strange and monstrous practices of iniquity and all their heinous acts of impiety aimed at the subversion of the statutes of nature. Thus should those who took their place as inhabitants gain instruction from the evil fate of others and learn from their history the lesson that if they emulate deeds of vice[a] they will suffer the same doom, but if they pay honour to a life of virtue they will possess the heritage appointed to them and be ranked not as settlers but as native-born.

We have shewn, then, that the Sheaf was an offering 171
both of the nation's own land and of the whole earth, given in thanks for the fertility and abundance which the nation and the whole human race desired to enjoy. But we must not fail to note that there are many things of great advantage represented by the offering. First, that we remember God, and what thing more perfectly good can we find than this? Secondly, that we make a requital, as is most fully due, to Him Who is the true cause of the good harvest. For the 172
results due to the husbandman's art are few or as good

taught by actual facts, *cf. Mos.* ii. 268 *τοῦτ' ἀπέβαινεν ἔργοις*, (*b*) emulate their actions.

ὀλίγα καὶ τὸ μηδέν, αὔλακας ἀναστεῖλαι ἢ περισκάψαι καὶ γυρῶσαι φυτὸν ἢ βαθῦναι τάφρον ἢ τὰς περιττὰς ἐπιφύσεις ἀποτεμεῖν ἤ τι τῶν ὁμοιοτρόπων ἐργάσασθαι, τὰ δ' ἐκ φύσεως ἀναγκαῖα πάντα καὶ χρήσιμα, γονιμώτατον ἔδαφος, εὔυδρα χωρία πηγαῖς καὶ ποταμοῖς αὐθιγενέσι καὶ χειμάρροις καὶ ἐτησίοις ὄμβροις καταρδόμενα, ἀέρος εὐκρασίαι ζωτικωτάταις αὔραις ἐπιπνέοντος, αἱ σπαρτῶν καὶ φυτῶν ἰδέαι μυρίαι· τί γὰρ τούτων ἄνθρωπος ἢ
173 εὗρεν ἢ ἐγέννησεν; ἡ μὲν οὖν γεννήσασα φύσις τῶν ἰδίων ἀγαθῶν οὐκ ἐφθόνησεν ἀνθρώπῳ, ζῴων δὲ τῶν θνητῶν ἡγεμονικώτατον αὐτὸν εἶναι ὑπολαβοῦσα, διότι λόγου καὶ φρονήσεως κεκοινώνηκεν, ἀριστίνδην εἵλετο καὶ πρὸς μετουσίαν τῶν ἰδίων ἐκάλεσεν· ὑπὲρ ὧν ἄξιον ἐπαινεῖσθαί τε καὶ θαυμάζεσθαι τὸν ἑστιάτορα θεὸν τὴν ὡς ἀληθῶς ἑστίαν γῆν ἅπασαν ἀεὶ πλήρη παρέχοντα τῶν οὐκ ἀναγκαίων μόνον ἀλλὰ καὶ ⟨τῶν πρὸς⟩ τὸν ἁβρο-
174 δίαιτον βίον. πρὸς δὲ τούτοις τὸ μὴ δεῖν εὐεργετῶν ἀλογεῖν· ὁ γὰρ πρὸς τὸν ἀνεπιδεᾶ καὶ ἑαυτοῦ ⟨πλήρη⟩[1] θεὸν εὐχάριστος γένοιτ' ἂν καὶ πρὸς ἀνθρώπους ἐξεθισθείς, οἳ μυρίων ὅσων ἐνδεεῖς
175 εἰσιν. κρίθινον δὲ τὸ τῆς ἀπαρχῆς δράγμα, πρὸς τὴν τῶν ὑποβεβηκότων ἀνυπαίτιον χρῆσιν· ἐπειδὴ γὰρ οὔτ' εὐαγὲς ἦν ἐκ πάντων ἀπάρχεσθαι, τῶν πλείστων πρὸς ἡδονὴν μᾶλλον ἢ τὴν ἀναγκαίαν χρῆσιν γεγονότων, οὔθ' ὅσιον ἀπολαῦσαι καὶ μετασχεῖν τινος τῶν πρὸς ἐδωδὴν

[1] On Cohn's insertion of πλήρη see note *a*.

as nothing, furrows drawn, a plant dug or ringed around, a trench deepened, excessive overgrowth lopped, or other similar operations. But what we owe to nature is all indispensable and useful, a soil of great fruitfulness, fields irrigated by fountains or rivers, spring-fed or winter torrents, and watered by seasonable rains, happily tempered states of the air which sends us the breath of its truly life-giving breezes, numberless varieties of crops and plants. For which of these has man for its inventor or parent?
No, it is nature, their parent, who has not grudged to 173
man a share in the goods which are her very own, but judging him to be the chiefest of mortal animals because he has obtained a portion of reason and good sense, chose him as the worthiest and invited him to share what was hers to give. For all this it is meet and right that the hospitality of God should be praised and revered, God Who provides for His guests the whole earth as a truly hospitable home ever filled not merely with necessaries, but with the means of
luxurious living. Further, we learn not to neglect 174
benefactors, for he who is grateful to God, Who needs nothing and is His own fullness,[a] will thus become accustomed to be grateful to men whose needs are
numberless. The sheaf thus offered is 175
of barley, shewing that the use of the inferior grains is not open to censure. It would be irreverent to give first-fruits of them all, as most of them are made to give pleasure rather than to be used as necessaries, and equally unlawful to enjoy and partake of any

[a] Cohn supports his insertion of πλήρη from *Leg. All.* i. 44 αὐτὸς ἑαυτοῦ πλήρης ὁ θεός, *cf. De Mut.* 27. Without it the text "having no need of Himself" might not be impossible, but would give a conception for which I know no parallel in Philo.

μὴ ἐν οἷς εὐπρεπὲς καὶ θέμις εὐχαριστήσαντας, τὸ δευτερείοις τροφῆς τετιμημένον εἶδος, κριθήν, ἀπάρχεσθαι προσέταξεν ὁ νόμος· ὁ γὰρ τοῦ σίτου ⟨καρπὸς⟩ τὰ πρεσβεῖα ἔλαχεν, οὗ πάλιν τὴν ἀπαρχὴν ἐπιφανεστέραν οὖσαν εἰς ἐπιτηδειότερον ἀνατίθεται καιρόν, οὐ προεκφοιτῶν ἀλλ' ἐν τῷ παρόντι ταμιευόμενος ὑπὲρ τοῦ καὶ τὰς εὐχαριστίας ἡρμόσθαι χρόνων τεταγμέναις περιόδοις.

176 XXX. Τοσαύτας ἔχουσα προνομίας, ὁπόσας ἔδειξεν ὁ νόμος, ἡ ἐπὶ τῷ δράγματι πανήγυρις προέορτός ἐστιν, εἰ δεῖ τἀληθὲς εἰπεῖν, ἑτέρας ἑορτῆς μείζονος· ἀπὸ γὰρ ἐκείνης ἡμέρα πεντηκοστὴ καταριθμεῖται ἑπτὰ ἑβδομάσιν, [ἐφ' αἷς][1] ἱερὸν ἀριθμὸν ἐπισφραγιζομένης μονάδος, ἥτις ἐστὶν ἀσώματος θεοῦ εἰκών, ᾧ κατὰ τὴν μόνωσιν ἐξομοιοῦται. τοῦτο μὲν δὴ πρῶτον κάλλος ἐπι-
177 δείκνυται πεντηκοντάς. ἕτερον δὲ μηνυτέον· θαυμαστὴ καὶ περιμάχητός ἐστιν ἡ φύσις ⟨αὐτῆς⟩ διά τε τἄλλα καὶ ἐπειδὴ συνέστηκεν ἐκ τοῦ στοιχειωδεστάτου καὶ πρεσβυτάτου τῶν ἐν οὐσίαις περιλαμβανομένων,[2] ὥς φασιν οἱ ἀπὸ τῶν μαθημάτων, ὀρθογωνίου τριγώνου· μήκει μὲν γὰρ αἱ

[1] MS. ἑβδόμη ἑβδομάς: Nicetas ἑπτὰ ἑβδομάδες. ἐφ' αἷς is omitted in Nicetas, Cohn substitutes for it ἀφέσεως. For a discussion of the text as a whole see App. pp. 627-628.

[2] MS. παραλαμβανομένων.

---

[a] There is no mention of barley in Lev. xxiii. As Josephus, *Ant.* iii. 250, says the same, the use of barley had probably become a general practice, which Philo by a slip of memory ascribes to the law.

[b] Or "privileges." If note *b* on § 162 is right, the προνομίαι consist in this, that the Sheaf is the first to exhibit all the virtues which accompany thanksgiving and have been enumerated in the preceding sections. Certainly in no other

form of food for which thanks had not been offered in the proper and rightful manner. And therefore the law ordained[a] that the first-fruit offerings should be made of barley, a species of grain regarded as holding the second place in value as food. For wheat holds the first place and as the first-fruit of this has greater distinction, the law postponed it to a more suitable season in the future. It does not anticipate matters, but puts it in storage for the time being, so that the various thank-offerings may be adjusted to their appointed dates as they recur.

XXX. The festival of the Sheaf, which has all 176
these grounds of precedence,[b] indicated in the law, is also in fact anticipatory of another greater feast. For it is from it that the fiftieth day is reckoned, by counting seven sevens, which are then crowned with the sacred number by the monad,[c] which is an incorporeal image of God, Whom it resembles because it also stands alone. This is the primary excellence exhibited by fifty, but there is another which should
be mentioned. One reason among others which 177
makes its nature so marvellous and admirable is that it is formed by what the mathematicians tell us is the most elemental and venerable of existing things,[d] namely, the right-angled triangle. In length its

sense does the law give *προνομία* to a rite which is disposed of in a few verses in Leviticus and not mentioned elsewhere in the Pentateuch.

[c] *i.e.* the addition of 1 turns 49 into the sacred number 50. The use of *ἐπισφραγίζεται* in § 211 is exactly similar.

[d] Lit. " of what is included in existences." The same view of 50 as the sum of the squares of the sides of the primary right-angled triangle appears in *De Vit. Cont.* 65, where it is called the *ἁγιώτατος καὶ φυσικώτατος* of numbers. See also *Mos.* ii. 80 and note. For other references see Zeller, *Presocratic Philosophy* (Eng. Trans.), i. 429 f.

τοῦδε πλευραὶ τριῶν οὖσαι καὶ τεσσάρων καὶ πέντε συμπληροῦσιν ἀριθμὸν τὸν δώδεκα, τοῦ ζῳοφόρου κύκλου παράδειγμα, διπλασιασθείσης ἑξάδος τῆς γονιμωτάτης, ἥτις ἐστὶν ἀρχὴ τελειότητος, ἐκ τῶν ἰδίων συμπληρουμένη μερῶν, οἷς[1] ἐξισοῦται· δυνάμει δ', ὡς ἔοικεν, ἀπογεννῶσι τὸν πεντηκοστὸν διὰ τοῦ τρὶς τρία καὶ τετράκις τέσσαρα καὶ πεντάκις πέντε, ὥστε ἀναγκαῖον εἶναι λέγειν τοσούτῳ ⟨κρείττω⟩ δωδεκάδος[2] εἶναι πεντηκοντάδα
178 ὅσῳ καὶ τὸ δυνάμει τοῦ μήκει.[3] εἰ δὲ τοῦ ἐλάττονος εἰκών ἐστιν ἡ καλλιστεύουσα τῶν ἐν οὐρανῷ σφαῖρα ἡ ζῳοφόρος, τίνος ἂν εἴη παράδειγμα τὸ κρεῖττον, ἡ πεντηκοντάς, ἢ πάντως ἀμείνονος φύσεως; περὶ ἧς οὐ καιρὸς λέγειν· αὔταρκες[4] γὰρ ἐν τῷ παρόντι σεσημειῶσθαι τὴν διαφορὰν ὑπὲρ τοῦ μὴ ἐν παρέργῳ προηγούμενον ἔργον τίθεσθαι.

179 Πρόσρησιν δ' ἔλαχεν ἡ κατὰ τὸν πεντηκοστὸν ἀριθμὸν ἐνισταμένη ἑορτὴ πρωτογεννημάτων, ἐν ᾗ δύο ἐζυμωμένους ἄρτους ἐκ πυροῦ γεγονότας ἔθος προσφέρειν ἀπαρχὴν σίτου, τῆς ἀρίστης τροφῆς. ὠνομάσθη δὲ πρωτογεννημάτων ἢ διότι, πρὶν εἰς τὴν ἀνθρώπων χρῆσιν ἐλθεῖν τὸν ἐπέτειον καρπόν, τοῦ νέου σίτου τὸ πρῶτον γέννημα καὶ ὁ πρῶτος παραφανεὶς καρπὸς ἀπαρχὴ προσάγεται—
180 δίκαιον γὰρ καὶ ὅσιον τὴν μεγίστην λαβόντας παρὰ θεοῦ δωρεὰν ἀφθονίαν ἀναγκαιοτάτης ὁμοῦ καὶ ὠφελιμωτάτης ἔτι δὲ καὶ ἡδίστης τροφῆς μήτε ἀπολαῦσαι μήτε συνόλως σπάσαι, πρὶν ἀπάρξασθαι τῷ χορηγῷ, διδόντας μὲν οὐδέν, αὐτοῦ γὰρ τὰ πάντα καὶ κτήματα καὶ δωρεαί, διὰ ⟨δὲ⟩ βραχέος

[1] MS. ἡμερῶν αἷς.
[2] MS. δεκάδος.
[3] MS. τοῦ δυνάμει τὸ μῆκος.
[4] MS. αὐτάρκως.

sides are 5, 3, 4, of which the sum is twelve, the pattern of the zodiac cycle, the duplication of the highly prolific six, which is the starting-point of perfection since it is the sum of the factors which produce it through multiplication. But we find that the sides when raised to the second power, *i.e.* $3 \times 3 + 4 \times 4 + 5 \times 5$, make 50, so that we must say that 50 is superior to 12 in the same degree as the
second power is superior to the first. And if the 178
lesser of these is represented by the most excellent of the heavenly spheres, the zodiac, the greater, namely 50, must be the pattern of some quite superior form of existence. But a discussion of this would be out of place at this point. It is quite enough for the present to call attention to the difference, so as to avoid treating a prominent fact as of secondary importance.

The feast which is held when the number 50 is 179
reached has acquired the title of "first-products."[a] On it it is the custom to bring two leavened loaves of wheaten bread for a sample offering of that kind of grain as the best form of food. One explanation of the name, "Feast of First-products," is that the first produce of the young wheat and the earliest fruit to appear is brought as a sample offering before
the year's harvest comes to be used by men. It is 180
no doubt just and a religious duty that those who have received freely a generous supply of sustenance so necessary and wholesome and also palatable in the highest degree should not enjoy or taste it at all until they have brought a sample offering to the Donor, not indeed as a gift, for all things and possessions and gifts are His, but as a token, however small,

[a] See on i. 183.

συμβόλου παραφαίνοντας εὐχάριστον καὶ θεοφιλὲς ἦθος πρὸς τὸν χαρίτων μὲν ἀνεπιδεᾶ συνεχεῖς δὲ
181 καὶ ἀενάους χάριτας ἄρδοντα—ἢ διότι κατ᾽ ἐξοχὴν πρῶτον καὶ ἄριστον γέννημα ὁ τοῦ σίτου καρπός ἐστιν, ἐν δευτέρᾳ τάξει τῶν ἄλλων καταριθμουμένων ὅσα σπαρτά· καθάπερ γὰρ ἄρχων ⟨μὲν⟩ ἐν πόλει, κυβερνήτης δ᾽ ἐν νηὶ πρῶτος εἶναι λέγεται, τῷ τὸν μὲν κατὰ πόλιν, τὸν δὲ κατὰ ναῦν ἀφηγεῖσθαί τε καὶ προφέρειν, τὸν αὐτὸν τρόπον καὶ ὁ τοῦ σίτου καρπὸς ὀνόματι συνθέτῳ πρωτογέννημα ὠνομάσθη διὰ τὸ πάντων ἄριστος εἶναι τῶν σπειρομένων· ἔδει γὰρ αὐτὸν καὶ τοῦ ζῴων ἀρίστου
182 τροφὴν εἶναι. ἐζυμωμένοι δ᾽ εἰσὶν οἱ ἄρτοι, τοῦ
[295] | νόμου ζύμην ἐπὶ τὸν βωμὸν ἀναφέρειν ἀπειπόντος, οὐχ ἵνα διαμάχῃ τις ᾖ ἐν τοῖς προστατтομένοις, ἀλλ᾽ ὑπὲρ τοῦ τρόπον τινὰ δι᾽ ἑνὸς εἴδους λαβεῖν τε καὶ δοῦναι, λαβεῖν μὲν τὴν ἀπὸ τῶν προσφερόντων εὐχαριστίαν, δοῦναι δὲ εὐθὺς ἀνυπερθέτως τὰ κομιζόμενα τοῖς προσφέρουσιν, οὐ μὴν ὥστε
183 χρῆσθαι· χρήσονται γὰρ τοῖς ἅπαξ καθιερωθεῖσιν οἷς ἔξεστί τε καὶ ἐφίεται, ἔξεστι δὲ τοῖς ἱερωμένοις, οἳ τῶν προσαγομένων τῷ βωμῷ ὅσα μὴ ὑπὸ τοῦ ἀσβέστου πυρὸς ἀναλίσκεται τὴν μετουσίαν ἔλαβον φιλανθρωπίᾳ νόμου δοθεῖσαν ἢ μισθὸν ὑπηρεσιῶν[1] ἢ γέρας ἀγώνων, οὓς ὑπὲρ εὐσεβείας ἀθλοῦσιν, ἢ κλῆρον ἱερόν, τοῦ κατὰ τὴν χώραν μὴ τὸν αὐτὸν

[1] MS. μισθῶν ἢ ὑπηρεσιῶν.

---

[a] This is the only sense I can give to ἔδει γάρ ("it had to be"). Heinemann "bestimmt," but would not this be ἔμελλε?

[b] Lev. ii. 11, *cf.* above i. 291. The meaning of what follows seems to be that the prohibition is waived in this case, because the loaves, though given to the Lord (Lev. xxiii. 20),

by which they show a disposition of thankfulness and loyalty to Him Who, while He needs no favours, sends the showers of His favours in never-failing constancy.
Another reason for the name may be that wheaten 181
grain is pre-eminent as the first and best product, all the other sown crops ranking in the second class in comparison; for as an archon in a city or a pilot in a ship are said to be the first because they regulate the course of the city or the ship, as the case may be, so wheaten grain has received the compound name of "first-product" because it is the best of all the cereals, which it would not be,[a] unless it were also
the food used by the best of living creatures. The 182
loaves are leavened in spite of the prohibition[b] against bringing leaven to the altar, not to produce any contradiction in the ordinances, but to ensure that so to speak there shall be a single kind, both for receiving and giving. By receiving I mean the thanksgiving of the offerers, by giving the immediate return without any delay to the offerers of what they bring,
though not for their own use. For food that has 183
once been consecrated will be used by those who have the right and authority, and that right belongs to those who act as priests who through the beneficence of the law have the right to partake of any thing brought to the altar which is not consumed by the undying fire—a privilege granted either as a payment for officiating or as a prize for the contests which they endure in the cause of piety, or a sacred allotment in lieu of land, in the apportionment of

are also received back from Him ("they shall be holy to the Lord for the priest that offers them"). It seems to be assumed that therefore they must be brought in the most palatable form, *cf.* § 184, presumably because it is a festal occasion, as the unleavened shew-bread was also eaten by the priests.

τρόπον ταῖς ἄλλαις φυλαῖς τὸ ἐπιβάλλον μέρος
184 διανειμάμενοι.[1] σύμβολον δ' ἐστὶ καὶ
ἄλλων ἡ ζύμη δυεῖν· ἑνὸς μὲν ἐντελεστάτης καὶ
ὁλοκλήρου τροφῆς, ἧς οὐκ ἔστιν εὑρεῖν ἐν τῇ καθ'
ἡμέραν χρήσει κρείττονα καὶ λυσιτελεστέραν·
κράτιστος δὲ καὶ ὁ τοῦ σίτου καρπὸς ἐν σπαρτοῖς,
ὡς ἁρμόττειν ὑπὲρ τοῦ ἀρίστου ποιεῖσθαι τὴν
185 ἀρίστην ἀπαρχήν. ἕτερον δὲ συμβολικώτερον· πᾶν
τὸ ἐζυμωμένον ἐπαίρεται· χαρὰ δὲ ψυχῆς ἐστιν
εὔλογος ἔπαρσις· ἐπ' οὐδενὶ δὲ τῶν ὄντων μᾶλλον
χαίρειν πέφυκεν ἄνθρωπος ἢ εὐπορίᾳ καὶ ἀφθονίᾳ
τῶν ἀναγκαίων· ἐφ' οἷς ἄξιον γεγηθότας εὐχαριστεῖν, ποιουμένους ἀοράτου τῆς περὶ τὴν
διάνοιαν εὐπαθείας αἰσθητὴν διὰ τῶν ἐζυμωμένων
186 ἄρτων εὐχαριστίαν. ἄρτοι δ' εἰσὶν ἀλλ'
οὐ σῖτος[2] ἡ ἀπαρχή, διὰ τὸ μηδὲν ἔτι ἐνδεῖν τῶν εἰς
ἀπόλαυσιν τροφῆς, σίτου γεγονότος· λέγεται γὰρ
ὅτι τῶν σπαρτῶν ἁπάντων τελευταῖος ὁ πυρὸς
γεννᾶσθαι πέφυκε καὶ πρὸς ἄμητον παρίστασθαι.
187 δύο δ' εἰσὶν ἄριστα δυοῖν χρόνων χαριστήρια, τοῦ
τε παρεληλυθότος, ἐν ᾧ τῶν ἐξ ἐνδείας καὶ λιμοῦ
κακῶν οὐκ ἐπειράθημεν ἐν εὐετηρίᾳ διάγοντες,
καὶ τοῦ μέλλοντος, διότι τὰς εἰς αὐτὸν χορηγίας
καὶ παρασκευὰς εὐτρεπισάμεθα καὶ γέμοντες χρη-

[1] MS. δανεισάμενοι, which Cohn retains, holding that it can bear the sense of acquiring (*Hermes*, 1908, p. 200). It may be objected to the correction (Tischendorf's) that no example is given of the middle in this sense, but it is a natural extension.

[2] Cohn brackets ἀλλ' οὐ σῖτος. See note *b*.

---

[a] See App. p. 628.

[b] Cohn's rejection of ἀλλ' οὐ σῖτος as "a foolish insertion"

which they had not received their proper share like
the other tribes. But leaven is also a 184
symbol for two other things: in one way it stands for food in its most complete and perfect form, such that in our daily usage none is found to be superior or more nourishing, and as wheat-meal is superior to that of the other seed crops, its excellence demands that the offering made in recognition of it
should be of the same high quality. The other point 185
is more symbolical. Everything that is leavened rises, and joy is the rational elevation or rising of the soul.[a] And there is nothing that exists which more naturally gives a man joy than the possession in generous abundance of necessaries. Such rightly call forth gladness and thanksgiving in those who by the leavened loaves give outward expression to the invisible sense of well-being in their hearts.
The offering takes the form of loaves 186
instead of wheaten meal,[b] because when the wheat has come there is nothing still missing in the way of appetizing food. For we are told that of all the seed crops, wheat is the last to spring up and be
ready for harvesting. And these thank-offerings of 187
the best kind are two in number for the two kinds of time, the past and the future; for the past, because our days have been spent in abundance, free from the experience of the evils of want and famine; for the future, because we have laid by and prepared resources to meet it, and are full of bright

rests on the ground that the antithesis is between the wheaten loaves and other kinds of grain. I think he misapprehends the point, which is that when the harvest is completed by the reaping of the wheat, the offering naturally takes the form in which it is actually consumed. I suspect that Philo connects ἄρτος and ἄρτιος.

στῶν ἐλπίδων ταμιευόμεθα τὰς τοῦ θεοῦ δωρεὰς εἰς τὴν καθ' ἡμέραν προφέροντες[1] αἰεὶ δίαιταν, ὅσων ἂν ⟨ᾖ⟩ χρεία κατὰ νόμους τῆς οἰκονομικῆς ἀρετῆς.

188 XXXI. Ἑξῆς ἐστιν ἱερομηνία, καθ' ἣν ἅμα ταῖς ἀναγομέναις θυσίαις ἐν τῷ ἱερῷ σαλπίζειν ἔθος· ἀφ' οὗ καὶ "σαλπίγγων" ἐτύμως ἑορτὴ προσαγορεύεται, διττὸν λόγον ἔχουσα, τὸν μὲν ἴδιον τοῦ ἔθνους, τὸν δὲ κοινὸν ἀνθρώπων ἁπάντων· ἴδιον μὲν ὑπόμνησιν τεραστίου καὶ μεγαλουργηθέντος ἔργου, καθ' ὃν χρόνον τὰ λόγια τῶν νόμων ἐθεσπί-
189 ζετο· τότε γὰρ ἀπ' οὐρανοῦ φωνὴ σάλπιγγος ἐξήχησεν, ἣν εἰκὸς ἄχρι τῶν τοῦ παντὸς φθάσαι περάτων, ἵνα καὶ τοὺς μὴ παρόντας καὶ μόνον οὐκ ἐν ἐσχατιαῖς κατοικοῦντας διὰ τοῦ συμβεβηκότος ἡ πτοία ἐπιστρέψῃ λογισαμένους, ὅπερ εἰκός, ὅτι τὰ οὕτως μεγάλα μεγάλων ἀποτελεσμάτων ἐστὶ σημεῖα· τί δὲ μεῖζον ἢ ὠφελιμώτερον εἰς ἀνθρώπους ἐλθεῖν ἐδύνατο τῶν γενικῶν νόμων, οὓς προεφήτευσεν ὁ θεός, οὐ δι' ἑρμηνέως καθάπερ τὰ ἐν
190 εἴδει νόμιμα; τοῦτο μὲν ἐξαίρετον τοῦ ἔθνους· κοινὸν δὲ πρὸς πάντας ἀνθρώπους ἐκεῖνο· ἡ σάλπιγξ ὄργανόν ἐστι πολέμου καὶ πρὸς τὴν κατ'
[296] ἐχθρῶν | ἐφόρμησιν, ὁπότε καιρὸς εἴη συμπλέκεσθαι καὶ πρὸς ἀνάκλησιν, ὁπότε διακρίνεσθαι δέοι πρὸς τὰ οἰκεῖα ἐπανελευσομένους στρατόπεδα. ἔστι δὲ καὶ ἕτερος θεήλατος πόλεμος, ὅταν ἡ φύσις ἐν ἑαυτῇ στασιάσῃ, τῶν μερῶν ἀντεπιτιθεμένων ἀλλήλοις, ἰσότητος εὐνομωτάτης πλεονεξίᾳ τοῦ

[1] MS. προσφέροντες.

hopes while we dispense and bring out for daily use the gifts of God as they are needed by the rules of good economy.[a]

XXXI. Next comes the opening of the sacred 188
month,[b] when it is customary to sound the trumpet in the temple at the same time that the sacrifices are brought there, and its name of "trumpet feast" is derived from this. It has a twofold significance, partly to the nation in particular, partly to all mankind in general. In the former sense it is a reminder of a mighty and marvellous event which came to pass when the oracles of the law were given from
above. [c] For then the sound of the trumpet pealed 189
from heaven and reached, we may suppose, the ends of the universe, so that the event might strike terror even into those who were far from the spot and dwelling well nigh at the extremities of the earth, who would come to the natural conclusion that such mighty signs portended mighty consequences. And indeed what could men receive mightier or more profitable than the general laws which came from the mouth of God, not like the particular laws,
through an interpreter? This is a signific- 190
ance peculiar to the nation. What follows is common to all mankind. The trumpet is the instrument used in war, both to sound the advance against the enemy when the moment comes for engaging battle and also for recalling the troops when they have to separate and return to their respective camps. And there is another war not of human agency when nature is at strife in herself, when her parts make onslaught one on another and her law-abiding sense of equality

[a] See App. p. 628.

[b] See on *De Dec.* 159, and *cf.* i. 186. [c] See Ex. xix. 16.

191 ἀνίσου κρατηθείσης. ὑπ᾽ ἀμφοτέρων δὲ τῶν πολέμων φθείρεται τὰ ἐπίγεια, πρὸς μὲν ἐχθρῶν δενδροτομίαις, δῃώσεσιν, ἐμπρήσεσι τροφῶν καὶ πεδίων σταχυηφορούντων, ὑπὸ δὲ τῶν κατὰ φύσιν αὐχμοῖς, ἐπομβρίαις, νοτίων βίαις πνευμάτων, φλογώσεσι ταῖς ἀφ᾽ ἡλίου, χιονώδει περιψύξει, τῆς ἁρμονίας τῶν ἐτησίων ὡρῶν περιηκούσης εἰς ἀναρμοστίαν, ἕνεκά μοι δοκῶ τῆς οὐ κατὰ μικρὸν ἐπιπολαζούσης ἀλλ᾽ ἀθρόῳ φορᾷ κεχυμένης ἀ-
192 σεβείας, παρ᾽ οἷς ἂν ταῦτα γίνηται. διὰ τοῦτο καθάπερ[1] ἐπώνυμον ἑορτὴν ὀργάνου πολεμικοῦ σάλπιγγος ἀπέφηνεν ὁ νόμος, ἐπ᾽ εὐχαριστίᾳ τοῦ εἰρηνοποιοῦ θεοῦ καὶ εἰρηνοφύλακος, ὃς καὶ τὰς ἐν ταῖς πόλεσι καὶ τὰς ἐν τοῖς μέρεσι τοῦ παντὸς στάσεις ἀνελὼν εὐθηνίας καὶ εὐετηρίας καὶ τῶν ἄλλων ἀγαθῶν ἀφθονίαν ἀπειργάσατο, μηδὲν ἐμπύρευμα καρπῶν φθορᾶς ἐάσας ζωπυρηθῆναι.

193 XXXII. Μετὰ δὲ τὴν τῶν σαλπίγγων ἄγεται νηστεία ἑορτή. τάχα ἄν τις εἴποι τῶν ἑτεροδόξων καὶ ψέγειν τὰ καλὰ μὴ αἰδουμένων· ἑορτὴ δ᾽ ἐστὶ τίς, ἐν ᾗ μὴ συμπόσια καὶ συσσίτια καὶ ἑστιατόρων καὶ ἑστιωμένων θίασος καὶ πολὺς ἄκρατος καὶ τράπεζαι πολυτελεῖς καὶ χορηγίαι καὶ παρασκευαὶ τῶν ἐν δημοθοινίᾳ πάντων εὐφροσύναι τε καὶ κῶμοι σὺν ἀθύρμασι καὶ τωθασμοῖς καὶ παιδιὰ μετ᾽ αὐλοῦ καὶ κιθάρας καὶ τυμπάνων τε καὶ κυμβάλων καὶ τῶν ἄλλων ὅσα ⟨κατὰ⟩ τὸ παραλελυμένον καὶ ἐκτεθηλυμμένον εἶδος μουσικῆς δι᾽
194 ὤτων ἐγείρει τὰς ἀκαθέκτους ἐπιθυμίας; ἐν γὰρ

[1] Perhaps, as Tischendorf, καθάπερ ⟨εἶπον⟩.

[a] *Cf*. i. 186.

is vanquished by the greed for inequality. Both 191
these wars work destruction on the face of the earth.
The enemy cut down the fruit-trees, ravage the
country, set fire to the foodstuffs and the ripening ears
of corn in the open fields, while the forces of nature
use drought, rainstorms, violent moisture-laden winds,
scorching sun-rays, intense cold accompanied by
snow, with the regular harmonious alternations of
the yearly seasons turned into disharmony, a state
of things in my opinion due to the impiety which does
not gain a gradual hold but comes rushing with the
force of a torrent among those whom these things
befall. And therefore the law instituted this feast 192
figured by that instrument of war the trumpet, which
gives it its name, to be as a thank-offering to God the
peace-maker and peace-keeper, Who destroys faction
both in cities and in the various parts of the universe
and creates plenty and fertility and abundance of
other good things and leaves the havoc of fruits without a single spark to be rekindled.

XXXII. The next feast held after the "Trumpets" 193
is the Fast.[a] Perhaps some of the perversely minded
who are not ashamed to censure things excellent will
say, What sort of a feast is this in which there are no
gatherings to eat and drink, no company of entertainers or entertained, no copious supply of strong
drink nor tables sumptuously furnished, nor a generous display of all the accompaniments of a public
banquet, nor again the merriment and revelry with
frolic and drollery, nor dancing to the sound of flute
and harp and timbrels and cymbals, and the other
instruments of the debilitated and invertebrate kind
of music which through the channel of the ears
awaken the unruly lusts? For it is in these and 194

τούτοις καὶ διὰ τούτων, ὡς ἔοικε, τὸ εὐφραίνεσθαι
τίθενται ἀγνοίᾳ τῆς πρὸς ἀλήθειαν εὐφροσύνης· ἣν
ὀξυδερκεστάτοις ὄμμασιν ἰδὼν ὁ πάνσοφος Μωυσῆς
τὴν νηστείαν ἑορτὴν ἀνεῖπε καὶ ἑορτῶν τὴν
μεγίστην πατρίῳ γλώττῃ "σάββατα σαββάτων"
αὐτὴν ὀνομάσας, ὡς δ' ἂν Ἕλληνες εἴποιεν, ἑβδομάδα ἑβδομάδων καὶ ἁγίων ἁγιωτέραν, διὰ πολλά·
195 πρῶτον μὲν ⟨δι'⟩ ἐγκράτειαν, ἣν ἀεὶ
καὶ πανταχοῦ παραγγέλλων ἐν ἅπασι τοῖς κατὰ
βίον ἐπιδείκνυσθαι πράγμασι διά τε γλώττης καὶ
γαστρὸς καὶ τῶν μετὰ γαστέρα νυνὶ δὲ διαφερόντως
κελεύει περιέπειν, ἐξαίρετον ἡμέραν ἀναθεὶς αὐτῇ·
σιτίων γάρ τις καὶ ποτῶν μαθὼν ἀλογεῖν τῶν
οὕτως ἀναγκαίων τίνος οὐκ ἂν ὑπερίδοι τῶν περιττῶν, ἃ γέγονεν οὐ διαμονῆς καὶ σωτηρίας ἕνεκα
196 μᾶλλον ἢ βλαβερωτάτης ἡδονῆς; δεύτερον δὲ ἐπειδὴ πᾶσα ἀνάκειται λιταῖς καὶ ἱκεσίαις,
περὶ μηδὲν ἕτερον ἄχρις ἑσπέρας ἐξ ἑωθινοῦ τῶν
ἀνθρώπων σχολὴν ἀγόντων ἢ δεητικωτάτας εὐχάς,
αἷς σπουδάζουσι τὸν θεὸν ἐξευμενίζεσθαι παραίτησιν
ἁμαρτημάτων ἑκουσίων τε καὶ ἀκουσίων αἰτού-
μενοι καὶ χρηστὰ ἐλπίζοντες, οὐ δι' ἑαυτοὺς ἀλλὰ
διὰ τὴν ἵλεω φύσιν τοῦ συγγνώμην πρὸ κολάσεως
197 ὁρίζοντος. τρίτον δὲ διὰ τὸν καιρόν, ἐν
ᾧ συμβέβηκε τὴν νηστείαν ἄγεσθαι· κατὰ γὰρ
τοῦτον ἤδη συγκεκόμισται πάντα ὅσα δι' ἔτους
ἤνεγκεν ἡ γῆ. τὸ μὲν οὖν εὐθὺς ἐμφορεῖσθαι τῶν
γεγονότων ἀπληστίας ὑπέλαβεν ἔργον εἶναι, τὸ δὲ
νηστεῦσαι καὶ τροφῆς μὴ προσάψασθαι παντελοῦς

---

[a] So LXX, in Lev. xvi. 31 and xxiii. 32. In E.V. "a sabbath of solemn rest."

through these that men, in their ignorance of what true merriment is, consider that the merriment of a feast is to be found. This the clear-seeing eyes of Moses the ever wise discerned and therefore he called the fast a feast, the greatest of the feasts, in his native tongue a Sabbath of Sabbaths,[a] or as the Greeks would say, a seven of sevens, a holier than the holy. He gave it this name for many reasons.

First, because of the self-restraint which it entails; 195
always and everywhere indeed he exhorted them to shew this in all the affairs of life, in controlling the tongue and the belly and the organs below the belly, but on this occasion especially he bids them do honour to it by dedicating thereto a particular day. To one who has learnt to disregard food and drink which are absolutely necessary, are there any among the superfluities of life which he can fail to despise, things which exist to promote not so much preservation and permanence of life as pleasure with all its powers of mischief? Secondly, because 196
the holy-day is entirely devoted to prayers and supplications, and men from morn to eve employ their leisure in nothing else but offering petitions of humble entreaty in which they seek earnestly to propitiate God and ask for remission of their sins, voluntary and involuntary, and entertain bright hopes looking not to their own merits but to the gracious nature of Him Who sets pardon before chastisement.

Thirdly, because of the time at which the celebration 197
of the fast occurs, namely, that when all the annual fruits of the earth have been gathered in. To eat and drink of these without delay would, he held, shew gluttony, but to fast and refrain from taking them as food shews the perfect piety which teaches

εὐσεβείας, ἥτις ἀναδιδάσκει τὴν διάνοιαν μὴ πε-
ποιθέναι τοῖς εὐτρεπισθεῖσι καὶ παρεσκευασμένοις
ὡς ὑγείας ἢ ζωῆς αἰτίοις· ταῦτα γὰρ καὶ παρόντα
198 πολλάκις ἔβλαψε καὶ μὴ παρόντα ὤνησε. μόνον
οὐκ ἄντικρυς, κἂν μηδὲν τῇ φωνῇ φθέγγωνται τὸ
παράπαν, οἱ μετὰ τὴν συγκομιδὴν τῶν καρπῶν
ἀπεχόμενοι σιτίων καὶ ποτῶν ἐκβοῶσι ταῖς ψυχαῖς
καί φασι ταῦτα· τὰς μὲν τῆς φύσεως χάριτας
εἰλήφαμεν ἄσμενοι καὶ ταμιευόμεθα, φθαρτὸν δὲ
οὐδὲν ἐπιγραφόμεθά ποτε τῆς ἡμετέρας διαμονῆς
αἴτιον, ἀλλὰ τὸν γεννητὴν καὶ πατέρα καὶ σωτῆρα
τοῦ τε κόσμου καὶ τῶν ἐν κόσμῳ θεόν, ᾧ καὶ διὰ
τούτων καὶ ἄνευ τούτων τρέφειν θέμις καὶ δια-
199 φυλάττειν. ἰδοὺ γοῦν καὶ τοὺς ἡμετέρους προγόνους μυριάσι πολλαῖς ἐρήμην ἀτριβῆ καὶ πᾶσαν
ἄγονον διεξιόντας γενεᾶς βίον ἔτη τεσσαράκοντα
[297] | διέθρεψεν ὡς ἐν βαθυγειοτάτῃ καὶ εὐφορωτάτῃ
χώρᾳ, πηγὰς μὲν τότε πρῶτον ἀνατεμὼν εἰς
ἄφθονον ποτοῦ χρῆσιν, ὕων δὲ τροφὴν ἐξ οὐρανοῦ
μήτε πλείονα μήτ᾽ ἐλάττονα τῆς διεξαρκούσης εἰς
ἑκάστην ἡμέραν, ἵνα ἀταμιεύτοις χρώμενοι τοῖς
ἀναγκαίοις μὴ πωλῶσιν ἀψύχων, ὧν ἂν ἐθησαυρί-
σαντο, τὰς ἀγαθὰς ἐλπίδας, ἀλλὰ μικρὰ φροντίζοντες τῶν χορηγουμένων τὸν χορηγὸν θαυμάζωσι
καὶ προσκυνῶσι καὶ τοῖς ἁρμόττουσιν ὕμνοις καὶ
200 εὐδαιμονισμοῖς γεραίρωσιν. ἡ δὲ ἡμέρα
τῆς νηστείας ἄγεται νόμου προστάξει δεκάτῃ
μηνὸς ἀεί. διὰ τί δὲ ἐν τῇ δεκάτῃ; ὡς ἐν τοῖς
περὶ αὐτῆς λόγοις ἠκριβώσαμεν, ὀνομάζεται μὲν

---

[a] By θέμις is meant, perhaps, that it is in accordance with the law of His being. But the application of the word to

the mind not to put trust in what stands ready prepared before us as though it were the source of health and life. For often its presence proves injurious and its absence beneficial. Those who abstain from food 198
and drink after the ingathering of the fruits cry aloud to us with their souls, and though their voices utter no sound, their language could hardly be plainer. They say, "We have gladly received and are storing the boons of nature, yet we do not ascribe our preservation to any corruptible thing, but to God the Parent and Father and Saviour of the world and all that is therein, Who has the power and the right[a] to nourish and sustain us by means of these or without these. See, for example, how the many thousands 199
of our forefathers as they traversed the trackless and all-barren desert, were for forty years, the life of a generation, nourished by Him as in a land of richest and most fertile soil; how He opened fountains unknown before to give them abundance of drink for their use; how He rained food from heaven, neither more nor less than what sufficed for each day, that they might consume what they needed without hoarding, nor barter for the prospect of soulless stores[b] their hopes of His goodness, but taking little thought of the bounties received rather reverence and worship the bountiful Giver and honour Him with the hymns and benedictions that are His due." By order of the law the 200
fast is held on the tenth day. Why on the tenth? As has been shewn in our detailed discussion of that

God is strange, and I do not know of any exact parallel. οὐ θέμις, as in Plato, *Ap.* 21 B οὐ γὰρ δήπου ψεύδεταί γε· οὐ γὰρ θέμις αὐτῷ, is not quite the same.

[b] Lit. "the lifeless things which they would have stored."

ὑπὸ σοφῶν ἀνδρῶν παντέλεια, περιέχει δ' ἐν αὐτῇ τὰς ἀναλογίας πάσας, τήν τε ἀριθμητικὴν καὶ τὴν ἁρμονικὴν καὶ τὴν γεωμετρικήν, καὶ προσέτι τὰς ἁρμονίας, ἐπίτριτον τὴν διὰ τεσσάρων καὶ ἡμιόλιον τὴν διὰ πέντε καὶ διπλασίαν τὴν διὰ πασῶν καὶ τετραπλασίαν τὴν δὶς διὰ πασῶν, ἔχει δὲ καὶ τὸν ἐπόγδοον λόγον, ὡς εἶναι πλήρωμα τῶν κατὰ μουσικὴν θεωρημάτων τελειότατον, ἀφ' οὗ καὶ
201 ὠνόμασται παντέλεια. τὴν οὖν σιτίων καὶ ποτῶν ἔνδειαν προστέταχε κατ' ἀριθμὸν τέλειον καὶ πλήρη γίνεσθαι τῆς δεκάδος διὰ τὰς τοῦ ἀρίστου τῶν ἐν ἡμῖν ἀρίστας τροφάς, ἵνα μηδεὶς ὑπολάβῃ λιμὸν τὸ πάντων ἀφορητότατον κακῶν εἰσηγεῖσθαι τὸν ἱεροφάντην, ἀλλὰ τῆς εἰς τὰς τοῦ σώματος δεξαμενὰς φερομένης ἐπιρροῆς ἀνακοπὴν βραχεῖαν.
202 οὕτως γὰρ ἔμελλε διαυγὲς καὶ καθαρὸν τὸ ἀπὸ τῆς λογικῆς πηγῆς [εἰς καθαρὸν] ἐπὶ ψυχὴν φέρεσθαι νᾶμα λείως, ἐπειδήπερ αἱ συνεχεῖς καὶ ἐπάλληλοι τροφαὶ κατακλύζουσαι τὸ σῶμα καὶ τὸν λογισμὸν προσεπισύρουσιν, εἰ δ' ἐπισχεθεῖεν, εὖ μάλα στηριχθεὶς ὡς ἐπὶ ξηρᾶς ἀτραποῦ καὶ λεωφόρου τὴν πορείαν ἄπταιστον δυνήσεται ποιεῖσθαι τῶν
203 θέας καὶ ἀκοῆς ἀξίων ἐφιέμενος. ἄλλως τε ἁρμόττον ἦν, τῶν εἰς εὐθηνίαν ἁπάντων κατὰ νοῦν κεχωρηκότων ἐπὶ τελείοις καὶ πλήρεσιν ἀγαθοῖς, ἐν εὐετηρίᾳ καὶ χορηγιῶν ἀφθονίᾳ λαβεῖν ἐνδείας ὑπόμνησιν ἀποχῇ σιτίων καὶ ποτῶν καὶ λιτὰς καὶ ἱκεσίας ποιεῖσθαι, ἅμα μὲν ὑπὲρ τοῦ μὴ εἰς ἀληθῆ πεῖραν ἐλθεῖν ἀπορίας τῶν ἀναγκαίων, ἅμα δὲ κα

---

[a] *Cf. De Dec.* 20, 21. But the "detailed discussion" probably refers to a lost treatise on numbers. *Cf. Mos.* ii. 11 τῇ περὶ ἀριθμῶν πραγματείᾳ, and *De Op.* 52.

number,[a] it is called by the learned the all-perfect,
and embraces all the progressions, arithmetical, harmonic and geometrical, and further the harmonies,
the fourth, the fifth, the octave and the double
octave, representing respectively the ratios 4 : 3,
3 : 2, 2 : 1 and 4 : 1, and it also contains the ratio of
9 : 8, so that it sums up fully and perfectly the leading truths of musical science, and for this reason it has
received its name of the all-perfect. In ordaining 201
that this privation of food and drink should be based
on the full and perfect number 10, he intended to
prescribe the best possible form of nourishment for
the best part of us. He did not wish anyone to suppose that as their instructor in the mysteries he was
advocating starvation, the most intolerable of sufferings, but only a brief stoppage in the influx which
passes into the receptacles of the body. For this 202
would ensure that the stream from the fountain of
reason should flow pure and crystal-clear with smooth
course into the soul, because the constantly repeated
administrations of food which submerge the body
sweep the reason away as well, whereas if they are
checked, that same reason stoutly fortified can in
pursuit of all that is worth seeing and hearing make
its way without stumbling as upon a dry firm causeway. Besides, it was meet and right when every- 203
thing has shewn abundance as they would have it,
and they enjoy a full and perfect measure of goodness, that amid this prosperity and lavish supply of
boons, they should by abstaining from food and drink
remind themselves of what it is to want, and offer
prayers and supplications, on the one hand to ask
that they may never really experience the lack of
necessities, on the other to express their thankfulness

εὐχαριστοῦντας, ὅτι ἐν ἀγαθῶν περιουσίᾳ μέμνηνται κακῶν οὐ γενομένων. τούτων μὲν δὴ ἅλις.

204 XXXIII. Τελευταία δ' ἐστὶν ἑορτὴ τῶν ἐνιαυσίων προσαγορευομένη σκηναί, καιρὸν ἔχουσα τὸν μετοπωρινῆς ἰσημερίας· ἐξ οὗ δύο παρίσταται, τό τε δεῖν ἰσότητα τιμᾶν ἀνισότητα ἐχθραίνοντας—ἡ μὲν γὰρ δικαιοσύνης ἐστίν, ἡ δὲ ἀδικίας ἀρχή τε καὶ πηγή, καὶ ἡ μὲν ἀσκίου φωτός, ἡ δὲ σκότους συγγενής—καὶ τὸ προσήκειν μετὰ τὴν ἁπάντων καρπῶν τελείωσιν εὐχαριστεῖν τῷ τελεσφόρῳ θεῷ
205 καὶ πάντων τῶν ἀγαθῶν αἰτίῳ. τὸ γὰρ μετόπωρον, ὡς καὶ αὐτὸ δήπου δηλοῖ τοὔνομα, καιρὸς ὁ μετὰ τὴν ὀπώραν ἐστὶν ἤδη συγκεκομισμένην, καὶ φόρους τοὺς ἐτησίους καὶ δασμοὺς τοὺς ἀναγκαίους εἰσενηνοχότων ⟨τῶν⟩ σπαρτῶν τε καὶ τῶν δένδρων καὶ τῆς γῆς ὅσας[1] τροφὰς ἐγέννησε ταῖς τῶν ἀμυθήτων ζῴων ἰδέαις ἡμέρων τε καὶ ἀγρίων ἀφθόνως παρεσχημένης, οὐ μόνον εἰς τὴν ἐν χερσὶ καὶ πρόσκαιρον ἀπόλαυσιν ἀλλὰ καὶ τὴν ὕστερον διὰ τὸ προμηθὲς τῆς φιλοζῴου φύσεως.
206 καὶ μὴν ἐν σκηναῖς προστέτακται διαιτᾶσθαι τὸν χρόνον τῆς ἑορτῆς, ἤτοι διὰ τὸ μηκέτι εἶναι χρεία[ι] ἐν ὑπαίθρῳ διάγειν τὰ περὶ γεωργίαν ἐκπονοῦντας, οὐδενὸς μὲν ὑπολειφθέντος ἔξω, πάντων δὲ καρπῶν ἐναποκειμένων σιροῖς καὶ τοιουτοτρόποις χωρίοις διὰ τὰς εἰωθυίας βλάβας παρακολουθεῖν ἔκ τε
207 φλογώσεως ἡλιακῆς καὶ φορᾶς ὑετῶν—ὅτε μὲν γὰρ ἐν πεδίοις ἐστὶ τὰ τρέφοντα, μὴ συγκλεισά-

[1] MS. ὅσα.

because in such wealth of blessings they remember the ills they have been spared. Enough on this matter.

XXXIII. The last of the annual feasts, called 204
Tabernacles, recurs at the autumn equinox.[a] From this we may draw two morals. The first is, that we should honour equality and hate inequality, for the former is the source and fountain of justice, the latter of injustice. The former is akin to open sunlight, the latter to darkness. The second moral is, that after all the fruits are made perfect, it is our duty to thank God Who brought them to perfection and is the source of all good things. For autumn, or after- 205
fruitage, is, as also the name clearly implies, the season after the ripe fruit has been gathered in, when the sown crops and the fruit-trees have paid their annual toll and bounden tribute, and the land has richly provided all that it yields for the sustenance of the various kinds of animals without number, both tame and wild, sustenance not only to be enjoyed on the spot and for the moment, but also in the future, through the foresight of nature, the friend of all that lives. Further, the people are commanded, during 206
the time of the feast, to dwell in tents.[b] The reason of this may be that the labour of the husbandmen no longer requires that they should live in the open air, as nothing is now left unprotected but all the fruits are stored in silos or similar places to escape the damage which often ensues through the blazing sunshine or storms of rain. For when the crops which 207
feed us are standing in the open field, you can only watch and guard the food so necessary to you, by

[a] *Cf.* i. 189.
[b] See Lev. xxiii. 40-43.

μενος θαλαμαίου γυναικὸς τρόπον ἀλλὰ προελθὼν ἐπιμελητὴς καὶ φύλαξ εἶ σὺ τῶν ἀναγκαίων· κἂν ὑπαιθρίῳ διατελοῦντί σοι προσπίπτῃ κρυμὸς καὶ θάλπος, εἰσὶν ἔφεδροι ⟨καὶ⟩ σκιαὶ τὰ λάσια τῶν δένδρων, οἷς ὑποστείλας τὴν ἀφ' ἑκατέρου δυνήσῃ βλάβην εὐμαρῶς ἐκφυγεῖν· ὅταν δ' οἱ καρποὶ πάντες εἰσκομίζωνται, συνεισέρχου στεγανωτέρας διαίτης ἐφιξόμενος πρὸς ἀνάπαυλαν ἀντὶ καμάτων οὓς γεωπονῶν ὑπέμεινας· ἢ δι' ὑπόμνησιν τῆς τῶν προγόνων μακρᾶς ὁδοιπορίας, ἣν δι' ἐρήμου ποιούμενοι βαθείας σκηναῖς πολυετῆ
208 χρόνον καθ' ἕκαστον σταθμὸν ἐνδιῃτῶντο. προσήκει δὲ καὶ ἐν πλούτῳ πενίας μεμνῆσθαι καὶ ἀδοξίας ἐν δόξῃ καὶ ἐν ἡγεμονίαις ἰδιωτικοῦ σχήματος καὶ ἐν εἰρήνῃ κινδύνων τῶν ἐν πολέμῳ καὶ ἐπὶ γῆς χειμώνων τῶν κατὰ θάλασσαν καὶ ἐν πόλεσιν ἐρημίας· ἡδονὴ γὰρ οὐκ ἔστι μείζων ἢ ἐν ταῖς ἄγαν εὐπραγίαις ἔννοιαν ἔχειν παλαιῶν ἀτυχη-
209 μάτων. πρὸς δὲ τῇ ἡδονῇ καὶ ὄφελος οὐ μικρὸν εἰς ἀρετῆς ἄσκησιν ἐγγίνεται· λαβόντες γὰρ πρὸ ὀφθαλμῶν τό τε εὖ καὶ τὸ χεῖρον καὶ τὸ μὲν ἀπεωσμένοι καρπούμενοι δὲ τὸ ἄμεινον ἐξ ἀνάγκης εὐχάριστοι γίνονται τὸ ἦθος καὶ πρὸς εὐσέβειαν παρορμῶνται φόβῳ τῆς πρὸς τἀναντία μεταβολῆς. ὅθεν καὶ ἐπὶ τοῖς παροῦσιν ἀγαθοῖς τὸν θεὸν ᾠδαῖς καὶ λόγοις γεραίρουσι καὶ ὑπὲρ τοῦ μηκέτι πειραθῆναι κακῶν λιπαροῦσι καὶ ἱκεσίαις ἐξευμενί-
210 ζονται. πάλιν δὲ ἡ ταύτης τῆς ἑορτῆς ἀρχὴ πεντεκαιδεκάτῃ μηνὸς ἐνίσταται, διὰ τὴν

coming out and not shutting yourself up like a woman who never stirs outside her quarters. And if while you remain in the open air you encounter extreme cold or heat, you have the thick growth of the trees waiting to shade you, and sheltered under them you can easily escape injury from either source. But when all the fruits are being gathered in, come in yourself also to seek a more weatherproof mode of life and hope for rest in place of the toils which you endured when labouring on the land.

[a] Another reason may be, that it should remind us of the long journeyings of our forefathers in the depths of the desert, when at every halting-place they spent
many a year in tents. And indeed it is well in wealth 208
to remember your poverty, in distinction your insignificance, in high offices your position as a commoner, in peace your dangers in war, on land the storms on sea, in cities the life of loneliness. For there is no pleasure greater than in high prosperity
to call to mind old misfortunes. But besides giving 209
pleasure, it is a considerable help in the practice of virtue. For people who having had both good and ill before their eyes have rejected the ill and are enjoying the good, necessarily fall into a grateful frame of mind and are urged to piety by the fear of a change to the reverse, and also therefore in thankfulness for their present blessings they honour God with songs and words of praise and beseech Him and propitiate Him with supplications that they may never repeat
the experience of such evils. Again, the 210
beginning of this feast comes on the fifteenth day of the month for the same reason as was given when

[a] This is the reason assigned in Leviticus, *l.c.*

λεχθεῖσαν καὶ ἐπὶ τῆς ἐαρινῆς ὥρας αἰτίαν, ἵνα μὴ μεθ' ἡμέραν μόνον ἀλλὰ καὶ νύκτωρ πλήρης ὁ κόσμος ᾖ τοῦ φύσει παγκάλου φωτός, ἡλίου καὶ σελήνης κατ' ἐκείνην τὴν ἡμέραν ἀλλήλοις ἐπ-
[298] ανατελλόντων αὐγαῖς ἀδιαστάτοις, ἃς[1] | μεθόριον οὐ
211 διακρίνει σκότος. ἑπτὰ δὲ ἡμέραις ὀγδόην ἐπισφραγίζεται καλέσας " ἐξόδιον " αὐτήν, οὐκ ἐκείνης, ὡς ἔοικε, μόνον τῆς ἑορτῆς, ἀλλὰ καὶ πασῶν τῶν ἐτησίων, ὅσας κατηριθμησάμην καὶ διεξῆλθον· τελευταία γάρ ἐστι τοῦ ἐνιαυτοῦ καὶ
212 συμπέρασμα. τάχα μέντοι καὶ πρῶτος κύβος, ὀγδοάς, ἐπενεμήθη ⟨τῇ⟩ ἑορτῇ διὰ τόδε· τῆς μὲν δυνάμει στερεᾶς οὐσίας ἐστὶν ἀρχὴ κατὰ τὴν ἀπὸ τῶν ἀσωμάτων μετάβασιν, τῆς δὲ νοητῆς συμπέρασμα· τὰ δὲ νοητὰ ταῖς παραυξήσεσι πρὸς
213 τὴν στερεὰν φύσιν * * *.[2] καὶ ἡ μετοπωρινὴ μέντοι ἑορτή, καθάπερ εἶπον, πλήρωμά τι καὶ συμπέρασμα τῶν ἐντὸς ἐνιαυτοῦ πασῶν ἔοικεν

[1] MS. and Nicetas αἷς.
[2] For the missing verb Cohn suggests μεταβαίνει or πληροῦται.

---

[a] *i.e.* § 155.
[b] One would expect ἰσημερίας or the omission of ὥρας, in which case ἑορτῆς would be understood. And so Heinemann, " Frühlingsfest." But ὥρας may be justified perhaps on the ground that §§ 151 f. dealt rather with the spring as a whole than with the equinox in particular.
[c] See Lev. xxiii. 36, Num. xxix. 35. This is " the last day, the great day of the feast " in John vii. 37. The word ἐξόδιον is used both in Leviticus and Numbers ; E.V. " solemn assembly," but in R.V. marg. " closing festival."
[d] For the general idea *cf. De Op.* 98, where plane geometry (γεωμετρία) and solid geometry (στερεομετρία) are identified respectively with things incorporeal and corporeal, though the equation of ἀσώματα to νοητά is something of an extension.

we were speaking [a] of the season of spring,[b] namely that the glorious light which nature gives should fill the universe not only by day but also by night, because on that day the sun and moon rise in succession to each other with no interval between their shining, which is not divided by any borderland of darkness.
As a crown to the seven days he adds an eighth,[c] 211
which he calls the "closing," not meaning apparently that it is the closing of that feast only, but also of all the yearly feasts which I have enumerated and described. For it is the last in the year and forms
its conclusion. Perhaps also the number 212
eight, the first cubic number, was assigned to the feast for the following reason: it is the beginning of the higher category of solids, marking where we pass from the unsubstantial and bring to its conclusion the category of the conceptual which rises to the solid
in the scale of ascending powers.[d] And indeed the 213
autumn festival, being as I have said a sort of complement [e] and conclusion of all the feasts in the year,

By δυνάμει, represented in the translation by "higher," he means, perhaps, that solidity is gained by raising to a higher power in the mathematical sense = παραυξήσεσι below. But this technical use is generally, if not always, confined to the second power or square (as in § 177) and the meaning may be less technical = "in nature" or "value." παραυξήσεσι is taken by Heinemann to mean the increase from 7 to 8. My preference for the rendering given above rests on the use of the plural (unless this may be accounted for by the plural νοητά). As I understand it, 1 = the point, 2 = the line, 4 = the superficies, and 8 = the solid. So in *De Op.* 91, 93 and 94 παραυξηθείς and παραύξων are used of the processes by which 1 is raised by multiples of 2 to 64, and 3 to 729. See further App. p. 628.

[e] Here the word πλήρωμα, used in § 200 in the sense of sum or fullness, = that which fills up. For examples of both these senses see L. & S. revised.

εἶναι σταθερώτερον καὶ παγιώτερον, τὰς ἀπὸ τῆς χώρας προσόδους εἰληφότων ἤδη καὶ μηκέτ' ἐνδοιασμοῖς τοῖς περὶ φορᾶς καὶ ἀφορίας πλαζομένων καὶ δεδιότων· ἀνίδρυτοι γὰρ αἱ γεωπόνων φροντίδες, ἄχρις ἂν οἱ καρποὶ συγκομισθῶσι, διὰ τὰς ἐφέδρους ἀπὸ μυρίων ὅσων ἀνθρώπων τε καὶ θρεμμάτων ζημίας.

214 Ταῦτα ἐπὶ πλέον ἐμήκυνα διὰ τὴν ἱερὰν ἑβδόμην ἐπιδείξασθαι βουλόμενος, ὅτι πάσας τὰς ἐτησίους ἑορτὰς συμβέβηκεν ὡς ἂν ἀπογόνους ἑβδομάδος εἶναι μητρὸς λόγον ἐχούσης[1] * * *
ἀφροσύναι καὶ εὐφροσύναι, καὶ διότι ἐν πανηγύρεσι καὶ ἱλαρῷ βίῳ τέρψεις ἀμέτοχοι συννοίας καὶ κατηφείας συνίστανται σώματα καὶ ψυχὰς ἀναχέουσαι, τὰ μὲν[2] τῷ ἁβροδιαίτῳ, τὰς δὲ τῷ φιλοσοφεῖν.

215 XXXIV. Ἔστι δέ τις παρὰ ταύτας ἑορτὴ μὲν οὔ, ἑορτώδης δὲ[3] πανήγυρις, ἣν καλοῦσι "κάρταλον" ἀπὸ τοῦ συμβεβηκότος, ὡς μικρὸν ὕστερον ἀποδείξομεν. τὸ μὲν οὖν μὴ ἑορτῆς ἔχειν ἀξίωμα καὶ

[1] With λόγον ἐχούσης Nicetas's excerpts come to an end, and the rest of the treatise depends solely on M and does not appear in Mangey at all. For the lacuna Heinemann suggests something like the following: "<but it is prescribed that people should enjoy themselves at the feasts" (Lev. xxiii. 40 and elsewhere) "because> folly and joy <are irreconcilable opposites>." It is certainly quite possible that some lost clause or clauses ended up with <ἐναντία> ἀφροσύναι καὶ εὐφροσύναι (*cf.* the same antithesis in § 49), but the rest of Heinemann's suggestion does not seem to me suitable. Apart from these three words, which may have intruded through some now inexplicable accident, the whole section reads like a continuous apology for the length at which the fourth commandment is treated compared with the third and fifth, the defence being (1) the sanctity of seven (διὰ τὴν ἱερὰν ἑβδόμην); (2) the intrinsic value of the feasts (καὶ διότι ἐν . . .). If something has really been lost I should rather suppose

seems to have more stability and fixity, because the people have now received their returns from the land and are no longer perplexed and terrified by doubts as to its fertility or barrenness. For the anxious thoughts of the husbandman are never settled till the crops are gathered in, so numberless are the men and animals from whom they are liable to suffer harm.

All this long exposition is due to my regard for the 214
sacred seventh day, and my wish to shew that all the yearly feasts prove to be as it were the children of that number which stands as a mother . . . scenes of folly and joy . . . and because the festal assemblies and the cheerful life which they afford bring delights that are free from all anxiety and dejection, and spread exhilaration both in the body and in the soul, in the body by the comfortable way of living, in the soul by the study of philosophy.

XXXIV. [a] But besides these we have what is not a 215
feast, but is a general ceremony of a festal character called the Basket, a name which describes what takes place, as we shall shortly shew.[b] That it has not the prestige and standing of a feast is clear for many

[a] Here Cohn begins a fresh numeration of chapters. See Gen. Introd. p. xviii.

[b] See Deut. xxvi. 1-11. *Cf. De Som.* ii. 272.

---

that it continued μητρὸς λόγον ἐχούσης with "to those who feast" (or "to feasts conducted") "religiously, and not with folly, for folly and joy are incompatible." This certainly presupposes that Nicetas had the same corruption before him as we have, but I know no reason to the contrary.

[2] MS. τοῖς μὲν.

[3] MS. ἑορτὴ μὲν θεοῦ ἑορτῆς, which Cohn prints as <οὐχ> ἑορτὴ μὲν θεοῦ, ἑορτῆς δὲ <συγγενὴς>. The text adopted here is that suggested by Heinemann (partly from Holwerda). For ἑορτώδης *cf.* § 216.

τάξιν δῆλον ἐκ πολλῶν· οὔτε γὰρ τοῦ ἔθνους ἐστὶν ὡς πάνδημος, οἵα τῶν ἄλλων ἑκάστη, οὔτε τι τῶν προσαγομένων ἢ προσφερομένων ἐπὶ τὸν βωμὸν καθαγιάζεται παραδιδόμενον τῷ ἀσβέστῳ πυρὶ καὶ ἱερῷ, οὔθ' ἡμερῶν ἀριθμὸς ὃν χρὴ ⟨ταύτην⟩
216 ἑορτάζειν εἴρηται. XXXV. τὸ δ' ἑορτώδη τύπον ἔχειν καὶ ἐγγὺς ἵστασθαι[1] πανηγυρικῆς ἰδέας[2] εὐμαρῶς κατίδοι τις ἄν. ἕκαστος γὰρ τῶν ἀγροὺς καὶ κτήσεις ἐχόντων ἀφ' ἑκάστου τῶν ἀκροδρύων εἴδους ἀγγεῖα πληρώσας, καθάπερ ἔφην, ἃ προσαγορεύουσι καρτάλους, ἀπαρχὴν τῆς εὐκαρπίας εἰς τὸ ἱερὸν κομίζει γεγηθὼς καὶ στὰς ἀντικρὺ τοῦ βωμοῦ δίδωσι τῷ ἱερεῖ, τὸ πάγκαλον καὶ θαυμάσιον ᾆσμα διεξιών, εἰ δὲ μὴ τύχοι μεμνημένος, ἀκούων παρὰ τοῦ ἱερέως μετὰ προσοχῆς
217 πάσης. ἔστι δὲ τοιόνδε ᾆσμα· "Συρίαν ἀπέβαλον[3] οἱ ἀρχηγέται τοῦ γένους ἡμῶν καὶ μετανέστησαν εἰς Αἴγυπτον. ὀλίγος ὄντες ἀριθμὸς ηὐξήθησαν εἰς πλῆθος ἔθνους. οἱ ἀπόγονοι μυρία κακωθέντες ὑπὸ τῶν ἐγχωρίων, οὐδεμιᾶς ἔτι φαινομένης ἐξ ἀνθρώπων ἐπικουρίας, ἐγένοντο θεοῦ ἱκέται κατα-
218 φυγόντες ἐπὶ τὴν ἐξ αὐτοῦ βοήθειαν. προδεξάμενος τὴν ἱκεσίαν ὁ πᾶσι τοῖς ἀδικουμένοις εὐμενὴς τοὺς μὲν ἐπιτιθεμένους κατέπληξε σημείοις καὶ τέρασι καὶ φάσμασι καὶ τοῖς ἄλλοις ὅσα κατ' ἐκεῖνον τὸν χρόνον ἐθαυματουργεῖτο, τοὺς δ' ἐπηρεαζομένους καὶ πάσας ὑπομένοντας ἐπιβουλὰς ἐρρύσατο, οὐ μόνον εἰς ἐλευθερίαν ἐξελόμενος,

[1] MS. ἑστιᾶσθαι.
[2] MS. ἀδείας, which Cohn retains, though suggesting ἰδέας.

reasons. For it does not affect the nation as a united whole like each of the others, nor do we find any victim being brought or led to the altar and then sacrificed and given over to be consumed by the sacred and unquenchable fire, nor is there any specified number of days during which the feast is to last.
XXXV. But that it has a festal character and nearly 216
approaches the form of a general ceremony [a] can be easily seen. For every person who possesses farms or landed estates takes some of every kind of fruit and fills receptacles which, as I have said, are called baskets, and brings them with joy as a sample offering of his rich fruit-harvest, to the temple, and there standing opposite the altar, gives them to the priest. Meanwhile he recites this beautiful and admirable canticle, or if he does not remember it, he listens
with all attention while the priest repeats it. The 217
sense of this canticle is as follows : " The founders of our race abandoned Syria and migrated to Egypt and, though few in number, increased to a populous nation. Their descendants suffered wrongs without number from the inhabitants, and when no further assistance from men appeared forthcoming, became
suppliants of God and sought refuge in His help. He 218
Who is kindly to all the wronged accepted their supplication and confounded their assailants with signs and wonders and portents and all the other marvels that were wrought at that time, and saved the victims of outrage who were suffering all that malice could devise, and not only brought them forth

[a] Presumably because though there is no general assembly everybody has to do it at some time.

It is difficult to see what ἀδεία can mean in connexion with the ceremony here described. [3] MS. ἀπέβαλλον.

219 ἀλλὰ καὶ χώραν πάμφορον δούς. ἀπὸ τῶν ταύτης καρπῶν, εὐεργέτα, σοὶ φέρομεν τὴν ἀπαρχήν, εἰ δὴ θέμις εἰπεῖν ἐστι κομίζειν τὸν λαμβάνοντα· σαὶ γάρ, ὦ δέσποτα, χάριτες καὶ δωρεαὶ τὰ πάντα, ὧν ἀξιωθέντες ἐναβρυνόμεθα καὶ ἐνευφραινόμεθα τοῖς ἀπροσδοκήτοις ἀγαθοῖς, ἅπερ οὐκ ἐλπίσασιν
220 ἡμῖν ἔδωκας.'' XXXVI. τὸ ᾆσμα τοῦτο σχεδὸν ἀπὸ θέρους ἐνισταμένου μέχρι μετοπώρου λήγοντος ἀδιαστάτως ὑφ' ἑτέρων καὶ ἑτέρων ᾄδεται δυσὶ καιροῖς, ὁλοκλήρῳ μέρει ἡμίσει τοῦ ἐνιαυτοῦ, διὰ τὸ μὴ πάντας ἀθρόους κατὰ ῥητὴν προθεσμίαν τὰ ὡραῖα δύνασθαι κομίζειν, ἀλλ' ἄλλοτε ἄλλους, ἔστι δ' ὅτε καὶ τοὺς αὐτοὺς ἀπὸ τῶν αὐτῶν χωρίων.[1]
221 ἐπειδὴ γὰρ τῶν καρπῶν οἱ μὲν θᾶττον οἱ δὲ βραδύτερον πεπαίνονται, καὶ διὰ τὰς τῶν τόπων διαφορὰς ἀλεεινοτέρων ἢ κρυμωδεστέρων ὄντων καὶ διὰ μυρίας ἄλλας αἰτίας, εἰκότως ἀόριστός ἐστι καὶ ἀπερίγραφος ὁ χρόνος τῆς τῶν ἀκροδρύων ἀπαρχῆς
222 ἐπὶ μήκιστον ἐκτεινόμενος. ἡ δὲ τούτων χρῆσις ἐπιτέτραπται τοῖς ἱερεῦσιν, ἐπεὶ γῆς μὲν ἀποτομὴν οὐκ ἔλαχον οὐδὲ προσοδευομένας κτήσεις, κλῆροι δ' εἰσὶν αὐτοῖς αἱ παρὰ τοῦ ἔθνους ἀπαρχαὶ ἀντὶ τῶν λειτουργιῶν, ἃς μεθ' ἡμέραν καὶ νύκτωρ ὑπομένουσι.

223 XXXVII. Τοσαῦτα μὲν περὶ ἑβδομάδος καὶ τῶν εἰς αὐτὴν ἀναφερομένων ἔν τε ἡμέραις καὶ μησὶ καὶ ἐνιαυτοῖς καὶ περὶ ἑορτῶν, αἳ συγγένειαν ἔχουσι

[1] Cohn, followed by Heinemann, proposes either to strike out αὐτούς, or read κατὰ τοὺς αὐτοὺς <χρόνους τοὺς>. See note *a*.

[a] See note 1. The second of these suggestions, which is what Heinemann actually translates, seems to me quite

into freedom, but gave them a land fertile in every
way. Of the fruits of this land we present a sample 219
offering to Thee, our Benefactor, if indeed we may
speak of presenting that which we receive. For all
these things, good Master, are Thy boons and gifts,
and as Thou hast judged us worthy of them, we
take pride and delight in the unexpected blessings
which Thou hast given us beyond all our hopes." 220
XXXVI. This canticle is used continually by a
succession of worshippers from early summer to late
autumn, through the two seasons which constitute a
complete half of the year. For the whole population
cannot in a body bring the fruits of the season at a
fixed time, but must do so at different times, and this
may even be the case with the same persons coming
from the same places.[a] For since some of the fruits 221
ripen more quickly than others, both because of the
difference of the situation which may be warmer or
colder, and for a multitude of other reasons, naturally the time when this sample of the fruits is due
cannot be exactly defined or limited, but extends
over a very considerable period. These offerings 222
are assigned for the use of the priests, because they
have no territory allotted to them, nor property which
brings them income, and their heritage consists of
the offerings of the nation in return for the religious
duties imposed upon them by night and day.

XXXVII. I have now completed the discussion of 223
the number seven and of matters connected with days and months and years that have reference to that number, and also of the feasts which are associ-

pointless. I understand the text to mean that the same growers may find their fruits ripening at different times in different years. This of course in itself would prevent a fixed date for the ceremony.

πρὸς ἑβδομάδα, διεξῆλθον ἑπόμενος εἱρμῷ τῶν προκειμένων κεφαλαίων κατὰ τὴν ἐν λόγοις ἀκολουθίαν. ἐπισκέψομαι δ' ἑξῆς τὸ ἑπόμενον, ὃ περὶ γονέων ἀναγέγραπται τιμῆς.

224 XXXVIII. Τέτταρα εἴδη πρότερον ὑπειπών, ἃ καὶ τῇ τάξει καὶ τῇ δυνάμει πρῶτα ἦν ὡς ἀληθῶς, τό τε περὶ μοναρχίας ᾗ μοναρχεῖται ὁ κόσμος, καὶ τὸ περὶ τοῦ μηδὲν ἀπεικόνισμα καὶ μίμημα δημιουργεῖν θεοῦ, καὶ τὸ περὶ τοῦ μὴ ψευδορκεῖν ἢ συνόλως μάτην ὀμνύναι, καὶ τὸ περὶ τῆς ἱερᾶς ἑβδόμης, ἅπερ σύμπαντα τείνει πρὸς εὐσέβειαν καὶ ὁσιότητα, μέτειμι ἐπὶ τὸ πέμπτον τὸ περὶ γονέων τιμῆς, ὅ, καθάπερ ἐν τοῖς ἰδίᾳ περὶ αὐτοῦ λόγοις
225 ἔδειξα, μεθόριον ἀνθρωπείων τε καὶ θείων. οἱ γὰρ γονεῖς μεταξὺ θείας καὶ ἀνθρωπίνης φύσεώς εἰσι μετέχοντες ἀμφοῖν· ἀνθρωπίνης μέν, ὡς ἔστι δῆλον, ὅτι καὶ γεγόνασι καὶ φθαρήσονται, θείας δ' ὅτι γεγεννήκασι καὶ τὰ μὴ ὄντα εἰς τὸ εἶναι παρήγαγον· ὅπερ γάρ, οἶμαι, θεὸς πρὸς κόσμον, τοῦτο πρὸς τέκνα γονεῖς, ἐπειδὴ ὡς ἐκεῖνος τῷ μὴ ὑπάρχοντι ὕπαρξιν κατειργάσατο, καὶ οὗτοι μιμούμενοι καθ' ὅσον οἷόν τε τὴν ἐκείνου δύναμιν τὸ γένος ἀθανα-
226 τίζουσιν. XXXIX. ἄξιοι δ' οὐ διὰ τοῦτο μόνον τιμῆς πατήρ τε καὶ μήτηρ, ἀλλὰ καὶ δι' ἕτερα πλείω. παρ' οἷς γὰρ λόγος ἀρετῆς ἐστί, πρεσβύτεροι νεωτέρων προκρίνονται καὶ διδάσκαλοι γνωρίμων καὶ εὐεργέται τῶν εὖ πεπονθότων καὶ ἄρχοντες
227 ὑπηκόων καὶ δεσπόται δούλων. ἐν μὲν οὖν τῇ ἀμείνονι τάξει κρίνονται γονεῖς, πρεσβύτεροι γὰρ

[a] Here begins the fifth commandment. Again a fresh numeration of chapters in Cohn.
[b] *i.e. De Dec.* 106-120.

ated with it. In this I have followed the order of the principal heads set before us as the sequence of the subjects demanded. I now proceed to the next head, in which we find recorded a statement of the honour due to parents.

XXXVIII. [a]In my previous remarks I have sketched 224
the four divisions which both in order and importance stand undoubtedly first. They comprise the assertion of the absolute sovereignty by which the universe is governed, the prohibition against making any image or likeness of God and against perjury or vain swearing in general and the doctrine of the sacred seventh day, all of them tending to promote piety and religion. I now proceed to the fifth, which states the duty of honouring parents, a matter which, as I have shewn in the discussion devoted to this in particular,[b] stands on the border-line between the human and the divine. For parents are midway between 225
the natures of God and man, and partake of both; the human obviously because they have been born and will perish, the divine because they have brought others to the birth and have raised not-being into being. Parents, in my opinion, are to their children what God is to the world, since just as He achieved existence for the non-existent, so they in imitation of His power, as far as they are capable, immortalize the race. XXXIX. And a father and mother de- 226
serve honour, not only on this account, but for many other reasons. For in the judgement of those who take account of virtue, seniors are placed above juniors, teachers above pupils, benefactors above beneficiaries, rulers above subjects, and masters above servants. Now parents are assigned a place 227
in the higher of these two orders, for they are seniors

εἰσι καὶ ὑφηγηταὶ καὶ εὐεργέται καὶ ἄρχοντες καὶ δεσπόται, ἐν δὲ τῇ ἐλάττονι υἱοὶ καὶ θυγατέρες, νεώτεροι γὰρ καὶ μαθηταὶ καὶ εὖ πεπονθότες ὑπήκοοί τε καὶ δοῦλοι. ὡς δ' οὐδὲν τούτων κατέψευσται, δῆλον μὲν ἐκ τῆς ἐναργείας[1]· αἱ δ' ἐκ λόγου πίστεις ἔτι μᾶλλον ἐπισφραγιοῦνται
228 τὴν ἀλήθειαν. XL. λέγω τοίνυν, ὅτι τὸ ποιοῦν τοῦ γινομένου καὶ τὸ αἴτιον οὗπέρ ἐστιν αἴτιον ἀεὶ πρεσβύτερόν ἐστιν· οἱ δὲ γεννήσαντες αἴτιοι καὶ δημιουργοὶ τρόπον τινὰ τῶν γεννηθέντων εἰσί· καὶ οἱ μὲν ὑφηγητῶν ἔχουσι τάξιν, ὅσαπερ ἂν εἰδότες τυγχάνωσι τοὺς παῖδας ἐκ πρώτης ἀναδιδάξαντες ἡλικίας, καὶ οὐ μόνον τὰ περὶ τὰς ἐπιστήμας ἀσκοῦσι καὶ νεάζουσιν ἐναποματτόμενοι λογισμοὺς ἀκμάζουσι παίδων,[2] ἀλλὰ καὶ τὰ ἀναγκαιότατα τῶν πρὸς αἱρέσεις καὶ φυγάς, αἱρέσεις μὲν ἀρετῶν, φυγὰς δὲ κακιῶν καὶ τῶν
229 κατ' αὐτὰς ἐνεργειῶν. εὐεργέται μέντοι τίνες ἂν εἶεν μᾶλλον ἢ παίδων γονεῖς, οἳ καὶ μὴ ὄντας εἰργάσαντο[3] καὶ αὖθις τροφῆς ἠξίωσαν καὶ μετὰ ταῦτα παιδείας τῆς κατά τε σῶμα καὶ ψυχήν,
230 [καὶ] ἵνα μὴ μόνον ζῶσιν, ἀλλὰ καὶ εὖ ζῶσι; τὸ

[1] MS. ἐνεργείας.

[2] The text here is well-nigh hopeless, and Cohn's treatment of it in *Hermes*, 1908, p. 202, is unsatisfactory. He places ἀσκοῦσι καὶ νεάζουσιν in brackets (which I have removed) as glosses (surely odd glosses) to ἀκμάζουσι, and apparently takes the next words as = "impressing thoughts on those of the children who are in their prime" (so also Heinemann). But this use of ἀκμάζουσι παίδων for τοῖς ἀκμάζουσι τῶν παίδων, which he himself says is "scarcely correct," seems to me impossible. For a tentative suggestion see App. pp. 628-629.

[3] I suggest μὴ ὄντας <ὄντας> εἰργάσαντο. See note *b*.

and instructors and benefactors and rulers and masters: sons and daughters are placed in the lower order, for they are juniors and learners and recipients of benefits and subjects and servants.
That none of these statements is false is self-evident, but logical proofs will ratify their truth still further.
XL. I say, then, that the maker is always senior to the 228
thing made and the cause to its effect, and the begetters are in a sense the causes and the creators of what they beget. They are also in the position of instructors because they impart to their children from their earliest years everything that they themselves may happen to know, and give them instruction not only in the various branches of knowledge which they impress upon their young minds,[a] but also on the most essential questions of what to choose and avoid, namely, to choose virtues and avoid vices and the activities to which they lead.
Further, who could be more truly called benefactors 229
than parents in relation to their children? First, they have brought them out of non-existence;[b] then, again, they have held them entitled to nurture and later to education of body and soul, so that they may have not only life, but a good life. They have 230

[a] The translation does not do more than give the general sense. See note 2.

[b] Or "brought them out of non-existence into existence." See note 3. As the words stand in the text they should mean "made them to be non-existent," for ἐργάζομαι does not appear to be used absolutely = "create." On the other hand, ἐργάζεσθαί τινά τι = "to render a person something" (adjective) is a known construction used by Philo, *e.g. De Agr.* 58 τὸν λαὸν . . . φιλήδονον . . . ἐργάσηται, *cf. Quod Deus* 43, *De Sac.* 48. If corrected as suggested, the phrase "made non-existent persons existent" is quite parallel to τὰ μὴ ὄντα εἰς τὸ εἶναι παρήγαγον in § 225 and elsewhere.

μὲν οὖν σῶμα διὰ τῆς γυμναστικῆς καὶ ἀλειπτικῆς ὠφέλησαν εἰς εὐτονίαν τε καὶ εὐεξίαν σχέσεις τε καὶ κινήσεις εὐμαρεῖς, οὐκ ἄνευ ῥυθμοῦ καὶ τοῦ πρέποντος, τὴν δὲ ψυχὴν διά τε γραμμάτων καὶ ἀριθμῶν γεωμετρίας τε καὶ μουσικῆς καὶ τῆς συμπάσης φιλοσοφίας, ἣ τὸν νοῦν εἰσῳκισμένον θνητῷ σώματι μετέωρον αἴρουσα παραπέμπει μέχρις οὐρανοῦ καὶ τὰς ἐν αὐτῷ μακαρίας καὶ εὐδαίμονας φύσεις ἐπιδείκνυται, ζῆλον ἅμα καὶ πόθον ἐνεργαζομένη τῆς ἀτρέπτου καὶ ἐναρμονίου τάξεως, ἣν οὐδέποτε λείπουσι πειθόμεναι τῷ
231 ταξιάρχῳ. πρὸς δὲ ταῖς εὐεργεσίαις καὶ τὴν ἐφ᾿ οἷς ἐγέννησαν ἀρχὴν ἔλαβον, οὐχ ὥσπερ ἐν ταῖς πόλεσι κατὰ κλῆρον ἢ χειροτονίαν, ὡς αἰτιᾶσθαι δύνασθαι τὸν μὲν ὀλίσθῳ τύχης γενόμενον, οὐ σὺν λογισμῷ, τὴν δὲ ὄχλου, πράγματος ἀνεξετάστου καὶ ἀνεπισκέπτου, φορᾷ, γνώμῃ δὲ ἀρίστῃ καὶ τελειοτάτῃ τῆς ἄνω φύσεως, ᾗ[1] καὶ τὰ θεῖα καὶ τὰ ἀνθρώπινα σὺν δίκῃ πρυτανεύεται.
232 XLI. διὰ τοῦτ᾿ ἔξεστι τοῖς πατράσι καὶ κακηγορεῖν[2] [πρὸς] τοὺς παῖδας καὶ ἐμβριθέστερον νουθετεῖν καί, εἰ μὴ ταῖς δι᾿ ἀκοῶν ἀπειλαῖς ὑπείκουσι, τύπτειν καὶ προπηλακίζειν καὶ καταδεῖν. ἂν μέντοι γε καὶ πρὸς ταῦτα ἀφηνιάζωσι τῇ ῥύμῃ τῆς ἀνιάτου μοχθηρίας ἀπαυχενίζοντες, ἐπέτρεψεν ὁ νόμος καὶ μέχρι θανάτου κολάζειν, ἀλλ᾿ οὐκέτι

[1] MS. ἡ. [2] MS. κατηγορεῖν.

---

[a] Including the lower instruction in reading and writing and the higher in literature, called respectively *γραμματιστική* and *γραμματική*, *De Cong.* 148.

[b] *i.e.* perhaps by setting them to degrading tasks. Heine-

benefited the body by means of the gymnasium and the training there given, through which it gains muscular vigour and good condition and the power to bear itself and move with an ease marked by gracefulness and elegance. They have done the same for the soul by means of letters[a] and arithmetic and geometry and music and philosophy as a whole which lifts on high the mind lodged within the mortal body and escorts it to the very heaven and shews it the blessed and happy beings that dwell therein, and creates in it an eager longing for the unswerving ever-harmonious order which they never forsake because they obey their captain and marshal.

But in addition to the benefits they 231
confer, parents have also received authority over their offspring. That authority is not obtained by lot nor voting as it is in the cities, where it may be alleged that the lot is due to a blunder of fortune in which reason has no place, and the voting to the impetuosity of the mob, always so reckless and devoid of circumspection, but is awarded by the most admirable and perfect judgement of nature above us which governs with justice things both human
and divine. XLI. And therefore fathers have the 232
right to upbraid their children and admonish them severely and if they do not submit to threats conveyed in words to beat and degrade them[b] and put them in bonds. And further if in the face of this they continue to rebel, and carried away by their incorrigible depravity refuse the yoke, the law permits the parents to extend the punishment to death, though here it requires more than the father alone or

mann aptly quotes Plato, *Laws* 866 E προπηλακισθέντες λόγοις ἢ καὶ ἀτίμοις ἔργοις.

μόνῳ πατρὶ ἢ μόνῃ μητρί, διὰ τὸ μέγεθος τῆς τιμωρίας, ἣν οὐκ ἄξιον ὑφ᾿ ἑνὸς ἀλλ᾿ ὑπ᾿ ἀμφοῖν δικασθῆναι· συμφρονῆσαι γὰρ οὐκ εἰκὸς ἐπ᾿ ἀναιρέσει τοῦ παιδὸς ἑκάτερον τῶν γονέων, μὴ βαρυνόντων καὶ καθελκόντων τῶν ἀδικημάτων ὁλκῇ τινι βεβαίῳ νικώσῃ τὴν ἐκ φύσεως ἐν-
233 ιδρυμένην πάγιον εὔνοιαν. ἀλλ᾿ οὐκ ἀρχὴν μόνον καὶ ἡγεμονίαν τὴν ἐπὶ τέκνοις ἀλλὰ καὶ δεσποτείαν γονεῖς ἔλαχον κατ᾿ ἄμφω τὰς ἀνωτάτω θεραπόντων κτήσεως ἰδέας, τήν τε ἐπ᾿ οἰκότριψι καὶ ἀργυρωνήτοις· πολυπλασίους τε γὰρ τῆς ἀξίας τιμὰς[1] κατατιθέασιν εἴς τε παῖδας καὶ ὑπὲρ παίδων τιτθαῖς καὶ παιδαγωγοῖς καὶ διδασκάλοις, δίχα τῶν εἰς ἐσθῆτας καὶ τροφὰς καὶ τὴν ἄλλην ἐπιμέλειαν ὑγιαινόντων τε καὶ καμνόντων ἐκ πρώτης ἡλικίας μέχρι τελείας· οἰκότριβές τε ἂν εἶεν οἱ μὴ μόνον οἴκοι γεννηθέντες ἀλλὰ καὶ [οἱ] ὑπὸ τῶν τῆς οἰκίας δεσποτῶν συνεισενεγκάντων τὰ πρὸς γένεσιν φύσεως θεσμοῖς εἰσφορὰν ἀναγκαίαν.

234 XLII. τοσούτων οὖν ὑπαρχόντων ἄξιον ⟨ἐπαίνου⟩ μὲν οὐδὲν δρῶσιν οἱ τιμῶντες ⟨τοὺς⟩ γονεῖς, ἐπεὶ καὶ ἕν τι τῶν εἰρημένων αὐταρκέστατον εἰς σεβασμὸν αὐτοὺς προκαλέσασθαι, ψόγου δὲ καὶ κατηγορίας καὶ τῆς ἀνωτάτω δίκης οἱ μήθ᾿ ὡς πρεσβυτέρους αἰδούμενοι μήθ᾿ ὡς ὑφηγητὰς ἀποδεχόμενοι μήθ᾿ ὡς εὐεργέτας ἀμοιβῆς ἀξιοῦντες μήθ᾿ ὡς ἄρχουσι πειθαρχοῦντες μήθ᾿ ὡς δεσπότας
235 εὐλαβούμενοι. πατέρα, οὖν φησι, μετὰ θεὸν καὶ

[1] MS. τιμῆς.

---

[a] See Deut. xxi. 18-21. Philo's language suggests a more independent action on the part of the parents than Deuteronomy. See App. p. 629.

the mother alone.[a] So great a penalty should be the sentence, not only of one of them but of both. For it is not to be expected that both the parents would agree to the execution of their son unless the weight of his offences depressed the scale strongly enough to overcome the affection which nature has firmly established in them.
233 But parents have not only been given the right of exercising authority over their children, but the power of a master corresponding to the two primary[b] forms under which servants are owned, one when they are home-bred, the other when they are purchased. For parents pay out a sum many times the value of a slave on their children and for them to nurses, tutors and teachers, apart from the cost of their clothes, food and superintendence in sickness and health from their earliest years until they are full grown. "Home-bred" too must they be who are not only born in the house but through the masters of the house, who have made the contribution enforced by the statutes of nature in giving them birth.[c]
234 XLII. With all these facts before them, they do not do anything deserving of praise who honour their parents, since any one of the considerations mentioned is in itself quite a sufficient call to shew reverence. And on the contrary, they deserve blame and obloquy and extreme punishment who do not respect them as seniors nor listen to them as instructors nor feel the duty of requiting them as benefactors nor obey them as rulers nor fear them as masters.
235 Honour therefore, he says, next to God thy father and thy mother,

[b] See on § 82.

[c] Does this imply that the *οἰκότριβες* were assessed in determining the *εἰσφορά*, as *ἀργυρώνητοι* naturally would be?

μητέρα τίμα δευτερείοις τοῖς γέρασιν ἀναδουμένους, ἅπερ ἡ φύσις ἀπένειμεν αὐτοῖς ἀθλοθετοῦσα. τιμήσεις δ' [ἐπ'] οὐδενὶ μᾶλλον ἢ πειρώμενος ἀγαθός τε εἶναι καὶ δοκεῖν εἶναι, ὧν τὸ μὲν τὴν ἄτυφον καὶ ἄπλαστον ἀρετὴν ἐπιζητεῖ, τὸ δὲ τὴν σὺν ὑπολήψει χρηστῇ καὶ τῷ παρὰ τῶν
236 συνόντων ἐπαίνῳ. μικρὰ γὰρ τῶν ἰδίων φροντίζοντες ὠφελειῶν τέλος εὐδαιμονίας νομίζουσι τὴν τῶν παίδων καλοκἀγαθίαν, δι' ἣν καὶ τοῖς προστασσομένοις θελήσουσιν ὑπακούειν ἐκεῖνοι καὶ ἐν ἅπασι καταπειθεῖς εἶναι τοῖς δικαίοις καὶ συμφέρουσιν· οὐδὲν γὰρ ἀλλότριον ἀρετῆς ὁ ταῖς ἀληθείαις[1] ὑφηγήσεται πατὴρ παιδί.

237 XLIII. Τεκμηριώσαιτο δ' ἄν τις τὴν πρὸς γονεῖς εὐσέβειαν οὐ μόνον ἐκ τῶν εἰρημένων, ἀλλὰ κἀκ τῆς πρὸς τοὺς ἥλικας ἐκείνων ἀποδοχῆς.[2] ὁ γὰρ πρεσβύτην καὶ πρεσβύτιδα οὐδὲν γένει προσήκοντας αἰδούμενος ἔοικέ πως ὑπομιμνήσκεσθαι πατρός τε καὶ μητρὸς καὶ ἀποβλέπων ὥσπερ εἰς ἀρχέτυπα
238 τεθηπέναι[3] τὰς εἰκόνας ἐκείνων. ὅθεν ἐν τοῖς ἱεροῖς γράμμασιν οὐ μόνον προεδρίας ἐξίστασθαι διείρηται νέους πρεσβύταις, ἀλλὰ καὶ παριοῦσιν ὑπανίστασθαι πολιὰν γήρως αἰδουμένους, εἰς ὅπερ ἐλπὶς ἀφ-
239 ικέσθαι τοὺς προνομίας τοῦτ' ἀξιοῦντας. παγκάλως δέ μοι κἀκεῖνο νενομοθετῆσθαι δοκεῖ· φησὶ γάρ· "ἕκαστος πατέρα τε ἑαυτοῦ καὶ μητέρα φοβείσθω,"

[1] Cohn suspects the wording and conjectures ὁ τῆς ἀληθείας <ἐρῶν>, but the form has already occurred and been accepted in i. 97 and *De Ios.* 38.

[2] MS. ἀποχῆς.

[3] MS. τεθεικέναι.

[a] See Lev. xix. 32, "Thou shalt rise up before the hoary head, and honour the face of the old man." The LXX has

who are crowned with a laurel of the second rank assigned to them by nature, the arbitress of the contest. And in no way wilt thou honour them as well as by trying both to be good and to seem good, to be good by seeking virtue simple and unfeigned, to seem good by seeking it accompanied by a reputation
for worth and the praise of those around you. For 236
parents have little thought for their own personal interests and find the consummation of happiness in the high excellence of their children, and to gain this the children will be willing to hearken to their commands and to obey them in everything that is just and profitable ; for the true father will give no instruction to his son that is foreign to virtue.

XLIII. But the proof of filial piety may be given 237
not only in the ways above mentioned, but also by courtesy shewn to persons who share the seniority of the parents. One who pays respect to an aged man or woman who is not of his kin may be regarded as having remembrance of his father and mother. He looks to them as prototypes and stands in awe of
those who bear their image. And therefore in the 238
Holy Scriptures the young are commanded not only to yield the chief seats to the aged but also to give place to them as they pass,[a] in reverence for the grey hairs that mark the age to which they may hope to
attain who judge it worthy of precedence. Admirable 239
too, as it seems to me, is that other ordinance where he says, "Let each fear his father and mother." [b]

ἀπὸ προσώπου πολιοῦ ἐξαναστήσῃ, which Philo might easily take to mean "rise up away from," *i.e.* make room for him. He need not be supposed to be claiming scriptural authority for yielding the chief seats, but mentions it as the universally accepted mark of respect.

[b] See Lev. xix. 3.

φόβον πρὸ εὐνοίας τιθείς, οὐχ ὡς πρὸς ἅπαν
ἄμεινον, ἀλλ' ὡς πρὸς τὸν παρόντα καιρὸν χρησι-
μώτερόν τε καὶ λυσιτελέστερον. πρῶτον μὲν γὰρ
τοῖς παιδευομένοις καὶ νουθετουμένοις ἄφροσιν
εἶναι συμβέβηκεν· ἀφροσύνη δ' οὐκ ἄλλῳ ἢ φόβῳ
θεραπεύεται· δεύτερον δ' ἁρμόττον οὐκ ἦν νομοθέτου παραγγέλμασι τοὺς παῖδας εὔνοιαν διδά-
σκεσθαι τὴν πρὸς γονεῖς, ἣν αὐτοκέλευστον ἡ
φύσις ἐξ ἔτι σπαργάνων [δὲ][1] ταῖς ψυχαῖς τῶν
240 οὕτως ἡνωμένων κατὰ γένος ἐνιδρύσατο. διὸ
φιλίαν μὲν τὴν πρὸς τοὺς γεννήσαντας ὡς αὐτομαθῆ
καὶ αὐτοδίδακτον καὶ προστάξεως οὐ δεομένην
ἀπέλιπε, φόβον δὲ προστάττει διὰ τοὺς εἰωθότας
ῥᾳθυμεῖν· ἐπειδὴ γὰρ γονεῖς παῖδας ὑπερβαλλούσῃ
χρώμενοι φιλοστοργίᾳ περιέπουσι καὶ πάντοθεν
ἐκπορίζοντες αὐτοῖς τἀγαθὰ χαρίζονται μηδένα
πόνον ἢ κίνδυνον ὑπερτιθέμενοι, δυνάμεσιν ὁλκοῖς
εὐνοίας[2] συνδεδεμένοι, τὸ λίαν φιλόστοργον αὐτῶν
οὐ δέχονταί τινες ἐπ' ὠφελείᾳ, τρυφὴν καὶ χλιδὴν
ἐζηλωκότες καὶ θαυμάζοντες μὲν τὸν ὑγρὸν βίον,
διαρρέοντες δὲ κατά τε σῶμα καὶ ψυχήν, καὶ
μηδὲν μέρος ἐῶντες ὀρθοῦσθαι ταῖς οἰκείαις δυνάμεσιν, ἃς ὑποσκελίζοντες καὶ ἐκνευρίζοντες οὐκ
ἐρυθριῶσιν ἕνεκα τοῦ μὴ δεδιέναι τοὺς σωφρο-
νιστὰς πατέρας καὶ μητέρας, ἐνδιδόντες καὶ
241 ἐπιχαλῶντες ταῖς ἰδίαις ἐπιθυμίαις. ἀλλὰ καὶ
τούτοις ἀναγκαῖον παραινεῖν, ὅπως εὐτονωτέραις
καὶ ἐμβριθεστέραις χρώμενοι νουθεσίαις θερα-
πεύσωσι τὸν τῶν παίδων ῥοῦν, καὶ τοῖς παισίν,

[1] MS. ἐξαιτεῖ σπαργάνων δὲ.
[2] MS. ὅρκοις εὐνοίαις.

Here he sets fear before affection, not as better in every way, but as more serviceable and profitable for the occasion which he has before him. For in the first place, persons subject to instruction and admonition are in fact wanting in sense, and want of sense is only cured by fear. Secondly, it would not be suitable to include in the enactments of a lawgiver an instruction on the duty of filial affection, for nature has implanted this as an imperative instinct from the very cradle in the souls of those who are thus united
by kinship.[a] And therefore he omitted any mention 240
of love for parents because it is learned and taught by instinct and requires no injunction, but did enjoin fear for the sake of those who are in the habit of neglecting their duty. For when parents cherish their children with extreme tenderness, providing them with good gifts from every quarter and shunning no toil or danger because they are fast bound to them by the magnetic forces of affection, there are some who do not receive this exceeding tenderheartedness in a way that profits them. They pursue eagerly luxury and voluptuousness, they applaud the dissolute life, they run to waste both in body and soul, and suffer no part of either to be kept erect by its proper faculties which they lay prostrate and paralyzed without a blush because they have never feared the censors they possess in their fathers and mothers
but give in to and indulge their own lusts. But these 241
parents also must be exhorted to employ more active and severe admonitions to cure the wastage of their children, and the children also that they may stand

[a] See App. p. 629.

ὅπως εὐλαβῶνται τοὺς γειναμένους[1] δεδιότες καὶ ὡς ἄρχοντας καὶ ὡς φύσει δεσπότας· μόλις γὰρ οὕτως ἀδικεῖν ὀκνήσουσι.

242 XLIV. Τὰ μὲν δὴ κατὰ τὴν προτέραν δέλτον πέντε κεφάλαια νόμων καὶ ὅσα τῶν κατὰ μέρος εἰς ἕκαστον ἐλάμβανε τὴν ἀναφορὰν διεξῆλθον. χρὴ δὲ καὶ τὰς ὁρισθείσας ἐπὶ τῇ τούτων παρα-
243 βάσει τιμωρίας δηλῶσαι. κοινὸς μὲν οὖν ἐστι κατὰ πάντων θάνατος, δι' ἣν[2] ἔχει τἀδικήματα πρὸς ἄλληλα συγγένειαν. αἰτίαι δὲ τῆς δίκης διάφοροι. ἀρκτέον δ' ἀπὸ τοῦ τελευταίου τοῦ πρὸς γονεῖς, ἐπειδὴ καὶ περὶ αὐτοῦ λόγος ἔναυλος. ἐάν, φησί, τις τυπτήσῃ πατέρα ἢ μητέρα, καταλευέσθω· πάνυ δικαίως· οὐ γὰρ θέμις ζῆν τῷ προπηλακίζοντι
244 τοὺς τοῦ ζῆν αἰτίους. ἀλλ' ἔνιοι τῶν εὐπαρύφων καὶ νομοθετῶν πρὸς δόξας ἀπιδόντες μᾶλλον ἢ τὴν ἀλήθειαν ἐκομψεύσαντο κατὰ πατροτυπτῶν ὁρίσαντες χειρῶν ἀποκοπήν, ὑπὲρ τοῦ παρὰ τοῖς εἰκαιοτέροις καὶ ἀνεξετάστοις εὐδοκιμῆσαι νομίζουσιν ἁρμόττον εἶναι τὰ μέρη οἷς ἐτύπτησαν τοὺς
245 γονεῖς ἀκρωτηριάζεσθαι. ἔστι δ' εὔηθες τοῖς ὑπηρετηκόσι πρὸ τῶν αἰτίων δυσχεραίνειν, τὴν γὰρ

[1] So Holwerda for MS. τοὺς γινομένους, for which Cohn conjectured τοὺς <τοῦ ζῆν αἰτίους> γενομένους.
[2] MS. δι' ὅν.

[a] See Ex. xxi. 15, "Let him be surely put to death" (LXX θανάτῳ θανατούσθω). Philo quotes it in *De Fuga* 83 with τελευτάτω. As stoning is the common form of execution in the Pentateuch and is definitely mentioned as the method to be used in the case of the disobedient son, the discrepancy is not remarkable.

in awe of those who begot them, fearing them both as rulers and masters. For only so, and that hardly, will they shrink from wrongdoing.

XLIV. I have now discussed the five heads of the 242
laws belonging to the first table, and all the particular enactments which may be classed under each of the five. But I must also state the penalties
decreed for transgression of them. The result of 243
the close affinity which the offences have to each other is that they all have a common punishment, namely, death, but there are different reasons for this punishment. We should begin with the last commandment, on the behaviour due to parents, since our discussion of it is fresh in our minds. He says "if anyone strikes his father or mother, let him be stoned."[a] This is quite just, for justice forbids that he should live who maltreats the authors of his
life. But some dignitaries and legislators who had 244
an eye to men's opinions rather than to truth, have decreed that striking a father should be punished by cutting off the hands, a specious refinement[b] due to their wish to win the approval of the more careless or thoughtless, who think that the parts with which the offenders have struck their parents should be
amputated.[c] But it is silly to visit displeasure on the 245
servants rather than on the actual authors, for the

[b] The common meaning of κομψεύω as applied to clever or subtle words and actions (Heinemann, "in spitzfindiger Weise"), *cf. De Mig.* 75, does not fit in well with the next words, which represent the practice as a concession to the thoughtless. The feeling expressed in it may be either that the officials disguise their real feelings or that the course adopted is less coarse and drastic than capital punishment, or perhaps a combination of both these.

[c] On the evidence for the existence of this law see App. pp. 629-630.

ὕβριν οὐ χεῖρες ἀλλὰ διὰ χειρῶν ὑβρισταὶ δρῶσιν, οὓς ἀναγκαῖον κολάζειν· εἰ μὴ καὶ τοὺς ἀνδροφονήσαντας ξίφει μεθετέον ὑπερόριον τὸ ξίφος ῥίψαντας, καὶ τοὐναντίον τοῖς ἀριστεύσασιν ἐν πολέμῳ τιμὰς οὐ δοτέον, ἀλλὰ ταῖς ἀψύχοις παν-
246 τευχίαις, δι' ὧν ἠνδραγαθίσαντο· μὴ καὶ τῶν ἐν γυμνικοῖς ἀγῶσι στάδιον ἢ δίαυλον ἢ δόλιχον νενικηκότων ἢ πυγμὴν ἢ παγκράτιον σκέλη καὶ χεῖρας αὐτὸ μόνον[1] ταινιοῦν ἐπιχειρήσουσιν ὅλα τὰ σώματα τῶν ἀθλητῶν παρέντες; γέλως μέντ' ἂν εἴη τὰ τοιαῦτ' εἰσηγεῖσθαι, ⟨τὰ⟩ ὧν οὐκ ἄνευ κολάζοντας ἢ τιμῶντας, δέον τοὺς αἰτίους· οὐδὲ γὰρ μουσικὴν ἐπιδεικνύμενόν τινα δι' αὐλῶν ἢ λύρας καὶ σφόδρα κατορθοῦντα παραμειψάμενοι τὰ
247 ὄργανα κηρυγμάτων καὶ τιμῶν ἀξιοῦμεν. τί οὖν ἔδει πατροτύπτας, ὦ γενναῖοι νομοθέται, χειροκοπεῖν; ἢ ἵνα πρὸς τῷ εἶναι μηδὲν χρήσιμοι τὸ παράπαν καὶ δασμὸν οὐκ ἐτήσιον ἀλλ' ἐφήμερον ἀναπράττωσι παρὰ τῶν ἠδικημένων τροφὰς ἀναγκαίας ἅτε πορίζειν ἀδυνατοῦντες; οὐ γὰρ σιδήρειος πατήρ ἐστί τις οὕτως, ὡς λιμῷ περιϊδεῖν θνῄσκοντα υἱόν, καὶ ταῦτα χρόνῳ τῆς ὀργῆς ἀμαυρουμένης.
248 κἂν μὴ ἐπενέγκῃ μέντοι χεῖρας, κακηγορῇ δ' οὓς χρέος ἀναγκαῖον εὐφημεῖν ἢ καὶ τρόπῳ ἑτέρῳ δρᾷ τι τῶν ἐπ' ἀτιμίᾳ γονέων, θνῃσκέτω· κοινὸς γὰρ

[1] MS. αὐτῶν μόνον.

---

[a] See Ex. xxi. 16 (17), Lev. xx. 9, E.V. "curseth," but R.V. margin "or revileth." In the latter half of the sentence he perhaps alludes to Deut. xxvii. 16, "Cursed be he that setteth light by (LXX ἀτιμάζων) his father or his mother."

outrage is not committed by the hands but by the persons who used their hands to commit it, and it is these persons who must be punished. Otherwise, when one man has killed another with a sword, we should cast the sword out of the land and let the murderer go free, and conversely, honour should be given, not to those who have distinguished themselves in war, but to the lifeless equipments and weapons which were the instruments of their exploits.
In the case of the victors in the athletic contests, 246
whether at the single or the double course or the long race or the boxing or the general contest, will they try to garland the legs and hands only and disregard the bodies of the athletes as a whole? It would surely be ridiculous to introduce such practices and give to the indispensable accompaniments the punishments or honours which should be given to the responsible persons. For similarly, in musical exhibitions, when anyone makes a highly successful performance on the flute or lyre, we do not pass him by and adjudge the laudatory announcements
and honours to the instruments. Why then, you 247
grand legislators, should we cut off the hands of those who strike a father? Or is your object that the offenders, besides being quite useless, may levy a tribute not annually, but daily, on those whom they have wronged, because they are unable to provide the sustenance they need. For no father is so ironhearted as to allow his son to starve to death, particularly as his anger grows faint as time goes on.
And even if while making no assault with his hands 248
he uses abusive language to those to whom good words are owed as a bounden duty, or in any other way does anything to dishonour his parents, let him die.[a] He

ἐχθρὸς καί, εἰ δεῖ τἀληθὲς εἰπεῖν, δήμιος ἁπάντων· ἐπεὶ[1] τίνι γένοιτ' ἂν εὐμενὴς ἄλλῳ ὁ μηδὲ τοῖς αἰτίοις τοῦ ζῆν, δι' οὓς εἰς γένεσιν ἦλθεν, ὧν ἐστι προσθήκη;

249 XLV. Πάλιν δ' ὁ τὴν ἱερὰν ἑβδόμην βέβηλον ἀποφήνας τὸ γ' ἐπ' αὐτὸν ἧκον μέρος ὑπόδικος ἔστω θανάτου. τοὐναντίον γὰρ τοῖς βεβήλοις καὶ πράγμασι καὶ σώμασι καθαρσίων εὐπορητέον εἰς τὴν ἀμείνω μεταβολήν, ἐπειδὴ "φθόνος," ὥς ἔφη τις, "ἔξω θείου χοροῦ βαίνει." τὸ δὲ τολμᾶν τὰ καθωσιωμένα παρακόπτειν καὶ παραχαράττειν ὑπερ-
250 βάλλουσαν ἀσέβειαν ἐμφαίνει. κατὰ τὴν παλαιὰν ἐκείνην ἐξ Αἰγύπτου μετανάστασιν ἡνίκα δι' ἐρήμης ἀτριβοῦς ἅπασα ἡ πληθὺς ὡδοιπόρει, γενομένης ἑβδόμης[2] αἱ μὲν τοσαῦται μυριάδες, ὅσας ἐδήλωσα πρότερον, ἐν ταῖς σκηναῖς κατὰ πολλὴν ἡσυχίαν διέτριβον, εἷς δ' οὐχὶ τῶν ἠμελημένων καὶ ἀφανῶν ὀλίγα φροντίσας τῶν διατεταγμένων καὶ χλευάσας τοὺς φυλάττοντας ἐξῄει μὲν ἐπὶ φρυ-
251 γανισμόν, ἔργῳ δ' εἰς παρανομίας ἐπίδειξιν. καὶ ὁ μὲν ὑπέστρεφεν ἀγκαλίδα ἀγαγών, οἱ δὲ τῶν

[1] MS. ἐπὶ. [2] MS. ἑβδομάδος.

---

[a] See Ex. xxxi. 14, 15.

[b] See note on *Quis Rerum* 242.

[c] Plato, *Phaedrus* 247 A, a quotation again made in *Quod Omnis Probus* 13, and with many echoes elsewhere, *e.g.* i. 320. See note on *De Fuga* 62.

[d] See Num. xv. 32-36. *Cf. Mos.* ii. 213 ff. [e] § 146.

[f] Heinemann, ignoring οὐχί, translates "one of the obscure and little esteemed," and adds in a note that Philo has inferred his insignificance either from his collecting firewood, or from the absence of any mention of his name. If this is not mere inadvertence, he must have considered that οὐχί should be expunged. But his explanations of the man's

is the common and indeed the national enemy of all. For who could find kindness from him who is not kind even to the authors of his life, through whom he has come into existence and to whom he is but a supplement?

XLV. Again, let him who has turned the sacred 249
seventh day into a profane thing, as far as lies in his power, be sentenced to death.[a] For on the contrary we ought to be rich in ways of purifying things profane, both material and immaterial,[b] to change them for the better, since, as it has been said, "envy has no place in the divine choir."[c] But to dare to debase and deface the stamp of things consecrated shews the utmost height of impiety. There is an incident 250
which occurred during the great migration from Egypt in ancient days while the whole multitude was journeying through the pathless wilderness.[d] The seventh day had come, and all those myriads, how numerous I have stated in an earlier place,[e] were staying very quietly in their tents, when a single person of a rank by no means mean or insignificant,[f] regardless of the orders given and mocking at those who maintained them, went out to gather firewood, but actually succeeded[g] in displaying his disobedience to the law. He returned bringing an armful, 251

insignificance are very unconvincing, and, as the MSS. of Philo do not shew as much tendency to insert negatives as they do to omit them, the text may stand, though I know of no explanation of Philo's statement that the offender was of high rank.

[g] Or "with the result that he displayed." This is perhaps an unusual meaning for *εἰς*. Heinemann gives "with the intention of shewing," but this would need *ἐξῄει λόγῳ μέν* rather than *ἐξῄει μέν*. He says that the same motive is suggested in § 213 of the parallel account, but misinterprets, I think, the sense of the phrase used there. See my note.

σκηνῶν ἐκχυθέντες,[1] καίτοι παρατεθηγμένοι, νεώτερον οὐδὲν ἕνεκα τοῦ περὶ τὴν ἡμέραν ἱεροπρεποῦς εἰργάσαντο, πρὸς δὲ τὸν ἄρχοντα ἀγαγόντες τὸ ἀσέβημα μηνύουσιν· ὁ δ' εἰς εἱρκτὴν ἀποθέμενος, ἐκπεσόντος λογίου καταλεύειν τὸν ἄνθρωπον, ἐκδίδωσι τοῖς πρῶτον θεασαμένοις εἰς ἀπώλειαν. ὡς γάρ, οἶμαι, πῦρ ἐναύειν[2] ἑβδόμαις οὐκ ἐπιτέτραπται—δι' ἣν πρόσθεν αἰτίαν εἶπον—, οὕτως οὐδὲ τὰ πυρὸς ἐκκαύματα συλλέγειν.

252 XLVI. Τοῖς μάρτυρα καλοῦσιν ἐπὶ μὴ ἀληθεῖ θεὸν ὥρισται δίκη θανάτου· προσηκόντως· οὐδὲ γὰρ ἄνθρωπος τῶν μετρίων ἀνέξεταί ποτε παρακληθεὶς συνεπιγράψασθαι ψεύδεσιν, ἀλλ' ἐχθρὸν ἄπιστον ὑπολαβεῖν ἄν μοι δοκεῖ τὸν εἰς ταῦτα
253 προτρέποντα. ὅθεν ῥητέον· τὸν ὀμνύντα μάτην ἐπ' ἀδίκῳ θεὸς ὁ τὴν φύσιν ἵλεως οὔποτε τῆς αἰτίας ἀπαλλάξει δυσκάθαρτον καὶ μιαρὸν ὄντα, κἂν διαφύγῃ τὰς ἀπ' ἀνθρώπων τιμωρίας. διαδράσεται δ' οὐδέποτε· μυρίοι γὰρ ἔφοροι, ζηλωταὶ νόμων, φύλακες τῶν πατρίων ἀκριβέστατοι, ⟨τοῖς⟩

[1] MS. ἐκκαυθέντες. [2] MS. ἐν δυοῖν.

---

[a] In the parallel account persons who have gone out to pray in the wilderness catch the Sabbath-breaker in the act. As Heinemann points out, we have in the two accounts two different answers to the question how they discovered the crime when they should have been staying in the tents.

[b] In Numbers "all the congregation."

[c] *i.e.* in § 65.

but the others, pouring out from the tents,[a] though greatly enraged refrained from violence on account of the sanctity of the day, but took him to the ruler and reported the impious deed. The ruler put him in custody, but when the divine pronouncement had been given out that he should be stoned, he surrendered him to those who had first seen him[b] to be done to death. For the prohibition against lighting a fire on the seventh day, the reason for which I have stated earlier,[c] applies equally, I presume, to collecting the means for kindling fire.

XLVI. For persons who call God to witness to an 252
untruth, death is the appointed punishment,[d] quite rightly. For not even a man, if he is of a decent sort, will tolerate an invitation to join in subscribing to an untruth, but would in my opinion regard anyone who urged him to this course as an enemy unfit to be trusted. And therefore we must declare that God, 253
though His nature is to be merciful, will never free from guilt him who swears falsely[e] to an injustice, a miscreant almost beyond possibility of purification, even if he evades the chastisements of men. And these he will never escape; for there are thousands who have their eyes upon him full of zeal for the laws, strictest guardians of the ancestral institutions,

[d] Philo has no scriptural authority for death as a punishment for breaking the third commandment, which he here confines to perjury, and indeed this was recognized in § 27. His argument, as appears in § 254, is that the sentence of death for the lighter shews that it must have been intended for the heavier offence.

[e] Not, I think, "lightly," "thoughtlessly," as Heinemann ("leichtfertig"). The sense of "falsely" is not uncommon in classical Greek. Philo uses μάτην to bring it into connexion with the ἐπὶ ματαίῳ of the commandment, and to suggest that perjury is included in "taking in vain."

ἐπὶ καταλύσει[1] τι δρῶσιν ἀμειλίκτως ἔχοντες· εἰ μὴ ἄρα ἐπὶ μὲν ἀτιμίᾳ πατρὸς ἢ μητρὸς φονᾶν[2] ἄξιον, ἐπὶ δ' ὀνόματι τῷ καὶ αὐτῆς εὐκλεεστέρῳ σεμνότητος ὑπ' ἀσεβῶν ἀτιμουμένῳ μετριώτερον
254 οἰστέον. ἀλλ' οὐχ οὕτως ἐστί τις ἀνόητος, ὡς ἕνεκα τῶν ἐλαττόνων κτείνων τοὺς αἰτίους ἐπὶ τοῖς μείζοσιν ἐᾶν· μεῖζον δ' ἀσέβημα τοῦ πρὸς γονεῖς κακηγορουμένους[3] καὶ ὑβριζομένους τὸ περὶ τὴν ἱερὰν πρόσρησιν θεοῦ γενόμενον ἐκ ψευδορκίας.
255 Εἰ δὲ ὁ μὴ προσηκόντως ὀμνὺς ὑπαίτιος, πόσης ἄξιος τιμωρίας ὁ τὸν ὄντως ὄντα θεὸν ἀρνούμενος καὶ τοὺς γεγονότας πρὸ τοῦ πεποιηκότος τιμῶν καὶ μὴ μόνον γῆν ἢ ὕδωρ ἢ ἀέρα ἢ πῦρ, τὰ στοιχεῖα τοῦ παντός, ἢ πάλιν ἥλιον καὶ σελήνην καὶ πλάνητας καὶ ἀπλανεῖς ἀστέρας ἢ τὸν σύμπαντα οὐρανόν τε καὶ κόσμον σέβειν ἀξιῶν, ἀλλὰ καὶ ὅσα θνητοὶ δημιουργοὶ κατεσκεύασαν ξύλα καὶ λίθους, ἅπερ
256 εἰς ἀνθρωποειδεῖς τύπους ἐμορφώθη; τοιγάρτοι καὶ αὐτὸς ἐξομοιούσθω τοῖς χειροκμήτοις· θέμις γὰρ μὴ μετέχειν ψυχῆς τὸν τὰ ἄψυχα τιμήσαντα, καὶ μάλιστα φοιτητὴν γενόμενον Μωυσέως, οὗ πολλάκις ἤκουσε λέγοντός τε καὶ προφητεύοντος τὰς ἱερωτάτας καὶ καταθέους ἐκείνας ὑφηγήσεις·

[1] MS. ἀκριβέστεροι ἐπὶ καταλεύσει. Cohn's emendation of καταλεύσει to καταλύσει, *sc.* τῶν πατρίων, is certain. For the rest he suggested ἀκριβέστατοι <ἐπὶ τοῖς> ἐπὶ καταλύσει. The form here adopted (see Grégoire, *Hermes*, 1909, p. 313), or possibly <τοῖς τῶν>, seems preferable.

[2] MS. φόνον.

[3] MS. κατηγορουμένους.

[a] Philo seems to take as his authority for the death sentence

merciless to those who do anything to subvert them. Otherwise we must suppose that while it is right to seek the death of one who dishonours a father or a mother, more moderation should be shewn when impious men dishonour the name which is more glorious than majesty itself. Yet none is so foolish 254
as to visit the lesser offences with death and spare those who are guilty of the greater; and the sacrilege involved in reviling or outraging parents is not so great as that committed by perjury against the sacred title of God.

But if he who swears a wrongful oath is guilty, how 255
great a punishment[a] does he deserve who denies the truly existing God and honours created beings before their Maker, and thinks fit to revere, not only earth or water or air or fire, the elements of the All, or again the sun and moon and planets and fixed stars, or the whole heaven and universe, but also the works of mortal craftsmen, stocks and stones, which they have fashioned into human shape? And there- 256
fore let him too himself be made like unto these works of men's hands. For it is right that he who honours lifeless things should have no part in life, especially if he has become a disciple of Moses and has often heard from his prophetic[b] lips those most holy and godly instruc-

on the breach of the first commandment Deut. xvii. 2-5, where the false gods are described in much the same way as here, and on breaches of the second Ps. cxv. 8, where instead of the A.V. "they that make them are like unto them" the LXX has ὅμοιοι γένοιντο, "may they become like."

[b] Lit. "both speaking and prophesying," meaning perhaps that though it is Moses speaking he is also God's spokesman, or that sometimes he speaks in his own person and sometimes as the spokesman. The words that follow, though primarily reproducing Ex. xxiii. 13, are, as "often" shews, intended to represent Moses' teaching elsewhere.

ὄνομα θεῶν ἑτέρων μήτε τῇ ψυχῇ παραδέξῃ εἰς ὑπόμνησιν μήτε φωνῇ διερμηνεύσῃς, ἀλλ' ἑκάτερον, νοῦν καὶ λόγον, μακρὰν τῶν ἄλλων διαζεύξας ἐπίστρεψον πρὸς τὸν πατέρα καὶ ποιητὴν τῶν ὅλων, ἵνα καὶ φρονῇς περὶ μοναρχίας τὰ ἄριστα καὶ κάλλιστα καὶ λέγῃς τὰ πρέποντα καὶ λυσιτελέστατα σαυτῷ τε καὶ τοῖς ἀκουσομένοις.

257 XLVII. Αἱ μὲν οὖν κατὰ τῶν παραβαινόντων τοὺς πέντε χρησμοὺς τιμωρίαι δεδήλωνται. τὰ δὲ προκείμενα τοῖς φυλάττουσιν αὐτοὺς ἆθλα, καὶ εἰ μὴ ῥηταῖς προστάξεσι μεμήνυκεν ὁ νόμος, ἀλλά
258 τοι δι' ὑπονοίας ἐμφαίνεται. τὸ μὲν οὖν μὴ νομίζειν θεοὺς ἑτέρους μηδὲ χειρόκμητα θεοπλαστεῖν μηδὲ ψευδορκεῖν ἑτέρου γέρως χρεῖον οὐκ ἔστιν· αὐτὸ γάρ, οἶμαι, τὸ ταῦτα ἐπιτηδεύειν ἄριστον καὶ τελεώτατόν ἐστι γέρας· ἐπὶ τίνι γὰρ δύναιτ' ἄν τις ἡσθῆναι μᾶλλον ἀληθείας ἐρῶν ἢ τῷ ἑνὶ προσκεῖσθαι θεῷ καὶ τῆς τούτου θεραπείας ἀδόλως
259 καὶ καθαρῶς περιέχεσθαι; καλῶ δὲ μάρτυρας, οὐχ οἵτινες θεραπεύουσι τῦφον, ἀλλὰ τοὺς ἀπλανῆ ζῆλον ἐζηλωκότας, παρ' οἷς ἀλήθεια τιμᾶται· φρονήσεώς τε γὰρ ἆθλον αὐτὴ ἡ φρόνησις καὶ δικαιοσύνη καὶ ἑκάστη τῶν ἄλλων ἀρετῶν ἑαυτῆς ἐστι γέρας. ἡ δ' ὥσπερ ἐν χορῷ καλλιστεύουσα καὶ κατάρχουσα πασῶν ὁσιότης[1] πολὺ πλέον ἐστὶν ἑαυτῆς καὶ ἀγώνισμα καὶ ἆθλον, παρέχουσα καὶ τοῖς χρωμένοις εὐδαιμονίαν καὶ τοῖς τούτων παισὶ καὶ ἐγγόνοις εὐπραγίας ἀναφαιρέτους.

260 XLVIII. πάλιν γε μὴν τοῖς τὴν ἱερὰν ἑβδόμην

[1] MS. ὁσιοτήτων.

[a] LXX, Ex. xxiii. 13, ἀναμνήσεσθε, E.V. "make no mention," which may have been intended by the Greek translator.

tions, " Do not admit the name of other gods into thy soul to remember it,[a] nor give expression to it with thy voice. Keep both thy mind and thy speech far apart from these others, and turn to the Father and Maker of all, that thy conceptions of His sole sovereignty may be the best and the noblest, and thy words such as are suitable and most profitable to
thyself and to them that shall hear thee." 257
XLVII. We have now explained the punishments inflicted on those who transgress the five oracles. But the guerdons awaiting those who keep them,
even if not stated by the law in actual words of the 258
injunctions, yet may be seen to underlie them. The refusal to acknowledge other gods, or to deify the works of men's hands, or to commit perjury, needs no other reward. For surely the practice of such abstinence is in itself the best and most perfect reward. For where can any lover of truth find greater pleasure than by devoting himself to the one God
and embracing his service in guilelessness and 259
purity? I call to witness not such as serve vanity but those who are inspired with a zeal which never goes astray, those among whom truth is honoured. For wisdom is itself the guerdon of wisdom, and justice and each of the other virtues is its own reward.[b] And much more is she, who as in a choir is the fairest and the queen of the dance—religion[c]—her own prize and guerdon, providing happiness to those who cherish her and to their children and children's
children blessings of welfare which can never be 260
taken from them. XLVIII. Again, the experience of those who keep the seventh day is that

[b] See App. p. 630.
[c] Or " holiness."

φυλάττουσι συμβαίνει περὶ δύο τὰ ἀναγκαιότατα
ὠφελεῖσθαι, σῶμα καὶ ψυχήν, τὸ μὲν ἀναπαύλαις
ἐκ τῶν συνεχῶν καὶ ἀτρύτων πόνων, τὴν δ'
ὑπολήψεσιν ἀρίσταις περὶ θεοῦ ὡς κοσμοποιοῦ καὶ
ἐπιμελουμένου ὧν ἐγέννησε· καὶ ⟨γὰρ⟩ τὰ σύμπαντα ἐτελεσφόρησεν ἑβδομάδι. δῆλον οὖν ἐκ
τούτων, ὅτι τὴν ἑβδόμην τιμῶν αὐτὸς εὑρίσκεται
261 τιμήν. ὁμοίως μέντοι καὶ ὁ τοὺς γονεῖς
ἀποδεχόμενος μὴ θηράσθω τι πλέον· εὑρήσει γὰρ
σκοπῶν ἐν αὐτῷ τῷ ἔργῳ τὸ ἆθλον. οὐ μὴν ἀλλ'
ἐπειδὴ τῶν προτέρων τεσσάρων κεφαλαίων, ἃ
θειοτέρας ἔλαχε μοίρας, ἔλαττον τοῦτ' ἐστὶ διὰ τὸ
θνητῶν ἐφάπτεσθαι, παρηγόρησεν εἰπών· "τίμα
πατέρα καὶ μητέρα, ἵνα εὖ σοι γένηται καὶ ἵνα
262 μακροχρόνιος γένῃ," δύο γέρα τιθείς· ἓν μὲν
μετουσίαν ἀρετῆς, τὸ γὰρ εὖ ἡ ἀρετὴ ἢ οὐκ ἄνευ
ἀρετῆς, ἕτερον δέ, εἰ δεῖ τἀληθὲς εἰπεῖν, ἀθανασίαν
διὰ πολυχρονίου ζωῆς καὶ βίου μακραίωνος, ὃν καὶ
μετὰ σώματος θρέψεις ψυχῇ κεκαθαρμένῃ τελείᾳ
καθάρσει βιῶν. ταῦτα μὲν οὖν ἀποχρώντως λέλεκται, τὰ δ' ἐν τῇ δευτέρᾳ δέλτῳ μετὰ ταῦτα
καιροῦ διδόντος ἐπισκεψόμεθα.

---

[a] For the same play on τιμή, "honour," and τιμή, "value," *cf. Quod Deus* 169 f.

[b] Or "when opportunity offers." See on iii. 6 (App.).

both body and soul are benefited in two most essential ways. The body is benefited by the recurrence of respite from continuous and wearisome toil, the soul by the excellent conceptions which it receives of God as the world-maker and guardian of what He has begotten. For He brought all things to their completion on the seventh day. These things shew clearly that he who gives due value [a] to the seventh day gains value [a] for himself. So too indeed he who 261
shews respect to his parents should not seek anything further, for if he look he will find his guerdon in the action itself. However, since this commandment, inasmuch as it is concerned with mortal things, is inferior to the first four heads whose province is nearer the divine, He gave encouragement with the words, "Honour thy father and thy mother, that it may be well with thee and that thy time may be long." Here He names two rewards : one is the pos- 262
session of virtue, for "well" is virtue or cannot exist without virtue, the other in very truth is salvation from death given by prolonged vitality and agelong life which thou wilt keep thriving even while in the body, if thou live with a soul purged clean of all impurity.

This part of the subject has now been sufficiently discussed. We will proceed in due season [b] to examine the contents of the second table.

INTRODUCTION TO *DE SPECIALIBUS LEGIBUS*, III

This treatise opens with an impassioned lamentation over the public business and troubles, which have debarred Philo in the past from his beloved studies, and an expression of his thankfulness that he now has some respite (1-5).

The Sixth (LXX) Commandment. We begin with some general thoughts on the need of continence even in marriage, and the gravity of the crime of adultery (7-11). Intercourse with a mother is mentioned with horror, and Philo traces to this practice the troubles rife among the Persians (12-19). But the law condemns no less marriage with a step-mother (20-21), with a sister (22-25), and forbids it with others less closely related, such as a wife's sister (26-28), and with an alien (29). It also strictly refuses to allow a woman who has been divorced and then married another to return to her first husband (31-31). There must be no intercourse during menstruation (32-33), and Philo himself disapproves of marriage with a woman known to be barren (34-36).

Graver matters are pederasty, popularly treated with a favour which Philo deplores (37-42), and bestiality which he illustrates with the story of Pasiphaë (48-50). A harlot, too, is worthy of death (51).

Speaking of adultery itself, he gives a full account of the test laid down in Numbers for the suspected wife (52-63). The penalties for rape or seduction of a widow or maiden are stated (64-71), and also for intercourse with a maiden betrothed to another (72-78), and for slander by a husband impugning the virginity of his bride (79-82).

The Seventh (LXX) Commandment. Murder is sacrilege and deserves the utmost penalty (83-85), and attempted murder is as bad (86-87). Murderers must not be allowed sanctuary in the temple (88-91). While unpremeditated homicide may be less heinous (92), no mercy must be shewn to poisoners (93-99), and with them may be classed magicians, though there is a higher magic (100-103). Returning to the subject of unpremeditated homicide, as in a sudden quarrel, he notes the law which enacted that if the sufferer did not die at once, his opponent would not suffer the extreme penalty (104-107). From the law as stated in the LXX, that a miscarriage caused by a blow was a capital crime if the child was fully formed (108-109), he draws the inference that the exposure of infants is murder, and inveighs very feelingly against the cruelty of the practice (110-119).

He then turns to the law which enables the involuntary homicide to fly to the "Cities of Refuge." He dwells on the hint given in Exodus, that the death of the man thus killed was divinely ordained, and suggests that these Levitical Cities were privileged because of the conduct of the Levites in slaughtering the calf-worshippers, which story he repeats at length (120-129). In connexion with this he discusses the meaning of the provision that the homicide must remain there till the death of the high priest (130-136).

Next we have laws dealing with cases where death is caused by a master beating a slave (137-143), or by a vicious bull left unguarded (144-146), or a pit left uncovered (147-148), or a roof left without a parapet (149).

The insistence of the law that murder must be punished with death is emphasized by the order that the body is to be prominently exhibited for a time (150-152).

No one is to suffer death as a substitute for the criminal, and here he enlarges on the cruelty shewn in attempts to extort taxes from the relatives of the debtors, and in laws which inflict death on the families of political offenders (153-168).

We now come to assaults not actually causing death. The decree in Deuteronomy that the woman who makes an indecent assault is to lose her hand gives rise to reflections on the modesty demanded of women (169-177), followed by an allegorical interpretation of the law (178-180). Punishment for violence must correspond with the crime (181-183). The law of "an eye for an eye" leads to a disquisition on sight as the channel of wisdom (184-191), and the eye as expressing the phases of the mind (192-194), though the law is modified in the case of a slave. Similarly "a tooth for a tooth" is justified by the indispensability of the teeth for maintaining life (195-204).

In conclusion he recurs to murder itself and argues that by holding contact with a corpse to cause uncleanness, the law shews its horror of the crime of taking life.

Γʹ

ΠΕΡΙ ΤΩΝ ΑΝΑΦΕΡΟΜΕΝΩΝ ΕΝ ΕΙΔΕΙ ΝΟΜΩΝ ΕΙΣ ΔΥΟ ΓΕΝΗ ΤΩΝ ΔΕΚΑ ΛΟΓΙΩΝ, ΤΟ ΕΚΤΟΝ ΚΑΙ ΤΟ ΕΒΔΟΜΟΝ, ΤΟ ΚΑΤΑ ΜΟΙΧΩΝ ΚΑΙ ΠΑΝΤΟΣ ΑΚΟΛΑΣΤΟΥ ΚΑΙ ΤΟ ΚΑΤΑ ΑΝΔΡΟΦΟΝΩΝ ΚΑΙ ΠΑΣΗΣ ΒΙΑΣ

1
[299] I. *Ἦν ποτε χρόνος, ὅτε φιλοσοφίᾳ σχολάζων καὶ θεωρίᾳ τοῦ κόσμου καὶ τῶν ἐν αὐτῷ τὸν καλὸν καὶ περιπόθητον καὶ μακάριον ὄντως νοῦν*[1] *ἐκαρπούμην, θείοις ἀεὶ λόγοις συγγινόμενος καὶ δόγμασιν, ὧν ἀπλήστως καὶ ἀκορέστως ἔχων ἐνευφραινόμην, οὐδὲν ταπεινὸν φρονῶν ἢ χαμαίζηλον οὐδὲ περὶ δόξαν ἢ πλοῦτον ἢ τὰς σώματος εὐπαθείας ἰλυσπώμενος, ἀλλ' ἄνω μετάρσιος ἐδόκουν ἀεὶ φέρεσθαι κατά τινα τῆς ψυχῆς ἐπιθειασμὸν καὶ συμπεριπολεῖν ἡλίῳ καὶ σελήνῃ καὶ σύμπαντι οὐρανῷ τε*
2 *καὶ κόσμῳ. τότε δὴ τότε διακύπτων ἄνωθεν ἀπ' αἰθέρος καὶ τείνων ὥσπερ ἀπὸ σκοπιᾶς τὸ τῆς διανοίας ὄμμα κατεθεώμην τὰς ἀμυθήτους θεωρίας τῶν ἐπὶ γῆς ἁπάντων καὶ εὐδαιμόνιζον ἐμαυτὸν ὡς ἀνὰ κράτος ἐκπεφευγότα τὰς ἐν τῷ θνητῷ βίῳ*

[1] Mangey *βίον*. See note *a*.

[a] I hardly think that *νοῦν* can be right. It is true that Philo often uses *νοῦς τῶν ὅλων* or *νοῦς τοῦ παντός* as an

BOOK III

ON THE PARTICULAR LAWS WHICH COME UNDER TWO OF THE TEN GENERAL COMMANDMENTS, NAMELY THE SIXTH AGAINST ADULTERERS AND ALL LICENTIOUSNESS AND THE SEVENTH AGAINST MURDERERS AND ALL VIOLENCE

I. There was a time when I had leisure for philo- 1
sophy and for the contemplation of the universe and its contents, when I made its spirit [a] my own in all its beauty and loveliness and true blessedness, when my constant companions were divine themes and verities, wherein I rejoiced with a joy that never cloyed or sated. I had no base or abject thoughts nor grovelled [b] in search of reputation or of wealth or bodily comforts, but seemed always to be borne aloft into the heights with a soul possessed by some God-sent inspiration, a fellow-traveller with the sun and moon and the
whole heaven and universe. Ah then I gazed down 2
from the upper air, and straining the mind's eye beheld, as from some commanding peak, the multitudinous world-wide spectacles of earthly things, and blessed my lot in that I had escaped by main force

equivalent for God, *e.g.* i. 18 above. But could he say *ἐκαρπούμην θεόν*? For Mangey's suggestion of *βίον cf.* *εὐδαίμονα βίον ἐδύναντο καρποῦσθαι*, *De Op.* 156 and *De Som.* ii. 74.

[b] Or "wallowed." More exactly "wriggled"; *cf. De Dec.* 149.

3 κῆρας. | ἐφήδρευε δ᾽ ἄρα μοι τὸ κακῶν ἀργαλεώ-
[300] τατον, ὁ μισόκαλος φθόνος, ὃς ἐξαπιναίως ἐπιπεσὼν οὐ πρότερον ἐπαύσατο καθέλκων πρὸς βίαν ἤ με καταβαλεῖν εἰς μέγα πέλαγος τῶν ἐν πολιτείᾳ φροντίδων, ἐν ᾧ φορούμενος οὐδ᾽ ὅσον ἀνανήξασθαι
4 δύναμαι. στένων δ᾽ ὅμως ἀντέχω τὸν ἐκ πρώτης ἡλικίας ἐνιδρυμένον τῇ ψυχῇ παιδείας ἵμερον ἔχων, ὃς ἔλεόν μου καὶ οἶκτον ἀεὶ λαμβάνων ἀνεγείρει καὶ ἀνακουφίζει. διὰ τοῦτον ἔστιν ὅτε τὴν κεφαλὴν ἐπαίρω καὶ τοῖς τῆς ψυχῆς ὄμμασιν ἀμυδρῶς μὲν —τὸ γὰρ ὀξυδερκὲς αὐτῶν ἡ τῶν ἀλλοκότων πραγμάτων ἀχλὺς ἐπεσκίασεν— ἀλλ᾽ ἀναγκαίως γοῦν περιβλέπομαι τὰν κύκλῳ καθαρᾶς καὶ ἀμιγοῦς
5 κακῶν ζωῆς σπάσαι γλιχόμενος. εἰ δέ μοι καὶ ἐξ ἀπροσδοκήτου βραχεῖα γένοιτο εὐδία καὶ γαλήνη θορύβων τῶν ἐν πολιτείᾳ, ὑπόπτερος ἐπικυματίζω μόνον οὐκ ἀεροπορῶν, αὔραις τῆς ἐπιστήμης καταπνεόμενος, ἥ με πολλάκις ἀναπείθει δραπετεύειν συνημερεύσοντα αὐτῇ καθάπερ ἀπὸ δεσποτῶν ἀμειλίκτων, οὐκ ἀνθρώπων μόνον ἀλλὰ καὶ πραγμάτων ἀλλαχόθεν ἄλλων χειμάρρου τρόπον ἐπ-
6 εισχεομένων. ἀλλὰ γὰρ καὶ ἐπὶ τούτοις θεῷ προσῆκον εὐχαριστεῖν, ὅτι καίτοι κατακλυζόμενος οὐκ ἐγκαταπίνομαι βύθιος, ἀλλὰ καὶ τοὺς τῆς ψυχῆς ὀφθαλμούς, οὓς ἀπογνώσει τινὸς χρηστῆς ἐλπίδος ᾠήθην[1] ἤδη πεπηρῶσθαι, διοίγω καὶ φωτὶ τῷ σοφίας ἐναυγάζομαι μὴ πάντα τὸν βίον τῷ σκότῳ παραδοθείς. ἰδού γέ τοι τολμῶ μὴ μόνον

[1] MSS. τινὲς . . . ᾠήθησαν (Mangey ᾠήθην ἂν).

[a] See App. p. 631.

from the plagues of mortal life. But, as it proved, my 3
steps were dogged by the deadliest of mischiefs, the
hater of the good, envy, which suddenly set upon me
and ceased not to pull me down with violence till it
had plunged me in the ocean of civil cares,[a] in which
I am swept away, unable even to raise my head above
the water. Yet amid my groans I hold my own, for, 4
planted in my soul from my earliest days I keep the
yearning for culture which ever has pity and compassion for me, lifts me up and relieves my pain. To this I owe it that sometimes I raise my head and with the soul's eyes—dimly indeed because the mist of extraneous affairs has clouded their clear vision—I yet make shift[b] to look around me in my desire to inhale a breath of life pure and unmixed with evil.
And if unexpectedly I obtain a spell of fine weather 5
and a calm from civil turmoils, I get me wings and ride the waves and almost tread the lower air, wafted by the breezes of knowledge which often urges me to come to spend my days with her, a truant as it were from merciless masters in the shape not only of men but of affairs, which pour in upon me like a torrent
from different sides. Yet it is well for me to give 6
thanks to God even for this,[c] that though submerged I am not sucked down into the depths, but can also open the soul's eyes, which in my despair of comforting hope I thought had now lost their sight, and am irradiated by the light of wisdom, and am not given over to lifelong darkness. So behold me

[b] For this idiomatic use of ἀναγκαίως = "as best I can" see note on *Quod Det.* 160.

[c] καὶ ἐπὶ τούτοις is better taken as explained by ὅτι κτλ. than as referring to the last sentence. The metaphor of the open eye goes back to § 4. For this and for the general sense of these sections see App. pp. 631-632.

τοῖς ἱεροῖς Μωυσέως ἑρμηνεύμασιν ἐντυγχάνειν, ἀλλὰ καὶ φιλεπιστημόνως διακύπτειν εἰς ἕκαστον καὶ ὅσα μὴ γνώριμα τοῖς πολλοῖς διαπτύττειν καὶ ἀναφαίνειν.

7 II. Ἐπεὶ δὲ τῶν δέκα λογίων, ἅπερ αὐτὸς ἔχρησεν ὁ θεὸς ἄνευ προφήτου καὶ ἑρμηνέως, πέντε μὲν εἴρηται τὰ χαραχθέντα ἐν τῇ προτέρᾳ δέλτῳ καὶ ὅσα τῶν κατὰ μέρος συνέτεινεν εἰς ταῦτα, δεῖ δ᾽ ἐν τῷ παρόντι καὶ τὰ λοιπὰ τὰ κατὰ τὴν ἑτέραν δέλτον ὡς οἷόν τε ἄριστα συνυφῆναι, πειράσομαι πάλιν καθ᾽ ἕκαστον τῶν γενῶν ἐφ-
8 αρμόζειν τοὺς ἐν εἴδει νόμους. ἐν δὲ τῇ δευτέρᾳ δέλτῳ πρῶτον γράμμα τοῦτ᾽ ἐστίν· "οὐ μοιχεύσεις," ὅτι, οἶμαι, πανταχοῦ τῆς οἰκουμένης μέγα πνεῖ ἡ ἡδονὴ καὶ οὐδὲν μέρος τὴν δυναστείαν αὐτῆς ἐκπέφευγεν, οὐ τῶν κατὰ γῆν, οὐ τῶν κατὰ θάλατταν, οὐ τῶν ἐν ἀέρι· χερσαῖά τε γὰρ καὶ
[301] πτηνὰ καὶ ἔνυδρα πάντα διὰ πάντων τέθηπε | καὶ περιέπει καὶ τοῖς ἐπιτάγμασιν αὐτῆς ὑπείκει πρός τι βλέμμα καὶ νεῦμα ἀφορῶντα κἂν εἰ φρυάττοιτο ὑπ᾽ ἀλαζονείας ἀσμενίζοντα καὶ μόνον οὐ φθάνοντα τὰς προστάξεις ὀξύτητι καὶ ἀνυπερθέτῳ τάχει τῶν
9 ὑπηρεσιῶν. ἔχει μὲν οὖν καὶ ἡ κατὰ φύσιν ἡδονὴ πολλὴν καὶ πολλάκις μέμψιν, ὅταν ἀμέτρως καὶ ἀκορέστως χρῆταί τις αὐτῇ, καθάπερ οἱ περὶ ἐδωδὴν ἄπληστοι, κἂν εἰ μηδὲν τῶν ἀπαγορευομένων προσφέροιντο, καὶ οἱ φιλογύναιοι συνουσίαις ἐπιμεμηνότες καὶ λαγνίστερον ὁμιλοῦντες γυναιξὶν
10 οὐκ ἀλλοτρίαις ἀλλὰ ταῖς ἑαυτῶν. ἡ δὲ μέμψις σώματός ἐστι μᾶλλον ἢ ψυχῆς κατὰ τοὺς πολλούς,[1]

[1] κατὰ τοὺς πολλοὺς is omitted by several MSS.

daring, not only to read the sacred messages of Moses, but also in my love of knowledge to peer into each of them and unfold and reveal what is not known to the multitude.

II. Since out of the ten oracles which God gave 7
forth Himself without a spokesman or interpreter, we have spoken of five, namely those graven on the first table, and also of all the particular laws which had reference to these, and our present duty is to couple with them those of the second table as well as we can, I will again endeavour to fit the special laws
into each of the heads. The first[a] commandment in 8
the second table is "Thou shalt not commit adultery." It comes first, I think, because pleasure is a mighty force felt throughout the whole inhabited world, no part of which has escaped its domination, neither the denizens of land nor of sea nor of the air, for in all three elements beasts, fowls and fishes all alike treat her with profound respect and deference and submit to her orders, look to her every glance or nod, accept contentedly even the caprices of her arrogance and almost anticipate her commands, so promptly and instantaneously do they hasten to render their services. Now even natural pleasure is often greatly 9
to blame when the craving for it is immoderate and insatiable, as for instance when it takes the form of voracious gluttony, even though none of the food taken is of the forbidden kind, or again the passionate desire for women shewn by those who in their craze for sexual intercourse behave unchastely, not with
the wives of others, but with their own. But the 10
blame in most of these cases rests less with the soul

[a] So LXX in Ex. xx., though not in Deut. v. *Cf. De Dec.* 121.

πολλὴν μὲν ἔχοντος εἴσω φλόγα, ἣ τὴν παραβληθεῖσαν τροφὴν ἐξαναλίσκουσα ἑτέραν οὐκ εἰς μακρὰν ἐπιζητεῖ, πολλὴν δὲ ἰκμάδα, ἧς τὸ ῥοῶδες διὰ τῶν γεννητικῶν ἀποχετεύεται κνησμοὺς καὶ ὀδαξησμοὺς ἐμποιοῦν καὶ γαργαλισμοὺς ἀπαύστους.

11 τοὺς δὲ [καὶ][1] γυναιξὶν ἄλλων καὶ ἔστιν ὅτε οἰκείων καὶ φίλων ἐπιμεμηνότας καὶ ἐπὶ λύμῃ τῶν πλησίον ζῶντας, ὅλα γένη πολυάνθρωπα κιβδηλεύειν ἐπιχειροῦντας καὶ τὰς μὲν ἐπὶ γάμοις εὐχὰς παλιμφήμους τὰς δὲ ἐπὶ τέκνοις ἐλπίδας ἀτελεῖς ἀπεργαζομένους, ἀνίατον νόσον ψυχῆς νοσοῦντας, ὡς κοινοὺς ἐχθροὺς ἅπαντος ἀνθρώπων γένους κολαστέον θανάτῳ, ὡς μήτε ζῶντες ἐν ἀδείᾳ πλείους διαφθείροιεν οἴκους μήτε διδάσκαλοι γένοιντο ἑτέρων, οἷς τὰ πονηρὰ τῶν ἐπιτηδευμάτων ζηλοῦν ἐπιμελές.

12 III. Εὖ μέντοι καὶ τὰ ἄλλα τὰ περὶ τὰς ὁμιλίας ὁ νόμος διετάξατο. κελεύει γὰρ οὐ μόνον ἀλλοτρίων ἀπέχεσθαι γυναικῶν, ἀλλὰ καὶ χηρευουσῶν[2] αἷς οὐ
13 θέμις συνέρχεσθαι. τὸ Περσικὸν ἔθος εὐθὺς ἀποστραφεὶς καὶ μυσαξάμενος ἀπεῖπεν ὡς μέγιστον ἀνοσιούργημα· μητέρας γὰρ οἱ ἐν τέλει Περσῶν

[1] I have followed Heinemann against Cohn in expunging καί. It is inserted by only one MS.

[2] Cohn χηρευουσῶν <μητρυιῶν>, after which he places a comma which is here expunged. See note *c*.

---

[a] For the death penalty for adultery see Lev. xx. 10, Deut. xxii. 22.

[b] This list of prohibited unions follows, as Heinemann notes, the order of Lev. xviii. Some of them appear also in Lev. xx. and Deut. xxii.

[c] Or perhaps "women who have not a husband," *femmes seules*, thus including not merely mothers and stepmothers,

than with the body, which contains a great amount both of fire and of moisture ; the fire as it consumes the material set before it quickly demands a second supply ; the moisture is sluiced in a stream through the genital organs, and creates in them irritations, itchings and titillations without ceasing.

It is not so with men who are mad to possess the 11
wives of others, sometimes those of their relations and friends, who live to work havoc among their neighbours, who go about to bastardize wholesale widespread family connexions, to turn their prayers for married happiness into a curse and render their hopes of offspring fruitless. Here it is the soul which is incurably diseased. Such persons must be punished with death[a] as the common enemies of the whole human race, that they may not live to ruin more houses with immunity and be the tutors of others who make it their business to emulate the wickedness of their ways.

III. Excellent also are the other injunctions laid 12
down by the law on the relation of the sexes.[b] It commands abstinence not only from the wives of others but also from widows[c] in cases where the union
is forbidden by the moral law. To the Persian 13
custom it at once shows its aversion and abhorrence and forbids it as a very grave offence against holy living.[d] For the Persian magnates marry their

but all the prohibited relations which follow. Cohn's insertion of μητρυιῶν is indefensible, as clearly it is mothers rather than stepmothers who are primarily under consideration. But no insertion is required. αἷς . . . συνέρχεσθαι is a natural way of describing unions which, though not adulterous, are incestuous.

[d] Lev. xviii. 7 ff. For the Persians' practice see App. p. 632.

τὰς ἑαυτῶν ἄγονται καὶ τοὺς φύντας ἐκ τούτων εὐγενεστάτους νομίζουσι καὶ βασιλείας, ὡς λόγος,
14 τῆς μεγίστης ἀξιοῦσιν· οὗ τί ἂν γένοιτο δυσσεβέστερον ἀνοσιούργημα; πατρὸς εὐνὴν τετελευτηκότος, ἣν ἄψαυστον ὡς ἱερὰν ἐχρῆν φυλάττεσθαι, καταισχύνειν, γήρως δὲ καὶ μητρὸς αἰδῶ μὴ λαμβάνειν, τὸν αὐτὸν τῆς αὐτῆς υἱὸν καὶ ἄνδρα γίνεσθαι καὶ πάλιν τὴν αὐτὴν τοῦ αὐτοῦ καὶ γυναῖκα καὶ μητέρα, καὶ τοὺς ἀμφοῖν παῖδας τοῦ μὲν πατρὸς ἀδελφούς, υἱωνοὺς δὲ τῆς μητρός, καὶ τὴν μὲν ὧν ἔτεκε μητέρα τε καὶ μάμμην, τὸν δὲ ὧν ἐγέννησεν ἐν ταὐτῷ πατέρα τε καὶ ὁμομήτριον
15 ἀδελφόν. ταῦτ'[1] ἐπράχθη τὸ παλαιὸν καὶ παρ' Ἕλλησιν ἐν Θήβαις ἐπὶ τοῦ Λαΐου παιδὸς
[302] Οἰδίποδος καὶ ἐπράχθη κατ' ἄγνοιαν, | οὐχ ἑκουσίῳ γνώμῃ, καὶ ὅμως τοσαύτην κακῶν φορὰν ἤνεγκεν ὁ γάμος, ὡς μηδὲν ἐλλειφθῆναι τῶν εἰς τὴν ἀνω-
16 τάτω βαρυδαιμονίαν. πολέμων τε γὰρ ἐμφυλίων καὶ ξενικῶν διαδοχαὶ καθάπερ κλῆρος παισὶ καὶ ἐκγόνοις παρὰ πατέρων καὶ προγόνων ἀπελείπετο καὶ πορθήσεις πόλεων τῶν ἐν τῇ Ἑλλάδι μεγίστων ἐγίνοντο καὶ φθοραὶ[2] στρατιωτικῶν δυνάμεων ἐγχωρίων τε καὶ τῶν κατὰ συμμαχίαν ἀφικνουμένων καὶ ἡγεμόνων τῶν παρ' ἑκατέροις ἀρίστων ἐπάλληλοι φθοραὶ[2] καὶ διὰ τὰς περὶ κράτους [καὶ][3]

[1] Cohn prints ἀδελφόν—ταῦτ', regarding what follows as a continuance of the sentence which begins with πατρὸς εὐνὴν.

[2] The duplication of φθοραὶ has been justly suspected. Mangey proposed to substitute φόνοι for the first φθοραὶ, Heinemann thought it better to omit it.

[3] καὶ should be omitted. κράτος ἀρχῆς is a common expression in Philo, *e.g.* *Mos.* i. 96, 307.

mothers and regard the children of the marriage as nobles of the highest birth, worthy, so it is said, to
hold the supreme sovereignty. What form of un- 14
holiness could be more impious than this: that a father's bed, which should be kept untouched as something sacred, should be brought to shame: that no respect should be shown for a mother's ageing years: that the same man should be son and husband to the same woman, and again the same woman wife and mother to the same man: that the children of both should be brothers to their father and grandsons to their mother: that she should be both mother and grandmother of those whom she bore and he both father and half-brother of those whom he begot?

Even, among the Greeks these things 15
were done in old days in Thebes in the case of Oedipus the son of Laïus. They were done in ignorance, not by deliberate intention, and yet the marriage produced such a harvest of ills that nothing was wanting
that could lead to the utmost misery. For a succes- 16
sion of wars civil and foreign was left to be passed on as a heritage to children and descendants from their fathers and ancestors.[a] The greatest cities in Greece were sacked, and armed forces both of natives and allied contingents were destroyed: the bravest leaders on both sides fell one after the other; brothers slew brothers in the deadly feud engendered by

[a] The reference is not only to the war of the *Seven against Thebes*, caused by the rivalry of the two sons of Oedipus, but also to the later war of the Epigoni (the sons of the first set of chieftains), which might be regarded as indirectly caused by the curse of Oedipus, and in which Thebes according to the legend was sacked. *Cf.* Diodorus, iv. 66. The whole section, however, is a great exaggeration of the ordinary tradition.

ἀρχῆς ἀσυμβάτους ἔχθρας ἀδελφοκτονίαι, δι᾿ ἃς οὐ μόνον αἱ συγγένειαι καὶ πατρίδες ἀλλὰ καὶ ἡ πλείστη μοῖρα τοῦ Ἑλληνικοῦ παντὸς ἐξεφθάρη πανωλεθρίᾳ· κεναὶ γὰρ αἱ πρότερον εὔανδροῦσαι πόλεις οἰκητόρων μνημεῖα τῶν τῆς Ἑλλάδος συμφορῶν ὑπελείφθησαν, ἀτυχὴς θέα τοῖς ὁρῶσιν.

17 οὐ μὴν οὐδὲ Πέρσαι, παρ᾿ οἷς ταῦτα ἐπιτηδεύεται, τῶν παραπλησίων κακῶν ἀμοιροῦσιν· ἀεὶ γὰρ ἐν στρατείαις καὶ μάχαις εἰσὶ κτείνοντες καὶ κτεινόμενοι καὶ τοτὲ μὲν τοὺς πλησιοχώρους κατατρέχοντες τοτὲ δὲ τοὺς ἐπανισταμένους ἀμυνόμενοι· πολλοὶ δὲ πολλαχόθεν ἐπανίστανται, τοῦ βαρβαρικοῦ μὴ πεφυκότος ἠρεμεῖν· πρὶν γοῦν καταλυθῆναι τὴν ἐν χερσὶ στάσιν, ἑτέρα φύεται, ὡς μηδένα τοῦ ἔτους ὑπεξῃρῆσθαι καιρὸν εἰς ἡσυχίαν, ἀλλὰ καὶ θέρους καὶ χειμῶνος μεθ᾿ ἡμέραν καὶ νύκτωρ ὁπλοφορεῖν, πλείω χρόνον ἐν τοῖς στρατοπέδοις ἐν ὑπαίθρῳ ταλαιπωροῦντας ἢ ἐν ταῖς πόλεσιν οἰκοῦντας διὰ πολλὴν ἔνδειαν εἰρήνης.

18 ἐῶ λέγειν τὰς τῶν βασιλέων μεγάλας καὶ ὑπερόγκους εὐπραγίας, οἷς ἀγώνισμα πρῶτον εὐθὺς ἅμα τῇ παραλήψει τῆς ἡγεμονίας τὸ μέγιστον ἄγος, ἀδελφοκτονία, μαντευομένων τὴν ἐκ τῶν ἀδελφῶν γενησομένην ἴσως ἐπίθεσιν ὑπὲρ τοῦ δοκεῖν

19 εὐλόγως κτείνειν. ἅπερ μοι δοκεῖ πάντα συμβαίνειν διὰ τὰς ἀναρμόστους υἱῶν πρὸς μητέρας ὁμιλίας, τῆς ἐφόρου τῶν ἀνθρωπείων δίκης ἀμυνομένης τῶν ἀνοσιουργημάτων τοὺς ἀσεβοῦντας· ἀσεβοῦσι δ᾿ οὐχ οἱ δρῶντες μόνον, ἀλλὰ καὶ ὅσοι τοῖς δρῶσιν ἑκουσίῳ γνώμῃ συνεπιγράφονται.

20 τοσαύτην δὲ ὁ ἡμέτερος νόμος φυλακὴν

ambition for sovereign power. In consequence not
only families and independent territories, but also
the largest part of the Greek world perished involved
in the general destruction. For cities formerly well
populated were left stripped of their inhabitants as
monuments of the disasters of Greece, a sinister sight
to contemplate. Nor are the Persians 17
either who follow these practices exempt from similar
troubles, for they are always engaging in campaigns
and battles, slaying and being slain.[a] Sometimes
they are attacking the neighbouring populations,
sometimes defending themselves against insurrection.
For of insurgents many appear from many quarters,
as the barbarian nature can never remain in quietude.
Thus before the sedition of the hour is put down
another springs up, so that no season of the year is
reserved for a tranquil life, but summer and winter,
day and night they are bearing arms, and so rarely
does peace reign that they spend more time enduring
the hardships of encampment in the open air than
dwelling in their cities. I put on one side the great 18
and magnificent triumphs of kings whose first exploit
when they succeed to the throne is that worst of
sacrileges fratricide—murders which they try to
vindicate as reasonable by predicting that their
brothers will probably attack them. All these things 19
appear to me to be the result of the ill-matched
matings of sons with mothers. For justice who
watches over human affairs avenges the unholy deeds
on the impious, and the impiety extends beyond the
perpetrators of the deed to those who voluntarily
range themselves with the perpetrators.
But such careful precautions has our law taken in 20

[a] See App. pp. 632-633.

πεποίηται τοῦ πράγματος, ὥστε οὐδὲ προγονῷ τελευτήσαντος πατρὸς ἄγεσθαι μητρυιὰν ἐφῆκε, διά τε τὴν εἰς τὸν πατέρα τιμὴν καὶ διότι μητρυιᾶς καὶ μητρὸς ὄνομα συγγενές, εἰ καὶ μὴ τὸ τῆς
21 ψυχῆς συνῳδὸν πάθος· ὁ γὰρ ἀλλοτρίας ἀπέχεσθαι διδαχθείς, ὅτι μητρυιὰ προσερρήθη, πολὺ μᾶλλον ἀφέξεται τῆς φύσει μητρός· καὶ εἴ τις διὰ τὴν
[303] ἐπὶ τῷ πατρὶ μνήμην αἰδεῖται τὴν ἐκείνου | ποτὲ γενομένην γυναῖκα, δῆλός ἐστιν ἕνεκα τῆς εἰς ἀμφοτέρους τοὺς γονεῖς τιμῆς οὐδὲν βουλευσόμενος ἐπὶ τῇ μητρὶ νεώτερον, ἐπεὶ καὶ σφόδρα ἐστὶν εὔηθες ἡμίσει μέρει τοῦ γένους χαριζόμενον ὁλοκλήρου καὶ παντελοῦς ὀλιγωρεῖν δοκεῖν.

22 IV. Ἑξῆς ἐστι παράγγελμα μηδ' ἀδελφὴν ἐγγυᾶσθαι, πάνυ σπουδαῖον καὶ συντεῖνον εἰς ἐγκράτειαν ὁμοῦ καὶ εὐκοσμίαν. ὁ μὲν οὖν Ἀθηναῖος Σόλων ὁμοπατρίους ἐφεὶς ἄγεσθαι τὰς ὁμομητρίους ἐκώλυσεν, ὁ δὲ Λακεδαιμονίων νομοθέτης ἔμπαλιν τὸν ἐπὶ ταῖς ὁμογαστρίοις γάμον ἐπιτρέψας τὸν
23 πρὸς τὰς ὁμοπατρίους ἀπεῖπεν· ὁ δὲ τῶν Αἰγυπτίων χλεύην ⟨θέμενος⟩[1] τὴν ἑκατέρων εὐλάβειαν ὡς ἡμίεργα διατατομένων εὐφόρησεν[2] εἰς ἀσέλγειαν, ἐπιδαψιλευόμενος δυσθεράπευτον κακὸν σώμασι καὶ ψυχαῖς ἀκρασίαν καὶ παρασχὼν ἄδειαν ἁπάσας ἀδελφὰς ἄγεσθαι, τάς τε ἰδίας τοῦ ἑτέρου τῶν

[1] A verb has evidently been lost. Cohn's insertion of *θέμενος* is justified by *χλεύην τίθεσθαι* in several places, *e.g. Mos.* i. 190.

[2] Cohn suspects this word, for which impossible variants are given in some MSS., and suggests *ἐφώρμησεν*. I think the word as given in the translation (or possibly "blossomed into") is natural and appropriate.

---

[a] Lev. xviii. 8.

these matters that it has not even permitted the son of a first marriage to marry his stepmother after the death of his father,[a] both on account of the honour due to his father and because the names of mother and stepmother are closely akin, however different are the feelings called up by the two words.[b] For he 21
who has been taught to abstain from another's wife because she is called his stepmother, will *a fortiori* abstain from taking his natural mother; and if the memory of his father makes him respect her who was once his father's wife, the honour which he pays to both his parents will certainly keep him from entertaining the idea of violating his mother in any way. For it would be the height of folly while acknowledging the claims of a half parentage to appear to treat with contempt the full and complete whole.

IV. Next comes a prohibition against espousing 22
a sister, a very excellent rule tending to promote both continence and outward decency.[c] Now Solon the lawgiver of the Athenians permitted marriage with half-sisters on the father's side but prohibited it when the mother was the same.[d] The lawgiver of the Lacedaemonians, on the other hand, allowed the second but forbade the first. But the lawgiver 23
of the Egyptians poured scorn upon the cautiousness of both, and, holding that the course which they enjoined stopped half-way, produced a fine crop of lewdness. With a lavish hand he bestowed on bodies and souls the poisonous bane of incontinence and gave full liberty to marry sisters of every degree whether they belonged to one of their brother's parents or

[b] The allusion is to the hostility constantly connected with the name μητρυιά. See examples in L. & S.

[c] Lev. xviii. 9, xx. 17.

[d] See App. p. 633.

γονέων, τοῦδε ἢ τοῦδε, καὶ τὰς ἐξ ἀμφοῖν καὶ τὰς
οὐ νεωτέρας μόνον ἀλλὰ καὶ πρεσβυτέρας καὶ
ἰσήλικας· καὶ δίδυμοι γὰρ πολλάκις ἐγεννήθησαν,
οὓς ἡ μὲν φύσις ἅμα τῇ γενέσει διήρτησε καὶ
διέζευξεν, ἡ δ' ἀκολασία καὶ φιληδονία εἰς κοινωνίαν
ἐκάλεσεν ἀκοινώνητον καὶ ἁρμονίαν ἀνάρμοστον.
24 ἅπερ ἐκμυσαξάμενος ὁ ἱερώτατος Μωυσῆς ὡς
ἀλλότρια καὶ ἐχθρὰ πολιτείας ἀνεπιλήπτου καὶ
προτρέποντα καὶ ἀλείφοντα πρὸς τὰ αἴσχιστα τῶν
ἐπιτηδευμάτων ἀνὰ κράτος ἀπεῖπεν ἀδελφῇ συνέρχεσθαι, εἴτε ἐξ ἀμφοῖν εἴτε καὶ μόνου γένοιτο τοῦ
25 ἑτέρου. τί γὰρ δεῖ τὸ τῆς αἰδοῦς κάλλος αἰσχύνειν;
τί δ' ἀχρωμάτους κατασκευάζειν παρθένους, ἃς
ἐρυθριᾶν ἀναγκαῖον; τί δὲ τὰς πρὸς τοὺς ἄλλους
ἀνθρώπους κοινωνίας καὶ ἐπιμιξίας ἐπέχειν εἰς
βραχὺ χωρίον τὸ ἑκάστης οἰκίας συνωθοῦντας μέγα
καὶ λαμπρὸν ἔρνος[1] ἐκτείνεσθαι καὶ χεῖσθαι δυνάμενον εἰς ἠπείρους καὶ νήσους καὶ τὴν οἰκουμένην
πᾶσαν; αἱ γὰρ πρὸς τοὺς ὀθνείους ἐπιγαμίαι
καινὰς ἀπεργάζονται συγγενείας τῶν ἀφ' αἵματος
26 οὐκ ἀποδεούσας. V. ὧν χάριν πολλὰς
καὶ ἄλλας ὁμιλίας ἐκώλυσε προστάξας μὴ θυγα-
τριδῆν, μὴ υἱιδῆν, μὴ τηθίδα πρὸς πατρὸς ἢ μητρός,
μὴ θείου ἢ υἱοῦ ἢ ἀδελφοῦ γυναῖκα γενομένην
ἐγγυᾶσθαι, μηδ' αὖ προγονὴν ἢ χήραν ἢ παρθένον

[1] MSS. ἔργον, for which Mangey and Cohn substitute γένος. I have adopted ἔρνος (my own correction), as favoured both by the sense and the *ductus literarum*.

---

[a] See App. p. 633.

[b] Philo prohibits the marriage of brother and sister (a practice which, it must be remembered, was adopted by the dynasty of the Ptolemies, which he did not regard with disfavour, *cf. Mos.* ii. 30) on the grounds (1) that it outrages

to both, and not only if they were younger than their brothers but also if they were older or of the same age.[a] For twins are often born who, although separated and disunited by nature at birth, enter at the call of concupiscence and voluptuousness into a partnership and wedlock which are neither in the true sense of the words. These practices our most 24
holy Moses rejected with abhorrence as alien and hostile to a commonwealth free from reproach and as encouragements and incitements to the vilest of customs. He stoutly forbade the union of a brother with a sister whether both her parents were the same as his or only one.[b] For modesty is lovely, why put it 25
to shame? Maidens must blush, why drive the hue from their cheeks? Why hamper the fellow-feeling and inter-communion of men with men by compressing within the narrow space of each separate house the great and goodly plant which might extend and spread itself over continents and islands and the whole inhabited world? For intermarriages with outsiders create new kinships not a wit inferior to blood-relationships. V. On this principle 26
he prohibits many other unions,[c] not allowing marriage with a son's daughter or a daughter's daughter, nor with an aunt whether paternal or maternal, nor with one who has been wife to an uncle or son or brother, nor again with a stepdaughter whether

family decency; (2) tends to prevent intermarriage with less closely related families.

[c] All these degrees of relationship are mentioned in Lev. xviii 10-16, except that there the prohibition against marriage with the paternal uncle's wife does not seem to be extended, as here implied, to the maternal uncle's wife. In the parallel passage, xx. 20, the R.V. has "uncle's wife" simply, but Philo would read in the LXX τῆς συγγενοῦς αὐτοῦ.

ζώσης μὲν τῆς γυναικὸς—ἄπαγε—ἀλλὰ μηδ' ἀποθανούσης· δυνάμει γὰρ ὅ γε πατρῳὸς πατὴρ ὀφείλων τὴν ἐκ τῆς γυναικὸς ἐν τάξει θυγατρὸς
27 τίθεσθαι. πάλιν δύο ἀδελφὰς ἄγεσθαι τὸν αὐτὸν
[304] οὐκ ἐπιτρέπει, οὔτ' ἐν τῷ αὐτῷ | οὔτ' ἐν διαφέρουσι χρόνοις, κἂν τύχῃ τις ἣν προέγημεν ἀπεωσμένος· ζώσης γὰρ ἔτι τῆς συνοικούσης, εἴτε[1] καὶ ἀπηλλαγμένης, ἐάν τε χηρεύῃ ἐάν τε καὶ ἑτέρῳ γαμηθῇ, τὴν ἀδελφὴν οὐχ ὅσιον ὑπέλαβεν ἐπὶ τὰ τῆς ἠτυχηκυίας παρέρχεσθαι, προδιδάσκων τὰ συγγενικὰ δίκαια μὴ λύειν μηδ' ἐπιβαίνειν πταίσμασι τῆς οὕτως ἡνωμένης κατὰ γένος μηδ' ἐναβρύνεσθαι καὶ ἐντρυφᾶν θεραπευομένην ὑπὸ τῶν ἐχθρῶν ἐκείνης καὶ ἀντιθεραπεύουσαν αὐτούς.
28 ἐγείρονται γὰρ ἐκ τούτων χαλεπαὶ ζηλοτυπίαι καὶ δυσπαρηγόρητοι φιλονεικίαι φορὰς ἀμυθήτους ἐπάγουσαι κακῶν· ὅμοιον γὰρ ὡς εἰ καὶ τὰ μέρη τοῦ σώματος τῆς κατὰ φύσιν ἁρμονίας ἐκστάντα καὶ κοινωνίας στασιάζοι πρὸς ἄλληλα, ὃ νόσους ἀνιάτους ἀπεργάζεται καὶ φθοράς· ἀδελφαὶ δέ, εἰ καὶ διαιρετὰ μέρη γεγόνασιν, ἀλλ' οὖν ἁρμόζονται καὶ ἑνοῦνται φύσει καὶ συγγενείᾳ μιᾷ· ἡ δὲ

[1] Perhaps read εἰ. See note *b*.

---

[a] In these two sections Philo follows closely Lev. xviii. 18, "thou shalt not take a woman to her sister to be a rival to her, to uncover her nakedness beside the other in her lifetime." The LXX for "rival," ἀντίζηλος, suggests even better than the R.V. the idea of jealousy which Philo stresses. Nothing is said in Leviticus of the deceased wife's sister, nor by Philo, though his argument suggests that he would not object to it He also says nothing about marriage with a brother's wife, though that is forbidden in *v.* 16. Possibly he did not see how to reconcile it with the express injunction

widow or unmarried, I need not say while the wife is alive, heaven forbid, but even after her death. For the stepfather is virtually a father whose duty is to set his wife's daughter in the same position as his own. Again, he does not allow the same man to 27
marry two sisters either at the same or at different times, even if the person in question has repudiated the one he married first.[a] For while she is still alive either as his consort or divorced,[b] whether she is remaining in widowhood or has married another, he considered that the law of holiness required that the sister should not take the position which the wife has lost by her misfortune, but should learn not to set at nought the rights of kinship, nor use as a stepping-stone the fallen state of one so closely united to her by birth, nor bask at ease while enjoying and returning the caresses of her sister's enemies. For from this source grow grave jealousies and bitter 28
feuds bringing with them train upon train of evils without number. For it is just as if the parts of the body were to renounce their natural partnership and place in the system and engage in strife with each other, thus producing incurable diseases and fatalities. Sisters though made as separate parts of the system are fitted into it and formed into a single whole by nature and identity of parentage.

of such a marriage, "to raise up seed to the brother," in Deut. xxv. 5 ff.

[b] If εἰ is read for εἴτε (see note 1), the meaning will be "while his (former) partner is alive, even though she has been divorced." This certainly best suits the rest of the sentence, which is confined to the case of the divorced wife. On the other hand it strains the meaning of the present participle τῆς συνοικούσης and leaves out of consideration τῷ αὐτῷ χρόνῳ above, which clearly contemplates the possibility of bigamy.

ζηλοτυπία, πάθος ἀργαλεώτατον, ἀπορρήττουσα χαλεπὰ καινουργεῖ κακὰ καὶ δυσίατα.

29 ἀλλὰ μηδὲ ἀλλοεθνεῖ, φησί, κοινωνίαν γάμου συντίθεσο, μή ποτε μαχομένοις ἔθεσιν ὑπαχθεὶς ἐνδῷς καὶ τῆς πρὸς εὐσέβειαν ὁδοῦ λάθῃς διαμαρτὼν πρὸς ἀνοδίαν ἐκτραπείς· καὶ τάχα μὲν αὐτὸς ἀνθέξεις ἐκ πρώτης ἡλικίας ἡρματισμένος ὑποθήκαις ἀρίσταις, ἃς οἱ γονεῖς κατεπᾴδοντες ἀεὶ τοὺς ἱεροὺς νόμους ὑφηγοῦντο· δέος δὲ οὐ μικρόν ἐστι περὶ υἱῶν καὶ θυγατέρων, ἴσως γὰρ δελεασθέντες νόθοις πρὸ γνησίων ἔθεσι κινδυνεύουσι τὴν τοῦ ἑνὸς θεοῦ τιμὴν ἀπομαθεῖν, ὅπερ ἐστὶν ἀρχὴ καὶ τέλος τῆς ἀνωτάτω βαρυδαιμονίας.

30 Ἐὰν δέ, φησίν, ἀνδρὸς ἀπαλλαγεῖσα γυνὴ καθ' ἣν ἂν τύχῃ πρόφασιν ἑτέρῳ γημαμένη πάλιν χηρεύσῃ, ζῶντος ἢ καὶ τετελευτηκότος τοῦ δευτέρου, μὴ ἐπανίτω πρὸς ἄνδρα τὸν πρότερον, ἀλλὰ πᾶσι τοῖς ἄλλοις ἔνσπονδος μᾶλλον ἢ τῷδε γενέσθω, θεσμοὺς παραβᾶσα τοὺς ἀρχαίους, ὧν ἐξελάθετο
31 φίλτρα καινὰ πρὸ τῶν παλαιῶν ἑλομένη. πρὸς δὲ συμβάσεις εἴ τις ἐθέλει χωρεῖν ἀνὴρ τῇ τοιαύτῃ

---

[a] Ex. xxxiv. 16, Deut. vii. 3 (here, as also in §§ 30, 31, Philo digresses from his interpretation of the prohibitions in Lev. xviii.). Though the prohibition in both Exodus and Deuteronomy is against intermarriage with the conquered Canaanites, the motive assigned, viz. fear of contamination with heathenism, is naturally regarded as making it a general ordinance. Josephus also appeals to it in condemnation of Solomon, *Ant.* viii. 191.

[b] Deut. xxiv. 4, where such an act is described as an abomination before the Lord, and defiling (LXX) the land. Though no penalty is mentioned, Philo, perhaps not un-

And jealousy is a most troublesome passion, creating if it breaks out grave evils unknown before and
hardly to be cured. [a] But also, he says, 29
do not enter into the partnership of marriage with a member of a foreign nation, lest some day conquered by the forces of opposing customs you surrender and stray unawares from the path that leads to piety and turn aside into a pathless wild. And though perhaps you yourself will hold your ground steadied from your earliest years by the admirable instructions instilled into you by your parents, with the holy laws always as their key-note, there is much to be feared for your sons and daughters. It may well be that they, enticed by spurious customs which they prefer to the genuine, are likely to unlearn the honour due to the one God, and that is the first and the last stage of supreme misery.

Another commandment is that if a woman after 30
parting from her husband for any cause whatever marries another and then again becomes a widow, whether this second husband is alive or dead, she must not return to her first husband but ally herself with any other rather than him, because she has broken with the rules that bound her in the past and cast them into oblivion when she chose new love-ties
in preference to the old.[b] And if a man is willing to 31
contract himself with such a woman, he must be

reasonably, interprets these strong phrases as describing an act deserving the death penalty, but is hard put to justify it. Apparently he understands the text as meaning that the remarriage shews that there was no real reason for the divorce. The woman is therefore " defiled " and an adulteress, and he not only a " pander," but an adulterer, either because he has connived at her adultery or perhaps because to marry an adulteress is in itself adultery. See further, App. p. 633.

γυναικί, μαλακίας καὶ ἀνανδρίας ἐκφερέσθω δόξαν, ἐκτετμημένος τῆς ψυχῆς τὸ βιωφελέστατον, μισοπόνηρον πάθος, ὑφ' οὗ καὶ τὰ οἴκων καὶ τὰ πόλεων πράγματα κατορθοῦται, καὶ δύο τὰ μέγιστα τῶν ἀδικημάτων εὐφόρως[1] ἀπομαξάμενος, μοιχείαν τε καὶ προαγωγειαν· αἱ γὰρ αὖθις καταλλαγαὶ μηνύματ' εἰσὶ τοῦ ἑκατέρου· θανάτου δίκην τινέτω σὺν τῇ γυναικί.

32 [305] VI. | Φορὰ τῶν μηνιαίων ὁπότε γένοιτο, μὴ ψαυέτω γυναικὸς ἀνήρ, ἀλλὰ τὸν χρόνον ἐκεῖνον ὁμιλίας ἀνεχέτω νόμον φύσεως αἰδούμενος καὶ ἅμα προδιδασκόμενος μὴ ἀτελεῖς γονὰς ἀκαίρου καὶ ἀμούσου χάριν ἡδονῆς προΐεσθαι· ὅμοιον γὰρ ὡς εἴ τις γεωπόνος ὑπὸ μέθης ἢ φρενοβλαβείας πυροὺς καὶ κριθὰς εἰς λίμνας καὶ χειμάρρους ἀντὶ πεδίων σπείροι, ξηραῖς γὰρ γενομέναις ταῖς ἀρούραις καταβάλλεσθαι χρὴ τὸν σπόρον εἰς

33 εὐκαρπίαν. καθαίρει δὲ καὶ ἡ φύσις ἑκάστῳ μηνὶ τὴν μήτραν οἷά τινα θαυμαστὴν ἄρουραν, ἧς τὸν καιρὸν ἀγαθοῦ γεωργοῦ τρόπον ἐπιτηρητέον, ἵν' ἔτι μὲν ἐπικλυζομένης ἐπέχοι τὸν σπόρον—λήσεται γὰρ τῇ φορᾷ κατασυρεὶς[2] ὑπὸ τῆς ὑγρότητος τοὺς σπερματικοὺς τόνους οὐ χαλασθεὶς[2] μόνον ἀλλὰ καὶ εἰς ἅπαν ἐκλυθείς[2]· οὗτοι δ' εἰσὶν οἱ ἐν τῇ μήτρᾳ τῷ τῆς φύσεως ἐργαστηρίῳ ζῳοπλαστοῦντες καὶ

[1] MSS. εὐφυῶς.

[2] MSS. mostly λήσεται γὰρ ἡ σπορὰ κατασυρεῖσα . . . χαλασθεῖσα . . . ἐκλυθεῖσα. Cohn follows F (supported by the Armenian), which has τῇ φορᾷ, though combined with the impossible feminine participles.

---

[a] Lev. xviii. 19 (*cf.* Ezekiel, xviii. 6). Here Philo resumes his interpretation of Lev. xviii. and, except for §§ 34-36, con-

saddled with a character for degeneracy and loss of manhood. He has eliminated from his soul the hatred of evil, that emotion by which our life is so well served and the affairs of houses and cities are conducted as they should be, and has lightly taken upon him the stamp of two heinous crimes, adultery and pandering. For such subsequent reconciliations are proofs of both. The proper punishment for him is death and for the woman also.

VI. Whenever the menstrual issue occurs, a man 32
must not touch a woman, but must during that period refrain from intercourse and respect the law of nature.[a] He must also remember the lesson that the generative seeds should not be wasted fruitlessly for the sake of a gross and untimely pleasure. For it is just as if a husbandman should in intoxication or lunacy sow wheat and barley in ponds or mountain-streams instead of in the plains, since the fields should become dry before the seed is laid in them.
Now nature also each month purges the womb as if 33
it were a cornfield—a field with mysterious properties, over which, like a good husbandman, he must watch for the right time to arrive. So while the field is still inundated he will keep back the seed, which otherwise will be silently swept away by the stream, as the humidity not only relaxes, but utterly paralyses the seminal nerve-forces, which in nature's laboratory, the womb, mould the living creature and with consummate craftsmanship perfect

tinues it in the same order to the end of § 53. He omits *vv.* 20, 21, the first denouncing simple adultery, already dealt with, the second against offering children to Moloch, which has no connexion with his present subject, even if he understood it, which is hardly possible, as the LXX has "give thy seed to serve the ruler."

τῶν μερῶν ἕκαστον σώματός τε καὶ ψυχῆς ἀκρότητι τέχνης τελεσιουργοῦντες—, εἰ δ' ἐπίσχοι τὰ μηνιαῖα, θαρρῶν ἤδη γόνιμα κατασπείροι μηκέτι φθορᾶς τῶν καταβληθησομένων δεδιώς.

34 Ὀνειδιστέον καὶ τοῖς σκληρὰν καὶ λιθώδη γῆν ἀροῦσιν· οὗτοι δὲ τίνες ἂν εἶεν ἢ οἱ στείραις συνερχόμενοι γυναιξί; θήρᾳ γὰρ αὐτὸ μόνον ἡδονῆς ἀκράτορος ὡς οἱ[1] λαγνίστατοι τὰς γονὰς ἑκουσίῳ γνώμῃ διαφθείρουσιν· ἐπεὶ τίνος ἄλλου χάριν ἐγγυῶνται τὰς τοιαύτας; οὐ μὴν δι' ἐλπίδα τέκνων ἣν ἴσασιν ἐξ ἀνάγκης ἀτελῆ γενησομένην, ἀλλὰ δι'
35 ὑπερβάλλοντα οἶστρον καὶ ἀκρασίαν ἀνίατον. ὅσοι μὲν οὖν ἄγονται κόρας ἀγνοίᾳ τοῦ πῶς ἕξουσιν εὐθὺς εὐτοκίας ἢ τοὐναντίον, ὁπόταν χρόνῳ μακρῷ ὕστερον ἐκ τῆς ἀγονίας αἰσθανόμενοι στείρας αὐτὰς μὴ ἀποπέμπωνται, συγγνώμης εἰσὶν ἐπάξιοι συνηθείας, βιαστικωτάτου πράγματος, ἡττώμενοι καὶ φίλτρα ἀρχαῖα συμβιώσει μακρᾷ ταῖς ψυχαῖς
36 ἐνεσφραγισμένα λύειν ἀδυνατοῦντες. ὅσοι δὲ προδεδοκιμασμένας ἑτέροις ἀνδράσιν ὡς εἰσὶν ἄγονοι μνῶνται συῶν τρόπον ἢ τράγων ὀχεύοντες αὐτὸ μόνον, ἐν ἀσεβῶν στήλαις ἐγγραφέσθωσαν ὡς ἀντίπαλοι θεοῦ· τῷ μὲν γὰρ ἅτε φιλοζῴῳ καὶ φιλανθρώπῳ δι' ἐπιμελείας τῆς πάσης ἐστὶ σωτηρίαν καὶ μονὴν τοῖς γένεσιν ἅπασιν ἐργάζεσθαι, οἱ δ' ἅμα τῇ καταβολῇ σβέσιν τοῖς σπέρμασι τεχνάζοντες ἐχθροὶ τῆς φύσεως ὁμολογουμένως εἰσίν.

[1] So Cohn for the ὅσοι of most MSS. F, however, has οἱ (= οἵ), which may be right, οἱ λαγνίστατοι being the common belated epithet, "lecherous people that they are."

each part both of body and soul. But if the menstruation ceases, he may boldly sow the generative seeds, no longer fearing that what he lays will perish.

[a] They too must be branded with reproach, who 34
plough the hard and stony land. And who should they be but those who mate with barren women? For in the quest of mere licentious pleasure like the most lecherous of men they destroy[b] the procreative germs with deliberate purpose. For what other motive can they have in plighting themselves to such women? It cannot be the hope of offspring, a hope which they know must necessarily fail to be realized; it can only be an inordinate frenzy, and incontinence past all
cure. Those who marry maidens in ignorance at the 35
time of their capacity or incapacity for successful motherhood, and later refuse to dismiss them, when prolonged childlessness shews them to be barren, deserve our pardon. Familiarity, that most constraining influence, is too strong for them, and they are unable to rid themselves of the charm of old affection imprinted on their souls by long companionship. But those who sue for marriage with women 36
whose sterility has already been proved with other husbands, do but copulate like pigs or goats, and their names should be inscribed in the lists of the impious as adversaries of God. For while God in His love both for mankind and all that lives spares no care to effect the preservation and permanence of every race, those persons who make an art of quenching the life of the seed as it drops, stand confessed as the enemies of nature.

[a] Philo has not, nor does he claim to have, any biblical authority for these three sections. See App. pp. 633-634.
[b] Or "waste."

37 VII. Ἐπεισκεκώμακε δὲ ταῖς πόλεσιν ἕτερον
πολὺ τοῦ λεχθέντος μεῖζον κακόν, τὸ παιδεραστεῖν,
ὃ πρότερον μὲν καὶ λεχθῆναι μέγα ὄνειδος ἦν, νυνὶ
δ' ἐστὶν αὔχημα οὐ τοῖς δρῶσι μόνον, ἀλλὰ καὶ |
[306] τοῖς πάσχουσιν, οἳ νόσον θήλειαν νοσεῖν ἐθιζόμενοι
τάς τε ψυχὰς καὶ τὰ σώματα διαρρέουσι μηδὲν
ἐμπύρευμα τῆς ἄρρενος γενεᾶς ἐῶντες ὑποτύφεσθαι,
περιφανῶς οὕτως τὰς τῆς κεφαλῆς τρίχας ἀνα-
πλεκόμενοι καὶ διακοσμούμενοι καὶ ψιμμυθίῳ καὶ
φύκεσι καὶ τοῖς ὁμοιοτρόποις τὰς ὄψεις τριβόμενοι
καὶ ὑπογραφόμενοι καὶ εὐώδεσι μύροις λίπα
χριόμενοι—προσαγωγὸν γὰρ μάλιστα ἐν τοῖς τοιούτοις τὸ εὐῶδες ἐν ἅπασι τοῖς εἰς εὐκοσμίαν
ἠσκημένοις—, καὶ τὴν ἄρρενα φύσιν ἐπιτηδεύσει
τεχνάζοντες εἰς θήλειαν μεταβάλλειν οὐκ ἐρυθριῶσι.
38 καθ' ὧν φονᾶν ἄξιον νόμῳ πειθαρχοῦντας, ὃς
κελεύει τὸν ἀνδρόγυνον τὸ φύσεως νόμισμα[1] παρα-
κόπτοντα νηποινεὶ τεθνάναι, μηδεμίαν ἡμέραν
ἀλλὰ μηδ' ὥραν ἐώμενον ζῆν, ὄνειδος αὐτοῦ καὶ
οἰκίας καὶ πατρίδος ὄντα καὶ τοῦ σύμπαντος
39 ἀνθρώπων γένους. ὁ δὲ παιδεραστὴς ἴστω[2] τὴν
αὐτὴν δίκην ὑπομένων, ἐπειδὴ τὴν παρὰ φύσιν
ἡδονὴν διώκει καὶ τὰς πόλεις τό γε ἐπ' αὐτὸν ἧκον
μέρος ἐρήμους καὶ κενὰς ἀποδείκνυσιν οἰκητόρων
διαφθείρων τὰς γονὰς καὶ προσέτι τῶν μεγίστων
κακῶν, ἀνανδρίας καὶ μαλακίας, ὑφηγητὴς καὶ

[1] MSS. τὰ φύσει (φύσεως) νόμιμα (ὄργανα).
[2] MSS. ἔστω.

---

[a] Lev. xviii. 22, xx. 13. *Cf.* the similar treatment of the vice, *De Abr.* 135, 136, and also *De Vit. Cont.* 59-62, following on an adverse criticism of Plato's *Symposium*. The wording here is also very similar to i. 325 above, though there it is

VII. Much graver than the above is another evil, 37
which has ramped its way into the cities, namely pederasty.[a] In former days the very mention of it was a great disgrace, but now it is a matter of boasting not only to the active but to the passive partners who habituate themselves to endure the disease of effemination, let both body and soul run to waste, and leave no ember of their male sex-nature to smoulder. Mark how conspicuously they braid and adorn the hair of their heads, and how they scrub and paint their faces with cosmetics and pigments and the like, and smother themselves with fragrant unguents. For of all such embellishments, used by all who deck themselves out to wear a comely appearance, fragrance is the most seductive. In fact the transformation of the male nature to the female is practised by them
as an art and does not raise a blush. These persons 38
are rightly judged worthy of death by those who obey the law, which ordains that the man-woman who debases the sterling coin of nature should perish unavenged, suffered not to live for a day or even an hour, as a disgrace to himself, his house, his native land and
the whole human race. And the lover of such may 39
be assured that he is subject to the same penalty. He pursues an unnatural pleasure and does his best to render cities desolate and uninhabited by destroying[b] the means of procreation. Furthermore he sees no harm in becoming a tutor and instructor in the

[a] ...ased on Deut. xxiii. 1, and the expulsion of such persons from the congregation, here on Lev. xx. 13, where the death penalty is prescribed for *both* offenders (see §§ 38, 39 below). See also App. p. 634.

[b] Or again "wasting," as in § 34. But here at least the thought may be the same as in *De Abr.* 135, where the pederast is supposed to become impotent.

διδάσκαλος ἀξιοῖ γενέσθαι τοὺς νέους ὡραΐζων
καὶ τὸ τῆς ἀκμῆς ἄνθος ἐκθηλύνων, ὃ πρὸς ἀλκὴν
καὶ ῥώμην ἀλείφειν ἁρμόττον ἦν, καὶ τελευταῖον
ὅτι κακοῦ τρόπον γεωργοῦ τὰς μὲν βαθυγείους
καὶ εὐκάρπους ἀρούρας χερσεύειν ἐᾷ μηχανώμενος
ἐπ᾽ αὐταῖς ἀγονίαν, ἐξ ὧν δ᾽ οὐδὲν βλάστημα
προσδοκᾶται τὸ παράπαν, εἰς ταῦτα πονεῖται μεθ᾽
40 ἡμέραν τε καὶ νύκτωρ. αἴτιον δ᾽ οἶμαι τὸ παρὰ
πολλοῖς τῶν δήμων ἀκρασίας καὶ μαλακίας ἆθλα
κεῖσθαι· τοὺς γοῦν ἀνδρογύνους ἔστιν ἰδεῖν διὰ
πληθυούσης ἀγορᾶς ἀεὶ σοβοῦντας κἀν ταῖς ἑορταῖς
προπομπεύοντας καὶ τὰ ἱερὰ τοὺς ἀνιέρους διειλη-
χότας καὶ μυστηρίων καὶ τελετῶν κατάρχοντας
41 καὶ ⟨τὰ⟩ Δήμητρος ὀργιάζοντας. ὅσοι δ᾽ αὐτῶν
τὴν καλὴν νεανιείαν προσεπιτείνοντες εἰς ἅπαν
ὠρέχθησαν μεταβολῆς τῆς εἰς γυναῖκας καὶ τὰ
γεννητικὰ προσαπέκοψαν, ἁλουργίδας ἀμπεχόμενοι
καθάπερ οἱ μεγάλων ἀγαθῶν αἴτιοι ταῖς πατρίσι
προέρχονται δορυφορούμενοι, τοὺς ὑπαντῶντας
42 ἐπιστρέφοντες. εἰ δ᾽ ἦν ἀγανάκτησις οἵα παρὰ
τῷ ἡμετέρῳ νομοθέτῃ κατὰ τῶν τὰ τοιαῦτα
τολμώντων καὶ ὡς κοινὰ τῶν πατρίδων ἄγη καὶ
μιάσματα δίχα συγγνώμης ἀνῃροῦντο, πολλοὺς ἂν
ἑτέρους συνέβαινε νουθετεῖσθαι· αἱ γὰρ τῶν προ-
καταγνωσθέντων ἀπαραίτητοι τιμωρίαι ἀνακοπὴν
οὐ βραχεῖαν ἐργάζονται τοῖς ζηλωταῖς τῶν ὁμοίων
ἐπιτηδευμάτων.

---

[a] The translation supposes that the idea is the same as i

grievous vices of unmanliness and effeminacy by pro-
longing the bloom[a] of the young and emasculating the
flower of their prime, which should rightly be trained
to strength and robustness. Finally, like a bad
husbandman he lets the deep-soiled and fruitful fields
lie sterile, by taking steps to keep them from bearing,
while he spends his labour night and day on soil from
which no growth at all can be expected. The reason 40
is, I think, to be found in the prizes awarded in many
nations to licentiousness and effeminacy. Certainly
you may see these hybrids of man and woman continually strutting about through the thick of the
market, heading the processions at the feasts,
appointed to serve as unholy ministers of holy things,
leading the mysteries and initiations and celebrating
the rites of Demeter.[b] Those of them who by way of 41
heightening still further their youthful beauty have
desired to be completely changed into women and
gone on to mutilate their genital organs, are clad in
purple like signal benefactors of their native lands,
and march in front escorted by a bodyguard, attract-
ing the attention of those who meet them. But if 42
such indignation as our lawgiver felt was directed
against those who do not shrink from such conduct,
if they were cut off without condonation as public
enemies, each of them a curse and a pollution of his
country, many others would be found to take the
warning. For relentless punishment of criminals
already condemned acts as a considerable check on
those who are eager to practise the like.

i. 325 τὸ τῆς ὥρας ταμιεύοντας ἄνθος ἵνα μὴ ῥᾳδίως μαραίνοιτο. But the phrase is strange; Heinemann gives "die jungen Leute sich herausputzen lässt." Two MSS. have τοῦ γένους, which Mangey would correct to τοὺς γένυς (*genas venustans*).

[b] See App. p. 634.

43
[307] VIII. | Ἀλλὰ γὰρ ἔνιοι τὰς Συβαριτῶν καὶ τὰς
ἔτι λαγνιστέρων ἐπιθυμίας ζηλώσαντες τὸ μὲν
πρῶτον ὀψοφαγίαις καὶ οἰνοφλυγίαις καὶ ταῖς
ἄλλαις ταῖς γαστρὸς καὶ τῶν μετὰ γαστέρα
ἡδοναῖς ἐνησκήθησαν, εἶτα δὲ κορεσθέντες ἐξ-
ύβρισαν—ὕβριν γὰρ κόρος γεννᾶν πέφυκεν—, ὡς
ὑπὸ φρενοβλαβείας λυττᾶν καὶ ἐπιμεμηνέναι μηκέτ'
ἀνθρώποις εἴτ' ἄρρεσιν εἴτε θηλείαις ἀλλὰ καὶ
ἀλόγοις ζῴοις, ὥσπερ ἐν Κρήτῃ φασὶ τὸ παλαιὸν
τὴν γυναῖκα Μίνω τοῦ βασιλέως ὄνομα Πασιφάην·
44 ταύρου γὰρ ἐρασθεῖσαν καὶ τῷ πάθει σφαδᾴζουσαν
ἕνεκα τῆς περὶ τὴν ὁμιλίαν ἀπογνώσεως—ἀπο-
τυγχανόμενος γὰρ ἔρως οὐ μετρίως ἐπιτείνεται—
Δαιδάλῳ τὴν κατέχουσαν συμφορὰν ἀνενεγκεῖν,
ὃς ἦν τῶν κατ' αὐτὸν ἄριστος δημιουργός· τὸν δὲ
πάνυ δεινὸν ὄντα ταῖς ἐπινοίαις τὰ ἀθήρατα θηρᾶν
δούρειον κατασκευάσαι βοῦν καὶ διὰ τῆς ἑτέρας
πλευρᾶς ἐνθεῖναι τὴν Πασιφάην, τὸν δὲ ταῦρον
ὁρμήσαντα ὡς ἐπὶ ζῷον συγγενὲς ἐπιβαίνειν·
ἐγκύμονα δὲ γενομένην χρόνοις ὕστερον ἀποτεκεῖν
45 μιξόθηρα τὸν ἐπικαλούμενον Μινώταυρον. εἰκὸς
δὲ καὶ ἄλλας ἔσεσθαι Πασιφάας, ἀχαλινώτων
ἐωμένων τῶν παθῶν, καὶ οὐ γυναῖκας μόνον ἀλλὰ
καὶ ἄνδρας ἐπιμανήσεσθαι θηρίοις, ἐξ ὧν γενήσεσθαι
τέρατα παλίμφημα, μηνύματα τῆς ἀνθρώπων
ὑπερβαλλούσης βδελυρίας· δι' ἣν ἴσως καὶ αἱ τῶν
ἀνυπάρκτων καὶ μεμυθευμένων ἀγένητοι φύσεις
Ἱπποκενταύρων καὶ Χιμαιρῶν καὶ τῶν ὁμοιο-
46 τρόπων ἔσονται. τοσοῦτον δ' ἄρα τὸ
προμηθὲς ἐν τοῖς ἱεροῖς νόμοις ἐστίν, ὥσθ' ὑπὲρ

---

[a] Lev. xviii. 23; xx. 15-16; Ex. xxii. 19.

VIII. Even worse than this is the conduct of some 43
who have emulated the lusts of the Sybarites and those of others even more lascivious than they. These persons begin with making themselves experts in dainty feeding, wine-bibbing and the other pleasures of the belly and the parts below it. Then sated with these they reach such a pitch of wantonness, the natural offspring of satiety, that losing their senses they conceive a frantic passion, no longer for human beings male or female, but even for brute beasts.[a] So according to the story did Pasiphaë the wife of King
Minos long ago in Crete.[b] She was enamoured of a 44
bull, but had no hope of obtaining its company. Consequently wild with passion, for amorousness is vastly intensified by unsuccess, she reported the trouble under which she was labouring to Daedalus, who was the best craftsman of his time. His masterly skill in devising plans for capturing the uncaptured enabled him to construct a wooden cow, into which he introduced Pasiphaë through one of its sides, and the bull supposing it to be a living animal of its own kind, charged and mounted it. She became pregnant, and in the course of time bore a half-beast called the
Minotaur. Probably, if passions are suffered to go 45
unbridled, there will be other Pasiphaës, and not only women but also men will be frantically in love with wild beasts, which will produce unnatural monsters to serve as monuments of the disgusting excesses of mankind; whence possibly the Hippocentaurs and Chimeras and the like, forms of life hitherto unknown and with no existence outside mythology, will come
into being. Actually so great is the pro- 46
visions made in the law to ensure that men should

[b] *Cf.* Diodorus, iv. 77.

τοῦ μηδεμίαν ἔκθεσμον ὁμιλίαν ἀνθρώπους προσίεσθαι διείρηται μηδὲ κτῆνος ἐᾶν ὑπό τινος
ἑτερογενοῦς ὀχεύεσθαι· τράγον οὐδεὶς ἐάσει ποιμὴν
Ἰουδαῖος ἐπιβαίνειν ἀμνάδι οὐδὲ κριὸν χιμαίρᾳ
οὐδὲ βοῦν ἵππῳ, εἰ δὲ μή, δώσει δίκας ὡς φύσεως
δόγμα λύων, ᾗ τὰ ἀνωτάτω γένη διατηρεῖν ἐπιμελὲς
47 οὐ νοθευόμενα. τοὺς ὀρεῖς ἔνιοι μὲν ἁπάντων
ὑποζυγίων προτιμῶσιν, ἐπειδὴ τὰ σώματα αὐτοῖς
πέπηγε καὶ σφόδρα νενεύρωται, κἀν τοῖς ἱππο-
φορβίοις καὶ ταῖς ἱπποστάσεσιν ὄνους ὑπερμεγέθεις,
οὓς προσαγορεύουσι κήλωνας, ἀνατρέφουσιν, ἵνα
ταῖς θηλείαις ἐπιβαίνωσι πώλοις, αἳ δὴ μικτὸν
ζῷον ἀποτίκτουσιν ἡμίονον, ἧς παρὰ φύσιν τὴν
γένεσιν εἰδὼς ἀνὰ κράτος ἀπεῖπε Μωυσῆς καθ-
ολικωτέρᾳ προστάξει, τοῖς ἀνομοιογενέσι μὴ ἐφεὶς
48 ὀχεύειν ἢ ὀχεύεσθαι. προὐνόησε μὲν οὖν ἀναλόγως
τοῦ πρέποντος καὶ ἀκολούθου τῇ φύσει, μακρόθεν
δ' ὡς ἀπὸ σκοπῆς ἐσωφρόνισεν ἀνθρώπους, ἵν' ἐκ
τῶνδε προμαθόντες ἄνδρες ὁμοῦ καὶ γυναῖκες
49 ἀνέχωσιν ὁμιλιῶν ἐκνόμων. ἐάν τε οὖν ἀνὴρ
ὀχεύῃ τετράπουν ἐάν τε γυνὴ ὑπὸ τετράποδος
ὀχεύηται, θνῃσκέτωσαν καὶ οἱ ἄνθρωποι καὶ τὰ
[308] τετράποδα, οἱ μὲν ὅτι ὑπὲρ τοὺς | ὅρους ἀκρασίας
αὐτῆς ἤλασαν εὑρεταὶ γενόμενοι παρηλλαγμένων
ἐπιθυμιῶν καὶ ὅτι ἡδονὰς ἀηδεστάτας ἐκαινούργη-
σαν, ὧν καὶ ἡ διήγησις αἰσχίστη, τὰ δὲ ὅτι τοιούτοις ὀνείδεσιν ὑπηρέτησε καὶ ἵνα μηδὲν ἢ τέκῃ

[a] Lev. xix. 19, where the prohibition is joined with others against sowing different seeds in a field and combining two stuffs in a garment. *Cf.* Deut. xxii. 9-11.

[b] Mules, however, are several times mentioned, evidently without reproach, in the O.T., *e.g.* Is. lxvi. 20, 1 Kings i. 33.

[c] See note *b* on § 63 below.

admit no unlawful matings, that it ordains that even cattle are not to be crossed with others of a different species.[a] No Jewish shepherd will allow a he-goat to mount a ewe or a ram a she-goat, or a bull a mare, or if he does he will be punished as an offender against the decree of nature, who is careful to preserve the primary species without adulteration. It is true that 47
some people value mules above all other beasts of burden, because their bodies are compact and exceedingly muscular, and accordingly in horse-stables or other places where horses are kept they rear donkeys of huge size to which they give the name of "Celons" to copulate with the female colts, who then give birth to a hybrid animal, the mule or half-ass. But Moses, recognizing that the way in which this animal is produced contravenes nature, stringently forbade it under the wider order by which he refused permission for animals of either sex to breed with those of an unlike species.[b] In making this 48
provision he considered what was in accord with decency and conformity to nature, but beyond this he gave us as from some far-off commanding height[c] a warning to men and women alike that they should learn from these examples to abstain from unlawful forms of intercourse. Whether, then, it is the man 49
who uses a quadruped for this purpose, or the woman who allows herself to be used, the human offenders must die and the beasts also; the first because they have passed beyond the limits of licentiousness itself by evolving abnormal lusts, and because they have invented strange pleasures than which nothing could be more unpleasing, shameful even to describe; the beasts because they have ministered to such infamies, and to ensure that they do not bear or beget any

ἢ γεννήσῃ παλίμφημον, οἷα εἰκὸς ἐκ τοιούτων
50 μιασμάτων· ἄλλως τε οἷς καὶ βραχὺ μέλει τοῦ
πρέποντος οὐκέτ᾿ ἂν χρήσαιντο τοῖς θρέμμασιν
εἰς οὐδεμίαν τῶν περὶ βίον ὑπηρεσίαν, μυσαττό-
μενοι καὶ ἀποστρεφόμενοι καὶ τὴν ὄψιν αὐτὴν
δυσχεραίνοντες καὶ νομίζοντες ὧν ἂν προσάψαιτο
κἀκεῖνα εὐθὺς ἀκάθαρτα εἶναι· τὰ δὲ μηδαμῇ
χρήσιμα τῷ βίῳ ζῆν εἰ καὶ λυσιτελὲς[1] ἀλλ᾿ οὖν
περιττὸν "ἄχθος γῆς," ὥς εἶπέ τις.
51 IX. Πάλιν πόρνην ἡ κατὰ Μωυσῆν οὐ παραδέχεται πολιτεία κοσμιότητος καὶ αἰδοῦς καὶ
σωφροσύνης καὶ τῶν ἄλλων ἀρετῶν ἀλλοτρίαν, ἣ
ἀναπιμπλᾶσα τὰς ψυχὰς ἀνδρῶν ὁμοῦ καὶ γυναικῶν
ἀκολασίας τὸ μὲν τῆς διανοίας ἀθάνατον κάλλος
αἰσχύνει, τὴν δὲ τοῦ σώματος ὀλιγοχρόνιον εὐ-
μορφίαν προτιμᾷ, παραρριπτοῦσα μὲν αὑτὴν τοῖς
ἐπιτυχοῦσι, τὴν δ᾿ ὥραν ὥσπερ τι τῶν ὠνίων ἐπ᾿
ἀγορᾶς πιπράσκουσα, καὶ ἐπὶ μὲν θήρᾳ τῶν νέων
ἕκαστα λέγει τε καὶ πράττει, τοὺς δὲ ἐραστὰς
ἀλείφει κατὰ ἀλλήλων αἴσχιστον ἆθλον αὑτὴν
προτιθεῖσα τοῖς τὸ πλέον εἰσενεγκοῦσιν. ὡς λύμη
καὶ ζημία καὶ κοινὸν μίασμα καταλευέσθω, τὰς
τῆς φύσεως διαφθείρασα χάριτας, ἃς ἥρμοττε
καλοκἀγαθίᾳ προσεπικοσμῆσαι.

[1] Mangey reads (with A) οὐ ζῆν εἶναι λυσιτελές, περιττὸν ὄντα γῆς ἄχθος (most MSS. insert ὄντα). See note *a*.

---

[a] The text as here translated makes some sort of sense, if we take λυσιτελές = something that has a monetary value. The text adopted by Mangey from A (see note 1), is much

monstrosity of the kind that may be expected to spring from such abominations. Besides, even people 50
who care little for seemliness would not continue to use their cattle for any purpose serviceable to their life, but would regard them with abhorrence and aversion, disliking the very sight of them and thinking that even what they touch, that too must become unclean. And, when things serve no purpose in life, their survival, even if it can be turned to some account,[a] is just a superfluity, "cumbering the earth," as the poet puts it.[b]

IX. Again, the commonwealth of Moses' institution 51
does not admit a harlot,[c] that stranger to decency and modesty and temperance and the other virtues. She infects the souls both of men and women with licentiousness. She casts shame upon the undying beauty of the mind and prefers in honour the short-lived comeliness of the body. She flings herself at the disposal of chance comers, and sells her bloom like some ware to be purchased in the market. In her every word and deed she aims at capturing the young, while she incites her lovers each against the other by offering the vile prize of herself to the highest bidder. A pest, a scourge, a plague-spot to the public, let her be stoned to death—she who has corrupted the graces bestowed by nature, instead of making them, as she should, the ornament of noble conduct.

clearer (the infinitive *εἶναι* may be defended as continuing the construction after *νομίζοντες*). As Mangey and A have it, it omits *ἀλλ' οὖν*, but this might be retained in the sense of "nay indeed," *i.e.* the survival is not merely unprofitable, but actually burdensome.

[b] See on i. 74.

[c] Deut. xxiii. 17, which, however, does not suggest death as the penalty. See App. p. 634.

52 X. [1]Μοιχείας δὲ τὰς μὲν ἢ αὐτοφώρους ἢ ἐναργέσιν ἐλέγχοις πιστουμένας ὑπαιτίους ἀπέφηνεν ὁ νόμος, τὰς δὲ καθ' ὑπόνοιαν οὐκ ἐδικαίωσεν ἐξετάζεσθαι πρὸς ἀνθρώπων, ἀλλὰ εἰς τὸ τῆς φύσεως ἤγαγε δικαστήριον, ἐπειδήπερ ἄνθρωποι μὲν τῶν ἐμφανῶν ἐπιγνώμονες, θεὸς δὲ καὶ τῶν ἀδήλων, ᾧ μόνῳ δυνατὸν ψυχὴν ἐναργῶς θεά-
53 σασθαι. φησὶν οὖν τῷ ὑπονοήσαντι ἀνδρί· γραψάμενος πρόκλησιν εἰς τὴν ἱερόπολιν ἴθι σὺν τῇ γυναικὶ καὶ καταστὰς ἐπὶ τῶν δικαστῶν ἀπογύμνωσον τὸ παραστάν σοι τῆς ὑπονοίας πάθος, μὴ ὡς ἄν τις συκοφάντης ἢ κακοτεχνῶν ὑπὲρ τοῦ πάντως περιγενέσθαι, ἀλλ' ὡς ἄν τις τῆς ἀληθείας
54 ἀκριβὴς ἐξεταστὴς ἄνευ σοφιστείας. ἡ δὲ γυνὴ δύο κινδύνους ὑπομένουσα, τὸν μὲν ὑπὲρ ψυχῆς,
[309] τὸν δὲ | αἰσχύνης βίου, παντὸς ἀργαλεώτερον θανάτου, κρινάτω παρ' αὐτῇ τὸ πρᾶγμα, κἂν μὲν καθαρεύῃ, θαρροῦσα ἀπολογείσθω, εἰ δὲ ὑπὸ τοῦ συνειδότος ἐλέγχοιτο, καταδυέσθω, προκάλυμμα τῶν ἁμαρτημάτων αἰδῶ ποιησαμένη· τὸ γὰρ μέχρι
55 τέλους ἀναισχυντεῖν ὑπερβολὴ κακίας. ἐὰν δὲ ἀμφήριστα ᾖ τὰ λεχθέντα καὶ μηδέτερον καθέλκῃ μέρος, ἴτωσαν εἰς τὸ ἱερόν, καὶ ὁ μὲν ἀνὴρ στὰς ἀντικρὺ τοῦ βωμοῦ, παρόντος τοῦ κατ' ἐκείνην τὴν ἡμέραν ἱερωμένου, δηλούτω τὴν ὑπόνοιαν, ἅμα καὶ κομίζων ἄλευρον κρίθινον, εἶδός τι θυσίας ὑπὲρ τῆς γυναικός, εἰς ἔνδειξιν τοῦ μὴ κατ' ἐπήρειαν ἀλλ' ἀπὸ γνώμης ὑγιοῦς κατ' ἐνδοιασμὸν

[1] mss. heading Περὶ μοιχαλίδος.

X. Adulteries detected on the spot or established by 52
clear evidence are condemned by the law. But when they are a matter of suspicion, the law did not think good to have them tried by men, but brought them before the tribunal of nature. For men can arbitrate on open matters, but God on the hidden also, since He alone can see clearly into the soul. [a] So the 53
law says to the husband who suspects his wife, "Draw up a formal challenge and come to the holy city with your wife and standing before the judges lay bare the suspicion which troubles you, not in the spirit of a false accuser or malicious schemer, set on winning at any cost, but of one who would strictly test the truth without sophistry. The woman who is threatened with two dangers, 54
one of losing her life, the other of bringing shame on her past (and this is a thing far more grievous than death), must judge the matter in her heart, and if she is pure, plead her cause with good courage, but if her conscience convicts her, make her submission and use her ashamedness to palliate her sins. For shamelessness carried to the end is the culmination of wickedness. But if the statements 55
of the two are inconclusive, and do not turn the scale to either side, let them go to the temple and let the man standing opposite the altar, in the presence of the priest officiating on that day, explain his suspicion. At the same time he should bring barley-meal, as a kind of sacrifice on behalf of the woman, to shew that the accusation is not made in wanton spite, but with honest intentions

[a] For §§ 53-62 see Num. v. 12-31, which Philo follows fairly closely, except that the law does not provide for a previous hearing before judges as in §§ 53, 54.

56 εὔλογον αἰτιᾶσθαι. ὁ δὲ ἱερεὺς λαβὼν προτεινέτω τῇ γυναικὶ καὶ τοὐπίκρανον ἀφελών, ἵν' ἐπικρίνηται γεγυμνωμένη τῇ κεφαλῇ, τὸ τῆς αἰδοῦς περιῃρημένη σύμβολον, ᾧ ταῖς εἰς ἅπαν ἀναιτίοις ἔθος χρῆσθαι. μήτε δὲ ἔλαιον μήτε λιβανωτὸς ὡς ἐπὶ τῶν ἄλλων θυσιῶν παρέστω, διὰ τὸ μὴ ἐπὶ χαρτοῖς ἀλλ' ἄγαν ὀδυνηροῖς τὴν θυσίαν μέλλειν ἐπι-
57 τελεῖσθαι. κρίθινον δ' ἐστὶ τὸ ἄλευρον, ἴσως ἐπειδὴ ὑπαμφίβολός ἐστιν ἡ ἀπὸ κριθῆς τροφὴ καὶ ἀλόγοις ζῴοις καὶ ἀτυχέσιν ἀνθρώποις ἐφαρμόζεται,[1] σύμβολον τοῦ τὴν μεμοιχευμένην οὐδὲν θηρίων διαφέρειν, ὧν ἀδιακρίτους εἶναι καὶ ἀνεπιστάτους τὰς ὀχείας συμβέβηκε, τὴν δὲ καθαρεύουσαν τῶν ἐγκλημάτων τὸν οἰκεῖον ἀνθρώπων
58 βίον ἐζηλωκέναι. λαβὼν δέ, φησίν, ὁ ἱερεὺς κεραμεοῦν ἀγγεῖον ἐγχείτω καθαρὸν ὕδωρ ἐκ πηγῆς ἀρυσάμενος καὶ ἐπιφερέτω βῶλον γῆς ἐκ τοῦ κατὰ τὸ ἱερὸν ἐδάφους· ἅπερ οἶμαι καὶ αὐτὰ συντείνειν πρὸς τὴν ἔρευναν τῆς ἀληθείας διὰ συμβόλων, τὸ μὲν κεραμεοῦν ἀγγεῖον πρὸς τὸ μεμοιχεῦσθαι, διὰ τὸ εὐκάτακτον, θάνατος γὰρ ἡ κατὰ μοιχῶν δίκη, ἡ δὲ γῆ καὶ τὸ ὕδωρ πρὸς τὸ καθαρεύειν τῆς αἰτίας, ἐπειδὴ δι' ἀμφοτέρων αἱ γενέσεις καὶ αὐξήσεις καὶ τελειώσεις ἁπάντων.
59 ὅθεν ἑκάτερον οὐκ ἀπὸ σκοποῦ καὶ τοῖς ὀνόμασιν

[1] MSS. ἐφαρμόζεσθαι.

---

[a] By εἶδος he may mean that this oblation, though called θυσία in the text, is not of the ordinary kind. In the E.V. the words are "he shall bring her offering for her"; in LXX "he shall bring the (or "his") gift about her." As he regards the oblation as made by the man and not by the woman, he appends this explanation of his motives.

and is founded on reasonable doubt.[a] The priest 56
taking the offering hands it to the woman and removes her kerchief, in order that she may be judged with her head bared and stripped of the symbol of modesty, regularly worn by women who are wholly innocent. But there must be no oil nor frankincense, as in the other sacrifices, because the intention of the sacrifice to be performed on this occasion is
not joyful but exceedingly painful.[b] The meal used 57
is of barley, perhaps because as a foodstuff it is of somewhat doubtful merit, suited for irrational animals and men in unhappy circumstances, and thus is a symbol that the adulteress is quite on a par with wild beasts, which copulate without discrimination or due consideration, while the wife who is innocent of the charges brought against her has emulated the life
which is fitted to human beings. The priest, it 58
continues, will take an earthen vessel, pour into it pure water which he has drawn from a spring, and put in a clod of earth got from the ground on which the temple stands.[c] These likewise, I consider, refer symbolically to the quest for the truth. The act of adultery is signified by the earthen vessel because of its fragility, since death is the punishment decreed for adulterers ; innocence of the charge by the earth and water, since both these are factors in the birth
and growth and consummation of all things. And 59
therefore the terms used in both cases make an

[b] In Numbers the reason of the absence of oil and frankincense is that "it is a sacrifice of jealousy, a sacrifice of memorial calling sin to remembrance," which assumes the guilt of the accused more than Philo is willing to do.

[c] Or "on the floor of the temple." LXX, "the earth," E.V. "the dust."

ἐπεκόσμησε, τὸ μὲν ὕδωρ εἰπὼν δεῖν "καθαρὸν"
λαμβάνειν καὶ "ζῶν," ἐπεὶ ἀνυπαίτιος ἡ γυνὴ
καθαρεύει τὸν βίον καὶ ζῆν ὀφείλει, τὴν δὲ γῆν
οὐκ ἀπὸ τοῦ τυχόντος ἀλλ' ἀπὸ τοῦ ἱεροῦ ἐδάφους,
ὅπερ ἀναγκαῖον ἀρετᾶν, ὡς καὶ γυναῖκα τὴν
60 σώφρονα. τούτων δὲ προευτρεπισθέντων, ἡ μὲν
ἀκατακαλύπτῳ τῇ κεφαλῇ τὸ κρίθινον ἄλευρον
κομίζουσα, καθάπερ ἐλέχθη, παρίτω, ὁ δὲ ἱερεὺς
[ἀντικρὺ] τὸ κεραμεοῦν ἀγγεῖον, ἐν ᾧ ὕδωρ ἐστὶ
61 καὶ γῆ, ⟨ἀντικρὺ⟩ στὰς ἐπιλεγέτω τάδε· "εἰ μὲν
τοὺς ἐπὶ γάμοις θεσμοὺς οὐ παραβέβηκας οὐδ'
ἀνὴρ ἕτερος ὡμίλησέ σοι καθυφεμένῃ τὰ πρὸς τὸν
[310] | νόμῳ[1] συνοικισθέντα δίκαια, ἀνυπαίτιος καὶ ἀθῷος
ἴσθι· εἰ δ' ὠλιγώρησας μὲν ἀνδρὸς καινὰς δὲ
ἐζήλωσας[2] ἐπιθυμίας ἢ ἐρασθεῖσα ἢ ἐρασθέντι
ἐνδοῦσα, τὰ ἀναγκαιότατα καὶ φίλτατα προδοῦσα
καὶ νοθεύσασα, μὴ ἀγνόει πάσαις ἀραῖς ἔνοχος
γεγενημένη, ὧν τὰ δείγματα ἀναφανεῖς ἐπὶ τοῦ
σώματος. ἴθι δὴ ἔκπινε ποτὸν ἐλέγχου, ὃ τὰ
κεκρυμμένα νῦν καὶ ἀδηλούμενα ἀπαμφιάσει καὶ
62 ἀπογυμνώσει." ταῦτα γράψας ἐν χαρτιδίῳ καὶ
ἀπαλείψας τῷ κατὰ τὸ ἀγγεῖον ὕδατι προτεινέτω
τῇ γυναικί· ἡ δὲ πιοῦσα ἀπαλλαττέσθω προσ-
δοκῶσα ἢ σωφροσύνης ἆθλον ἢ ἀκολασίας τὴν
ἀνωτάτω τιμωρίαν. εἰ μὲν γὰρ σεσυκοφάντηται,
σπορὰν καὶ γένεσιν τέκνων ἐλπιζέτω τῶν ἐπὶ

[1] MSS. νόμον. [2] MSS. ζηλώσασα.

[a] So LXX. E.V. and Hebrew merely "holy." In Num. xix. 17, where the E.V. has "running water," the LXX has ζῶν.

[b] So, as the sequel shews, rather than "conviction," though

appropriate addition to the picture. The water, it says, must be taken "pure" and "living,"[a] since if the woman is guiltless her conduct is "pure" and she deserves to "live"; the earth is taken not from any chance place but from the "holy" ground, which must needs be capable of fertility, as also must the chaste wife. When these preliminaries are completed, 60
the woman is to come forward with her head uncovered, bringing the barley-meal, as has been said, and the priest holding the earthen vessel with the earth and water in it stands fronting her and pronounces as follows: "If thou hast not transgressed 61
the lawful usages of marriage, if no other man has had intercourse with thee, suffered by thee in abandonment of thy duties to the legitimate partner of thy home, be clear of guilt and its consequences. But if thou hast set at naught thy husband and eagerly gratified thy new desires, seized with love for another or surrendering to his love, betraying and debasing the closest and fondest ties, be well assured that thou hast laid thyself open to every curse, and the signs of their fulfilment thou wilt exhibit in thy body. Come then, drink the draught of testing[b] which will uncover and lay bare what is now hidden in secrecy." He will 62
then write these words on a piece of paper and after blotting them out in the water in the vessel, proffer it to the woman, and when she has drunk she will depart expecting either reward for her chastity or extreme punishment for her incontinence. For if she has been falsely accused she may hope to conceive and bear children and pay no heed to her fears and

that is the meaning of the LXX ἐλεγμοῦ followed by "that brings the curse." E.V. "the water of bitterness that causeth the curse."

στειρώσει καὶ ἀγονίᾳ φόβων καὶ φροντίδων ἀλογοῦσα· εἰ δ' ἐστὶν ἔνοχος, ἐφεδρεύσοντα ἴστω γαστρὸς ὄγκον οἰδούσης καὶ πιμπραμένης καὶ τῶν περὶ μήτραν δεινὴν κάκωσιν, ἣν καθαρὰν οὐκ ἠξίωσε διατηρεῖν ἀνδρὶ τῷ κατὰ πάτρια γήμαντι.
63 τοσαύτην δ' ἔχει πρόνοιαν ὁ νόμος τοῦ μηδὲν ἐπὶ γάμοις νεωτερίζεσθαι, ὥστε καὶ τοὺς συνιόντας εἰς ὁμιλίαν ἄνδρας καὶ γυναῖκας κατὰ τοὺς ἐπὶ γάμοις θεσμούς, ὅταν εὐνῆς ἀπαλλάττωνται, οὐ πρότερον ἐᾷ τινος ψαύειν ἢ λουτροῖς καὶ περιρραντηρίοις χρῆσθαι, πόρρωθεν μοιχείας ἀνείργων καὶ τῶν ἐπὶ μοιχείαις ἐγκλημάτων.

64 XI. Ἐὰν δέ τις χήραν ἀποθανόντος ἀνδρὸς ἢ καὶ διαζευχθεῖσαν ἄλλως βιασάμενος αἰσχύνῃ, κουφότερον ἢ κατὰ μοιχείαν ἁμάρτημα δρῶν, ἥμισυ σχεδὸν ἐκείνου, τῆς μὲν θανάτου τιμωρίας ἀφείσθω, βίαν δὲ καὶ ὕβριν καὶ ἀκολασίαν καὶ θράσος τὰ αἴσχιστα ὡς κάλλιστα ἀποδεξάμενος κατηγορείσθω καὶ ὅ τι χρὴ παθεῖν ἢ ἀποτῖσαι τιμάτω[1] τὸ δικαστήριον ἐπ' αὐτῷ.

65 [2]Ἀδελφὸν μὲν καὶ συγγενὲς ἀδίκημα μοιχείας φθορά, καθάπερ ἐκ μητρὸς μιᾶς, ἀκολασίας, φύντα[3]·

[1] MSS. τιμάσθω. [2] MS. heading Περὶ φθορᾶς.

[3] For the solecism φύντα Mangey suggests φῦσα, but this does not suit μιᾶς.

[a] Lev. xv. 18.

[b] Lit. "forbidding from afar." The same word (or μακρόθεν) is used in the same way § 47 above, and again §§ 48, 117. *Cf.* also iv. 104, *De Virt.* 137.

[c] Philo neither has nor claims any biblical authority for this section. He is about to describe the pentateuchal law about the rape or seduction of a virgin, and feels that the similar offence in the case of a married woman who is now without a husband must call for punishment or redress. Whether what he says reflects the practice of his time (see

apprehensions of sterility or childlessness. But if she is guilty she may be sure that the fate awaiting her is an unwieldy belly, swollen and inflamed, and terrible suffering all round the womb, which she has not cared to keep pure for the husband who married her according to ancestral custom. So careful is the 63
law to provide against the introduction of violent changes in the institution of marriage that a husband and wife, who have intercourse in accordance with the legitimate usages of married life, are not allowed, when they leave their bed, to touch anything until they have made their ablutions and purged themselves with water.[a] This ordinance extends by implication to a prohibition[b] of adultery, or anything which entails an accusation of adultery.

XI. If anyone dishonours by violence a woman 64
widowed by the death of her husband or through any other form of separation, the crime he commits is less serious than in adultery, of which it may be said to be the half.[c] The penalty of death should not be enforced in his case: but since he has accepted as highly honourable such vile things as violence, outrage, incontinence and effrontery, he must be indicted and the court must determine for him the penalty he should suffer or the compensation he should pay.

The corruption[d] of a maiden is a criminal offence 65
closely akin to adultery, its brother in fact, for both spring as it were from one mother, licentiousness, to

Goodenough, p. 90), or merely what he feels would be right, seems to me quite uncertain.

[d] Ex. xxii. 16, 17; Deut. xxii. 28, 29. The first passage deals rather with seduction ("entice," ἀπατήσας); the second with rape ("lay hold on her," βιασάμενος). The right of the father to refuse his consent to the marriage does not appear in the second passage.

ἣν ἔνιοι τῶν εἰωθότων εὐπρεπέσιν ὀνόμασι τὰ αἰσχρὰ ἐπικοσμεῖν ἔρωτα ὀνομάζουσι τἀληθὲς ὁμολογεῖν ἐρυθριῶντες. ἀλλ᾿ ὅμως, εἰ καὶ συγγενές, οὐ παντάπασιν ὅμοιον, τῷ τὸ ἀδίκημα μὴ εἰς πλείους χωρεῖν οἰκίας, ὡς ἐπὶ τῆς μοιχείας συμβέβηκεν, ἀλλ᾿ εἰς μίαν συνῆχθαι τὴν τῆς
66 παρθένου. λεκτέον οὖν τῷ κόρης ἀστῆς ἐπιθυμοῦντι· "προπέτειαν καὶ θράσος ἀναίσχυντον ἢ τὰς ἐπ᾿ ἐνέδρᾳ πάγας ἤ τι τῶν ὁμοιοτρόπων, ὦ
[311] | οὗτος, ἀποστραφεὶς μήτε ἀναφανδὸν μήτε λάθρα
67 πονηρὸς ἐξετασθῇς. ἀλλ᾿ εἴπερ ἄρα τι τῇ ψυχῇ πέπονθας πρὸς τὴν παῖδα οἰκεῖον, ἴθι πρὸς τοὺς γονεῖς αὐτῆς, ἐὰν ζῶντες τυγχάνωσιν, εἰ δὲ μή, πρὸς τοὺς ἀδελφοὺς ἢ ἐπιτρόπους ἢ ἄλλους κυρίους, καὶ ἀπογυμνώσας τὸ σεαυτοῦ πάθος, ὡς χρὴ τὸν ἐλεύθερον, αἴτει πρὸς γάμον καὶ παρακάλει μὴ
68 ἀνάξιος νομισθῆναι. σκαιὸς γὰρ οὐδεὶς ἂν οὕτως γένοιτο τῶν ἐπιμελουμένων τῆς παιδός, ὡς ἐναντιωθῆναι πρὸς λιπαρεστέρας δεήσεις, καὶ μάλιστά γε ἐπειδὰν ἐξετάσας ἀνευρίσκῃ μὴ κατεψευσμένον ἢ ἐπιπόλαιον ἄλλως τὸ πάθος ἀλλ᾿ ἐπαληθεῦον καὶ
69 παγίως ἐνιδρυμένον." ἐὰν δέ τις λυττῶν καὶ μεμηνώς, ἅπασι τοῖς ἐκ λογισμοῦ πολλὰ χαίρειν φράσας, δυναστείαν τὸν οἶστρον καὶ τὴν ἐπιθυμίαν ὑπολαβών, νόμου βίαν, ὥς φασί τινες, προτιμοτέραν θέμενος, ἁρπάζῃ καὶ φθείρῃ ταῖς ἐλευθέραις ὡς θεραπαίναις χρώμενος, τὰ πολέμου δρῶν ἐν εἰρήνῃ,
70 πρὸς τοὺς δικαστὰς ἀγέσθω. κἂν μὲν ᾖ πατὴρ τῇ βιασθείσῃ, βουλευέσθω περὶ ἐγγύης τῆς πρὸς[1] τὸν ἐφθαρκότα· εἶτα ἐὰν μὲν ἀνανεύῃ, προικιζέτω

[1] MSS. περὶ.

which some whose way it is to bedizen ugly things with specious terms, ashamed to admit its true nature, give the name of love. Still the kinship does not amount to complete similarity, because the wrong caused by the corruption is not passed on to several families as it is with adultery, but is concentrated in
one, that of the maiden herself. Our advice then to 66
one who desires a damsel of gentle birth should be this : " My good sir, have nothing to do with reckless and shameless effrontery or treacherous snares, or anything of the kind, and do not either openly or
secretly prove yourself a rascal. But if you have, 67
heart and soul, centred your affections on the girl, go to her parents, if they are alive, or, if not, to her brothers or guardians or others who have charge of her, lay bare before them the state of your affections, as a free man should, ask her hand in marriage and plead that you may not be thought unworthy of her.
For none of those who have had the care of the girl 68
would behave so stupidly as to set himself in opposition to the increasing earnestness of your entreaties, particularly if, on examination, he finds that your affections are not counterfeited nor superficial, but are
genuine and firmly established." But if anyone in 69
furious frenzy will have nothing to say to the suggestions of reason, but regarding wild passion and lust as sovereign powers and giving the place of honour to violence above law, as the saying goes, turns to rapine and ravishment and treats free women as though they were servant-maids, acting in peace as he might in war-time, he must be brought
before the judges. And if the victim of the violation 70
has a father he must consider the question of espousing her to the author of her ruin. If he refuses, the

τὴν παῖδα ὁ φθορεὺς ἄλλως ζημιούμενος χρήμασιν, ἐὰν δὲ συναινῇ καὶ συνεπιγράφηται, μηδὲν ὑπερτιθέμενος ἀγέσθω προῖκα πάλιν τὴν ἴσην ὁμολογῶν καὶ μήτε ἀναδύεσθαι τὴν ἐξουσίαν ἐχέτω μήτε παραιτεῖσθαι, καὶ δι᾿ αὐτόν, ἵνα μὴ λαγνείας ἕνεκα δοκῇ μᾶλλον ἢ κατ᾿ ἔρωτα νόμιμον ἐφθαρκέναι, καὶ διὰ τὴν κόρην, ἵν᾿ αὐτῆς τὸ περὶ τὴν πρώτην σύνοδον ἀτύχημα παρηγορηθῇ βεβαιοτάτῳ γάμῳ,
71 ὃν οὐδὲν ἄλλο τι ἢ θάνατος διαζεύξει. ἐὰν δὲ πατρὸς ὀρφανὴ τυγχάνῃ, πρὸς τῶν δικαστῶν ἐρωτάσθω, εἴτε βούλεται συνοικεῖν εἴτε μή· ἐάν τε δὲ συναινῇ ἐάν τε ἀρνῆται, τὰ αὐτὰ γινέσθω ἃ ἂν καὶ ἐπὶ ζῶντι διωμολογήθη τῷ πατρί.

72 XII. [1]Μεθόριόν τινες ὑπολαμβάνουσιν ἀδίκημα εἶναι φθορᾶς καὶ μοιχείας ὑπογάμιον, ὅταν ὁμολογίαι μὲν ὑπερεγγυήσωσι, μήπω δὲ τῶν γάμων ἐπιτελεσθέντων ἕτερος ἀπατήσας τις ἢ καὶ βιασάμενος εἰς ὁμιλίαν ἔλθῃ. παρ᾿ ἐμοὶ δὲ κριτῇ μοιχείας καὶ τοῦτ᾿ ἐστὶν εἶδος· αἱ γὰρ ὁμολογίαι γάμοις ἰσοδυναμοῦσιν, αἷς ἀνδρὸς ὄνομα καὶ γυναικὸς καὶ

[1] MS. heading Περὶ ὑπογαμίου.

---

[a] Or perhaps "to dismiss her" (at a later time). *Cf.* the examples of παραιτεῖσθαι in the sense of "divorce" in L. & S. This will correspond with Deuteronomy, "he may not put her away all his days," as well as with Philo's words at the end of the section.

[b] Philo has no biblical authority for this section. It is curious that the guardians whose consent has to be obtained for the ordinary marriage of an orphan do not appear here.

[c] For §§ 72-78 see Deut. xxii. 23-27.

[d] The curious word ὑπογάμιον occurs only here. The suggestion in the translation is that it is formed on the analogy of the not uncommon use of ὑπό = "just before." But except

seducer must give a dowry to the girl, his punishment being thus limited to a monetary fine, but if the father consents to the union, he must marry her without any delay and agree to give the same dowry as in the former case, and he must not be at liberty to draw back, or to make difficulties.[a] This is in the interest both of himself, to make the rape appear due to legitimate love rather than to lasciviousness, and of the girl, to give her for the misfortune, which she has suffered at their first association, the consolation of a wedlock so firmly established that nothing but death will undo it. [b] If 71
she has lost her father, she must be asked by the judges whether she wishes to consort with the man or not. And whether she agrees or refuses, the terms agreed upon must be the same as they would have been if her father were alive.

XII. [c] Some consider that midway between the cor- 72
ruption of a maiden and adultery stands the crime committed on the eve of marriage,[d] when mutual agreements have affianced the parties beyond all doubt, but before the marriage was celebrated, another man, either by seduction or violence, has intercourse with the bride. But this too, to my thinking, is a form of adultery. For the agreements, being documents containing the names of the man and woman, and the other particulars

for the epic adjectives ὑπηοῖος and ὑποδείελος, I cannot find any analogous compounds. However, ὑπὸ γάμον would be an easy correction. The general opinion seems to be that the ὑπό suggests "secret" or "illicit," and presumably this is the idea in Mangey's "interceptus concubitus," and L. & S.'s "illicit intercourse with a betrothed person." Also the word seems to be regularly regarded as a substantive. It seems to me more likely that it is an adjective agreeing with ἀδίκημα.

73 τὰ ἄλλα τὰ ἐπὶ συνόδοις ἐγγράφεται. ὧν χάριν καταλεύειν ὁ νόμος ἀμφοτέρους προσέταξεν, ἐάν γε ἀπὸ μιᾶς καὶ τῆς αὐτῆς γνώμης ἐπιθῶνται τοῖς ἀδικήμασι συμφρονήσαντες· οὐχ οἷόν τε γὰρ μὴ ἀπὸ τῶν αὐτῶν ὁρμηθέντας βουλευμάτων νομίζεσθαι
74 συναδικεῖν, οὐ συναδικοῦντας. παρὰ γοῦν τὰς
[312] τῶν τόπων διαφορὰς | αὔξεσθαι συμβέβηκε καὶ μειοῦσθαι τἀδίκημα· μεῖζον μὲν γάρ, ὡς εἰκός, ἐστίν, εἰ πραχθείη κατὰ πόλιν, ἔλαττον δέ, εἰ τειχῶν ἔξω κατ' ἐρημίαν· ἐνταῦθα μὲν γὰρ βοηθὸς οὐδὲ εἷς ἐστι τῇ παιδὶ πάνθ' ὅσα ὑπὲρ τοῦ διατηρῆσαι τὴν παρθενίαν ἄψαυστον καὶ ἀνεπιβούλευτον λεγούσῃ τε καὶ δρώσῃ, ἐν ἄστει δὲ βουλευτήρια, δικαστήρια, στρατηγῶν, ἀγορανόμων, ἀστυνόμων, ἄλλων ἀρχόντων ὅμιλοι μεγάλοι καὶ
75 σὺν τούτοις ὁ δῆμος. ἔστι γὰρ ἔστιν ἐν ἑκάστου τῇ ψυχῇ, κἂν ἰδιώτης τυγχάνῃ, μισοπόνηρον πάθος, ὃ διακινηθὲν ἀποδείκνυσι τὸν ἔχοντα κατ' ἐκεῖνον τὸν χρόνον ὑπέρμαχον καὶ προαγωνιστὴν αὐτο-
76 κέλευστον τοῦ δόξαντος ἠδικῆσθαι. XIII. τῷ μὲν οὖν διαπραξαμένῳ τὴν βίαν ἕπεται δίκη πανταχοῦ, μηδὲν ἐκ τῆς τῶν χωρίων διαφορᾶς εὑρισκομένῳ πρὸς ἐπανόρθωσιν ὧν ὕβρισε καὶ παρηνόμησε· τῇ δὲ παιδί, καθάπερ ἔφην, τοτὲ μὲν ἔλεος καὶ συγγνώμη τοτὲ δὲ ἀπαραίτητος τιμωρία παρ-
77 ακολουθήσει. καὶ περὶ ταύτης μέντοι πολυπραγμονητέον τῷ δικαστῇ μὴ πάντ' ἐπὶ τοὺς τόπους ἀναφέροντι· δύναται γὰρ καὶ κατὰ μέσην τὴν πόλιν

[a] Deuteronomy makes no suggestion of a documentary form of betrothal, though it speaks of a "bill of divorcement" (xxiv. 3). But Philo naturally reads into it the practice of his own time. See App. pp. 634-635.

needed for wedlock, are equivalent to marriage.[a]
And therefore the law ordains that both should 73
be stoned to death, if, that is, they set about their misdeeds by mutual agreement with one and the same purpose. For if they were not actuated by the same purpose, they cannot be regarded as fellow-criminals, where there was no such fellowship.
Thus we find that difference of situation makes the 74
criminality greater or less. Naturally it is greater if the act is committed in the city and less if it is committed outside the walls and in a solitude. For here there is no one to help the girl, though she says and does everything possible to keep her virginity intact and invulnerable, while in the town there are council-chambers and law-courts, crowds of controllers of districts,[b] markets and wards, and other persons in
authority and with them the common people. For 75
assuredly there is in the soul of every man, however undistinguished he may be, a detestation of evil, and if this emotion is roused, no outside influence is then needed to turn its possessor into a champion ready to do battle for anyone who to all appearance has been
wronged. XIII. As for the man who perpetrated the 76
violation, justice pursues him everywhere, and difference of situation lends him no help to make good his outrageous and lawless conduct. It is not so with the girl. In the one case pity and forgiveness attend her, as I have said, in the other inexorable
punishment. And indeed her position demands care- 77
ful inquiry from the judge who must not make everything turn upon the scene of the act. For she may have been forced against her will in the heart of the

[b] Or "nomes." See on i. 55.

ἄκουσα βεβιάσθαι καὶ ἔξω τῆς πόλεως ἑκοῦσα πρὸς ἔκθεσμον ὁμιλίαν ἐνδοῦναι. διὸ παρατετηρημένως καὶ σφόδρα καλῶς ἀπολογούμενος ὑπὲρ τῆς ἐν ἐρημίᾳ φθειρομένης φησὶν ὁ νόμος· "ἐβόησεν ἡ νεᾶνις, καὶ ὁ βοηθήσων οὐκ ἦν αὐτῇ," ὥστε, εἰ μήτε ἐβόησε μήτε ἠναντιώθη, βουλομένη δὲ συναπῆρε, γένοιτ᾿ ἂν ἔνοχος, σόφισμα τοῦ βεβιάσθαι
78 δοκεῖν προστησαμένη τὸν τόπον. καὶ μὴν ἐν πόλει τί γένοιτ᾿ ἂν ὄφελος τῇ πάντα μὲν ἐθελούσῃ ποιεῖν ὑπὲρ τῆς ἰδίας ἐπιτιμίας, ἀδυνατούσῃ δὲ ἕνεκα τῆς περὶ τὸν ὑβριστὴν ἰσχύος; τί γάρ, εἰ μετὰ τῶν ἄλλων[1] καταδήσειεν ἢ τὸ στόμα ἀποφράξειεν, ὡς μηδὲ φωνὴν ῥῆξαι δύνασθαι, γένοιτ᾿ ἂν ὄφελος ἐκ τῶν συνοικούντων; τρόπον γάρ τινα ἥδε μὲν ἐν πόλει διατρίβουσα κατ᾿ ἐρημίαν ἐστὶν ἅτε βοηθῶν ἔρημος, ἡ δέ, κἂν μηδεὶς παρατυγχάνῃ, τῷ ἑκοῦσα συναπᾶραι λέγοιτ᾿ ἂν οὐδὲν διαφέρειν τῆς ἐν ἄστει.

79 XIV. Εἰσὶ δέ τινες περὶ τὰς ὁμιλίας ἀψίκοροι, γυναικομανεῖς ἐν ταὐτῷ καὶ μισογύναιοι, συγ-

[1] Some MSS. μετὰ τῶν κάλων, which Mangey adopted, translating "cum funibus." But such a use of μετά seems hardly possible. Cohn at first suggested μετά<γων ἄποθεν> τῶν. But see note *a*.

---

[a] Lit. "the others," *i.e.* those others whose help would be required to bind and gag her before she could cry out. Perhaps, however, τῶν ἄλλων is neuter, *i.e.* "besides the rest of his violence"; translate, "if he further proceeds to bind her." Cohn, who originally suggested the correction mentioned in note 1, came to the conclusion (*Hermes*, 1908, p. 205) that this solution was satisfactory. He compares *De Dec.* 69.

city, and she may have surrendered voluntarily to unlawful embraces outside the city. And therefore the law in defending the case of a woman deflowered in a solitude is careful to add the very excellent proviso: "The damsel cried out and there was none to help her;" so that if she neither cried out nor resisted but co-operated willingly, she will be found guilty, and her use of the place as an excuse is merely a device to make it seem that she was forced.
Again what help would be available in the city to one 78
who was willing to use all possible means to protect her personal honour, but was unable to do so because of the strength which the ravisher could bring to bear? If he should bind her with the help of others[a] and gag her mouth so that she could not utter a sound, what help could she get from the neighbours? In a sense such a one, though living in a city, is in a solitude, being solitary so far as helpers are concerned. The other, even if no one was present to help, may be said, in view of her willing cooperation, to be in exactly the same position as the offender in the town.

XIV. [b] There are some persons who show fickleness 79
in their relations to women, mad for them and loath-

[b] For §§ 79-83 see Deut. xxii. 13-21. Philo's account makes no mention of the "tokens of virginity." Also there is no allusion to the order that if the case is given against the wife she is to be stoned. This is perhaps because the real subject of these sections is the misconduct of husbands who make treacherous attempts to get rid of unwanted wives. Still, the omission is curious. Apart from the concealment, the misconduct of the woman is not, or need not be, *ὑπογάμιον*, and falls under the head of *φθορά*, which Philo has treated as an *ἀτύχημα* to the maiden rather than a crime (§ 70). One would expect an explanation of why the extreme penalty was required.

κλύδων καὶ μιγάδων ἠθῶν ἀνάπλεῳ, οἳ ταῖς πρώταις εὐθὺς ὁρμαῖς ἐνδιδόντες, ὁποῖαί περ ἂν οὖσαι τυγχάνωσιν, ἃς ἡνιοχεῖν δέον ἀχαλινώτους ἐῶσιν, ἀπερισκέπτως καὶ ἀπροοράτως σώμασιν ὁμοῦ καὶ πράγμασιν ἐπεμπίπτοντες τυφλῶν τρόπον, ἅτε ῥύμῃ καὶ φορᾷ βιαίῳ συνωθοῦντες καὶ ἀνατρέποντες, οὐκ
80 ἐλάττω ὧν διατιθέασι πάσχουσι. περὶ ὧν τάδε νομοθετεῖται· κόρας οἱ ἀγόμενοι νόμῳ καὶ γάμους θύσαντές τε καὶ ἑστιαθέντες, μηδὲν οἰκεῖον ἐπὶ ταῖς γαμεταῖς πάθος σῴζοντες, ἀλλ' ὑβρίσαντες |
[313] καὶ ὡς ἑταίραις ταῖς ἀσταῖς προσενεχθέντες, ἐὰν διάζευξιν τεχνάζωσι μηδεμίαν ἀπαλλαγῆς πρόφασιν ἀνευρίσκοντες, εἶτ' ἐπὶ τὸ συκοφαντεῖν τραπόμενοι σπάνει φανερῶν ἐγκλημάτων πρὸς τὰ ἀφανῆ τρέπωσι τὰς αἰτίας καὶ παρελθόντες κατηγορῶσιν, ὅτι παρθένοις δόξαντες συνεληλυθέναι γυναῖκας ἐν ταῖς πρώταις ὁμιλίαις ἐφώρασαν, ἀθροιζέσθω μὲν ἡ γερουσία πᾶσα πρὸς τὴν κρίσιν, παρίτωσαν δὲ οἱ τῶν κατηγορουμένων γονεῖς ἀπολογησόμενοι περὶ
81 κοινοῦ κινδύνου. κίνδυνος γὰρ οὐ ταῖς θυγατράσι μόνον περὶ τῆς τῶν σωμάτων ἁγνείας ἐστίν, ἀλλὰ καὶ τοῖς ἐπιμεληταῖς, οὐ μόνον ὅτι εἰς τὸν ἀναγκαιότατον τῆς ἀκμῆς καιρὸν οὐ παρετήρησαν, ἀλλ' ὅτι καὶ ὡς παρθένους τὰς ὑφ' ἑτέρων ἐφθαρμένας

---

[a] The causal clause introduced by ἅτε may look forward and give the reason why they suffer as they have done to others. It seems to me better to take it as looking backwards and giving the reason why they stumble over everything. For σώματα καὶ πράγματα see note on *Quis Rerum* 242 (vol. iv. p. 573).

ing them at the same time, each of them a mass of chaotic and promiscuous characteristics. They give way in a moment to their first impulses of any and every kind and let them go unbridled instead of reining them in as they should. They run about wildly and violently, pushing about and upsetting everything material or immaterial, with the result that like blind men without eyes to see before or around they tumble over them and suffer in the same measure as they have meted.[a] For these 80
people the law lays down as follows: In the case of persons who take maidens in lawful matrimony and have celebrated the bridal sacrifices and feasts, but retain no conjugal[b] affection for their wives, and insult and treat these gentlewomen as if they were harlots—if such persons scheme to effect a separation, but finding no pretext for divorce resort to false accusation and through lack of matters of open daylight shift the charges to secret intimacies and bring forward an incriminating statement that the virgins whom they supposed they had married were discovered by them, when they first came together, to have lost their virginity already—then the whole body of elders will assemble to try the matter and the parents will appear to plead the cause in which all are endangered. For the danger affects 81
not only the daughters whose bodily chastity is impugned, but also their guardians, against whom the charge is brought not only that they failed to watch over them at the most critical period of adolescence, but that the brides they had given as virgins had been dishonoured by other men, and thereby the bride-

[b] *i.e.* suitable to the intimate relation. *Cf.* the use of *οἰκεῖον πάσχειν*, § 67.

ἐνεγύησαν ἀπατῶντες καὶ φενακίζοντες τοὺς λαμ-
82 βάνοντας. εἶτα ἐὰν περιγένωνται τοῖς δικαίοις, τιμάτωσαν οἱ δικασταὶ κατὰ τῶν ψευδεῖς αἰτίας πλαττομένων χρημάτων ζημίας καὶ τὰς διὰ πληγῶν εἰς τὰ σώματα ὕβρεις καὶ—τὸ πάντων ἐκείνοις ἀηδέστατον—τὴν τῶν γάμων βεβαίωσιν, ἐὰν ὑπομένωσιν αἱ γυναῖκες ἔτι τοῖς τοιούτοις συνοικεῖν· ταῖς μὲν γὰρ ἐφίησιν ὁ νόμος θελούσαις καὶ μένειν καὶ ἀπαλλάττεσθαι, τοὺς δὲ οὐδετέρου κυρίους ἀπέφηνεν, ἀνθ' ὧν ἐσυκοφάντησαν.

83 XV. [1]Ὄνομα μὲν ἀνδροφονία κατὰ τοῦ κτείναντος ἄνθρωπον ἐπιφημίζεται, τὸ δ' ἀληθὲς ἔργον ἐστὶν ἱεροσυλία καὶ ἱεροσυλιῶν ἡ μεγίστη, διότι τῶν ἐν κόσμῳ κτημάτων καὶ κειμηλίων οὐδὲν οὔτε ἱεροπρεπέστερον οὔτε θεοειδέστερόν ἐστιν ἀνθρώπου· * * *[2] παγκάλης εἰκόνος πάγκαλον ἐκμαγεῖον ἀρχετύπου λογικῆς ἰδέας παραδείγματι τυπωθέν.
84 τὸν οὖν ἀνδροφόνον εὐθὺς ἀσεβῆ καὶ ἀνοσιουργὸν ὑποληπτέον, ἀνοσιουργημάτων καὶ ἀσεβημάτων δρῶντα τὸ μέγιστον, ὃν ἀμείλικτα ἐργασάμενον

[1] MS. heading Κατὰ ἀνδροφόνων.

[2] The insertion of ὅς ἐστι (Mangey), or ἔστι γὰρ (Cohn), will make the sentence grammatical. But quite possibly the text as it stands may be due to a slip of Philo, the eye being caught by the nominatives οὐδὲν, etc. *Cf.* φύντα, § 65.

---

[a] There is no biblical authority for this right of the slandered women, nor according to Heinemann any rabbinical tradition. It may be regarded as a slip of memory, perhaps induced by the similar liberty allowed to the seduced maidens in § 71.

[b] At this point Philo turns to the sixth (his seventh) commandment, and this takes up the rest of the treatise. The transition is abrupt (though not more so than that from the first to the second commandment in i. 21) and suggests that

grooms were cheated and deceived. Then, if the 82
justice of their cause prevails, the judges must assess the punishments due to these concoctors of false charges. This will consist of monetary fines, bodily degradation in the form of stripes, and what is most distasteful of all to the culprits, confirmation of the marriage, if, that is, the women can bring themselves to consort with such persons.[a] For the law permits the wives to stay or separate as they wish, but deprives the husbands of any choice either way, as a punishment for their slanderous accusations.

XV. [b]The term murder or manslaughter is used to 83
signify the act of one who has killed a human being, but in real truth that act is a sacrilege,[c] and the worst of sacrileges ; seeing that of all the treasures which the universe has in its store there is none more sacred and godlike than man, the glorious cast of a glorious image, shaped according to the pattern of the archetypal form of the Word.[d] It follows necessarily that 84
the murderer must be regarded as an offender against piety and holiness, both of which are violated in the highest degree by his action. For his merciless con-

he may himself have headed these chapters with the words of the commandment, as he must have done with the ninth in iv. 41.

[c] *Cf. De Dec.* 132, 133. The other argument against murder used there, viz. that it is against the law of nature which has made man a social creature, is not repeated here.

[d] Philo is following his regular interpretation of κατ' εἰκόνα θεοῦ, *i.e.* that man was made in the likeness of God's image, *i.e.* the Logos, which is εἰκών to God, but παραδεῖγμα to man. *Cf.* particularly *De Som.* i. 76, and examples given in note there. λογικῆς here = of the Logos; *cf.* § 207 below. Philo also has in mind Gen. ix. 6, "whoso sheddeth man's blood, by man shall his blood be shed, for in the image of God made he man."

ἀναιρετέον, ἐπειδὴ[1] μυρίων θανάτων ἐπάξιος ὢν ἕνα
ὑπομένει διὰ τὸ τῆς τιμωρίας ἀθάνατον[2] εἰς πλῆθος
μὴ πεφυκυίας συναύξεσθαι· χαλεπὸν δὲ οὐδέν, εἰ
85 ταὐτὸν οἷς διέθηκέ τις πείσεται. καίτοι πῶς ἐστι
ταὐτόν, εἰ καὶ χρόνοις καὶ πράξεσι καὶ βουλήμασι
καὶ προσώποις διαλλάττει; ἢ οὐχὶ τὸ μὲν χειρῶν
ἄρχειν ἀδίκων ἐστὶ πρότερον, τὸ δ' ἀμύνεσθαι
ὕστερον; καὶ ἀνδροφονία μὲν παρανομώτατον, ἡ δὲ
κατὰ ἀνδροφόνων κόλασις νομιμώτατον; καὶ ὁ μὲν
κτείνας ἐκπεπλήρωκε τὴν ἐπιθυμίαν ὃν προῄρητο
ἀνελών, ὁ δὲ πεπονθὼς ἅτε γεγονὼς ἐκποδὼν οὔτ'
ἀντιδιαθεῖναι οὔτ' ἀντεφησθῆναι δυνατός ἐστι; καὶ
[314] ὁ μὲν ἐπιβουλεύειν αὐτοχειρίᾳ | πέφυκε δι' ἑαυτοῦ,
τῷ δ' ἀτελὴς ἡ ἐπέξοδος, εἰ μὴ συγγενεῖς ἢ φίλοι
προαγωνίσαιντο λαβόντες τοῦ πάθους οἶκτον;
86 Ἐάν τις ἐπανατείνηται ξίφος, ὥστε ἀποκτεῖναι,
κἂν μὴ ἀνέλῃ, ἔνοχος ἔστω προαιρέσει γεγονὼς
ἀνδροφόνος, εἰ καὶ μὴ τὸ τέλος τῇ γνώμῃ συν-
έδραμε. τὰ δ' αὐτὰ πασχέτω, κἂν σὺν τέχνῃ τις
ἐξ ἐνέδρας, οὐ θαρρῶν ἄντικρυς ἐπιχειρεῖν, βουλεύῃ

[1] I suggest εἰ καὶ δὴ: Cohn καίτοι. The difficulty of logic in "because" would be eased if ἀμειλίκτως is inserted before ἀμείλικτα, the thought being that since he can have only one death, that must be inflicted without mercy. Even so, however, "although" is to be expected. For εἰ καὶ δὴ *cf.* εἰ καί, § 86, and εἰ δή, § 132.

[2] This is certainly corrupt. The simplest emendation, as it seems to me, will be to suppose some word lost before ἀθάνατον, which will then be taken with πλῆθος. The word which I should suggest is ἑνικὸν, the regular term in grammar for the "singular" opposed to "πληθυντικόν" plural; *cf.* ἑνικῶς, *De Dec.* 43. See further App. p. 635.

---

[a] For death as a penalty for killing a man see Ex. xxi. 12; Lev. xxiv. 17, 21; Num. xxxv. 16-21, 30-31; besides Gen. lx. 6.

duct he must be put to death,[a] though indeed it is a thousand deaths that he deserves instead of the one which he suffers, because his punishment being necessarily single cannot grow into a plurality in which death has no place.[b] And there is no hardship if he suffers the same as he has done; and yet how can it 85
be called the same when the times, the actions, the motives and the persons are different? Is it not the fact that the unprovoked wrong comes earlier and the punishment for it later; that murder is entirely lawless and the punishment for murder entirely lawful; that the slayer has satisfied his desire with the blood which he purposed to shed while his victim, being removed from the scene, can neither retaliate nor feel the pleasure which retaliation gives; that the former can work his will single-handed and as sole agent, while to the latter any counter-stroke is only possible if his friends and kinsmen in pity for his misfortune make his cause their own?

If anyone threatens the life of another with a 86
sword, even though he does not actually kill him, he must be held guilty of murder in intention, although the fulfilment has not kept pace with the purpose.[c] The same should be the lot of anyone who craftily lies in wait, and, though not daring to attack outright,

[b] The translation follows the suggestion in note 2. The πλῆθος is ἀθάνατον because if a punishment can be repeated it is "deathless" in the sense that it does not involve death.

[c] Philo is here giving his interpretation of Ex. xxi. 14, as it is in the LXX. Where the E.V. has "if a man come presumptuously upon his neighbour to slay him with guile," the LXX has ἐπιθῆται, which Philo understands to mean "if he attack him, even if he does not succeed." This appears from *De Conf.* 160, where he takes the same text as shewing that the intention to kill is the same as actually killing, because the word used is ἐπιτίθεσθαι, not ἀναιρεῖν. See App. p. 635.

καὶ μηχανᾶται δολερῶς τὸν φόνον· ἐναγὴς γὰρ καὶ οὗτος εἰ καὶ μήπω ταῖς χερσὶν ἀλλά τοι τῇ ψυχῇ
87 καθέστηκεν. ὥσπερ γάρ, οἶμαι, πολεμίους οὐ μόνον τοὺς ἤδη ναυμαχοῦντας ἢ πεζομαχοῦντας ἀλλὰ καὶ τοὺς εἰς ἑκάτερον παρεσκευασαμένους καὶ τὰς ἑλεπόλεις ἐφιστάντας τοῖς λιμέσι καὶ τείχεσι, κἂν μήπω συμπλέκωνται, κρίνομεν, οὕτως καὶ ἀνδροφόνους χρὴ νομίζειν οὐ τοὺς κτείναντας αὐτὸ μόνον ἀλλὰ καὶ τοὺς πάντα δρῶντας εἰς τὸ ἀνελεῖν ἢ φανερῶς ἢ λάθρα, κἂν μὴ τὸ ἀδίκημα ὦσιν
88 εἰργασμένοι. ἐὰν δὲ καὶ ὑπὸ δειλίας ἢ θράσους, μαχομένων καὶ ἐπιλήπτων παθῶν, καταφυγεῖν τολμῶσιν εἰς τὸ ἱερὸν ὡς ἀσυλίαν εὑρησόμενοι, κωλυτέον· κἂν φθῶσι[1] παρεισδύντες, ἐκδοτέον ἐπ᾽ ἀναιρέσει τοιαῦτα ἐπιλέγοντας, ἀσυλίαν ἀνιέροις τὸ ἱερὸν μὴ παρέχεσθαι. πᾶς γὰρ ὁ ἀνίατα δρῶν ἐχθρὸς θεῷ· ἀνδροφόνοι δὲ ἀνίατα δρῶσιν, ἐπεὶ καὶ οἱ ἀνδροφονηθέντες ἀνίατα πε-
89 πόνθασιν. ἢ τοῖς μὲν μηδὲν ἡμαρτηκόσιν, ἕως ἂν ἀπολούσωνται καὶ περιρρανάμενοι καθαρθῶσι τοῖς εἰωθόσι καθαρσίοις, ἄβατος ὁ νεώς ἐστι, τοὺς δὲ ἐνόχους ἀνεκπλύτοις ἄγεσιν, ὧν τὰ μιάσματα οὐδεὶς ἀπονίψει χρόνος, ἄξιον ἐπιφοιτᾶν καὶ ἐνδιατρίβειν τοῖς ἕδεσιν, οὓς οὐδ᾽ ἂν οἰκία δέξαιτο
90 κοσμίων ἀνδρῶν οἷς μέλει τῶν ὁσίων; XVI. προσ-

[1] So Heinemann. Cohn ὀφθῶσι with two MSS. The rest have φθάνωσι, which (or φθῶσι) gives the better sense.

---

[a] For §§ 88-91 see Ex. xxi. 14, "thou shalt take him from mine altar that he may die."

plots and schemes to shed blood treacherously, for he too is under the curse in his soul at least even though
his hands are innocent as yet. For just as not only 87
those who fight battles by sea or land, but also those who have made preparations for either and planted their engines to command our harbours and walls are judged by us to be our enemies, even though there is no engagement as yet, so too in my opinion should we regard as murderers, not merely those who have slain but also those whose every action aims at destroying life either openly or secretly, even though they have not carried out the crime.
And if through cowardice or effrontery, two antagon- 88
istic but equally culpable emotions, they venture to take refuge in the temple, hoping to obtain an asylum there, they must be prevented from entering; and if they manage to slink in, they must be handed over for execution with a declaration to the effect that the holy place does not provide asylum for the unholy.[a] Everyone whose actions are irremediable is an enemy of God, and the actions of murderers are irremediable, as are also the calamities which the murdered have
sustained. If those who have committed no sin are 89
forbidden access to the sanctuary, until they have bathed and purged themselves with purifying water according to the customary rites, is it fitting that the sacred building should be the resort and abode of men labouring under the curse of ineffaceable crimes, the pollution of which no length of time will wash away —men who would not be admitted into the dwelling-houses of decent people who take any thought for
what the law of holiness[b] permits or forbids? XVI. So 90

[b] ὅσιος is perhaps used here in the common Attic sense of what is allowable and therefore almost = βέβηλος.

τιθέντας οὖν ἀδικήματα ἀδικήμασιν, ἀνδροφονίᾳ παρανομίαν καὶ ἀσέβειαν, ἀναγκαῖον ἀπάγειν δώσοντας δίκην, τοὺς ὡς ἔφην ἄξια μυρίων θανάτων, οὐχ ἑνός, εἰργασμένους. ἄλλως τε τοῖς συγγενέσι καὶ φίλοις τοῦ δολοφονηθέντος ἀποκεκλείσεται τὸ ἱερόν, εἰ ὁ ἀνδροφόνος ἐνδιατρίβοι, μὴ ἂν ὑπομείνασιν εἰς ταὐτόν ποτε ἐλθεῖν· ἄτοπον δὲ ἑνὸς ἕνεκα πολλοὺς καὶ τοῦ παρανομωτάτου τοὺς παρανομηθέντας ἐξελαύνεσθαι, οἳ πρὸς τῷ μηδὲν ἁμαρτεῖν ἔτι καὶ πένθος πρόωρον ἀνεδέξαντο.
91 τάχα μέντοι καὶ τὰ μακρὰν ὀξυωπίᾳ λογισμοῦ
[315] πεφυκὼς ἐμβλέπειν | προὐνόησε μὴ φόνον ἐν τῷ ἱερῷ γενέσθαι κατὰ τὰς ἐπιφοιτήσεις τῶν τοῦ σφαγέντος ἐπιτηδείων, οὓς στοργή, πάθος ἀδούλωτον, ὥσπερ τοὺς ἐνθουσιῶντας καὶ κατεχομένους προκαλέσεται μόνον οὐκ αὐτοχειρίᾳ κτεῖναι τὸν ἀνδροφόνον· οὗ γενομένου συμβήσεταί τι τῶν ἀνοσιωτάτων, αἵματι γὰρ ἀνδροφόνων αἷμα θυσιῶν ἀνακραθήσεται, τὸ καθωσιωμένον[1] τῷ μὴ καθαρῷ. διὰ μὲν δὴ ταῦτα κελεύει καὶ ἀπ᾽ αὐτῶν τῶν βωμῶν ἐκδοῦναι τὸν ἀνδροφόνον.

92 XVII. Ἀλλ᾽ οἱ μὲν ξίφεσιν ἢ δορατίοις ἢ βέλεσιν ἢ ξύλοις ἢ λίθοις ἤ τισιν ὁμοιοτρόποις ἀναιροῦντες

[1] So or καθοσιωμένον most MSS. S has τῶν καθοσιωμένων, which Cohn adopts (correcting the ο to ω).

as they have added crimes to crimes and capped murder with defiance of the law and impiety, these malefactors whose deeds, as I have said, deserve not one but a thousand deaths must be carried off to pay the penalty. Another consideration is that the temple will remain closed ground to the friends and kinsmen of the victim of treachery, if the murderer makes it his abode, since they would never bring themselves to come under the same roof as he. And it would be preposterous that a single person, a transgressor of the worst kind, should cause the banishment of the many sufferers from his transgression, who not only have committed no sin but have sustained a sad and untimely bereavement. It may 91
well be also that Moses, who in the keenness of his mental vision could look into the distant future, took steps to provide that the visits of the slain man's relatives should not lead to bloodshed in the temple. For family affection is an emotion which cannot be kept in bondage, and as with persons possessed by fanaticism it will incite them to slay him almost on the spur of the moment,[a] and the result of this will be a profanation of the gravest sort. For the blood of the murderer will mix with the blood of the sacrifices, the impure with the consecrated. These are the reasons why he ordered the murderer to be handed over from the altar itself.

XVII. But those who take another's life with swords 92
or spears or javelins or staves or stones or anything else

[a] The dictionaries do not suggest this meaning for αὐτοχειρία and αὐτόχειρ as a variant to the ordinary meaning of "with one's own hand"; but the sense here seems to require such a modification. To suggest that the injured persons would like to do the act almost with their own hands seems feeble. Still more is this the case in § 96.

δύνανται μὴ προβεβουλευμένοι μηδ' ἐκ πολλοῦ παρ' αὐτοῖς λελογισμένοι τὸ ἄγος, ἐκ ταὐτομάτου διακινηθέντες καὶ θυμῷ δυνατωτέρῳ χρησάμενοι λογισμοῦ, δρᾶσαι τὸν φόνον, ὡς ἡμίεργον τὴν πρᾶξιν εἶναι, τῆς διανοίας μὴ προκατεσχημένης ἐκ μακροῦ
93 τοῖς μιάσμασιν. εἰσὶ δὲ ἕτεροι πονηρότατοι, χερσὶ καὶ γνώμαις ἐναγεῖς, οἱ μάγοι καὶ φαρμακευταί, σχολὴν καὶ ἀναχώρησιν ἐνδιδόντες αὑτοῖς πρὸς καιρίους ἐπιθέσεις καὶ τέχνας καὶ μηχανὰς πολυτρόπους ἀνευρίσκοντες ἐπὶ ταῖς τῶν
94 πλησίον συμφοραῖς. ὅθεν κελεύει φαρμακευτὰς καὶ φαρμακίδας μηδεμίαν ἡμέραν ἀλλὰ μηδ' ὥραν ἐπιβιοῦν, ἀλλ' ἅμα τῷ ἁλῶναι τεθνάναι, μηδεμιᾶς ἐγγινομένης προφάσεως εἰς ἀναβολὴν καὶ ὑπέρθεσιν τῆς τιμωρίας· τοὺς μὲν γὰρ ἄντικρυς ἐπιβουλεύοντας δύναιτ' ἄν τις φυλάξασθαι, τῶν δὲ κρύφα συντιθέντων καὶ σκευωρούντων τὰς ἐπιθέσεις
95 φαρμακείαις οὐ ῥᾴδιον τὰς τέχνας συνιδεῖν. ἀναγκαῖον οὖν, ἃ μελλήσουσι δι' αὐτοὺς ἕτεροι ποθεῖν, τοὺς δρῶντας προδιαθεῖναι. καὶ γὰρ ἄλλως ὁ μὲν ἐμφανῶς ξίφει κτείνων ἤ τινι ὅπλῳ τῶν ὁμοιοτρόπων καθ' ἕνα καιρὸν ὀλίγους ἀνελεῖ, φαρμάκοις δὲ θανασίμοις μυρίους ὅσους τὴν ἐπιβουλὴν

---

[a] See Num. xxxv. 16-18, where we have the same enumeration of weapons (iron, stone, wood), the use of which constitutes murder, followed later (*vv.* 22, 23) by the proviso that if the death was not caused through enmity, it is not murder, though this refers rather to accidental than, as Philo seems to construe it, to unpremeditated slaying He resumes the subject in § 104. At present his point is that poisoning cannot possibly have such an excuse.

[b] Philo's main authority for these two sections is Ex. xxii. 18, where, while the A.V. has "thou shalt not suffer a witch

of the kind may not act on premeditation[a]; they may not have long pondered the abomination in their hearts; they may have been moved by a momentary instinct and allowed their anger to overpower their reason when they did the fatal deed. If so, theirs is but a half action, since the mind has not been under the control of the polluting influences from some far
earlier time. [b] But there are others, the 93
worst of villains, accursed both in hand and will, the sorcerers and poisoners, who provide themselves with leisure and retirement to prepare the onslaughts they will make when the right time comes,[c] and think out multiform schemes and devices to harm their neighbours. And therefore he orders that poisoners, male 94
or female,[d] should not survive for a day or even an hour, but perish as soon as they are detected, since no reason can be given for delay or for postponing their punishment. Hostile intentions if undisguised can be guarded against, but those who secretly frame and concoct their plans of attack with the aid of poisons employ artifices which cannot easily be
observed. The only course, then, is to anticipate them 95
by meting to the actors the treatment which others may expect to suffer through their acts. For apart from other considerations the slayer who openly uses a sword or any similar weapon will make away with a few on one particular occasion, but if he mixes an injection of deadly poison with some articles of food

(R.V. "sorceress") to live," the LXX has *φαρμακοὺς οὐ περιποιήσεις*. The word *φαρμακός* is applied to sorcerers as well as poisoners, as Philo himself implies in § 102, where see note.

[c] Or possibly "deadly," as in § 106.

[d] Does this suggest that Philo had an inkling or had been informed that the Hebrew word which the LXX translated by *φαρμακούς* was actually feminine?

οὐ προαισθανομένους ἐδωδίμοις τισὶν ἀναμίξας καὶ
96 συνανακερασάμενος. ἤδη γοῦν πολυάνθρωπα συσσίτια καθ᾿ ἑταιρείαν συνεληλυθότων ἐπὶ τοὺς αὐτοὺς
ἅλας καὶ τὴν αὐτὴν τράπεζαν ἐν σπονδαῖς ἄσπονδα
ἔπαθεν ἐξαίφνης διαφθαρέντα καὶ θάνατον ἀντ᾿
εὐωχίας ἀντηλλάξατο. διὸ προσήκει κατὰ τῶν
τοιούτων καὶ τοὺς ἐπιεικεστάτους καὶ τοὺς
μετριοπαθεστάτους φονᾶν, μόνον οὐκ αὐτόχειρας
γινομένους καὶ νομίζοντας εὐαγὲς εἶναι τὸ μὴ
97 ἑτέροις τὴν τιμωρίαν ἐπιτρέπειν ἀλλ᾿ ἑαυτοῖς. πῶς
γὰρ οὐκ ἔστι πάνδεινον, διὰ τροφῆς ἣ τοῦ ζῆν
αἰτία καθέστηκε θάνατον τεχνάζειν καὶ τοῖς φύσει
τροφίμοις φθοροποιὸν ἐνεργάζεσθαι μεταβολήν, ἵνα
τινὲς διὰ φυσικὴν ἀνάγκην ἐπ᾿ ἐδωδὴν καὶ πόσιν
ἰόντες, οὐ προϊδόντες τὴν ἐνέδραν, ὡς σωτήρια
98 προσῶνται τὰ πανωλεθρίας αἴτια; τὴν δ᾿ αὐτὴν
ὑπομενέτωσαν τιμωρίαν, κἂν [εἴ] τινες θανάσιμα
μὴ συντιθέντες τὰ δι᾿ ὧν μακραὶ κατασκευάζονται
[316] | νόσοι προσφέρωσι· θάνατοι γὰρ πολλάκις αἱρε-
τώτεροι νόσων εἰσὶ καὶ μάλιστα τῶν τοιούτων,
αἳ μήκεσι χρόνων ἀποτείνονται καὶ τέλος ἔχουσιν
οὐκ αἴσιον· δυσίατα γὰρ ἤδη καὶ παντελῶς
ἀθεράπευτα τὰ ἐκ φαρμακειῶν ἀρρωστήματα.
99 χαλεπώτερα μέντοι συμβαίνειν φιλεῖ τῶν ἐν τοῖς
σώμασι καὶ ⟨τὰ⟩ περὶ τὰς ψυχὰς πάθη τῶν ἐπι-
βουλευομένων· ἐκστάσεις γὰρ καὶ παραφροσύναι

---

[a] Goodenough, who translates this passage, p. 105, gives the meaning more literally, "suffer in the libation something which should have no connexion with it." But the idea of "truce," is inextricably bound up with "libation" in σπονδή and still more in ἄσπονδος.

his victims who have no foreknowledge of the plot
will be counted by thousands. We have certainly 96
heard of banquets where sudden destruction has fallen upon a great assemblage of guests drawn by comradeship to eat of the same salt and sit at the same board, to whom the cup of peace has brought the bitterness of war[a] and festivity has been changed into death. And therefore it is right that even the most reasonable and mild-tempered should seek the blood of such as these, that they should lose hardly a moment in becoming their executioners,[b] and should hold it a religious duty to keep their punishment in
their own hands and not commit it to others. For 97
surely it is a horror of horrors to manufacture out of the food which is the source of life an instrument of death, and to work a destructive change in the natural means of sustenance, so that when the compulsion of nature sends them to take food and drink they do not see the pitfall that lies before them and put to their lips what will annihilate the existence which they
think it will preserve. The same punishment must 98
be suffered by any who, although the compounds which they make are not deadly, purvey what will set up chronic diseases.[c] For death in many cases is preferable to diseases, particularly such as drag on through long periods of time without any favourable termination. For maladies caused by poisoning have been found difficult to cure and sometimes entirely
unamenable to treatment. However, the bodily 99
troubles of the sufferers from these machinations are often less grievous than those which affect their souls. Fits of delirium and insanity and intolerable frenzy

[b] See note on αὐτοχειρία, § 91.

[c] See App. p. 635.

καὶ ἀφόρητοι μανίαι κατασκήπτουσι, δι᾿ ὧν ὁ νοῦς, ὃν μεγίστην ἀπένειμεν ἀνθρώπων γένει δωρεὰν ὁ θεός, κακούμενος πάσας κακώσεις, ὅταν ἀπογνῷ τὰ σωτήρια, μετανίσταται καὶ μετοικίζεται τὸ τῆς ψυχῆς φαυλότερον εἶδος ὑπολειπόμενος ἐν τῷ σώματι, τὸ ἄλογον, οὗ καὶ τὰ θηρία μετέσχηκεν, ἐπειδὴ πᾶς ὁ ἐρημωθεὶς λογισμοῦ τοῦ κρείττονος μέρους ψυχῆς μεταβέβληκεν εἰς θήρειον φύσιν, κἂν ἔτι μένωσιν οἱ τοῦ σώματος χαρακτῆρες ἀνθρωπόμορφοι.

100 XVIII. Τὴν μὲν οὖν ἀληθῆ μαγικήν, ὀπτικὴν ἐπιστήμην οὖσαν, ᾗ τὰ τῆς φύσεως ἔργα τρανοτέραις φαντασίαις αὐγάζεται, σεμνὴν καὶ περιμάχητον δοκοῦσαν εἶναι, οὐκ ἰδιῶται μόνον ἀλλὰ καὶ βασιλεῖς καὶ βασιλέων οἱ μέγιστοι καὶ μάλιστα οἱ Περσῶν διαπονοῦσιν οὕτως, ὥστ᾿ οὐδένα φασὶν ἐπὶ βασιλείαν δύνασθαι παραπεμφθῆναι παρ᾿ αὐτοῖς, εἰ μὴ πρότερον τοῦ μάγων γένους κεκοι-

101 νωνηκὼς τυγχάνοι. ἔστι δέ τι παράκομμα ταύτης, κυριώτατα φάναι κακοτεχνία, ἣν μηναγύρται καὶ βωμολόχοι μετίασι καὶ γυναίων καὶ ἀνδραπόδων τὰ φαυλότατα, περιμάττειν καὶ καθαίρειν κατεπαγγελλόμενα καὶ στέργοντας μὲν εἰς ἀνήκεστον ἔχθραν μισοῦντας δὲ εἰς ὑπερβάλλουσαν εὔνοιαν ἄξειν ὑπισχνούμενα φίλτροις καὶ ἐπῳδαῖς τισιν, εἶτα τοὺς ἀπλάστοις καὶ ἀκακωτάτοις ἤθεσι κεχρημένους ἀπατᾷ τε καὶ ἀγκιστρεύεται, μέχρις ἂν τὰς μεγίστας προσλάβωσι συμφοράς, δι᾿ ἃς οἰκείων καὶ συγγενῶν ὅμιλοι μεγάλοι καὶ πολυάνθρωποι

---

[a] *Cf. Quod Omn. Prob.* 74, where the magic of the Persians

swoop down upon them, and thereby the mind, the greatest gift which God has assigned to human kind, is subject to every sort of affliction, and when it despairs of salvation it takes its departure and makes its home elsewhere, leaving in the body the baser kind of soul, the irrational, which the beasts also share. For everyone who is left forsaken by reason, the better part of the soul, has been transformed into the nature of a beast, even though the outward characteristics of his body still retain their human form.

XVIII. Now the true magic,[a] the scientific vision by 100
which the facts of nature are presented in a clearer light, is felt to be a fit object for reverence and ambition and is carefully studied not only by ordinary persons but by kings and the greatest kings, and particularly those of the Persians, so much so that it is said that no one in that country is promoted to the throne unless he has first been admitted[b] into the
caste of the Magi. But there is a counterfeit of this, 101
most properly called a perversion of art,[c] pursued by charlatan mendicants and parasites and the basest of the women and slave population, who make it their profession to deal in purifications and disenchantments and promise with some sort of charms and incantations to turn men's love into deadly enmity and their hatred into profound affection. The simplest and most innocent natures are deceived by the bait till at last the worst misfortunes come upon them and thereby the wide membership which unites great companies

is described in almost the same words as here. See App. pp. 635-636.

[b] Or "made a partner with," *i.e.* "has learnt their lore." But this would seem to need the dative. The genitive, at any rate in Philo, is regularly applied to the thing shared.

[c] For the use of κακοτεχνία see note on *De Mut.* 151.

κατὰ μικρὸν ὑπορρέοντες ἀψοφητὶ ταχέως ἐξ-
102 εφθάρησαν. εἰς ἅπερ, οἶμαι, πάντα ἀπιδὼν ὁ ἡμέτερος νομοθέτης οὐκ ἐᾷ τὰς κατὰ φαρμακευτῶν εἰς ὕστερον ἀναβάλλεσθαι δίκας, παραχρῆμα τὰς τιμωρίας ἀναπράττειν κελεύσας· αἱ γὰρ ὑπερθέσεις τοὺς μὲν ὑπαιτίους ἐνευκαιρεῖν τοῖς αὐτοῖς ἀδικήμασι παρορμῶσιν ἅτε θανατῶντας,[1] τοὺς δὲ εἰς τὸ παθεῖν ὑπόπτους φοβερωτέρου δέους ἀναπιμπλᾶσι, τὴν ἐκείνων ζωὴν θάνατον αὐτῶν εἶναι
103 νομίζοντας. καθάπερ οὖν ἔχεις καὶ σκορπίους | καὶ
[317] ὅσα ἰοβόλα, πρὶν δακεῖν ἢ τρῶσαι ἢ συνόλως ἐφορμῆσαι, θεασάμενοι μόνον χωρὶς ὑπερθέσεως κτείνομεν, προφυλαττόμενοι διὰ τὴν ἐνυπάρχουσαν αὐτοῖς κακίαν τὸ μηδὲν παθεῖν, τὸν αὐτὸν τρόπον καὶ ἀνθρώπους ἄξιον τιμωρεῖσθαι, οἳ φύσεως ἐπιλαχόντες ἡμέρου διὰ τὴν κοινωνίας αἰτίαν, λογικὴν ψυχήν,[2] ἐπιτηδεύσει πρὸς θηρίων ἀτιθάσων ἀγριότητας μετέβαλον ἐν ἡδονῇ καὶ ὠφελείᾳ τῇ πάσῃ τιθέμενοι τὸ κακῶς ποιεῖν ὅσους ἂν δύνωνται.

104 XIX. Τοσαῦτ' ἐν τῷ παρόντι περὶ φαρμακευτῶν ἀποχρώντως λελέχθω. προσήκει μέντοι μηδὲ τοῦτ' ἀγνοεῖν, ὅτι καιροὶ συμπίπτουσιν ἀβούλητοι πολ-

[1] Cohn, who originally suggested ἅτε θανατοῦντας, later in a note to Heinemann's translation declared the words to be an interpolation. See note *c* and App. pp. 636-637.

[2] So Cohn following Mangey for MSS. πηγήν. I follow them without doubt. Is λογικὴ πηγή in the sense of the "fountain of reason," *i.e.* containing reason, as a periphrasis for the mind or soul, impossible?

of friends and kinsmen falls gradually into decay and is rapidly and silently destroyed. All these things our 102
lawgiver had in view,[a] I believe, when he prohibited any postponement in bringing poisoners to justice and ordained that the punishment should be exacted at once.[b] For postponement encourages the culprits to use the little time they have to live [c] as an opportunity for repeating their crimes, while it fills those who already have misgivings as to their safety with a still more horrifying fear, as they think that the survival of the poisoners means death to themselves. So 103
just as the mere sight of vipers and scorpions and all venomous creatures even before they sting or wound or attack us at all leads us to kill them without delay as a precaution against injury necessitated by their inherited viciousness, in the same way it is right to punish human beings who though they have received a nature mellowed through the possession of a rational soul, whence springs the sense of fellowship, have been so changed by their habits of life that they shew the savageness of ferocious wild beasts and find their only source of pleasure and profit in injuring all whom they can.

XIX. Enough has been said for the present on the 104
subject of poisoners, but we must not fail to observe that occasions often arise unsought in which a man

[a] Philo here clearly implies that he sees that the magical arts described in the previous section fall under the head of the crime denounced in Ex. xxii. 18 φαρμακοὺς οὐ περιποιήσεις.

[b] Philo finds this meaning in οὐ περιποιήσεις. The verb might properly be used of a person temporarily reprieved.

[c] Lit. "to make the best of their opportunities since they are about to die," if the text is to stand, on which see App. pp. 636-637. Cohn's first suggestion of ἅτε θανατοῦντας, meaning, I suppose, "since they are murderous people," seems to me impossibly weak.

λάκις, ἐν οἷς ἀνδροφονεῖ τις οὐκ ἐπὶ τοῦτ᾽ ἐλθὼν ἢ παρεσκευασμένος, ἀλλ᾽ ἐξαπιναίως ἁρπασθεὶς ὑπ᾽ ὀργῆς, ἀνηκέστου καὶ ἐπιβούλου πάθους, ὃ καὶ τὸν ἔχοντα καὶ ⟨τὸν⟩ καθ᾽ οὗ γίνεται τὰ μέγιστα
105 βλάπτει. προελθὼν γὰρ ἔστιν ὅτε εἰς ἀγορὰν ἕνεκα πραγματείας ἐπειγούσης, ἐντυχών τινι προπετεστέρῳ κακηγορεῖν ἢ τύπτειν ἐπιχειροῦντι ἢ καὶ αὐτὸς ἄρξας τῆς πρὸς ἐκεῖνον διαφορᾶς, συμπλοκῆς γενομένης, ὑπὲρ τοῦ διαζευχθῆναι καὶ θᾶττον ἐκφυγεῖν ἢ πὺξ ἔπαισε τῇ χειρὶ ἢ λίθον ἀράμενος
106 ἔρριψε· καιρίως δὲ τῆς πληγῆς ἐνεχθείσης, εἰ μὲν εὐθὺς θνήσκοι, καὶ ὁ παίσας θνησκέτω τὰ ἴσα οἷς διέθηκε παθών· ἐὰν δὲ παραχρῆμα μὲν ἐκ τῆς πληγῆς μὴ τελευτήσῃ, νόσῳ δὲ χρήσηται καὶ κλινήρης γενόμενος ἐπιμελείας τυχὼν τῆς προσηκούσης αὖθις ἐξαναστῇ καὶ προέλθῃ, κἂν μὴ ποσὶν ἀρτίοις πως δύνηται βαδίζειν ἀλλ᾽ ὑπερειδόντων τινῶν ἢ καὶ βακτηρίᾳ σκηριπτόμενος, διττὰς ὁ παίσας ἐκτινέτω ζημίας, τὴν μὲν εἰς ἀργίας ἐπανόρθωσιν, τὴν δ᾽ ἀντὶ τῶν ἰατρείων.
107 καταθεὶς δ᾽ ἀπηλλάχθω τῆς ἐπὶ τῷ θανάτῳ τιμωρίας, κἂν ὕστερον ὁ τὴν πληγὴν λαβὼν τελευτήσῃ· τάχα γὰρ οὐκ ἀπὸ τῆς πληγῆς, ἐπειδὴ ῥᾴων γενόμενος εἰς περίπατον προῆλθεν, ἀλλὰ καθ᾽ ἑτέρας αἰτίας, αἳ καὶ τοὺς ὑγιεινοτάτους τὰ σώματα πολλάκις ἐξαίφνης ἐπιθέμεναι διέφθειραν.

---

[a] For §§ 105-107 see Ex. xxi. 18, 19. Observe that Philo does not really follow up the idea suggested in the preceding section and still more clearly in § 92, viz. that manslaughter committed in sudden anger is only a "half action," and presumably, therefore, to be punished less severely. For if the other dies on the spot the penalty is still death, and if he dies later, the remission of the penalty is only justified by the

commits murder without having come with this purpose in his mind or with any preparations, but has been carried away by anger, that intractable and malignant passion so highly injurious both to him who entertains it and to him against whom it is directed. [a] Sometimes a man goes to the market-place 105
through stress of business ; he meets another of the more headstrong kind who sets about abusing or striking him, or it may be that he himself begins the quarrel ; then when they have set to, he wishes to break off and escape quickly ; he smites the other with his clenched fist or takes up a stone and throws it. Suppose that the blow strikes home, then if his 106
opponent dies at once, the striker too must die and be treated as he has treated the other, but if that other is not killed on the spot by the blow, but is laid up with sickness and after keeping his bed and receiving the proper care gets up again and goes abroad, even though he is not sound on his feet and can only walk with the support of others or leaning on a staff, the striker must be fined twice over, first to make good the other's enforced idleness and secondly to compensate for the cost of his cure.[b] This 107
payment will release him from the death-penalty, even if the sufferer from the blow subsequently dies. For as he got better and walked abroad, his death may be due not to the blow but to other causes which often suddenly attack and put an end to persons whose bodily health is as sound as possible.

uncertainty that the death was due to the blow. See on § 120 (App. pp. 637-638).

[b] E.V. "only he shall pay for the loss of his time and shall cause him to be thoroughly healed." Philo follows closely the wording of the LXX, πλὴν τῆς ἀργίας αὐτοῦ ἀποτίσει καὶ τὰ ἰατρεῖα.

108 Ἐὰν δὲ συμπλακεὶς γυναικί τις ἐγκύῳ πληγὴν
ἐμφορήσῃ κατὰ τὴν γαστέρα, ἡ δὲ ἀμβλώσῃ, ἐὰν μὲν ἄπλαστον καὶ ἀδιατύπωτον τὸ ἀμβλωθὲν τύχῃ, ζημιούσθω, καὶ διὰ τὴν ὕβριν καὶ ὅτι ἐμποδὼν ἐγένετο τῇ φύσει ζῳογονῆσαι τὸ κάλλιστον τεχνιτευούσῃ καὶ δημιουργούσῃ ζῷον, ἄνθρωπον· εἰ δὲ ἤδη μεμορφωμένον, ἁπάντων μελῶν τὰς οἰκείους
109 τάξεις καὶ ποιότητας ἀπειληφότων, θνῃσκέτω. τὸ
γὰρ τοιοῦτον ἄνθρωπός ἐστιν, ὃν ἐν τῷ τῆς φύσεως ἐργαστηρίῳ διεχρήσατο μήπω καιρὸν εἶναι νομι-
[318] ζούσης εἰς φῶς προαγαγεῖν, ἐοικὸς ἀνδριάντι | ἐν
πλαστικῇ κατακειμένῳ, πλέον οὐδὲν ἢ τὴν ἔξω παραπομπὴν καὶ ἄνεσιν[1] ἐπιζητοῦντι.

110 XX. Διὰ ταύτης τῆς προστάξεως καὶ ἕτερόν τι
μεῖζον ἀπηγόρευται, βρεφῶν ἔκθεσις, ὃ παρὰ πολλοῖς τῶν ἄλλων ἐθνῶν ἕνεκα τῆς φυσικῆς ἀπ-
111 ανθρωπίας χειρόηθες ἀσέβημα γέγονεν. εἰ γὰρ τοῦ
μηδέπω ταῖς ὡρισμέναις τῶν καιρῶν περιόδοις ἀποκυηθέντος προνοητέον, ὡς μὴ ἐξ ἐπιβουλῆς τι δεινὸν πάθοι, πῶς οὐχὶ μᾶλλον τοῦ τελειογονηθέντος καὶ ὥσπερ εἰς ἀποικίαν ἣν ἔλαχον ἄνθρωποι προπεμφθέντος ἐπὶ τῷ μεταλαχεῖν τῶν τῆς φύσεως δωρεῶν, ἃς ἀνίησιν ἐκ γῆς καὶ ὕδατος καὶ ἀέρος καὶ οὐρανοῦ, παρέχουσα τῶν μὲν οὐρανίων τὴν

[1] Cohn suggests ἄφεσιν.

[a] Ex. xxi. 22. Here Philo follows the LXX, which differs seriously from the Hebrew. There the words "so that her fruit depart, and yet no mischief follow," appear to mean (see Driver) that the woman does not die or suffer permanent injury from the miscarriage, and the question of the complete formation or not of the child does not appear at all. LXX ἐὰν . . . ἐξέλθῃ τὸ παιδίον μὴ ἐξεικονισμένον.

[b] See App. p. 637.

[a] If a man comes to blows with a pregnant woman 108
and strikes her on the belly and she miscarries, then, if the result of the miscarriage is unshaped and undeveloped, he must be fined both for the outrage and for obstructing the artist Nature in her creative work of bringing into life the fairest of living creatures, man.[b] But, if the offspring is already shaped and all the limbs have their proper qualities and places in
the system, he must die, for that which answers to 109
this description is a human being, which he has destroyed in the laboratory of Nature who judges that the hour has not yet come for bringing it out into the light, like a statue lying in a studio requiring nothing more than to be conveyed outside and released from confinement.[c]

XX. This ordinance carries with it the prohibition 110
of something else more important, the exposure of infants,[d] a sacrilegious practice which among many other nations, through their ingrained inhumanity,
has come to be regarded with complacence. For if 111
on behalf of the child not yet brought to the birth by the appointed conclusion of the regular period thought has to be taken to save it from disaster at the hands of the evil-minded, surely still more true is this of the full-born babe sent out as it were to settle in the new homeland assigned to mankind, there to partake of the gifts of Nature. These gifts she draws from earth and water and air and heaven.

[c] See App. p. 637.

[d] The exposure of children is nowhere expressly forbidden in the law, though doubtless it would fall under the general head of murder as Philo himself suggests in § 118, and Josephus presumably held when he says, *Contra Ap.* ii. 202, that it was forbidden by the law. The LXX mistranslation of Ex. xxi. 22 comes in happily to help Philo to clinch the point.

θέαν, τῶν δὲ ἐπιγείων τὸ κράτος καὶ τὴν ἡγεμονίαν, καὶ πάσαις μὲν χορηγοῦσα ταῖς αἰσθήσεσιν ἄφθονα τὰ πάντων, τῷ δὲ νῷ καθάπερ μεγάλῳ βασιλεῖ τὰ μὲν διὰ τούτων ὡς ἂν δορυφόρων ὅσα αἰσθητά, τὰ
112 δ' ἄνευ τούτων ὅσα λόγῳ καταληπτά; τοσούτων οὖν ἀποστεροῦντες ἀγαθῶν τοὺς παῖδας οἱ τροφεῖς, ἅμα τῇ γενέσει τούτων μηδενὸς μεταδιδόντες, ἴστωσαν νόμους φύσεως καταλύοντες καὶ τὰ μέγιστα κατηγοροῦντες αὐτῶν, φιληδονίαν, μισανθρωπίαν, ἀνδροφονίαν καὶ—τὸ χαλεπώτατον ἄγος—
113 τεκνοκτονίαν. φιλήδονοι μὲν γάρ, εἰ μὴ σπορᾶς ἕνεκα τέκνων καὶ τοῦ διαιωνίσαι τὸ γένος συνέρχονται γυναιξὶν ἀλλὰ θηρώμενοι συῶν ἢ τράγων τρόπον τὴν ἐξ ὁμιλίας ἀπόλαυσιν· μισάνθρωποι δὲ τίνες ἂν εἶεν μᾶλλον ἢ οἱ τῶν γεννηθέντων ἐχθροὶ καὶ ἀμείλικτοι δυσμενεῖς; εἰ μή τις οὕτως ἐστὶν ἠλίθιος, ὡς ὑπολαβεῖν ὅτι πρὸς τοὺς ἀλλοτρίους ἔνσπονδοι γένοιντ' ἂν οἱ τοὺς ἡνωμένους κατὰ γένος
114 ἔκσπονδα εἰργασμένοι. τάς γε μὴν ἀνδροφονίας καὶ τεκνοκτονίας ἐναργεστάταις βεβαιοῦνται πίστεσιν οἱ μὲν αὐτόχειρες γινόμενοι καὶ τὴν πρώτην εἰσπνοὴν τῶν βρεφῶν πιέζοντες καὶ ἀναθλίβοντες ὑπὸ ὠμότητος καὶ δεινῆς ἀναλγησίας, οἱ δὲ εἰς ποταμὸν ἢ θαλάττης βυθὸν ἀφιέντες, ὅταν ἀπαιωρήσωσιν
115 ἄχθος, ἵνα θᾶττον τῷ βάρει καταφέρηται· οἱ δ' ἐπ' ἐρημίαν κομίζουσιν ἐκθήσοντες, ὡς μὲν αὐτοί φασιν, ἐλπίδι σωτηρίας, ὡς δὲ τἀληθὲς ἔχει, πρὸς ἀνιαροτάτας συμφοράς· ὅσα γὰρ ἀνθρωπίνων σαρ-

[a] *πάντων* apparently refers to earth, air, and water summed up in *τὰ ἐπίγεια*. The *οὐράνια* are not given to *all* the senses.

Of heavenly things she grants the contemplation, of earthly things the sovereignty and dominion. She bestows in abundance on all the senses what every element contains,[a] on the mind, as on a mighty king, through the senses as its squires, all that they perceive, without them all that reason apprehends. If 112
the guardians of the children cut them off from these blessings, if at their very birth they deny them all share in them, they must rest assured that they are breaking the laws of Nature and stand self-condemned on the gravest charges, love of pleasure, hatred of men, murder and, the worst abomination of all, murder of their own children. For they are pleasure-lovers 113
when they mate with their wives, not to procreate children and perpetuate the race, but like pigs and goats in quest of the enjoyment which such intercourse gives. Men-haters too, for who could more deserve the name than these enemies, these merciless foes of their offspring? For no one is so foolish as to suppose that those who have treated dishonourably their own flesh and blood will deal honourably with strangers. As to the charges of murder in general 114
and murder of their own children in particular the clearest proofs of their truth is supplied by the parents. Some of them do the deed with their own hands; with monstrous cruelty and barbarity they stifle and throttle the first breath which the infants draw or throw them into a river or into the depths of the sea, after attaching some heavy substance to make them sink more quickly under its weight. Others 115
take them to be exposed in some desert place, hoping, they themselves say, that they may be saved, but leaving them in actual truth to suffer the most distressing fate. For all the beasts that feed on human

κῶν ἅπτεται θηρία, μηδενὸς ἀνείργοντος, ἐπιφοιτᾷ καὶ εὐωχεῖται τῶν βρεφῶν, καλῆς θοίνης, ἣν οἱ μόνοι κηδεμόνες καὶ πρὸ τῶν ἄλλων σῴζειν ὀφείλοντες, πατὴρ καὶ μήτηρ, προὔθεσαν· καὶ τὰ λείψανα μέντοι προσεπιλιχμῶνται τῶν οἰωνῶν οἱ σαρκοβόροι καταπτάντες, ὅταν μὴ προαίσθωνται· αἰσθόμενοι γὰρ καὶ περὶ τῶν ὅλων[1] πρὸς τοὺς χερ-
116 [319] σαίους θῆρας κονίονται. φέρε δ' οὖν | τῶν ὁδῷ παριόντων τινὰς ἡμέρῳ κινηθέντας πάθει λαβεῖν οἶκτον καὶ ἔλεον τῶν ἐκτεθέντων, ὡς ἀνελέσθαι τε καὶ τροφῆς μεταδοῦναι καὶ τῆς ἄλλης ἐπιμελείας ἀξιῶσαι· ταυτὶ τὰ οὕτως χρηστὰ ἔργα τί νομίζομεν; ἆρ' οὐ τῶν γεννησάντων εἶναι καταδίκην,[2] εἴ γ' οἱ μὲν ἀλλότριοι τὰ γονέων, οἱ δὲ γονεῖς οὐδὲ τὰ τῶν ἀλλοτρίων εἰς εὔνοιαν ἐπετήδευσαν;

117 Πόρρωθεν οὖν τὴν βρεφῶν ἔκθεσιν ἀπεῖπε δι' ὑπονοιῶν θάνατον, ὡς ἔφην, ὁρίσας κατὰ τῶν αἰτίων ἀμβλώσεως τὰ μεμορφωμένα ἤδη κυϊσκούσαις· καίτοι τὰ μὲν ἔτι κατὰ γαστρὸς προσεχόμενα τῇ μήτρᾳ τῶν κυουσῶν εἶναι μέρη λέγεται παρά τε φυσικοῖς ἀνδράσιν, οἷς ὁ θεωρητικὸς διαπονεῖται βίος, καὶ παρὰ ἰατρῶν τοῖς δοκιμωτάτοις, οἳ τὴν ἀνθρώπου κατασκευὴν διηρεύνησαν τά τ' ἐν ὄψει καὶ τὰ ἀφανῆ μετ' ἐπιμελείας ἐξ ἀνατομῆς ἀκριβώσαντες, ἵν', εἰ χρεία τις γένοιτο θεραπείας, μηδὲν ἀγνοίᾳ παρολιγωρηθὲν αἴτιον μεγάλου

[1] MSS. καὶ πρὸ τῶν ὁδῶν or καὶ τῶν ὅλων.
[2] MSS. καταδίκη or καταδίκας.

[a] The word ἀνελέσθαι probably carries with it the technical

flesh visit the spot and feast unhindered on the infants, a fine banquet provided by their sole guardians, those who above all others should keep them safe, their fathers and mothers. Carnivorous birds, too, come flying down and gobble up the fragments, that is, if they have not discovered them earlier, for, if they have, they get ready to fight the beasts of the field
for the whole carcase. But suppose some passing 116
travellers, stirred by humane feeling, take pity and compassion on the castaways and in consequence raise them up,[a] give them food and drink, and do not shrink from paying all the other attentions which they need, what do we think of such highly charitable actions? Do we not consider that those who brought them into the world stand condemned when strangers play the part of parents, and parents do not behave with even the kindness of strangers?

So Moses then, as I have said, implicitly and in- 117
directly forbade the exposure of children, when he pronounced the sentence of death against those who cause the miscarriage of mothers in cases where the foetus is fully formed. No doubt the view that the child while still adhering to the womb below the belly is part of its future mother is current both among natural philosophers whose life study is concerned with the theoretical side of knowledge and also among physicians of the highest repute, who have made researches into the construction of man and examined in detail what is visible and also by the careful use of anatomy what is hidden from sight, in order that if medical treatment is required nothing which could cause serious danger

sense of "taking up" or acknowledgment by the father. Lat. *tollere*. See L. & S.

118 κινδύνου γένηται. τὰ δ' ἀποκυηθέντα τῆς τε συμφυΐας ἀπέζευκται καὶ διυφειμένα καθ' αὑτὰ ζῷα γέγονεν οὐδενὸς ἐπιδεᾶ τῶν ὅσα συμπληρωτικὰ τῆς ἀνθρωπίνης φύσεώς ἐστιν, ὥστε ἀνενδοιάστως ἀνδροφόνον εἶναι τὸν βρέφος ἀναιροῦντα, τοῦ νόμου μὴ ἐπὶ ταῖς ἡλικίαις ἀλλ' ἐπὶ τῷ γένει παρα-
119 σπονδουμένῳ δυσχεραίνοντος. εἰ μέντοι καὶ ἡλικιῶν ἔδει προμηθεῖσθαι, δοκεῖ μοί τις ἂν δεόντως ἀγανακτῆσαι μᾶλλον ἐπὶ τοῖς ἀναιροῦσι βρέφη· πρὸς μὲν γὰρ τοὺς τελείους μυρίαι προφάσεις εὔλογοι προσκρουσμάτων τε καὶ διαφορῶν, τοῖς δὲ κομιδῇ νηπίοις ἄρτι παρεληλυθόσιν εἰς φῶς καὶ τὸν ἀνθρώπινον βίον οὐδ' ἐπιψεύσασθαι κατηγορίαν ἀκακωτάτοις οὖσιν ἐνδέχεται. διὸ πάντων ὠμότατοι καὶ ἀνηλεέστατοι κριθεῖεν ἂν οἱ ἐπαποδυόμενοι ταῖς τούτων ἐπιβουλαῖς, οὓς ἐχθαίρων ὁ ἱερὸς νόμος ἐνόχους ἀπεφήνατο.

120 XXI. [1]Τὸν μὴ ἑκουσίῳ γνώμῃ τοῦ κτείναντος ἀναιρεθέντα φησὶν ὁ ἱερὸς νόμος παραδεδόσθαι ὑπὸ θεοῦ χερσὶν ἀνδροφόνοις, τῇ μὲν ἀπολογούμενος ὑπὲρ τοῦ δόξαντος ἀνελεῖν ὡς ἔνοχον ἀνελόντος—
121 μὴ γὰρ ἄν ποτε τὸν ἵλεω καὶ συγγνώμονα θεὸν ἐπ' ἀναιρέσει τόν γε ἀναίτιον ἐκδοῦναι, ἀλλ' ὅστις τὰς μὲν παρὰ ἀνθρώποις κρίσεις εὐμηχάνως ἕνεκα τοῦ πολυτρόπου διαδιδράσκει, πρὸς δὲ τὸ τῆς φύσεως ἀχθεὶς ἀφανὲς δικαστήριον ἑάλω, ἐν ᾧ μόνῳ

[1] mss. heading Περὶ ἀκουσίου φόνου.

[a] See note (App.) on § 109.

[b] Ex. xxi. 13. E.V "If a man lie not in wait, but God deliver him into his hand," *i.e.* if he is killed by accident (Driver), "then I will appoint thee a place whither he shall flee." For the first words the LXX has "he that did not

should be neglected through ignorance. But when 118
the child has been brought to the birth it is separated from the organism with which it was identified and being isolated and self-contained becomes a living animal, lacking none of the complements needed to make a human being.[a] And therefore infanticide undoubtedly is murder, since the displeasure of the law is not concerned with ages but with a breach of faith to the race. Though indeed, if 119
age had to be taken into consideration, infanticide to my mind gives a greater cause for indignation, for in the case of adults quarrels and differences supply any number of reasonable pretexts, but with mere babes, who have just passed into the light and the life of human kind, not even a false charge can be brought against such absolute innocence. Therefore those who gird themselves up to conspire against such as these must be judged to be the cruellest and most ruthless of men. The holy law detests them and has pronounced them worthy of punishment.

XXI. The holy law describes the man who has been 120
slain without the deliberate intention of him who did the deed as having been delivered by God into the manslayer's hands.[b] In this phrase it is partly defending one who has admittedly taken the life of another on the ground that it was the life of a guilty person. For it assumes that a merciful and forgiving 121
God would never surrender an innocent man to be done to death but only one who having been enabled by his resourcefulness to make a skilful escape from the justice of men has been arraigned and condemned in the invisible court of Nature, that court in which

intend it" (ὁ δὲ οὐχ ἑκων). For Philo's conception of ἀκούσιος φόνος see App. pp. 637-638.

τἀληθὲς ἀκραιφνέστατον ὁρᾶται, λόγων τέχναις οὐκ ἐπισκιαζόμενον, οὐδὲ γὰρ λόγους τὴν ἀρχὴν παραδέχεται βουλήματα ἀπαμπίσχον καὶ διανοίας ἀφανεῖς εἰς τοὐμφανὲς ἄγον—, τῇ δὲ καὶ τὸν ἀνελόντα φόνῳ μὲν οὐ ποιῶν ὑπόδικον ἅτε θείᾳ κρίσει δόξαντα ὑπηρετῆσαι, μιάσματι δὲ ἀδηλουμένῳ καὶ
[320] βραχεῖ πάντως, ὃ παραιτητὸν καὶ | συγγνωστόν
122 ἐστι. χρῆται γὰρ ὁ θεὸς τοῖς ὀλίγα καὶ ἰάσιμα διαμαρτάνουσι κατὰ τῶν μέγιστα καὶ ἀνίατα ἠδικηκότων ὑπηρέταις κολάσεως, οὐκ ἐκείνους ἀποδεχόμενος, ἀλλ' ὡς ἂν ὄργανα παραλαμβάνων ἐπιτήδεια πρὸς τιμωρίαν, ἵνα μηδεὶς ὅλῳ βίῳ καθαρὸς ὢν καὶ ἐκ καθαρῶν φόνου, κἂν δικαιότατος
123 ᾖ, προσάψηται. φυγὴν οὖν κατὰ τοῦ κτείναντος ἀκουσίως ὥρισεν, οὐχ ὅπῃ τύχοι οὐδ' εἰς ἀεί· πόλεις μὲν γὰρ ἓξ ἀπένειμεν, ὀγδόην μοῖραν ὧν ἔλαχεν ἡ ἱερωμένη φυλή, τοῖς ἁλοῦσιν, ἃς ἀπὸ τοῦ συμβεβηκότος ὠνόμασε "φυγαδευτηρίων"[1]· χρόνον δὲ τῆς φυγῆς τὸν βίον τοῦ ἀρχιερέως προσενομοθέτησε κάθοδον μετὰ τὴν ἐκείνου τελευτὴν ἐπιτρέπων.

124 XXII. αἰτία δὲ τούτου μὲν[2] προτέρα ἥδε· ἡ λεχθεῖσα φυλὴ τὰς πόλεις εἴληφεν ἆθλον ἀνδροφονίας εὐαγοῦς, ἣν ἀριστειῶν ὅσαι πώποτε γεγόνασιν ἐπιφανεστάτην καὶ μεγίστην ὑποληπτέον.

[1] MSS. φυγαδευτήριον (-ου) (-α).

[2] The μὲν seems out of place. I suggest τούτου <ἡ> μέν.

[a] *i.e.* setting the slayer to be His executioner, God marks him as one of a less worthy type. Philo is assigning a reason for the φυγή, which he regards rather as a sentence of banishment than as an escape from vengeance.

truth is seen in perfect purity, which is not beclouded by verbal artifices, since it never accepts words at all but unveils motives and brings hidden intentions into open daylight. Partly, too, it lays the manslayer under the imputation, not indeed of murder, since he is held to have been the minister of divine judgement, but of a defilement of little note and quite insignificant, for which pardon may well be asked
and granted.[a] For in inflicting chastisement on 122
offenders whose deeds have been evil beyond all remedy God uses as His ministers those whose sins are few and easily remedied, though He does not show approval of them but merely takes them as suitable instruments of vengeance. For He would not wish that anyone whose whole life is stainless and his lineage also should set his hand to homicide
however justly deserved. He therefore sentenced the 123
involuntary manslayer to go into exile, but not just anywhere nor yet for all time. For He assigned to persons convicted under this head six cities, an eighth part of those allotted to the consecrated tribe,[b] a fact recorded in the name of "cities of refuge" which He gave to them, and by a further edict He limited the time of banishment to the life of the high priest, after whose death the exile should be permitted to return.[c]

XXII. [d] The first reason for this is as 124
follows: the aforesaid tribe received the cities as a reward for a righteous slaughter which we must regard as the most illustrious act of heroism that has

[b] Num. xxxv. 6, 11-15.

[c] *Ibid.* 28.

[d] For §§ 124-127 see Ex. xxxii. Philo here recurs to the story which he has already told at length in *Mos.* ii. 159 ff. and 270 ff., to say nothing of shorter accounts in *De Ebr.* 67, and above, i. 79.

125 ἡνίκα γὰρ ὁ προφήτης εἰς τὸ περιμηκέστατον καὶ ἱερώτατον τῶν κατ᾿ ἐκεῖνον τὸν τόπον ὀρῶν ἀνακληθεὶς ἐθεσπίζετο τὰ γένη τῶν ἐν εἴδει νόμων καὶ πλείους ἦν ἀφανὴς ἡμέρας, οἱ μὴ τὰς φύσεις εἰρηνικοὶ τῶν ἐξ ἀναρχίας κακιῶν[1] πάντα κατέπλησαν καὶ τέλος προσέθηκαν ἀσέβειαν· τὰς μὲν ἀρίστας καὶ καλὰς ὑφηγήσεις περὶ τῆς τοῦ ὄντως ὄντος θεοῦ τιμῆς χλευάσαντες, ταῦρον δὲ κατασκευασάμενοι χρυσοῦν, Αἰγυπτιακοῦ μίμημα τύφου, θυσίας ἀνῆγον ἀθύτους καὶ ἑορτὰς ἀνεόρτους καὶ χοροὺς ἀχορεύτους ἐπετέλουν σὺν ᾠδαῖς καὶ ὕμνοις
126 ἀντὶ θρήνων. ἡ δὲ λεχθεῖσα φυλὴ πάνυ χαλεπῶς ἐνεγκοῦσα τὴν αἰφνίδιον ἐκδιαίτησιν καὶ ζήλῳ πυρωθεῖσα διὰ μισοπόνηρον πάθος, ὑπόπλεῳ πάντες ὀργῆς, μεμηνότες, ἐνθουσιῶντες, ὡς ἀφ᾿ ἑνὸς συνθήματος ὁπλισάμενοι, διττὴν μεθύοντας μέθην, τὴν μὲν ἀσεβείᾳ, τὴν δὲ οἴνῳ, μάλα καταφρονητικῶς ἐπιστροφάδην ἀνῄρουν, ἀπὸ τῶν οἰκειοτάτων καὶ φιλτάτων ἀρξάμενοι, φίλον καὶ συγγένειαν ἓν τὸ θεοφιλὲς εἶναι νομίζοντες· καὶ βραχεῖ μέρει ἡμέρας τέσσαρες πρὸς ταῖς εἴκοσι χιλιάδες ἀνῃρέθησαν, ὧν αἱ συμφοραὶ τοὺς συναπονοεῖσθαι μέλλοντας ἐνουθέτησαν, δέει τοῦ μὴ τὰ παραπλήσια
127 παθεῖν. ταύτην τὴν στρατείαν ἐθελουργὸν καὶ αὐτοκέλευστον ὑπὲρ εὐσεβείας καὶ ὁσιότητος τῆς[2]

[1] MSS. κακῶν.
[2] MSS. τὴν.

[a] This certainly is the sense required for this passive (or middle?) of θεσπίζω, but no other examples seem forthcoming, unless *De Abr.* 262 οὓς Μωυσῆς ἐθεσπίσθη, is to be taken in the sense of "was inspired to give" instead of "prophesied." See note there.

ever been achieved. When the prophet, summoned 125
up to the highest and most sacred mountain in that region, was receiving[a] from God the heads which sum up the particular laws, and had disappeared for several days, the born enemies of peace had diffused through every part of the camp the vices that spring up in the ruler's absence and had crowned them with impiety. They mocked at the most excellent and admirable injunctions which bade them honour the truly existing God, constructed a golden bull in imitation of the vanity of Egypt, offered sacrifices which were no sacrifices, held feasts which were no feasts and danced dances of death with songs and
hymns which should have been dirges.[b] Then this 126
same tribe, sorely distressed at the sudden backsliding and fired with zeal by their heart-felt hatred of evil, every man of them filled with rage, frenzied, possessed, took arms as if at one signal,[c] and despising all thoughts of danger mowed down their foes drunk with the twofold intoxication of impiety and wine. They began with their nearest and dearest, for they acknowledged no love nor kinship but God's love, and in the space of a few hours 24,000[d] had fallen whose fate served as a warning through fear that they might suffer the like to those who were on the brink of
sharing their delusion. This campaign, waged spon- 127
taneously and instinctively on behalf of piety and

[b] Much the same phraseology as in *Mos.* ii. 162, except that there the χόρους coupled with ἵστασαν signifies the dancers rather than, as here, the dances.

[c] The same phrase as in *Mos.* ii. 170.

[d] A slip for 3000 (given correctly *De Ebr.* 67 and *Mos.* ii. 274), induced by confusion with Num. xxv. 9, where Philo saw a similar slaughter rather than a plague. See *Mos.* i. 304 and note.

εἰς τὸν ὄντως ὄντα θεὸν γενομένην οὐκ ἄνευ μεγάλων κινδύνων τοῖς ἀραμένοις τοὺς ἀγῶνας αὐτὸς
ὁ πατὴρ τῶν ὅλων ἀπεδέξατο καὶ τοὺς ἀνελόντας
δικάσας παρ' αὐτῷ καθαροὺς εἶναι παντὸς ἄγους |
[321] καὶ μιάσματος ἱερωσύνην τῆς ἀνδραγαθίας τούτοις
128 ἀντιδωρεῖται. XXIII. τὸν οὖν ἀκούσιον
δράσαντα φόνον κελεύει φυγεῖν εἰς ἐνίας ὧν ἔλαχον
οὗτοι πόλεις ἕνεκα παρηγορίας καὶ ὑπὲρ τοῦ μὴ
ἀπογινώσκειν τὴν εἰς ἅπαν ἀσφάλειαν, ὑπομιμνη-
σκόμενον ἐκ τοῦ τόπου τὸ ἄφοβον καὶ λογιζόμενον,
ὅτι τοῖς ἑκουσίως ἀπεκτονόσιν οὐ μόνον ἀμνηστία
δέδοται ἀλλὰ καὶ γέρα μεγάλα καὶ περιμάχητα καὶ
πολλῆς εὐδαιμονίας, εἰ δὲ τούτοις, πολὺ μᾶλλον
τοῖς μὴ ἐκ προνοίας ἀνελοῦσιν, εἰ καὶ μηδὲν τῶν
ἐπὶ τιμῇ, ἀλλ' αὐτὸ γοῦν τὸ πανύστατον, μὴ
ἀνταναιρεθῆναι· δι' οὗ παρίσταται τὸ μὴ πᾶσαν
ἀνδροφονίαν ἐπίληπτον ἀλλὰ τὴν σὺν ἀδικίᾳ μόνην
εἶναι, καὶ τῶν ἄλλων ἐπαινετὴν μὲν τὴν κατὰ πόθον
καὶ ζῆλον ἀρετῆς, οὐ ψεκτὴν δὲ τὴν ἀκούσιον.
129 ἥδε μὲν αἰτία προτέρα λελέχθω, δευτέραν δ' αὐτίκα μηνυτέον· βούλεται ὁ νόμος τὸν
ἀκουσίως ἀποκτείναντα διασῴζειν, εἰδὼς γνώμῃ
μὲν οὐκ ἔνοχον χερσὶ δὲ ὑπηρετήσαντα τῇ τῶν
ἀνθρωπίνων ἐφόρῳ δίκῃ πραγμάτων· ἐφεδρεύουσι
γὰρ ἐχθροὶ φονῶντες οἱ τοῦ τεθνεῶτος ἀγχιστεῖς,
οἳ δι' ὑπερβάλλοντα οἶκτον καὶ πένθος ἀπαρηγόρη-

---

[a] The first reason for the choice of the Levitical cities was that their history shewed that homicide was not necessarily a crime. The second was that their superior sanctity made them a more secure refuge.

holiness towards the truly existing God and fraught with much danger to those who undertook it, was approved by none other than the Father of all Who took it upon Himself to judge the cause of those who wrought the slaughter, declared them pure from any curse of bloodguiltiness and gave them the priesthood as a reward for their gallantry.

XXIII. So then he bids the unintentional homicide 128
flee to some of the cities allotted to this tribe, there to gain consolation and be saved from despairing of salvation altogether. There the place will remind him of the fearless courage once shewn in the past; there he may reflect that those who shed blood intentionally received not only full pardon but also rewards great and much to be desired and fraught with abundant happiness; and that, if they fared thus, much more will those whose act was not premeditated receive, not indeed such privileges as confer honour, but at least the lowest and last that they do not pay for the blood they have shed with their own. This shews that not every kind of homicide is culpable but only that which entails injustice, and that as for the other kinds if it is caused by an ardent yearning for virtue it is laudable and if unintentional it is free from blame. No 129
more need be said about the first reason; we must proceed at once to explain the second.[a] The law wishes to preserve the unintentional homicide, as it recognizes that in intention he was free from guilt, and that with his hands he had been the servant of justice, the overseer of human affairs. It knows that watching and waiting for him are blood-thirsty enemies, the kinsmen of the dead man, urged on to vengeance by overwhelming pity and inconsolable

τον ἵενται πρὸς ἄμυναν ἀλόγῳ φορᾷ τἀληθὲς καὶ
130 τὸ φύσει δίκαιον οὐκ ἐξετάζοντες. ἐπέτρεψεν οὖν τῷ τοιούτῳ καταφεύγειν οὔτε εἰς ἱερὸν ἅτε μήπω κεκαθαρμένῳ οὔτε εἰς ἠμελημένον καὶ ἀφανὲς χωρίον, ἵνα μὴ ῥᾳδίως ἐκδοθῇ καταφρονηθείς, ἀλλ' εἰς ἱερόπολιν, ἥτις ἐστὶν ἱεροῦ καὶ βεβήλου τόπου μεθόριος, τρόπον τινὰ δεύτερον ἱερόν· αἱ γὰρ τῶν ἱερωμένων πόλεις σεμνότεραι τῶν ἄλλων εἰσίν, ἐφ' ὅσον, οἶμαι, καὶ οἰκήτορες οἰκητόρων ἐντιμότεροι· βούλεται γὰρ τῇ τῆς ὑποδεξαμένης προνομίᾳ βεβαιοτάτην ἀσφάλειαν περιποιῆσαι τῷ καταφυγόντι.

131 χρόνον δ', ὡς ἔφην, ὥρισε τῆς καθόδου τὴν τοῦ μεγάλου ἱερέως τελευτὴν αἰτίας ἕνεκα τοιᾶσδε· ὥσπερ ἑνὸς ἑκάστου τῶν δολοφονηθέντων οἱ συγγενεῖς εἰσιν ἔφεδροι τῆς κατὰ τῶν δολοφονησάντων δίκης καὶ τιμωρίας, οὕτως καὶ τοῦ σύμπαντος ἔθνους συγγενὴς καὶ ἀγχιστεὺς κοινὸς ὁ ἀρχιερεύς ἐστι, πρυτανεύων μὲν τὰ δίκαια τοῖς ἀμφισβητοῦσι κατὰ τοὺς νόμους, εὐχὰς δὲ καὶ θυσίας τελῶν καθ' ἑκάστην ἡμέραν καὶ τὰ ἀγαθὰ αἰτούμενος ὡς ὑπὲρ ἀδελφῶν καὶ γονέων καὶ τέκνων, ἵνα πᾶσα ἡλικία καὶ πάντα μέρη[1] τοῦ ἔθνους ὡς ἑνὸς σώματος εἰς μίαν καὶ τὴν αὐτὴν ἁρμόζηται κοινωνίαν εἰρήνης καὶ εὐνομίας ἐφιέμενα.
132 τοῦτον οὖν εὐλαβείσθω πᾶς ὁ ἀκουσίως ἀνελὼν ὡς ὑπέρμαχον καὶ προαγωνιστὴν τῶν ἀναιρεθέντων καὶ

[1] MSS. τὰ μέρη.

---

[a] Philo's explanations in §§ 131-136 of "till the death of the high priest" are (1) that the high priest, as representing the nation, is bound to inflict the punishment which the

grief, and so carried away by unreasoning passion that they do not inquire what is true or essentially just.
It therefore permitted such a one to fly for refuge, 130
not to the holy temple, since he had not yet been purged, nor yet to some obscure and insignificant place where he might easily be surrendered as one of little account, but to a holy city which comes midway between holy and profane ground and is in a sense a secondary temple. For the cities of the consecrated order compared with the others receive a higher reverence, corresponding, I consider, to the honour paid to their respective occupants. The law wished in fact to use the superior rank of the city which gave them shelter to put the safety of the fugitive on
the firmest possible footing. [a] When, as 131
I said, it appointed the death of the high priest as the date for the exile's return, it did so for some such reason as this. Just as each single individual who is wilfully murdered has kinsmen to inflict vengeance on the murderer, so too the whole nation has a kinsman and close relative common to all in the high priest, who as ruler dispenses justice to litigants according to the law, who day by day offers prayers and sacrifices and asks for blessings, as for his brothers and parents and children, that every age and every part of the nation regarded as a single body may be united in one and the same fellowship, making peace and good order
their aim. Everyone, then, who has slain another 132
unintentionally must fear the high priest as a champion and defender of the slain and keep himself

fugitive incurs by leaving his refuge; (2) that he is a theoretically perfect character and will therefore refuse to tolerate the presence of even the involuntary offender. In the first case the φυγή is regarded as a refuge, in the second as exile (as in § 123). See further App. p. 638.

εἴσω τῆς πόλεως εἰς ἣν κατέφυγε κατακεκλείσθω, |
[322] μὴ ἐπιθαρρῶν ἔξω προέρχεσθαι τειχῶν, εἰ δή τινα
ποιεῖται λόγον ἀσφαλείας καὶ τοῦ ζῆν ἀκινδύνως.
133 ὅταν οὖν λέγῃ " μὴ ἐπανίτω ὁ φυγάς, ἕως ἂν
ἀποθάνῃ ὁ ἱερεὺς ὁ μέγας," ἴσον τι τούτῳ φησίν·
ἕως ἂν ἀποθάνῃ ὁ πάντων κοινὸς ἀγχιστεύς, ᾧ
μόνῳ καὶ τὰ τῶν ζώντων καὶ τὰ τῶν τετελευτη-
134 κότων ἐφεῖται βραβεύειν. XXIV. τὴν
μὲν οὖν καὶ νεωτέρων ἀκοαῖς ἐφαρμόζουσαν αἰτίαν
τοιαύτην εἶναι συμβέβηκεν. ἣν δὲ πρεσβυτέροις καὶ
τελείοις τὸ ἦθος θέμις ἀναφέρειν, ἥδ' ἐστί· τῶν μὲν
ἑκουσίων ἀδικημάτων αὐτὸ μόνον ἰδιώτας καθαρεύειν ἐφείσθω, λεγέτω δ' εἰ βούλεταί τις καὶ
τοὺς ἄλλους ἱερεῖς, ἀμφοτέρων δ' ἑκουσίων τε καὶ
ἀκουσίων κατὰ τὸν ἐξαίρετον λόγον τὸν ἀρχιερέα.
135 προσάπτεσθαι γὰρ αὐτῷ μιάσματος τὸ σύνολον οὐ
θεμιτόν, οὔτ' ἐκ προνοίας οὔτε κατὰ τροπὴν τῆς
ψυχῆς ἀβούλητον, ἵνα ἱεροφάντης ὢν κοσμῆται καθ'
ἑκάτερον, διανοίᾳ τε χρώμενος ἀνεπιλήπτῳ καὶ
136 εὐπραγίᾳ βίου, ᾧ μηδὲν ὄνειδος πρόσεστι. τῷ δὴ
τοιούτῳ γένοιτ' ἂν ἀκόλουθον ὑποβλέπεσθαι καὶ
τοὺς ἀκουσίως ἀπεκτονότας οὐχ[1] ὡς ἐναγεῖς,
ἀλλ' οὐχ ὡς καθαροὺς καὶ παντὸς ἀμετόχους
ἁμαρτήματος, καὶ εἰ τὰ μάλιστα τοῖς τῆς φύσεως

[1] Cohn expunged the οὐχ, quite wrongly, I think; see note *b*.

---

[a] While the second explanation has something in common with the allegorical interpretation in *De Fuga* 108 f., it is difficult to see why as it stands it is more suitable for older ears than the other. Perhaps the idea is that it involves the theological and somewhat mystical distinction between voluntary and involuntary sins on which Philo often dwells in his allegorical disquisitions, *cf. e.g. De Ebr.* 125.

shut up within the city in which he has taken refuge, never venturing to shew himself outside the walls, that is, if he sets any value on his safety, or on a life secure from danger. When, then, he says that the 133
exile must not return till the death of the high priest, it is as much as to say till the death of the common kinsman of all, who alone has authority to arbitrate on the rights both of the living and the dead.

XXIV. Such is the reason which we find suitable to 134
younger ears, but for elders and those whose character is fully developed there is another which may properly be given.[a] For laymen it may be allowed that it is enough to keep undefiled from voluntary misdeeds only, and anyone who likes may say the same of the other priests, but he must make an exception of the high priest and agree that he needs to be innocent of the involuntary as well as the voluntary. The contact with pollution of any kind is forbidden 135
to him, whether it is the result of definite purpose or of some movement of the soul which he has not willed, for only so can he take his place as revealer in both aspects, his motives blameless and his life so fortunate that no stigma attaches to it. It is a 136
necessary consequence that such a one should include in the objects of his displeasure the unintentional homicides, regarding them not indeed as accursed,[b] but yet not pure or free from sin of every kind, however much they are admitted to have ministered to

[b] Cohn's rejection of οὐχ, though accepted by Heinemann, seems to me unreasonable. ἐναγεῖς is a strong word, and to negative it perfectly agrees with the description of unintentional homicide as a pollution of little note (§ 121). Apart from this, ἀλλά does not suit the parallelism, which Cohn's text demands, between ἐναγεῖς and οὐ καθαρούς.

ὑπηρετῆσαι βουλήμασιν ἔδοξαν τισαμένης διὰ τούτων τοὺς ἀναιρεθέντας, ὧν ἀφανῶς αὐτὴ[1] δικάσασα παρ' ἑαυτῇ θάνατον κατέγνω.

XXV. Ταῦτα μὲν ἐπ' ἐλευθέροις καὶ ἀστοῖς· ἑξῆς δὲ καὶ περὶ οἰκετῶν νομοθετεῖται βιαίως ἀναιρεθέντων.

137 [2]Θεράποντες τύχῃ μὲν ἐλάττονι κέχρηνται, φύσεως δὲ τῆς αὐτῆς μεταποιοῦνται τοῖς δεσπόταις. τῷ δὲ θείῳ νόμῳ κανὼν τῶν δικαίων ἐστὶν οὐ τὸ τῆς τύχης ἀλλὰ τὸ τῆς φύσεως ἐναρμόνιον. διὸ προσήκει τοὺς κυρίους μὴ κατακόρως χρῆσθαι ταῖς ἐξουσίαις κατὰ τῶν οἰκετῶν, ἀλαζονείαν καὶ ὑπεροψίαν καὶ δεινὴν ὠμότητα ἐπιδεικνυμένους· ταῦτα γὰρ οὐκ ἔστι δείγματα ψυχῆς εἰρηνικῆς ἀλλ' ὑπὸ ἀκρασίας τὸ ἀνυπεύθυνον ζηλούσης κατὰ
138 τυραννικὴν δυναστείαν. ὁ γὰρ τὴν μὲν ἰδίαν οἰκίαν ὥσπερ ἄκραν ἐπιτειχίσας, παρρησίας δὲ τῶν ἔνδον μηδενὶ μεταδιδούς, ἀλλὰ πρὸς ἅπαντας ἠγριωμένος ὑπὸ τῆς ἐμφύτου τάχα δὲ καὶ ἐπιτετηδευμένης μισανθρωπίας, τύραννός ἐστιν ἐλάττοσι παρα-
139 σκευαῖς χρώμενος. ἐξ ὧν διελέγχεται μὴ στησόμενος ἐπὶ τῶν αὐτῶν, εἰ μειζόνων λάβοιτο χρημάτων· διαβήσεται γὰρ εὐθὺς ἐπὶ πόλεις τε καὶ χώρας καὶ ἔθνη τὴν αὑτοῦ πατρίδα προδουλωσάμενος εἰς ἔνδειξιν τοῦ μηδενὶ μέλλειν τῶν ἄλλων
140 ὑπηκόων ἡμέρως προσφέρεσθαι. σαφῶς οὖν ὁ τοιοῦτος ἴστω μὴ τὴν τοῦ συνεχῶς καὶ εἰς πολλοὺς
[323] ἁμαρτάνειν | ἄδειαν ἕξων· ἐναντιώσεται γὰρ ἡ

[1] So MSS.: Cohn corrects to αὕτη. In view of the common conjunction between αὐτός and the reflexive, I think the MS. reading is preferable.

[2] MS. heading Κατὰ τῶν οἰκέτας κτεινόντων.

Nature's will, who has used them as instruments of vengeance against those who have fallen by their hands, condemned to death in the secret tribunal where she sits as sole judge.

XXV. What has been said applies to free-born persons of citizen rank; the enactments which follow deal with slaves whose death is caused by violence.

[a] Servants rank lower in fortune but in nature can 137
claim equality with their masters, and in the law of God the standard of justice is adjusted to nature and not to fortune. And therefore the masters should not make excessive use of their authority over slaves by showing arrogance and contempt and savage cruelty. For these are signs of no peaceful spirit, but of one so intemperate as to seek to throw off all responsibility and take the tyrant's despotism for its model. He who has used his private house as a 138
sort of stronghold of defiance and allows no freedom of speech to any of the inmates, but treats all with the brutality created by his native or perhaps acquired hatred for his fellow-men, is a tyrant with smaller resources. By his use of them he gives proof that he 139
will not stay where he is, if he gets more wealth into his hands, for he will pass on at once to attack cities and countries and nations, after first reducing his own fatherland to slavery, a sign that he will not deal gently with any of his other subjects. Such a one 140
must clearly understand that his misconduct cannot be prolonged or widely extended with immunity, for he will have for his adversary justice, the hater

[a] Presumably these are non-Israelites, *cf.* ii. 123. For the sentiments expressed *cf.* ii. 69. For the following sections see Ex. xxi. 20, 21.

μισοπόνηρος αὐτῷ δίκη, ἡ βοηθὸς καὶ ὑπέρμαχος τῶν ἀδικηθέντων, ἣ λόγον καὶ εὐθύνας αὐτὸν τῆς
141 περὶ τοὺς πεπονθότας συμφορᾶς ἀπαιτήσει· κἂν ἄρα φάσκῃ πληγὰς ἕνεκα νουθεσίας ἐντεῖναι μὴ διανοηθεὶς ἀνελεῖν, οὐκ εὐθὺς βαδιεῖται γεγηθώς, ἀλλ' εἰς δικαστήριον ἀπαχθεὶς παρ' ἀκριβέσι λογισταῖς τῆς ἀληθείας ἐξετασθήσεται, πότερον ἑκὼν ἀπέκτεινεν ἢ ἄκων· κἂν ἐπιβεβουλευκὼς ἀνευρίσκηται γνώμῃ ἀνοσίῳ, θνῃσκέτω, μηδὲν παρόσον δεσπότης ἐστὶ κερδαίνων εἰς τὸ σωθῆναι.
142 ἐὰν δὲ μὴ εὐθὺς ἐκ τῶν πληγῶν οἱ τυπτηθέντες ἀναιρεθῶσιν, ἀλλὰ βιώσωσιν ἡμέραν μίαν ἢ καὶ δύο, μηκέθ' ὁμοίως ὁ δεσπότης ὑπόδικος ἔστω φόνου, πλεονέκτημα εἰς ἀπολογίαν πεπορισμένος τὸ μήτε παραχρῆμα τύπτων ἀνελεῖν μήθ' ὕστερον, ἔχων κατὰ τὴν οἰκίαν, ἀλλὰ ζῆν ἐάσας ὅσον βιοῦν οἷοί τε ἦσαν χρόνον, εἰ καὶ παντάπασιν ὀλίγον· χωρὶς τοῦ μηδένα οὕτως ἠλίθιον εἶναι, ὡς λυπεῖν ἕτερον
143 ἐπιχειρεῖν, ἐν οἷς αὐτὸς ἀδικηθήσεται. κτείνων δέ τις οἰκέτην πολὺ πρότερον ἑαυτὸν βλάπτει, ὑπ-

---

[a] The thought of justice as the adversary and the legal process described in the next section probably spring from a misunderstanding of Ex. xxi. 20. There, where the E.V. has "he shall surely be punished," the LXX has *δίκῃ ἐκδικηθήσεται*. Philo, misunderstanding, as often, the Hebrew idiomatic way of strengthening the verb, takes this to mean "he shall be condemned by justice." He also interprets this to imply the death-penalty, though the text points rather to a fine (see Driver, *ad loc.*).

of evil, the defender and champion of the ill-used, who will call upon him to give an account for the unhappy condition of the sufferers.[a] And if he 141
alleges that the stripes he inflicted were meant as a deterrent and not with the intention of causing death, he shall not at once depart with a cheerful heart, but will be brought before the court, there to be examined under strict investigators of the truth as to whether he meant to commit homicide or not; and if he is found to have acted with intentional wickedness and with malice aforethought he must die, and his position as master will avail him nothing to escape the sentence. [b] But if the 142
sufferers do not die on the spot under the lash but survive for one or perhaps two days, the situation is different and the master is not to be held guilty of murder. In this case he is provided with a valuable plea, namely that he did not beat them to death at the time nor yet later when he had them in his house, but suffered them to live as long as they could, even though that was quite a short time. Furthermore he may argue that no one is so foolish as to try to harm another when he himself will be wronged thereby. And it is true that anyone who kills a slave 143
injures himself far more, as he deprives himself of

[b] Ex. xxi. 21, "Notwithstanding if he continue (LXX διαβιώσῃ, "survive") a day or two, he shall not be punished; for he is his money." Philo understands the first part of this to mean that the master will be acquitted on the grounds that if he had intended to kill the slave he would have done so at once. The last words, "for he is his money," which probably mean that the master will not be fined, as he anyhow loses his property, are construed as a plea that he cannot have intended to destroy a valuable possession. Philo fails to observe that the plea would have been equally applicable if the slave had died on the spot.

ηρεσιῶν τε ἃς παρὰ ζῶντος εἶχε στερόμενος καὶ τὴν τιμὴν ζημιούμενος καὶ πλείστην ἴσως. ἐὰν μέντοι θανάτου πεπραχὼς ἄξια τυγχάνῃ, πρὸς τοὺς δικαστὰς ἀγέτω καὶ δηλούτω τὸ ἀδίκημα, τοὺς νόμους κυρίους ποιῶν τῆς τιμωρίας ἀλλὰ μὴ ἑαυτόν.

144 XXVI. [1]Ἐάν τινα ταῦρος ἀναπείρας ἀποκτείνῃ, καταλευέσθω—ἀσφαγὴς γὰρ ἱερείοις—καὶ ἄβρωτα ἔστω τὰ τούτου κρέα. διὰ τί; ὅτι τροφὴν ἢ προσόψημα τροφῆς ἀνθρώπων γίνεσθαι τὰ τοῦ

145 κτείναντος ἄνθρωπον οὐχ ὅσιον. ἐὰν δὲ ὁ τοῦ κτήνους κύριος ἄγριον εἰδὼς καὶ ἀτίθασον μήτε καταδήσῃ μήτε κατακλείσας φυλάττῃ, τύχῃ δὲ καὶ παρ' ἑτέρων πεπυσμένος ὅτι οὐκ ἔστι χειρόηθες, ἄφετον ἐάσας ἐκνέμεσθαι ὥσπερ αἴτιος ὑπόδικος ἔστω· καὶ τὸ μὲν ἀναπεῖραν αὐτίκα θνῃσκέτω, ὁ δὲ κύριος προσαναιρείσθω ἢ λύτρα καὶ σῶστρα κατατιθέσθω, τὸ δὲ δικαστήριον ὅ τι χρὴ παθεῖν ἢ ἀποτῖσαι διαγνώσεται. εἰ μέντοι δοῦλος ὁ ἀναιρεθεὶς εἴη, τὴν τιμὴν ἐπανορθούσθω τῷ δεσπότῃ.

146 ἐὰν δὲ μὴ ἄνθρωπον ἀλλὰ | κτῆνος ἀναπείρῃ, τὸ

[324] τεθνηκὸς ὁ τοῦ κτείναντος λαβὼν δεσπότης τὸ ὅμοιον ἀποτισάτω, [διότι τὸ ἀνήμερον τοῦ ἰδίου

[1] MS. heading Κατὰ ζῴων ἀλόγων ἃ παραίτια γίγνεται θανάτου.

---

[a] For §§ 144-146 see Ex. xxi. 28-32 and 35, 36.

[b] The stoning is probably to avoid contact, *cf.* Ex. xix. 13, "no hand shall touch him but he shall surely be stoned or

the service which he receives from him when alive and loses his value as a piece of property, which may be possibly very considerable. When the slave has committed some act worthy of death his master should bring him before the judges and state the offence, thus leaving the decision of the penalty with the laws instead of keeping it in his own hands.

XXVI. [a] If a bull gores a man and kills him, it must 144
be stoned,[b] since it is not fit to be slaughtered as a sacrifice, and its flesh must not be eaten. Why is this? It is required by the law of holiness that the flesh of an animal that has killed a man should not be used as a foodstuff for men or to make their food more palatable. If the owner of the animal knowing 145
that it is savage and wild has not tied it up nor kept it shut up under guard,[c] or if he has had information from others that it is unmanageable, he must be held guilty as responsible for the death by allowing it to range at large. And while the aggressive animal is to be put to death at once, the owner must also forfeit his life or else redeem it by a ransom, what punishment he must suffer or what compensation he must pay being left to the decision of the court. If, however, it is a slave who is killed, he must make good his value to the owner and if it has gored not a man 146
but one of the live-stock, here too the owner of the beast which has caused its death must pay like for

shot through" (with a dart). Philo seems to understand it that any animal killed in the ordinary way is suitable for sacrifice.

[c] So E.V. "hath not kept him in." The LXX has ἀφανίσῃ αὐτόν = "removed" or "kept him out of the way." Heinemann notes that here Philo is nearer to the Hebrew than to the LXX. But this may be merely accidental. His interpretation of ἀφανίσῃ is a very natural one.

προαισθανόμενος οὐκ ἐφυλάξατο· κἂν αὐτὸ μέντοι τὸ θρέμμα ἀλλότριον ἀνέλῃ, πάλιν ὅμοιον ἀποτινέτω,][1] χάριν εἰδὼς ἐπὶ τῷ μὴ πλείονα ζημίαν ὑπομένειν ἄρξας ἐπηρείας.

147 XXVII. [2]Ὀρύγματα γῆς εἰώθασί τινες εὖ μάλα βαθύνειν ἢ φλέβας πηγαζούσας ἀναστέλλοντες ἢ πρὸς ὑποδοχὴν ὀμβρίου ὕδατος, εἶθ' ὑπονόμους εὐρύναντες ἀφανεῖς, δέον τὰ στόμια ἢ περιοικοδομῆσαι ἢ περιπωμάσαι, κατά τινα δεινὴν ῥᾳθυμίαν ἢ φρενοβλάβειαν ἐπ' ὀλέθρῳ τινῶν εἴασαν ἀχανῆ.
148 ἐὰν οὖν τις τῶν ὁδῷ παριόντων μὴ προαισθόμενος κατὰ κενοῦ ἐπιβὰς ἐνεχθῇ καὶ τελευτήσῃ, ἐπιγραφέσθωσαν οἱ βουλόμενοι ὑπὲρ τοῦ τετελευτηκότος πρὸς τοὺς τὸ ὄρυγμα ποιησαμένους καὶ τιμάτω τὸ δικαστήριον ὅ τι χρὴ παθεῖν ἢ ἀποτῖσαι. ἐὰν δὲ θρέμμα κατενεχθὲν ἀποθάνῃ, τὴν ἀξίαν τιμὴν ὡς ζῶντος ἐπανορθούσθωσαν τῷ δεσπότῃ τὸ νεκρὸν
149 αὐτοὶ λαβόντες. ἀδελφὸν δὲ καὶ συγγενὲς ἀδίκημα δρῶσι τῷ λεχθέντι καὶ ὅσοι κατασκευάζοντες οἰκίας ἰσόπεδα καταλείπουσι τὰ τέγη, περιστεφανοῦν θωρακίοις δέον ὑπὲρ τοῦ μή τινα κατακρημνισθῆναι λαθόντα· φόνον γάρ, εἰ δεῖ τἀληθὲς εἰπεῖν, δρῶσι,

1 The words in brackets only appear in two MSS. See note *a*.
2 MS. heading Περὶ ὀρυγμάτων.

---

a Ex. xxi. 36, "pay bull for bull." Philo, I think, rightly interprets this to pay compensation enough to buy another bull (or whatever the animal killed is), not as Goodenough, to hand over his own (and vicious) bull to the other. The words expunged by Cohn (see note 1), "because having foreknowledge of the savageness of his own animal he has not taken precautions; and if it kills the beast of another, he must pay the like as compensation," are absurdly super-

like,[a] taking the dead animal for his own, and be thankful that as the original cause of the wanton mischief he does not suffer a greater loss.[b]

XXVII. [c] It is a common practice with some people 147
to dig deep holes in the ground either when they are opening veins of spring water or making receptacles for the rain water. Then after widening the tunnels out of sight, instead of walling the mouths in or covering them up with a lid as they should, through some fatal carelessness or mental aberration they leave them
gaping as a death-trap. If, then, some person walking 148
along does not notice them in time but steps on a void and falls down and is killed, anyone who wishes may bring an indictment on behalf of the dead man against the makers of the pit, and the court must assess what punishment they must suffer or what compensation they must pay. But if anyone of the cattle falls down and is killed, they must make good to the owners the value of the animal as if it were
alive and keep the dead body for themselves.[d] Of the 149
same family as the above is the offence committed by those who in building their houses leave their roofs flat instead of ringing them in with parapets to prevent anyone being precipitated unawares over the edge. Indeed they are to the best of their ability

fluous. Cohn (*Hermes*, 1908, p. 206) also considers that the Greek has faults of which Philo would not have been guilty.

[b] Philo passes over the case (*v.* 36) where the bull has not been known to be vicious, when the two owners divide the loss between them.

[c] For §§ 147-148 see Ex. xxi. 33, 34, which, however, legislates for cases where death is thus caused to an animal, not to a man. See App. p. 638.

[d] Deut. xxii. 8, where, though no penalty is prescribed, it is implied that the omission will constitute bloodguiltiness (LXX ποιήσεις φόνον). See App. pp. 638-639.

κἂν μηδεὶς ὑποσυρεὶς ἀποθάνῃ, τό γε ἐπ' αὐτοὺς ἧκον μέρος. κολαζέσθωσαν οὖν ἐν ἴσῳ τοῖς ἀχανῆ τὰ στόμια τῶν ὀρυγμάτων καταλείπουσι.

150 XXVIII. Λύτρα παρὰ ἀνδροφόνου, ὃν δέον τεθνάναι, διαγορεύει ὁ νόμος μὴ ἐξεῖναι λαμβάνειν ἐπὶ μειώσει τῆς τιμωρίας ἢ ὑπαλλαγῇ φυγῆς ἀντὶ θανάτου· αἵματι γὰρ αἷμα καθαίρεται, τῷ τοῦ

151 κτείναντος τὸ τοῦ ἐπιβουλευθέντος. ἐπεὶ δ' ὅρον οὐκ ἔχουσιν οἱ πονηροὶ τὰς φύσεις τοῦ πλημμελεῖν, ἀλλ' ἀεὶ μεγαλουργοῦσι προσυπερβάλλοντες καὶ τὰς κακίας ἐπιτείνουσι καὶ διαίρουσι πρὸς τὸ ἄμετρον καὶ ἀπερίγραφον, μυρίους μὲν θανάτους, εἴπερ οἷόν τε ἦν, ὥρισεν ἂν κατ' αὐτῶν ὁ νομοθέτης· ἐπεὶ δὲ τοῦτ' οὐκ ἐνεδέχετο, τιμωρίαν ἄλλην προσδιατάττεται κελεύων τοὺς ἀνελόντας ἀνασκολοπίζεσθαι.

152 καὶ τοῦτο προστάξας ἀνατρέχει πάλιν ἐπὶ τὴν αὑτοῦ φιλανθρωπίαν, ἡμερούμενος πρὸς τοὺς ἀνήμερα εἰργασμένους, καί φησι· μὴ ἐπιδυέτω ὁ ἥλιος ἀνεσκολοπισμένοις, ἀλλ' ἐπικρυπτέσθωσαν γῇ πρὸ δύσεως καθαιρεθέντες. ἦν γὰρ ἀναγκαῖον τοὺς ἅπασι τοῖς μέρεσι τοῦ κόσμου πολεμίους μετεωρίσαντας εἰς τοὐμφανὲς ἐπιδείξασθαι μὲν αὐτοὺς

[a] Num. xxxv. 31, 32. In the second of these verses, where the E.V. has "ye shall take no ransom for him that is fled to his city of refuge, that he should come again to dwell in the land until the death of the priest," the LXX has οὐ λήψεσθε λύτρα τοῦ φυγεῖν εἰς πόλιν κτλ., which might easily be wrongly taken to mean "ye shall not accept a ransom so that he shall fly." Philo's phrase in "substitute banishment for death" suggests that he did take it so, meaning presumably that the voluntary homicide might purchase a leave to use the city of refuge.

murderers, even if no one is killed by the force of the fall. They must receive the same penalty as those who leave the mouths of their pits wide open.

XXVIII. [a] The law forbids the acceptance of 150
ransom-money from a murderer deserving of death, in order to mitigate his punishment or substitute banishment for death, for blood is purged with blood,[b] the blood of the wilfully murdered with the blood
of the slayer. Since there are no bounds to the in- 151
iquities of evil natures, and they are ever committing a superabundance of enormities and extending and exalting their vices beyond all measure and all limit, the lawgiver would, if he could, have sentenced them to die times beyond number. But since this was impossible he ordained another penalty as an addition,
and ordered the manslayers to be crucified.[c] Yet 152
after giving this injunction he hastened to revert to his natural humanity and shews mercy to those whose deeds were merciless when he says "Let not the sun go down upon the crucified but let them be buried in the earth before sundown."[d] For while it was necessary that the enemies of every part of the universe should after punishment be set on high and

[b] *Ibid. v.* 33 "the land shall not be purged from the blood shed upon it but by the blood of him that shed it."

[c] Or simply "hanged up." But in the other two places where Philo uses the word, *De Post.* 61 and *De Som.* ii. 213, it is definitely coupled with nailing, and he probably understood the κρεμάσητε ἐπὶ ξύλου of the LXX to mean "affix to something wooden," as also did Paul in Gal. iii. 13. Probably he understood that it is only the corpse of the malefactor which is so affixed, though he does not make it absolutely clear.

[d] Deut. xxi. 22, 23. Philo treats the text very freely. It does not enjoin the "hanging," but merely that if it is done, the body shall be buried the same day. Nor is it specified that it is a punishment for murderers in particular.

ἡλίῳ καὶ οὐρανῷ καὶ ἀέρι καὶ ὕδατι καὶ γῇ |
[325] κολασθέντας, πάλιν δὲ εἰς τὸν νεκρῶν χῶρον
ὑποσῦραί τε καὶ καταχῶσαι, ὅπως μὴ τὰ ὑπὲρ γῆν
μιαίνωσι.
153 XXIX. Παγκάλως μέντοι κἀκεῖνο διατέτακται,
πατέρας ὑπὲρ υἱῶν μὴ ἀποθνήσκειν μηδ᾽ υἱοὺς
ὑπὲρ γονέων, ἀλλ᾽ ἕκαστον τῶν ἄξια θανάτου
δεδρακότων αὐτὸν ἰδίᾳ μόνον ἀναιρεῖσθαι, διὰ τοὺς
ἢ βίαν τοῦ δικαίου προτιμῶντας ἢ πάνυ φιλο-
154 στόργους. οὗτοι μὲν γὰρ διὰ περιττὴν καὶ ὑπερβάλλουσαν εὔνοιαν ἐθελήσουσι πολλάκις ἄσμενοι
προαποθνήσκειν, αὑτοὺς ἐπιδιδόντες ὑπὲρ τῶν
ἐνόχων οἱ ἀνυπαίτιοι, μέγα κέρδος νομίζοντες τὸ
μὴ ἐπιδεῖν κολαζομένους ἢ τοὺς γεννήσαντας υἱοὶ
ἢ τοὺς παῖδας γονεῖς, ὡς ἀβίωτον καὶ παντὸς
ἀργαλεώτερον θανάτου τὸν αὖθις χρόνον βιωσό-
155 μενοι. πρὸς οὓς λεκτέον· "ἡ εὔνοια ὑμῶν οὐκ
ἔχει καιρόν, τὰ δ᾽ ὅσα μὴ ἐν καιρῷ ψέγεται
δεόντως, ἐπεὶ καὶ τὰ καίρια ἐπαινεῖται. χρὴ
μέντοι φιλεῖν τοὺς ἄξια φιλίας δρῶντας, πονηρὸς
δ᾽ οὐδεὶς πρὸς ἀλήθειαν φίλος. συγγενεῖς δὲ καὶ
ἐν συγγενέσι φίλους καλουμένους ἠλλοτρίωσαν αἱ
μοχθηρίαι πλημμελοῦντας· συγγένεια γὰρ οἰκειοτέρα
τῆς πρὸς αἵματος ἡ πρὸς δικαιοσύνην καὶ πᾶσαν
ἀρετὴν ὁμολογία, ἣν ἐκλιπών τις οὐκ ἐν ὀθνείοις
καὶ ξένοις μόνον ἀλλὰ καὶ ἐν ἀσπόνδοις ἐχθροῖς
156 ἀναγράφεται. τί οὖν κατεψευσμένον ὄνομα εὐνοίας
ὅ τι χρηστὸν καὶ φιλάνθρωπόν ἐστιν ὑποδύεσθε,
τἀληθῆ μαλακίαν καὶ ἀνανδρίαν παρακαλυπτόμενοι;
ἢ οὐκ ἄνανδροι τὰς φύσεις, παρ᾽ οἷς οἴκτου λο-

---

[a] Deut. xxiv. 16.

exhibited to the sun and heaven and air and water and earth, it was equally necessary that they should be thrust down into the place of the dead and there entombed, that nothing above the earth might be polluted by them.

XXIX. Another excellent ordinance is that fathers 153
should not die for their sons nor sons for their parents, but each person who has committed deeds worthy of death should suffer it alone and in his own person.[a] This order has in view those who either set violence before justice or are strongly influenced by family affection. These last in their excessive and over- 154
whelming devotion will often be willing and glad to sacrifice their guiltless selves for the guilty and die in their stead. They count it a great gain to be spared from seeing, parents their children and sons their parents, undergoing a punishment which they feel will make their after-life intolerable and more painful than any death. To these we should answer 155
"your devotion is mistimed and the mistimed deserves censure just as the rightly timed deserves praise. It is right indeed to shew friendship to those whose actions are worthy of friendship, but no evil-doer is a true friend. Those whom we call our kinsfolk or within the circle of kinsmen our friends are turned into aliens by their misconduct when they go astray; for agreement to practise justice and every virtue makes a closer kinship than that of blood, and he who abandons this enters his name in the list not only of strangers and foreigners but of mortal enemies. Why, 156
then, under the false name of devotion do you assume to be all that is kind and humane and cloak the realities, your weakness and unmanliness? For unmanly is the nature you shew in letting compassion

γισμὸς ἡττᾶται; καὶ ταῦθ᾽ ἵνα διπλοῦν ἀδίκημα δράσητε, τοὺς μὲν ὑπαιτίους ῥυόμενοι τῆς τιμωρίας, αὐτοὺς δ᾽ ἐπὶ μηδενὶ μεμφθέντας τὸ παράπαν οἰόμενοι δεῖν ἀντ᾽ ἐκείνων κολάζειν;"

157 XXX. ἀλλ᾽ οὗτοι μὲν ὑποτίμησιν ἔχουσι τὸ μηδὲν[1] θηρᾶσθαι ἐπ᾽ ὠφελείᾳ καὶ τὸ λίαν πρὸς τοὺς ἐγγυτάτω γένους φιλόστοργον, ὑπὲρ ὧν τῆς
158 σωτηρίας ἀποθνῄσκειν ἄσμενοι διανοοῦνται. τοὺς δὲ ὠμοθύμους καὶ τὴν φύσιν θηριώδεις τίς οὐκ ἂν προβάλοιτο τῶν οὐ λέγω μετρίων ἀλλὰ καὶ τῶν μὴ σφόδρα ἀτιθάσων τὴν ψυχήν, οἳ ἢ λάθρα τεχνάζουσιν ἢ ἐπιθαρροῦσι φανερῶς ἑτέροις ἀνθ᾽ ἑτέρων τὰς μεγίστας ἐπανατείνεσθαι συμφοράς, φιλίαν ἢ συγγένειαν ἢ κοινωνίαν ἤ τι ὁμοιότροπον ἐπ᾽ ὀλέθρῳ τῶν οὐδὲν ἠδικηκότων προφασιζόμενοι; καὶ ταῦτα δρῶσιν ἔστιν ὅτε μηδὲν πεπονθότες δεινόν, ἕνεκα δὲ πλεονεξίας ἢ ἁρπαγῆς.

159 πρώην τις ἐκλογεὺς φόρων ταχθεὶς παρ᾽ ἡμῖν, ἐπειδή τινες τῶν δοξάντων ὀφείλειν διὰ πενίαν ἔφυγον δέει τιμωριῶν ἀνηκέστων, γύναια τούτων
[326] | καὶ τέκνα καὶ γονεῖς καὶ τὴν ἄλλην γενεὰν ἀπαγαγὼν πρὸς βίαν, τύπτων καὶ προπηλακίζων καὶ πάσας αἰκίας αἰκιζόμενος, ἵν᾽ ἢ τὸν φυγόντα μηνύσωσιν ἢ τὰ ὑπὲρ ἐκείνου καταθῶσιν οὐδέτερον δυνάμενοι, τὸ μὲν ὅτι ἠγνόουν, τὸ δ᾽ ὅτι οὐχ ἧττον τοῦ φυγόντος ἀπόρως εἶχον, οὐ πρότερον ἀνῆκεν,

[1] MSS. μηδενὸς.

overcome your reason, only to commit a double wrong in trying to deliver the guilty from chastisement and in thinking it right that you should be punished in their stead when no blame at all has
been cast upon you." XXX. Still these 157
can plead in their defence that they seek no profit and are moved by exceeding affection for their nearest of kin, to save whom they propose
cheerfully to lay down their lives. But the other 158
kind, the cruel of heart and bestial of nature, would be spurned, I need not say by all respectable people, but by any who are not thoroughly uncivilized in soul. I mean those who either secretly and craftily or boldly and openly threaten to inflict the most grievous sufferings on one set of persons in substitution for another and seek the destruction of those who have done no wrong on the pretext of their friendship or kinship, or partnership, or some similar connexion, with the culprits. And they sometimes do this without having suffered any grievous harm but merely
through covetousness and rapine. An 159
example of this was given a little time ago in our own district by a person who was appointed to serve as a collector of taxes. When some of his debtors whose default was clearly due to poverty took flight in fear of the fatal consequences of his vengeance, he carried off by force their womenfolk and children and parents and their other relatives and beat and subjected them to every kind of outrage and contumely in order to make them either tell him the whereabouts of the fugitive or discharge his debt themselves. As they could do neither the first for want of knowledge, nor the second because they were as penniless as the fugitive, he continued this treatment until while

ἢ βασάνοις καὶ στρέβλαις τὰ σώματα κατατείνων ἀποκτεῖναι κεκαινουργημέναις ἰδέαις θανάτου·
160 ἄμμου σπυρίδα πλήρη βρόχοις ἐκδησάμενος ἀνήρτα κατὰ τῶν αὐχένων, βαρύτατον ἄχθος, ἱστὰς ἐν ὑπαίθρῳ κατὰ μέσην ἀγοράν, ἵν᾿ οἱ μὲν ἀθρόαις τιμωρίαις, ἀνέμῳ καὶ ἡλίῳ καὶ τῇ ἀπὸ τῶν παριόντων αἰσχύνῃ καὶ τοῖς ἐκκρεμαμένοις ἄχθεσι, βιαζόμενοι χαλεπῶς ἀπαγορεύωσιν, οἱ δὲ θεώμενοι
161 τὰς τούτων τιμωρίας προαλγῶσιν· ὧν ἔνιοι τρανότερον τῆς διὰ τῶν ὀφθαλμῶν τὴν διὰ τῆς ψυχῆς λαβόντες αἴσθησιν, ὡς ἐν τοῖς ἑτέρων σώμασιν αὐτοὶ κακούμενοι, τῷ βίῳ προαπετάξαντο ξίφεσιν ἢ φαρμάκοις ἢ ἀγχόναις, μεγάλην ὡς ἐν κακοπραγίαις νομίζοντες ἐπιτυχίαν τὴν ἄνευ βασάνων
162 τελευτήν· οἱ δὲ μὴ φθάσαντες ἑαυτοὺς διαχρήσασθαι καθάπερ ἐν ταῖς τῶν κλήρων ἐπιδικασίαις, κατὰ στοῖχον ἤγοντο οἱ ἀπὸ τοῦ γένους πρῶτοι καὶ μετ᾿ αὐτοὺς δεύτεροι καὶ τρίτοι μέχρι τῶν ὑστάτων· καὶ ὁπότε μηδεὶς λοιπὸς εἴη τῶν συγγενῶν, διέβαινε τὸ κακὸν καὶ ἐπὶ τοὺς γειτνιῶντας, ἔστι δ᾿ ὅτε καὶ ἐπὶ κώμας καὶ πόλεις, αἳ ταχέως ἔρημοι καὶ κεναὶ τῶν οἰκητόρων ἐγένοντο μετανισταμένων καὶ σκεδαννυμένων ἔνθα λήσεσθαι προσεδόκων.
163 ἀλλ᾿ οὐδὲν ἴσως θαυμαστόν, εἰ φορολογίας ἕνεκα βάρβαροι τὰς φύσεις, ἡμέρου παιδείας ἄγευστοι, δεσποτικοῖς πειθαρχοῦντες ἐπιτάγμασι τοὺς ἐτησίους ἀναπράττουσι δασμούς, οὐ μόνον ἐκ τῶν οὐσιῶν ἀλλὰ καὶ ἐκ τῶν σωμάτων, ἄχρι καὶ ψυχῆς τοὺς κινδύνους ἐπιφέροντες ὑπὲρ ἑτέρων

wringing their bodies with racks and instruments of torture he finally dispatched them by newly-
invented methods of execution. He filled a large 160
basket with sand and having hung this enormous weight by ropes round their necks set them in the middle of the market-place in the open air, in order that while they themselves sank under the cruel stress of the accumulated punishments, the wind, the sun, the shame of being seen by the passers-by and the weights suspended on them, the spectators of their
punishments might suffer by anticipation. Some of 161
these, whose souls saw facts more vividly than did their eyes, feeling themselves maltreated in the bodies of others, hastened to take leave of their lives with the aid of sword or poison or halter, thinking that in their evil plight it was a great piece of
luck to die without suffering torture. The others 162
who had not seized the opportunity to dispatch themselves were brought out in a row, as is done in the awarding of inheritances, first those who stood in the first degrees of kinship, after them the second, then the third and so on till the last. And when there were no kinsmen left, the maltreatment was passed on to their neighbours and sometimes even to villages and cities which quickly became desolate and stripped of their inhabitants who left their homes and dispersed to places where they expected to remain unobserved.

Yet perhaps it is not to be wondered at 163
if uncivilized persons who have never had a taste of humane culture, when they have to collect the revenue in obedience to imperious orders levy the annual tributes not only on property but on bodies, and even on the life when they bring their terrors to bear upon
these substitutes for the proper debtors. Indeed in 164

164 ἑτέροις. ἤδη δὲ καὶ οἱ τῶν δικαίων ὅροι καὶ κανόνες, αὐτοὶ οἱ νομοθέται, πρὸς δόξαν μᾶλλον ἢ πρὸς ἀλήθειαν ἀπιδόντες, τῶν ἀδικωτάτων ὑπέμειναν γενέσθαι, κελεύσαντες τοῖς μὲν προδόταις τοὺς παῖδας συναναιρεῖσθαι, τοῖς δὲ τυράν-
165 νοις τὰς ἐγγυτάτω πέντε οἰκίας. διὰ τί; φαίην ἄν· εἰ μὲν γὰρ συνεξήμαρτον, καὶ συγκολαζέσθωσαν, εἰ δὲ μήτε κατεκοινώνησαν μήτε ζηλωταὶ τῶν ὁμοίων ἐγένοντο μήτε ταῖς τῶν οἰκείων εὐτυχίαις ἐπαρθέντες ἐνηδυπάθησαν, τίνος χάριν ἀναιρεθήσονται; ἢ δι' ἓν τοῦτο μόνον, ὅτι συγγενεῖς εἰσι;
[327] γένους γὰρ ἢ | παρανομημάτων αἱ τιμωρίαι;
166 χρηστῶν ἴσως ὑμεῖς, ὦ σεμνοὶ νομοθέται, τῶν οἰκείων ἐλάχετε· μοχθηροὶ δ' εἴπερ ἐγένοντο, δοκεῖτέ μοι μηδ' ἂν εἰς νοῦν ποτε βαλέσθαι τὰς τοιαύτας προστάξεις, ἀλλὰ καὶ γράφοντας ἑτέρους δυσχερᾶναι, διὰ τὴν τοῦ μηδὲν ἀνήκεστον παθεῖν προφυλακὴν * * *[1] τὸν ἐν ἀσφαλεῖ βίῳ διάγοντα μετὰ τῶν κινδυνευόντων σκοπεῖν καὶ ἐν ταῖς ἴσαις κακοπραγίαις ἐξετάζεσθαι· τὸ μὲν γὰρ ἔχει δέος, ὃ φυλαττόμενός τις οὐδ' ἂν ἕτερον περιΐδοι, τὸ δ'

[1] The text here is very difficult I have not altered the form printed by Cohn, who, as also Mangey, supposed a lacuna after προφυλακὴν, but I doubt whether the error lies here. Something like τὸν διάγοντα ἐν ἀσφαλεῖ βίῳ is required as subject to παθεῖν, for the legislator is not supposed to be guarding against his own ruin, but that of his relations. If σκοπεῖν is omitted, or some other infinitive = ἁλῶναι dependent on κινδυνευόντων substituted, and μὴ inserted before ἐξετάζεσθαι, the sentence, though very awkward, will be translatable. In that case ἐξετάζεσθαι is co-ordinate with παθεῖν and the sense as given in the translation. Heinemann, accepting the lacuna, suggested filling it by δεινὸν γάρ, *i.e.* "it would be terrible to see the safe man in such a plight," but this, I think, would require ἐξεταζόμενον.

the past the legislators themselves, who are the landmarks and standards of justice, have not shrunk from acting as such[a] to the greatest injustice. With an eye to men's opinions rather then to truth they have ordained that the fate of traitors and tyrants should be shared by the children in the first case and by the next five families in the second.[b]
Why, one might ask? If they were companions in 165
error let them also be companions in punishment, but if they had no association with the others, never followed the same objects, never let elation at the success of their kinsmen tempt them to a life of ease and pleasure, why should they be put to death? Is their relationship the one sole reason? Then is it birth or lawless actions which
deserve punishment? Probably you, most reverend 166
lawgivers, had worthy people for relations. If they had been bad, I do not think the idea of such enactments would have entered your minds. Indeed you would have been indignant if others had proposed them, for you would have taken precautions that the man who lives in safety should not suffer ruin with those who run into danger, nor be set on a level with them in misfortune.[c] Of the two situations[d] one involves a danger which you would guard against and not allow another to incur: the other has nothing to

[a] τῶν ἀδικωτάτων depends on ὅροι καὶ κανόνες understood.

[b] Heinemann impossibly translates "die fünf nächsten Verwandten ihres Hauses." For the law see App. pp. 639-640.

[c] The translation is based, as stated in note 1, on the conjecture that σκοπεῖν is to be omitted. Though the idea of the passage is fantastic, the general meaning seems clear, however uncertain the details of the text.

[d] I understand τὸ μέν "as having bad," τὸ δέ "as having good" relations.

ἐστὶν ἄφοβον, ὑφ' οὗ πολλάκις ἀνεπείσθησάν τινες ἀλογεῖν ἀνθρώπων ἀνυπαιτίων ἀσφαλείας.

167 Ταῦτ' οὖν ἐκλογισάμενος ὁ ἡμέτερος νομοθέτης καὶ τὰ παρὰ τοῖς ἄλλοις ἁμαρτήματα συνιδὼν ὡς φθοροποιὰ τῆς ἀρίστης πολιτείας ἀπεστράφη καὶ διεμίσησε [καὶ] τοὺς χρωμένους εἴτε ῥᾳθυμίαις εἴτε ἀπανθρωπίαις καὶ κακίαις καὶ οὐδέποτέ τινα τῶν συμβεβιωκότων ἐξέδωκεν ἐπὶ τιμωρίᾳ προσθήκην ποιησάμενος αὐτὸν ἀδικημάτων ἑτέρων.

168 διόπερ ἄντικρυς ἀπεῖπεν υἱοὺς ἀντὶ γονέων ἢ γονεῖς ἀντὶ υἱῶν ἀναιρεῖσθαι, δικαιώσας ὧν τὰ ἁμαρτήματα τούτων εἶναι καὶ τὰς τιμωρίας, εἴτε ζημίας χρημάτων εἴτε καὶ πληγὰς καὶ βιαιοτέρας ὕβρεις εἴτε τραύματα καὶ πηρώσεις καὶ ἀτιμίας καὶ φυγὰς καὶ ὅσα ἄλλα τῶν ἐπὶ δίκαις· ἑνὸς γὰρ τοῦ μὴ ἕτερον ἀνθ' ἑτέρου κτείνειν μνησθεὶς καὶ τὰ ἡσυχασθέντα προσπεριέλαβεν.

169 XXXI. [1]Ἀγοραὶ καὶ βουλευτήρια καὶ δικαστήρια καὶ θίασοι καὶ σύλλογοι πολυανθρώπων ὁμίλων καὶ ὁ ἐν ὑπαίθρῳ βίος διὰ λόγων καὶ πράξεων κατὰ πολέμους καὶ κατ' εἰρήνην ἀνδράσιν ἐφαρμόζουσι, θηλείαις δὲ οἰκουρία καὶ ἡ ἔνδον μονή, παρθένοις μὲν εἴσω κλισιάδων τὴν μέσαυλον ὅρον πεποιημέναις, τελείαις δὲ ἤδη γυναιξὶ τὴν αὔλειον.

[1] MS. heading Περὶ τοῦ μὴ ἀναισχυντεῖν γυναῖκας.

---

[a] At this point Philo, having hitherto discussed actions which lead, or are intended to lead, to the loss of human life, turns to the question of assaults which do not necessarily have, nor are intended to have, that result. That these should be included under his seventh commandment is perfectly rational, and indeed he has stated this in *De Dec.* 170. They may

fear and a sense of security often persuades people to neglect insuring the safety of the innocent.

So then our legislator took these things into con- 167
sideration and observing the errors current among other nations regarded them with aversion as ruinous to the ideal commonwealth; persons whose conduct shewed any kind of sloth or inhumanity or vice he detested and would not ever surrender anyone whose life had been passed in their company to be punished with them and thus made an appendix to the crimes of others. He therefore expressly forbade that sons 168
should be slain instead of fathers or fathers instead of sons. Thereby also he gave it as his judgement that persons who had sinned should be the persons who were punished, whether the punishment consisted of monetary fines or stripes and injurious treatment of a still more violent kind, or wounds and maiming and disfranchisement and exile or any other kind of sentence. For in the single statement that one man should not be killed instead of another he included also the cases which he left unmentioned.

XXXI. [a] Market-places and council-halls and law- 169
courts and gatherings and meetings where a large number of people are assembled, and open-air life with full scope for discussion and action—all these are suitable to men both in war and peace. The women are best suited to the indoor life which never strays from the house, within which the middle door is taken by the maidens as their boundary, and the outer door by those who have reached full womanhood. Organ- 170

involve other matters. Thus the law discussed in the next twelve sections, though it gives rise to a disquisition on female modesty, is primarily directed against an assault, just as the "eye for eye" of § 184 is preceded by the discussion of equal punishment in §§ 181 f.

170 διττὸν γὰρ πόλεων εἶδος, μειζόνων καὶ βραχυτέρων·
αἱ μὲν οὖν μείζους ἄστη καλοῦνται, οἰκίαι δ' αἱ
βραχύτεραι. τὴν δ' ἑκατέρων προστασίαν διειλή-
χασιν ἄνδρες μὲν τῶν μειζόνων, ἧς ὄνομα πολιτεία,
γυναῖκες δὲ τῶν βραχυτέρων, ἧς ὄνομα οἰκονομία.
171 μηδὲν οὖν ἔξω τῶν κατὰ τὴν οἰκονομίαν πολυ-
πραγμονείτω γυνὴ ζητοῦσα μοναυλίαν μηδ' οἷα
νομὰς κατὰ τὰς ὁδοὺς ἐν ὄψεσιν ἀνδρῶν ἑτέρων
ἐξεταζέσθω, πλὴν εἰς ἱερὸν ὁπότε δέοι βαδίζειν,
φροντίδα ποιουμένη καὶ τότε μὴ πληθυούσης
ἀγορᾶς, ἀλλ' ἐπανεληλυθότων οἴκαδε τῶν πλείστων,
ἐλευθέρας τρόπον καὶ τῷ ὄντι ἀστῆς ἐν ἠρεμίᾳ
[328] θυσίας | ἐπιτελοῦσα καὶ εὐχὰς εἰς ἀποτροπὴν
172 κακῶν καὶ μετουσίαν ἀγαθῶν. τὸ δὲ λοιδορου-
μένων ἢ συμπλεκομένων ἀνδρῶν ἐπεκθεῖν τολμᾶν
κατὰ πρόφασιν συμμαχίας ἢ βοηθείας γυναῖκας
ἐπίληπτον καὶ οὐ μετρίως ἀναίσχυντον, ἃς οὐδ'
ἐν πολέμοις καὶ στρατείαις καὶ τοῖς ὑπὲρ πάσης
τῆς πατρίδος κινδύνοις ἐδικαίωσεν ὁ νόμος ἐξετάζεσθαι, τὸ πρέπον ἰδών, ὅπερ ἀκίνητον ἀεὶ καὶ
πανταχοῦ φυλάττειν διενοήθη, νομίσας αὐτὸ τοῦτ'
εἶναι καθ' αὑτὸ νίκης καὶ ἐλευθερίας καὶ πάσης
173 ἄμεινον εὐτυχίας. ἐὰν μέντοι καὶ πυθομένη τις
ὑβρίζεσθαι τὸν ἄνδρα, πόθῳ τῷ πρὸς ἐκεῖνον
ἡττηθεῖσα φιλανδρίας, ὑπὸ τοῦ παραστάντος πάθους
ἐξορμῆσαι βιασθῇ, μὴ πλέον τῆς φύσεως ἀρρε-

[a] There was of course no Jewish temple in Alexandria. Philo may mean the synagogue, but surely no sacrifice could be offered there. It seems to me more probable that he is giving advice to the female population in general and does not feel any necessity to speak disrespectfully of their religious observances. But see App. p. 640.

[b] Lit. " a citizeness," carrying with it something of the idea

ized communities are of two sorts, the greater which we call cities and the smaller which we call households. Both of these have their governors; the government of the greater is assigned to men under the name of statesmanship, that of the lesser, known as household management, to women. A woman, 171
then, should not be a busybody, meddling with matters outside her household concerns, but should seek a life of seclusion. She should not shew herself off like a vagrant in the streets before the eyes of other men, except when she has to go to the temple,[a] and even then she should take pains to go, not when the market is full, but when most people have gone home, and so like a free-born lady[b] worthy of the name, with everything quiet around her, make her oblations and offer her prayers to avert the evil and gain the good.
The audacity of women who when men are exchang- 172
ing angry words or blows hasten to join in, under the pretext of assisting their husbands in the fray, is reprehensible and shameless in a high degree. And so in wars and campaigns and emergencies which threaten the whole country they are not allowed to take their place according to the judgement of the law, having in view the fitness of things, which it was resolved to keep unshaken always and everywhere and considered to be in itself more valuable than victory or liberty or success of any kind. If indeed 173
a woman learning that her husband is being outraged is overcome by the wifely feeling inspired by her love for him and forced by the stress of the emotion to hasten to his assistance, she must not unsex herself by a boldness beyond what nature

of ἀστεῖος. *Cf.* ἀσταί τε καὶ ἀστεῖαι, *De Mig.* 99, also *De Cong.* 63.

νούσθω θρασυνομένη, μενέτω δὲ καὶ ἐν οἷς βοηθεῖ γυνή· πάνδεινον γάρ, εἰ βουλομένη τις ὑπεξελέσθαι τὸν ἄνδρα ὕβρεως ὑβρισθήσεται πρὸς ἑαυτῆς κατάπλεων ἀποφαινούσης τὸν ἴδιον βίον αἰσχύνης καὶ μεγάλων ὀνειδῶν τῶν ἐπ' ἀνιάτῳ θρασύτητι.
174 λοιδορήσεται γὰρ γυνὴ κατ' ἀγορὰν ῥῆμά τέ τι τῶν ἀπηγορευμένων φθέγξεται, ἑτέρου δὲ κακηγοροῦντος οὐκ ἀποδραμεῖται τὰ ὦτα ἐπιφράξασα; νυνὶ δὲ προβαίνουσί τινες, ὡς μὴ μόνον ὑπὸ γλωσσαλγίας ἐν ἀνδρῶν ὄχλῳ γυναῖκες[1] κακηγορεῖν καὶ προπηλακίζειν,[2] ἀλλὰ καὶ τὰς χεῖρας ἐπιφέρειν τὰς ὑφάσμασι καὶ ταλασίαις ἀλλ' οὐ πληγαῖς καὶ ὕβρεσι καθάπερ παγκρατιαστῶν καὶ πυκτῶν ἐνασκουμένας.
175 καὶ τὰ μὲν ἄλλα [οἰστὰ καὶ] φέρειν ἄν τις δύναιτο· χαλεπὸν δ' ἐκεῖνο, εἴ τις γυνὴ τοσοῦτον καταθρασύνοιτο, ὡς διαδράξασθαι τῶν τοῦ διαφερομένου γεννητικῶν· μὴ γάρ, παρόσον ἀνδρὶ βοηθοῦσα δοκεῖ τοῦτο πράττειν, ἀφείσθω, τῆς δ' ἄγαν θρασύτητος ἐπεχέσθω τίνουσα δίκην, ὑφ' ἧς αὐτὴ μὲν τὰ ὅμοια ἐξαμαρτάνειν ἐθέλουσα αὖθις οὐκ ἂν δύναιτο, τῶν δ' ἄλλων ὅσαι προπετέστεραι φόβῳ μετριάσουσιν· ἔστω δ' ἡ δίκη χειρὸς ἀποκοπὴ τῆς ἁψαμένης ὧν οὐ θέμις

[1] Cohn brackets γυναῖκες, or would transfer it to after προβαίνουσι. It seems to me in its antithetical position very idiomatic. Mangey's correction to γυναῖκας is, I think, inferior Greek.

[2] In the MSS. καὶ προπηλακίζειν is placed after ἐπιφέρειν.

[a] Deut. xxv. 11, 12. Philo appears at first sight to giv

permits but limit herself to the ways in which a woman can help. For it would be an awful catastrophe if any woman in her wish to rescue her husband from outrage should outrage herself by befouling her own life with the disgrace and heavy reproaches which boldness carried to an extreme entails. What, is a 174
woman to wrangle in the market-place and utter some or other of the words which decency forbids? Should she not when she hears bad language stop her ears and run away? As it is, some of them go to such a length that, not only do we hear amid a crowd of men a woman's bitter tongue venting abuse and contumelious words, but see her hands also used to assault—hands which were trained to weave and spin and not to inflict blows and injuries like pancratiasts and boxers. And while all else might be 175
tolerable, it is a shocking thing, if a woman is so lost to a sense of modesty, as to catch hold of the genital parts of her opponent.[a] The fact that she does so with the evident intention of helping her husband must not absolve her.[b] To restrain her over-boldness she must pay a penalty which will incapacitate herself, if she wishes to repeat the offence, and frighten the more reckless members of her sex into proper behaviour. And the penalty shall be this—that the hand shall be cut off which has touched what decency forbids it to touch. The managers of gymnastic 176

approval to this law, and if he realizes that it is open to the same objections as he made to a similar enactment in ii. 244, he does not say so. Still one may perhaps see some hesitation. The phrase ἔστω δ' ἡ δίκη may not mean more than that the law says so. In § 178 of the literal explanation he merely says that is what is commonly given, not that it is true, and his preference for the allegorical is not disguised.

[b] So Deuteronomy, "Thine eye shall have no pity."

176 ἄξιον ἐπαινεῖν καὶ τοὺς τῶν γυμνικῶν ἀγώνων ἀθλοθέτας, οἳ τῆς θέας ἀνεῖρξαν γυναῖκας, ἵνα μὴ γυμνουμένοις ἀνδράσι παρατυγχάνουσαι τὸ δόκιμον αἰδοῦς νόμισμα παρακόπτωσιν ἀλογοῦσαι φύσεως θεσμῶν, οὓς ὥρισεν ἑκατέρῳ τμήματι τοῦ γένους ἡμῶν. οὐδὲ γὰρ ἄνδρας, ἀποτιθεμένων ἐσθῆτας γυναικῶν, ἐμπρεπὲς παρατυγχάνειν, ἀλλ' ἑκατέρους τὰς τῶν ἑτέρων ὄψεις ἐκτρέπεσθαι γυμνουμένων
177 τοῖς τῆς φύσεως βουλήμασιν ἑπομένους. εἶθ' ὧν ἡ ὄψις ἐπίληπτος, οὐ πολὺ μᾶλλον αἱ χεῖρες ὑπαίτιοι; ὀφθαλμοὶ μὲν γὰρ καὶ ἃ μὴ βουλόμεθα πολλάκις ὁρᾶν ἀπελευθεριάζοντες ἀποβιάζονται, χεῖρες δ' ἐν τῇ τῶν ὑπηκόων τάξει τεταγμέναι |
[329] μερῶν πειθαρχοῦσαι τοῖς ἡμετέροις ἐπιτάγμασιν ὑπηρετοῦσιν.

178 XXXII. Ἥδε μὲν αἰτία ἣ[1] παρὰ πολλοῖς εἴωθε λέγεσθαι· ἑτέραν δὲ ἤκουσα θεσπεσίων ἀνδρῶν τὰ πλεῖστα τῶν ἐν τοῖς νόμοις ὑπολαμβανόντων εἶναι σύμβολα φανερὰ ἀφανῶν καὶ ῥητὰ ἀρρήτων. ἦν δὲ τοιάδε· ψυχῆς, ὥσπερ ἐν ταῖς συγγενείαις, ἡ μέν ἐστιν ἄρρην καὶ πρὸς ἀνδρῶν, ἡ δὲ θήλεια καὶ πρὸς γυναικῶν· ἄρρην μὲν ἡ μόνῳ θεῷ προσκληροῦσα ἑαυτὴν ὡς πατρὶ καὶ ποιητῇ τῶν ὅλων καὶ πάντων αἰτίῳ, θήλεια δὲ ἡ ἐκκρεμαμένη τῶν ἐν γενέσει καὶ φθορᾷ καὶ ἀποτείνουσα καθάπερ χεῖρα τὴν δύναμιν αὐτῆς, ἵνα τυφλῶς τῶν ἐπιτυχόντων ἐφάπτηται, γένεσιν δεξιουμένη τὴν τροπαῖς ἀμυθήτοις χρωμένην καὶ μεταβολαῖς, δέον τὴν ἀμετάβλητον καὶ μακαρίαν καὶ τρισευδαίμονα θείαν

[1] Perhaps omit ἣ with one ms.

[a] See App. p. 640.

[b] The text is allegorized in substantially the same way in

competitions also deserve praise for debarring women from the spectacle,[a] in order that they may not be present, when men are stripping themselves naked, nor debase the sterling coin of modesty, by disregarding the statutes of nature which she has laid down for each section of our race. For men too cannot with propriety be present when women are taking off their clothes. Each sex should turn away from seeing the nakedness of the other and so comply
with what nature has willed. Surely, then, if it is 177
reprehensible for them to use their sight, their hands are far more guilty. For the eyes often take liberties and compel us to see what we do not wish to see, but the hands are ranked among the parts which we keep in subjection, and render obedient service to our orders.

XXXII. This is the explanation commonly and 178
widely stated, but I have heard another from highly gifted men who think that most of the contents of the law-book are outward symbols of hidden truths, expressing in words what has been left unsaid. This explanation was as follows.[b] There is in the soul a male and female element just as there is in families, the male corresponding to the men, the female to the women. The male soul assigns itself to God alone as the Father and Maker of the Universe and the Cause of all things. The female clings to all that is born and perishes ; it stretches out its faculties like a hand to catch blindly at what comes in its way, and gives the clasp of friendship to the world of created things with all its numberless changes and transmutations, instead of to the divine order, the immutable, the

De Som. ii. 68, 69, though the point of the "female soul" is not there brought out.

179 φύσιν. εἰκότως οὖν τὴν ἐφαψαμένην χεῖρα τῶν διδύμων ἀποκόπτειν διείρηται συμβολικῶς, οὐχ ὅπως ἀκρωτηριάζηται τὸ σῶμα στερόμενον ἀναγκαιοτάτου μέρους, ἀλλ' ὑπὲρ τοῦ τῆς ψυχῆς πάντας τοὺς ἀθέους ἐκτέμνειν λογισμοὺς ἐπιβάθρᾳ χρωμένους ἅπασιν ὧν γένεσίς ἐστι· δίδυμοι γὰρ σύμ-
180 βολον σπορᾶς καὶ γενέσεως. ἑπόμενος δ' ἀκολουθίᾳ φύσεως κἀκεῖνο λέξω, ὅτι μονὰς μέν ἐστιν εἰκὼν αἰτίου πρώτου, δυὰς δὲ παθητῆς καὶ διαιρετῆς ὕλης· ὃς ἂν οὖν δυάδα πρὸ μονάδος τιμήσῃ καὶ δεξιώσηται, μὴ ἀγνοείτω ⟨τὴν⟩ ὕλην ἀποδεχόμενος μᾶλλον ἢ θεόν. ἧς χάριν αἰτίας ἐδικαίωσεν ὁ νόμος ταύτην τὴν ἐπιβολὴν τῆς ψυχῆς ἀποκόπτειν οἷα χεῖρα· μεῖζον γὰρ οὐκ ἔστιν ἀσέβημα ἢ τῷ παθητῷ τὴν τοῦ δρῶντος ἀνατιθέναι δύναμιν.

181 XXXIII. Μέμψαιτ' ἄν τις δεόντως τοὺς ἀνόμοια τοῖς ἀδικήμασι τάττοντας ἐπιτίμια κατὰ τῶν εἰργασμένων, ζημίας χρημάτων ἐπ' αἰκίαις ἢ ἐπὶ τραύμασι καὶ πηρώσεσιν ἀτιμίας ἢ ἐπ' ἀνδροφονίαις ἑκουσίοις ἐλάσεις ὑπερορίους καὶ τὰς εἰς ἀεὶ φυγὰς ἢ δεσμοὺς ἐπὶ κλοπαῖς· τὸ γὰρ ἀνώμαλον καὶ ἄνισον ἐχθρὸν πολιτείας ζηλούσης τὴν ἀλήθειαν
182 ἰσότητος δὲ ὑφηγητὴς ὁ ἡμέτερος νόμος τὰ ὅμοια κελεύων τοὺς ἁμαρτάνοντας ὑπομένειν οἷς ἔδρασαν, ἐκ τῶν οὐσιῶν, ἐὰν περὶ τὰς οὐσίας ἀδικοπραγῶσι τῶν πλησίον, ἐκ τῶν σωμάτων, ἐὰν εἰς τὰ σώματα

---

[a] As noted on *De Som.* ii. δίδυμοι is the LXX translation of the word translated "secrets" in E.V.

[b] Heinemann "in natürlichem Zusammenhang." I hardly think φύσεως can bear this meaning. I understand it of the higher truths of nature, which the allegorist (ὁ φυσικός) contemplates. See note on *De Abr.* 99, and the references there given.

blessed, the thrice happy. Naturally therefore we 179
are commanded in a symbol to cut off the hand which has taken hold of the "pair,"[a] not meaning that the body should be mutilated by the loss of a most essential member, but to bid us exscind from the soul the godless thoughts which take for their basis all that comes into being through birth ; for the "pair" are a symbol of seed-sowing and birth. I will add 180
another thought, following where the study of nature leads me.[b] The monad is the image of the first cause, the dyad of matter passive and divisible. Therefore one who honours the dyad before the monad should not fail to know that he holds matter in higher esteem than God. It is for this reason that the law judged it right to cut off this tendency of the soul as if it were a hand, for there is no greater impiety than to ascribe to the passive element the power of the active principle.

XXXIII. The legislators deserve censure who 181
prescribe for malefactors punishments which do not resemble the crime, such as monetary fines for assaults, disfranchisement for wounding or maiming another, expulsion from the country and perpetual banishment for wilful murder or imprisonment for theft.[c] For inequality and unevenness is repugnant to the commonwealth which pursues truth. Our 182
law exhorts us to equality[d] when it ordains that the penalties inflicted on offenders should correspond to their actions, that their property should suffer if the wrongdoing affected their neighbour's property, and their bodies if the offence was a bodily injury,

[c] See App. p. 640.

[d] For the *ius talionis* see Ex. xxi. 24, Lev. xxiv. 19-21, Deut. xix. 21, and *cf.* Matthew v. 38.

ἐξαμαρτάνωσι κατὰ μέρη καὶ μέλη καὶ τὰς
[330] αἰσθήσεις· κἂν ἄχρι | μέντοι τῆς ψυχῆς ἐπιβου-
λεύσωσιν, εἰς ψυχὴν τιμωρεῖσθαι κελεύει· ὑπομένειν γὰρ ἀνθ᾿ ἑτέρων ἕτερα μηδεμίαν ἔχοντα
κοινωνίαν ἀλλὰ τοῖς εἴδεσιν ἀπηρτημένα κατα-
183 λυόντων νόμους ἐστίν, οὐ βεβαιούντων. ταυτὶ
δέ φαμεν τῶν ἄλλων [οὐχ] ὁμοίως ἐχόντων· οὐ
γὰρ ταὐτὸν ἀλλοτρίῳ καὶ πατρὶ πληγὰς ἐμφορῆσαι
οὐδὲ ἄρχοντα ἢ ἰδιώτην κακῶς εἰπεῖν οὐδὲ ἐργά-
σασθαί τι τῶν μὴ ἐφειμένων ἐν βεβήλοις ἢ ἱεροῖς
χωρίοις οὐδ᾿ ἐν ἑορταῖς καὶ πανηγύρεσι καὶ δημο-
τελέσι θυσίαις καὶ πάλιν ἐν ἡμέραις αἷς μηδὲν
πρόσεστι τῶν εἰς ἐκεχειρίαν ἢ καὶ συνόλως ἀπο-
φράσι, καὶ ὅσα ἄλλα τοιουτότροπα διερευνητέον
εἰς συναύξησιν ἢ μείωσιν κολάσεως.

184 Πάλιν ἐάν τις, φησίν, ὀφθαλμὸν οἰκέτου ἢ
θεραπαίνης ἐκκόψῃ, ἐλευθέρους ἀφιέτω. διὰ τί;
ὥσπερ τὴν τοῦ σώματος ἡγεμονίαν ἡ φύσις ἀνῆψε
κεφαλῇ χαρισαμένη καὶ τόπον οἰκειότατον ὡς
βασιλεῖ τὴν ἄκραν—ἄνω γὰρ αὐτὴν ἐπ᾿ ἀρχὴν
παραπέμψασα ἱδρύσατο καθάπερ ἀνδριάντι βάσιν
ὑποθεῖσα τὴν ἀπ᾿ αὐχένος ἄχρι ποδῶν ἅπασαν
ἁρμονίαν—, οὕτως καὶ τῶν αἰσθήσεων τὸ κράτος
ἀνέδωκεν ὀφθαλμοῖς· ὑπεράνω γοῦν καὶ τούτοις
ὡς ἄρχουσιν ἀπένειμεν οἴκησιν, βουληθεῖσα μὴ

---

[a] The translation assumes that the subject of ὑπομένειν is to be understood out of καταλυόντων κτλ. But perhaps in view of the ὑπομένειν above it may be better, though looser, to take it " that a man should suffer."

the penalty being determined according to the limb, part or sense affected, while if his malice extended to taking another's life his own life should be the forfeit. For to tolerate a system [a] in which the crime and the punishment do not correspond, have no common ground and belong to different categories, is to subvert rather than uphold legality. In saying this I 183
assume that the other conditions are the same, for to strike a stranger is not the same as to strike a father nor the abuse of a ruler the same as abuse of an ordinary citizen. Unlawful actions differ according as they are committed in a profane or sacred place, or at festivals and solemn assemblies and public sacrifices as contrasted with days which have no holiday associations or are even quite inauspicious.[b] And all other similar facts must be carefully considered with a view to making the punishment greater or less.

Again he says that if anyone knocks out the eye of 184
a manservant or maidservant he must set him or her at liberty.[c] Why is this? Just as nature conferred the sovereignty of the body on the head when she granted it also possession of the citadel as the most suitable position for its kingly rank, conducted it thither to take command and established it on high with the whole framework from neck to foot set below it, like the pedestal under the statue, so too she has given the lordship of the senses to the eyes. Thus to them too as rulers she has assigned a dwelling right above the others in her wish to give them

[b] *i.e.* (apparently) for religious observances. This seems somewhat different from the usual meaning of the phrase which signifies days on which secular business was forbidden = "dies nefasti." See App. p. 641.

[c] Ex. xxi. 26.

μόνον τοῖς ἄλλοις ἀλλὰ καὶ χωρίῳ περισημοτάτῳ
καὶ περιφανεστάτῳ τούτους γεραῖραι.
185 XXXIV. τὰς μὲν οὖν χρείας καὶ ὠφελείας, ἃς
παρέχουσι τῷ γένει ἡμῶν ὀφθαλμοί, μακρὸν ἂν
εἴη καταριθμεῖσθαι· μίαν δὲ τὴν ἀρίστην λεκτέον.
φιλοσοφίαν ὤμβρησε μὲν ὁ οὐρανός, ἐχώρησε δὲ ὁ
ἀνθρώπινος νοῦς, ἐξενάγησε δὲ ὄψις· πρώτη γὰρ
αὕτη κατεῖδε τὰς λεωφόρους ἐπ' αἰθέρος[1] ὁδούς.
186 ἀγαθῶν δέ, ὅσα πρὸς ἀλήθειαν ἀγαθά, πηγὴ
φιλοσοφία· ἧς ὁ μὲν ἀρυτόμενος εἰς κτῆσιν καὶ
χρῆσιν ἀρετῆς ἐπαινετός, ὁ δ' ἕνεκα πανουργίας
καὶ τοῦ κατασοφίσασθαί[2] τινα ψεκτός· ἔοικε γὰρ
ὁ μὲν ἀνδρὶ συμποτικῷ καὶ ἑαυτὸν καὶ τοὺς
συνεστιωμένους πάντας εὐφραίνοντι, ὁ δὲ τῷ τὸν
ἄκρατον εἰς παροινίαν καὶ ὕβριν ἑαυτοῦ τε καὶ τῶν
187 πλησίον ἐμφορουμένῳ. ὅτῳ δ' οὖν[3] τρόπῳ φιλοσοφίαν ἐξενάγησεν ὄψις, ἤδη λεκτέον. ἀναβλέψασα
εἰς αἰθέρα κατεῖδεν ἥλιον καὶ σελήνην καὶ πλάνητας
καὶ ἀπλανεῖς ἀστέρας, τὴν ἱεροπρεπεστάτην οὐρανοῦ
στρατιάν, κόσμον ἐν κόσμῳ, εἶτ' ἀνατολὰς καὶ
δύσεις καὶ χορείας ἐμμελεῖς καὶ τεταγμέναις
188 χρόνων περιόδοις συνόδους, ἐκλείψεις, ἐπιλάμψεις,
εἶτ' αὐξήσεις καὶ μειώσεις σελήνης, ἡλίου κινήσεις
τὰς κατὰ πλάτος, ἀπὸ μὲν τῶν νοτίων ἐπὶ τὰ
βόρεια προσιόντος, ἀπὸ δὲ τῶν βορείων ἐξανα-
[331] χωροῦντος | πρὸς τὰ νότια, εἰς καιρῶν τῶν ἐτησίων

[1] MSS. ἀπ' αἰθέρος. [2] MSS. καταψηφίσασθαι.
[3] MSS. γοῦν.

[a] See App. p. 641.

amongst other privileges the most conspicuous and
distinguished situation.[a] XXXIV. Now as 185
for the services and benefits which the eyes render
to the human race, it would take a long time to
enumerate them, but one, the best, must be mentioned. Philosophy was showered down by heaven
and received by the human mind, but the guide
which brought the two together was sight, for sight
was the first to discern the high roads which lead
to the upper air.[b] Now philosophy is the fountain 186
of good things, all that are truly good, and he who
draws from that spring deserves praise, if he does so
for the acquisition and practice of virtue, but blame,
if it is for knavish ends and to outwit another with
sophistry. For in the first case he resembles the
convivial man who makes himself and all his fellow-guests merry, in the second the drinker who swills
himself with strong wine, only to play the sot and
insult himself and his neighbours. Now let us 187
describe the way in which sight acted as guide to
philosophy; sight looked up to the ethereal region
and beheld the sun and moon and the fixed and
wandering stars, the host of heaven in all its sacred
majesty, a world within a world; then their risings
and settings, their ordered rhythmic marchings, their
conjunctions as the appointed times recur, their
eclipses, their reappearances; then the waxing and 188
waning of the moon, the courses of the sun from side
to side[c] as it passes from the south to the north and
returns from the north to the south, thus producing

[b] For this often repeated thought, originally, as has been noted before, derived from *Timaeus* 47 A, *cf.* i. 339 above, *De Abr.* 164 and *De Op.* 54 f. and notes.

[c] Lit. "along a broad space" (?), Heinemann "ausgedehnten," Mangey "transversos (motus)."

γένεσιν, οἷς[1] τὰ πάντα τελεσφορεῖται, καὶ πρὸς τούτοις μυρία ἄλλα θαυμάσια· καὶ περιαθρήσασα κατά τε γῆν καὶ κατὰ θάλατταν καὶ ἀέρα τάδε
189 πάντα τῷ νῷ μετὰ σπουδῆς ἐπεδείξατο. ὁ δ' ἅπερ οὐχ οἷός τ' ἦν δι' αὑτοῦ καταλαβεῖν διὰ τῆς ὁράσεως ἰδὼν οὐκ ἐπὶ τῶν ὁραθέντων αὐτὸ μόνον ἔστη, ἀλλ' ἅτε φιλομαθὴς καὶ φιλόκαλος, ἀγάμενος τὴν θέαν, λογισμὸν εἰκότα ἐλάμβανεν, ὅτι ταῦτα οὐκ ἀπαυτοματισθέντα συνέστη φοραῖς ἀλόγοις, ἀλλὰ διανοίᾳ θεοῦ, ὃν πατέρα καὶ ποιητὴν ὀνομάζειν θέμις, καὶ ὅτι οὐκ ἔστιν ἄπειρα, πεπέρασται δὲ ἑνὸς κόσμου περιγραφῇ, πόλεως τρόπον τῇ τῶν ἀπλανῶν ἐξωτάτω σφαίρᾳ περιλαμβανόμενα, καὶ ὡς ὁ γεννήσας πατὴρ νόμῳ φύσεως ἐπιμελεῖται τοῦ γενομένου, προνοούμενος καὶ τοῦ ὅλου καὶ
190 τῶν μερῶν. εἶτα προσεπεσκέψατο, τίς οὐσία τοῦ ὁρατοῦ καὶ εἰ πάντων ἡ αὐτὴ τῶν κατὰ τὸν κόσμον ἢ ἑτέρων ἑτέρα καὶ ἐκ τίνων ἕκαστα ἐτελέσθη, καὶ τὰς αἰτίας δι' ἃς ἐγένετο καὶ δυνάμεις αἷς συν-
191 έχεται καὶ πότερον αὗται σώματα ἢ ἀσώματοι. ἡ γὰρ περὶ τούτων καὶ τῶν παραπλησίων ἔρευνα τί ἂν ἄλλο ἢ φιλοσοφία προσαγορεύοιτο; τί δὲ τῷ σκοπουμένῳ ταῦτα θεῖτο ἄν τις οἰκειότερον ὄνομα ἢ φιλόσοφον; τὸ γὰρ περὶ θεοῦ σκοπεῖν καὶ κόσμου καὶ τῶν ἐν αὐτῷ κοινῶς ζῴων τε καὶ φυτῶν καὶ περὶ νοητῶν παραδειγμάτων καὶ πάλιν αἰσθητῶν ἀποτελεσμάτων καὶ τῆς καθ' ἕκαστον τῶν γεγονότων ἀρετῆς τε καὶ κακίας φιλομαθῆ

[1] MSS. ὡς.

the yearly seasons by which all things are brought to their consummation. Numberless other marvels did it behold, and after it had gazed around over earth and sea and the lower air, it made speed to
shew all these things to the mind. The mind, having 189
discerned through the faculty of sight what of itself it was not able to apprehend, did not simply stop short at what it saw, but, drawn by its love of knowledge and beauty and charmed by the marvellous spectacle, came to the reasonable conclusion that all these were not brought together automatically by unreasoning forces, but by the mind of God Who is rightly called their Father and Maker ; also that they are not unlimited but are bounded by the ambit of a single universe, walled in like a city by the outermost sphere of the fixed stars ; also that the Father Who begat them according to the law of nature takes thought for His offspring, His providence watching over both
the whole and the parts. Then it went on to inquire 190
what is the substance of the world which we see and whether its constituents are all the same in substance or do some differ from others ; what are the elements of which each particular part is composed, what are the causes which brought them into being, and what are the forces or properties which hold them together
and are these forces corporeal or incorporeal. We 191
may well ask what title we can give to research into these matters but philosophy and what more fitting name than philosopher to their investigator. For to make a study of God and the Universe embracing all that is therein, both animals and plants, and of the conceptual archetypes and also the works which they produce for sense to perceive, and of the good and evil qualities in every created thing—shews a dis-

καὶ φιλοθεάμονα καὶ τῷ ὄντι φιλόσοφον διάθεσιν
192 ἐμφαίνει. μέγιστον μὲν δὴ τοῦτο τῷ
βίῳ τῶν ἀνθρώπων ἀγαθὸν ὄψις παρέχεται· δοκεῖ
δέ μοι ταύτης ἠξιῶσθαι τῆς προνομίας, ἐπειδὴ
τῶν ἄλλων αἰσθήσεων συγγενεστέρα ψυχῇ καθ-
έστηκεν· ἅπασαι μὲν γὰρ τὴν πρὸς διάνοιαν
ἔχουσιν οἰκειότητα, αὕτη δὲ καθάπερ ἐν ταῖς
οἰκίαις τὴν ἐγγυτάτω γένους πρώτην καὶ ἀνωτάτω
193 τάξιν εἴληχε. τεκμηριώσαιτο δ' ἄν τις ἐκ πολλῶν·
τίς γὰρ οὐκ οἶδεν, ὅτι χαιρόντων μὲν ὀφθαλμοὶ
γανοῦνται καὶ μειδιῶσι, λυπουμένων δὲ συννοίας
γέμουσι καὶ κατηφείας; εἰ δὲ πλεονάζοι καὶ πιέζοι
καὶ ἀναθλίβοι τὸ ἄχθος, ἐκδακρύουσι καὶ κρα-
τούσης μὲν ὀργῆς οἰδοῦσι καὶ ὕφαιμον καὶ
πυρωπὸν ἐμβλέπουσιν, ἵλεων δὲ καὶ εὐμενές, εἰ
194 χαλάσαι ὁ θυμός. καὶ ἐν μὲν τῷ λογίζεσθαι
καὶ σκοπεῖν αἱ κόραι πεπήγασι τρόπον τινὰ συν-
εννοοῦσαι, τῶν δὲ εὐηθεστέρων ὑπ' ἠλιθιότητος
[332] πλάζεται καὶ ἡ ὅρασις οὐκ ἠρεμοῦσα· | καὶ συνόλως
τοῖς τῆς ψυχῆς πάθεσι συμπάσχουσιν ὀφθαλμοὶ
καὶ ταῖς ἀμυθήτοις τροπαῖς συμμεταβάλλειν πε-
φύκασι διὰ τὴν οἰκειότητα· δοκεῖ γάρ μοι μηδὲν
οὕτως ὁ θεὸς ἐμφανὲς ἀφανοῦς ἀπεργάσασθαι
μίμημα ὡς ὄψιν λογισμοῦ.
195 XXXV. Ἐάν τις οὖν εἰς τὴν ἀρίστην καὶ ἡγε-
μονικωτάτην τῶν αἰσθήσεων ὅρασιν ᾗ ἐπιβεβου-
λευκώς τῳ καὶ καταφανῇ μὲν ἐλευθέρου ὀφθαλμὸν
ἐκκόψας, τὰ αὐτὰ ἀντιπασχέτω, δούλου δὲ μή·
οὐχ ὅτι συγγνώμης ἐστὶν ἄξιος ἢ ἔλαττον ἀδικεῖ,

---

[a] *i.e.* "to the mind," regarded as the head of the family.

[b] *Cf. De Abr.* 151 f.

[c] Philo reads Ex. xxi. 26 as limiting the previous verse,

position which loves to learn, loves to contemplate and is truly wisdom-loving or philosophical.

This is the greatest boon which sight bestowed on 192
human life, and I think that this pre-eminence has been awarded to it because it is more closely akin to the soul than the other senses. They are all of the same family as the mind, but, just as it is with families, the place which is closest in birth [a] and first
and highest, is held by sight. We may find many 193
proofs of this, for who does not know that when we rejoice the eyes are bright and smiling, when we are sad they are full of anxiety and dejection, and, if the burden is magnified and presses and crushes, they break out into tears; when anger prevails they swell and their look is bloodshot and fiery; when the
temper dies down it is gentle and kindly; when we 194
are reflecting or inquiring the pupils are set and seem to share our thoughts, while in persons of little sense their silliness makes their vision roaming and restless. In general the emotions of the soul are shared by the eyes, and as it passes through its numberless phases they change with it, a natural consequence of their affinity.[b] Indeed it seems to me that nowhere else in God's creations is the inward and invisible so well represented by the outward and visible as reason is by sight.

XXXV. If, then, anyone has maliciously injured 195
another in the best and lordliest of his senses, sight, and is proved to have struck out his eye, he must in his turn suffer the same, if the other is a free man,[c] but not if he is a slave. Not that the offender deserves pardon or is less in the wrong, but because

"eye for eye, tooth for tooth . . . but (δέ) if he strikes out the eye of a slave," etc.

ἀλλ' ὅτι πονηροτέρῳ χρήσαιτ' ἂν ὁ πεπονθὼς ἀντιπηρωθέντι τῷ δεσπότῃ, μνησικακήσοντι[1] τῆς συμφορᾶς τὸν ἀεὶ χρόνον καὶ ἀμυνουμένῳ καθ' ἑκάστην ἡμέραν ὡς ἐχθρὸν ἄσπονδον ἀφορήτοις καὶ βαρυτέροις τῆς δυνάμεως ἐπιτάγμασιν, οἷς
196 πιεζόμενος καὶ τὴν ψυχὴν ἀπορρήξει. προὐνόησεν οὖν ὁ νόμος τοῦ μήτε τὸν ἐπιβεβουλευκότα ἀθῷον ἀφεθῆναι μήτε τὸν πεπηρωμένον προσαδικηθῆναι κελεύσας, εἴ τις ἐκκόψειε θεράποντος ὀφθαλμόν,
197 ἀνενδοιάστως ἐλευθερίας μεταδιδόναι.[2] οὕτως γὰρ ὁ μὲν ἀνθ' ὧν ἔδρασε διττὴν ἐνδέξεται[3] ζημίαν, ἅμα τῇ τιμῇ καὶ τὴν ὑπηρεσίαν ἀφαιρεθείς, καὶ τρίτον ἑκατέρου τῶν λεχθέντων χαλεπώτερον, ἀναγκαζόμενος ἐν τοῖς μεγίστοις εὐεργετεῖν ἐχθρόν, ὃν ἴσως ηὔχετο κακοῦν ἀεὶ δύνασθαι, ὁ δὲ ἀνθ' ὧν ὑπέμεινε παρηγορίαν ἕξει διπλῆν, οὐ μόνον ἐλευθερωθεὶς ἀλλὰ καὶ ἀργαλέον καὶ ὠμὸν δεσπότην ἐκφυγών.

198 XXXVI. Προστάττει δὲ κἂν εἴ τις ὀδόντα θεράποντος ἐκκόψειεν, ἐλευθερίαν χαρίζεσθαι τῷ θεράποντι. διὰ τί; ὅτι ζωὴ μὲν τίμιον, ὄργανα δὲ ζωῆς ἐτεκτήνατο ἡ φύσις ὀδόντας, οἷς τὴν τροφὴν οἰκονομεῖσθαι συμβέβηκεν. ὀδόντες δὲ οἱ μέν εἰσι τομίαι τῷ τέμνειν σιτία καὶ ὅσα ἄλλα ἐδώδιμα,[4] διὰ τοῦτο ταύτης τῆς προσηγορίας

[1] MSS. μνησικακήσαντι. [2] MSS. μεταδιδότω or μεταδιδῶ.
[3] MSS. ἐνδείξεται or ἐνδέχεται *et alia*.
[4] The construction is somewhat difficult, as εἰσι τῷ τέμνειν =" are for the purpose of cutting " is hardly Greek. Heinemann and Cohn (doubtfully) suggest omitting διὰ τοῦτο with F. In this case it would be almost necessary to omit ταύτης also. If the text is kept, perhaps understand τροφὴν οἰκονομοῦντες from the sentence before.

if the master is mutilated as a punishment the injured slave will find him worse than before. He will harbour a perpetual grudge for his misfortune and avenge himself on one whom he regards as a mortal enemy by setting him every day to tasks of an intolerable kind and beyond his powers to cope with, the oppressive weight of which will break his spirit also. The law, therefore, provided 196
on the one hand that a master should not go unpunished for his malicious assault and on the other that the servant should not suffer further wrong in addition to the loss of his eye. It effected this by enacting that if anyone struck out his servant's eye he should without hesitation grant him his liberty, for 197
in this way the master will incur a double penalty; he will lose the value of the slave as well as his services, and a third affliction more severe than either of these two is that he will be forced to confer a benefit that touches his highest interest on an enemy whom he probably hoped to be able to maltreat indefinitely. The servant will receive a double solatium for his suffering; he is not only set at liberty but has escaped from a harsh and cruel master.

XXXVI. A further command is that if anyone 198
strikes out a servant's tooth he must grant him his liberty.[a] Why is this? Because life is precious and the means contrived by nature for the preservation of life are teeth by which the food is subjected to the processes necessary for dealing with it. Now the teeth are divided into the cutters and the grinders; the former do their part by cutting or biting the bread-stuffs and all other comestibles, whence their appropriate name of cutters, the latter by their

[a] Ex. xxi. 27.

ἀξιωθέντες, οἱ δὲ μύλαι τῷ τὰ διατμηθέντα εἰς
199 μείονα λεαίνειν δύνασθαι. παρ' ἣν αἰτίαν
ὁ ποιητὴς καὶ πατὴρ οὐδὲν εἰωθὼς δημιουργεῖν,
ὃ μὴ πρός τινι τέτακται χρείᾳ, τοὺς ὀδόντας οὐχ
ὥσπερ τῶν ἄλλων μερῶν ἕκαστον κατὰ τὴν πρώτην
γένεσιν εὐθὺς εἰργάζετο, διανοηθεὶς ὅτι βρέφει μὲν
γαλακτοτροφεῖσθαι μέλλοντι περιττὸν ἄχθος γενήσονται, μαστοῖς δὲ πηγάζουσιν, οἷς ἄρδεται ἡ
τροφή, χαλεπὴ ζημία κατὰ τὴν ὁλκὴν τοῦ γάλακτος
200 ὀδαξωμένοις. τὸν ἐπιτήδειον οὖν καιρὸν προ-
ϊδόμενος—ἔστι δ' οὗτος, ἡνίκα τὸ βρέφος ἀπότιτθον
γίνεται—τὴν ἔκφυσιν τῶν ὀδόντων, ἣν ἐταμιεύ-
σατο πρότερον, ἀνέφηνεν * * *[1] ἤδη τῆς τε-
λειοτέρας ἀνέχεσθαι τροφῆς ὀργάνων ὧν εἶπον
δεομένης τὴν διὰ τοῦ γάλακτος ἀποστρεφόμενον.
201 Ἐὰν οὖν τις εἴξας ἀλαζονείᾳ | θεράποντος ὀδόντα
[333] ἐκκόψῃ τὸν ὑπηρέτην καὶ ὑποδιάκονον τῶν ἀναγκαιοτάτων, τροφῆς τε καὶ ζωῆς, ἐλευθερούτω τὸν
ἀδικηθέντα, στερόμενος καὶ αὐτὸς τῆς ἐκ τοῦ
πεπονθότος λατρείας τε καὶ ὑπηρεσίας. ἰσότιμον
202 οὖν, φήσει[2] τις, ὀδοὺς ὀφθαλμῷ; πρὸς ἃ γέγονεν
ἑκάτερον, εἴποιμ' ἄν, ἰσότιμον, πρὸς μὲν τὰ ὁρατὰ
ὀφθαλμός, πρὸς δὲ τὰ ἐδώδιμα ὀδούς. εἰ δὲ καὶ
συγκρῖναί τις ἐθελήσει, σεμνότατον μὲν εὑρήσει
τῶν ἐν σώματι μερῶν ὀφθαλμὸν ἅτε θεωρὸν ὄντα
τοῦ σεμνοτάτου τῶν κατὰ τὸν κόσμον, οὐρανοῦ,
χρήσιμον δὲ ὀδόντα ὡς ἂν τροφῆς, τοῦ χρησιμω-

[1] Something is wanted to complete the construction. Cohn inserts ὅτε δύναται. I suggest ἐνὸν (impersonal participle) as more easily lost after ἀπέφηνεν.

[2] MSS. φησί.

capacity for reducing the bitten pieces into smaller particles. This is the reason why the 199
Maker and Father, Whose way is to frame nothing that does not serve some purpose, did not make the teeth straight away at birth like each of the other parts. He bore in mind that they would be a superfluous burden to the infant who would be fed on milk, and would also bring serious trouble to the breasts, the fountain through which the liquid sustenance flows, as they would be galled during the suction of the milk. He 200
looked forward, therefore, to the proper time, that is, to when the infant is weaned from the breast, and brought out that supplementary growth of teeth, which He hitherto kept in storage, only when the infant would refuse to take food in the form of milk and could bear the more mature kind which requires the instruments which I have mentioned.

If, then, anyone gives way to insolent presumption 201
and strikes out his servant's tooth which ministers obediently to his most essential needs, sustenance and survival, he must set at liberty the victim of his injustice and suffer himself the loss of the services and ministries of the injured party.[a] Is a tooth then,
I shall be asked, of the same value as an eye? They 202
are both, I should reply, of the same value for the purposes for which they were made, the eye being made for what is visible, the tooth for what is edible. And if anyone cares to compare these, he will find that the eye is the noblest of the body's members because it contemplates the heaven which is the noblest part of the universe, while the tooth is useful as the operator

[a] Thus the *ius talionis* is preserved, as both lose a servant.

τάτου πρὸς τὸ ζῆν, ἐργάτην· καὶ ὁ μὲν τὰς ὄψεις ἀποβαλὼν οὐ κεκώλυται βιοῦν, τῷ δὲ ἐκκοπέντι
203 τοὺς ὀδόντας ἐφεδρεύει θάνατος οἴκτιστος. εἰ δή τις ἐπιβουλεύει περὶ τὰ μέρη ταῦτα τοῖς οἰκέταις, μὴ ἀγνοείτω λιμὸν ἐν εὐθηνίᾳ καὶ εὐετηρίᾳ κατασκευάζων τούτοις χειροποίητον· τί γὰρ ὄφελος ἀφθονίαν μὲν εἶναι τροφῶν, τὰ δὲ πρὸς τὴν διοίκησιν αὐτῶν ὄργανα σεσυλῆσθαι καὶ ἀποβεβληκέναι χαλεπῶν ἕνεκα καὶ ἀμειλίκτων καὶ ὠμοθύμων
204 δεσποτῶν; διὰ τοῦτο καὶ ἑτέρωθι παρὰ χρεωστῶν ἀπαγορεύει δανεισταῖς μύλον ἢ ἐπιμύλιον ῥύσιον αἰτεῖν, ἐπειπὼν ὅτι ὁ τοῦτο δρῶν ψυχὴν ἐνεχυριάζει· ὁ γὰρ τὰ τοῦ ζῆν ὄργανα ἀφαιρούμενος ἐπ' ἀνδροφονίαν ἵεται, μέχρι καὶ ψυχῆς ἐπιβουλεύειν διανοηθείς.

205 Τοσαύτην δὲ πρόνοιαν ἐποιήσατο τοῦ μηδένα παραίτιόν τινι γενέσθαι θανάτου, ὡς καὶ τοὺς προσαψαμένους νεκροῦ σώματος, ὃ τελευτὴν ἐνδέδεκται τὴν κατὰ φύσιν, οἴεται δεῖν μὴ εὐθὺς[1] εἶναι καθαρούς, μέχρις ἂν περιρρανάμενοι καὶ ἀπολουσάμενοι καθαρθῶσιν. εἰς μέντοι τὸ ἱερὸν οὐδὲ τοῖς σφόδρα καθαροῖς ἐφῆκεν εἰσιέναι ἐντὸς ἡμερῶν

[1] Cohn, while retaining *εὐθὺς*, adds *excludendum videtur*. See note *c*.

---

[a] Deut. xxiv. 6. See App. p. 641.
[b] Numbers xix. 11 ff. Philo here, in concluding the treatise, leaves the discussion of acts of violence and recurs to murder in the proper sense. The argument in the next three sections is exactly similar to that of § 63, viz. that if a thing when

of what is most useful for maintaining life, namely food. Also anyone who has lost his sight is not thereby prevented from living, but one who has had his teeth struck out has only a most miserable death awaiting him. So if anyone takes steps to injure his 203
servants in this part of their bodies he must recognize that the effect of his act upon them is a famine artificially created in the midst of abundance and plenty. For what use have they for a generous supply of food if they have been robbed of the instruments needed for dealing effectively with it, lost to them through the actions of hard, cruel and merciless masters? And therefore elsewhere 204
the lawgiver forbids creditors to demand that their debtors should give their mill or upper mill-stone as a surety, and he adds that anyone who does so takes the life to pledge.[a] For one who deprives another of the instruments needed to preserve existence is well on the way to murder, since his hostile intentions extend to attacking life itself.

[b] So careful was the lawgiver to guard against any- 205
one helping to bring about the death of another that he considers that even those who have touched the corpse of one who has met a natural death must remain unclean [c] until they have been purified by aspersions and ablutions. Indeed he did not permit even the fully cleansed to enter the temple within

caused naturally and innocently produces defilement, how much more defiling must it be if caused in a sinful way!

[c] If εὐθύς is retained in its present position, it should mean they are not straight away (*i.e.* necessarily) clean, as might be expected since what they have done is natural and innocent. This is very strained. The sense to be expected is that they are *ipso facto* unclean, but this would be rather εὐθὺς μή. To omit the word would certainly simplify the sense.

ἑπτά, τρίτῃ καὶ ἑβδόμῃ κελεύσας ἀφαγνίζεσθαι.
206 ἔτι μέντοι καὶ τοῖς εἰσιοῦσιν εἰς οἰκίαν, ἐν ᾗ τετελεύτηκέ τις, προστάττει μηδενὸς ἅπτεσθαι, μέχρις ἂν ἀπολούσωνται καὶ τὰς ἐσθῆτας αἷς ἀμπίσχοντο προσαποπλύναντες· σκεύη δὲ καὶ ἔπιπλα καὶ ὅσα ἄλλα ἔνδον εἶναι συμβέβηκε πάνθ'
207 ὡς ἔπος εἰπεῖν ἀκάθαρτα ἡγεῖται. ψυχὴ γὰρ ἀνθρώπου τίμιον, ἧς μετανισταμένης καὶ μετοικιζομένης τὰ ἀπολειφθησόμενα πάντα μιαίνεται στερόμενα θείας εἰκόνος, ἐπειδὴ θεοειδὴς ὁ ἀνθρώπινος νοῦς πρὸς ἀρχέτυπον ἰδέαν, τὸν ἀνω-
208 τάτω λόγον, τυπωθείς. ἔστω δέ, φησίν, ἀκάθαρτα καὶ τὰ ἄλλα ὅσων ἂν ὁ ἀκάθαρτος προσάψηται, μετουσίᾳ τοῦ μὴ καθαροῦ μιαινόμενα. καθολικωτέραν δ' ἀπόφασιν ὁ χρησμὸς οὗτος ἔοικέ πως δηλοῦν, οὐκ ἐπὶ σώματος αὐτὸ μόνον ἱστάμενος, ἀλλὰ ἤθη καὶ τρόπους προσδιερευνώμενος
209 ψυχῆς. ἀκάθαρτος γὰρ κυρίως ὁ ἄδικος καὶ
[334] ἀσεβής, ὅτῳ μήτε τῶν ἀνθρωπίνων μήτε | τῶν θείων αἰδώς τις εἰσέρχεται, πάντα φύρων καὶ συγχέων διά τε τὰς ἀμετρίας τῶν παθῶν καὶ τὰς τῶν κακιῶν ὑπερβολάς, ὥστε ὧν ἂν ἐφάψηται πραγμάτων πάντ' ἐστὶν ἐπίληπτα τῇ τοῦ δρῶντος

[a] Philo's account differs from Numbers in that he implies that, except to get admission to the temple, a purification at

seven days and ordered them to purge themselves
on the third and seventh.[a] Further too, those who 206
enter a house in which anyone has died are ordered
not to touch anything until they have bathed themselves and also washed the clothes which they were wearing.[b] And all the vessels and articles of furniture, and anything else that happens to be inside, practically everything is held by him to be unclean.[c]
For a man's soul is a precious thing, and when it 207
departs to seek another home, all that will be left behind is defiled, deprived as it is of the divine image. For it is the mind of man which has the form of God, being shaped in conformity with the ideal archetype, the Word that is above all.
Everything else too, he says, that the unclean person 208
touches must be unclean, being defiled by its participation in the uncleanness.[d] This pronouncement may be thought to include a more far-reaching veto, not merely stopping short with the body but extending its inquiry to matters of temperament and
characteristics of soul. For the unjust and impious 209
man is in the truest sense unclean. No thought of respect for things human or divine ever enters his mind. He puts everything into chaos and confusion, so inordinate are his passions and so prodigious his vices, and thus every deed to which he sets his hand is reprehensible, changing in conformity with

the time is enough, and the man is then "fully cleansed." In Numbers everyone who touches the corpse is impure for seven days and requires the purging on the third and seventh. The exclusion from the temple only appears (*vv.* 13 and 20), in the words "whosoever . . . purifieth not himself defileth the tabernacle of the Lord."

[b] *Ibid. v.* 14: "washing the clothes," *v.* 19.

[c] *Ibid. v.* 15.

[d] *Ibid. v.* 22.

συμμεταβάλλοντα μοχθηρίᾳ· καὶ γὰρ κατὰ τοὐναντίον αἱ πράξεις τῶν ἀγαθῶν ἐπαινεταί, βελτιούμεναι ταῖς τῶν ἐνεργούντων ἀρεταῖς, ἐπειδὴ πέφυκέ πως τὰ γινόμενα τοῖς δρῶσιν ἐξομοιοῦσθαι.

[a] These last two sections are not really germane to the sub-

the worthlessness of the doer. For conversely all the doings of the good are laudable, gaining merit through the virtues of the agents in accordance with the general law that the results of actions assimilate themselves to the actors.[a]

ject. The point is introduced because of the spiritual lesson which can be drawn from it.

APPENDIX TO *DE DECALOGO*

§ 1. *For knowledge loves to learn*, etc. As stated in the footnote, the phrasing seems almost impossible. I can find no case where ἐπιστήμη bears a sense which could be coupled with φιλομαθής, or where διάνοια means an understanding which is above knowledge. The translators appear to be at a loss. Treitel has "wegen der auf den tieferen Sinn gerichteten Schriftforschung." But how can ἐπιστήμη = "Schriftforschung"? Mangey (perhaps translating the conjecture mentioned below) has "reconditae scientiae studio et curiosae." Yonge (probably translating Mangey) "natural love of more recondite and laborious study." The emendations mentioned are Mangey's δι' ὑπονοιῶν for πρὸς διάνοιαν, and Wendland's ἐπιστάσεως for ἐπιστήμης. If ἐπίστασις can = "intentio," this will give some sense, though it would be better if ὑπόνοιαν is accepted for διάνοιαν (ὑπόνοια sing. is used for "allegorizing" in *Spec. Leg.* ii. 257).

§ 21. *The arithmetical*, etc. This seems to be very loosely expressed. ἀναλογία does not carry with it the idea of a series like our "progression," but of an equality of ratio, and indeed it can only be properly (κυρίως) applied, as Nicomachus says, to the geometrical. It certainly cannot itself be said to exceed or be exceeded. Philo has stated it quite clearly in *De Op.* 108, in much the same words as are used in the translation. Possibly here also we should read ᾗ ⟨ὁ μέσος ὅρος⟩ ὑπερέχει, κτλ.

§ 30. *The categories.* Philo follows with little variation the two lists given by Aristotle in *Topica*, i. 9 and *Categoriae* 4 of the 10 categories. But he carries them away into a very different region from Aristotle's logical meaning of predicates or "classification of the manners in which assertions may be made of the subject." His reason for asserting that he has οὐσία, and his view of time and place (in Aristotle πότε and ποῦ) as the indispensables for all existence are quite foreign to Aristotle's thought, at any rate in drawing up this list.

§ 39. (Text of ὅτε δὲ προστάττων, etc.) Cohn deals with this passage in *Hermes*, 1903, pp. 502 f., but not very conclusively. The solution he would prefer is to omit ὅτε δὲ and to correct (with one MS.) ἰδίᾳ to ἰδίᾳ δ', a change which he bases largely on the improbability of such an hiatus as ἰδίᾳ ὡς. I do not feel competent to estimate the value of this last argument (see remarks on *Spec. Leg.* i. 90, App. p. 620). The omission of ὅτε δὲ has some support from one MS. (G), which has διαλέγεται ἑνὶ ἑκάστῳ προστάττων, κτλ. Of the rest, one has ἑνί, ὅτε δὲ, the others an obvious corruption of this, ἐνίοτε δὲ. No doubt with Cohn's changes the sentence is translatable. He, however, says that he cannot see the sense of τῶν ἐμφερομένων, which he justly remarks cannot mean, as Mangey takes it, "eorum qui adsunt." I think the sense given in the translation, which will also fit in with the form suggested by Cohn, does not present much difficulty. In the kind of oration which Philo has in mind definite instruction as to the steps to be taken (τὰ πρακτέα) would be only part of the contents.

§ 54. *They call air Hera.* This is first suggested by Plato, *Cratylus* 404 c (ἀήρ being an anagram of ἥρα) and was adopted by the Stoics. See particularly Diog. Laert. vii. 147, where Hera is the name given to the divine power in virtue of its extension (διάτασις) to the air, as Athena, Poseidon, Hephaestus and Demeter represent its extension to aether, sea, fire and earth. For other references see Index to *S. V.F.* So also Philo, *De Vit. Cont.* 3, where the name is supposed to be derived παρὰ τὸ αἴρεσθαι καὶ μετεωρίζεσθαι εἰς τὸ ὕψος.

§ 56. *Living on alternate days.* Or perhaps as Philo understands it "living (and dying) alternately every day," which is what the interpretation of the story by the hemispheres requires. So, too, in the other place where he alludes to the story, *De Som.* i. 150, since the antithesis there is between sleeping and waking. The only other passage where I have found this interpretation is in Sext. Emp. *Adv. math.* ix. 37 τὰ γὰρ δύο ἡμισφαίρια τό τε ὑπὲρ γῆς καὶ τὸ ὑπὸ γῆν Διοσκούρους οἱ σοφοὶ τῶν τότε ἀνθρώπων ἔλεγον.

§ 77. (Egyptian animal worship.) See Herodotus ii. 65-74. These chapters lay stress chiefly on cats (αἴλουροι) and crocodiles, but ibises and snakes are mentioned also. Juv. xv. 1-7 mentions crocodiles, ibises, apes, dogs and fishes.

On these lines Mayor has collected a number of illustrations, among them Philo, *Legatio* 139, where he speaks very briefly in the same sense as here. Neither Herodotus nor Juvenal mentions wolves and lions, and I see no other allusion to them in Mayor's quotations.

§ 88. ἐγὼ μέν γε. This is one of the small matters in which an earlier knowledge of the Palimpsest would apparently have led Cohn to alter his reading. His MSS. have μὲν, except M which has μὲν γὰρ, on the strength of which he printed μέν γε. The Palimpsest has μὲν οὖν, which he considers preferable. Unwilling or unable to judge, I have retained μέν γε with this warning.

§ 92. τὰ κενὰ τῶν. This emendation of μὲν αὐτῶν to κενὰ τῶν seems certain and will perhaps support my emendation of the same two words in *De Mig.* 164, where I have altered them to μελιττῶν.

§ 96. *Once a month.* The principal passages quoted in support of this are Herod. vi. 57, where he says that the Spartans made offerings to Apollo at every new moon and seventh day of the month, and Hes. *Op.* 770, where the seventh day is said to be sacred as Apollo's birthday. Also there are inscriptions in various places where ἑβδομαῖος and ἑβδομαῖον appear as epithets of Apollo or indicating feasts held in his honour. See references in L. & S. (revised).

Ibid. (σελήνην or θεὸν.) Cohn writing in *Hermes*, 1903, p. 548, before the discovery of the Palimpsest, had declared for σελήνην. His explanation of the corruption to θεὸν is that it arises from the scribes mistaking the astronomical symbol of the moon for $\overline{\Theta N}$ = θεόν. (This would be convincing if this symbol were as he describes it. On my present information it is rather C, while Θ = the sun.) *Prima facie* it does not seem impossible that in a country where the opening of the sacred and lunar month has to be distinguished from the civil the phrase " according to the goddess " might have been in such common use that Philo might employ it without much thought or scruple. See note on *Spec. Leg.* iii. 171. But the discovery that the Palimpsest actually has σελήνην certainly weights the evidence strongly in favour of it.

§ 106. προστάττεται for πρὸς τὰ πέντε, which may be presumed from Cohn's silence to be the reading of the Palimpsest as well as of the other MSS, is adopted by him on the grounds that TTETAI might easily be corrupted to ΠΕΝΤΕ, and that the Armenian version gives a similar sense "ut videtur." If this last is clearly established, the emendation may be accepted. Otherwise it is difficult to see why a word like *προστάττειν*, which perpetually recurs in these treatises, should be corrupted. The reading of G, *ἑνοῖ* ("unites") *πρὸς τὰ ἕτερα πέντε καὶ συνάπτει τῇ δευτέρᾳ*, looks, as he says, like an unsuccessful attempt to emend the passage. Perhaps we might consider as an alternative *προστεθέν τε*, "last of the first pentad in which are the most sacred things and added to it," *i.e.* "an appendage." Philo often uses *προσθήκη* with a sense of inferiority, *e.g. Spec. Leg.* ii. 248, and it would fitly describe the relation of the fifth to the first four commandments.

§ 116. (Filial affection of storks.) The currency of this idea is best shewn by the existence of the verb *ἀντιπελαργεῖν* = "to return kindness." Other mentions of it will be found in Aristotle, *Hist. Anim.* ix. 18, Aristophanes, *Av.* 1353 ff.; and the *φρονιμώτατοι οἰωνοί* of Sophocles, *El.* 1058, "who are careful to nourish those who gave them nurture," are no doubt the same.

§ 120. *Some bolder spirits.* One such is Hierocles the Stoic quoted by Stobaeus (Meineke, iii. p. 96), *οὓς* (*sc.* *γονεῖς*) *δευτέρους καὶ ἐπιγείους τινὰς θεοὺς οὐκ ἂν ἁμάρτοι τις, ἕνεκά γε τῆς ἐγγύτητος, εἰ θέμις εἰπεῖν, καὶ θεῶν ἡμῖν τιμιωτέρους.* Heinemann quotes Dikaiogenes (Fr. 5 Nauck), *θεὸς μέγιστος τοῖς φρονοῦσιν οἱ γονεῖς.* The ordinary Stoic view is given by Diog. Laert. vii. 120, that parents, brothers and sisters are to be reverenced next to the gods.

§§ 142-146. This disquisition on the four passions is thoroughly Stoic in substance and much of its phraseology is found elsewhere. Thus any passion is a *κίνησις ψυχῆς παρὰ φύσιν* (*S.V.F.* iii. 389, and elsewhere). So, too, pleasure is *ἔπαρσις ἄλογος* (*ibid.* 391). A passage which closely resembles this is Cic. *De Fin.* ii. 13 (*S.V.F.* iii. 404) "(Voluptatem) Stoici . . . sic definiunt: sublationem animi sine ratione, opinantis se magno bono frui." *πτοία*, which Philo associates with fear, is a characteristic of all four; (*λέγουσι*) *πᾶσαν πτοίαν πάθος εἶναι καὶ πᾶν πάθος πτοίαν* (*ibid.* 378), while *ἀγωνία* is a subdivision of *φόβος*, defined by Diog. Laert. vii. 112 as *φόβος ἀδήλου πράγματος* (*ibid.* 407). Also *ἐπιθυμία* is often an *ὄρεξις*, though none of the definitions quoted otherwise agree closely with Philo's. I have not found any parallels to his idea that desire differs from the others in being more voluntary.

For a shorter definition of the four see *Mos.* ii. 139.

§ 147. (Text at end of section.) Cohn in his description of the Palimpsest has an interesting if not quite convincing theory about this. In place of ἀμαυροῦνται καὶ θροῦ the Palimpsest has in the main body of the text ὁμάδου τε καὶ θροῦ beginning the next sentence, while ἀμαυροῦνται is set in smaller writing on the margin. Cohn's view is that ὁμάδου τε is the original text, and was corrupted in one or more MSS. to ἀμαυροῦνται, which was then set in others such as the Palimpsest as a marginal variant and finally ousted the real words. One may perhaps accept his theory about the corruption of ὁμάδου τε to ἀμαυροῦνται, which as he says is not indispensable to the construction, but his other argument that ὁμάδου τε is wanted to correspond to ὀφθαλμοί τε in the previous sentence seems questionable. "Both . . . and" are expressed by τε . . . καί, as well as by τε . . . τε.

§ 158. τὸ περὶ τῆς ἑβδομάδος. While there would be no great difficulty in this passage, where the virtues of the number are so prominent, in taking ἑβδομάς as = "the number seven," there can be no doubt that Philo does sometimes use it for the seventh day See notes on *Quis Rerum* 170, where we have ἀπραξία ascribed to it, and *Mos.* i. 205, where οὐδὲν ἐφεῖται δρᾶν ἐν αὐτῇ, *i.e.* on ἱερὰ ἑβδομάς. So, too, Jos. *Contra Apion.* ii. 282 τῆς ἑβδομάδος ἣν ἀργοῦμεν ἡμεῖς. This use is ignored in L. & S. (revised), which indeed has expunged the entry of older editions, "The seventh day, *Eccl.*"

On the other hand, ἑβδόμη below appears to be used for ἑβδομάς, as also in *Spec. Leg.* ii. 40 τῆς ἐν ἀριθμοῖς ἑβδόμης, and there are other instances in earlier treatises, where clearly the number and not the seventh day is under consideration, *e.g. De Op.* 116, *De Post.* 64. I leave to experts to consider whether a confusion of the two words may have been produced by varying interpretations of ζ′.

§ 159. ἱερομηνία. Except in *Mos.* ii. 23, where he is apparently referring to pagan use, Philo consistently uses this word to denote the first of Tishri or Feast of Trumpets (New Year's day in the civil year). Whether this usage is in accordance with its regular meaning in classical Greek is not clear to me. The general opinion seems to be that there it indicates a *period* during which, as stated in the note on *Mos. loc. cit.*, hostilities or legal proceedings are forbidden, not a particular day. See *Dict. of Ant.* and L. & S. (revised), where it is only given two meanings, " sacred month during which the great festivals were held and hostilities suspended," and (in the plural) "sacrifices offered during the sacred month." On the other hand Stephanus gives examples from Harpocration, Scholiasts, etc., which assert that it means a festal day, and that is what is suggested in *Mos. loc. cit.*, where it is contrasted with the single day fast of the Jews.

A scholiast on Pind. *Nem.* iii. 2, who says that ἱερομηνία is an abbreviation κατὰ σύντμησιν of ἱερονουμηνία "because the beginnings of months are sacred to Apollo," expresses, whatever his authority may be worth, the idea which had occurred to me in connexion with *Spec. Leg.* i. 180. I refer these points to the lexicographer. The entry in L. & S. is clearly inadequate.

APPENDIX TO *DE SPECIALIBUS LEGIBUS*, I

§ 2. (Circumcision in Egypt.) The original authority for this is Herodotus ii. 36. In itself it is not impossible that Philo, knowing little of the intimate practices of the Egyptians outside the Jewish and Hellenistic world, should take Herodotus for his authority. But in *Quaest. in Gen.* iii. 47, 48, where he gives the arguments for circumcision in much the same way as here, he adds that the Egyptians circumcised females as well as males and at the age of puberty, and neither of these did he find in Herodotus. The statement made here is supported by Diodorus i. 28, iii. 32. Josephus, *Contra Apion.* ii. 140 ff. says positively that the Egyptian priests were circumcised, but the fact that Apion, himself an Egyptian, appears to have ridiculed the Jews on this ground tells rather against it for the nation at large. See on the whole question Wendland in *Archiv für Papyrusforschung* ii. (1903) (referred to by Goodenough, p. 30).

§ 6. *The spirit force in the heart.* The doctrine and phraseology is Stoic. So "All the Stoics say that *τὸ ἡγεμονικόν* resides *ἐν ὅλῃ τῇ καρδίᾳ ἢ ἐν τῷ περὶ τὴν καρδίαν πνεύματι*," *S.V.F.* ii. 838. The *ἡγεμονικόν* itself is a *πνεῦμα* according to them, *ibid.* 96. For the question between the brain and the heart as the seat of the mind see §§ 213 f. below.

§ 25. "*Blind*" *wealth.* Philo in several places, *e.g.* ii. 23 below, *De Abr.* 25, contrasts the "seeing" with the "blind" riches, and in these passages he borrows the phrase from Plato, *Laws* 631 C *πλοῦτος οὐ τυφλὸς ἀλλ' ὀξὺ βλέπων*, though the thought is not quite the same, since with Plato the "seeing wealth" is wealth in the literal sense used wisely, with Philo wisdom or virtue itself. But here, where there is no such contrast and the stress is rather on the uncertainty of riches, *τοῦ λεγομένου* may refer rather to the fable, earlier than Plato, that Zeus made Plutus blind, so that he should distribute his gifts without regard to merit (see Aristophanes, *Plutus*).

§ 27. *Some assert . . . state of flux. Cf. e.g.* Plato, *Theaetetus* 160 D κατὰ μὲν Ὅμηρον καὶ Ἡράκλειτον καὶ πᾶν τὸ τοιοῦτον φῦλον οἷον ῥεύματα κινεῖσθαι τὰ πάντα, *Cratylus* 402 A λέγει που Ἡράκλειτος ὅτι πάντα χωρεῖ καὶ οὐδὲν μένει, καὶ ποτάμου ῥοῇ ἀπεικάζων τὰ πάντα λέγει ὡς δὶς ἐς τὸν αὐτὸν ποταμὸν οὐκ ἂν ἐμβαίης. Rather nearer to our passage is Aristot. *Physica* viii. 3, 253 b 9, φασί τινες (apparently the Heracleiteans) κινεῖσθαι τῶν ὄντων οὐ τὰ μὲν τὰ δ' οὔ, ἀλλὰ πάντα καὶ ἀεί, ἀλλὰ λανθάνειν τὴν ἡμετέραν αἴσθησιν.

§ 28. θεοὺς . . ὥσπερ ἀπὸ μηχανῆς. The phrase seems to me to suggest primarily the use of the supernatural as a facile way of getting out of a difficulty and to carry with it the idea of artificiality rather than suddenness and unexpectedness. The fact that the "machine" was employed to bring the god hovering over the stage is incidental, though it served to enhance the impression of something artificial and slightly ludicrous. To take the examples given in Stephanus, this is the sense in Plato, *Cratylus* 425 D ὥσπερ οἱ τραγῳδοποιοί, ἐπειδάν τι ἀπορῶσιν, ἐπὶ τὰς μηχανὰς καταφεύγουσι θεοὺς αἴροντες ("like the tragic poets who in any perplexity have their gods waiting in the air," Jowett), and in Aristotle, *Poetics* xv. 7. So in Plutarch, *Them.* 10 Themistocles employs oracles and divine signs ὥσπερ ἐν τραγῳδίᾳ μηχανὴν ἄρας. In Demosthenes, p. 1026. 1 Τιμοκράτης μόνος ἀπὸ τοσούτων, ὥσπερ ἀπὸ μηχανῆς, μαρτυρεῖ, the thought seems to be that he assumes the rôle of a superior being. In Plato (?), *Cleitophon* 407 A the point is different, viz. that the gods in these appearances are apt to rebuke the follies of humanity. In our passage and in ii. 165 the main idea seems to be artificiality.

§§ 33 f. The argument from design has been given in much the same form in *Leg. All.* iii. 97-99. For other statements of it see *S.V.F.* ii. 1009-1020, particularly Cic. *De Nat. Deorum*, ii. 16-17, iii. 26. *Cf.* also Cic. *Tusc.* i. 68 (referred to by Heinemann), *Pro Milone* 83, 84 and Xen. *Mem.* i. 4.

§ 55. (Lynching of apostates.) Two questions arise here, (1) whether the lynching so strongly recommended here and almost as explicitly in § 316 is in accordance with Deut., (2) whether it was customary or practicable in Philo's time. As to (1), in Deut. xiii. 6-11, which I take to be more to the point than *ibid.* 12-17 (enjoining the destruction of an apostate city), which Heinemann cites, the E.V. merely says, "thou shalt surely kill him; thine hand shall be first upon him to put him to death, and afterwards the hand of all the people." Philo would indeed find in the LXX, instead of "thou shalt surely kill him," "thou shalt surely report it" (ἀναγγέλλων ἀναγγελεῖς), which sounds more judicial. But in § 316 this is interpreted to mean that the report is to be sent round to summon the lovers of piety to assist in the execution. In Deut. xvii. 4-7 a careful inquiry is to be made when such a call is reported, and two or three witnesses are required. Heinemann thinks that Philo is not referring to these passages at all, but is merely extracting a general law from the case of Phinehas. I do not think this can be right, so far as Deut. xiii. is concerned, as in § 316 he formally expounds that passage. As for Deut. xvii., Philo if faced with it might reply that it does not suggest a formal trial, but that the self-constituted executioners before taking action must assure themselves that the charge is true, and that what he says here does not deny that.

As to (2), Goodenough (pp. 36 ff.) argues that the Acts (*e.g.* Stephen's execution and the attempts to stone Paul) shews that the Jews did sometimes inflict capital punishment without direct permission from the Roman government. He also cites 3 Maccabees vii. 10-15, which gives an account of a decree of Ptolemy Philopator empowering the Jews in Alexandria to put transgressors against the law to death (E.V. somewhat inaccurately "without warrant or special commission") (Greek ἄνευ πάσης βασιλικῆς ἐξουσίας ἢ ἐπισκέψεως). All this may be true, but hardly meets the case. Stephen was tried by the Sanhedrin; and the persons for whose execution Paul voted, Acts xxvi. 10, were presumably legally tried. And the Decree, even if historical, need not mean more than that Jewish constituted authorities might condemn independently of the king. But Philo's words, "Jury, council or any kind of magistrate at all," must surely include Jewish as well as Roman courts. That he should be seriously encouraging his fellow-Jews in Alexandria, where we know that the Jews had independent jurisdiction, to put apostates to death without any legal trial, seems to me almost impossible. But was it perhaps otherwise in other cities of the Dispersion, where the Jews had no such privileges and knew that the ordinary courts would not take cognizance of apostasy or heresy? Paul's experiences at Iconium and

Lystra possibly lend themselves to such a view. It is to Jews so circumstanced that this section is addressed if it has any practical bearing. Otherwise it must be regarded as a rhetorical way of saying that apostasy is so hateful a crime that to avenge it on the spot is not only pardonable but a duty.

§ 58. The connexion of this section, which comes in so oddly as it stands, would become much clearer, if we might suppose that some words had been lost at the end, as "such practices Moses absolutely forbids." In this case a new paragraph would begin with ἔνιοι δέ, linked with the preceding by the antithesis of the two bondages, but introducing the new subject of indirectly idolatrous practices. What he means by the "like principle" would then become quite clear. It may be noted that in Lev. xix. the prohibition of printing marks comes in directly after and is followed shortly by denunciation of divination and the like.

§§ 59 ff. Goodenough, pp. 37 f., observes that Philo ignores the passages in Leviticus which prescribe the death-penalty for some kinds of divination and only alludes to Deut. xvii. where we have no punishment prescribed but expulsion from the commonwealth and that only indirectly. In this he sees a reflection of the fact that public opinion would not have tolerated stoning such persons, while the Roman government always discouraged and in A.D. 16 expelled them from Italy. But he fails to note that Deut. provided Philo with a far more specific list of the forms of μαντική, on which he enlarges in the following section, and also that it leads on to the promise of the true divination, which is described in § 65.

§ 67. *Only one temple.* Cohn and Heinemann note that Josephus also gives the same reason for the one temple (*Contra Apion.* ii. 193, *Ant.* iv. 200). It does not follow that Josephus is dependent on Philo. The argument of the oneness of God, which Josephus supplements with the oneness of the Hebrew race, was an obvious argument against the attempts to build other temples like that of Leontopolis in the Dispersion.

§§ 71 f. The temple here described is of course Herod's temple (18 or 19 B.C.), elaborately described by Josephus, *Wars* v. and *Ant.* xv. Philo (Mangey ii. 646, an extract from *De Providentia*) speaks of something which he saw at Ascalon, when he visited that city in the course of a journey to "the temple of his fathers to pray and sacrifice." The passage does not in the least suggest that this was his only visit to Jerusalem, and he may have gone there often, though I cannot find authority for Edersheim's statement that he acted as envoy to carry the tributes (see § 78). But whether he went there once or oftener, there is not much sign of personal observation in his description of the building itself, which is very slight compared with Josephus's. Heinemann (*Bildung*, p. 16) notes an inaccuracy, viz. that the sanctuary stood in the "very middle," whereas the part in front was much larger than the part behind. However, that the description should be slight is natural enough. He is expounding the laws of the Pentateuch and these did not provide for the building which would be needed when the nation was settled in Palestine, as he himself observes in *Mos.* ii. 72, 73, but only for a portable sanctuary. This last with its furniture was fully described in *Mos.* ii. 74-108, and the omission of any such description here may be due to a feeling that this one part of the law had been definitely suspended.

§ 79. (The consecration of the Levites.) The idea that the Levites received consecration as a reward for slaughtering the idolaters is supposed to have been obtained by Philo from Ex. xxxii. 29, "consecrate yourselves to the Lord," where the Hebrew phrase is literally "fill your hands," which the LXX translates literally, but in the indicative, "ye have filled your hands." In Ex. xxviii. 41 (37) the same Hebrew phrase evidently meaning "consecrate" or "install" *is* translated in LXX by "thou shalt fill their hands." See Driver on both passages. In the other eight passages, however, cited by Driver from the Pentateuch, where the same phrase is used in the Hebrew, the LXX has a different verb, *τελειόω* with or without *χεῖρας*. It seems to me rather doubtful whether Philo would have seen consecration in the words "ye have filled your hands every man against his son," etc., and more likely that he found it rather in the words that follow, "that a blessing should be given you."

§ 80. *Redundant . . . excrescence.* The E.V. in Lev. xxi. 18 has "anything superfluous," which *prima facie* would seem to be represented here by *κατὰ πλεονασμὸν περιττεύσαντος*. But in the LXX the word in the list of defects corresponding to the Hebrew translated as "superfluous" is *ὠτότμητος*, "with a split ear." Is this one of the few cases where Philo seems somehow to have known the Hebrew? Heinemann does not notice the point.

§ 83. *εὐχάς = votive offerings.* If the word is genuine here, this must surely be the sense, as what requires an unhampered rapidity must be a concrete object. The word seems to be used in the LXX in this sense, Deut. xii. 6, 17, 26, but I cannot find that it is so used elsewhere by Philo or other authors. Stephanus only quotes it from inscriptions and L. & S. (revised) do not mention it at all. I have left the text as Cohn prints it, pending further knowledge as to what is exactly meant by the ? appended to R's εὐχὰς, or what the Armenian, which is extant for this part, has to say.

§ 90. (φῶς ἡλίου as R, or as Cohn φῶς, ἡλίου ἥλιος ?) Cohn's principal objection to the reading of what he considers the best authority, R, is that ἡλίου ἀνέλαμψεν is an inadmissible hiatus. I do not know how far this argument is valid. Cohn nowhere, so far as I know, formulates his doctrine of hiatus. On p. 197 of the article in *Hermes*, 1908, he gives examples of corrigenda, and amongst them is γάμον οὕτως for γάμου οὕτως, and γάμων ἁγνήν for γάμου ἄγνης. I do not understand how on these principles his own ἡλίου ἥλιος is to stand. It is no doubt an objection to R's reading that it does not account for the φῶς ἥλιος or φῶς ἥλιος δ' of the other MSS. Could not this be met by φῶς ἥλιός τ'? Mangey has ἥλιος διανέλαμψε, to which Cohn objects that there is no such word, *i.e.* it is not found in the dictionaries. This is no argument at all, see on *Mos.* i. 172. Words compounded with διά and ἀνά are fairly common, and the διά would have some point here.

§ 96. *ἱερωμένον.* Cohn, who printed ἱερώμενον (present of ἱεράομαι), later declared for the MSS. ἱερωμένον (perfect participle of ἱερόω), and this is followed in the translation. But except for the MSS., ἱερώμενον = "acting as priest," makes equally good sense.

§ 103. *Scars and prints.* Cohn quotes Seneca, *De Ira*, i. 16. 7, *S.V.F.* i. 215 "Nam ut dicit Zenon, in sapientis quoque animo, etiam cum vulnus sanatum est, cicatrix manet. Sentiet itaque suspiciones quasdam et umbras affectuum, ipsis quidem carebit." This is not quite the same. The figure of the scarred soul was familiar to Philo from *Gorgias* 524 E.

§ 146. The thought here, though differing in detail, bears in mind *Timaeus* 69 E, where the mortal soul is placed in the thorax, with its nobler part = θυμός divided by the midriff from the baser = ἐπιθυμία. The θυμός is settled nearer the head, in order that it may be under the control of the reason and join with it in restraining the lusts. The sequel in Plato is definitely quoted in § 149, where see footnote.

§ 172. δι' ἣν αἰτίαν . . . Cohn suggests completing this passage thus: δι' ἣν αἰτίαν τοῦτο προστέτακται αὐτίκα λεκτέον· ἐαρινῇ μὲν κτλ. That is, ἣν stands for τίνα or ἥντινα and introduces an indirect question. This is no doubt common in Greek and may be in Philo, though I have not noticed an example: ii. 251 is not as it stands parallel. On the other hand, it may be pure relative, and introduce something of which the preceding statement is the cause. So above, § 124, and ii. 51.

§ 180. *At the beginning of the year.* Though the Jewish sacred year began with Nisan in the spring, the civil year continued to begin with Tishri in the autumn. See article "Time" in Hastings' Biblical Dictionary, and *cf.* Jos. *Ant.* i. 81. Heinemann, however, says that Philo knows nothing of this, and is merely following the Macedonian calendar introduced into Egypt. He certainly seems to take it for granted, ii. 153, that the month of the autumnal equinox is the "first in the sun's revolution." He must, however, have known that in Ex. xxiii. 16 and elsewhere in the Law, the Feast of Tabernacles is said to occur at the "going out (ἔξοδος) of the year."

§ 208. *Fullness and Want*, etc. That with Heracleitus κόρος = ἐκπύρωσις and χρησμοσύνη = διακόσμησις is also stated by Hippolytus (quoted in Zeller, *Pres. Phil.* ii. p. 46, note 1), καλεῖ δὲ αὐτὸ (*sc.* τὸ πῦρ) χρησμοσύνην καὶ κόρον. χρησμοσύνη δέ ἐστιν ἡ διακόσμησις κατ' αὐτόν, ἡ δὲ ἐκπύρωσις κόρος. The thought is perhaps the same in Diog. Laert. ix. 8 (of Heracleitus), "that what tends to γένεσις is called war and strife, what tends to ἐκπύρωσις is agreement and peace."

§ 242. *Thirdly because . . . thrust from office.* The thought lying behind this somewhat illogical sentence may be this. In § 117 he has said that all priests, whether suffering from defects or not, were entitled to eat the sacred meats, and therefore it might be thought that the defective are included in "every male priest"; *cf.* Lev. vi. 29. But in *v.* 26 we have "the priest that offers it shall eat of it," and as the defective cannot offer the sacrifice "every male priest" must be taken to mean "such as are qualified by freedom of defect."

§ 273. (Footnote *a.*) It must be remembered of course that the temple which Hecataeus mentioned is Zerubbabel's temple, not Herod's, which Philo saw. But it may be presumed that in a matter like this the third temple would reproduce the second, about the details of which I understand that little is known.

§ 291. (Wasps bred from horses.) So Plutarch (*Cleomenes, ad fin.*) mentions the idea that bees are bred from the carcasses of oxen, wasps from horses, beetles from donkeys, and serpents from men.

§ 318. *What is pleasing to nature*, etc. Philo, I suspect, substituted the Stoic "nature" for "before the Lord thy God," because he sees in καλόν and ἀρεστόν Stoic phraseology. The Stoic identification of τὸ καλόν with the Good is of course one of their leading doctrines, but ἀρεστόν was also a term applied to τὸ ἀγαθόν and ἀρετή, *cf. S.V.F.* iii. 208 τὴν δ' ἀρετὴν πολλοῖς ὀνόμασι προσαγορεύουσι. ἀγαθόν τε γὰρ λέγουσιν αὐτὴν ὅτι ἄγει ἡμᾶς ἐπὶ τὸν ὀρθὸν βίον· καὶ ἀρεστὸν ὅτι δοκιμαστόν ἐστιν ἀνυπόπτως. So also *ibid.* 88.

§ 321. λόγων ποτίμων. This phrase, which occurs again in ii. 62 and several times in other treatises, is no doubt a reminiscence of *Phaedrus* (243 D), which has also been clearly, though rather loosely, quoted in the preceding section. In *Quod Omn. Prob.* 13 the same two passages from the *Phaedrus* are brought together in the same sentence. The connexion of πότιμοι λόγοι with Plato is brought out most clearly in *Leg. All.* ii. 32, where, as in Plato, they serve to wash away the briny taste (τὸ ἁλμυρόν).

§ 322. (Footnote 1.) I have adopted Cohn's reading from R with the alteration of πνευμάτων into αὐρῶν. But the fact that the sense which lies behind R's nonsensical διανέμοντες αὐτῶν is easily recovered does not, I think, make the reading of A and H unworthy of consideration. Their wording τὰς . . ἀέρος εὐκρασίας ἀνέμων τε corresponds with the parallel in *De Praem.* 41 ἀέρος καὶ πνευμάτων εὐκρασίας, while none of the other parallels corresponds with the form postulated by R.

§§ 327–end. (Errors attacked in these sections.) It seems to me, subject to correction by others more expert in such matters, that Philo in these allegorical interpretations is not alluding to particular schools, but to ways of thinking in general. The theory of Ideas, which he here rather unexpectedly adopts as an essential part of the true creed, was, I think, denied by the Stoics (*S.V.F.* i. 65), and in the full Platonic sense by Aristotle, but did any school of Philo's time hold it? The atheistical argument in § 330 that God has been invented to deter men more effectually from evil-doing is developed at length in an iambic poem (to which Mr. Angus has called my attention), attributed to the tyrant Critias, and quoted by Sext. Emp. ix. 54. But this again does not belong to a particular school. The Stoics sometimes identified νοῦς and θεός (see on iii. 1), and Heinemann, (*Bildung*, p. 176) quotes Sen. *Ep.* xxxi. 11, where the "animus rectus bonus" is said to be "deus in humano corpore hospitans." But this surely belongs to a region of thought different from Philo's description of the practical achievements of mind. The votaries of sense may at first sight suggest the Epicureans, who held that sensations are always true, though our judgements about them are fallible (Zeller, *Stoics and Epicureans*, Eng. trans. p. 402), but that again is different from Philo's disquisition on the practical value of the senses. (Heinemann, *loc. cit.* says that the doctrine of the divinity of αἴσθησις was ascribed to Diogenes, but I have been unable to trace the reference.)

My feeling is that by his fourth and fifth class Philo is simply speaking of the οἴησις which, as he constantly says, leads men to ascribe to themselves what belongs to God, and the division into mind and sense, a very reasonable division since human self-confidence divides itself between the two, is merely made to fit in with Ammon and Moab, which, on philological grounds, he identifies with the two.

§ 333. *Fourth and fifth class also.* Heinemann suggests with considerable probability that in *De Mut.* 205 τεθλασμένοι γὰρ τὰ γεννητικὰ τῆς διανοίας ἢ καὶ τελείως ἀποκοπέντες οἱ τὸν ἴδιον νοῦν καὶ τὴν αἴσθησιν ἀποσεμνύνοντες ὡς μόνα τῶν κατ' ἀνθρώπους αἴτια πραγμάτων, we should read ἀποκοπέντες <ἢ> οἱ, thus bringing into the allegory as here Deut. xxiii. 3, as well as the two preceding verses. The only objection to this is that it leaves the τεθλασμένοι and ἀποκοπέντες without any theological interpretation corresponding to the other classes. Possibly this might be met by inserting <οἱ ἄθεοι ἢ> instead of merely <ἢ>.

APPENDIX TO *DE SPECIALIBUS LEGIBUS*, II

§ 4. For the elliptical oath *cf.* Plato, *Gorgias* 466 E, Aristoph. *Frogs* 1374. Commentators have ascribed the first example to piety, but this is incompatible with Plato's use of the names of deities elsewhere and even in the same dialogue, and no such motive can be ascribed to Aristophanes. See Thompson's note on *Gorgias*, *loc. cit.*

§ 46. *Lightened by anticipation.* On the value of πρόληψις (*praemeditatio*) as alleviating λύπη (*aegritudo*) see the discussion in Cic. *Tusc. Disp.* iii. 24-34 and 52 f., where the opinion is represented as Cyrenaic in opposition to the Epicurean that it was futile to dwell on evils beforehand. But it was also to some extent a Stoic view, see *ibid.* and *S.V.F.* iii. 482, where Poseidonius (or Chrysippus?) is quoted as saying προενδημεῖν δεῖν τοῖς πράγμασι μήπω τε παροῦσιν οἷον παροῦσι χρῆσθαι.

§ 56. *Some give it the name of the "season."* For the Pythagorean application of καιρός to Seven see Aristotle, *Met.* i. 5. 985 b. They say ὅτι τὸ μὲν τοιονδὶ τῶν ἀρίθμων πάθος, τὸ δὲ τοιονδὶ ψυχὴ καὶ νοῦς, ἕτερον δὲ καιρός (quoted in Ritter and Preller, 65 d), and more explicitly Alexander Aphr. in *Met.* pp. 28, 29 καιρὸν δὲ πάλιν ἔλεγον τὸν ἑπτά. δοκεῖ γὰρ τὰ φυσικὰ τοὺς τελείους καιροὺς ἴσχειν καὶ γενέσεως καὶ τελειώσεως κατὰ ἑβδομάδας (quoted *ibid.* 78 c).

For Philo's more or less mystical use of the word, apart from the number seven, see his comments on Num. xiv. 9 ἀφέστηκεν ὁ καιρὸς ἀπ' αὐτῶν, ὁ δὲ κύριος ἐν ἡμῖν in *De Post.* 121 f., and *De Mut.* 265. In the first of these καιρός is the passing moment or opportunity which men impiously take for their God, in the second it is the God-sent opportunity which they fail to take.

§ 69. *No man being naturally a slave.* This is said to be a Stoic doctrine. But among the passages collected by Arnim, *S.V.F.* iii. 349-366, there is no other which lays down the principle so explicitly as this. The Stoic mind concentrates itself on the thought that only the wise are truly free and only the foolish or wicked truly slaves, and does not concern itself with the actual institution of slavery. That the rights of humanity do not extend to the unreasoning animals appears in Cic. *De Fin.* iii. 67 (quoting Chrysippus) "cetera nata esse hominum causa et deorum . . . ut bestiis homines uti ad utilitatem suam possint sine iniuria."

§ 73. *Since it is a general truth . . . sole good.* I do not see any exact parallels in *S.V.F.* 327-332 (which Heinemann cites) to the doctrine implied here that ideally there is no such thing as a foreigner (ἀλλότριος), but it accords with *De Ios.* 29 that the Megalopolis, the world, has a single πολιτεία and a single law in the λόγος φύσεως.

For the Stoic canon (Στωικὸν δόγμα *De Post.* 133) that μόνον τὸ καλὸν ἀγαθόν see note on *Quod Det.* 9 (App.) where, however, the statement that "no Greek passage seems to reproduce the dogma exactly in this form" must have been written under a misapprehension. There are several passages in *S.V.F.* (see Index) which exhibit it or its Latin equivalent "solum bonum esse quod honestum sit." Note particularly Diog. Laert. vii. 101 λέγουσι δὲ μόνον τὸ καλὸν ἀγαθὸν εἶναι, καθά φησιν Ἑκάτων καὶ Χρύσιππος.

§ 82. *Tribe* (or *deme*?) *and ward.* "The full citizens in Alexandria were those enrolled in tribes and demes. The important and constant element was the deme rather than the tribe and during the Ptolemaic and earlier Roman period it was customary, since the deme-names of Alexandria and Ptolemais differed, to describe a citizen of either city by his deme only. The tribe-names were more fluid, thus we know that Claudius sanctioned a proposal to name a tribe in his honour," Bell, *Camb. Mod. Hist.* x. p. 295. The evidence for this statement (from Papyri?) is not given, nor is it stated whether it applies equally to the πολίτευμα of the Jews. If nothing is known to the contrary, Philo's words suggest that it does.

It should be noted, however, that Philo found δῆμος as well as φυλή in Num. xxxvi. (see *v.* 6). Apparently, however, they are there convertible terms. E.V. has "the family of the tribe."

§ 91. (Depreciation of athletes and athletic training.) This is not uncommon, especially in contrast with military training. *Cf.* Quintilian, x. 1. 33, where the athlete's "tori" or fleshy protuberances are contrasted with the military "lacerti." Several parallels are quoted by Peterson in his note on that passage, bringing out the idea that the athlete's training did not fit him to endure the various hardships of the soldier's life. Philo may have the same idea here, though he does not bring in the contrast with the soldier.

For πιαινομένων *cf. Leg. All.* i. 98, where the athlete's diet is ἕνεκα τοῦ πιαίνεσθαι καὶ ῥώννυσθαι, and for πολυσαρκία see Lucian, *Dial. Mort.* x. 5 (quoted by Peterson), where an athlete πολύσαρκός τις ὤν nearly makes Charon's boat sink.

§ 125. ἡ προεστῶσα ἀρχὴ κτλ. In making this statement, and indeed in the whole section, Philo has no biblical authority and is simply giving what he considers to be just, based apparently on Attic (or Alexandrian ?) law. In Attic law the archon (who seems to be alluded to in ἡ προεστῶσα ἀρχή) had the general duty of caring for orphans and heiresses. See Lipsius, *Att. Recht.* p. 58, though this seems to mean only the obligation to see that the legitimate ἐπίτροποι performed their duty (*ibid.* p. 525). Philo's words here would naturally imply something more definite than this and are not easy to reconcile with iii. 67, where proposals of marriage to orphan maidens are to be addressed "to the brothers or guardians or others who have charge of her."

§ 133 and sequel to § 139. (The double portion of the first-born.) Goodenough, pp. 56 f., after giving evidence of the right of the eldest son to a double portion in Ptolemaic Egypt as well as in Greece, holds that Philo has no scriptural warrant for attesting this as a general Mosaic law, but quotes Deut. xxi. as the nearest thing he can find in scripture to a law which had forced itself on Jewish practice. It seems to me that Philo could reasonably find an acknowledgement of the claims of primogeniture in v. 17, "for he is the beginning of his children (LXX) and to him belong the rights of the first-born (πρωτοτοκεῖα)." That is to say, what the law forbids in this passage is that the repudiation of the mother, who in Philo's view is not only hated but discarded (ἀπηλλαγμένη § 139), should be allowed to cancel the acknowledged rights of her son.

There is more to be said for Heinemann's contention that the arguments in §§ 132-139 imply that what was stated as a general law in § 133 only obtained in the particular case here discussed. The third reason in particular (§ 139) might be taken to mean that the duplication of the portion of the first-born was a compensation for the wrongs he had already suffered. But this is not necessarily so. Philo may mean, as indeed he implies in the last sentence, that the law wishes to protect the just rights of both families and shews its intention by asserting the special right of the first-born.

§ 145. *The Crossing-feast.* I have not found in any authority which I have seen any light thrown on Philo's departure from the ordinary explanation of Passover. Josephus, *Ant.* ii. 313 explains πάσχα as meaning ὑπερβασία (so also later Aquila; see Driver on Ex. xii. 13). It must be remembered that the point is disguised in the LXX, which translates the noun *pésah* in xii. 21 and 27 by πάσχα, but the verb *pâsah* in *vv.* 13 and 27 by σκεπάω and ἐσκέπασε, in *v.* 23 by παρελεύσεται. That Philo was not alone in his opinion is shewn by his statement that others allegorized in the same way, for such an allegory could only be founded on the "crossing" interpretation. That he believed διάβασις to be the correct translation appears in *De Mig.* 25 τὸ πάσχα, τὸ δέ ἐστιν ἑρμηνευθὲν διάβασις.

Ibid. From noon till eventide. See Ex. xii. 6, Lev. xxiii. 5, Num. ix. 3, where the R.V. has "at even," (margin) Hebrew "between the two evenings." The LXX translates this in Ex. and Num. by πρὸς ἑσπέραν, but in Leviticus by ἀνάμεσον τῶν ἑσπερινῶν. "For this the traditional interpretation adopted by the Pharisees and Talmudists was that the 'first' evening was when the heat of the sun begins to decrease, about 3 P.M., and that the second evening began with sunset" (Driver on Ex. xii. 6). Philo's interpretation is in accordance with another opinion quoted by Driver, "that the sacrifice if offered before noon was not valid."

§ 162. *Directly after the first day.* The Hebrew "on the morrow after the Sabbath," translated by the LXX in Lev. xxiii. 11 by ἐπαύριον τῆς πρώτης though in *v.* 15 by ἐπαύριον τῶν σαββάτων, is said to have been diversely interpreted by the Pharisees and Sadducees (see Thackeray on Jos. *Ant.* iii. 250). The Pharisees, with whom Josephus as well as Philo agrees, understood it to mean the second day of Unleavened Bread. The Sadducees held it to be on the day after the Sabbath, which necessarily occurred at some time in the festal week.

§ 176. (Text of ἀπὸ . . . μονάδος.) M has ἀλλὰ γὰρ ἐκείνης ἡμέρα πεντηκοστὴ καταριθμεῖται ἑβδόμη ἑβδομάς, ἐφ' αἷς ἱερὸν ἀριθμὸν ἐπισφραγιζομένης μονάδος. Nicetas ἀπὸ γὰρ ἐκείνης τῆς ἡμέρας πεντηκοστὴ ἀριθμεῖται ἑπτὰ ἑβδομάδες ἱερὸν ἀριθμὸν ἐπισφραγιζομένης μονάδος. Nicetas's text is followed by Mangey with the correction of ἑβδομάδες to -δων. Nicetas's ἀπὸ is clearly right (see Lev. xxiii. 15, for reckoning Pentecost from the Sheaf) and the question between his τῆς ἡμέρας . . . ἀριθμεῖται . . . and M's ἡμέρα . . . καταριθμεῖται is unimportant, but his ἑβδομάδες is impossible ; Cohn's correction to ἑβδομάσι agrees, as he says, with the parallel in *De Dec.* 160, whereas Mangey's ἑβδομάδων will make the sacred number 49 instead of 50. Cohn's correction of ἐφ' αἷς to ἀφέσεως seems to me much more doubtful. In *De Cong.* 109 which he cites, and a similar passage in *De Mut.* 228, an allegory is founded on the connexion of "release" with the Jubile of the fiftieth year. Here we are talking of a different feast which, except for the number 50, has no connexion with the Jubile, and there is no further allusion to the idea of release. The corruption of ἑβδόμη ἑβδομὰς ἐφ' αἷς in M may have arisen (1) by an assimilation of ἑβδομάδες to the singular verb καταριθμεῖται, (2) by a variation of construction between a relative clause and a genitive absolute.

§ 185. *Joy is the rational elevation or rising of the soul.* This is the regular Stoic definition of χαρά, in contrast with ἡδονή. See *S.V.F.* iii. 431, 432. Each of the "good emotional states" (εὐπάθειαι) is distinguished from the corresponding πάθος by being εὔλογος. Thus εὐλάβεια ("cautiousness") is opposed to φόβος as being εὔλογος ἔκκλισις, Diog. Laert. vii. 116.

§ 188. *Rules of good economy.* Lit. "laws of economic virtue." According to the Stoics οἰκονομική or the knowledge of what is profitable to the household is an ἀρετή (*S.V.F.* iii. 267) and only the wise man is οἰκονομικός (*ib.* 567). So Philo, *Quaestio in Gen. iv. 165* "urbanitas (*i.e.* πολιτική) et oeconomia cognatae sunt virtutes." *Cf. De Ebr.* 91.

§ 212. *In the scale of ascending powers.* I have not found the compound παραύξησις (-άνω) in Plato or Nicomachus meaning "to raise to a higher power." But the uncompounded verb or noun is common in this sense. So in *Rep.* 528 B the square is the δευτέρα αὔξη and the cube the τρίτη αὔξησις. In 587 D κατὰ δύναμιν καὶ τρίτην αὔξην seems to mean "by squaring and cubing." In Nicomachus xi. 15, 9 being thrice 3 by another 3 αὔξεται ἐπ' ἄλλο διάστημα and becomes 27.

§ 228. (Text of καὶ οὐ μόνον . . . παίδων.) The simplest suggestion I can make for this is to correct λογισμοὺς to λογισμοῖς καὶ. Translate "impressing them on the minds of the children both in the earlier and in the riper stage of youth." This will make good sense, giving *three* stages of parental instruction—early childhood, boyhood, and later adolescence. But I lack authority for the antithesis implied between νεάζειν and ἀκμάζειν, and also while λογισμός = "reasoning faculty" or "mind" is quite common in Philo, I have not found it in the plural.

Another difficulty felt by Cohn, that οἱ μὲν just above has no following δὲ, which leads him to suggest that the end of the sentence has been lost, does not seem to be weighty. Philo begins no doubt with thinking of the parents as μέν and the children as δέ, but that he should forget to express the latter formally does not seem unlike him.

§ 232. (The disobedient son.) In Deut. xxi. the incorrigible son is brought before the "elders," after which (LXX) he is denounced to the "men of the city," who thereupon stone him. Nothing is said of any right of either the "elders" or the "men of the city" to examine the accusation, but the account savours more of a judicial proceeding than Philo's words suggest. And Heinemann (*ad loc.* and *Bildung*, pp. 251) and Goodenough, p. 69 ff., may be right in tracing here the influence of the Roman *patria potestas*, as also in the doctrine of parental **δεσποτεία** in the next sentence.

§ 239. *Secondly, it would not be suitable . . . by kinship.* Heinemann aptly quotes Seneca, *De Beneficiis*, iv. 17 "quomodo nulla lex amare parentes . . . iubet (supervacuum est enim, in quod imus, impelli)."

§ 244. (Penalty for striking a parent.) Heinemann quotes Seneca, *Controv.* ix. 4 "qui patrem pulsaverit manus ei praecidantur," which he calls a Roman law and also declares it to come from the Twelve Tables. Goodenough, accepting the first part of this, bases on it an argument that the εὐπάρυφοι of § 244 are definitely Roman officials. Such a law is certainly not found among any of the fragments of the Twelve Tables known to us, but there is no reason to think that it is a Roman law at all. Seneca's words are no evidence. The laws which form the basis of the several *controversiae* need not have and do not claim to have any foundation in fact. In this particular case the theme is as follows: The law is supposed to be as stated above. A "tyrant" has commanded two sons to strike their father. One commits suicide rather than do so; the other obeys the command. When the tyrant has fallen or in one version has been killed by the same son, the son is charged under this law and arguments are adduced by the debaters for and against exacting the penalty. The same law with practically the same theme is noted by a scholiast as used by the Greek rhetor Syrianus (Walz, *Rhet. Graeci*, iv. 467), and, with different themes attached, in the Declamations ascribed to Quintilian 358, 362, 372. Another of Seneca's *Controv.* (viii. 2) starts with a law that amputation of the hands is the penalty for sacrilege. Whether these imaginary laws prescribing the mutilation of the offending member (*cf.* Deut. xxv. 11, 12, and iii. 175, below) are based on some old tradition, or are the product of the inventiveness of the rhetoricians, it is impossible to say. The only code known to us which assigns this punishment for striking a father is the Babylonian code of Hammurabi (about 2000 B.C.), and this is hardly likely to have influenced either the rhetor or Philo. The common assumption in the schools that such legislation existed or had existed somewhere would be enough to make him embark without further inquiry on a demonstration of its injustice.

§ 259. *Each of the other virtues is its own reward.* The sentiment is of course implicit in the common Stoic aphorism that virtue is *αὐτὴ δι' αὑτὴν αἱρετός* and *αὐταρκὴς πρὸς εὐδαιμονίαν.* The most exact parallel quoted is *S.V.F.* iii. 45, from Servius, "Stoici dicunt virtutem esse pro praemio si nulla sint praemia."

APPENDIX TO *DE SPECIALIBUS LEGIBUS*, III

§ 3. *The ocean of civil cares.* I do not know that we know enough about the dates of Philo's writings to say that Heinemann's positive statement that this refers to the serious troubles of A.D. 38–41 described in the *In Flaccum* and *Legatio ad Gaium* is impossible. But it is at any rate uncertain. Apart from such matters as the apparently unsuccessful attempt to interfere with Jewish religion mentioned in *De Som.* ii. 123 (where see note in App.), and the oppression of the tax-collectors noted below (§§ 159 ff.), there must have been considerable friction in Alexandria caused by the special position of the Jewish *πολιτεία* long before the outbreak. It is this to which I understand the *φθόνος* to refer, rather than, as Goodenough, to the conventional idea of the jealousy of fate shewn to prosperity, an idea which does not seem to fit in well with the epithets *μισόκαλος* and *κακῶν ἀργαλεώτατον*.

§ 6. *Yet . . . even for this.* The meaning of §§ 1-6, when reduced to plain prose, is that the days when Philo could devote his whole powers to philosophy are far back in the past. He is now permanently engaged and sometimes absorbed in political business of a troublesome nature, but there are times when he can get some leisure for his favourite studies and use his philosophical insight (§ 4). There are indeed other times (§ 5) when he can shake off the shackles altogether and perhaps feel the inspiration which he described in *De Mig.* § 35. But this is not one of these times. His condition is that he can open his eyes as in § 4, though he cannot triumphantly ride the waves as in § 5; yet even for this he is thankful.

If it is asked why this eloquent outcry is introduced at this point, I think it is enough to say that it is a natural literary device marking that he is just halfway through his great subject. Such prologues at pauses in a long disquisition are not, I think, uncommon. They appear, for instance, in Quintilian. It is possible, though I think less probable, that it means to indicate that the work has actually been interrupted by civic troubles and that καιροῦ διδόντος at the end of the preceding treatise should be translated "when opportunity offers," with the suggestion that the opportunity will have to be waited for.

Goodenough's idea (p. 9), that the outcry is elicited by a feeling that the criminal and civil laws now to be treated forcibly remind him of his civic distractions, seems to me fanciful.

§ 13. (Persian incest.) See Clement Alex. *Strom.* iii. 2. 11, who cites the early historian Xanthus as saying μίγνυνται οἱ Μάγοι μητράσι καὶ θυγατράσι, and couples them with sisters. In *Paedagogus*, i. 7 he says the same of the Persians in general. Tertullian also in *Ad Nationes*, i. 15 and *Apol.* 9 repeats the statement on the authority of Ctesias, another early historian. Philo evidently assumes that these early authorities hold good for his own time, though he says nothing of the Magi, for whom elsewhere he expresses admiration (see on § 100 below). Compare on the other hand Sext. Emp. *Pyrrh. Hyp.* iii. 305 Πέρσαι δὲ καὶ μάλιστα αὐτῶν οἱ σοφίαν ἀσκεῖν δοκοῦντες, οἱ Μάγοι, γαμοῦσι τὰς μητέρας καὶ Αἰγύπτιοι τὰς ἀδελφὰς ἄγονται πρὸς γάμον. The charge against the Persians is often repeated in later writers (references in Mangey *ad loc.* and Commentator on Clement (Migne)).

§§ 17-18. (Persian civil troubles.) No suggestions are given by Heinemann as to what events, if any, Philo has in mind. Possibly he may have known of the troubles both before and after the succession of Darius Hystaspes and after the death of Xerxes, and a number of fratricides are recorded, beginning with the murder of Smerdis by Cambyses, and before or after the accessions of Darius Nothu and Ochus and Codomannus. See Rawlinson, *Fifth Grea Monarchy*. But his words fit better into more contemporar matters and he is more likely to be thinking of the late Parthian empire which absorbed the Persian. He was quit aware that the Parthians had conquered the Persians (*D Ios.* 136, *Quod Deus* 174), but he might, like Horace identify the two in a vague statement of this kind. Plutarch *Lucullus* 36 speaks of the Parthian power as weakened ὑπ ἐμφυλίων καὶ προσοίκων πολέμων at the time of Lucullus campaign (about 78 B.C.), and the civil war between Mithradates III and Orodes after their murder of their father Phraates, a war which ended with the victory of Orodes and the execution of his brother, would be well known to Philo.

§ 22. *Marriage with half-sisters on the father's side.* So Cimon married his *germana* (here=ὁμοπάτριος) *soror*, "nam Atheniensibus licet eodem patre natas uxores ducere," Corn. Nep. *Cim.* i. 2. Themistocles' daughter married her brother οὐκ ὄντα ὁμομήτριον, Plut. *Them.* 32. The scholiast on Aristophanes, *Nubes* 1372, where the poet denounces marriage with an ὁμομήτριος ἀδελφή, says that since marriage between ὁμοπάτριοι was lawful at Athens, the word is added εἰς αὔξησιν τοῦ ἀδικήματος. Philo is right in saying that there was such a law at Athens, whether dating from Solon or not. He does not say that it was a common practice, and when Plato, *Laws* 838 A, B puts brother and sister without adding ὁμομήτριος among the relations between which intercourse was not only unlawful but felt so strongly to be unlawful that most people had no desire for it, it is difficult to suppose that it was common.

No evidence appears to be forthcoming for Philo's statement about the Spartan law.

§ 23. (Egyptian marriage with sisters on both sides.) See Diod. Sic. i. 27, where the practice is said to be modelled on the marriage of Isis and Osiris, also the words of Sext. Emp. quoted in note on § 13. Goodenough cites for a later age from the Papyri a card of invitation issued by a mother for the marriage of one of her sons to a daughter.

§ 30. (Remarriage with a divorced wife). On this point Goodenough, pp. 85, 86 calls attention to the *Lex Iulia de adulteriis*, 18 B.C., which provides that among the things which that law punishes as adultery is "si adulterii damnatam sciens uxorem duxerit," *Dig.* iv. 37. 1. Assuming, then, that the remarriage shewed that the intermediate union was adultery, the offender would be liable under Roman law in Philo's time. Elsewhere (see references in *Dict. of Ant.*) condonation of adultery is treated under the same law as *lenocinium*. Is this the Latin equivalent for what Philo calls προαγωγεία? In Greek law this last was a capital crime, as Goodenough notes (though only perhaps if proved to be ἐπὶ μισθῷ. See Lipsius, *A.R.* p. 435).

§§ 34-36. Heinemann, *Bildung*, pp. 262-267, has a long

and careful discussion of the views expressed here by Philo, and less specifically in other places (*Quod Det.* 102, *De Ios.* 43, *Mos.* i. 28), as compared with Rabbinical and Greek opinion. The upshot of it is that Philo goes far beyond the latter at any rate. The only passage cited which at all approaches this is from Charondas (Stobaeus, *Flor.* ii. p. 184 Meineke). According to Zeller (*Stoics and Epicureans*, Eng. Trans. p. 303), the Stoics merely required chastity and moderation in marriage (including total abstinence from pregnant women).

§§ 37-38. Philo may also be bearing in mind Deut. xxiii. 17, where *ὁ πορνεύων* (E.V. "sodomite") is coupled with *πόρνη* as forbidden in Israel. *πορνεύων* and *πόρνος* seem regularly to mean a male prostitute rather than as in Heb. xii. 16 simply a fornicator. Though no punishment is prescribed in Deut., the fact that Philo seems to base the stoning of the *πόρνη* on this verse (see on § 81) shews that he would feel the same about the *πόρνος*.

§ 40. *Celebrating the rites of Demeter*, etc. I have not been able to find any evidence in support of this account of the prominence of male prostitutes in the mysteries of Demeter or similar rites; nor yet of the next sections describing the honours paid to the castrated. No doubt the Galli, the priests of Attis, were well known and also the votaries who castrated themselves in honour of Attis. See Frazer (*Adonis, Attis, and Osiris*, pp. 22 ff.), who also mentions the eunuch priests of Artemis of Ephesus, and the Syrian Astartē. But Philo can hardly be referring to these.

§ 51. (Death penalty for harlots.) This severity is in accordance with *De Ios.* 43, where Joseph is represented as saying "with us death is the penalty for harlots," but inconsistent with i. 81, where the repentant harlot may retain her civic rights and marry anyone except a priest, and presumably not merely escape death, but remain unpunished.

§ 72. *Documents containing the names, etc.* Heinemann, *Bildung*, p. 289, gives an excellent parallel from the Papyri. "The announcement of marriage" contains the names of the parties and of the parents of the wife, the amount of her dowry, the guarantee of the husband to make fitting provision, the promise of fidelity on both sides, and the penalties in the event of infringement.

Goodenough's theory (p. 92) that this *ὁμολογία* is regarded by Philo as justifying marital relations before the complete marriage, and that therefore ὑπογάμιον (or ὑπογάμιον ἀδίκημα) was *de facto* adultery seems to me to be negatived by the phrase in § 74 (which Goodenough passes over very lightly), that the girl has her virginity to defend. Clearly some people did not regard it as adultery, and, when Philo maintains the contrary, he seems to me to be upholding what he takes to be the view of Deuteronomy, which assigns the same punishment as for adultery, and speaks of the violator as having dishonoured (ἐταπείνωσε) his neighbour's wife. For the equivalence of betrothal to marriage see also i. 107, where it is implied that the betrothed is no longer a παρθένος, "even though her body is pure."

§ 84. τὸ τῆς τιμωρίας ἀθάνατον. Cohn (*Hermes*, 1908, p. 206) offers a solution of this corruption which perhaps is preferable to that suggested in the translation. He suggests that εἶδος or an equivalent word has fallen out, and that ἀθάνατον is the result of a gloss explanatory of εἶδος. The glossator wrote α′ (=ἕνα) θάνατον, and this having been re-embodied in the text in the form of ἀθάνατον ultimately ousted εἶδος.

In the first part of the sentence the suggestion of inserting ἀμειλίκτως is due to H. Grégoire in *Hermes*, 1909, p. 320, though he would place it between ἐργασάμενον and ἀναιρετέον.

§ 86. (Intention to kill.) Heinemann points out that in giving this interpretation to Ex. xxi. 14 ἐπιθῆται . . . δόλῳ, and extending it to cover βούλευσις in general, Philo is following Greek law, τὸν βουλεύσαντα ἐν τῷ αὐτῷ ἐνέχεσθαι καὶ τὸν χειρὶ ἐργασάμενον, Andocides i. 94.

§ 89. (Punishment of poisoners.) Heinemann and Goodenough point out that Philo's views on this subject are in accordance with the spirit of the *Lex Cornelia de sicariis et veneficis* (about 81 B.C.) which decreed punishment for preparing, having or selling poisons for the destruction of human life, as well as for actually using them. Josephus, *Ant.* iv. 279 is closer to the Roman law, as he expressly includes the possession of such poisons as criminal. Both authors apparently go beyond the *Lex Cornelia* in saying that poison intended to cause other injuries than death. (Jos. εἰς ἄλλας βλάβας πεποιημένον is on the same footing.)

§ 100. (The Magi and the true magic.) Mangey and others quote for the last part of the sentence Cic. *De Div.* i. 91 "Nec quisquam rex Persarum potest esse qui non ante Magorum disciplinam scientiamque perceperit."

As to what Philo understands by "true magic" I hazard the conjecture that he has in mind the distinction between "artificiosa divinatio" and "naturalis," a distinction which is made by the Stoic in the *De Div.*, and accepted by his opponent. The coincidence quoted above inclines one to think that both this passage and the substance of *De Div.* i. are based on some Stoic treatise (? Poseidonius). In the *De Div.* the "artificiosa" comprises haruspicy, augury, and the like, while the "naturalis" is limited to inspiration, such as oracles, and dreams. It seems to be equated in i. 90 with "ratio naturae quam φυσιολογίαν Graeci appellant." This agrees with our passage and with *Quod Omn. Prob.* 74, where the Magi are extolled as "researching in tranquillity into the works (or facts) of nature and by clearer visions receiving and giving revelations (ἱεροφαντοῦνταί τε καὶ ἱεροφαντοῦσι) of divine excellences." Further at the end of *De Div.* i. the Stoic, though he has defended the "artificiosa" in general, rejects the charlatan impostors in much the same tone as Philo takes in § 101. Compare also *Mos.* i. 277 where ἔντεχνος μαντική was inadequately translated by "his art of wizardry." Rather it means the "artificiosa" discarded for the "naturalis" of the prophetic spirit. It is an objection to this, but not I think a fatal objection, that either Philo or Cicero must have misunderstood the reference to the Magi. For in Cicero the Magi "augurantur et divinant," *i.e.* practise the "artificiosa."

Heinemann thinks that Philo is just adopting the accepted Stoic definition of μαντική as ἐπιστήμη οὖσα θεωρητικὴ καὶ ἐξηγητικὴ τῶν ὑπὸ θεῶν ἀνθρώποις διδομένων σημείων (*S.V.F.* ii. 1018, iii. 654), while giving the last words a "monotheistic" twist. He means, I suppose, that φύσις=(as often) θεός is substituted for θεῶν. In view of Philo's wholesale denunciation of μαντική in i. 59 ff. it seems to me improbable that he would accept this definition without more explanation than this.

It is possible, no doubt, that he is simply echoing the vague popular idea that there is a respectable as well as a disreputable magic, which we find also in the N.T. with the "wise men" from the east on the one hand and Simon and Elymas on the other, all described as μάγοι.

§ 102. θανατῶντας. The same sense for θανατᾶν, *i.e.* "to be about to die," is demanded certainly or preferably in *De Virt.* 34, *De Ex.* 159, and *De Aet.* 89. The word cannot be an interpolation in all these places; nor does Cohn raise any objection there. It is true that the accepted meaning of θανατᾶν is "to desire death," as in *Phaedo* 64 B. If here and elsewhere it carries the sense of imminence rather than desire, it is presumably on the analogy of verbs of sickness such as ὑδεριάω = "be dropsical" or ὀφθαλμιάω = "have sore eyes." In this way it may easily = "sick unto death," and thence pass on to being doomed to death from other causes than sickness. It is a pertinent objection that these verbs are in -ιάω rather than -άω, though indeed to add the vowel in each case in Philo would be less drastic than expunging the word. At any rate the positive fact for the lexicographer is that in these four places the MSS. of Philo exhibit θανατᾶν as = "being near to death." Possibly to these should be added i. 237, where θανατῶσαν νόσον is corrected by Cohn to θανατοῦσαν νόσον. That the disease itself is near to death (*cf.* "this sickness is not unto death") would be a fairly natural extension.

§ 108. *Both for the outrage, and for obstructing nature,* etc. Goodenough, pp. 113 f. points out that Josephus, *Ant.* iv. 278 mentions a double fine, (1) for diminishing the population; (2) compensation to the husband, and that Philo's two reasons, "nature" and ὕβρις, roughly correspond to these. He infers that Philo also contemplates a double fine. He may very likely have found the LXX ἐπιζήμιον ζημιωθήσεται καθότι ἂν ἐπιβάλῃ ὁ ἀνὴρ τῆς γυναικὸς δώσει μετὰ ἀξιώματος obscure.

§ 109. *A human being . . . from confinement.* Heinemann and Goodenough note a discrepancy between this and § 117, where Philo accepts the Stoic theory (*S.V.F.* ii. 806) that the child is not a separate living creature till it has left its mother's womb. I do not think there is any real discrepancy. Here he is stating what he considers to be implied by the LXX, *i.e.* that the child at this stage is (potentially) a human being. There he argues that while the Stoic theory may be true and is supported by hign authorities, the stricter law of the LXX seems to emphasize the sacredness of the infant and shews *a fortiori* how heinous is the destruction of the fully born. *Cf.* for a very similar argument *De Virt.* 137, 138.

§ 120. (Involuntary homicide.) What does Philo understand by this? In the Pentateuch it seems to mean accidental homicide, see particularly the example given in Deut. xix. 5 of the man killed by the slip of the head from his neighbour's axe. Nothing is said in these sections exactly in contradiction of this, though the *μὴ ἐκ προνοίας* in § 128 may point to a wider interpretation. But in §§ 92 and 104 we have had suggestions that he regards homicide, if committed in sudden anger or in an unpremeditated quarrel, as different from ordinary murder, though he does not follow this up (see notes on §§ 92 and 104). His view in fact seems much the same as that of Plato, who (*Laws* 866 D ff.) discusses the point and says that one who kills another in hot blood or unpremeditatedly is *οὐ παντάπασιν ἀκούσιος ἀλλ' εἰκὼν ἀκουσίου*. Philo's *ἡμίεργον* in § 92 is a rough equivalent of Plato's *εἰκών* ("likeness or shadow," Jowett) and indeed may be a reminiscence of it. That is to say, it is something between *ἀκούσιος* and *ἑκούσιος*. One may conjecture that he does not consider it worthy of death, but in face of the law of Ex. xxi. 18, 19, described in § 100, refrains from saying so.

§§ 131-136. *The death of the high priest.* Why the death of one high priest should abrogate the reasons assigned for the limit of the exile, when he is immediately succeeded by another, is not here discussed. The real explanation, as I understand from the commentators, is that the rights of the avenger of blood had to be limited, and that the succession of a new high priest, like the accession of a new sovereign, made a convenient limit. Philo himself in *De Fuga* 106 f. has pronounced the enactment, if literally taken, to be absurd, and therefore explains the death of the high priest as the death of the Logos in the soul.

§ 148. (Punishment in the case where a man is killed by falling into an unguarded pit.) Philo's statement in the face of the absence of any specific provision in the Law is regarded by Goodenough, p. 129 as clear evidence that he is here giving us the practice of the Jewish courts in Egypt. I think it is merely one of his reasonable inferences from analogous cases. By making the negligence punishable when an animal is killed, the law suggests that it is still more punishable in the case of a human being. What he says really amounts to saying that no one need think himself debarred from making a complaint to the court, which will then have to follow the principle laid down in the matter of the unguarded well, *i.e.* either death or a fine. He naturally hesitates to prescribe death in so many words, but evidently thinks it would be justified, as also in the case of the *φόνος* of the unguarded roof mentioned in § 149.

§ 149. (The unguarded roof.) It is noteworthy that Josephus,

Ant. iv. 284 also couples this with the unguarded pit, though they came from quite different parts of the Pentateuch, and this has sometimes (see Thackeray *ad loc.*) been regarded as one of the points which shew Josephus's dependence upon Philo. See vol. vi., Introd. p. xxii, note *e*. I think the analogy of the two is obvious enough to have struck both writers independently.

§ 164. (Traitors and tyrants, etc.) Heinemann in his note says positively that the latter law, *i.e.* against tyrants (in *Bildung*, p. 212, both laws, regarded as a single law), is an old Macedonian law. Goodenough accepts this and infers that it was probably continued in Ptolemaic Egypt and therefore known to Philo. All this has very slender foundation. Heinemann's authority is two passages (cited quite reasonably by Cohn as illustrations), one from Curtius Rufus vi. 42. 20, the other from Cicero, *De Inventione*, ii. 144. The first of these mentions in connexion with a plot against Alexander a "law of the Macedonians providing that the relations of a conspirator against the king should be put to death." Here it is relations (*propinqui*), not children, and an "insidiator" is not the same as a προδότης. Still there may be some connexion.

The second passage deals with a problem in the rhetorical schools. There are supposed to be two laws: one that the tyrannicide may claim *any* reward; another that the "five nearest relations of the tyrant shall be put to death." The example given is that of Alexander, tyrant of Pherae, who was murdered in 367 B.C., by his wife. By the first law she can claim the life of her son by him as the reward; by the second he must be put to death, and the arguments for either course are elaborately discussed by Cicero. As apparently Alexander's wife was acting in concert with her brother, who afterwards assumed the tyranny (Diod. xvi. 14), the question can hardly have arisen, and if it did, Pherae was presumably not under Macedonian jurisdiction. But it is quite unsafe to assume that such a law was in existence. The death of Alexander was a famous case of tyrannicide and a useful peg on which to hang one of the controversies, in which tyrannicide was a favourite subject, and to which historicity was a matter of complete indifference. Heinemann and Goodenough have fallen into the same error as on ii. 244, in mistaking these fictions of the schools for sober history; though it must not be assumed that because they are worthless as evidence, Philo had not some other ground, historical or traditional, for his statements.

§ 171. *The temple.* Possibly τὸ ἱερόν may have become in the διασπορά a conventional name for the synagogue as the best possible substitute for the temple, particularly in Alexandria where the synagogue is said to have been especially magnificent and famous (*Jewish Encyclopedia, s.v.* synagogue); and so too with the common collocation εὐχὰς καὶ θυσίας for the due performance of all religious rites possible.

On the strict seclusion of women indicated in this section Heinemann (*Bildung*, p. 234) quotes *In Flaccum* 89 (of the Jewish women in Alexandria) γύναια κατάκλειστα μηδὲ τὴν αὔλειον προερχόμενα καὶ θαλαμευόμεναι παρθένοι, though he points out that it reflects Greek rather than Jewish ideas.

Goodenough cites a passage from the female Pythagorean Phintys, quoted in Stobaeus (Meineke, iii. 64), which in some ways curiously resembles this, but shews less strictness. Phintys's lady may go out duly attended not only to public worship but to see spectacles (θεωρίαι) and to shop.

§ 176. (Exclusion of women from gymnastic competitions.) The only evidence for this known to me is their exclusion from the Olympic games mentioned in Aelian, *V.H.* x. 1, and Pausanias, v. 6. 7. Elsewhere Pausanias, vi. 20. 9 (if the text is right) states that virgins were not excluded.

§ 181. (Penalties not corresponding to the crimes.) Goodenough, p. 137 says that the list of punishments here given follows those provided in Greek law for the several crimes. This seems to be only partially correct. The punishment for αἰκία was a monetary fine, and murderers were apparently allowed to evade the death-penalty by flying the country. But the punishment for τραύματα ἐκ προνοίας, *i.e.* wounding intended to kill, which perhaps may be equated with Philo's τραύματα καὶ πηρώσεις, was banishment, not ἀτιμία, which is a loss of civil rights not entailing banishment. It seems to be true that theft might sometimes be punished by a few days' imprisonment as a supplement to a manifold restitution of the things stolen, but what Philo here means is imprisonment instead of such restitution. I do not see any reason to think that he refers to any particular body of legislation.

The references given by Goodenough to Lipsius are to pp. 646, 605-607, 440, to which add for wilful murder, 603-604.

§ 183. *ἀποφράδες ἡμέραι*. The idea suggested in the translation is that, as all religious rites are forbidden on these days, the action cannot desecrate them. Compare Lucian, *Pseudologistes* 12, where the performance of sacred rites is included among the things prohibited on the Apophrades. Something of the same sort appears in *Laws* 800 D, where Plato forbids the melancholy strains used at sacrifices as blasphemy and relegates them to the Apophrades.

It seems possible, however, that the contrast intended may be the opposite of this, namely that things which are lawful on the feast-days are intolerable at other times. Philo may be thinking of pagan usage around him and allude to the license allowed on public feast-days (*cf. De Cher.* 91 ff.). This will give *ἀποφράδες ἡμέραι* something more like its ordinary meaning. Days which are inauspicious for ordinary business will be still more inauspicious for unlawful actions.

§ 184. *The most conspicuous and distinguished situation.* Heinemann quotes Cic. *De Natura Deorum*, ii. 140 "oculi tanquam speculatores altissimum locum obtinent," but the thought there is somewhat different, rather of convenience than dignity, as it continues "ex quo plurima conspicientes fungantur suo munere."

§ 204. (The law of the millstone). Heinemann, who (*Bildung*, p. 430) gives *ἵεται ἐπ' ἀνδροφονίαν* the somewhat stronger sense of "aims at murder," considers Philo's comments to be a rhetorical exaggeration, and that no such murderous intention on the part of the creditors is suggested by a law which merely prohibits the attachment for debt of an indispensable article. (Such laws are paralleled in other legislations, indeed in the Common Law of England, see Adam Smith *ad loc.* Goodenough (p. 142) aptly cites out of the Papyri an example from the Ptolemaic law of Egypt, where a farmer's cattle and tools and a weaver's loom are mentioned.) But Philo gives a natural interpretation of the strong phrase *ψυχὴν ἐνεχυράζει*. It must be remembered that he only notes this law incidentally to strengthen his point of the criminality of destroying a man's teeth.

Printed in Great Britain by R. & R. CLARK, LIMITED, *Edinburgh*

THE LOEB CLASSICAL LIBRARY

VOLUMES ALREADY PUBLISHED

LATIN AUTHORS

Ammianus Marcellinus. J. C. Rolfe. 3 Vols.
Apuleius : The Golden Ass (Metamorphoses). W. Adlington (1566). Revised by S. Gaselee.
St. Augustine : City of God. 7 Vols. Vol. I. G. E. McCracken. Vol. II. W. M. Green. Vol. III. D. Wiesen. Vol. IV. P. Levine. Vol. V. E. M. Sanford and W. M. Green. Vol. VI. W. C. Greene.
St. Augustine, Confessions of. W. Watts (1631). 2 Vols.
St. Augustine : Select Letters. J. H. Baxter.
Ausonius. H. G. Evelyn White. 2 Vols.
Bede. J. E. King. 2 Vols.
Boethius : Tracts and De Consolatione Philosophiae. Rev. H. F. Stewart and E. K. Rand.
Caesar : Alexandrian, African and Spanish Wars. A. G. Way.
Caesar : Civil Wars. A. G. Peskett.
Caesar : Gallic War. H. J. Edwards.
Cato and Varro : De Re Rustica. H. B. Ash and W. D. Hooper.
Catullus. F. W. Cornish : Tibullus. J. B. Postgate ; and Pervigilium Veneris. J. W. Mackail.
Celsus : De Medicina. W. G. Spencer. 3 Vols.
Cicero : Brutus and Orator. G. L. Hendrickson and H. M. Hubbell.
Cicero : De Finibus. H. Rackham.
Cicero : De Inventione, etc. H. M. Hubbell.
Cicero : De Natura Deorum and Academica. H. Rackham.
Cicero : De Officiis. Walter Miller.
Cicero : De Oratore, etc. 2 Vols. Vol. I : De Oratore, Books I and II. E. W. Sutton and H. Rackham. Vol. II : De Oratore, Book III ; De Fato ; Paradoxa Stoicorum ; De Partitione Oratoria. H. Rackham.
Cicero : De Republica, De Legibus, Somnium Scipionis. Clinton W. Keyes.

Cicero: De Senectute, De Amicitia, De Divinatione. W. A. Falconer.
Cicero: In Catilinam, Pro Murena, Pro Sulla, Pro Flacco. Louis E. Lord.
Cicero: Letters to Atticus. E. O. Winstedt. 3 Vols.
Cicero: Letters to his Friends. W. Glynn Williams. 3 Vols.
Cicero: Philippics. W. C. A. Ker.
Cicero: Pro Archia, Post Reditum, De Domo, De Haruspicum Responsis, Pro Plancio. N. H. Watts.
Cicero: Pro Caecina, Pro Lege Manilia, Pro Cluentio, Pro Rabirio. H. Grose Hodge.
Cicero: Pro Caelio, De Provinciis Consularibus, Pro Balbo. R. Gardner.
Cicero: Pro Milone, In Pisonem, Pro Scauro, Pro Fonteio, Pro Rabirio Postumo, Pro Marcello, Pro Ligario, Pro Rege Deiotaro. N. H. Watts.
Cicero: Pro Quinctio, Pro Roscio Amerino, Pro Roscio Comoedo, Contra Rullum. J. H. Freese.
Cicero: Pro Sestio, In Vatinium. R. Gardner.
[Cicero]: Rhetorica ad Herennium. H. Caplan.
Cicero: Tusculan Disputations. J. E. King.
Cicero: Verrine Orations. L. H. G. Greenwood. 2 Vols.
Claudian. M. Platnauer. 2 Vols.
Columella: De Re Rustica, De Arboribus. H. B. Ash, E. S. Forster, E. Heffner. 3 Vols.
Curtius, Q.: History of Alexander. J. C. Rolfe. 2 Vols.
Florus. E. S. Forster; and Cornelius Nepos. J. C. Rolfe.
Frontinus: Stratagems and Aqueducts. C. E. Bennett and M. B. McElwain.
Fronto: Correspondence. C. R. Haines. 2 Vols.
Gellius. J. C. Rolfe. 3 Vols.
Horace: Odes and Epodes. C. E. Bennett.
Horace: Satires, Epistles, Ars Poetica. H. R. Fairclough.
Jerome: Select Letters. F. A. Wright.
Juvenal and Persius. G. G. Ramsay.
Livy. B. O. Foster, F. G. Moore, Evan T. Sage, A. C. Schlesinger and R. M. Geer (General Index). 14 Vols.
Lucan. J. D. Duff.
Lucretius. W. H. D. Rouse.
Martial. W. C. A. Ker. 2 Vols.
Minor Latin Poets: from Publilius Syrus to Rutilius Namatianus, including Grattius, Calpurnius Siculus,

Nemesianus, Avianus, with "Aetna," "Phoenix" and other poems. J. Wight Duff and Arnold M. Duff.
Ovid: The Art of Love and other Poems. J. H. Mozley.
Ovid: Fasti. Sir James G. Frazer.
Ovid: Heroides and Amores. Grant Showerman.
Ovid: Metamorphoses. F. J. Miller. 2 Vols.
Ovid: Tristia and Ex Ponto. A. L. Wheeler.
Petronius. M. Heseltine: Seneca: Apocolocyntosis. W. H. D. Rouse.
Phaedrus and Babrius (Greek). B. E. Perry.
Plautus. Paul Nixon. 5 Vols.
Pliny: Letters. Melmoth's translation revised by W. M. L. Hutchinson. 2 Vols.
Pliny: Natural History. 10 Vols. Vols. I-V and IX. H. Rackham. Vols. VI-VIII. W. H. S. Jones. Vol. X. D. E. Eichholz.
Propertius. H. E. Butler.
Prudentius. H. J. Thomson. 2 Vols.
Quintilian. H. E. Butler. 4 Vols.
Remains of Old Latin. E. H. Warmington. 4 Vols. Vol. I (Ennius and Caecilius). Vol. II (Livius, Naevius, Pacuvius, Accius). Vol. III (Lucilius, Laws of the XII Tables). Vol. IV (Archaic Inscriptions).
Sallust. J. C. Rolfe.
Scriptores Historiae Augustae. D. Magie. 3 Vols.
Seneca: Apocolocyntosis. *Cf.* Petronius.
Seneca: Epistulae Morales. R. M. Gummere. 3 Vols.
Seneca: Moral Essays. J. W. Basore. 3 Vols.
Seneca: Tragedies. F. J. Miller. 2 Vols.
Sidonius: Poems and Letters. W. B. Anderson. 2 Vols.
Silius Italicus. J. D. Duff. 2 Vols.
Statius. J. H. Mozley. 2 Vols.
Suetonius. J. C. Rolfe. 2 Vols.
Tacitus: Dialogus. Sir Wm. Peterson; and Agricola and Germania. Maurice Hutton.
Tacitus: Histories and Annals. C. H. Moore and J. Jackson. 4 Vols.
Terence. John Sargeaunt. 2 Vols.
Tertullian: Apologia and De Spectaculis. T. R. Glover; Minucius Felix. G. H. Rendall.
Valerius Flaccus. J. H. Mozley.
Varro: De Lingua Latina. R. G. Kent. 2 Vols.
Velleius Paterculus and Res Gestae Divi Augusti. F. W. Shipley.

VIRGIL. H. R. Fairclough. 2 Vols.
VITRUVIUS: DE ARCHITECTURA. F. Granger. 2 Vols.

GREEK AUTHORS

ACHILLES TATIUS. S. Gaselee.
AELIAN: ON THE NATURE OF ANIMALS. A. F. Scholfield. 3 Vols.
AENEAS TACTICUS, ASCLEPIODOTUS AND ONASANDER. The Illinois Greek Club.
AESCHINES. C. D. Adams.
AESCHYLUS. H. Weir Smyth. 2 Vols.
ALCIPHRON, AELIAN AND PHILOSTRATUS: LETTERS. A. R. Benner and F. H. Fobes.
APOLLODORUS. Sir James G. Frazer. 2 Vols.
APOLLONIUS RHODIUS. R. C. Seaton.
THE APOSTOLIC FATHERS. Kirsopp Lake. 2 Vols.
APPIAN'S ROMAN HISTORY. Horace White. 4 Vols.
ARATUS. *Cf.* CALLIMACHUS.
ARISTOPHANES. Benjamin Bickley Rogers. 3 Vols. Verse trans.
ARISTOTLE: ART OF RHETORIC. J. H. Freese.
ARISTOTLE: ATHENIAN CONSTITUTION, EUDEMIAN ETHICS, VIRTUES AND VICES. H. Rackham.
ARISTOTLE: THE CATEGORIES. ON INTERPRETATION. H. P. Cooke; PRIOR ANALYTICS. H. Tredennick.
ARISTOTLE: GENERATION OF ANIMALS. A. L. Peck.
ARISTOTLE: HISTORIA ANIMALIUM. A. L. Peck. 3 Vols. Vol. I.
ARISTOTLE: METAPHYSICS. H. Tredennick. 2 Vols.
ARISTOTLE: METEOROLOGICA. H. D. P. Lee.
ARISTOTLE: MINOR WORKS. W. S. Hett. "On Colours," "On Things Heard," "Physiognomics," "On Plants," "On Marvellous Things Heard," "Mechanical Problems," "On Indivisible Lines," "Situations and Names of Winds," "On Melissus, Xenophanes, and Gorgias."
ARISTOTLE: NICOMACHEAN ETHICS. H. Rackham.
ARISTOTLE: OECONOMICA AND MAGNA MORALIA. G. C. Armstrong. (With Metaphysics, Vol. II.)
ARISTOTLE: ON THE HEAVENS. W. K. C. Guthrie.
ARISTOTLE: ON THE SOUL, PARVA NATURALIA. ON BREATH. W. S. Hett.

THE LOEB CLASSICAL LIBRARY

Aristotle: Parts of Animals. A. L. Peck; Motion and Progression of Animals. E. S. Forster.
Aristotle: Physics. Rev. P. Wicksteed and F. M. Cornford. 2 Vols.
Aristotle: Poetics; Longinus on the Sublime. W. Hamilton Fyfe; Demetrius on Style. W. Rhys Roberts.
Aristotle: Politics. H. Rackham.
Aristotle: Posterior Analytics. H. Tredennick; Topics. E. S. Forster.
Aristotle: Problems. W. S. Hett. 2 Vols.
Aristotle: Rhetorica ad Alexandrum. H. Rackham. (With Problems, Vol. II.)
Aristotle: Sophistical Refutations. Coming-to-be and Passing-away. E. S. Forster; On the Cosmos. D. J. Furley.
Arrian: History of Alexander and Indica. Rev. E. Iliffe Robson. 2 Vols.
Athenaeus: Deipnosophistae. C. B. Gulick. 7 Vols.
Babrius and Phaedrus (Latin). B. E. Perry.
St. Basil: Letters. R. J. Deferrari. 4 Vols.
Callimachus: Fragments. C. A. Trypanis.
Callimachus: Hymns and Epigrams, and Lycophron. A. W. Mair; Aratus. G. R. Mair.
Clement of Alexandria. Rev. G. W. Butterworth.
Colluthus. *Cf.* Oppian.
Daphnis and Chloe. *Cf.* Longus.
Demosthenes I: Olynthiacs, Philippics and Minor Orations: I-XVII and XX. J. H. Vince.
Demosthenes II: De Corona and De Falsa Legatione, C. A. Vince and J. H. Vince.
Demosthenes III: Meidias, Androtion, Aristocrates, Timocrates, Aristogeiton. J. H. Vince.
Demosthenes IV-VI: Private Orations and In Neaeram. A. T. Murray.
Demosthenes VII: Funeral Speech, Erotic Essay, Exordia and Letters. N. W. and N. J. DeWitt.
Dio Cassius: Roman History. E. Cary. 9 Vols.
Dio Chrysostom. 5 Vols. Vols. I and II. J. W. Cohoon. Vol. III. J. W. Cohoon and H. Lamar Crosby. Vols. IV and V. H. Lamar Crosby.
Diodorus Siculus. 12 Vols. Vols. I-VI. C. H. Oldfather. Vol. VII. C. L. Sherman. Vol. VIII. C. B. Welles. Vols. IX and X. Russel M. Geer. Vols. XI and XII. F. R. Walton. General Index. Russel M. Geer.

DIOGENES LAERTIUS. R. D. Hicks. 2 Vols.
DIONYSIUS OF HALICARNASSUS: ROMAN ANTIQUITIES. Spelman's translation revised by E. Cary. 7 Vols.
EPICTETUS. W. A. Oldfather. 2 Vols.
EURIPIDES. A. S. Way. 4 Vols. Verse trans.
EUSEBIUS: ECCLESIASTICAL HISTORY. Kirsopp Lake and J. E. L. Oulton. 2 Vols.
GALEN: ON THE NATURAL FACULTIES. A. J. Brock.
THE GREEK ANTHOLOGY. W. R. Paton. 5 Vols.
THE GREEK BUCOLIC POETS (THEOCRITUS, BION, MOSCHUS). J. M. Edmonds.
GREEK ELEGY AND IAMBUS WITH THE ANACREONTEA. J. M. Edmonds. 2 Vols.
GREEK MATHEMATICAL WORKS. Ivor Thomas. 2 Vols.
HERODES. *Cf.* THEOPHRASTUS: CHARACTERS.
HERODOTUS. A. D. Godley. 4 Vols.
HESIOD AND THE HOMERIC HYMNS. H. G. Evelyn White.
HIPPOCRATES AND THE FRAGMENTS OF HERACLEITUS. W. H. S. Jones and E. T. Withington. 4 Vols.
HOMER: ILIAD. A. T. Murray. 2 Vols.
HOMER: ODYSSEY. A. T. Murray. 2 Vols.
ISAEUS. E. S. Forster.
ISOCRATES. George Norlin and LaRue Van Hook. 3 Vols.
ST. JOHN DAMASCENE: BARLAAM AND IOASAPH. Rev. G. R. Woodward, Harold Mattingly and D. M. Lang.
JOSEPHUS. 9 Vols. Vols. I-IV. H. St. J. Thackeray. Vol. V. H. St. J. Thackeray and Ralph Marcus. Vols. VI and VII. Ralph Marcus. Vol. VIII. Ralph Marcus and Allen Wikgren. Vol. IX. L. H. Feldman.
JULIAN. Wilmer Cave Wright. 3 Vols.
LONGUS: DAPHNIS AND CHLOE. Thornley's translation revised by J. M. Edmonds; and PARTHENIUS. S. Gaselee.
LUCIAN. 8 Vols. Vols. I-V. A. M. Harmon. Vol. VI. K. Kilburn. Vols. VII and VIII. M. D. Macleod.
LYCOPHRON. *Cf.* CALLIMACHUS.
LYRA GRAECA. J. M. Edmonds. 3 Vols.
LYSIAS. W. R. M. Lamb.
MANETHO. W. G. Waddell; PTOLEMY: TETRABIBLOS. F. E. Robbins.
MARCUS AURELIUS. C. R. Haines.
MENANDER. F. G. Allinson.
MINOR ATTIC ORATORS. 2 Vols. K. J. Maidment and J. O. Burtt.
NONNOS: DIONYSIACA. W. H. D. Rouse. 3 Vols.

PROCOPIUS: HISTORY OF THE WARS. H. B. Dewing. 7 Vols.
PTOLEMY: TETRABIBLOS. *Cf.* MANETHO.
QUINTUS SMYRNAEUS. A. S. Way. Verse trans.
SEXTUS EMPIRICUS. Rev. R. G. Bury. 4 Vols.
SOPHOCLES. F. Storr. 2 Vols. Verse trans.
STRABO: GEOGRAPHY. Horace L. Jones. 8 Vols.
THEOPHRASTUS: CHARACTERS. J. M. Edmonds; HERODES, etc. A. D. Knox.
THEOPHRASTUS: ENQUIRY INTO PLANTS. Sir Arthur Hort. 2 Vols.
THUCYDIDES. C. F. Smith. 4 Vols.
TRYPHIODORUS. *Cf.* OPPIAN.
XENOPHON: ANABASIS. C. L. Brownson.
XENOPHON: CYROPAEDIA. Walter Miller. 2 Vols.
XENOPHON: HELLENICA. C. L. Brownson. 2 Vols.
XENOPHON: MEMORABILIA AND OECONOMICUS. E. C. Marchant. SYMPOSIUM AND APOLOGY. O. J Todd.
XENOPHON: SCRIPTA MINORA. E. C. Marchant and G. W. Bowersock.

VOLUMES IN PREPARATION

GREEK AUTHORS

ARISTIDES: ORATIONS. C. A. Behr.
HERODIANUS. C. R. Whittaker.
LIBANIUS: SELECTED WORKS. A. F. Norman.
MUSAEUS: HERO AND LEANDER. T. Gelzer and C. H. Whitman.
THEOPHRASTUS: DE CAUSIS PLANTARUM. G. K. K. Link and B. Einarson.

LATIN AUTHORS

ASCONIUS: COMMENTARIES ON CICERO'S ORATIONS. G. W. Bowersock.
BENEDICT: THE RULE. P. Meyvaert.
JUSTIN–TROGUS. R. Moss.
MANILIUS. G. P. Gould.
PLINY: LETTERS. B. Radice.

DESCRIPTIVE PROSPECTUS ON APPLICATION

CAMBRIDGE, MASS. HARVARD UNIV. PRESS — LONDON WILLIAM HEINEMANN LTD